150 Heroes

For Beth

Thank you for your work to make this a better world.

Other books by Richard Lapchick

150
Heroes

PEOPLE IN SPORT
Who Make This a Better World

Richard Lapchick

with

Jessica Bartter Duffaut
Joslyn Dalton
Stacy Martin-Tenney
Austin Moss
Brian Wright
Jenny Yehlen

FITNESS INFORMATION TECHNOLOGY
A Division of the International Center
for Performance Excellence
West Virginia University
262 Coliseum, WVU-CPASS
PO Box 6116
Morgantown, WV 26506-6116

Library of Congress Card Catalog Number: 2010933013

ISBN: 978-1-935412-22-9

Cover photographs (wrapping around from back cover): Kyle Maynard, Courtesy of the National Consortium for Academics and Sports; Jason Ray, courtesy of UNC Athletics; Vivian Stringer, courtesy of Romanenko/Rutgers Athletics; Geno Auriemma, courtesy of University of Connecticut Athletics; Aaron Fotheringham, courtesy of Hardcore Sitting, LLC.; Katie Holloway, courtesy of Cal State Northridge Athletics; Gilbert Tuhabonye, courtesy of Holly Reed Photography.; film strip, © Nicola Gavin, bigstockphoto.com; basketball court © Jorge Gonzalez, istockphoto.com.

Cover Design: Bellerophon Productions
Typesetter: Bellerophon Productions
Production Editor: Aaron Geiger
Copyeditor: Aaron Geiger
Proofreader: Mark Slider
Printed by Data Reproductions Corporation

10 9 8 7 6 5 4 3 2 1

Fitness Information Technology
A Division of the International Center for Performance Excellence
West Virginia University
262 Coliseum, WVU-CPASS
PO Box 6116
Morgantown, WV 26506-6116
800.477.4348 (toll free)
304.293.6888 (phone)
304.293.6658 (fax)
Email: fitcustomerservice@mail.wvu.edu
Website: www.fitinfotech.com

This book is dedicated to Darryl Williams, who transformed the City of Boston from a symbol of hate to a symbol of brotherhood. His passing in 2010 was a great loss to the world but his legacy must continue in all of our hearts.

Contents

CHAPTER 3 ● Playing to Win in Life   157

CHAPTER 4 ● Transcending Sport to Help Society   195

CHAPTER 5 • Hurdlers Overcoming Obstacles   279

CHAPTER 6 • Creating a Better World   349

CHAPTER 7 • Fighting Racism   397

CHAPTER 8 • Creating a New
Game Plan for College Sport   421

CHAPTER 9 • Creating the Environment   461

CHAPTER 10 • Coming to America   499

Conclusion   563

Foreword

This volume contains portraits of 150 sports heroes who have been honored by the National Consortium for Academics and Sports during the past 25 years. Many are household names; others are less widely recognized, and some may only be known to those whose lives they directly touched. But all share one thing in common: they are gifted women and men who used the power and appeal of sport to enhance educational achievement and to affect meaningful social change; and they did so with dignity, courage, and integrity. By so doing, each helped to fulfill the mission of the NCAS.

Sports heroes seem to be in short supply these days. We read about coaches who compromise their own integrity by gambling, abusing alcohol, or misusing funds. We read about athletes who cheat by taking performance enhancing drugs, who are disloyal to their spouses, or who attack the very fans who come to see them play. But for every sordid story, there are coaches, athletic directors, general managers, and players who give far more to sport and to the world than sport gives to them. And so we have written this tribute to our 150 heroes who restore our belief in sport not only as games that entertain but also teach the virtues of discipline, teamwork, and an understanding and appreciation of diversity. These heroes used sport as a vehicle to reach out to people in need of help and so work to create a better and more just world.

It was our belief that sport has the power to create positive social change that led to the establishment of the National Consortium for Academics and Sports 25 years ago in Boston. One year earlier, Richard Lapchick and I had founded an organization we called the Center for the Study of Sport in Society at Northeastern University to deal with problems in intercollegiate sport at a time when student-athletes were routinely exploited by the very coaches who recruited them to their campuses. I was the Dean of Arts and Sciences at the

University, and I appropriated a small portion of my College's budget to support the Center. Richard gave up an important post at the United Nations for some modest secretarial assistance, an even more modest salary, and a small, windowless office. For him it was a labor of love; for me it was a very large gamble since if the Center failed, we would have been out of work. Happily, we were successful, so much so in fact, that we were able to hire Tom "Satch" Sanders as our Associate Director and expand the modest educational programs. We began with the New England Patriots, the Boston Bruins, and the Boston Red Sox, whose participating players worked to help at-risk student-athletes in area middle and high schools. We expanded into new initiatives that you will read about elsewhere in this volume and that exist unto the current day. When those programs attracted the interest of professors, coaches, and student-athletes in other colleges and universities, both in and beyond the Boston area, the idea of establishing a consortium was born.

Organizing the NCAS was no easy task. We were swimming upstream against a very strong current. Officials at some schools we contacted about becoming NCAS members said no politely; others weren't even polite. Anecdotally, I remember one conversation Richard, Satch, and I had with the athletic director of a large Midwestern university who smiled and nodded throughout our session. We left convinced his school would join. The next day we learned that he was nearly deaf without his hearing aid, and that he simply wanted to be cordial. And when he incorrectly concluded that our goal was to reform his athletic department, he wouldn't even acknowledge us anymore. But thankfully, a handful who saw value in the activist programs we were promoting signed on, and in 1985 the NCAS was born. Richard became its Executive Director, and I returned to my deanery.

Running any kind of consortium is a tricky business, since on the one hand it is necessary to give participating consortium members enough latitude to "do their own thing," while at the same time maintaining program coherence and consistency from one consortium member to another. Working with university personnel poses an even greater challenge given the institutional autonomy that characterizes American higher education, which, depending upon the needs of the moment, is either a blessing or a curse. And when one is dealing with schools as diverse as UC Berkeley, Temple, and William Patterson—who were three NCAS charter members—the challenge is even greater.

While we were gradually able to add staff, largely through the largesse of private foundations and federal agencies that provided support for our programs, the plain fact is that were it not for Richard Lapchick, NCAS would have died a quick and little-noticed death. Richard spent the better part of five years traveling the country, meeting with coaches, with faculty, with athletic directors, and with provosts and presidents selling the message of the Consortium. And through sheer force of personality, he got the job done.

Over time, Richard has become the social conscience of sport. While in those early years, his was a voice in the wilderness, he pressed his case that sport can and ought to help us overcome injustice, racism, poverty, and disease. And while he has been critical of those who use their position in sport only to aggrandize their own ends, his has not been the shrill voice of anger or the lament of despair. Rather, he has always shined an affirming light, celebrating excellence and criticizing only for the purpose of improvement.

Many of the problems that Richard and I identified when we formed the Center and the NCAS have been solved, their negative consequences muted. It is no longer acceptable for college coaches and athletic directors to exploit student-athletes. It still happens, of course, but when it does there are penalties and there is justice. The scourge of apartheid is no more. The doors to management positions in collegiate and professional sport are finally, if slowly, opening to women and people of color. And the governing bodies of sport who once shunned the NCAS now embrace us and the principles for which we stand.

Good timing? Perhaps. But it's been more than that. Richard would be the last to argue that he alone has been responsible for the important and dramatic social changes that have occurred in the sports world during the past 25 years. But it is or ought to be clear to anyone who cares that Richard has been in the vanguard of the effort to reform sport, and that no one has been more effective in ensuring that sport lifts up, encourages and inspires, that it helps us affirm the principles of justice and equality which are the foundations of our Republic.

Richard Lapchick has never won Olympic Gold. He has neither a Super Bowl nor World Series ring. But his contribution to the world of sport is every bit as important as those of even the most celebrated athletes whom we honor in this volume. In his own time and with his own voice, he has made a real and enduring difference. In essence then, this book of vignettes about 150 heroes is really a book about 151. And the last is truly first.

—Richard Astro
May 2010

Acknowledgments

I picked six individuals to help me compile the stories of these 150 heroes who make this a better world through sport because of their own commitment to using sport as an instrument for social change. It is with enormous appreciation that I tip my cap to our floor general, Jessica Bartter Duffaut and our teammates, Jenny Yehlen, Stacy Martin-Tenney, Brian Wright, Joslyn Dalton, and Austin Moss. Their intelligence and research and writing skills made this possible.

I also salute Philomena Pirolo and Maria Molina who had our back and supported us throughout the project.

Most importantly, I would like to thank my family which inspires me each day. My wife, Ann, our children Joe, Emily, Chamy and her husband Michael and grandchildren Taylor and Emma give me the energy to keep doing what I think needs to be done. I love them so much.

Finally, I thank everyone associated with the National Consortium for Academics and Sports for the past 25 awesome years. At the top of that list is my best friend who is himself a hero. Keith Lee is the COO of the NCAS. Then there are dear friends Tom Miller, our Chair of the NCAS Board, Robert Weathers, the Associate Director for Outreach, and chief academic officer Richard Astro. Keith, Robert, Richard, and I have been together all these 25 years. Jeff O'Brien and Suzi Katz have been with us for nearly two decades.

—Richard Lapchick

Introduction

by Richard Lapchick

Because of the work that we do in the National Consortium for Academics and Sports and the DeVos Sport Business Management Program we become all too aware of the problems that exist in sport. Each day we seem to read about a rule being violated, an athlete getting in trouble with drugs or arrested for sexual assault, steroid use in baseball, the NFL, or track and field, the threat that gambling poses to college sports, and agents recruiting young athletes with illegal monetary inducements. The list goes on and on. That is why it was so joyous for me when Dr. Taylor Ellis, the Dean of Undergraduate Education in the College of Business Administration at the University of Central Florida, came to my office in February of 2005.

I had just finished writing a book I called *New Game Plans for College Sport* and was frankly tired of writing. I vowed that I would not take up another book project for several years. Taylor changed all of that on the morning after the 2005 Consortium banquet. He came in, sat down, and said, "When I was a boy, I wasn't involved in school. I had no sense of direction or sense of purpose." He continued, "then someone gave me this book." Taylor placed the well-worn Barlow Meyers' *Real Life Stories: Champions All the Way*, published 45 years earlier, on my desk. He said, "About that time in my life somebody gave me this book about seven athletes and the obstacles they overcame to do great things in life. This book transformed my life and gave me a sense of direction and hope." Taylor said, "Every year you honor five or six such athletes at the Consortium's award banquet. You have to write a book about them." The seed for *150 Heroes* had been planted.

It was a no-brainer to think about undertaking the project in spite of my vow to the contrary. This book could be, I thought, a real celebration of sport. It could portray the power of sport to transform not only individuals, but their impact on society more generally. I ran through my head the names of all the award winners I could recall and knew that their stories would inspire people collectively who could not be in the presence of these people in the halls when we honored them.

With the 25th anniversary of the Consortium approaching, I enlisted the support of Jessica Bartter, who is the Assistant Director for Communications and Marketing of the National Consortium. We began to draw all of the names and addresses together and contact the previous award winners who were still alive. Their support for the project was overwhelmingly positive. We began to collect the biographical materials and stories that were the basis for the awards. We also asked Stacy Martin-Tenney, Jennifer Brenden Yehlen, Brian Wright, Joslyn Dalton, and Austin Moss all current or former graduate students in the DeVos Sport Business Management Program, to help write the individual stories.

Before discussing the sections of *150 Heroes: People in Sport Who Make This a Better World*, I must stress that there are obviously extraordinary leaders in sport who are not included here. This only includes people honored with Giant Steps Awards and who were inducted into the Hall of Fame of the NCAS. Thus such giants as Arthur Ashe, Wilma Rudolph, Rafer Johnson, and so many others are not in this book.

Our *Barrier Breakers* section includes well-known heroes. Three people named Robinson, one of whom was a legendary coach for 56 years at Grambling State. Jackie and Rachel not only broke down baseball's segregation but also did great deeds over the next six decades. Rachel carried on Jackie's legacy. Coaches Boone and Yoast were the real titans who integrated high school football in northern Virginia. Nancy Lieberman paved the way for other generations of athletes in college and professional women's basketball. Lee Elder was the first African-American to play in the Masters. Billy Mills, Phillip Castillo, Pamela White-Hanson, and Ryneldi Becenti were Native American athletes in a time when Native Americans rarely competed in sport. Donna Lopiano was a legendary player and women's athletic director in Texas and lifetime advocate for the opportunities of women in sport. Ernestine Bayer and Anita DeFrantz were pioneering rowers, one considered the mother of the sport, and the second, the first African-American medalist in the Olympics, a woman who stood up against an American president for his decision to boycott the Moscow Olympics and ultimately become the most powerful woman in sport as the Vice President of the International

Olympic Committee. Annie Boucher, a grandmother who rocked the college sports world as a student-athlete in her fifties. Dr. Roscoe C. Brown Jr., and Colonel Lawrence Roberts were Tuskegee Airmen who this nation is greatly indebted to. And finally, the greatest of all, Muhammad Ali, who stood tall for justice and human rights from the time he won an Olympic gold medal in 1960 through the opening of until the Muhammad Ali Center in Louisville, KY in the fall of 2005 and beyond.

Then there are a series of coaches described in the section *Coaching to Win in Life*, some known nationally, some known primarily to the people they touched directly, all who understood what sports were meant to be and then helped the young people under their charge to grow socially, athletically, and academically. Sometimes they did things in games to emphasize sportsmanship rather than the pursuit of victory. They come from urban areas and rural areas, from north and south, from California to Mississippi to Miami to St. Louis to Boston. They made their athletes winners in life.

Playing to Win in Life is about 10 individuals whose star quality as athletes gave them a platform to work towards contributing to a better society.

Transcending Sport to Help Society presents the stories of 25 athletes and coaches of such magnitude that a special section was devoted to them. They included the dominant softball player of her time, Dot Richardson; Kareem Abdul-Jabbar, perhaps the greatest big man in the history of the NBA; "Tiny" Archibald, one of the best little men in the history of the NBA; Dave Bing, former NBA star who become one of the most successful African-American entrepreneurs in America; Alan Page, the great Minnesota Viking football player who became a Minnesota Supreme Court justice; Dean Smith, the winningest coach in the history of men's basketball; Pat Summit, his equivalent in women's basketball; Joe Paterno, who at the time of this writing was still leading Penn State at 83 years old; former Senator Bill Bradley, a great New York Knicks player and Rhodes Scholar who eventually ran for president; Tom Osborne, the dynamic coach at Nebraska who became a U.S. Congressman; "Dr. J" Julius Erving, who transformed the game of basketball with his style; Jackie Joyner-Kersee, who perhaps was the greatest athlete of her generation; Lawrence Burton, former NFL player who helped build the legends of Boys Town; Geno Auriemma, one of the most successful coaches of all-time at the University of Connecticut who at the time of this writing was pummeling teams by double digits en route to an expected national championship; Coach Derek DeWitt who sacrificed a shutout game to Coach Dave Frantz by letting Jake Porter make the play of his life; Julie Foudy who captained the U.S. Women's Soccer team for 13 years while advocating for the rights of women and children; Dean and Diane Alford who started and run the dream-fulfilling and smile-producing Miracle League; Mallory Holtman and Liz Wallace who reminded this nation what true sportsmanship looks like in 2008; Travis Roy whose college hockey career lasted 11 seconds; Floyd Keith who currently leads the Black Coaches and Administrators advocating for social change; and Captain Ed Nicholson who runs Project Healing Waters which uses fly fishing as therapy for veterans.

Another section, *Hurdlers Overcoming Obstacles*, tells the story of 17 athletes who overcame great physical, emotional, and addictive barriers to demonstrate to all around them what the human spirit was capable of doing when it was determined to win in life.

The lives of the 14 athletes are portrayed in the section *Creating a Better World*. These athletes devoted an important part of their lives to having an impact on changing the social circumstances in which they found themselves to make it a better world for everybody. Most of the 14 are not household names, but their acts affected so many outside of their own households.

The *Fighting Racism* section discusses five athletes whose individual acts stood tall against racism: Dionte Hall, barely a teenager; Darryl Williams, a sophomore in a Boston high school; Michael Watson, just graduating from college; and David Lazerson and Richard Green, a Hasidic Jew and an African-American in Crown Heights that took on the forces of hate swirling around them.

The *New Game Plan for College Sport* section is on nine individuals who devoted a large part of their lives to making college sport live up to its ideals. They include two former college presidents, three athletics directors, an academic advisor, and three men who worked from outside of college sport to make it better inside.

The section on *Creating the Environment* discusses the 12 leaders who, through their own example, began to change how different sports organizations and entities could work towards making sport live up to its ideals. At the high school level, Dr. Clinton Albury in his own Florida school and H. Ross Perot in his state of Texas, led a movement for "No Pass, No Play"—raising the academic standards of high school athletes. At the pro level, Rich DeVos, the owner of the Orlando Magic, saw the power an individual franchise could have to infect a community with spirit and to do positive things through an enormously expansive philanthropic body of work. Also at the pro level, Jerry Reinsdorf, owner of MLB's Chicago White Sox and the NBA's Chicago Bulls, has been instrumental in advocating for the greater good of sport while leading from two different leagues. Lewis Katz and Raymond Chambers, owners of the New Jersey Nets, worked hard to earn money and have worked even harder to put it back into the community. Mike Ilitch, owner of the NHL's Red Wings and Little Caeser's Pizza, uses his power in sports to positively impact his community. After a 13-year professional playing career, "Satch" Sanders spent 18 years working with other pros easing their transition in and out of the NBA. At the Olympic level, Billy Payne, shared his Olympic dreams with his community by orchestrating the 1996 Summer Games in Atlanta. This section includes David Stern and Paul Tagliabue, two league commissioners and Gene Upshaw, a players association chief who showed that players and management could work together to better their game.

One of the most moving sections is *Coming to America* about the lives of five people who chose to leave their war-torn societies and move to America where they became fine student-athletes as well as storytellers about what drove them out of their countries and why Americans gave them hope. They came from Burundi, Sudan, Afghanistan, and Bosnia. They all came with courage.

150 Heroes concludes with stories about the legends that live on after their passing. Some were coaches, some were athletes, one a mascot, one an entrepreneur, philanthropist, and team owner—all made sport and society better than where they found it. Their spirit underlines the meaning of heroes.

Just as Taylor Ellis' book inspired him to go on to lead a meaningful and wonderful life, it is our hope at the National Consortium for Academics and Sports that those we have honored over the past 25 years will inspire all of the readers to understand what they can do to make this a better world and to help others believe in what they cannot see.

I

BARRIER BREAKERS

by Richard Lapchick

The term "barrier breaker" describes that rare individual who took down walls that previously had inhibited or barred a group of people from the equal opportunity that American society holds as the hallmark of democracy.

No name resonates more with this description than that of Jackie Robinson, who broke baseball's color barrier in 1947. By his side at the time, his wife Rachel helped keep his strength intact. After his early death, Rachel continued his legacy and created her own by helping hundreds of young African-American students attend college and succeed in a world where they were preordained to fail.

Herman Boone and Bill Yoast combined forces to lead the Titans of Alexandria, Virginia to a state football championship in their first year of coaching together. But their story is even more about the successful integration of their team in the 1960s in spite of tremendous opposition. Boone and Yoast became household names after the release of the movie *Remember the Titans*, which chronicles their remarkable story.

Billy Mills, Ryneldi Becenti, Phillip Castillo, and Pamela White-Hanson are four Native American athletes who broke barriers in their own sports and then went back to help younger Native Americans use sport to fight high drop out rates and alcoholism on Native American reservations. Becenti became the first Native American woman to play in the WNBA while Mills became the first and only American to win the 10,000-meter race in any Olympics.

Two female rowers who not only created opportunities for women in rowing, but inspired generations of women who followed them are Ernestine Bayer, considered the "mother of modern rowing," and Anita DeFrantz, the first African-American female to win a medal in the Olympics in her sport. DeFrantz subsequently led the protest against President Carter's boycott of the 1980 Olympics. She became a Vice President for the Los Angeles Organizing Committee in 1984. As a senior member of the IOC today, she is considered sport's most powerful woman.

Donna Lopiano, a great softball player, became a pioneering athletic director for the women's program at the University of Texas. For more than a decade, she led the Women's Sports Foundation in its barrier-breaking role for women and girls in sports.

Nancy Lieberman elevated the game of women's basketball in the 1970s at Old Dominion University and then throughout a distinguished professional career inhibited only by the lack of opportunities for women in basketball when she was at the height of her game.

Annie Boucher, already a grandmother, used the sport of tennis to help her achieve her high school and college degrees.

Lee Elder became the first African-American to play in The Master's golf tournament, and paved the way for Tiger Woods and other people of color.

Eddie Robinson, who led Grambling State University for 56 years, was the winningest coach in the history of the sport upon his retirement and had sent more players to the National Football League than any other coach in the history of college football.

Dr. Roscoe C. Brown Jr., and Colonel Lawrence Roberts were Tuskegee Airmen who this nation is greatly indebted to. Brown and Roberts piloted during the boom of American aviation and fought for democracy and freedom abroad despite not being treated as equals in their home country.

Finally, Muhammad Ali has led a life that is unparalleled in the world of sport. The Muhammad Ali Center in Louisville was recently opened as a living tribute to a man who, by his work in and outside the ring, gave hope to millions.

In their own time and in their own way, each of these distinguished women and men changed the face of sport and the societies in which they lived. Their work to make a better world should serve as a stimulus to inspire us to do more ourselves.

Rachel Robinson

Barrier Breakers

by Jessica Bartter Duffaut

Perhaps best known as the wife of Jackie Robinson, Rachel Robinson is a woman of countless achievements and accolades, both in her own right and those achieved jointly with her husband. She has earned the titles of civil rights leader, humanitarian, activist, author, teacher, nurse, and leader, though none of them came without opposition. And that was just in her free time as her life mainly consisted of being a wife and a mother. Strong, compassionate, loving, determined, elegant, and stylish are just a few of the words used to describe Mrs. Robinson.

Born in 1922, Rachel Isum was raised in Northern California before moving to Southern California to attend the University of California, Los Angeles in 1940. A shy, nursing student, she was soon introduced to the big man on campus, Jackie Robinson. Jackie was the first student to letter in four varsity sports at UCLA and did not go unnoticed by his fellow students. But Rachel was surprised to learn he, too, was shy. She also noted he was a serious man, proud to be a black man, with a warm smile, a pigeon-toed walk and extremely handsome looks. Needless to say, they felt an immediate connection and the courtship blossomed.[1]

After two years at UCLA, Rachel transferred to the UC San Francisco School of Nursing to become a registered nurse. Her days were filled with a full course load and eight-hour hospital shifts. After three years of this arduous schedule, Rachel graduated in June 1945 with the Florence Nightingale award for clinical excellence.

Two months later, her fiancé, Jackie Robinson, signed with the Brooklyn Dodgers, joining forces with Dodgers president and general manager Branch Rickey in a fight to change the world.

It has often been said, "Behind every strong man, there is a strong woman." Rickey took this to heart knowing the task he presented to Jackie of integrating Major League Baseball was going to face much adversity, confrontation, and perhaps failure. Rickey chose Jackie for his character and skill, and made him promise that he could silently endure the racially motivated physical and mental abuse that was sure to follow, but not before he asked Jackie if he had a girl. Though Rickey knew Jackie would need the support of a woman by his side to dilute the pain of deep rooted racial segregation, even Rickey could not have predicted Jackie would become "the target of racial epithets and flying cleats, of hate letters and death threats, of pitchers throwing at his head and legs, and catchers spitting on his shoes,"[2] as *Sports Illustrated* described two years later in 1947 when Jackie Robinson officially broke the color barrier in Major League Baseball. With Rachel's support and encouragement, Jackie responded to the provocation of racial insults and inequities that often included violence with his play on the field, earning the respect of his teammates and, in time, the opposition. Jackie even earned the National League Rookie of the Year title with 12 home runs, a league-leading 29 stolen bases and a .297 batting average along with the greatest achievement of all: social change.

Several teammates of Jackie's credited Rachel for being his co-pioneer and anchor and acknowledged her beauty and intellect that "replenished his strength and courage"[3] for the 10 years he competed in the big leagues. Jackie, himself, later wrote of Rachel as "Strong, loving, gentle and brave, never afraid to either criticize or comfort. When they try to destroy me, it's Rachel who keeps me sane."[4]

After Jackie's successful career as a professional athlete, his mission in life to help others and commit to a changed and more equitable America was only strengthened. Together, Rachel and Jackie thought their work could best be utilized in politics and in the civil rights movement. Most notably, the Robinsons supported Dr. Martin Luther King Jr., and even organized an outdoor jazz concert on their property to raise funds to be used as bail money for civil rights activists who had been jailed for their involvement in the movement.

For 26 years, the same concert was held the last Sunday every June in Connecticut and then in New York City.

After years of homemaking and raising their three children, Rachel returned to school to get her master's degree at New York University and later worked as a researcher and clinician at the Albert Einstein College of Medicine's Department of Social and Community Psychiatry. Five years later, Rachel became the Director of Nursing for the Connecticut Mental Health Center and as Assistant Professor of Nursing at Yale University. Her independence and self-sustaining capabilities proved vital to her existence at the untimely death of her husband in 1972. Early on, Rachel had "to learn to be both [her] selves without letting 'Mrs. Jackie Robinson' overshadow 'Rachel Robinson.'"[5]

Within weeks of the loss of Jackie, Rachel was faced with the challenge of taking over his business that was originally intended to be a construction company. Though new to the business world, Rachel decided the company lacked the resources to be the construction company Jackie envisioned but rather, was capable of being a real estate development company. Thus the Jackie Robinson Development Company was born. By 1980, 1,300 housing units were built for families of low to moderate incomes in Jackie's honor.

Rachel was so proud of her husband and what he had accomplished that she wanted to continue to improve society through Jackie's name. Although Jackie Robinson will always be remembered for being the first man to integrate baseball, she wanted to do something else that would carry on Jackie's legacy and continue to make a difference in society. Thus, the Jackie Robinson Foundation was created in 1973—a not-for-profit organization that provides leadership and education opportunities to academically gifted students of color with financial need. According to their website as of 2010, the Jackie Robinson Foundation distributed $21 million in scholarships to 1,400 students, enabling them to attend the college of their choice. The students chosen to carry on Jackie Robinson's legacy have sustained an impressive 97 percent graduation rate.

In 1997, Major League Baseball celebrated the 50ᵗʰ anniversary of the integration of baseball. According to *The New York Times*, Rachel reflected, "This anniversary has given us an opportunity as a nation to celebrate together the triumphs of the past and the social progress that has occurred. It has also given us an opportunity to reassess the challenges of the present. It is my passionate hope that we can take this reawakened feeling of unity and use it as a driving force so that each of us can recommit to equality of opportunity for all Americans."[6] While she is very proud to have helped so many over the years, it is important to her to see the process of change continue. Rachel Robinson's commitment to helping those in need, to the fight for racial equity and to bettering society in general, deserves a prominent and enduring place in our social history.

Notes

1. Rachel Robinson, *Jackie Robinson: An Intimate Portrait* (New York: Harry N. Abrams, Inc., 1996), 22.

2. William Nack, "The Breakthrough," SportsIllustrated.cnn.com, (May 5, 1997) http://sportsillustrated.cnn.com/vault/article/magazine/MAG1010023/1/index.htm, (accessed January 12, 2010).

3. Rachel Robinson, "Black Biography: Rachel Robinson," http://www.answers.com/topic/rachel-robinson, (accessed January 12, 2010).

4. Valentine's Day, "The Robinsons," The History Channel, http://www.history.com/content/valentine/great-romances/the-robinsons, (accessed December 9, 2005).

5. Rachel Robinson, *Jackie Robinson: An Intimate Portrait* (New York: Harry N. Abrams, Inc., 1996), 162.

6. Murray Chass, "Standing by Her Man, Always With Elegance" *The New York Times*, April 16, 1997.

Jackie Robinson

Barrier Breakers

by Jessica Bartter Duffaut

If his life was measured by his own words that "A life is not important except in the impact it has on other lives,"[1] Jackie Robinson's life was one of the most important of the 20th century. However, by account of all who knew him, that would be an understatement.

Robinson—who was an athlete, entrepreneur, civil rights activist, actor, author, father, and husband—is remembered by many as a spectacular ball player, but it was the mere fact that he stepped onto the field in a Brooklyn Dodgers uniform that had such an everlasting impact on the United States. In 1947, Robinson became the first African-American to play for any Major League Baseball team in the modern era. By donning the Dodgers uniform, Robinson integrated professional athletics and broke the color barrier that existed in Major League Baseball for decades. But Robinson could not have done it alone. It took the foresight of Branch Rickey, president and general manager of the Brooklyn Dodgers, to recognize that Robinson was an individual with the requisite determination and willpower to affect such social change. Rickey knew the task any player of color would face would be detrimental to one's spirit and play in the form of abuse and threats, but chose Robinson because he believed Jackie had sufficient strength and staying power to get the job done. Rickey challenged Robinson to endure the abuse in silence and fight back with his brilliant play on the field instead. And brilliant he was. In his debut season, Robinson had 12 home runs, a league-leading 29 stolen bases, and a .297 batting average that earned him National League Rookie of the Year as his team was crowned National League Champions and nearly beat their archrivals, the New York Yankees, in what is still considered one of the most exciting World Series ever played.

Robinson's accomplishments did not come about easily. He was forced to tolerate racial insults from the stands, was haunted by hate letters and death threats to himself and his family, and even suffered abuse from on the field where he was the target of many wild pitches and spiked cleats. In upholding his promise to Rickey, Robinson fought back on the diamond and used his unselfish team play and magnificent skills to earn the respect of his teammates and eventually the nation. In particular, he was befriended by shortstop Pee Wee Reese, himself a Southerner whose friendship helped mute the worst of the abuse. According to Rachel Robinson, Reese "went out of his way to convey his support publicly. His gestures dramatically demonstrated what an individual can do." [2]

In just his third season, Robinson was named the National League's Most Valuable Player. Robinson led the league in 1947 and 1949 in stolen bases. In 1949, he won the batting title with a .342 average. From 1949 to 1952, Robinson led second basemen in double plays and was named to the National League All-Star team every year from 1949 to 1954.

Stardom as an athlete was nothing new for Robinson, who lettered in baseball, track and field, football, and basketball in high school and college. He was the first to do so at the University of California, Los Angeles, but before UCLA, he attended Pasadena Junior College to be near his mother. Since track and field and baseball had the same season, Robinson managed to break his older brother's broad jump record of 25-feet $\frac{1}{2}$ inch and star in a baseball game in the same day. Robinson was named Most Valuable Player of the junior colleges in Southern California after leading his team to the state championship in baseball. After transferring to UCLA, Robinson earned All-American accolades for his accomplishments on the gridiron.

Unfortunately for UCLA athletics, Robinson was forced to leave college because of financial challenges. Robinson enjoyed a short stint with the Honolulu Bears playing semipro football but left Pearl Harbor just two days before the Japanese attack in 1942. Shortly thereafter, he received a draft notice and joined the armed forces to put his patriotism into action. But segregation was still commonplace in the military and Robinson felt he was fighting a war at home, rather than overseas. Robinson spoke out against racial injustices he witnessed in the military and stood up for his rights and those of other African-American soldiers. An intelligent man, Robinson was well aware when army regulations changed to outlaw racial discrimination on any vehicle operating on any army base. In 1944, when Robinson was ordered to the back of the bus by the driver, he refused, causing him to be court-martialed and eventually leading to his honorable discharge. His discharge was blamed on the bone chips in his ankle from football.

Upon leaving the military, without a college degree and with little experience in the working world, Robinson began his professional baseball career with the Kansas City Monarchs of the Negro Leagues. Rickey first discovered Robinson as a Monarch and called him to New York. Robinson's wife Rachel recalls that it was here, in 1945 during a role-playing session that, "Rickey subjected Jack to every form of racial attack he could imagine to test his strengths and prepare him for the ordeals sure to come."[3] Robinson believed Rickey was sincere and determined to rid baseball of its social inequalities and "promised that regardless of the provocation he would not retaliate in any way."[4] After suffering through an excruciatingly painful spring training in Central Florida, Robinson spent the next year with the Dodgers' AAA team, the Montreal Royals, while he and Rickey continued to expand their relationship. Robinson scored the winning run in the seventh game of the Little World Series in 1946, leading to his debut with the Brooklyn Dodgers on April 15, 1947 thus changing the face of baseball forever.

In 1949, Robinson decided to end his silence and become true to himself. After a decade of success with the Brooklyn Dodgers in which they went to six World Series and finally beat the Yankees in 1955, Robinson announced his retirement. His impact on our society in general and professional sports had been etched in stone, and Robinson had paved the way for many to follow to continue the journey to social equality that he initiated. Robinson recognized the magnitude of being the first, but knew that if he was not followed by more players of color in the big leagues, his accomplishment would be insignificant. As a sign of success for the great "social experiment,"[5] many other African-Americans were signed including teammates Don Newcombe, Joe Black, and Roy Campanella. The New York Giants quickly followed suit, signing Monte Irvin and Willie Mays, and the Cleveland Indians integrated the American League when they signed Larry Doby, followed by Luke Easter.

Robinson remained active after he finished playing. He opened a men's apparel shop in Harlem, served a radio station as the director of community activities and was vice president of Chock Full O'Nuts. Robinson balanced his business endeavors with his civic engagements. While still a ballplayer, Robinson marched with Dr.

Martin Luther King Jr. and his involvement in the civil rights movement only increased after retirement. In 1963, Jackie and his wife Rachel organized an outdoor jazz concert on their property to raise funds to be used as bail money for civil rights activists who had been jailed for their involvement in the movement. For 26 years, the same concert was held the last Sunday every June in Connecticut and New York. Robinson served on the board of directors of the NAACP for eight years and was one of their leaders in fundraising. Robinson traveled the country making appearances and demonstrating his support for numerous causes, proving one person can make a difference. In one of Robinson's last efforts to serve others, he established the Jackie Robinson Construction Company. The Construction Company's mission was to build homes for families with low and moderate incomes.

In 1972, Jackie Robinson's jersey, number 42, was retired alongside those of Roy Campanella and Sandy Koufax at Dodger Stadium in Los Angeles. Years later, number 42 was permanently retired throughout Major League Baseball. Indeed, after Mariano Rivera retires from the Yankees, no baseball player in MLB will ever wear his number again.

Sadly, Jackie Robinson lost his life to diabetes and heart disease on October 23, 1972. Though his life was tragically short, his impact on others will last forever. Today, Rachel Robinson recognizes that despite the progress that was made by her husband and so many others in so many hard fought battles, challenges and threats still remain. Yet, she hopes that we can look back on "Jack's triumphant struggle to cope with both the opportunities and the obstacles" while realizing that we "need not despair. The example of Jack's life shows that a fighting spirit and hard work can overcome great obstacles."[6]

Notes

1. The Official Site of Jackie Robinson, "Quotes," Jackie Robinson, http://www.jackierobinson.com/about/quotes.html, (accessed January 12, 2010).

2. Rachel Robinson, *Jackie Robinson: An Intimate Portrait* (New York: Harry N. Abrams, Inc., 1996), 75.

3. Ibid., 37.

4. Ibid.

5. Ibid., 38.

6. Ibid., 12.

Herman Boone and William Yoast

Barrier Breakers

by Jessica Bartter Duffaut

A follower of Dr. Martin Luther King, Herman Boone practiced King's civil rights beliefs in his everyday life as a high school teacher and football coach. So when the Supreme Court handed down a ruling that ended all state-imposed public school segregation in 1971 it is no surprise that Boone became a part of what some considered at the time to be a radical movement.

The Rocky Mountain, North Carolina native was one of 12 children in his family who grew a passion for sports early in life. After a successful career as an athlete, he accepted his first job at I.H. Foster High School in Virginia, where he taught and coached basketball, baseball, and football. He returned to North Carolina in 1961 to coach football at E.J. Hayes High School. In his nine years as head coach, Boone led his team to a record of 99 wins and just eight losses. His 1966 squad was named "The Number One Football Team in America" by the *Scholastic Coach's Magazine*. Despite the unmistakable success Boone enjoyed as a head coach, he was asked to sit as an assistant coach at Williamston High School in 1969. The chairman of the local school board was hoping Boone would accept the position to help assist Martin County integrate their schools, academically and athletically. Boone valued his experience and skill too highly to serve Williamston High as its "token black coach." His wife was carrying their third daughter at the time, so Boone quickly looked elsewhere for another opportunity to support his family. The opportunity arose in Alexandria, Virginia where Boone accepted the assistant coaching job at the all-black T.C. Williams High School.

A year later, Virginia, too, began integrating its public schools by combining T.C. Williams High School with one white school and another black school.[1] Boone heard through the grapevine that the T.C. Williams athletics director was looking for an African-American head coach to take over the consolidated football team and that he was hoping for Boone. As a man of values, Boone was not about to accept a job on the basis of his skin color after turning one down for the same reason just one year prior. After talking with the athletic director and confirming that he would be hired for his character and reputation as a coach, Boone was still reluctant. A man named William Yoast, head coach of the all-white Hammond High School, was a 20-year coaching veteran, a local favorite, and obvious next-in-line to be offered the position. Boone was apprehensive about taking a job where he would most likely feel unwelcome. After initially declining the offer, Boone was approached by members of the black community in Alexandria expressing their desire to have him prove to the rest of the community that a black man was perfectly capable of leading an integrated high school football team to success. Boone realized he was up for the challenge.[2]

Yoast was left feeling snubbed as a victim of politics. He decided to leave rather than spend the next year coaching under a man he viewed not as deserving as himself. On his way out, 10 returning players from Yoast's team signed a petition refusing to play without Yoast at the reigns of the team. All of them were willing to miss their senior season and potentially lose their chance at a college scholarship and degree. Yoast was in the coaching field for his love of football and for its ability to impact the lives of so many kids. As a coach, all he ever wanted to do was help as many kids as possible. For him, skin color was irrelevant. Remembering the roots of his passion, He quickly convinced his players to come back with him and promised they would make it through the season together. After Boone offered Yoast the defensive coordinator title, Yoast was back on board.

Boone and Yoast accepted the challenge together, determined to win football games. Yet they did not fully anticipate all the controversy that would arise, both on and off the field. Football players that were formerly cross-town rivals were suddenly teammates, both unaware of how—and some not interested in trying—to get along. Boone faced criticism from his assistant coaches, many of whom were formerly Yoast's assistant coaches, as well as community members, school boosters, parents, and even players. Even before the start of the season, neighbors made sure Boone and his family knew they were not welcome. In addition to signing a petition calling for the black family to leave the white neighborhood, neighbors just watched and laughed as a toilet bowl full of feces was thrust through the window of their house. Though he worried for the safety of his family, Boone knew the potential impact of sports and remained steadfast to win games in hopes the tone of the community would change.

Change in attitude on the 1971 T.C. Williams High School football team came from the top and trickled down. The mixed-race coaching staff put aside their differences and unified in an attempt at a winning season. Players eventually followed their lead and learned to get along on the field, while many even got along off the field and became friends. The sight of this and the increase in wins turned the community around as well. Boone's offense and Yoast's defense went on to have an undefeated season and a state championship, proving that color does not matter in the huddle. In the process, both coaches took the opportunity to teach the kids about more than just football. Boone and Yoast cared about each of their players as if they were their own sons and were genuinely concerned with their actions off the field. Boone earned the respect of many young white teenagers while Yoast did the same with his black players, something entirely new to Alexandria, Virginia. Likewise, their players and the community learned to respect one another.

Boone and Yoast's football team had such an impact on the city of Alexandria that the story of the Titans of T.C. Williams High was still being told decades later. A screenwriter named Gregory Allen Howard overheard the inspiring tale in a barber shop one day and believed it would make a great movie. Walt Disney Pictures produced the inspiring tale that cast Academy Award winner Denzel Washington as Coach Herman Boone and William Patton as Coach Bill Yoast. The real Boone and Yoast served producer Jerry Bruckheimer as consultants advising on the set, allowing for much of the movie to be true to real life. Released in 2000, *Remember the Titans* grossed over $115 million domestically.

Shortly after the movie was released, the players, coaches and cheerleaders of the championship team formed the 71 Original Titans Foundation. The Foundation is a nonprofit organization dedicated to helping high school students pursue post-secondary education. The original Titans wanted to give something back to their community in Alexandria and decided to raise scholarship money for T.C. Williams High School students by selling Titan memorabilia, giving talks and granting interviews about how their team members triumphed in spite of all of their differences. The "scholarships are provided to students who demonstrate leadership in the classroom and community, and promote harmony across all racial and social boundaries."[3]

After their controversial inaugural season together, Coach Boone remained head coach of the Titans for five more seasons before retiring in Alexandria. Coach Yoast served as his assistant for four more then coached elsewhere for 15 years. The release of the film inspired by their lives made them celebrities overnight, thus disrupting their retirements. Since the Hollywood fame, both have traveled the country giving countless speeches and presentations, both remaining as humble as ever. The movie has given Boone and Yoast the platform to better spread their message of justice, equality, and respect. They are proud to still have the honor of impacting the lives of children, the work to which they dedicated their lives nearly 40 years ago.

Notes

1. Christine Becker, "'Remember the Titans' Coaches to Address Congress of Cities," *Nation's Cities Weekly*, December 4, 2000.

2. Anonymous, "Reminiscences of the real-life coaches of 'Remember the Titans'," *New Pittsburgh Courier*, December 13, 2000.

3. Foundation Mission, "1971 Original Titans Foundation's Mission," 71 Original Titans, http://www.71originaltitans.com/mission1.asp, (accessed March 9, 2010).

Ryneldi Becenti

Barrier Breakers

by Jessica Bartter Duffaut

The National Collegiate Athletic Association (NCAA) estimates that only four-tenths of a percent of student-athletes during the 2007–08 academic year were American Indian/Alaskan Native. The percentage of Native American college student-athletes is less than half of the percentage of Native American college students and general populations of Native Americans, according to the 2000 Census. Can we attribute this discrepancy to the lack of visibility and support, the alcohol issue, gaming opportunities, or strong family obligations on the reservation? Some say all of the above, and while many Native Americans struggle off the reservation, a passion for basketball catapulted Ryneldi Becenti into successful collegiate and professional basketball careers outside the Navajo Reservation's boundaries.

Basketball's popularity on the Navajo Reservation breeds talent and enthusiasm for the sport. Yet, opportunities beyond high school are minimal. While college scouts can travel to several schools in one city in one day's time, they may have to travel several days to one school to visit one student-athlete on a reservation. Native Americans seldom leave their reservations to go to college. The lack of encouragement from the outside fuels the fire. The rare opportunities that arise are often turned down or forfeited because of the culture shock felt by young Native Americans while on a college campus. Professional athletic careers are even rarer and nonexistent in the Women's National Basketball Association (WNBA) until Ryneldi Becenti broke that barrier in 1993.

Becenti's career flourished with her courage to leave the reservation. She told *The Denver Post* that she knew to be "the best you have to play the best, and that means leaving to play African-Americans, Anglos, and others."[1] The sacrifice of leaving home was balanced by the opportunities she received elsewhere. After two successful seasons at Scottsdale Community College, where she became the team's first player to score 2,000 career points, Becenti joined the Sun Devils at Arizona State University (ASU). In just two seasons, Becenti recorded the second most assists in an ASU career with 396. She became the school record holder with 17 assists in one game, and the Pac-10 Conference record holder for her average of 7.1 assists per game.

In 1992 and 1993, Becenti accumulated several accolades including All-American honorable mention honors, All-Conference first team selections and four-time Pac-10 Player of the Week recognition. Becenti was honored to represent the United States, specifically the Navajo Reservation, by playing on the U.S. squad in the 1993 World Games. While each was a tremendous accomplishment, selection to the Phoenix Mercury of the WNBA was the most gratifying since it was a first for any Native American.

Becenti attributes her renowned basketball skills to her parents, who traveled to play in tournaments on the reservation nearly every weekend. Her mother even played competitively through the first six months of her pregnancy with Ryneldi, perhaps implanting the repetitive sound of a leather ball hitting wood in her destiny. Sadly, Becenti's mother passed away before her sophomore year in high school. She initially struggled with the thought of returning to the court without her mom in the stands, but Becenti quickly discovered basketball kept them "connected" as she always felt her mother's presence and would talk to her when she was on any basketball court.

Throughout college, however, Becenti was never short of support as her father missed only two home games in all four years. The two he missed were because of blizzards, which made even local travel virtually impossible. For every game, he and hundreds of other reservation residents traveled the five-and-a-half-hour drive to Arizona State University to witness the magic of one of their own. Another several hundred Navajos who lived in the Phoenix area also filled the arena. In total, Becenti's followers made up half the attendance, doubling the women's basketball attendance record at ASU. Becenti believes she would not have succeeded off the reservation if she didn't receive such support. In seeing her followers in the stands, a little bit of home was brought to her, helping Becenti fight the homesickness and isolation that she experienced living away from the reservation. It was the maroon and gold painted faces of her little brothers, the sight of her oldest brother in uniform straight off the Navy base in San Diego, the sound of her grandmother's hands clapping together, and the cheers of her fellow Native Americans that drove her to be her best.

After Becenti chased her dreams as far as they would go in the WNBA, she returned to Window Rock on the Navajo Reservation where she teaches and coaches girls' basketball. Ryneldi Becenti recognizes that for most young people, it is easier and more influential to look up to someone of their own race. She gladly accepts the responsibility as a role model and embraces the ability to show and educate other Native Americans to the opportunities available to them through basketball.

Note

1. Electa Draper, "Trying to turn the game into more than a dead end," *The Denver Post*, May 17, 2005.

Phillip Castillo

Barrier Breaker

by Jessica Bartter Duffaut

Sixty miles west of Albuquerque, New Mexico, 110 miles east of the Arizona border, surrounded by the reservations of the Laguna, Isleta, Canoncito, Navajo, Zuni, and Zia Indians, sits a small community of less than 3,000 Native Americans called Acoma Pueblo. Also known as "Sky City," Acoma Pueblo is a Native American community that was built atop a 367-foot sandstone mesa on 70 acres. It is believed to be the oldest community in the United States that has been continuously inhabited, perhaps since the 10th century.

It is on this plateau and surrounding villages that Phillip Castillo found his love for running. At the young age of six, Castillo entered in his first competitive race. He enjoyed it so much that he continued to compete in "fun runs" in the surrounding communities until high school. Some of his best practice was done in the 30-minute journey from his house to the home of his grandmother.

As a freshman in high school, Castillo recognized that he had the skill and interest in running, but in order to truly excel he had to commit himself to the cross country team. And excel he did. In just his sophomore season, Castillo placed second in the New Mexico High School State Championships. His high school was in the midst of discussions that involved cutting the track program due to a lack of funding, but his success in the state championships quickly changed their minds. After saving the program, Castillo enjoyed more success and in his senior year earned a spot at the National High School Championships. Castillo's speed and patience with long distances helped him pace right into an eighth place finish.

It was no surprise that collegiate athletic departments across the country began calling on Castillo after he finished eighth in the nation. Although Castillo was offered several fully paid recruiting trips, he was unfamiliar with the recruiting process and so he turned them all down. Castillo and his family were not aware that accepting such trips did not imply commitment to that school. Nonetheless, Castillo found the perfect school for him, Adams State College, where he enrolled in 1990. Adams State, in Alamosa, Colorado, had a strong NCAA Division II track and field program and was only a four-hour drive from Castillo's home.

In 1992, the Adams State men's cross country team had a perfect score at the NCAA Championships when the top five finishes were won by five of their runners only four seconds apart. Castillo and his teammates Peter DeLaCerda, David Brooks, Paul Stoneham, and Jason Mohr were the first to accomplish such a feat for Adams State.

Castillo also became the first Native American to win a NCAA Division II cross country title. Castillo wanted to ensure that he would not be the last. He began volunteering with an organization called Wings of America to share the joy he found in running with other Native American youth. Wings of America, an American Indian youth development program of the Earth Circle Foundation, Inc., was established in 1988 to reach Native American youth, one of the most at-risk populations in the United States. The founders, as well as Castillo, recognize running for its fundamental place in the spiritual and ceremonial traditions of Native Americans thus a running-based program was built as a way to reach Native American youth. Castillo coached the annual American Indian Running Clinic. With the help of Nike, Wings of America was able to bring prominent coaches, sports physicians, running club directors, Olympians, and collegiate athletes, like Castillo, to the Native American youth while presenting a camp experience that was informative and affordable. Castillo used running as a unique way to help teach Native American youth traditional Indian games, nutritional information, mental and physical training, and other useful skills.

If Castillo had not already earned the role model title in his community, his future success secured it. He went on to graduate after earning the All-American title an impressive nine times. After graduating, Castillo stayed at Adams State to earn his master's degree in health. He also continued to train. Castillo worked as a movie manager, waiter, and physical education teacher at an elementary school to make ends meet while he passionately continued to run. After earning his master's degree, Castillo learned of the opportunities that the United States Army offered someone like him. Castillo was attracted to the army's running program that allowed soldiers to train full-time while being paid. The Army also would pay off his student loans that totaled more than $30,000. So in 1998, Castillo enlisted and, after 17 vigorous weeks of training, he proudly graduated and became an infantry soldier.

In 1996, the State of Colorado asked for Castillo's assistance in carrying the Olympic torch across the state on its way to Atlanta. Castillo's focus, though, was on the 2000 Olympics because his hard work was starting to pay off after he qualified for the 2000 Olympic Trials in the marathon event. He was ranked 45th in the nation but finished 54th in the trials. While he didn't make it to the Olympics, Castillo is rightfully proud of his effort. Had he not dedicated himself for so many years, through countless arduous training sessions, Castillo would not have received the opportunities he did. He encourages youth to not be selfish with their talents and share them with their communities, much like he did.

For a few years, Castillo continued to train, eventually running in 20 marathons. His personal best was 2:19:19, averaging 5:19 for 26 miles. After his retirement from competitive racing in 2003, Castillo's role in life took on a new importance. As a second lieutenant in the U.S. Army, Castillo controls the lives of the 40 men that make up his platoon. He admits that, at times, his running routine of 140 miles a week was easier than some of the stresses of being a leader in the army. Yet, he wakes up each day committed to make the lives of his fellow service members, as well as the lives of his wife and three daughters, better. Castillo is proud to be a father, a Native American, and a soldier ready to fight for freedom for his family and fellow Americans. Phillip Castillo's life journey has showed him that taking risks is sometimes the only way we can achieve our dreams. He knows that leaving his reservation, as scary as it may have been, was necessary to follow his dreams, and he encourages today's Native American youth to never stop pursuing their passions, no matter where they may lead.

Pamela White-Hanson

Barrier Breaker

by Jessica Bartter Duffaut

On the 27,000 square miles of beautiful desert plains, consisting of breathtaking canyons, refreshing lakes and rivers, and luscious valleys that make up the Navajo Reservation and cross the borders of Arizona, New Mexico, and Utah, a young girl spread her wings and grew a passion for running long distances. Born and raised on the Navajo Reservation, Pamela White-Hanson joined the elite class of Native American athletes that leave their home and people in exploration of new experiences and greater opportunities.

White-Hanson's journey began at Adams State College, a NCAA Division II school and member of the Rocky Mountain Athletic Conference, located in Alamosa, Colorado. A severe case of plantar fasciitis—an overuse injury that affects the sole of the foot—almost prevented White-Hanson from fulfilling her dream to become a national champion, but this courageous student-athlete was determined. A diagnosis of plantar fasciitis meant the fibrous band of tissue connecting her heel bone to the base of her toes was inflamed causing intense pain in the heel of her foot. Typically, plantar fasciitis patients are prescribed rest, ice after activities, shoe inserts, and for the pain, anti-inflammatory drugs such as aspirin and ibuprofen. None of these standard treatments worked for White-Hanson's pain and her last option, in order to continue training, was surgery. The surgery involved a release of part of the plantar fascia, the long, flat ligament extending from her heel to her toes that previously had stretched irregularly, causing damage and inflammation through small tears in the ligament. The reconstructive surgery to eliminate White-Hanson's painful condition took two full years of recovery. The pain, surgery, and recovery time could not prevent White-Hanson from becoming a six-time All-American cross country runner and track and field athlete. Also, as a member of the Adams State cross country team, she led her team to three NCAA Division II National Championships. The three-time national champion managed to complete two undergraduate degrees in elementary education and exercise physiology in just four years despite her struggle to get healthy.

White-Hanson wanted to share her success with as many Native Americans as possible, and, in particular, hoped to show the youth of the Navajo Nation all that was possible outside the reservation borders, and that the Native American traditions need not be sacrificed in order to expand one's horizon. She began working for Wings of America, an American Indian youth development program of the Earth Circle Foundation, Inc. White-Hanson's involvement began as a coach for the annual American Indian Running Clinic. With the help of Nike, Wings of America was able to bring prominent coaches, sports physicians, running club directors, Olympians, and collegiate athletes together to present a camp that was informative and affordable. White-Hanson and other camp coaches taught traditional Native American games, a run-walk fitness program, nutritional education for a healthy lifestyle, mental and physical preparedness, and led a non-competitive 5K fun run to conclude the camp's activities while allowing the youth to put their new skills to work.

White-Hanson continued her work with Wings of America while she returned to Adams State College to obtain her master's degree in bilingual education of the Navajo language. She continued to run with the support of The Native American Sports Council (NASC) Sports Warriors while completing her graduate degree in 2000. In 2002, she married Brent Hanson and the couple soon moved to Arizona. The couple have "three beautiful boys who continue to keep [Pam] on the run."[2]

At one time, "it was inconceivable that within a generation the most widely spoken indigenous language in the United States would be dangerously at risk." But that assumption was "abruptly challenged in 1996 when testing revealed that only a small fraction of the Navajo children living in and around the community of Flagstaff could speak their native language."[3] In response, the Flagstaff Unified School District established a Navajo language revitalization program at Puente De Hozho in 2001. Since 2002, White-Hanson has been teaching Navajo at the trilingual elementary school in Flagstaff, Arizona. In Kindergarten, the students receive 90 percent of the academic instructions in Navajo and 10 percent in English. Then in first grade, the students are instructed in Navajo 80 percent of the time. From second to sixth grade, the students receive half their instructions in Navajo and the other half in English. White Hanson is the second-eldest of nine children so she has a natural inclination to educate youth and currently works with second and third graders at the magnet school. She said, "We are challenged daily to help students become global leaders. Our goal is to teach future leaders to become biliterate and bilingual in two languages."[4] White-Hanson is fluent in both Navajo and English and knows some French and a bit of Spanish. In 2010, she was honored as one of Arizona's RODEL Exemplary Teachers.

As a successful student-athlete, both in the classroom and on the field, White-Hanson was easy to admire. Today, her magnetic personality and welcoming smile encourages Native American youth to work hard and to succeed. Because of her incredible accomplishments as a student, athlete, and now as a teacher and mother, White-Hanson serves as a role model to youth who may had never before dreamed of leaving the Navajo Nation to pursue a college education.

Though many have tried, her success is hard to emulate, thus leaving Pamela White-Hanson and Phillip Castillo along with Billy Mills in an elite class of Native American runners spreading their wings beyond the reservation and into the hearts of so many young Native Americans.

Notes

1. Wings of America, "About Wings: Mission Statement," http://www.wingsof america.org/about/index.html, (accessed March 1, 2010).

2. Pamela White-Hanson, email to author, March 27, 2010

3. Puente de Hozho: Navajo Revitalization Project, "About Us," http://www.puente dehozho.org/about_us.htm, (accessed March 3, 2010).

4. Ibid.

Anita DeFrantz

Barrier Breakers

by Jessica Bartter Duffaut

Courtesy of LA84 Foundation.

Anita DeFrantz has lived a life defying the odds. She did not play sports as a child, despite the fact that she grew up in Hoosier basketball territory in Indiana. She rowed in college despite the fact that she was on an academic scholarship. She won an Olympic medal in rowing despite the fact that she had been introduced to the sport just five years prior. She defied President Jimmy Carter's 1980 Moscow Olympic boycott despite the fact that the United States Olympic Committee (USOC) had not previously contradicted any president's orders and sent Olympians into competition. She was elected vice president of the International Olympic Committee despite the fact that no female before her held that position. And that was just during the first 50 years of her life.

DeFrantz was born in Philadelphia but grew up in Indianapolis, where she learned a great deal of compassion and strength from her parents. Both her mother, who was a teacher, and her father, who ran an organization called Community Action Against Poverty, displayed commitments to youth, community, and education, and encouraged their daughter to do the same.

In 1970, DeFrantz enrolled at Connecticut College on an academic scholarship with no athletic intentions, but as a sophomore she discovered the sport of rowing. While walking on campus one day DeFrantz stopped to ask a man about the long, thin object he was carrying. The man, Bart Gulong, turned out to be the rowing coach and the object he was carrying was a rowing shell. DeFrantz's interest and 5-foot-11-inch build caused him to encourage her to participate in the new sport at Connecticut College. Though DeFrantz had never tried the sport before, she knew most of the girls who went out for the team would also be beginners; so she gave it a shot. Gulong had been right in predicting DeFrantz's athleticism and, shortly thereafter, suggested she consider training for the Olympics. At the time, DeFrantz was not even aware that rowing was an Olympic sport for women because it had just been chosen to make its debut in the next Olympics.

DeFrantz graduated with honors in 1974 with a bachelor's degree in political philosophy after competing at the collegiate level for three years. Her excellence in the rowing shell earned her a spot on the national team every year from 1975 until 1980. Coach Gulong's suggestion came to fruition as DeFrantz traveled to Montreal for the 1976 Olympic Games. Just five years after learning the sport, DeFrantz and the rest of the American team came in third place behind the East Germans and the Soviet Union in the Olympic debut of women's rowing. In the midst of Olympic training, DeFrantz applied to and enrolled in law school at the University of Pennsylvania. After graduating in 1977 and passing the bar exam, DeFrantz began practicing law representing children.

In October 1977, DeFrantz participated in her first of many changes involving the Olympic Committee. She and three other Olympians were summoned to testify regarding the rights of athletes. Their testimony helped produce the Amateur Sports Act of 1978, which restructured the way Olympic sports are governed in the United States.

While a bronze medal in the Olympics is nothing short of an amazing accomplishment, DeFrantz hoped to return to the 1980 Olympics and capture the gold. Her participation with the national team kept her in tiptop shape while simultaneously fulfilling her professional career as a lawyer. DeFrantz worked for a public interest law firm in Philadelphia that protected children before taking a year off in 1979 to focus on what would be her last Olympic opportunity. To DeFrantz's dismay, then-President Jimmy Carter announced in January 1980 that the United States planned to boycott the 1980 Olympics in Moscow because of the Soviet invasion of Afghanistan.

As a lawyer, DeFrantz immediately knew she and her teammates had rights as athletes. She did not want to stand by and watch President Carter strip away the athletes' Olympic dreams. DeFrantz believed the Olympics were pure of political confrontations between countries and that a boycott represented the exact opposite of the Olympic ideology. DeFrantz had been a member of the USOC's Athletes Advisory Council since her Olympic debut in 1976. She and other members pleaded with the USOC to defy President Carter's order and eventually filed suit to allow them the opportunity to compete. DeFrantz knew the USOC could enter a team regardless of President Carter's suggestions. Despite this, the Carter administration's threat to ruin the USOC's funding was taken seriously enough that DeFrantz, her teammates, and every other 1980 Olympic hopeful would have to wait another four more years.

Until the boycott decision was official in April 1980, DeFrantz continued to train, hoping for the best. She had become the face and name connected with the opposition to Carter's position and the associated unpatriotic accusations left her very unpopular, making her the recipient of disturbing hate mail. Though the suit was lost, DeFrantz's fight for athletes' rights was just beginning.

While the opposition DeFrantz presented made her disliked by many, she certainly attracted notice, not all of which was negative. In 1981, Peter Ueberroth hired her on the management team of the 1984 Summer Olympic Games scheduled to take place in Los Angeles. Ueberroth asked her to serve the Los Angeles Olympic Organizing Committee as liaison with the African nations and as chief administrator of the Olympic Village. DeFrantz is credited with helping to save the 1984 Summer Games by preventing African nations from boycotting after South African runner Zola Budd was allowed to run for Great Britain because her grandfather was British. At the time, apartheid had led to an international boycott of South African sports, which would have prevented Budd from competing at the Olympics. DeFrantz had the necessary credibility because she had actively opposed apartheid and had worked with Richard Lapchick and the American Coordinating Committee for Equality in Sport and Society (ACCESS) to keep South Africa out of international sports contests. Lapchick, who became a lifelong friend, calls Anita "one of sport's greatest leaders and heroes. She always stands up for justice." She has had many opportunities to do so.

DeFrantz was named vice president for the newly created Amateur Athletic Foundation (AAF) of Los Angeles, which was established from $93 million of the $230 million profit the 1984 Games produced. In 1987, she became president of the AAF, which has since changed its name to The LA84 Foundation. During the previous year, the International Olympic Committee (IOC) was looking to fulfill a

Courtesy of Anita DeFrantz.

1976 Montreal Olympics.

lifetime position and found 34-year-old DeFrantz. Her appointment makes her a voting member of the IOC until the age of 80, when the position will become honorary in 2032. DeFrantz is one of two Americans to represent the United States and was the first woman and the first African-American to do so. DeFrantz finally gained the platform necessary to make her case for athletes' rights.

In 1988, DeFrantz spoke out against the injustice she witnessed at the Olympic Games. Canadian Ben Johnson tested positive for performance-enhancing drugs after running the 100-meter dash in 9.79 seconds. DeFrantz refused to shy away from the controversy and spoke out publicly to fight for pure, drug-free Olympic competitions. Eight years and two Olympic Games later, DeFrantz continued to fight for clean sports by preventing the Atlanta Committee for the Olympic Games from using less expensive and not as concise drug testing methods for the 1996 Atlanta Games.

As a member of the IOC, DeFrantz made an impact fighting for athletes' rights and the purity of the Games. Yet, her commitment and intelligence made her worthy of a position with the IOC that exhibits more power. From 1992 until 2001, DeFrantz sat on the executive board and in 1997 she accomplished a feat no female had successfully done in the past—DeFrantz was named one of the four vice presidents of the IOC serving a four-year term. In the history of the IOC, which dates back to 1894, no woman had never held such a prestigious position.

DeFrantz, whose high school did not offer team sports for girls, has worked tirelessly to provide opportunities for underprivileged youth, ensuring opportunities exist for males and females alike. The LA84 Foundation is committed to the eight counties of Southern

California, but focuses mainly on Los Angeles. And while no child is turned away, special emphasis is placed on girls, ethnic minorities, those physically challenged and developmentally disabled, and other underserved community members. DeFrantz knows sports can change lives and bring many social and physical opportunities to children. Nonetheless, she is realistic with the children, informing them of their slim chances in becoming professional athletes and encouraging them to focus on their education. DeFrantz believes this message should also be carried by the coaches and has committed the LA84 to a special coaching education program since 1985. In its first 25 years of existence, DeFrantz has led the LA84 in its endeavors, committing more than $185 million to accomplish its mission that has benefitted 2 million boys and girls, more than 1,000 youth sports organizations, and trained over 50,000 coaches in Southern California.[1]

DeFrantz is active in several youth, sport, and legal organizations, including Kids in Sports, the NCAA Leadership Advisory Board, the Juvenile Law Center, The Knight Foundation Commission on Intercollegiate Athletics, the Institute for International Sport, and FISA (the International Rowing Federation). DeFrantz also sits on several different Olympic committees, utilizing her historic position to the fullest.

In 2004, then First Lady of California, Maria Shriver, created The Minerva Awards in an effort to honor women for their humanity and commitment to service. Shriver named the Awards after the Roman goddess portrayed on the California State Seal who represents both a warrior and a peacemaker. Shriver chose four special women whose stories she believed would inspire others in the community, state, and nation. Fittingly, DeFrantz was a 2005 recipient of The Minerva Awards.

The great-great-granddaughter of a Louisiana plantation owner and one of his slaves, Anita DeFrantz has proven herself to be a true leader. She has achieved many firsts, both for her family and for our nation. This internationally-known figure has put so many before herself persistently. She truly is a warrior and a peacemaker.

Note

1. LA84 Foundation About Us, "Mission: Life Ready Through Sport," LA84 Foundation, http://www.la84foundation.org/who/who_frmst.htm, January 25, 2010.

Ernestine Bayer

Barrier Breaker

by Jessica Bartter Duffaut

Competitive sport opportunities for women in the 1920s and 30s were scarce, and participation in recreational sports was generally discouraged. In 1928, the Olympics sponsored a mere three sports for women: track and field, swimming, and gymnastics. In 1931, Major League Baseball Commissioner Judge Kenesaw Mountain Landis banned women from professional baseball. In 1933, softball was as much of a man's sport as it was a woman's. Female involvement in sport was limited to sitting in the stands. Women were expected to remain on the sidelines and cheer for their men. Fortunately, the 1930s were also a time for pioneers; a handful of brave women entered uncharted territory to play the games—that until then—they could only watch. Ernestine Bayer was one such pioneer.

Ernestine Bayer met the love of her life in 1927 when she was 18 years old. His name was Ernest, and coincidentally, they were both often called Ernie. Ernest and Ernestine eloped in 1928 and kept their marriage a secret for almost nine months. Ernest was an oarsman and was training for the 1928 Olympic Games. Rowing in the 1928 Olympics was limited to men. The sport even condemned marriage, suggesting that men lost their strength and devotion to rowing after getting hitched. Thus, Ernest and Ernestine kept their marriage a secret to avoid hurting Ernest's Olympic chances.

Ernestine watched her husband train on the Schuylkill River in Philadelphia. Ernest trained as hard as ever and earned his spot on the coxless-four crew American team. He traveled to Amsterdam aboard the SS *Roosevelt* to represent his country in the 1928 Games. After defeating Italy in the semi-finals, the American team lost the gold medal to Great Britain. When he returned home, silver medal in hand, the Bayers announced their marriage.

After watching her husband train day after day for years, Ernestine noticed a woman take a boat out on the river and row on her own. This was highly frowned upon, particularly among many male rowers, but it inspired Ernestine. She wondered why more women did not row. Ernestine did not wonder long before she decided to take action. Ernestine asked Ernie if she, too, could give rowing a try, to which he informed her that women simply do not row. But she persisted and he eventually let her take his boat out for herself. She recalled that a majority of his male rowing friends and team-mates "wouldn't speak to him" after that, and, "When they did talk, they'd tell him girls had no right to be out on the river rowing."[1]

Soon thereafter, Ernestine was determined to turn this recreational sport into a competitive option for women. Thus, she founded the Philadelphia Girl's Rowing Club in 1938, the first women's rowing organization in the country. Just two years prior, Sally Sterns became the first woman coxswain of a male rowing team at Rollins College. Now Sterns and thousands of other women would have new opportunities for women's teams thanks to Ernestine Bayer. Her pivotal action has led many to consider Ernestine the mother of women's rowing.

Ernestine organized races at the Philadelphia Girl's Rowing Club and in 1939 won the Independence Day Race on the Schuylkill River in a coxless-two-seater. In the 1940s and 50s, she competed in every event she was allowed to enter. As her grew older, Ernestine continued to compete in masters rowing tournaments. In 1992 at the age of 83, Bayer won the Head of Charles of the women's veteran singles. At the age of 86, Ernestine set a world indoor rowing record for women ages 80–89 with a time of 11:14.0. With her handicap, she finished well ahead of all but two of her competitors in the 60 and over age group. While many of her competitors were young enough to be children of hers, her real daughter, Tina Bayer, sat cheering in the stands pushing her mother through the last grueling moments.[2] It is no surprise that Ernest and Ernestine's daughter Tina shared their love for rowing. Together, they traveled the world watching and competing in the sport they loved.

Women's rowing was finally debuted in the 1976 Montreal Olympic Games. Ernestine was asked to sit on the first U.S. Women's Olympic Committee. While she was already a legend to many, Ernestine's place in sporting history was secured after the establishment of Olympic rowing. She was the first women to be inducted into the National Rowing Hall of Fame in 1984. Ernestine says the thrill of her life was being asked to fill the No. 2 seat of the 1984 Olympic Gold Medal Women's Eight.

In 1997, Ernestine lost the love of her life and partner in her journey to establish rowing. Ernestine spread Ernest's ashes on the Schuylkill where they had enjoyed so many peaceful days on the water. Yet, Ernestine's passion for rowing remained and she was crowned World Masters Champion in 2000. Ernestine went on to organize and win countless races into her early 90s.

U.S. Rowing renamed their Woman of the Year Award as the Ernestine Bayer Award because of her outstanding contributions to rowing. Each year, the Award is given to another woman who demonstrates Ernestine Bayer's dedication, determination, and love for rowing.

The seemingly-ageless athlete suffered a stroke in 2003. Her strong will and competitive spirit helped her recover enough to return to the water, rowing in a double. But in July of 2005, Ernestine suffered a second stroke that left her paralyzed on one side and unable to speak. The rowing world and female athletes of every sport lost a heroic pioneer on September 10, 2006 when Ernestine Bayer died from complications with pneumonia at the age of 97.

Notes

1. Richard Goldstein, "Ernestine Bayer, 97, Pioneer in Rowing, Dies," *The New York Times*, September 29, 2006.

2. Amy Nutt, "Going nowhere fast," *Sports Illustrated*, January 27, 1997.

Dr. Donna Lopiano

Barrier Breakers

by Jessica Bartter Duffaut

Courtesy of Donna Lopiano.

There are many important benefits for young girls who participate in sports, yet there are counter pressures in our society that discourage young girls from being strong and active. For years, marketers have pushed a girly, subordinate demeanor of women, discouraging young girls from being tough and independent. Donna Lopiano ignored such pressures as a child. While many young girls growing up in the 1950s and 1960s viewed sport as a man's game and preferred to watch, Lopiano could always be found playing with the boys. In fact, she did not even notice the difference between her and her neighborhood playmates until her gender denied her a spot on a Little League team that had actually recruited her at age 11.

For the previous six years, she had spent hours after school perfecting her baseball pitches against the side of her family's house. She idolized Mickey Mantle, Whitey Ford, and Don Drysdale, and dreamt of pitching for the New York Yankees.[1] When she was lined up at the field to get her uniform, another Little Leaguer's father pulled out the rule book and demanded Lopiano be taken off the team because the rules stated that no girls were allowed. That very team went on to win the Little League World Series without her.

Lopiano was hurt by the exclusion and the subsequent pain drove her to work even harder toward success. She did not appreciate being told she could not pursue her dream and has worked tirelessly over the past four decades to prevent the same from happening to other young, impressionable girls.

Until she was old enough to stand up for the injustices in women's sports, Lopiano was forced to conform to the standard that males play baseball and females play softball. Lopiano learned to execute her powerful pitches with an underhand release and quickly excelled on the softball mound. In 1963, Lopiano was discovered by the Raybestos Brakettes, an amateur softball team for whom she played until 1972. During her 10 seasons, Lopiano earned All-American honors nine times and was named MVP three times. Her force from the mound led to a .910 winning percentage with 183 games won and just 18 games lost. In 817 innings pitched she struck out 1,633 opponents at the plate. A force at the plate herself, Lopiano twice led her team in batting average with .316 and .367. In addition to sharpening her softball skills, her career with the Brakettes provided her with the opportunity to travel and explore other parts of the world. By the time she was 18, she had already toured France, Hong Kong, India, and Australia playing the game she loved.[2]

One of the most amazing aspects of Lopiano's amateur softball career is that it spanned over her high school, collegiate, and post-graduate educations. In between long practices, intense training, international travel, and national championships, Lopiano managed to graduate from Stamford High School, Southern Connecticut State University with a bachelor's degree in physical education, and the University of Southern California, where she earned her master's and doctoral degrees. Lopiano's career as a Raybestos Brakette also did not interfere with her success on the field hockey, volleyball, and basketball teams. Including her amateur career, she played in 26 national championships in the four sports. The success she earned as an athlete led her to coaching positions for collegiate men's and women's volleyball, women's basketball, and women's softball programs.

At just 28 years old, Lopiano was hired by the University of Texas at Austin, as the director of intercollegiate athletics for women. Her energetic attitude and high standards appealed to the selection committee. Lopiano put pressure on the coaches both on and off the field. In her first 10 years, she went through 16 coaches in eight different sports. She made it clear to her staff that winning was a priority as well as education. Lopiano warned coaches that their jobs depended on whether or not their teams were top 10 programs. Lopiano also stressed that their jobs were equally dependent on the success their student-athletes achieved in the classroom. Within the first year that she began holding her coaches accountable for their student-athletes' academic performance, the athletic department's mean SAT score increased by 100 points. During her 17 years at UT Austin, the

Longhorns graduated 95 percent of its women athletes who completed their athletic eligibility. Athletically, Lopiano's Longhorns were equally successful. Eighteen National Championships (Association for Intercollegiate Athletics for Women [AIAW] and National Collegiate Athletic Association [NCAA]), 62 Southwest Conference Championships, more than 300 All-Americans, and over a dozen Olympians made Lopiano's women's program a dominant one in collegiate athletics. Her program's success was a direct result of her philosophy—that money and coaches were the two key ingredients for a collegiate program. Lopiano believed that if she adequately funded the program then she could attract the best coaches who would accept her demands, athletically and academically.[3] By attracting the best coaches, Lopiano predicted the best athletes would follow. Lopiano developed her department's budget from $57,000 in 1975 to almost $3 million in 1987.[4]

While the short-term numbers prove Lopiano's success, she made great strides for women's sports in the long run. A pioneer for her time, Lopiano has served females everywhere with her advocacy for Title IX of the Education Amendments of 1972, a federal law that prohibits discrimination on the basis of sex in all education programs and activities receiving federal funds. Title IX is commonly referred to for its impact on sports, but it also pertains to drama, band, and other extracurricular student activities. Title IX is credited with increasing female involvement in sport more than tenfold. In 1970, only one in every 27 high school girls played varsity sports compared to one in every 2.5 girls 30 years later. Title IX has led to increased funding and support for women's sports, bringing the ratio of girls playing much closer to the ratio of boys in sports, which is equal to one in every two. Lopiano was instrumental in implementing Title IX at UT Austin, pushing equal rights for women, something she was denied in her youth.[5]

Lopiano moved to the Women's Sports Foundation (WSF) in April of 1992 to continue her advocacy for female athletes' rights. The WSF is a 501(c)(3) nonprofit organization that was founded in 1974 by tennis legend Billie Jean King to advance the lives of girls and women through sports and physical activity. The Foundation's programs, services, and initiatives are dedicated to participation, education, advocacy, research, and leadership for women's sports.

In her 15 years as executive director, Lopiano secured funding for girls' and women's sport programs and educated the public and corporations about the importance of women's health and gender equality in sport. Lopiano believes the 1996 Summer Olympics was a celebration of Title IX, showing the first generation of success stories in gymnast Kerri Strug, sprinter Gail Devers, softball player Dot Richardson, swimmer Amy Van Dyken, and basketball player Lisa Leslie who all took home gold medals. Young girls everywhere suddenly had female role models in the sports world despite the lack of professional athletic opportunities for females in the United States. Individuals and parents under the age of 40 are also of the Title IX generation and have been a major influence on children, according to Lopiano, by encouraging both sons and daughters to participate in sports.

The Sporting News named Lopiano one of "The 100 Most Influential People in Sports"; *College Sports* magazine ranked her among "The 50 Most Influential People in College Sports"; *Ladies Home Journal* named her one of "America's 100 Most Important Women"; and she was named as one of the century's greatest sportswomen by *Sports Illustrated Women*. She is an inductee of the National Sports Hall of Fame, the National Softball Hall of Fame, and the Texas Women's Hall of Fame. In honor of her many contributions to women in athletics at the University of Texas, the crew team christened the Varsity Eight shell "Donna A. Lopiano" in April 2005. Lopiano sat on the United States Olympic Committee's executive board for many years and was awarded the 2005 International Olympic Committee (IOC) Women and Sport Trophy. Since 2000, the IOC Women and Sport Trophy has been awarded annually to a person or organization in recognition of their outstanding contributions to developing, encouraging, and strengthening the participation of women and girls in physical and sports activities, in coaching, and in administrative, journalism, and media positions.

In August 2007, Lopiano announced her retirement from the Women's Sports Foundation. In 2008, she founded Sports Management Resources (SMR), a consulting firm specializing in educational sport. As president of SMR, Lopiano is helping athletics directors solve integrity, growth, and development challenges in their respective athletics departments. A champion athlete in her own right,

Donna Lopiano is similarly considered a champion of equal opportunity for women in sports. Her educational advocacy of ethical conduct garnering gender equality in sports made Lopiano a pioneer whose bravado, intelligence, and determination have left an everlasting—and feminine—effect on American sports.

Notes

1. Alexander Wolff, "Prima Donna: Women's Athletic Director Donna Lopiano Has Taken the Bull by the Horns at Texas," *Sports Illustrated*, December 17, 1990.

2. Ibid.

3. Ibid.

4. Texas Woman's University, "Texas Women's Hall of Fame: Donna Lopiano," http://www.twu.edu/twhf/tw-lopiano.htm, August 18, 2004 (accessed July 27, 2005).

5. Women's Sports Foundation, "Title IX and Race in Intercollegiate Sport," http://www.womenssportsfoundation.org/cgi-bin/iowa/issues/disc/article.html?record=955, June 23, 2003 (accessed April 2, 2008).

Nancy Lieberman

Barrier Breakers

by Brian Wright

At the tender age of seven, Nancy Lieberman knew that she would make athletic history. Born into the basketball-crazed city of Brooklyn, New York, Lieberman developed a deep love and passion for the game. Her talents on the court were discovered at an early age, but due to the negative stereotypes about women's sports, Lieberman was often discouraged from participating. Women and girls were discouraged from playing competitive sports, and those who decided to play sports were perceived as a "tomboys." As a child, Lieberman's mother had gone as far as to puncture one of her basketballs in an attempt to discourage Lieberman from pursuing her aspirations. Although these stereotypes challenged Lieberman's goals of becoming a professional basketball player, they never discouraged her, as she was confident that she would make history in sports.

Lieberman disregarded all the negative feedback she received about playing sports and continued to develop her skills. She took her game to the outdoor courts and gyms of Harlem and competed with some of the best young players in the city. Lieberman did not only compete with the boys, she dominated them. She developed a knack for the game along with a rugged and tough style of play which differentiated her from other players in the city. Playing hard and tough became second nature for Lieberman. Standing at 5-foot-10, Lieberman was able to tower over her smaller opponents and use her physical style of play to outmatch and overpower them. In her sophomore year of high school Lieberman earned a reputation around New York City as one of the best basketball players in the city and was invited to the ABAUSA's National Team Trials. This trial invitation was unprecedented in women's basketball due to her young age but her amazing talent was too attractive for the team to pass up. As a 15-year-old high school student, Lieberman earned one of the prestigious 12 team member spots and was named to the USA National Team. Lieberman would continue her basketball success in the years to come, helping the USA National Team win gold and silver medals in the World Championships and Pan American Games of 1975 and 1979, respectively. On the first ever women's Olympic basketball team, Lieberman contributed a great deal to her team's silver medal performance and was the youngest basketball player in Olympic history to ever win a medal. Lieberman had competed at the highest levels of international basketball competition at age 18, even before she ever set foot on a college campus.

Lieberman chose Old Dominion University to pursue her higher education. Lieberman, or "Lady Magic" as she was often called for her flashy passes and brilliant scoring drives, continued to amaze spectators while performing in college. At Old Dominion, Lieberman helped the women's basketball program grow into a national powerhouse. She led them to a National Women's Invitational Tournament Championship in 1977, and back-to-back AIAW National Championships in 1978 and 1979. In her final two seasons at Old Dominion, Lieberman and company achieved a 72-2 record. She was a two-time winner of the Wade Trophy which honors the nation's best women's basketball performer for their academic achievement, community service, and on-court performances, along with the Broderick Award, honoring the nation's best collegiate female athlete. Lieberman was honored with both of these awards in consecutive years, which is a feat still unmatched today in women's collegiate athletics. Upon graduating from college, Lieberman was regarded not only as one of the best female athletes to ever play college basketball, but also as one of the best collegiate basketball players ever on a men's or women's team.

Lieberman hoped to play on the U.S. women's team in the 1980 Olympics in Moscow, but a boycott by President Jimmy Carter and the USA Olympic teams would deny her this opportunity. Though disappointed, Lieberman agreed with the decision to withdraw from the Games because of the Soviet Union's invasion into Afghanistan. In 1980, Lieberman entered the Women's Basketball League (WBL) draft and was selected by the Dallas Diamonds. In her first season with the Diamonds, Lieberman led them to their first and only Championship series appearance. Though the Diamonds would eventually lose the five-game series, Lieberman had made her mark on the league and franchise.

In an effort to help another female activist for the advancement of women's sports, Lieberman took a leave of absence from the Diamonds to become a personal trainer to tennis great Martina Navratilova. Through the demanding physical workouts by Lieberman and the tennis instruction from received from Renee Richards, Navratilova's game took off and she regained her ranking as the #1 female tennis player in the world. She returned to the Diamonds in the 1984 season as a member of the newly formed Women's American Basketball Association (WABA). In the 1984–85 WABA season Lieberman led the team to the Championship while earning Most Valuable Player honors, averaging 27 points per game. Lieberman was again leading by example in excellence on the court for women playing at the highest level of sport. Lieberman deeply desired to show women, young and old, that they could make a good living in sports. In 1986, Lieberman made history once again by becoming the first woman to join a men's professional basketball team. She joined the Springfield Fame of the United States Basketball League (USBL), and played an entire season with them before leaving to play for the Long Island Knights the following season. In 1988, Lieberman made her final move as she joined the Washington Generals on a World Tour with the storied Harlem Globetrotters. Such sports career decisions were unprecedented thus far, and played a very significant role in promoting the visibility of women playing professional sports in the United States.

In 1988, Lieberman became the color commentator for NBC during the Olympic Games in Seoul, Korea. Lieberman covered the women's Olympic basketball team on their way to winning a second gold medal. Lieberman would later go on to write two books, one on her life story as an athlete, and the other on the evolution of women's basketball with Robin Roberts of ESPN and ABC.

As a player Lieberman was a pioneer for women's sports. As an analyst at the Olympic Games Lieberman promoted women's sports and, in 1993, she was rewarded by becoming the first woman inducted into the New York City Basketball Hall of Fame. Not long after, Lieberman was inducted into the Naismith Basketball Hall of Fame for her great accomplishments on the court. In 1997, with the conception of the Women's National Basketball Association (WNBA), Lieberman felt that this was the league that she had dreamt of as a child and she wanted to be a part of the inaugural season. At age 38, Lieberman decided to return to the court and take part in the historical opening season of the WNBA. Lieberman trained and was the 15th overall selection in the WNBA draft by the Phoenix Mercury.

Lieberman entered the season as the oldest player in the League, but her experience and leadership on and off the court paid dividends for the Mercury as she helped lead them to the regular season Western Conference Championship and the semi-finals of the WNBA playoffs. The home fan attendance of the Mercury also was evidence of Lieberman's ability to attract fans to women's sports just as she had done her entire life. The Mercury achieved a league high average of 13,000 fans per game.

In 1998, Lieberman decided to move into a front office executive position of General Manager and Head Coach of the expansion WNBA Detroit Shock franchise. Lieberman was very successful in this endeavor as well leading the Shock to a winning record in its first season, as well as a coveted trip to the WNBA playoffs. Throughout her illustrious career as an athlete, analyst, coach, and executive, Lieberman has been very successful not only for herself but for the advancement of women's sports as a whole. The growth of women's sports, particularly basketball, can be directly linked to her courage and desire to achieve more for women within the world of sports.

On July 24, 2008, Nancy Lieberman shockingly signed a seven-day contract with WNBA team the Detroit Shock. At age 50, Lieberman broke her own prior record of the oldest player to play in a WNBA game.[1] On August 13, 2008 Lieberman was part of an inaugural class inducted into the Hampton Road Sports Hall of Fame honoring athletes, coaches, and administrators who made contributions to Southeast Virginia. Continuing with her theme of breaking down barriers for women in basketball, on November 4, 2009 Lieberman was hired to be head coach the National Basketball Development League (NBDL) affiliate of the Dallas Mavericks. Lieberman is the first female to ever serve as a head coach in the NBDL.

Through her lifetime of success on the court, as well as her commitment to women's sports off the court, Lieberman has fulfilled her early age promise of making history in sports.

Note

1. "Basketball Hall of Famer Nancy Lieberman Makes History with On-Court Appearance with Detroit Shock," PR Newswire. July 25, 2008, http://www.highbeam.com/doc/1G1-181796566.html, (accessed February 27, 2010).

Annie Boucher

Barrier Breaker

by Jessica Bartter Duffaut

A student-athlete with nine years of competitive playing experience in their sport may be considered a seasoned veteran, ready for the challenges of the college elite. And if the student-athlete was a self-taught, 44-year-old mother and grandmother who did not begin playing until the age of 37, those nine years of experience would certainly come in handy.

Annie Boucher, a Jamaican native, moved to New York City in her early 20s with her daughter Sandra. Day in and day out, Boucher worked hard, nine-to-five as a keypunch operator for Paine Webber, and 24 hours a day as a single parent raising her daughter. One summer day in 1978, a fit, confident woman dressed in tennis gear caught Boucher's eye. Boucher, attracted to the healthy persona portrayed by the stranger, stopped the woman to ask where she was headed. The stranger's answer compelled Boucher to run upstairs to her apartment, rummage through her closet for a tennis racket, and follow the woman to the neighborhood courts. The tennis racket, which she had purchased years prior for five dollars, finally got its first use on the court.

It only took six months of self-motivated practice for Boucher to make the finals of the neighborhood tennis tournament. There she met the "best female player in the neighborhood,"[1] Camille Bodden. Boucher took her opponent point-by-point and did not pay attention to the score, mainly because she did not know how to keep score in tennis. Her concentration was only broken when the score keeper, Camille Bodden's father, yelled at her to say, "You've won the match already; you don't have to serve anymore."[2] Boucher achieved the first of many goals tennis had now presented to her.

Boucher continued her hard work and practice after her day job and on weekends for several years. Encouraged by her daughter's marriage and the support of other tennis companions, Boucher earned her GED in 1986 through an adult education center in Queens. Boucher had previously dropped out of high school in her homeland of Jamaica before going to England to attend nursing school. But before she was certified, Boucher became pregnant and after four years on her own, relocated to New York City.

Realizing a new avenue in life, Boucher continued to pursue her education and enrolled in Queensborough Community College. Ready to take her academics seriously once and for all, Boucher was reluctant to participate in extracurricular activities including her new passion, tennis. Yet, the classes proved to be easy enough for Boucher to handle and she joined the tennis team that fall. In fact, Boucher also joined the basketball team in the winter and the softball team in the spring. Boucher enjoyed early success at Queensborough. She was quickly named captain of the tennis team and went undefeated at the No. 1 singles and doubles position with a 9-0 record. The 44-year old was an instant star, stunning many in the stands and her opponents.

In academia, Boucher found the subject of psychology to be her calling. Facing a challenging academic load, she decided to put her athletics on hold for a year. Eventually, like every student-athlete must inevitably learn, Boucher realized she could once again balance the academics with athletics and joined the tennis team in her third year at Queensborough. As if she had never left, she repeated her undefeated run at No. 1 singles and doubles until the final match of the season. During that match, up 5-0, 4-0, she broke her ankle as she chased down her opponent's shot. The pins and screws needed to repair her ankle ended her athletic career at Queensborough. But they did not prevent her from winning Team MVP honors and the Queensborough's Outstanding Female Athlete award. And like a true student-athlete, Boucher was most pleased with her 3.2 GPA.

Inspired by her new found love for psychology, Boucher enrolled in a four-year university to continue her studies and complete her degree. At Alfred University, Boucher was also able to continue her athletic excellence. In her first year of competition since the ankle injury, Boucher went 3-4, helping the team to a 3-4 record. The next year, Boucher earned an impressive 9-1 record, assisting the Saxons with an undefeated season, a first for Alfred University tennis. To keep her skills sharp, she often practiced with the men's tennis team during the off-season.

After graduating from Alfred University in 1992 with a bachelor's degree in psychology, Boucher moved to Jamaica, New York where she resides with her husband, Chet Turnquest. The couple have a daughter, Sandra Nkrumah and a grandson, Haki Nkrumah. Haki followed his grandmother to Alfred University where he played tennis as well.

Boucher jumped over many hurdles to achieve such great accomplishments, but the most remarkable impact has been on her opponents and fellow student-athletes who were nothing but inspired when meeting her, despite the fact that she most likely beat them. Her story reinforces the saying "better late than never" and proves that with desire and commitment, age is irrelevant to success.

Notes

1. Stephanie Scheer, "Grandma's on the varsity," *Sports Illustrated*, December 16, 1991.

2. Ibid.

Lee Elder

Barrier Breaker

by Jessica Bartter Duffaut

In 1975, it had been 29 years since Kenny Washington integrated the National Football League, 28 years since Jackie Robinson integrated Major League Baseball, and 25 years since Nat "Sweetwater" Clifton integrated the National Basketball Association. In each case, their historic achievements could not have been possible without help from others. Dan Reeves signed Washington, Branch Rickey signed Robinson, and Joe Lapchick signed Clifton. But nobody with ample power had spoken out enough against the injustices of country club practices and the game of golf remained segregated for many years after the other major leagues opened their doors. In 1962, Charlie Sifford became the first African-American to play on the Professional Golfers' Association (PGA) of America Tour. But golf remained a game of tradition and invitation only events and the most prestigious tournament, The Masters, excluded whomever they wished, particularly African-Americans. The Masters has been held at the Augusta National Golf Course in Georgia since 1934 and kept all-white for over 40 years until a man named Lee Elder stepped up to the tee box for the first time, leading the way for change.

Elder was introduced to golf as a nine-year old when he began caddying to earn money for food. His love for golf grew as a teenager when he got a job as a caddy for Alvin C. Thompson. While Thompson had the skills to succeed on the PGA Tour, the possible earnings were not nearly as high as the money he earned, challenging golfers on courses across the country. As a black man, Elder was not permitted in many of the country clubs where he caddied, so he negotiated competitions for Thompson with other caddies out in the caddyshack. Often, Thompson bet that he and his caddy could beat any two golfers at a club and they usually did. Elder picked up many pointers from Thompson and could drive the ball a great distance. He even snuck onto the back holes of a segregated course in Dallas, Texas where he caddied most often to practice with clubs he borrowed from a course manager. Despite Elder's ability to drive impressive yardage, he believed he could make more money as a caddy than as a golfer with the United Golf Association, the all-black golf tour.

Elder later joined the Army where he earned acclaim for his golf skills. In 1961, in his late twenties, Elder finally joined the United Golf Association and dominated the tour, making a name for himself. Six years later, Elder joined the PGA to compete on the tour. Pete Brown and Charlie Sifford had won on the tour, yet neither were invited or voted by past Champions to play in the most prestigious golf event, The Masters. Presumably, the lack of opportunities was upholding the long-standing tradition of whites only at Augusta National. Finally in 1972, The Masters Tournament began automatically inviting all PGA Tour winners, opening the door for a new face in the game of golf.[1]

Sadly, in a country built on apartheid, Elder was able to integrate golf in South Africa before doing so in the United States. In 1971, Elder was invited to play at the South African PGA Tournament, the first integrated tournament in South Africa. Though Elder wanted to make history, he wanted to make sure that it meant more than just a game. Elder agreed to golf in South Africa only after being assured that the gallery would be integrated and that he and his wife would be permitted to stay and go wherever they chose.[2] While he made monumental strides, Elder was not content with the social change he instigated in South Africa and was intent on seeing the same in the United States. And change he saw on April 21, 1974, when he sank an 18-foot putt on the fourth hole of a sudden death playoff to win the Monsanto Open in Pensacola, Florida, qualifying him for The Masters, the first African-American to do so. Elder was 40 years old in his first Masters Tournament when he shot a 74 and 78 on opening day, missing the cut by five shots. Yet, Elder won with the significance of the event. Elder made history by walking on the course in 1975. He returned to the Masters Tournament again in 1977 and every year until 1983. During that time, he made the cut twice. Though he never walked off the course with the prized green jacket, Elder carved a path for others to follow. At the time, Augusta National Golf Club had no members of color and did not for more than a decade following Elder's inaugural competition.[3]

Elder also became the first African-American to golf with the American team in the Ryder Cup in 1984. The Ryder Cup matches up the best American golfers with those of Europe, a competition that has been played every year since 1927.

Elder left the PGA Tour and in 1984 joined the Senior Tour where he dominated for years. Elder won the Suntree Senior Classic and the Hilton Head Seniors International in 1984, the Denver Post Championship, the Merrill Lynch/Golf Digest Commemorative, the Digital Seniors Classic and the Citizens Union Senior Golf Classic in 1985, and the Merrill Lynch/Golf Digest Commemorative in 1986 and the Gus Machado Classic in 1988.

Elder has been witness to too many injustices in his lifetime and does his best to take a stand whenever possible. He has spoken out against the lack of opportunities for women and minorities in golf. The Lee Elder National Junior Golf Program was started to promote the game to minority youth. The junior program taught basic instructions and golf etiquette to youth who, most likely, would not otherwise have the opportunity to play golf.[4] Elder remains troubled by the lack of people of color playing golf. Indeed, a lack of awareness and opportunity in golf for inner-city children keeps the percentage of those young people involved disturbingly low. Elder's program was developed to help lead the way and to increase the number of African-Americans teeing up on courses across the country. Lee Elder fought tirelessly to earn his spot in golf's history. The path he paved was long overdue but this pioneer's best reward is to see it followed over and over.

Notes

1. Rana L. Cash, "Lee Elder: 25 years ago a ground-breaking moment at Augusta," *Knight Ridder Tribune*, April 5, 2000.

2. "Lee Elder," West Virginia University, www.wvu.edu/~physed/blacksports/fall 2002/leeelder.htm, (accessed August 30, 2005).

3. Randall Mell, "Lee Elder said it's time for Augusta to change policy on women," *South Florida Sun-Sentinel*, September 17, 2002.

4. Jim Nelson, "Lee Elder National Junior Golf Program provides opportunities for area youth," *Indianapolis Recorder*, June 14, 1997.

Eddie Robinson

Barrier Breakers

by Richard Lapchick

Eddie Robinson's coaching career at Grambling State University in deep, rural Louisiana lasted through 11 presidents and three wars. Grambling was home to Coach and his wife, Doris, for 66 years. They were married that long and he coached for 56 years—all at the same institution! When he retired in November 1997, many people in America stood up and took note for the first time of the winningest coach in the history of college football. In the African-American community, he was very likely the best known coach in America and was surely the most beloved. However, institutionalized racial barriers kept Robinson a secret from most of white America outside of the world of sports. By the time he died in 2007, his passing had become a national day of mourning.

Initially a coach in a segregated society, Eddie Robinson helped football transcend race in the America he loved and treasured. I co-authored his autobiography in the hope that it would help Americans of every color and in every corner of our country discover the full meaning of the life of this great son of America. At a time when so many coaches and players seemed ready to extol their own virtues, Robinson was always reluctant to discuss any of his victories or records. I had to drag game stories out of him because he wanted to talk about his players and fellow coaches as men. He wanted to talk about life and philosophy, which was a pure pleasure for me to listen to. Nonetheless, getting him to talk about himself was very difficult.

In his autobiography, *Never Before, Never Again*, Coach Robinson wrote, "They said I would never be able to reach my third grade dream of coaching football. I saw a coach then, he looked so good and his boys seemed to worship him. The fact that he was their hero was written all over their faces. That was the life I wanted. Seventy years later I ended a 56-year ride as a college head coach!"[1]

He knew that life had changed dramatically in America. "I know life isn't easy for young people now. They face all these challenges that my generation didn't have. When I was growing up in Jackson and Baton Rouge, children weren't killing each other; crack didn't exist; I never heard of steroids; most families had a mother and father. Many of today's student-athletes were raised in poverty and despair. They know that some white people will decide who they are just because of what they look like. Yes, indeed, life is hard today."[2]

After achieving one of sports' most incredible records with his 400th win in 1995, Coach Eddie Robinson said, "I wish I could cut up all of these victories into 400 pieces and give them to all the players and assistant coaches I have had. They are the ones who truly deserve the credit."[3] Now that I know him, I see that these words were coming straight from his heart.

The stories about his retirement brought new exposure for Coach in communities where his messages of tradition, loyalty, family, and racial understanding are desperately needed. Eddie Robinson began to become a household name after every major newspaper and TV station featured him on multiple occasions throughout the 1997 season. Viewers and readers caught glimpses of his wisdom and his wit, finally revealing the genius of this great American leader who happened to be a coach and happened to be African-American.

Never a public crusader for civil rights, Coach courageously challenged racism in his own way by proving that a black man could be a great football coach, and simultaneously exhibit tenacity and determination as he led adolescents into manhood. Thirty years later, many of today's civil rights leaders hail Eddie Robinson's life in the same breath as that of Jackie Robinson's. The Reverend Jesse Jackson told me, "Eddie Robinson has always been a hero in my eyes. Without question, he is an ambassador for our people, not only African-Americans, but all of the Americans. That's why I have such respect for Coach Robinson."

In 1941, he assumed the role of mentor, role model, father, and counselor to his student-athletes both on and off the field. Grambling and college coaching were never the same. Nor were the thousands of young men who played for Coach Robinson. He guided the once obscure Grambling State Tigers to national and international acclaim while helping to produce championship teams and players. But it was never about just training athletes. Robinson believed that as a coach he had many more responsibilities than just teaching the mechanics of football. The career-related accomplishment of which Coach is proudest of is that 80 percent of his players graduated in a sport where the national average during his tenure had been less than 45 percent. At a time when most head coaches today delegate caring for student-athletes to assistants, Coach Robinson spent 56 years personally going into the athletic dorm with his now famous cow bell at 6:30 a.m. each weekday to be sure his men were awake and ready to go to class. Coach has proven the power of an individual to make a huge difference in the lives of young people. Some have gone on to become lawyers and doctors. Joseph B. Johnson became Grambling's president. Raymond Jetson became a Louisiana State Representative.

Coach Robinson helped motivate men at Grambling to succeed on and off the field. Under Robinson's leadership, Grambling became one of the most productive training camps for professional football; more than 300 of his players went to pro camps. More than 200 have made the active rosters in the NFL. Three have been inducted in the NFL Hall of Fame. Many of his former players have become coaches themselves. Several players were, like their coach, pioneers for African-American athletes: Tank Younger was the first player drafted from an historically black college; Buck Buchanan was the first African-American to be selected as the NFL's number one draft choice; James Harris was the first African-American starting quarterback; and Doug Williams was the first African-American quarterback to start and win a Super Bowl.

Of all of his accomplishments, he maintains that his greatest achievements are that he has had only one wife and one job for over 56 years. Robinson came to Grambling in 1941 just months after marrying Doris, his sweetheart since he was 14! The marriage was a great love story.

They held hands throughout six decades. I saw this whenever I was with them and it was moving. I was told on many occasions, "Listen, Rich, I have to go now to have lunch with Doris," or, "It's time for dinner with Doris." At first I thought he might just be tired from hours of talking to me. But then we would always pick it up at 10:00 p.m. and go until 1:00 a.m. For years I believed I didn't know any man who loved his wife as much as I did. I may have met him that first night with Coach.

In spite of the racial barriers that surrounded his life, Coach somehow maintained a positive attitude about opportunity in America for people of all colors. Coach said, "I'm just trying to be a good American . . . when the Man calls me up to Him, I want to be ready to answer the call . . . I want to hear God say, 'Eddie, you have been a good person, a good husband and father, a good friend, a good coach and a good American.' That would, in the end, be the best measure of my life if I live up to it."[4]

Looking back at the issue of race, Coach wrote, "We made extraordinary statements to break stereotypes: Buchanan was the first Grambling player picked in the first round of the NFL draft in 1963. Grambling won 17 SWAC championships and nine National Black Championships. The Howard Cosell documentary on Grambling in 1968 had black and white sports fans calling me a 'great football coach.' As we traveled across the South, we tried to use Grambling green (dollars) to quietly integrate hotels and restaurants. None of my players or coaches were seen at demonstrations in the 1960s. We made our own. The civil rights movement was helping to change the laws. Our goal was to help to change attitudes."[5]

When he was 18 and tried to buy a ticket for an LSU game in Baton Rouge, he was told they did not sell tickets to blacks. The language, of course, was not so polite. When Coach died in 2007, his body lay in state in Baton Rouge, the first African-American afforded that honor. Coach Robinson changed Louisiana and America.

I will never forget that 9.500 people attended his funeral at Grambling. I was honored to be one of nine people to give a eulogy. Willie Davis spoke before me. He asked all of Coach's players to stand. Nearly 2,000 men from the 1940s, 50s, 60s, 70s, 80s, and 90s stood tall. This was his legacy that after all these years, all these people wanted to come to this remote spot in deep rural Louisiana to thank their coach. Never before, never again.

In 2010, the Eddie Robinson Museum opened on a frigid winter day on Grambling's campus. I was happy to go there with my dear friend, Keith Lee. The Museum is a fitting tribute and captures the history so well. Now the children of those former players can come learn about the Coach their dads talked about.

Legendary Penn State Coach Joe Paterno talked of Robinson's historic contributions to the game of college football, "Nobody has ever done or will do what Eddie Robinson has done for this game. Our profession will never be able to repay Eddie Robinson for what he has done for the country and the profession of football."[6]

Muhammad Ali said, "They call me the greatest. I know that the greatest football coach who ever stepped foot on the field is Coach Robinson. I have admired what he has done in turning boys into men. He is a credit to sport and to humanity."[7]

Notes

1. Eddie Robinson with Richard Lapchick, *Never Before, Never Again*, (New York: St. Martin's Press, 1999), 2.
2. Ibid.
3. Ibid., 217.
4. Ibid, 252–53
5. Ibid., 5–6.
6. Ibid., back cover.
7. Ibid.

Muhammad Ali

Barrier Breakers

by Richard Lapchick

Considered brash and bold when he was young, Muhammad Ali became a messenger of peace for the United Nations. He was considered to be the athlete who most divided the races after he proclaimed allegiance to the Black Muslims and proclaimed that he would not go to Vietnam to fight. Ali has undoubtedly become the public figure who helps unite people across racial groups and makes people feel comfortable when they are in the presence of people who do not look like themselves.

Ali is a person of such personal magnitude that a 96,000-square foot Muhammad Ali Center was opened in the fall of 2005 in Louisville to commemorate the life of this giant. Ali captured the public's attention with his great athletic skills. By the time he was 18, he had won six Kentucky Golden Gloves Championships, two National Golden Gloves Championships and two National AAU titles. Barely 18, he won the gold medal in the 1960 Rome Olympics. In coming home, Ali faced the ugly reality of racism in America. After a public parade welcomed him back to Louisville, Ali went into a restaurant and was refused service.

With that as the backdrop, Ali trained hard to try to win the World Heavyweight Championship. Facing a menacing Sonny Liston as a 7-to-1 underdog, Cassius Clay upset the champion and took the title in 1964. Within 24 hours, he announced that he had become a member of the Nation of Islam and was changing his name from Cassius Clay to Cassius X. His polarization from the media and white America began. He soon took the name of Muhammad Ali.

Ali refused induction into the United States Army. He said he refused to fight, because, "I ain't got no quarrel with them Vietcong."[1] That action seemed to erect concrete barriers. He soon lost his boxing licenses all across America. Stripped of his championship, Ali was unable to fight for nearly three years. Ali became a spokesperson on college campuses against the war in Vietnam as it became more and more unpopular.

Ali won his case in the Supreme Court and his boxing career resumed. He beat Jerry Quarry in 1970 and then lost to Joe Frazier in 1971. In the meantime, the most heralded match of Ali's career, "The Rumble in the Jungle," was being prepared in Zaire against George Foreman, who came in as a 3-to-1 favorite. It was in this fight that Ali invented his famous "rope-a-dope" strategy that tired Foreman out and allowed Ali to beat Foreman and reclaim the championship. After winning the "Thrilla in Manila" in the third fight with Frazier, Ali, dancing on top of the world, was upset in a stunning match by Olympic champion Leon Spinks. Ali won the rematch becoming the only heavyweight to win the championship three times. Ali closed his long career which started at age 12 and ended at 39 with 56 victories, and only five defeats.

In retirement, Ali tirelessly traveled the world, winning friends and working for peace, serving as an ambassador for presidents to release hostages. Muhammad Ali has won the admiration of generations of people, even those who never saw him box. During this period, he met his fourth wife, Lonnie, who had lived nearby Ali when she was a child in Louisville. She has been his angel. Lonnie is always by his side and is his most loyal ally and best friend.

I have to relate some personal experiences with Ali whom I first met in the 1960s.

Ali was in Boston in 1997 when the verdict in the civil case of O.J. Simpson was rendered. At present, America's odyssey with and against O.J. Simpson may finally faded from view. But at that time it was red-hot and ugly. Almost simultaneously, the continued resurgent star of Muhammad Ali, which began with the opening ceremonies of the Olympics, seemed very much on the sports horizon. It is ironic that we have dealt in such personal depth in such different ways with two of our nation's greatest African-American athletes.

The publication of *Healing*, Ali's book with Thomas Hauser and the release of *When We Were Kings*, then a new documentary about Ali's historic "Rumble in the Jungle" in Zaire, brought Ali to city after city to talk about racial healing. In most cases, Lonnie Ali talked to the students assembled at each school. Gyms were packed with young people from elementary school through high school. They had all been prepared so they could understand what Muhammad Ali had done to make their principals and teachers so excited that Ali could actually be coming to their school. I was informed that students were drilled about his artistic boxing career, his stand against the Vietnam War and his work for civil rights of African-Americans. All were true and provided great perspective.

Whenever Muhammad Ali was sighted entering a gym, pandemonium broke out. Even children who didn't know the history were simply swept away by the stature and charisma of this man who has been slowed by Parkinson's syndrome but whose mind is as sharp as ever.

Moments built on one another to create a level of enthusiasm and anticipation that few students or their teachers had ever experienced. The first school was the Hennigan Elementary School. They had gifts for Ali, and one fifth grader had written a poem that he was "the greatest and not Ali." Ali called him forth and did an Ali Shuffle that not many believed he had in him. He has so many thoughts and emotions inside which he mostly expresses without words.

My then seven-year old, Emily, first met Ali when she was a very shy five-year old. She was standing with my wife, Ann, when Ali caught her eye from the other side of a table. This girl, who takes 15 to 20 minutes to warm up to friends she hadn't seen for a week, flew across the room and jumped into his open arms. That was 1995.

We went to dinner with the Ali family on the second night of his stay in Boston. It was Muhammad, Lonnie, their son Assad, Ann, Emily, noted photographer Howard Bingham, and Henry Louis Gates of Harvard's Afro-American Studies Department. We were the guests of the LoConte family at the great Italian eatery in Boston's North End, known simply as LoConte's.

It was early in the evening, which happened to be the night of President Clinton's State of the Union Address. The evening was so special to be with the Ali's that no one thought of trying to hear the President. Then a waiter came to our table to say that the jury was coming back with O.J. Simpson's civil case verdict. Professor Gates asked if there was a TV to watch the verdict. An old black and white set was promptly brought out.

I observed Ali as he watched intently, but without expression, as to what he hoped for in a verdict. Everything went against O.J.

this time. We turned the TV off and resumed the conversations around the table.

Ali drew a picture for Emily. She made him a valentine. Emily and Assad sent notes to each other. It was one of those nights that I know I will always remember.

I listened to the news on the way home. Commentators speculated that this new verdict would further divide the races in America as they said it had in the criminal case. I wondered how commentators were still blind to how huge the racial divide has been, with or without the O.J. Simpson case.

I thought long and hard that night about these two African-American men. Both had incredible athletic careers. Both became beloved by the public and crossed over racial lines. Simpson seemed to spend his life trying to prove that there was no divide between the races. Ali's legacy included standing up as a proud black man, emphasizing boldly—as no other athlete has done so forcefully—that race does matter.

It seems ironic that now one of them roams free but lives in disgrace in the eyes of the majority of Americans, accused of dividing the races. The other, who once was accused of dividing the races because he stood so tall as a black American, now brings people of all racial groups together by preaching "healing" and appealing to everyone, irrespective of race, religion, or age.

Ann and I went to the 2009 Major League Baseball Civil Rights Weekend in Cincinatti, where Muhammad was being honored. He looked tired. We wondered if he was slowing down at age 67. Then I had dinner with him and Lonnie in Phoenix in November and he looked great. He was charming, funny, and as sharp as ever. Lonnie said their travel schedule was as extensive as always. I was not surprised when Muhammad and Lonnie appealed for help for the Haitian victims of the earthquake on the concert to help raise funds for that horrible tragedy.

As a young boxer, Muhammad Ali called himself "The Greatest." Now the world calls him "The Greatest" more than five decades after he won his gold medal. Yes, Muhammad Ali is still "The Greatest." And he always will be in my book.

Note

1. Page 2 staff, "Significant moments in sports and war," http://espn.go.com/page2/s/list/warandsports.html, (accessed March 24, 2010).

Billy Mills

Barrier Breakers

by Stacy Martin-Tenney

Billy Mills is one of track and field's greatest heroes and his victory in the 10,000-meter final of the 1964 Tokyo Olympiad is one of the most inspiring stories of all time. Mills is not a hero for winning a race or a gold medal, although winning gold certainly took heroic efforts. He is a hero for what he endured prior to that race, how he won that race, and for the impact he has made on the global community since that race.

When Billy Mills toed the starting line at the Olympic final of the 10,000 meters, anxiousness, belief, and adrenaline accompanied him. He started those fateful 25 laps keeping up with the pack and progressing into a world record pace that favorite Ron Clarke of Australia had set, but soon he started to fall into the back of the pack with the slower runners. Billy Mills had a powerful belief in his ability during that race and it propelled him forward on the long, hard journey to catch the leaders. He exerted an exorbitant amount of energy on that journey, far more than he would have if he had been able to maintain the early pace and rhythm of the leaders. It was a true come from behind effort with an impressive level of determination and grit.

With only two laps to go, Mills was with Clarke and Tunisia's Mohammad Gammoudi. The bell rang to signify the final lap of the race. Mills and Clarke were running shoulder to shoulder with 400 meters to go. Mills was on the outside shoulder of Clarke, who was hugging lane one and pushing Mills away from him. Then Gammoudi surged through the hole Clarke created by pushing Mills, and further jostled Mills who was pushed all the way past lane three on the curve. Mills fell back into fourth place after he traversed four-lane widths back across the track toward Clarke and Gammoudi. Mills recounted, "Momentarily I was going to quit, but only because I empowered my mind over four years, 100 times a day, 1,000 times a week— visualizing imagery that at one moment in time, the body, mind and spirit worked as one—I couldn't quit." [1] He began fighting against self-doubt and disbelief in order to win.

Soon, Mills passed the third place runner and began to close on Clarke, who was attempting to pass Gammoudi. The memorable broadcaster, Dick Banks, shouted, "And here comes Billy Mills!"[2] Mills came off the curve into the final stretch and overtook Clarke and Gammoudi to win Olympic Gold in the 10,000 meters. His efforts on his final lap resulted in a 59.8 second split despite the jockeying for lane position that brought his winning time to 28 minutes and 24.4 seconds—a new Olympic Record at that time. At last, his dream had come true; his vision became reality. "At that one fleeting moment in time, you're the very best in the world. You can't describe it. You feel it. I hope someday everybody has the opportunity to reach within himself or herself and pull out a very special gift that they have and fulfill it," he said.[3]

Billy Mills is an Oglala Lakota (Sioux) Native American and he was not only the first Native American to win the Olympic Gold in the 10,000 meters, but also the first and only American to win the 10,000-meter race in any Olympic competition.

Mills' come-from-behind win was awe-inspiring, but the true testament was his resiliency. Shortly after the 1964 Games, the emergence of African nation dominance in distance running began and still owns the sport today. Mills was not a favorite, in fact, he ran in borrowed shoes because team officials only supplied shoes to athletes whom they had deemed potential winners. A reporter asked Ron Clarke after the race if he was worried about Mills from the beginning and Clarke was quoted, "Worry about him? I never even heard of him."[4]

Mills might have appeared to be an upset but in his own mind—he had planned to win this race all along. Mills employed the same techniques that are touted today to train his mind for that race—visualization, journaling, and believing that one will achieve their goals. Some may have said it was a lucky guess, but Mills planned to win at Tokyo, and he planned to run a 28:25:00. He knew he was a world-class runner—the rest of the world just didn't know yet. He had to overcome a two-minute barrier to achieve this goal, so he set out measurable goals and determined that he would improve each lap in order to make up the two-minute deficit in Tokyo. He achieved his goal. After Tokyo, he continued racing and continued on his path to set the world record for the six-mile run in 1965, as well as the US record for both the 10,000-meter and the three-mile races. By the time he had finished his career, Mills had earned seven American records. He was inducted into the 1984 class of the U.S. Olympic Hall of Fame for his performance at the 1964 Olympiad. His accolades earned him an induction into the United States Track and Field Hall of Fame, the National Distance Running Hall of Fame, the Kansas Hall of Fame, the San Diego Hall of Fame, United States Marine Corps Sports Hall of Fame, and the National High School Hall of Fame.

Almost more impressive than his résumé of honors, is what he endured to achieve his dreams. Mills was born in 1938 on the Pine Ridge Indian Reservation in South Dakota, historic site of the Wounded Knee Massacre. Billy was bi-racial, born to a white mother and Sioux father. He was not accepted by either culture and forced to renounce one in the presence of the other. Billy's mother died when he was only 8 years old and so his father became the driving influence in his life. He was still treated as a "mixed-blood" by the Native Americans and struggled to feel any self-worth. His father encouraged his son to dream and urged that the pursuit of those dreams would be the very thing that healed him. "My dad told me, 'Son, you have broken wings.' He asked, 'How do you feel?' I felt angry. I had lost my mom when I was eight. I felt hatred. My dad said, "You have a whole lot of self-pity. All of these things will destroy you. You have to look deeper to where dreams lie. You find the dreams below the anger."[5]

Mills began to run. "Running did not give me an identity. It gave me tranquility. I grew up half-Indian and half-white. In the full-blooded Indian world, they would call me a word that meant half-breed. In the white world, they called me an Indian. Neither of those cultures knew me, and when I ran I felt tranquil and in balance with Mother Earth." Billy Mills' Lakota name, Makata Taka Hela, means, "love your country" or more traditionally translated, "respects the earth." Unfortunately, at age 12, Billy was orphaned and sent to a state-supported Native American boarding school in Kansas.[6]

He pursued his studies and his passion for running. In the summers he worked. "On a typical day we were biking, walking, or running an average of 50 miles a day just to play . . . It was just the lifestyle. I went biking 15 miles just to go fishing, 30 miles round trip," he said.[7] Running was his respite from the pain.

One summer, he thought that he and his friend had found a perfect job cleaning grain elevators, until no one in town would rent them a room. One kind farmer let the boys stay in a couple of wrecked cars he had parked next to a creek and provided clean water for drinking. "So I picked out a Hudson Hornet, one I could stretch out in the back seat. My friend picked out a Cadillac. He always liked Cadillacs."[8]

Mills earned a full athletic scholarship to the University of Kansas for track and field. Leaving the seclusion of the reservation and boarding school was a difficult experience, but one that no doubt prepared him for the challenges that he would one day overcome. "I experienced more cultural shock going from Pine Ridge to the University of Kansas and rejection than I have in the now 83 different countries."[9] Even a teammate would harass him with racist comments like "You're not so fast, chief."[10] He was rejected by the social fraternity system on campus and most of the girls, but then he met Patricia Harris. She was enamored with his sweet, compassionate soul and they married only a year after they met.

Mills earned the first diploma in his family, and after graduation, he enlisted in the Marine Corp. "I was constantly told and challenged [by my father] to live my life as a warrior. As a warrior, you assume responsibility for yourself. The warrior humbles himself. And the warrior learns the power of giving."[11] He became a proud, United States Marine Lieutenant, but quietly harbored his Olympic dreams. It was a mentor, Earl "Tommy" Thomson, that he met through the marines that fueled Mills' passion to pursue his dream of running in the Olympic Games. Thomson mentored Mills through 18 months of training before making the team and continued to press Mills on his goals as they prepared for Tokyo. Thomson was the 1920 Olympic Gold Medalist in the 110-meter high hurdles and knew what kind of focus was required for such a physical and mental undertaking. Mills flourished under Thomson's tutelage.

Mills has concentrated his efforts on fighting poverty and other challenges the Native American communities face, especially the youth. Billy identifies his focus as teaching Global Unity Through Global Diversity. His storied running career and passion for humanitarianism fuel his teachings and motivational speeches. He aims to inspire the American Indian Youth who face rejection through lessons of self-empowerment. Mills is the national spokesman for Running Strong for American Indian Youth, a non-profit organization that identifies its mission as helping communities with self-sufficiency programs, youth activities, and cultural identity projects. At Pine Ridge alone, the organization has generated a youth and wellness center, a clinic for diabetics, and an agricultural development program for over 500 families. "My involvement with community service work has been one of the most inspiring and rewarding experiences I have had. I act because I hold true to our Lakota belief, 'We are all related.' And we all must act."[12]

A few privileged individuals have had the honor to chronicle Mills' life and impact on sport and the Native American community. The 1984 movie "Running Brave" was based on his victory and the film's producer, Ira Englander, said it was the "first to be truly representative of what Indian life is like."[13] The editors of *Indian Country Today* stated in their 2001 article, "Appreciating Billy Mills," that "Long-distance running is a particularly Native sport, requiring speed and stamina and evoking a type of forward-movement concentration that is often meditative. For many tribes, it is a spiritual activity that complements important traditional ceremonies. Mills is an Olympic champion who not only set a record, instilling a deep and abiding pride in his own people, but who throughout his life has sustained an ongoing commitment to help his people that is in itself nothing short of Olympian."

Billy Mills has shared his warrior spirit, kind soul, and God-given gift with anyone interested in his story. He recently stated, "A key factor in overcoming the obstacles we face today is by incorporating our traditional virtues and values in a contemporary way. Only when the virtues and values of our culture, tradition, and spirituality are transformed into a present day power that permeates our social and economic fabric, will we meet our truly great warriors of the 21st century."[14] He is not just a hero to the sport of track and field; he is a hero to his Sioux Nation, to the United States of America, and to the global society. His victory was inspiring in 1964, but it is the life he has led that has inspired a nation and the world to cheer.

Notes

1. Kay Humphrey/*Indian Country Today*, "Billy Mills delivers a message of empowerment, hard work," *Indian Country Today*, http://www.indiancountrytoday.com/archive/28220949.html, (accessed March 21, 2010).

2. Frank Coffey, "Olympian Billy Mills; Long may he run; Part Two," *Indian Country Today* (Lakota Times), August 13, 2003.

3. Kay Humphrey/*Indian Country Today*, "Billy Mills delivers a message of empowerment, hard work," *Indian Country Today*, http://www.indiancountrytoday.com/archive/28220949.html, (accessed March 21, 2010).

4. Jenna Sumara, "BILLY MILLS: Overlooked Hero of Running, The Olympic Legend," December 14, 2006, http://www.thefinalsprint.com/2006/12/billy-mills-the-olympic-legend/, (accessed March 21, 2010).

5. Mark Johnson, "Unlikely Olympic champ finds tranquility in running," *The Milwaukee Journal Sentinel*, October 27, 2005.

6. Running Past, "Billy Mills," http://www.runningpast.com/billy_mills.htm, (accessed March 21, 2010).

7. Kay Humphrey/*Indian Country Today*, "Billy Mills delivers a message of empowerment, hard work," *Indian Country Today*, http://www.indiancountrytoday.com/archive/28220949.html, (accessed March 21, 2010).

8. Matt Moline, "Running with a passion Olympic gold medalist Billy Mills tells Horton students to find a positive, constructive activity they can enjoy in life," *The Topeka Capital-Journal*, August 25, 2000.

9. Kay Humphrey/*Indian Country Today*, "Billy Mills delivers a message of empowerment, hard work," *Indian Country Today*, http://www.indiancountrytoday.com/archive/28220949.html, (accessed March 21, 2010).

10. Frank Coffey, "Olympian Billy Mills; Long may he run; Part One," *Indian Country Today (Lakota Times)*, August 6, 2003.

11. Running Past, "Billy Mills," http://www.runningpast.com/billy_mills.htm, (accessed March 21, 2010).

12. Billy Mills, "Honor each other through service and action," *Indian Country Today*, January 16, 2009, http://www.indiancountrytoday.com/opinion/37731194.html, (accessed March 21, 2010).

13. Catherine Heer, "1964 Olympic Gold Medal Winner Billy Mills Recalls His Struggle to Overcome Prejudice," *The Harvard Crimson*, April 24, 1984.

14. Billy Mills, "Honor each other through service and action," *Indian Country Today*, January 16, 2009, http://www.indiancountrytoday.com/opinion/37731194.html, (accessed March 21, 2010).

Colonel Lawrence Roberts and Dr. Roscoe C. Brown Jr.

Barrier Breakers

by Richard Lapchick

The Tuskegee Airmen, America's first African-American military airmen, are legendary heroes. Like so many before them who were not allowed to serve their country in such a capacity, the Tuskegee Airmen all had a passion to serve the United States with everything they had, including risking their lives. In doing so, they saved the lives of many white airmen at the conclusion of World War II while helping us win the war.

Coming from all over America, many airmen were college graduates or undergraduates. All were rigorously trained to be an Army Air Corps flying squadron or their ground support unit.

These airmen were trained at Tuskegee Army Air Field (TAAF) in Tuskegee, Alabama. Their inaugural class began in July 1941, completing their preparations in March 1942. Between 1941 and 1946, nearly one thousand pilots graduated. More than 450 served in combat in North Africa, Sicily, and Italy from April 1943 through July 1944 when they were transferred to the 332nd Fighter Group in the 15th Air Force.

Like most African-Americans, the Airmen fought to offset the effects of racism and stereotypes at home and overseas. These airmen battled against Germany and Italy in World War II and against racism at home. Like other soldiers of color after the war, African-American airmen returned to the United States and faced continued racism as if they were never part of the war effort.

None of this stopped their heroism in the fighting. The Airmen successfully escorted bombers during World War II. They only lost a small number of bombers to enemy fire in more than 200 combat missions. Books have been written, documentaries and movies have been made to acknowledge the remarkable achievements of the Tuskegee Airmen.

When we inducted the Airmen into the NCAS Hall of Fame, we chose two men to represent all of them. Dr. Roscoe C. Brown Jr., served as Squadron Commander of the 100th Fighter Squadron of the 332nd Fighter Group. He left the military in 1945.

Brown flew his first combat mission, escorting B-24 bombers over the Ploesti oil fields in Romania, in August 1944 and ultimately completed 68 combat missions flying the P-51 Mustang, escorting B-24 and B-17 bombers over Germany, Austria, and the Balkans and conducting low altitude strafing missions over enemy airfields and rail yards.

Arguably the height of his military career occurred when, on March 24, 1945, Brown became the first 15th Air Force fighter pilot to shoot down the ME-262 jet fighter, while escorting B-17 bombers over Berlin, Germany on the 15th Air Force's longest mission. This led to the 332nd Fighter Group's selection

Dr. Roscoe C. Brown with Robin Roberts (daughter of Colonel Lawrence Roberts) of ABC's Good Morning America at the 2007 NCAS Banquet and Hall of Fame induction.

Courtesy of the National Consortium for Academics and Sports.

to receive the Presidential Unit Citation—the highest honor bestowed upon a combat unit. The 332nd's successful combat record, which included the downing of 111 enemy aircraft in flight and 150 on the ground, was a principal factor in President Truman's decision to integrate the Armed Services in 1948. Brown also downed an FW-190 German fighter and was awarded the Distinguished Flying Cross (DFC) and the Air Medal with eight Oak Leaf Clusters.

Brown earned his PhD from New York University, and had a remarkable career in higher education. For over 25 years, he was a full-time Professor at NYU, where he founded and directed NYU's Institute of Afro-American Affairs. He served as President of Bronx Community College of The City University of New York (CUNY). He also created the Center for Urban Education Policy at the CUNY

Graduate School and University Center and served as its Director since 1993.

Colonel Lawrence Roberts was the second person chosen to represent the Tuskegee Airmen at the NCAS banquet where his daughter, Robin Roberts, and his wife, Lucimarian, accepted the induction in his place.

Col. Roberts helped to break racial barriers in the U.S. military as one of the military's first black pilots. Roberts entered the U.S. Army Air Corps as a private and retired as a colonel. He graduated from the trainings at the Tuskegee Army Air Field to prepare him for combat. Roberts graduated from the program as second lieutenant and was assigned to the 477th Medium Bombardment Group and later to the 332nd Fighter Wing.

Col. Roberts flew Piper Cubs, Boeing B-25 bombers, C-54 transports, and F-86 fighter jets, but World War II ended before he flew in combat. Roberts served in Vietnam, where he won one of three Legion of Merit medals. He served in both technical and command assignments in the United States, Japan, Canada, Turkey, and Vietnam.

Roberts received 19 service medals and awards. Among them was the Legion of Merit with two Oak Leaf Clusters, the Joint Service Commendations Medal, the United States Air Force Commendation Medal, and the Distinguished Service Order and Air Service Medal, received from the Republic of Vietnam.

Roberts was deeply involved in both his church and his community. In October 2004, Roberts passed away from a heart attack at the age of 81. He and his wife had three children in addition to Robin: Lawrence E. Roberts II, Dorothy Roberts McEwen, and Sally-Ann Roberts Craft.

On March 29, 2007, The Tuskegee Airmen were awarded the Congressional Gold Medal in recognition of their service. Dr. Brown attended the ceremony in the U.S. Capitol Rotunda.

2

COACHING TO WIN IN LIFE

by Richard Lapchick

Coaching is among the most rewarding careers a man or woman can undertake. A coach leads, trying to teach teams skills and the concept of working together to pursue a common goal. For many coaches, the only goal is to win and they do so consistently and brilliantly. For others, the goals are more expansive, more permanent. These coaches teach sportsmanship, teamwork, the ability to win and lose with equal grace, the concern for a teammate, leadership, and the many health benefits of sport, all of which are as or more important than win-loss records. This is a section about 21 coaches who have done just that and whom we honor in *Coaching to Win in Life*.

Willie Davis, unable to finish his own education, was asked to step beyond his janitorial role in Louisiana to lead junior high school teams that had no coaches. He won titles and taught the children under his charge about the value of education by example.

Jim Ellis took a group of mostly African-American swimmers in an urban environment into pools and competitions that had traditionally been reserved for white youngsters. He built champions of color in a sport where there were few before.

Jack Aker, a seasoned Major League Baseball player, took his skills in the off-season to Native American reservations to teach the game to young people who would otherwise never have had the opportunity to play baseball. Aker, a Native American himself, was one of the few Native American players in the history of Major League Baseball.

Dorothy Gaters took a group of girls in Chicago and together they performed miracles. Many of her players, most from Chicago's most poverty stricken area, have gone on to play professionally in Europe and in the United States.

Bert Jenkins survived the brutality of the Nazi régime as a heroic American soldier who came home an amputee. Rising to new challenges, he became the winningest high school basketball coach in the history of the sport in Mississippi.

Until her own health concerns forced her to the bleachers, Marian Washington led Kansas University for three decades on the sidelines of the basketball court, producing a group of outstanding female scholar-athletes and championship teams.

Vivian Stringer led three different teams to the Final Four over the course of her extraordinary career. Like Washington, there are legions of women across America who value what Stringer did for them as individual human beings more than the games they won on the court under her leadership.

Carolyn Peck showed that age does not matter as the youthful basketball coach led Purdue to a National Championship. After guiding the Orlando Miracle to success in the WNBA, she rebuilt the University of Florida's women's team.

Mike Sheppard created a legacy as baseball coach at Seton Hall University for nearly three decades where he led his team to countless wins on the field and produced a group of men who still look back to their coach as teaching them the most valuable of life's lessons.

Rob Hamilton converted a group of underachieving Boston youth and emphasized the importance of their being scholar-athletes and not just city athletes.

Bob Shannon led his East St. Louis high school team to championships in one of the most violent and poverty-stricken communities in the country. In the process, he saved the lives of his players and as well as producing winning teams.

Ken Carter was made famous by the movie "Coach Carter" because he forced his basketball players to produce in the classroom before he allowed them back on the court. His fame with his players preceded the national recognition afforded him after the release of the movie.

Beverly Kearney, a highly decorated track and field athlete and coach, sent a powerful message to her athletes as she coached from a hospital bed, then with a walker, leading her women to the 2005 National Championship.

Jennifer Rizzotti, one of the best college basketball players from the University of Connecticut went on to play professionally and coach in college simultaneously.

Willie Stewart led the Anacostia High School football team against opponents on the field and in the streets for decades. With Stewart's guidance, players learned of opportunities beyond the poverty, drugs, and the violence of Washington, D.C.

Sonny Hill, known as "Mr. Basketball," has dedicated his life to youth basketball in Philadelphia. For nearly 40 years, Hill's basketball leagues have helped Philadelphia become a basketball mecca.

After averaging 40 points per game in high school, Jody Conradt coached for more than 30 years offering her talented instructions on the basketball court in the state of Texas.

More than half of Kay Yow's 38-year career coaching basketball was spent fighting breast cancer. She fought for her health on and off the court while earning a winning record of 737-344 before her passing in 2009. Almost 1,500 people attended her funeral.

Ron Hunter, the men's basketball coach at IUPUI, had his first pedicure in 2008 in preparation for his barefoot coaching debut. Hunter partnered with Samaritan's Feet to raise awareness and money for the nearly 300 million impoverished children worldwide who have never owned a pair of shoes.

Joe Ehrmann, an NFL player in his heyday was described as someone who "ate quarterbacks for lunch" starting using love and respect to teach football after ending his professional career. He has spent three decades mentoring and leading young men and women to be responsible members of society and their families.

Glenn Johnson is a retired Chicago Public School teacher who leads the football student-athletes at Dunbar Vocational Career Academy off the streets. Many of his student-athletes come from the notoriously violent Englewood neighborhood and have to take multiple buses in order to get to school each day. Dunbar sometimes is little more than a safe haven for students to get a couple of warm meals.

As the title of this chapter suggests, these coaches have focused their careers on the life lessons they could teach in the gym as much as, if not more than, they did on earning championship titles.

Willie Davis

Coaching to Win in Life

by Richard Lapchick and Joslyn Dalton

The story of Willie Davis' life and work is remarkable. For years, Davis was employed at Arthur F. Smith Junior High School in Alexandria, Louisiana where he worked as a custodian. He was also a coach. Everyday Davis mopped the halls, washed the windows, mowed the lawn, and cleaned the toilets. And when his work was done, he grabbed his whistle and coached. Davis gave all he had to his work as a custodian and a coach, but more importantly he used the lessons he learned in life to inspire thousands of students.

Several years ago when there was a shortage of coaches at the school, the head girls' basketball coach asked Davis if he would help with the team. Davis was thrilled by the idea, but since he did not have a college degree and could not be certified to work as a coach, the school was unable to compensate Davis for his work. A couple of years later, Davis would be rewarded for his efforts by being named head coach of the boys' seventh and eighth grade basketball team and the head football coach. For his work as coach of the boys' teams, the school paid Davis an additional $900 a year. The money, however, did not matter to Davis. He just loved the game and working with youth.

On the court, Davis, or "Coach D" as his student-athletes preferred to call him, led Arthur F. Smith to three District titles in six years. Coach D even guided the team to a 34-game winning streak on his way to a 101-21 career record. More importantly, off the court and field Davis made sure his students got the education he never had the opportunity to complete. In his high school days, Davis' father passed away forcing Davis to drop his basketball career in order to work and support his family. Davis was able to graduate from high school, but decided to stay in Alexandria to continue supporting his family. He worked tirelessly in a variety of cleaning jobs before settling down at Arthur F. Smith Junior High School.

There are several reasons why Davis has been so successful. The first in Davis' mind is his love for his three children. He said that it is his understanding of them that has helped him to become a father figure to many of his athletes.

Davis' model for success is really quite simple: a belief in God first, books second, and basketball third. Davis' starters were known for their straight-A report cards. By using lessons from his own life and constantly setting a positive example for his student-athletes, Davis transformed his life from custodian to educator. Davis taught his student-athletes values and discipline, preached the importance of education, and in the end, translated all the positive messages into a winning basketball program for Arthur F. Smith Junior High School.

Davis became a celebrity around Alexandria. He has been featured in *Sports Illustrated* and on HBO's *Real Sports with Bryant Gumbel*. Hollywood has a movie in development based on Davis' life that will star John Cusack and Halle Berry. Actor and rapper Ice Cube will play the role of Coach D. In the down economy, they have struggled to find the funding for the movie. The rights to Davis' life story have been purchased for the motion picture, but Revolution Studio was in a holding pattern as of early 2010. They are looking for funding from HBO or Q-Vision in order to keep his story alive. Whether or not the movie becomes a reality, Davis does not plan on changing. "I've told my kids as I've coached them, be the same person whether you are making 50 cents or five dollars," he said.[1]

The national exposure Davis received for his impact at Arthur F. Smith caught the attention of a philanthropist who was inspired to anonymously donate funds for much-needed athletic equipment for the school. The donor also offered to pay for Davis to attend college. In his first online course at Northwestern State University where he is studying education, Davis earned a B grade. Davis is determined to earn his degree so that he can become a certified teacher and coach. While he hopes to accomplish this feat one day, his priorities remain with his family and the youth he coaches. "I might give out at times but I never give up. I am going to reach my goal with education," he said with confidence.[2]

In 2002, Davis left Arthur F. Smith for a position with the Alexandria Recreational Department. Coaching remained his passion. Smith students missed the man they said that everyone wanted to be around because he was an inspiration.

When Cenla Christian Academy in Pineville, Louisiana opened its doors in 2006, Davis was chosen to lead the inaugural season for the Lions. He continued to prove his expertise as a coach, taking the Lions to the first round of the state playoffs. Davis was named Coach of the Year by the high school. Outside of the school setting, Davis took a job working for Alexandria's low income housing project and has been working to start a basketball league for its youth. Furthermore, he desires to become involved with handicapped kids in the greater Alexandria community. "I would like to take five or so kids and help them get involved. Even just throwing or rolling balls around, that is what I would really like to do," he said.[3]

Most of all, Davis is known for the interest he takes in each student and the time he spends getting to know everyone. Willie Davis' journey has been nothing short of remarkable. And perhaps the most remarkable thing about it is we know there are even more lives that he will touch in the years ahead.

Notes

1. Willie Davis, interview with Joslyn Dalton, March 31, 2010.
2. Ibid.
3. Ibid.

James "Jim" Ellis

Coaching to Win in Life

by Joslyn Dalton

As an African-American swimmer competing collegiately for Cheyney University in the 1960s, it was clear to Jim Ellis how racially and economically separated he was from the rest of the swimming community. After all, for most of the 20th century, American pools were segregated. Even if there had been no racial barriers, economic limitations remained for many people of color. Private swim clubs often had elaborate facilities and were quite expensive. As a result, swimming had always been a predominantly white, upper-class sport.

Ellis' own experience as an outsider to the swimming community inspired him to seek more diversity in the sport he loved. With the civil rights era booming around him, upon graduating he chose coaching as his avenue for social change. A native of Pittsburgh, Pennsylvania, Ellis began to teach young, inner-city athletes how to swim as a coach for the Philadelphia Department of Recreation in 1971. By 1973, he started the country's first all-African-American swim team and named it the Sayre Aquatics Club. Seven years later, his responsibilities for the city increased when he was put in charge of a new facility, the Marcus Foster Pool. Ellis transferred his swim team to this new location and renamed his group PDR.

In over three decades under Ellis' watchful eye, PDR has gone from anonymity to national prominence. During this period, PDR has produced countless champions at the national and international level including the Junior Olympics, Junior Nationals, and United States Nationals. With multiple swimmers qualifying for the Olympic Trials, the success of PDR's swimmers attracted white, suburban kids by the mid-1990s. Always an advocate of diversity, Ellis welcomed the new swimmers to his team. While Ellis is proud of his most accomplished swimmers, he also finds special encouragement in the large number of his athletes who have earned college scholarships. As a high school math teacher in the Philadelphia School District, Ellis has always placed an emphasis on academics.

Ellis' coaching style is centered more on teaching discipline than simply improving fundamentals. In developing the mantra, "Beat them in the pool," he has encouraged his athletes to avoid fighting ignorance with ignorance.[1] As an example of the discrimination Ellis and his team often faced, he distinctly remembers being approached at a swim meet by angry parents who yelled, "You [blacks] have basketball, you have track, you have football, you have boxing. Now you want swimming!"[2] Ellis has exemplified how to handle such prejudices by reminding his athletes, "Racism is racism, and when you react to it in a negative way by lashing out, you're just as bad as being a racist yourself."[3] Over the years, Philadelphia has benefited from Ellis' influence in the community, his team's success in the swimming pool, and at integrating the sport. Ellis has watched as among his swimmers respect and friendships have formed across social, racial, gender, economic, and cultural boundaries.

Throughout his quest to teach African-American children how to swim competitively, Ellis has endured an upstream battle. USA Swimming membership statistics continue to demonstrate that the sport is predominantly white. A study in 2008 revealed 58 percent of black children and 56 percent of Hispanic children are unable to swim, compared to the 31 percent of white children who also can't swim. Furthermore, black children drown at a rate almost three times the average overall rate. USA Swimming has increasingly become involved with trying to diversify the sport. It was only in 2000 that the United States had its first African-American male swimmer compete at the Olympic Games, and in 2004, its first African-American female. Ellis has played a vital role in developing the Minority Outreach Swim Camp held at the Olympic Training Center in Colorado Springs. Regardless of such advances, less than two percent of USA Swimming's nearly 252,000 members who swim competitively are black.

Despite the continued obstacles, Ellis' impact has been significant. In fact, in 2007 a major motion picture based on his career and life was released. For his part, Ellis was surprised to find that his story would be made into a film considering that PDR was hardly publicized in the media despite its monumental success. "No newspapers or local media covered us, it's swimming, despite years and years of national success," he said. "I don't know if race was involved. But we had kids who achieved above and beyond what anyone thought."[4] *Pride*, set in the early 1970s, showcased the lives of the young PDR swimmers, full of hardship and prejudice, before revealing the uplifting and soulful story of one coach's impact. Starring Academy Award nominee Terrence Howard as Ellis, the Lionsgate film opened in national and international box offices on March 23, 2007.

Despite insurmountable odds, through his work with PDR, Jim Ellis has proved that African-American swimmers can in fact develop into competitive swimmers and contribute to the growth of the sport. With the hopes of one day seeing Philadelphia build a facility that can accommodate 800 inner-city kids, Ellis remains at a pool roughly half the size of a 50-meter Olympic-sized pool. "I'm still here, 35 years later with my little hole in the wall, watching my kids swim," he said. Even if all he had was a bathtub, Jim Ellis will continue to make a splash for diversity in hopes that one day "pride" will beat out prejudice.

Notes

1. Joseph Santoliquito, "Movie to document swim coach's efforts," Special to ESPN.com, February 9, 2007, http://sports.espn.go.com/espn/blackhistory2007/news/story?id=2759883, (accessed March 25, 2010).

2. Nancy Greenleese, "Philadelphia Teacher Has Been Making Poor Black Kids Into Competitive Swimmers for 35 Years," Voice of America News, June 11, 2007, http://www1.voanews.com/english/news/a-13-2007-06-11-voa32-66561217.html, (accessed March 25, 2010).

3. Joseph Santoliquito, "Movie to document swim coach's efforts," Special to ESPN.com, February 9, 2007, http://sports.espn.go.com/espn/blackhistory2007/news/story?id=2759883, (accessed March 25, 2010).

4. Ibid.

Jack Aker

Coaching to Win in Life

by Joslyn Dalton

Throughout Jack Aker's 11-year playing career in Major League Baseball, it seemed as though he spent as much time packing as he did pitching. A journeyman reliever, Aker found himself in a number of different jerseys since first signing with the Kansas City Athletics in 1964 at the age of 23. During his professional career, he played for the A's, Seattle Pilots, New York Yankees, Chicago Cubs, Atlanta Braves, and New York Mets. An outfielder when he entered the minor leagues, coaches saw promise in his powerful arm and decided to switch him to pitcher. Although he was initially pegged as a starter, his throwing technique converted him to a reliever. "I was one of the 10 or 12 guys who began to define what a closer was," he said.[1]

Aker's most successful major league season came in 1966 while he was playing for the Kansas City A's. He went 8-4 and reached an ERA of 1.99. His 32 saves broke the record at that time, a true testament for the newness of the closing position. For his efforts, the American League recognized him as the Fireman of the Year.

Aker also received notoriety when he was selected as the American League player representative for the players union. Upon retiring in 1974, he had played 495 games, accumulated 123 saves and a lifetime ERA of 3.28. Over the next 10 years, he remained in professional baseball as a minor league manager for the Mets. He also spent two years as a pitching coach for the Cleveland Indians and the Atlanta Braves. After nearly 30 years in the game, Aker decided to blaze a new path in 1988.

As a way to share his vast knowledge with aspiring young ballplayers, Aker founded Jack Aker Baseball, Inc. Organizing camps, clinics, and private instruction for individuals and teams throughout the country, Aker has coached a number of players who have gone on to achieve success in baseball. However, it is for Native American children, a group unlikely to have much exposure to the big leagues, in which Aker has developed a special interest.

Of Native American descent himself, Aker dedicates two weeks each spring to those he calls, "America's forgotten children."[2] Since 1994, he has used a grant from the National Indian Youth Leadership Project to interact with children residing on Navajo, Hopi, and Zuni reservations in the Southwest. Aker focuses on where he feels he is needed most, remote areas with little or no organized athletics and an absence of male role models. Historically, these reservations have been plagued by drug and alcohol abuse. Teen suicide is above the national rate. It is here that Aker uses baseball to reach and positively impact children.

Aker invites both boys and girls to his clinics. He has found the Native American children to be tough. "I hit a pop-up that landed squarely on the head of one little 10-year old," he said. "None of the parents ran for an ambulance or an attorney. The boy giggled and the other kids were laughing so hard they rolled in the dirt"[3]

Far from well-manicured fields with plush green grass, white bases, and a clean home plate, most Native American kids play on gravel and clay dirt. Many do not even own a glove. In hopes that they will continue to play after he leaves, Aker gives out a baseball to each participating child. In comparison with the majority of the kids Aker works with, the children on the reservations carry modest goals. His discussions with them stretch far beyond the game. "After the clinic I sit them down and talk about working hard, staying in school, and steering clear of drugs and alcohol," Aker shared. "I tell them to find something to devote themselves to. Not necessarily baseball, but something they can be passionate about."[4]

Notes

1. Brad Barth, "Much-Swapped Reliever Settles in LI to Instruct," January 1, 1999, http://www.antonnews.com/roslynnews/1999/01/01/sports/, (accessed March 23, 2010).

2. Bill Retherford, "Where are they now?" July 19, 2004, http://www.baseballsavvy.com/archive/w_aker.html, (accessed March 24, 2010).

3. Ibid.

4. Ibid.

Dorothy Gaters

Coaching to Win in Life

by Joslyn Dalton

Young athletes often dream of making it to the collegiate or professional ranks. Similarly, in the realm of coaching, one's career is frequently defined by the prestige of a big-time university or professional organization. Yet for Dorothy Gaters, the high school stage is big enough.

As a 1964 graduate of Chicago's John Marshall Metropolitan High School, Gaters has stayed with the school and community in which she was raised. After the assassination of Martin Luther King Jr. in 1968, she watched firsthand as her west suburb neighborhood become infused with riots. Once a thriving community, Maywood, Illinois quickly became plagued with poverty. Still suffering in a poor school district, throughout the years Marshall High has become a goldmine for Gaters.

Early into her teaching career, Gaters believed her young students would benefit from extracurricular activities as a way to help keep them in school. Girls' sports were limited at the time. No girls' basketball program was offered at Marshall. Gaters was determined to see this change. When no one else stepped up to the challenge, Gaters precariously took on the position as Marshall's first head girls' basketball coach. She had no prior coaching experience. Over the weeks that followed, Gaters picked the minds of local coaches, listened to television commentators, and watched as many basketball games as possible, teaching herself the game and how she would coach it. She became consumed by the notion of Marshall developing a strong basketball presence throughout Illinois. In a matter of three decades, Gaters would rewrite her state's record books en route to becoming a legendary coach.

In January 2009, Gaters longevity was rewarded as she won her 900th career victory. She also has received notoriety as the winningest coach in the State of Illinois. Upon the completion of her 34th season, her teams have reached the state tournament more than 20 times, collecting a record-total of eight state championships and three runner-up finishes. Gaters has won over 90 percent of her games. She has produced 17 high school All-Americans, as well as 17 professional players. She credits her own coaching success to the talent of the girls she has worked with. "You need talent to win. Some of these coaches think they invented the wheel. The reason we have maintained our success is that we have been very privileged to have so many great athletes."[1]

One of her former players, Cappie Pondexter, played for Rutgers University and became the 2006 Big East Player of the Year. As the second overall WNBA draft pick, Pondexter joined the Phoenix Mercury where she later became an All-Star, league Champion, and WNBA Most Valuable Player. When asked about her high school coach, Pondexter credited Gaters diligence. "She's a hard worker. She expects your best, but she expects a lot out of herself as well. She's kind of a perfectionist."[2]

As of 2009, the Illinois Basketball Coaches Association had named Gaters their "Coach of the Year" eight times. In 1998, she was awarded the National STUDENT-Athlete Day Giant Steps Award. She has been enshrined into five halls of fame including the Women's Basketball Hall of Fame, the Illinois Basketball Coaches Association Hall of Fame, and the Chicago Public League Basketball Coaches Association Hall of Fame. In an effort to honor those who have had tremendous influence on high school basketball and to provide them with a national stage to be acknowledged, Gaters was a 2009 recipient of the Morgan Wooten Lifetime Achievement Award.

Recognition has been slow to catch up with Gaters. Colleges first began paying attention to her coaching prowess through recruiting her senior star players in the mid-1990s. She was encouraged to bring her coaching strengths to the collegiate level after a successful stint as an assistant coach at the 1986 U.S. Olympic Festival, as well as the 1992 WBCA Girls' High School All-America Game. Although many would have seen it as an opportunity to escape the poverty of west side Chicago, Gaters remained committed to Marshall. Her tireless efforts to prove her inner-city program could compete with the best of the state would not come to an end.

As a tool to foster academic achievement, the graduation rates of Gaters' players have surpassed that of Marshall's regular student body. Always an educator, Gaters' role expanded at Marshall when she became the school's athletic director in 2005. Consistent throughout the years, she expects that her players hold high regard for their teachers. Her mission has been to build healthy, well-rounded girls who contribute positively to the community. In doing so, she created the Dr. Martin Luther King Jr. Dream Classic National Basketball Shoot-Out as a way to honor Dr. King through healthy competition. Starting with 10 girls' teams in 2001, the MLK Dream Classic grew rapidly to 66 teams by 2010.

Known as the "queen of girls' basketball," Dorothy Gaters has achieved an amount of success at the high school level that has stretched far beyond anyone's expectations.[3] With many of her past athletes following in her coaching footsteps, her impact will continue to influence numerous communities and countless young girls long after she steps away from the game. Until then, Gaters remains hard at work continuing to nurture and build the reputation of the dominate program she created.

Notes

1. Patrick McGavin, "Dorothy Gaters," https://www.chicagobusiness.com/cgi-bin/article.pl?article_id=21748, (accessed March 5, 2010).

2. Ibid.

3. Larry Gross, "Maywood to honor Marshall high school's Dorothy Gaters," http://www.chicagodefender.com/article-1407-maywood-to-honor-marshall-high-schoolrss-dorothy-gaters.html, (accessed March 5, 2010).

Bert Jenkins

Coaching to Win in Life

by Joslyn Dalton

In the world of sports, phrases such as "going to war" or "battling it out" are often used as expressions to exemplify high stakes competition. In the excitement of a sporting event, it is easy for a person who has not experienced both to confuse sport with war. Mississippi's Bert Jenkins knows the two are vastly different. Throughout his childhood, Jenkins dreamed of becoming a star athlete. An avid sports fan, Jenkins played basketball in high school and tried out at Mississippi State during his freshman year in college. Although he didn't make the team, Jenkins' passion for basketball did not abate. Instead, he got to work developing his skills in anticipation of try-outs the following year. In the meantime he focused on his studies, pursuing a passion for literature and writing, which was passed on by his mother, an English teacher.

At the age of 18, Jenkins' plans were interrupted and his life took an unexpected detour when he was drafted for World War II. Immediately he was shipped overseas to train in England. Only days following D-Day, Jenkins' and his 313th infantry regiment of the 79th division arrived on Utah Beach at Normandy. During their first night on shore, Jenkins and his comrades were barraged by German bombs and shrapnel that rained down from the sky. Over the months that followed, the 313th infantry regiment fought without rest.

"It was January 5, 1945, two weeks after the Battle of the Bulge in what we called the Battle of the Southern Bulge," Jenkins remembers thinking back to the moment that changed his life forever.[1] With enemy gunfire swirling around him, a bullet made its way deep inside Jenkins' leg. He crawled for his life, managing to drag himself into a ditch for protection. Shortly thereafter, he passed out from the excruciating pain and tremendous blood loss. At sunrise the next day, Jenkins was captured by German troops and later shipped to a prisoner of war camp. He was immediately taken into surgery upon his arrival. Lying on the operating table, Jenkins dreamed—days of basketball flashed in his mind as he pleaded for his leg with the German surgeon who was readying his amputation equipment. Waking up the next day in severe pain, Jenkins saw that his leg was gone, along with any chance at a playing career.

Of the months that followed, Jenkins has little memory. "I have had doctors tell me that the shock and trauma of the amputation and the fact that I was a young kid is why my memory was gone," he said. Numb to the world, Jenkins never experienced the feeling of being liberated when the war came to a close. "I recovered my memory after the war ended. I was in a hospital in France and all of a sudden I was riding home with my parents."[2]

Upon his arrival home, Jenkins made the decision not to focus on his limitations. Instead, he opened his mind to the possibilities that awaited him. He went back to school. Once in college, he never let up, even taking classes through the summer. He graduated with his bachelor's degree from the University of Southern Mississippi in 1948 and earned his master's in English from the University of Alabama in 1949.

Still passionate about sports, but unable to play, Jenkins decided that the next best thing he could do was coach. He took a teaching and coaching job at Gulfport Junior High School in 1950. He moved to Gulfport High School in 1961 and began teaching 11th grade English while coaching basketball and football. After five years of coaching both, he decided to focus exclusively on basketball.

Throughout his 28 years at Gulfport High, Jenkins developed a reputation across the state of Mississippi as an elite high school basketball coach. His unprecedented success included seven state championships and 13 conference titles. With 25 seasons of at least 20 wins, 18 seasons with 30 wins, and three seasons with 40 wins, Jenkins achieved an impressive career record of 866 wins and 180 losses. Jenkins proved that his abilities far overshadowed what would seem to have been a disability. For 19 years, including six of the seven state championships seasons, Jenkins managed the sidelines with his good friend and assistant coach, Gerald Austin. "Sitting on the bench with Jenkins, I would make a suggestion and he would take it, go with it, make it work, and then give me credit for it," Austin shared.[3]

Austin remembered Jenkins' coaching style as being very detailed and direct. He admired Jenkins for his ability to understand the changing dynamics of athletes. "(Jenkins) was willing to change with the times, not only in his basketball philosophy but in dealing with the young people," Austin said.[4]

Jenkins was further known for his game analysis, his ability to lead a team, and his adherence to his core values. During one season he kicked his star player off his team due to repeated misbehavior. With other juniors and seniors threatening to quit if the removed player could not rejoin the team, Jenkins held his ground as 11 varsity players ultimately left the team. With only junior varsity players available to fill in, Jenkins team ended the season with a losing record, but the experience was gratifying. "We had fun in every game. Every game was like a state championships for those boys," Jenkins recalls.[5] As a testament to his coaching prowess, the following year his young team improved significantly and capped their second season on varsity as Mississippi State Champions.

In addition to Jenkins' evolving coaching style, he has been a staunch advocate for improved race relations in Mississippi. He took this stance at a time when it was unpopular. Regardless of pressures around him, Jenkins was always open to integrating his team. With the support of his beloved wife, Lilian, who goes by Lil, he was able to reach out to minority kids from low-income households. "He and Lil bought clothes for kids, gave them rides, made sure they got to doctors appointments. He did a lot of things for students, even non-basketball players, which most people don't know about," recalled Austin. "Lil paid for their medicine, even took one kid to Houston, Texas to see a specialist a couple of times," added Jenkins.[6]

When Jenkins first met his future wife at a basketball event, he described it as love at first sight. Although it took her a bit of time to feel the same way, the two have made quite the team together. Jenkins considers Lil's support for Gulfport to have been tremendous. "She was our trainer, she was a scorekeeper, she took care of our uniforms, she kept the concession stand," he said. "I don't know if we could have had that much success without her."[7]

When asked how his experience in World War II affected the way he coached, Jenkins explained that the impact could be seen through his work ethic, even during the offseason. "Other coaches were off hunting and fishing, doing their hobbies. I remember another coach saying he didn't mind when his team was eliminated because he could go play golf," Jenkins said. "I couldn't do that. When my team was eliminated, we started practicing the very next day."[8]

Jenkins achievements brought him both local and national recognition. Along with having Gulfport High School name their gymnasium after him, Jenkins was awarded many honors. The Mississippi Association of Coaches, National High School Athletic Coaches Association, Babe McCarthy Tip-off Club and Scholastic named him their Coach of the Year on multiple occasions. He was also inducted into the Mississippi Sports Hall of Fame, as well as the Mississippi Association of Coaches Hall of Fame. In 1989, the NCAA awarded Jenkins as the National High School Coach of the Year.

Sports Illustrated named Jenkins one of Mississippi's 50 greatest 20th century sports figures in 1999. That same year he was announced as a Giant Steps Award winner by the National Consortium for Academics and Sports and was invited to the White House to be recognized by President Bill Clinton. The Bert Jenkins Scholarship at Mississippi State was established in 2010 by Jenkins daughter, Ann Campbell.

Following retirement in 1989, Jenkins has enjoyed traveling. With the support and assistance of his wife and children, in 2009 Jenkins was able to return to some of the historic battlefields on which he fought during the war. Jenkins visited Utah and Omaha Beach before paying his respects at the Luxembourg American Cemetery. Although it can be difficult to travel, he and his wife have taken an annual trip for the past 20 years to Orlando, Florida to watch the Atlanta Braves' spring training.

In 2005, Jenkins and his wife moved to Hattiesburg, Mississippi. Since the amputation, Jenkins has experienced a great deal of continuing pain and the move allowed him to be closer to his hospital. Stemming from a nomination by his doctors, Jenkins was chosen for the annual "Making A Difference Award" by Endo Pharmaceuticals Inc. Jenkins and Lil continue to go to the hospital's Wellness Center three days a week and have become fast friends with their fellow workout partners. In his spare time, Jenkins enjoys reading and writing poetry about the war. He has developed a personal library of over 400 books and takes the most pleasure in novels.

Bert Jenkins' life story is anything but fiction. As an athlete, student, solider, teacher, and coach, Jenkins' service has influenced those both within and outside the sphere of sports. While his bravery in World War II alone makes him a hero, it is his determination to press forward in spite of life's setbacks that makes him a true champion.

Notes

1. Bert Jenkins, interview, March 26, 2010.
2. Ibid.
3. Gerald Austin, interview, March 26, 2010.
4. Ibid.
5. Bert Jenkins, interview, March 26, 2010.
6. Ibid.
7. Ibid.
8. Ibid.

Marian Washington

Coaching to Win in Life

by Joslyn Dalton

Marian Washington has accomplished what she first set out to do. With an honest and humble outlook, her life's mission has been to make a difference in the lives of young people. Specifically, she wanted to use the domain of athletics to help cultivate good character as well as develop athletic talent. A fearless pioneer, Washington has changed the landscape of sports for women.

As a competitive athlete, Washington was raised in West Chester, Pennsylvania. Sensational in seven different sports during high school, her talent elevated her game to the collegiate level. Washington attended West Chester State University where she reached AAU All-American status twice while leading her team to an undefeated season and national title the first year the sport had a recognized championship. Washington took advantage of the opportunities Title IX provided as her desire to continually improve women's athletics was fostered.

Pursuing her love for basketball, Washington stayed in the game after her playing career ended at West Chester State. Before graduating with her master's degree in biodynamics and administration from the University of Kansas, Washington became the head women's basketball coach for KU in 1974. The program started in 1968 and she was its fourth coach. In her first season, she posted a winning record while her responsibilities grew beyond basketball. Between 1974 and 1979, Washington became the first and only Director of Women's Athletics at the University of Kansas. She took KU's women's athletic program to new heights. Notably, she founded the KU women's track and field team in 1974 and served as its head coach for one year.

Although Kansas took advantage of Washington's expertise off the basketball court, they benefited tremendously from her coaching guidance on the court. In 31 years as head coach for the Lady Jayhawks, Washington accumulated a 560-363 (.607) record. Her teams reached the 20-win mark 17 times. She led them to seven league crowns, six conference tournament championships, two post-season WNIT tournaments, 11 postseason NCAA Tournaments, and two Sweet Sixteen appearances. She produced four All-American players and three academic All-Americans.

With a month to go before the regular 2003–04 season, Washington shocked the basketball community with her sudden retirement. At the age of 57, unspecified health issues were cited as the reason for her departure from the game. "When you are in this business for as long as I have been, you tend to dismiss yourself because your commitments are to your players, your university, and your program," she shared in a press conference with her athletic director, Lew Perkins.[1] Perkins responded by reminding the public that Washington was a pioneer, a leader, and a mentor. He felt it was not a business for Washington, but a passion.

Washington was named Conference Coach of the Year for three seasons. Her coaching talent and zeal for the game made her the first African-American to serve as head coach for a U.S. team that competed internationally. She made history again becoming the first African-American to coach on an Olympic women's basketball staff in 1996 when the USA won Olympic gold.

Washington's impact on women's basketball catapulted her to a variety of additional roles. She has been a member of the national officiating committee and the Kodak All-American selection committee. She served on the board of directors for the Women's Basketball Coaches Association and was the first female to be elected president of the Black Coaches Association (BCA), now known as the Black Coaches and Administrators. Admiration from her peers was evident as she was the first person elected to serve consecutive terms in this position.

In 1991, Washington received the Carol Eckman Award given to outstanding coaches who demonstrate the character of Eckman— sportsmanship, honesty, courage, ethical behavior, dedication to purpose, and commitment to the student-athlete. Before dying from cancer, Eckman coached several future NCAA Division I coaches during her tenure at West Chester State, including Washington.

In 1995, the National Consortium for Academics and Sports presented Washington with a Giant Steps Award. *Ebony Magazine* also took notice of Washington's distinguished career by choosing her as a recipient of their Outstanding Black Women in Sports Award. On two separate occasions the BCA named Washington the Coach of the Year. In 2004, she received the BCA's Lifetime Achievement Award. Following her retirement, Washington became a 2004 inductee for the Women's Basketball Hall of Fame.

Since leaving the game for health reasons, Washington continues to impact others through an Internet-based fitness program. "It's still difficult to not want to be out there and coach on the floor, because I've always enjoyed motivating," she said. "Now, I want to help motivate people toward a better, healthier lifestyle."[2] Through an interactive, virtual journey capitalizing on Washington's expertise, people are invited to enter the total amount of steps they take doing everyday tasks at www.trackandfitness.com.

In devoting her entire head coaching career to one university, Washington became a legend in the tradition-rich history of Kansas basketball. Various recognitions and countless awards reveal the significance of Washington's coaching legacy. Since leaving the sidelines, the life mission of Marian Washington continues through her unique involvement in the sport and fitness community.

Notes

1. Kevin Haskin, "Washington takes leave of absence" *Topeka Capital Journal*, January 30, 2004.

2. Mechelle Voepel, "Former KU coach Washington finds another way to motivate people," http://traditionofexcellence.wordpress.com/2008/04/21/former-ku-coach-washington-finds-another-way-to-motivate-people/, (accessed March 3, 2010).

C. Vivian Stringer

Coaching to Win in Life

by Joslyn Dalton

Known as a record setting women's coach, C. Vivian Stringer's achievements stem far beyond the boundaries of the basketball court. With a reputation that rests in her ability to take mediocre programs to magnificent prominence, Stringer has simultaneously turned personal setback into professional accomplishment.

On the court, Stringer is a staple, the first coach—male or female, black or white—to lead three different universities to the NCAA Final Four. Stringer guided Cheyney University in 1982, the University of Iowa in 1993, and Rutgers University both in 2000 and 2007. Throughout her entire career, Stringer has divided her time between the same three schools. Her teams have qualified for 22 out of 28 NCAA tournaments, including nine regional finals. In 39 seasons as a head coach, Stringer became the eighth coach all-time to accumulate over 800 wins while also being named the third winningest women's coach of all time. At the end of the 2008–09 season Stringer's career record was 825-280.

Stringer began her head coaching career in 1971 at the historically-black Cheyney University located outside of Philadelphia. Anxiously waiting for the effects of Title IX, Stringer's underdog team competed for the first-ever women's basketball national championship in 1982. Despite a loss to Louisiana Tech, the following season the Cheyney Wolves began to earn immense popularity in front of packed stands—a sight uncommon for the women's game at the time.

Stringer's drive was relentless. After 12 successful seasons at Cheyney, Stringer wanted to challenge herself with a move to the

Big Ten Conference. Joining an underperforming program at the University of Iowa, Stringer's impact was immediate. After only two seasons, her Hawkeyes became an NCAA Second Round Team. The following year they reached the Regional Finals. During the tenth year of Stringer's guidance, Iowa made the coveted trip to the NCAA Final Four.

Stringer's success impacted more than her players. She had become a driving force in changing the landscape of women's basketball. Coaching a defensive style of game that filled the seats of the Carver-Hawkeye Arena, the unprecedented amount of popularity from the fans helped Iowa become the first women's basketball team to ever record an advanced sellout game.

Completing 12 seasons at the University of Iowa, Stringer moved east for the opportunity to turn a New Jersey team into what she considered the "Jewel of the East."[1] Joining the sidelines for Rutgers University in 1995, Stringer once again immediately impacted her school. Within five seasons—half the time it took her at Iowa—Stringer propelled the Lady Knights to the 2000 NCAA Final Four.

A tribute to Stringer's coaching prowess is a look at the journey of her 2006–07 squad. Void of senior leadership, five freshmen grappled with the suffocating defensive system that Stringer brought to Rutgers. She disciplined and molded her team and eventually her young players stopped fighting the system. Finally playing in harmony, Stringer took an otherwise hopeless team to the NCAA National Championships. The first team in school history to play in the finals, Rutgers fell shy of victory leaving Stringer's résumé void of a national title.

Throughout her magnificent coaching run, Stringer exemplified the life lesson of her youth growing up in Edenborn, Pennsylvania. She admired her father's dedication to his family and to his work at a local coal mine. "Work hard and don't look for excuses," she was told by her parents, "and you can achieve anything."[2]

Stringer learned not to shy away from difficulty. The sport of basketball was not offered to girls while Stringer was in high school. She enjoyed competing with the boys whenever possible. Since she was not allowed to play basketball, Stringer decided to become a cheerleader in order to be as close to the game as possible. She fought her high school's administration for a spot on the all-white cheerleading squad and prevailed by making room for herself on the sidelines.

The untimely death of Stringer's father came when she was only 19 years old. Her mother pushed forward, finding work to care for her six children on her own. Seeing her mother as the family breadwinner, Stringer admired the strength of her mother.

Obstacles in Stringer's personal life remained consistent once she began her coaching career. While at Cheney, Stringer's 14-month-old daughter was diagnosed with spinal meningitis the weekend of the national basketball championship. Learning that her only daughter would never walk or talk again, Stringer managed to stay focused while guiding her team to the finals.

Stringer's second trip to the NCAA finals was also personally challenging. On Thanksgiving Day in 1991, Stringer's 47 year-old husband suffered a massive heart attack that took his life. The sudden loss of her support system shook Stringer as she was left with two sons and her sick daughter. A grief-filled heart competed for her energy, yet still relentless to defeat, Stringer was able to lead her 1993 team to the finals.

In a more public battle, Stringer addressed the racist and sexist comments of radio personality, Don Imus, which hit the airwaves the day following Rutgers NCAA title game loss to Tennessee in 2007. Speaking out against his racist and sexist remarks Stringer said it was not about the players "as black or nappy-headed. It's about us as a people. When there is not equality for all, or when there has been denied equality for one, there has been denied equality for all." She further said that her athletes worked diligently in the classroom and accomplished much on the court, bringing smiles and pride to the state of New Jersey. She called the words of Imus "deplorable, despicable, abominable, and unconscionable," adding, "It hurts me."[3] Stringer's graceful reaction was not a surprise coming from someone who spent years mustering the strength to strive forward in the throngs of adversity.

Stringer's prowess as a leader has earned her a multitude of awards. She was recognized as the National Coach of the Year in 1982, 1988, and 1993. In 2003, *Sports Illustrated* named her one of the "101 Most Influential Minorities in Sports." A recipient of the Lifetime Achievement Award from the Black Coaches Association (now Black Coaches and Administrators), Stringer is a seven-time finalist for the Naismith National Coach of the Year Award.

Stringer joined the Women's Basketball Hall of Fame in 2001, the Center for the Study of Sport in Society Hall of Fame in 2005, and the International Women's Sports Hall of Fame in 2006. In light of the controversy surrounding Imus' remarks in 2007, the National Consortium for Academics and Sports (NCAS) named Stringer and her team the inaugural winners of the Eddie Robinson Leadership Award. Executive Director for the NCAS, Dr. Richard Lapchick said of Coach Stringer and her team that "they took adversity and turned it into another victory. The dignity they showed America forced us as a nation to look at all the ways we objectify and demean women. They may be helping us to change the culture."[4]

Prior to 2008, Stringer considered one of her most memorable events and honors to have come when Nike in Beaverton, Oregon named its second child development center after her. Yet one year later, after nearly four decades of work and dedication, Stringer was inducted into the Naismith Memorial Basketball Hall of Fame. Upon receiving her award, she acknowledged previous Hall of Famer, John Chaney, who coached and befriended Stringer during her days at Cheyney. "Most of what I know about basketball—most of what I know and understand about people—I learned from him."[5]

Respect for Stringer's career is widespread beyond her extensive collegiate experience. Most notably, Stringer was an assistant coach in 2004 for the gold-medal U.S. Olympic Team. Prior to the news of her daughter's illness and the death of her husband, Stringer was heavily involved with USA Basketball. She was an assistant coach for the 1980 USA Jones Cup Team that earned the bronze medal. In 1984, she helped coach the silver medalist U.S. World University Games Team. Stringer led the U.S. World Championship Qualifying Team to gold in 1989, and gained Pan American Games experience in 1991.

Off the sidelines, Stringer has used her expertise as a noted administrator in the development of the Women's Basketball Coaches Association. She has spent time serving on the Kay Yow/WBCA Cancer Fund Board of Directors. In a more private matter, Stringer herself overcame a bout with breast cancer during her coaching career.

Stringers ability to teach young women through her life's example continues to significantly impact her players and those who know her closely and from a far. In her memoir, *Standing Tall*, her story of strength, perseverance, and determination has been able to reach those outside the confines of the basketball court. Still in pursuit of a coveted national title, to many, C. Vivian Stringer is already considered a champion.

Notes

1. Rutgers (W) Official Website, "Player Bio: C.Vivian Stringer," The Official Site of Rutgers's Women's Basketball http://www.scarletknights.com/basketball-women/coaches/stringer.asp, (accessed January 15, 2009).

2. C. Vivian Stringer with Laura Tucker. *Standing Tall: A Memoir of Tragedy and Triumph,* Maryland: Crown, 2008.

3. Associated Press, "Rutgers women's team, coach speaks out," http://sports.espn.go.com/ncw/news/story?id=2831636, (accessed January 15, 2010).

4. "Eddie Robinson Leadership Award Announced," The Official Site of Rutgers Athletics, http://www.scarletknights.com/basketball-women/news/release.asp?prID=5312, (accessed January 15, 2010).

5. Michael J. Fensom, "Rutgers coach C. Vivian Stringer still struggling to come to terms with Hall of Fame enshrinement," www.nj.com/rutgerswomen/index.ssf/2009/09/rutgers_womens_basketball_coac.html, (accessed January 15, 2010).

Carolyn Peck

Coaching to Win in Life

by Joslyn Dalton

Carolyn Peck loved to play basketball. During her senior year of high school in Jefferson City, Tennessee, she was named the state's Miss Basketball after averaging 35 points and 13.2 rebounds per game. Standing 6-foot-4, her towering size and raw talent caught the attention of college recruiters. Peck took her services to Vanderbilt University where she played from 1985 to 1988, averaging 10.6 points and 5.8 rebounds per game. Throughout her career, she blocked a total of 180 shots—a record that stood long after she graduated with a degree in communication.

After graduating, Peck passed up the opportunity to play professionally in Spain. Instead, she began working as a television marketing consultant and pharmaceutical sales representative. After two years away from basketball, she realized how deep her passion for the game extended. She returned to the court to play professionally in Italy before joining a team in Japan. In her second season with her new team, Peck's squad captured the League Championship.

In 1993, Peck moved back to her home state and became an assistant coach for the legendary Pat Summitt. Coaching woman's basketball at the University of Tennessee proved to be a great experience for Peck as she was able to quickly develop her coaching skills.

Unable to take on a larger coaching role at Tennessee, Peck's next assistant coaching stop was at the University of Kentucky in 1995. The following season, Peck joined Nell Fortner who had just replaced former head coach, Lin Dunn at Purdue University. During her time as an assistant coach, Peck helped guide the Boilermakers to a share of the Big Ten Championship and a run to the second round of the NCAA tournament. At the conclusion of the season, Fortner landed the head coaching position of the U.S.A. Women's basketball team for the 2000 Summer Olympics. With Fortner's exit, Peck became Purdue's third head coach in three seasons.

Peck enjoyed success during her first season as a head coach. The Boilermakers went 23-10, finishing with an Elite Eight appearance. Yet after one season, Peck was enticed with a new coaching offer, this time for the WNBA. Pat Williams, senior executive vice president of a new Orlando-based team asked her to be his head coach and general manager. It was a dream of Peck's to coach in the NBA. When the offer to coach in the WNBA came along, she could not refuse. After only one year of experience as a head coach, she accepted the job offer.

When Peck shared the news with her team, she was not prepared for how angry they became. The upcoming seniors, who would have four coaches in four years, were especially upset. "We'd stayed and played for her because we believed in what she wanted to do," said senior Stephanie McCarty. "Now she was going to leave? We didn't want to be just stepping-stones for people. I felt betrayed, and I told her so."[1]

As a compromise, Peck agreed to coach one additional year with the Boilermakers before making her move to Orlando. Although a separation between Peck and her team had formed, a season-opening upset of top-ranked Tennessee helped the Boilermakers reunite. Summitt, who was experiencing a 46-game winning streak, was shocked by the 78-68 loss to her former assistant. Purdue went on to notch a 28-1 regular season record in route to winning the NCAA National Championship. In each of their six tournament games, the Boilermakers won by at least 10 points.

As of 2009, Peck is the only African-American, Division I coach to win a national title. She was named the Women's Basketball Coach of the Year by the Associated Press, as well as Big Ten Coach of the Year. The New York Athletic Club chose her as their first woman and first African-American to win the Winged Foot Award, an honor bestowed on the best coach in college basketball. In addition to Peck's coaching recognition, her Boilermakers made history by becoming the only Big Ten school to have won a national championship in women's basketball.

Two weeks following her 62-45 championship game win over Duke, Peck moved to Florida where she assumed the head coaching position of the Orlando Miracle. Peck was 32 years old. Although she endured criticism because of her young age and lack of experience, she proved resilient as she guided the team to a tie for second place in the Eastern Conference. The Miracle qualified for the playoffs in 2000 after having just missed them the year before. During her three-year span with the team, the Miracle's overall record was 44-52.

With her contract with the Miracles at an end, Peck returned to college basketball and became the eighth head coach of the University of Florida. In five seasons, she posted a 72-76 record from the 2002–03 season through the 2006–07 season. In her second year, she was responsible for the greatest one-season turnaround in Florida's history. Ranked as the third-toughest schedule in the country, UF played 11 nationally-ranked teams in route to winning 10 more games in 2003–04 than the year before.

Under Peck's leadership, the Gators enjoyed two berths to the NCAA tournament and one to the WNIT. In her 2005–06 season, Peck guided the Gators to two upsets when they defeated number two-ranked LSU and number five-ranked Tennessee, becoming the second unranked team to ever defeat the Lady Vols in Knoxville. The win marked the second time Peck beat Summitt.

Off the court, during Peck's time at the helm, the Gators amassed 31 SEC Academic Honor Roll accolades. During her two years with Purdue, eight different players combined for 11 Academic All-Big Ten honors, while Stephanie White was named the GTE Academic All-American of the Year.

After suffering through a 14-game losing streak and 9-22 record during the 2006–07 season, former University of Florida basketball player Amanda Butler replaced Peck as the Gators' head coach. In all, Peck has accumulated 12 years of experience in the SEC, five as a head coach, three as an assistant, and four as a player. Additionally, she was an assistant coach for the silver medalist 1997 U.S. Jones Cup Team and the gold medalist 2004 U.S. Junior World Championship Team.

Experienced and knowledgeable, ESPN hired Peck in 2007 as a basketball analyst. During her time with the company, she has covered men's and women's college basketball, as well as NBA and WNBA games. Peck's latest role has provided her with new insight. "Being a coach, you're more concerned with your team only," she said. "When broadcasting, you have the challenge of making sure you're giving out correct information, you're promoting the sport."[2]

Women's basketball has benefited greatly from the involvement of Carolyn Peck. As a successful player, multi-level coach, and experienced commentator, she has transcended the sport. Throughout her career, she has kept her eyes open to exciting new opportunities; a mentality she summed up when she said, "Be careful what you wish for, because when it comes along, you're going to have to make a decision. It might never come along again."[3]

Notes

1. Leigh Montville, "Miracle Worker," CNNSI.com, June 14, 1999, http://sports illustrated.cnn.com/vault/article/magazine/MAG1016155/index.htm, (accessed March 10, 2010).

2. Jessica Collins, "Catching Up With ESPN Basketball Analyst Carolyn Peck," *SportsBusiness Daily*, July 31, 1999, http://www.sportsbusinessdaily.com/article/132 169, (accessed March 10, 2010).

3. Leigh Montville, "Miracle Worker," CNNSI.com, June 14, 1999, http://sports illustrated.cnn.com/vault/article/magazine/MAG1016155/index.htm, (accessed March 10, 2010).

Mike Sheppard Sr.

Coaching to Win in Life

by Joslyn Dalton

Baseball has always been a family affair for Mike Sheppard. At the age of three, he tragically lost his mother. Shortly thereafter, he was sent to live with his grandmother, leaving his grief-stricken father behind to take on life as a widower. When Sheppard was old enough to head to school, his grandmother took him back to his father who, by then, had settled into living life as a bachelor. It took time for Sheppard and his father to become reacquainted with one another. Although they had little in common at first, baseball became the common thread that wove their father-son relationship together. "He didn't coach, but he loved baseball," Sheppard remembers.[1]

Courtesy of S.R. Smith/Seton Hall Athletics.

Living with his father allowed Sheppard the opportunity to see firsthand how to persevere from hardship and commit to hard work. His father always told him, "Never lose your hustle," which became Sheppard's anthem throughout his playing and coaching career.[2] Excelling in football and wrestling in high school for Seton Hall Prep, it was Sheppard's talent as a baseball catcher that took him to the next level. He earned a scholarship to Seton Hall University to play for Owen T. Carroll. While in school, Sheppard knew his education was salient to his overall well-being as a young man. He studied health and physical education with the hopes of one day becoming head coach of a baseball program. He also was diligent about service and spent three years in the Marine Corps.

In 1974, Sheppard was offered his dream job. His loyalty never strayed from Seton Hall. Growing up across the street from the University, he walked 800 yards to both high school and college. When asked to be the head coach of Seton Hall University, he wasted little time accepting the position. Located just miles from the "house that Ruth built," Sheppard began building one of his own.

Sheppard's run at Seton Hall was a lifelong journey which would culminate in his recognition as the greatest baseball coach in the school's history, scoring 998 career victories. As of 2009, he was ranked 50th on the NCAA's all-time winningest list which includes Divisions I, II, and III coaches. Sheppard recorded 28 winning seasons and took his team to the NCAA College World Series on two occasions. Eighty of his athletes have gone on to play professionally, with 30 in the major leagues, including Charlie Puleo, John Morris, Pat Pacillo, Craig Biggio, Rick Cerone, Jason Grilli, Matt Morris, Mo Vaughn, and John Valentin.

A true testament to his coaching prowess, Sheppard produced seven first-round draft picks, all of whom were not skilled enough to be drafted out of high school. He masterfully taught his players the art of hitting and pitching, but more importantly, he taught them discipline. Craig Biggio, a second baseman for the Houston Astros, in 2007 became the ninth MLB player to log 3,000 hits while playing every game for a single team. Looking back at his Seton Hall University days, he is thankful for what Sheppard instilled in him. "When I was there (1985–87), I didn't understand him like I understand him now. When you're 18 years old and go away from home, you think you know everything," Biggio reminisced. "You know nothing. In college you need somebody to step on your toes once in awhile. Otherwise, you'll get away with murder," he said.[3] As proud as Sheppard is for his MLB stars, he finds it equally rewarding to follow his past players as they have become CEOs, presidents, and successful businessmen.

A major part of Sheppard's discipline involved his expectations in the classroom. An associate professor of Education, he wanted his athletes to get their degrees. NCAA rules required student-athletes to obtain a 2.0 grade point average (GPA) by their senior year. For Sheppard's young men, he required his student-athletes maintain a 2.5 if they were going to be allowed to compete. "I wanted to travel a lot for games. I didn't want to take kids out of class who were having trouble with their studies," he said.[4] Sheppard worked off the field to help his students. He scheduled mandatory study halls for his freshmen and sophomores along with any player below the

2.5 GPA mark. He also established a "Monitoring System of Athletics" through which Seton Hall faculty members issued monthly reports on the baseball team's performance in the classroom, attendance, and grades. "I was hell on wheels when it came to going to class," Sheppard said. "If I found out a guy cut class and we were traveling to a game, I'd throw him off the bus. Even if he was scheduled to pitch, I'd throw him off the bus!"[5] Sheppard's "Monitoring System of Athletics" became a model for all sports programs at the University.

As the winningest coach in Seton Hall University history, Sheppard has collected numerous honors. He is a three-time Big East Coach of the Year, two-time AACBC District Coach of the Year, and four-time NJCBA Coach of the Year. In 1989, the National Consortium for Academics and Sports chose Sheppard as a Giant Steps Award recipient for his efforts both on the field and in the classroom. He earned the McQuaid Medal in 1990, an award given for 20 years of academic and athletic service to the Seton Hall community. In 1996, he was inducted into the Seton Hall Athletic Hall of Fame as well as the Newark Athletic Hall of Fame. In 2003, he was awarded Seton Halls' Most Valuable Pirate Award and in 2004, Seton Hall retired his jersey number 17. For his most recent achievement, the American Baseball Coaches Association Hall of Fame has chosen Sheppard as a 2011 inductee.

Following his retirement in 2003, Sheppard was named Seton Hall's Head Coach Emeritus. He continues to go to practices, he travels for games with the team, and visits the office on a daily basis. "I try to make myself available to people, to give advice to parents and players when they ask for it," he said.[6] Away from his duties for the Pirates, Sheppard has maintained an active role in the baseball community. Founded in 1974, Sheppard began the family owned and operated Hustler's Baseball School, the oldest continuous baseball school in the New Jersey area. Since 1983, he has been the Chairman of the Essex County American Legion Baseball. He also serves as the Commissioner of the Atlantic Baseball Confederation Collegiate League.

Health issues have occasionally slowed Sheppard down. After experiencing a debilitating stroke at the age of 62, Sheppard beat the odds by recovering and making his way back to the dugout. In 2001, he underwent open heart surgery and recently he was diagnosed with leukemia. Through it all, Sheppard knows what it has meant to have his players' support. "If you take care of the kids, they come back and take care of you," he shared. Throughout his setbacks, Sheppard has left little room for excuses, saying, "It has all made me stronger." He also believes his circumstances have helped him teach humility to his athletes. "Humility is a trait that is played down too much today," he said. "But if you are humble in victory that actually makes you a stronger person."[7]

Sheppard makes sure he and his wife, Phyllis, leave space on their calendars to take part in one of their favorite activities, watching their 13 grandchildren participate in sports. "They play field hockey, soccer, football, basketball, swimming, baseball . . . you name it!" he said.[8] Sport is what has woven together the fabric of the Sheppard family. All three of Sheppard's sons coach baseball. His eldest, Mike Sheppard Jr., is currently the head coach for Seton Hall Preparatory High School, a program that has annually been ranked as number one in the country. John Sheppard is the head coach for Morristown-Beard Crimson High School in Northwest Jersey as well as the school's athletic director. Rob Sheppard succeeded his father as the head coach for Seton Hall University in 2003. He has already been recognized by the New Jersey Collegiate Baseball Association as a Division I Coach of the Year. Sheppard's son-in law, Ed Blankmeyer, who also happens to be Sheppard's first recruit to play at Seton Hall University, has been the head baseball coach for St. John's University for over 15 seasons.

Mike Sheppard Sr. has left his imprint on the world of college baseball both on the field and in the classroom. When asked what young coaches should know when going into the profession, Sheppard shared, "Love the game and take care of your players. It's more than just coaching."[9]

Notes

1. Mike Sheppard, interview with author, March 30, 2010.
2. Ibid.
3. Sullivan, Tara. "Seton Hall's Good Sheppard," *The Record*, May 10, 1998.
4. Mike Sheppard, interview with author, March 30, 2010.
5. Ibid.
6. Ibid.
7. Ibid.
8. Ibid.
9. Ibid.

Robert Hamilton

Coaching to Win in Life

by Stacy Martin-Tenney

Robert Hamilton's experience on the basketball court as a student-athlete inspired him to return to the game, this time on the sideline. He initiated a call to action for parents, teachers, coaches, and students to get involved in an athlete's life. His hope is for those athletes to develop into scholars largely due to the personal interest that someone takes in them. In the inner city of Boston, too many children do not feel that anyone cares about them. It was a struggle to survive, let alone succeed, at least until Rob Hamilton came to town. He issued a challenge to those groups so vitally important to a young person's success with the Coaches Academic Leadership League, also known as CALL.

The Leadership League was organized around what Hamilton called the Academic Guardian program, which named a teacher at the school to be responsible for the student-athlete's academic welfare. This component is essential to classroom achievement because it eliminated the blame game that teachers and coaches often play over the responsibility of a player's grades. The academic guardian was in charge of monitoring all of the athlete's class work through frequent progress reports. The accountability and ownership that each instructor felt about his or her student-athlete created a bond that existed on and off the court. Academic guardians soon became fixtures in the bleachers at home games. The student-athletes finally received the attention and caring devotion that some of them had been lacking. CALL prompted parents to become more involved in their children's lives as well, and, of course, the coach was calling plays on and off the court to show his commitment to his team. The League was a way to round out the responsibility of teachers to the development of a young mind.

Hamilton was an assistant basketball coach at Brandeis University shortly after graduating from Middlebury College, but then he moved to the frontlines of tomorrow, the high school arena. He began teaching and coaching at Umana Technical High School, now

Umana Middle School, in the inner city of East Boston. He followed that with a coaching stint at Charlestown High School where he also implemented CALL. It involved all of the same elements of guardians, involvement, and academic progress reports. Charlestown was laying a foundation then for the basketball powerhouse that they are today. Often in high schools limited resources cause bickering among athletic teams, especially between the boys and girls basketball teams over court time. At Charlestown, there was harmony. Hamilton let the girls' team practice first, while his boys' team went to the library for study hall. In this way he could guarantee completed course work, because he was watching. The team was successful and in pursuit of the State Championship.

Hamilton is a reserved and unassuming man, but his voice carries far beyond gymnasiums. He answered his call to leadership as the president of the Boston High School Basketball Coaches Association. Hamilton utilized the resources he had available to establish Project LEAD, which was an outgrowth of CALL that focused on the key principle of class attendance. The first hurdle is usually getting young adults to actually be present in class, before they can begin to learn. He negotiated a deal with Converse to provide a pair of sneakers for each student-athlete in the city of Boston who met the 90 percent class attendance requirement. Project LEAD opened doors for children without many other opportunities by simply asking them to enter a classroom.

Hamilton knew that he could reach children through basketball, but an official school season was much too short. He created and directed an AAU basketball league called Boston Prep. It wasn't the typical AAU league concerned with skill, talent, and, of course, winning. Boston Prep had a coach, as well as an MIT student, who worked with the student-athletes. Hamilton negotiated an agreement with a Kaplan Learning Center for an MIT student to teach SAT prep courses to his team. Boston Prep had skill, talent, and they were winners in the classroom and on the court.

Hamilton received the Giant Steps Award as a coach in 1988, just seven years after his college graduation. According to him, it changed his life. The recognition that came from the award broadened his horizons as he realized how much more he could accomplish in the world. The personal recognition of goals set Hamilton on a new path in sports, one that moved him further from the game and into the boardroom. His creative thinking and intimate knowledge of the sport landed him a job as the Marketing Director of Reebok Basketball. His dedication and hard work quickly produced dividends for him. He became solely responsible for a young Shaquille O'Neal from Louisiana State University, escorting the present NBA superpower around the globe on world tours and beginning to cultivate Shaquille's brand and image. His executive status sent him on business trips to factories in the Pacific as well. While traveling internationally, Hamilton learned a great deal about the world. The breadth of knowledge that he held now was invaluable, but he missed being in direct contact with the children.

He quenched the thirst for direct connection to the student-athletes by accepting the coaching position at Massachusetts College of Liberal Arts, a small Division III school. At some point in everyone's life they seem to return to where they started. When they get there they can judge where they have been and where they are going. Hamilton was born in the Berkshires near North Adams, where MCLA is located, so for him it was a homecoming. Hamilton instituted the CALL program there, too. He mandated study halls and academic progress from his student-athletes and implemented aggressive tracking systems to keep them on course for graduation. During this time a number of the NCAA's member institutions had violated its rules. MCLA, however, was certainly not on its list. In fact, it was setting a positive example for other schools. Athletes deserve ethical treatment in regard to their personal welfare. They should not be abused by the system as a means to a win. Hamilton and his Trailblazers had a 100 percent graduation rate and they were blazing a trail through academics.

Hamilton believes that the true reflection of a man's success is in his home. His son, Onaje is a reflection of his father's triumphs in the greatest possible way. Hamilton executed the CALL and LEAD programs to get his student-athletes scholarships to college, and his son lived those programs at home and at school. Onaje attended Yale and by his sophomore season was listed as a 2nd team All-Conference performer. Onaje embraced his father's beliefs in education and helping those people around him. Hamilton's reflection seems as clear as a mirror image.

His involvement in sports has certainly encompassed all of the arenas from high school to college to professional. Rob Hamilton has challenged athletes over the years to be scholars. As a coach he is content with winning seasons, but as a person he celebrates high GPAs and SAT scores. When he tells his story, the milestones he recounts about his players are where they attended college and what their test scores were, not their scoring averages. Hamilton has blended academics and athletics into a success story for dozens, indeed, hundreds of young people.

Bob Shannon

Coaching to Win in Life

by Joslyn Dalton

Blemished with rundown liquor stores and abandoned strip malls, the forsaken community of East St. Louis rests in the heart of the Illinois floodplain, across from the Mississippi River. In the 1980s, city trash collected in backyards and vacant lots before the decision was made to have it go up in smoke. Years later, charcoal remnants can be found smeared on poorly painted buildings, and the stench of rotten garbage still lingers in the thick summer air of East St. Louis. For years, the community, a population dominated primarily by blacks, has struggled to grasp onto hope.

Bob Shannon first arrived to East St. Louis when things were in slightly better shape. A high school football coach looking for work, he decided to take the assistant position at Lincoln High in 1971. Five years later, he moved to East St. Louis Senior High as the head football coach of the Flyers. The football field where he held practice had anything but freshly cut glass and finely painted lines. Instead, spectators who came to Shannon's field were greeted with a reminder from the school, "No Drugs, Alcohol, or Guns Allowed." It was clear that the deterioration of the city was taunting its youth.

Shannon knew he needed a special group of players to survive at East St. Louis High. From 1976 until the start of the 1995 season, he searched for boys with influential instincts to play on his teams. Leadership became the fundamental premise of his coaching philosophy. Along with the threats of gangs and drug dealers, family life also served as a distraction for his players. Broken homes and absent parents left students to raise themselves. Still, with a quarter of the town's adult population unemployed and two thirds of the total population on public aid, Shannon's relentless faith in the inner city youth he coached became his consuming passion.

Through sport, Shannon was able to spark a sense of optimism in East St. Louis. The growth of his football team became a bright light for a community left largely in the dark. The physical prowess and street-smart toughness of his players helped turn the Flyers into a perennial national powerhouse. Over his 20 years as head coach, he amassed a career record of 194 wins and 35 losses. The dominance of East St. Louis High was rewarded with six Illinois state titles and two national championships in 1985 and 1989. A string of 44 continuous wins highlighted the success of Shannon's program.

Although Shannon hooked his athletes with football, he reached them with education. More than 100 of his players went to college on athletic scholarships, a few making it into the National Football League. "Football here has never been just about winning," Shannon said. "It's been a road out for these kids."[1] Shannon understood what it meant to search for a more promising path. During his childhood, he used sport as the medium to transcend his challenging circumstances. Along with his 10 siblings, Shannon worked hard at a variety of manual labor jobs such as picking cotton and harvesting pecans. It was through his work delivering fancy furniture for the wealthy that he was exposed to what it meant to have money. Mesmerized by the luxurious lifestyle of the people who employed him, Shannon decided he would go to college in order to give himself a chance at such opportunity.

He knew no one who had attended college, yet on his own he discovered that sports could be his ticket. A standout on the football field, he achieved an athletic scholarship and the chance to play quarterback for Tennessee State. Although he left college for a brief stint in the NFL, he returned to school to finish his degree in Education. The first from his family to graduate college, Shannon's accomplishment allowed him to take a teaching and coaching job in East St. Louis. Watching his athletes experience affluent neighborhoods during football games on the road, he understood what stirred beneath the surface. "We just worked that much harder, took pride in showing the world that kids from East St. Louis could learn and achieve, just like those suburban kids," he said, teaching them that education, not drug dealing, would financially liberate them.[2]

By 1992, Shannon had transformed from a young boy with big dreams into a symbol of hope for the community around him. While on his campaign, President Bill Clinton met Shannon during a speaking engagement at East St. Louis High School. Clinton admired Shannon and saw a great deal of promise in him. He nationally recognized Shannon for his efforts, choosing him as one of the 53 Faces of Hope. Shannon appeared on television shows such as *60 Minutes* and became the focus for Kevin Horrigan's book, *The Right Kind of Heroes*. Never quick to become wrapped up in fame, Shannon continued to keep his eye on the prize, East St. Louis' drifting youth.

As an outspoken coach, Shannon became increasingly concerned with the internal financial strategy of his school district. A $10 million deficit surfaced around 1993, revealing that corruption was hard at work. Even though Illinois had been providing the East St. Louis school district with 80 percent of the district's overall budget, $58 million a year, the school's officials were unable to account for the millions of missing dollars. Teachers had been laid off, class sizes expanded, school supplies vanished, and fire alarms stopped working. Educational theorist Jonathan Kozol considered East St. Louis one of country's poorest school districts. Shannon was repeatedly denied basic funds for his football program, forcing him to beg for equipment on behalf on his players. Understanding his school was participating in unethical behavior, he took it upon himself to trace the money trail.

Speculations of corruption traveled throughout the town. The news turned from rumor to reality when in 1994, Illinois started monitoring the school's finances, finding monumental errors and under the table payouts. Shannon finally collected documented proof of how funds that were supposed to be used for food for his football team were hoarded by the school's athletic director, Arthur May. Prior to his 1995 season, Shannon announced that he wanted to become the school's athletic director. In doing so, he felt he could help overcome the unethical behavior of May. While exposing the corruption that besieged the school, Shannon paid the price for taking a stand. Under immense pressure from the school board, he began to consider leaving East St. Louis High. He became afraid that he was bringing more harm than good to his football team. "As much as I love coaching, they thought I'd never be able to walk away," Shannon said.[3] While he was supposed to have time to think over whether or not he would stay or leave, the school board swiftly met in a special meeting to vote 6-0 for his resignation. In standing up for his values and for the rights of the young men he coached, Shannon was forced out of his coaching position with the Flyers.

East St. Louis High had misplaced more than finances during the last portion of Shannon's career. After taking time off, he took the head coaching position for Christian Brother's College High

School (CBC) in East St. Louis. He coached for the Cadets from 1999 to 2007, collecting a record of 56 wins and 39 losses. Even though CBC offered him a 3,000-seat stadium with artificial turf and a state-of-the-art press box, Shannon's heart still beat for the misguided youth at his old school.

Over the years, East St. Louis High has remained dominate on the national scale. According to Rod Kloeckner, a local sportswriter, the program will always be good. "It's a football factory started under Bob Shannon," he said.[3] Kloeckner also added that East St. Louis remains a rampant community consumed with poverty. Yet with the exposure brought forth from Shannon, the Flyers football team has gained tremendous support from anonymous donors and a Booster Club. Today, the team plays on a manicured field under big, expensive lights. Even with such physical advancements, few have forgotten where this program came from. Shannon's efforts are still admired by the community; 15 years after the school drove him away. "Everyone knows his name, face, and the history of the East St. Louis High football program," Kloeckner said.[4] While the new stadium has become the jewel of the city, its diamond has always been Bob Shannon.

Notes

1. Darcy Frey, "Sidelined," *Sports Illustrated*, October 30, 1995, http://sportsillustrated.cnn.com/vault/article/magazine/MAG1007324/index.htm, (accessed March 25, 2010).

2. Ibid

3. Rod Kloeckner, interview with author, March 30, 2010.

4. Ibid.

Ken Carter

Coaching to Win in Life

by Joslyn Dalton

Student-athletes can easily experience difficulty balancing academics and athletics if they do not have a sufficient support system in place. For Ken Carter, a close knit family provided the structure he needed to excel in both. With two involved parents, seven sisters, and one brother, Carter's life was rooted in deep values and the discipline of hard work. Born in Fernwood, Mississippi, Carter moved to the troubled city of Richmond, California at the age of 12. He became a star basketball player for the Richmond High School Oilers from 1973 to 1977. Setting all-time school records for scoring, assists, and steals, Carter averaged 23.3 points per game and earned All-League honors his senior year. He also found success on the baseball diamond as a shortstop for the Oilers.

While shining in sports, Carter remained committed to his schoolwork. After graduating high school, he attended George Fox University in Oregon where he played basketball. His passion for entrepreneurship led him to take e-commerce classes at Contra Costa College in San Pablo, California, which was close to Richmond. While Carter was excelling in college, his adolescent neighborhood was deteriorating. Drug use and unemployment were rampant. In spite of these difficulties, Carter returned home after finishing school, where he operated his family's sporting goods store and eventually opened his own barbershop and salon.

In 1997, Richmond High was desperate for change. The school's student achievement record, which ranked in the bottom 10 percent of California high schools, was failing along with the school's basketball program. During the two decades that followed Carter's glory days as a player, Richmond had not produced a winning season. Alarmed by the worsening conditions at his old high school, Carter embraced the opportunity to once again walk the halls of Richmond High. Along with taking a position as a math teacher, he accepted the head coaching position for the boys' basketball team. His impact would be immediate.

Carter was concerned with more than just the Oilers success on the court. He worked tirelessly to give the school an external face-lift by cleaning up trash and scrubbing away graffiti. He knew it was imperative that his athletes become disciplined in their schoolwork. He had all of his players sign a contract, promising to maintain a 2.3 grade point average. His student-athletes were also responsible for sitting in the front of the classroom, studying 10 hours a week, turning in homework on time, dressing in formal attire on game days, and addressing their elders as "sir" and "madam" as a sign of respect. Carter expected discipline and he got results. Despite improving his players' demeanor off the court, Carter's teams were slow to progress on the court. After two seasons of struggles, the Oilers began to finally see improvement under their new coach. During the third season under Coach Carter, the team went undefeated through its first 13 games, and was widely seen as contenders for a state championship. At one point, Carter's team was ranked third among California's Division III high schools. As the team started to rack up wins, the community began to take note.

Although his young men were thriving on the court, 15 of his 45 players were failing to keep up with their contractual agreements in the classroom. On January 4, 1999, during the middle of the season, Carter decided to make a point. He padlocked the doors of Richmond's gymnasium. Instead of practicing, he sent all of his athletes to the library for tutoring. "I wanted them to understand the message that they could create options for themselves," he reflected years later. "If they did not want to continue in the lifestyle they were in and if they wanted to accomplish moving to the next level, they would have to make their main focus their studies."[1]

In the eight days that followed Carter's lockout, he continued to prevent his team from practicing and even from playing in two games, ending the Oilers' undefeated season. The school's principal at the time, Haidee Foust-Whitemore, was supportive of Carter's decision. Looking back she said, "The bottom line is that he was trying to get the kids up to par, get them working up to their potential."[2] At the time however, Carter took a great deal of heat from basketball boosters, school officials, coaches from other teams, and some parents. Controversy over the way he went about making a point to his players boiled. Eventually, Principal Foust-Whitemore and athletic director Roy Rogers decided to end the lockout. In their first game back, the Oilers won 61-51 against St. Elizabeth High School, yet by February 11, 1999, some of Carter's players continued to not live up to their contract. Instead of cancelling games, this time Carter held his players accountable by benching those who were performing poorly in the classroom. "For some reason, our young men are starting to slip away," he said.[3] Richmond High ended the season 19-5, losing in the second round of the district playoffs.

Carter's tactics and message ended up reverberating throughout the country. He was interviewed on *Today, Good Morning America, All Things Considered*, and in several major newspapers. He even took his platform to the steps of California's State Capitol on November 1, 2000 for a project he named "Scooting for Schools and Education." On a human-powered kick scooter, Carter made his way from Richmond to Sacramento. His goal was to raise the awareness of state officials to the inadequacies of California's educational system, while simultaneously gaining the attention of the nation. "I was scooting for better quality education for all children," he said. "I wanted to not only get the attention of the students and teachers, but the parents, neighbors, relatives, and lawmakers."[4] Carter's radical efforts were rewarded. Richmond High received building enhancements and computers from the Office of the Secretary of Education.

Having used sport as the vehicle to generate social change, Carter embraced the opportunity to carry the torch for the 2002 Olympic Games in Salt Lake City, Utah. "It was a privilege and honor, especially since the only way to participate in the event was to have been nominated and voted for by others that felt your contributions to the community were as noteworthy as the Olympics itself," he shared.[5] That same year, Carter decided to leave Richmond High, venturing into a new sport, Slam Ball, which combines basketball, football, and gymnastics on a floor-level trampoline surface. In the inaugural season of the new league, he led The Rumble to a national title.

Over the years, Carter has been recognized with countless awards. He was a 2000 recipient of *CityFlight Newsmagazine*'s "Ten Most Influential African Americans in the Bay Area." Additionally, he has the Harvard Club's Distinguished Secondary Educator Award, NAACP's Impact Citizen of the Year Award, California State Lottery/

Governor Gray Davis' Heroes in Education Award, Willie Brown's Leadership Award, California's Unsung Heroes Award, and the A.N.G. Californian Boy's Coach of the Year Award to his credits.

Ever since the "Great Lockout," Carter has gained access to a variety of entrepreneurial endeavors. The owner and operator of Prime Time Publications and Prime Time Sports, Carter also became an author and motivational speaker. To develop and promote educational training and mentoring programs for minority youth, he started the non-profit organization, Coach Ken Carter Foundation. In 2005, Paramount Pictures released a film called *Coach Carter*, which depicted the real-life events of the 1999 Richmond Oilers team including the now infamous lockout. With Samuel L. Jackson as Carter, the passion, intensity, and commitment of the legendary coach was evident. "It's a combination of *Rudy*, *Stand and Deliver*, *Lean on Me*, *Hoosiers* and *Seabiscuit*, Carter said.[6] He was on set everyday and worked with the writers and producers. The film topped American box offices the week of its first release, grossing over $29 million.

Carter has chosen to place many of his entrepreneurial profits back into the Richmond community. In 2009, he introduced his biggest project to date, an unconventional boarding school named the Coach Carter Impact Academy. Located in Marlin, California, Carter hopes the Academy will attract troublemakers and under-achievers who are ready for change as well as straight-A students who want a deeper experience. "Kids today need a high challenge," he said. "If you set the bar low, they'll hit it. If you set the bar high, they'll hit it."[7]

Despite the Hollywood fame and public attention, Carter's commitment to the advancement of society's youth is unending. In placing high expectations on his players as well as political figures, he undoubtedly has put high expectations on himself. Through the countless chapters and different scenes of his life, Coach Ken Carter has made the most of his leading role.

Notes

1. James Anderson, "Rumble Coach Ken Carter: An Impact Deeper Than Just SlamBall," http://coachcarter.com/rumble-coach-ken-carter-an-impact-deeper-than-just-slamball/, (accessed March 29, 2010).

2. Jeff Merron, "How Real is the Reel 'Coach Carter?'" Special to ESPN.com, January 25, 2005, http://sports.espn.go.com/espn/page3/story?page=merron/coachcarter, (accessed March 29, 2010).

3. Ibid.

4. James Anderson, "Rumble Coach Ken Carter: An Impact Deeper Than Just SlamBall," http://coachcarter.com/rumble-coach-ken-carter-an-impact-deeper-than-just-slamball/, (accessed March 29, 2010).

5. Ibid.

6. Ibid.

7. J.B. Smith, "Coach Carter's Sequel: A Marlin boys' school," http://coachcarter.com/2009/07/23/hello-world/, (accessed March 29, 2010).

Beverly Kearney

Coaching to Win in Life

by Jessica Bartter

Beverly Kearney at the National Consortium for Academics and Sports' 2005 Giant Steps Awards Banquet and Hall of Fame Induction Ceremony

After she slowly stammered up the steps and across the stage, each foot carefully placed in front of the next with the help of a cane on either side, she finally arrived at the podium. She leaned over to the microphone and said, "I want you all to know that I have two canes, but I really only need one . . . deep down inside I'm a diva and I couldn't wear my sneakers so I had to kind of compromise a little in order to wear my dress shoes."[1] The 450 guests, each on edge as they watched the star of the evening struggle to the stage to accept her award, roared with laughter. It wasn't just Beverly Kearney's gorgeous smile that warmed their hearts, but the resiliency that resounded as soon as she spoke to them. A tear rolled down my smiling face as I sat in the very back of the banquet hall enthralled by the emotion a perfect stranger could bring to me.

A perfect stranger is perhaps a bit of an exaggeration. For the previous 10 months I had repeatedly read Kearney's story and watched the heart-wrenching television specials that introduced her to me. Kearney was the recipient of the National Consortium for Academics and Sports' Coach Award in honor of National STUDENT-Athlete Day in 2005. As one of the event coordinators, the anticipation of meeting her was overwhelming and to my great pleasure and emotion, she did not disappoint my expectations.

The preeminent coach hails from Bradenton, Florida. While life for Kearney didn't come easy, even as a child, she has made the most of every situation, capitalizing on expecting nothing but the best from herself. Kearney was the sixth of seven children her mother had with five different men. As the situation would suggest, her father was not a big contributor to her childhood. Kearney refused to let her absent father, alcoholic mother, and surroundings of drugs and prostitution determine her fate. Instead, Kearney blazed her own path—and quickly!

In high school, the track and field athlete was recruited to the basketball team for her speed. Girls basketball began in 1974 at her high school and by 1975, Kearney was a member of the team. Her high school basketball coach said the guard's speed gave her the ability to steal the ball and make easy layups but her shooting skills left something to be desired.

During her senior year, Kearney had to deal with the sudden death of her mother. She turned to Joan Falsone, a former assistant athletic director for county schools, who encouraged Kearney to enroll at Florida's Hillsborough Community College in 1977. The National Junior College All-American talent was then welcomed at Auburn University. As an Auburn Tiger, she earned two AIAW All-American honors, Auburn Athlete of the Year and team MVP. In 1980, she qualified for the U.S. Olympic Trials in the 200 meters.

Upon earning her bachelor's degree in social work, Kearney sought work as a social worker until Falsone suggested the coaching field. Kearney's athletic talent was unquestionable, but her coaching success was only a vision of Falsone's. Kearney's later coaching success would prove Falsone to be a visionary.

Kearney did her time to learn the ins and outs of the coaching profession while she earned her master's degree in adapted physical education at Indiana State University where she served the track team as a graduate assistant. She then did a two-year stint at the University of Toledo, where she held her first head coach title. From Toledo, Kearney accepted the top assistant coach title at the University of Tennessee because the track powerhouse was irresistible, despite the step backward in job titles. Tennessee was just a stepping-stone to the powerhouse Kearney would later build at the University of Texas, after she made another stop as the University of Florida's head coach. Again Kearney wasted no time in reaching her goal, and in just her fifth year at the helm of UF, the Gators won the 1992 NCAA Division I Indoor title. Kearney became the first black female track and field head coach to win a NCAA Division I National Championship and just the third black head coach ever to win any NCAA title, following John Thompson's 1984 basketball title with Georgetown University and Tina Sloan Green's 1984 women's lacrosse title with Temple University.

The University of Texas couldn't help but take notice of the thriving coach and quickly wooed Kearney to join the Longhorns. The relationship has proved prosperous for both since her first season of 1993. When Kearney started her 18th season at UT in 2009–10, she already had led the Longhorns to six NCAA National Championships and 19 conference titles. Twenty-four current UT records have been set under Kearney's tutelage. Several of her student-athletes have gone on to win a total of nine Olympic medals since 1992.

While 2008 marked a big birthday for Bev, as she is endearingly called, it was not age that kept her from quickly entering the stage that evening in 2005. The 50-year old, who could easily pass for someone in her 30s, was critically injured in a car crash that left her one of three survivors in a five-person, single-car crash. While headed to Disneyworld on December 26, 2002, the vehicle Kearney was riding in crossed the median of Interstate 10 before rolling several times. Alcohol was not involved. Kearney, who was not wearing a seatbelt, was thrown from the vehicle. She suffered a critical back injury and underwent five hours of surgery to repair her vertebrae. Nonetheless, Kearney was lucky to be alive. She was traveling with two friends, Ilrey Sparks and Michelle Freeman, Freeman's mother Muriel Wallace, and Sparks' two-year-old daughter Imani. Sadly, Ilrey Sparks and Muriel Wallace did not survive the accident. The accident left Kearney with paralyzing injuries and a huge responsibility; Bev became the legal guardian and caregiver for Imani Sparks. They both live with fellow survivor Michelle Freeman.

After two more surgeries in a month's time, Kearney coached from her hospital bed, watching tapes, and writing notes and orders for her assistant coaches to pass along to the team. Like all else she participates in, Kearney gave 100 percent to her physical therapy and has steadily improved since early 2003. She joined the team on the field in a wheelchair just three months after the accident. Her character and leadership was already inspiring to her young student-athletes, but without words, her presence inspired them immeasurably more. Though doctors worried Kearney would never use her legs again, she boldly stood on April 5, 2003 to the amazement and joy of the 20,000 athletes and spectators of the Texas Relays. After steadying herself with one arm, she flashed that gorgeous Bev smile and raised the other arm with a classic Longhorn hand signal. Marcus Sedberry, a University of Nebraska sprinter who was competing that day, delayed his warm-up in anticipation of what she promised she would do three months prior. The sight of her standing nearly brought Sedberry to tears. "The 2003 Texas Relays was a remarkable event," he remembers. "The competition was great as usual, but the competition was overshadowed by the anticipation of Coach Bev standing for the first time since her accident. When she stood up, it sent a deafening roar across the entire Mike A. Myers Stadium. Regardless of what school you were affiliated with or cheering for, you were on your feet cheering and applauding the courage and determination Coach Bev showed at that moment."[2]

Kearney steadily progressed from the wheelchair to a walker, then two canes, until she was down to just one cane in 2005, a feat that encouraged her to give away her wheelchair. While her balance is still not what it used to be, Kearney finds it easiest to get around in her scooter for long hauls. She credits Michelle Freeman, fellow survivor and the driver of the car that crashed, for her on-going care and support. In addition to living with Kearney and Sparks, Freeman is a volunteer coach with UT and has been a constant caregiver to Kearney since 2002.

Kearney's commitment to inspiring the lives of youth and improving the community led her to found the "Pursuit of Dreams" a non-profit organization charged with developing mentoring relationships to help people achieve their mental, physical, and spiritual goals. The organization's motto is "Independently we make a difference, collectively we make change."[3]

While Kearney's coaching accomplishments are stand-alone amazing, the personal tragedy she has faced makes her success even more astounding. Most importantly, Kearney has hundreds of more student-athletes to influence and titles to win in her years to come. Two goals remain unconquered on Kearney's list: professionally, to win the triple crown (winning an indoor and outdoor track and field title, and the cross country title in a single year); and personally, to wiggle her toes. Something tells me that when she does wiggle her toes for the first time in years, her student-athletes will be so inspired, they will easily bring home the triple crown. Or, perhaps, it will happen the other way around. Either way, Beverly Kearney has already proven she can accomplish anything she puts her mind, heart, and faith into.

Notes

1. Beverly Kearney, Acceptance Speech, The National Consortium for Academics and Sports' 7th Annual Giant Steps Awards Banquet and Hall of Fame Induction Ceremony, Orlando, FL, February 21, 2005.

2. Marcus Sedberry, interview with author, April 30, 2008.

3. Pursuit of Dreams, "About Us," Pursuit of Dreams Foundation, http://www .bevkearneypursuitofdreams.com/?page_id=110, (accessed March 26, 2010).

Jennifer Rizzotti

Coaching to Win in Life

by Jessica Bartter Duffaut

To say that Jennifer Rizzotti led a double life is a true but somehow contradictory statement. Rizzotti juggled her professional playing career with her college coaching career, both in the sport that she loves—basketball. While this balancing act was difficult, Rizzotti could not see choosing between the game she loved to play and the game she loved to coach.

In 1996 while starring at the University of Connecticut, Rizzotti was recognized by the Associated Press as the National Player of the Year, was a two-time Kodak All-American first team selection, received the Wade Trophy for college basketball's outstanding senior player, and was named Big East Player of the Year. A true testament to the "student" in student-athlete, she was a GTE/CoSIDA Women's Basketball Academic All-American and the Big East Women's Basketball Scholar-Athlete of the Year. As a Husky, Rizzotti started every game—135 straight—during her four-year career. Her career was highlighted by UConn's two Final Four appearances and 1995–96's 35-0 undefeated and National Championship season. The University of Connecticut was the first team to complete a perfect season since Texas went 34-0 in 1985–86. Upon graduation, Rizzotti left the Huskies as the season and career record holder in assists and steals, averaging 11.4 points per game, and totaling 637 assists and 349 steals. More than a decade later, at the start of the 2008–09 season, Rizzotti remained second on both the assists and steals record lists for a season and a career. To date, no one has been able to surpass her single-game assists record of 10.[1]

Rizzotti continued to surpass expectations and astonish audiences as a pro. Rizzotti began her professional career with the American Basketball League's (ABL) New England Blizzard, where she earned All-Star appearances for two of her three seasons. In her ABL debut, Rizzotti took an elbow just above the eye, drawing blood, before the clock counted down the first two minutes of the game. As Rizzotti headed to the locker room for a Band-Aid, she knew she would be back. In the second quarter, Rizzotti returned with seven stitches, entered the game, and led a 25-2 New England scoring run enroute to a 100-73 victory. Despite missing most of the first quarter, Rizzotti finished the game with eight points and five assists, and she inspired her teammates through her intensity, hustle, and dedication.

After the ABL folded, Rizzotti was drafted by the Women's National Basketball Association's (WNBA) Houston Comets in the fourth round, where she and her teammates earned the 1999 WNBA Championship. Rizzotti later joined the Cleveland Rockers where she spent three years and went on to win another WNBA Championship.

In the midst of her success as a professional athlete, Rizzotti was offered the women's basketball head coaching position at the University of Hartford, just 12 days after her first WNBA Championship. At only 25, she was the youngest Division I women's basketball coach in the country. Rizzotti was as successful as a coach as she was as a player. In just her third year as the Hawks' leader, Rizzotti coached the team to their first-ever America East Championship and NCAA Tournament appearance. In her fifth season in 2003–04, Hartford won a school record 18 games. Rizzotti's juggling act proved fruitful for both careers—playing and coaching.

In 2004, Rizzotti began a new journey with her husband and assistant coach, Bill Sullivan—building a family. As she coached the 2004–05 season through her pregnancy, Rizzotti focused on saving her energy for the games and practices. While she predicted her patience would increase after becoming a mother, her intensity did not lessen. Hartford broke its school record and won 22 games and earned their second America East title that year. The Hawks also broke records for conference victories with 13 and the best home record in school history with an almost perfect 15-1 record. Rizzotti gave birth to son Holden in 2005.

The following year, in 2005–06, she led the Hawks to their first-ever victory in the NCAA Tournament and advanced to the final 32 teams in the nation. They again broke records for conference victories with 15 wins, team victories with 27, and a school-best 15-game winning streak during regular season play. Without missing a beat, Rizzotti gave birth to her second son, Conor, in 2008 while leading her team to tremendous success.

As Rizzotti began her eleventh season as head coach in 2009–10, she had four conference tournament titles and four NCAA tournament appearances under her belt. With Rizzotti at the helm, the team has gained national prominence.

Rizzotti is a testament to the observation that sport offers participants leadership opportunities by learning about themselves and their teammates. While some athletes make great players, and others make great coaches, Rizzotti has accomplished both. Of course, her athletic prowess contributed to her success, but it was as much her intelligence, leadership skills, dedication, self-discipline, motivation, and genuine care for the players with whom she played and those she coaches that accounts for her distinctive career. On coaching, she said, "I love it. I love the challenge of it, working with kids every day, setting goals for myself and the program. I feel it was what I was meant to do."[2]

Notes

1. University of Connecticut Athletics, "2008–09 Women's Basketball Media Guide," http://www.uconnhuskies.com/datadump/WBasketball/2009/Media%20Guide/99-116.pdf, (accessed March 10, 2010).

2. Frank Litsky, "Staley and Rizzotti have been there and done that," *New York Times*, March 19, 2006.

Willie Stewart

Coaching to Win in Life

by Richard Lapchick

Coach Willie Stewart was a leader for Anacostia High School in Washington, D.C., where life on the streets is more menacing than any opposing athletic team. From 1976 to 1980, he first coached at Eastern High School in D.C. before transferring to Anacostia from 1981 to 2009. Throughout his 41-year coaching career, Stewart captured 15 East Division Football Championships and seven District of Columbia Interscholastic Athletic Association Championships. More impressive than his wins was the environment from which his young athletes played. Many wonder what kept Stewart at Anacostia, located in one of the worst neighborhoods in the United States just blocks from Capitol Hill. A community stricken with poverty, drugs, and violence, Stewart and his assistants worked for low pay. For years his players wore uniforms and shoes he received from the University of the District of Columbia and until 2004, they never played home games in a real stadium.

Stewart drove his players to school in the morning and home from practice at night. He made sure they studied to overcome the long odds society laid down for Anacostia students to graduate and go to college. Often turning down more lucrative college offers, he recognized the dearth of African-American male role models for inner-city youth.

Stewart's uncommon concern for the welfare of his players and their communities was evident. He worked tirelessly to save young lives. In 2003, he said, "During my 25 some years of coaching, I have lost close to 20 athletes to gun violence."[1] In each somber incident, Stewart brought the entire Anacostia football team to the funeral hoping to make them realize it could have been them lying in the coffin if they did not change their behavior. In 1994 alone, four of his players were shot, one of them fatally. Stewart's familiarity with gun violence and his dedication to prevention led him to the Alliance for Justice in 2003. Stewart was the first coach to jump on board with a public education campaign known as Coaches Against

Gun Violence. Along with Stewart, seven other Washington, D.C. coaches agreed to dedicate one of their football games to victims of gun violence. Each of the eight games included a special ceremony where city officials, students, athletes, faculty, community members, and others were educated about gun violence prevention.

One of Stewart's many success stories involves Lovell Pinkney. In 1989, Pinkney was in the 10th grade when Stewart took notice of his continuing absences from class and football practice. Suspecting the worst, he searched for and found Pinkney hanging on street corners dealing drugs. Stewart tried over and over to make Pinkney realize he had a future in football and that he didn't need to sell drugs to get by. Deep down inside, Stewart knew that path Pinkney had chosen would most likely lead to jail or death. After all, in Stewart's first 12 years of coaching he had already lost eight players to drug-related killings. Yet, like many teenagers, Pinkney didn't believe it could happen to him, until he narrowly survived a drive-by shooting that convinced him to stop selling crack once and for all. Once Stewart had his full attention, he coached Pinkney into the Player of the Year for Washington, D.C. as a senior. Pinkney's play earned him a spot as a University of Texas Longhorn. In 1995, he was the fourth round pick in the NFL chosen by the St. Louis Rams. Today, he realizes he would not be where he is without Coach Stewart's guidance. Because just one person cared about him, he escaped a dead-end future and possible premature death. Pinkney learned the power one individual can have and hopes to do for other athletes what Stewart did for him.

"These are the kids who need the guidance, not the college kids," Stewart told me. "You can't save everybody, but I still try." The young men at Anacostia High School learned more than just football from Stewart. They learned the importance of academics from their mentor. Furthermore, Stewart inspired them to realize that success in athletics comes with a sense of responsibility and that they need to come back to help others.

In April 2005, Stewart was asked to testify for the House Reform Committee regarding the use of steroids. He provided testimony alongside Paul Tagliabue, NFL Commissioner, Gene Upshaw, then-Executive Director of the NFLPA, and Steve Courson, former NFL player as well as doctors, professors, and other coaches. Stewart explained to the Committee that many young student-athletes admire professional athletes and believe that performance enhancing drugs are the quickest way to emulate them despite the accompanying risks. He disclosed that he had suspected steroid use in two of his players over the years and that his suspicions proved true in one case. Just two weeks prior to his testimony, one of Stewart's former student-athletes died of kidney failure at age 28. Based upon that experience, Stewart has made it a point to encourage other coaches to become familiar with steroid abuse and to warn their athletes about its dangers.

Stewart's impact on the community of Anacostia has been extraordinary. His genuine interest in his student-athletes accounted for the saving of countless human lives. Stewart used football to show troubled teens a way out of poverty, drugs, and violence and into a better life. His lessons extended beyond the big plays, throwing tips, and tackling techniques; they also dealt with life beyond the field and emphasized education, compassion, discipline, and feelings of self-worth.

In spite of Stewart's impact, a first-year Anacostia principal who had not been at the school long enough to see or understand the influence of Stewart, sent a letter to Stewart asking him to step down in 2009. An iconic figure to the world of sports in the D.C. area, Stewart was shocked. So too were his current and former players. Cato June, the 1997 All-Met Defensive Player of the Year at Anacostia and current NFL player, was disappointed. "(D.C. football) is not a powerhouse, like Florida, Texas, or California. We've got different problems. We're just trying to get kids to come to practice," he said. "That's what Stew did. He kept them there."[2]

Bill McGregor, head coach for a neighboring high school, was also perplexed. "(Stewart is) a great man, a great coach, a great community leader," McGregor said when he heard the news. "It's not about wins and losses with Willie; it never was. It's all about the kids he's saved."[3]

Prior to being let go, Coach Willie Stewart was honored by the Center for the Study of Sport and Society alongside Coach Tom Osborne and Muhammad Ali in 1994. As Ali watched, awaiting his turn to be inducted into Sport and Society's Hall of Fame he turned to me to reflect on Osborne and Stewart: "That's what coaching should be all about." Ali said it best and coming from "The Greatest" is perhaps the highest accolade of all.

Notes

1. Maria Feit, "Anacostia Football Coach Joins 'Coaches Against Gun Violence,'" Alliance for Justice, October 10, 2003, http://www.afj.org/news_and_press/press_release_collection/collection/press_anacostiacoach.html, (accessed August 30, 2005).

2. Alan Goldenbach, "Reflecting on Willie Stewart," *The Washington Post.com*, December 16, 2009, http://voices.washingtonpost.com/prepspost-dc/2009/12/reflecting_on_willie_stewart.html, (accessed March 31, 2010).

3. Ibid.

Sonny Hill

Coaching to Win in Life

by Richard Lapchick

I have been hearing about Sonny Hill for almost four decades. Anyone who has any Philadelphia connection knows the legend who has built a legacy of saving children's lives through basketball. "Get them off the streets and they will have a better chance in life," he said.[1] Today, such ideas are more common. Most of them are built on what Sonny Hill started so many years ago. He was the architect and the innovator for the concept that has allowed some young children to have a floor built on the despair they otherwise see as a daily reality; a roof over the things they dream about that they cannot see.

He is known as Sonny "Mr. Basketball" Hill and has dedicated his life to youth basketball in Philadelphia. For nearly 40 years, Hill's basketball leagues have been an outlet for Philadelphia's inner city where he is as an influential leader. We honored Hill with a Giant Steps Award in 2009. He has a real presence in a room. Dashingly dressed, handsome, and with a vibrant smile, he lights up small and big rooms alike. He is at once humble and charismatic and is a great storyteller. And he has some stories to tell. Seventy-three when he got the award in 2009, no one who saw him thought he was more than 60 years old.

He was a genuine star player in college and in the Eastern League who, like so many other African-Americans, played in the era when the NBA was integrated but still did not have many African-Americans on their teams. Many argued that there was a "quota" system to limit the number of African-Americans. People who saw him play said he clearly had the talent to be in the NBA. Ironically, he never got that chance in a league that now is the most progressive professional sport by far for opportunities for people of color on and off the court. The 5-foot-9 Hill never had the same opportunity as today's African-American players to play in the NBA. He did, however, have a great part in paving the way for other African-American players today.

While Hill's exceptional on-the-court talent was on display in his college days and in the Eastern Basketball League, it is off the court where Hill broke down long-locked doors. At CBS, he was the first black commentator for NBA games. "Ahead of his time," said Marc Narducci, longtime NBA reporter at the *Philadelphia Inquirer.* "The first analyst who actually dissected the game for viewers."[2]

In 1968, Hill founded the Sonny Hill Community Involvement League, which continues to provide youth with discipline, guidance, and direction. The league runs each year with divisions ranging from middle school through adult. His leagues have provided thousands of kids an opportunity and his dedication and tireless efforts have led to Philadelphia becoming one of the best basketball cities in the country.

In addition to basketball-related people who influenced Hill, Sonny credits the relationships that he has developed over the years with Jackie Robinson, Dr. Martin Luther King Jr., and legendary boxers Joe Louis and Sugar Ray Robinson.

Because the history of his time as a player had Hill on the periphery of the game, he never had a chance to be voted into the Naismith Basketball Hall of Fame as a player. But in 2008 he was on the grand stage of the Hall as co-recipient of the Mannie Jackson Basketball Human Spirit Award along with NBA Hall of Famer, David Robinson.

His passion for the game of basketball drove Hill to become the man who was honored by the Hall of Fame for his contributions to life more than for his plentiful basketball skills. Hill's programs are credited with keeping hundreds of kids alive, and of keeping them out of gangs. He started The Sonny Hill League in 1968 as a way to pull children back from the gang warfare common in so many cities across America. Rebecca Goodman wrote that, "It was a way of saying, if they play in the Sonny Hill League, they could cross the gang turfs."[3]

The Sonny Hill League is a safe haven and, at the same time, a learning center. There is a mandatory tutoring program for all league participants. He had everyone tested before each season to objectively see which program they should attend. Hill told me it was very basic: "You had to go to class to play. There were no exceptions. We wanted these kids to realize they could do more than play basketball. We brought in speakers with all kinds of careers to show them what was possible."[4]

Hill, who has his own show every Sunday on WIP Sport Radio and serves as executive advisor for the Philadelphia 76ers, has presided over making Philadelphia a virtual basketball mecca, starting by co-founding the Charles Baker Memorial League, summer home of many of the NBA elite—from Wilt Chamberlain to Bill Bradley to Ray Allen—for nearly 50 years. He has received an honorary doctorate from Temple University and was named one of the "100 Most Influential Minorities in Sports" by *Sports Illustrated*.

Notes

1. Sonny Hill, interview with the author, October 2009.

2. Steve Young, "Sonny Hill: Humanitarian Hall of Famer—Making Basketball, Practice for the Real World," August 6, 2008, http://www.huffingtonpost.com/steve-young/sonny-hill-humanitarian-h_b_117390.html, (accessed March 25, 2010).

3. Rebecca Goodman, "Profile: Sonny Hill," Official Website of the Philadelphia 76ers, http://www.nba.com/sixers/features/drive_profile_sonnyhill_070731.html, (accessed March 25, 2010).

4. Sonny Hill, interview with the author, October 2009.

Jody Conradt

Coaching to Win in Life

by Stacy Martin-Tenney

Jody Conradt pioneered women's college athletics and has been a cornerstone in women's basketball. Her contribution to the women's game is legendary, having coached the first undefeated Division I National Championship team in women's basketball in 1986. With that win, she changed the game, and became the coach to emulate. She coached for 31 seasons at the University of Texas at Austin. Her lifetime coaching record across her 38 cumulative seasons amassed 900 wins and only 306 losses.

Conradt learned her passion for winning at a young age as an athlete herself in her hometown of Goldthwaite, Texas. She averaged 40 points a game for Goldthwaite High School when she played from 1955 to 1959, in a town where sports were an integral part of the daily life. She attended Baylor University and played on the school's first varsity team. Her 20 points a game were a staple for the Bears and her determination and hard work earned her four varsity letters. She obtained a bachelor's degree and master's degree in physical education from Baylor and eventually was hired at Waco Midway High School as a physical education teacher. Her mentor, M.T. Rice, was one of the state's most successful girl's basketball coaches. He asked Conradt to help coach the team and that was when she fell in love with coaching basketball.

Her next move was to Sam Houston State, where the love of the game was the only thing she received for her coaching services in 1969. It was the beginning of her collegiate coaching career and still during a time when women played six-on-six instead of the more strenuous boys' game of five-on-five. Only two women were allowed to play the full court. Conradt expected the best from her players and they delivered. By the time she left Sam Houston her basketball coaching record was 74-23, while she also coached volleyball and track and field. Her multitasking did not end at Sam Houston. She was hired at University of Texas at Arlington in 1973 as the women's basketball coach, volleyball coach, and softball coach. Her record for basketball during her three-year tenure was 43-39.

In 1976, Conradt was hired at the University of Texas at Austin to develop a women's program during a time where women's sports were severely underrepresented and collegiate athletics were on the heels of Title IX being passed. Jody Conradt was the right person for the job. She quickly led her team to the top of the national ranks with a Top 20 finish in her first year, Top 15 in her second year, Top 5 in her third year, and an impressive 33-4 record her fourth year, which earned her a National Coach of the Year title. She led her teams to six consecutive Association for Intercollegiate Athletics for Women tournament appearances, cementing the Longhorn's position at the top of women's college basketball. In 1982, Texas joined the National Collegiate Athletic Association and Conradt continued to flourish as a coach that developed powerhouse teams.

In 1986, Conradt had built her program to be a performance machine. The team went undefeated all the way to the NCAA Division I Championship and became the first ever undefeated Division I championship team. During her time at Texas, Conradt was no stranger to the NCAA Tournament, achieving 11 Sweet 16 births in 21 NCAA Tournament Appearances. Her only title was in 1986, but she took her team all the way to the Final Four in 1987 and 2003.

In 1992, she was asked to serve as the interim Women's Athletic Director for the University of Texas since the position was vacated by Donna Lopiano, their first full-time athletic director. It was a difficult time for the university as it was facing a lawsuit under Title IX for inequalities in the number of women's teams funded by the University. Conradt's leadership led to a settlement of the lawsuit and the creation of varsity soccer, softball, and rowing programs for women. Conradt assumed the full-time position as Women's AD in 1993, but retained her head coaching role with the basketball team. "Being AD was never my dream job, but it was the right thing to do at the time," said Conradt. "I feel extreme loyalty to this university and that is what I was asked to do."[1] As usual, Conradt did more than just the job, she excelled.

Under her leadership, Texas Women's Athletics saw one of its most successful periods ever. Track and field won four national championships and tennis picked up two more. Texas also made the transition from the former Southwest Conference to the Big 12 Conference during Conradt's tenure. Texas had earned 39 conference championships before the Southwest Conference dissolved, 19 of those titles belong to Conradt's basketball teams. Conradt sums up her impact best, "We've come a long way. In 1992, we were in the Southwest Conference and we were being sued to add opportunities for women. Since then, we have added three sports that have gained national prominence, moved to a new conference, and continued to be a broad-based successful athletic program."[2] In 2001, Conradt resigned as the Women's AD so that she could pursue coaching full time rather than juggling it with the responsibilities as AD. "The most difficult thing was standing in front of the president and saying I can't do this. I came in as a basketball coach and I want to leave as a basketball coach."[3]

Associate Athletic Director, Chris Plonsky, who works on both men's and women's athletics at Texas assumed Conradt's AD responsibilities in the interim. She commended Conradt for her service to the university in both roles. "She has performed an unbelievable task for nine years, probably far beyond what anyone expected," Plonsky said. "She did the right thing then, and I think this is the right thing now. I know the operation of the basketball no doubt had to have been infringed upon with her double duty. But it was the right thing for the University, and putting Jody in the leadership role got us through a real tumultuous period."[4] Jody Conradt wanted to leave as a basketball coach and she wanted to return to her team and coach with passion and commitment, because her 20-13 record wasn't good enough for her. She calls coaching women's basketball at Texas her dream job. "My goal is to get this program back to national prominence and leave feeling a real sense of accomplishment," said Conradt. "That doesn't mean I have set a timetable on coaching but that does mean I am not going to have another job. This is it, this is what I want to do."[5]

Conradt's passion paid off and she took her team to the 2003 National Championship Final Four. Her career has left her with many accolades. She was the first women's coach to record 700 wins and then she raced Pat Summitt to record 800 wins, and before her career was over, she reached 900 wins. Conradt's commitment to coaching made her the first woman to coach 100 basketball games. She earned four Coach of the Year awards throughout her career in addition to conference coach of the year recognition. Her success as a coach earned her a spot in the Naismith Basketball Hall of Fame and the Women's Basketball Hall of Fame. Her most impressive honor, however, is that she was committed to her players and their future after basketball and she graduated 99 percent of her players over 31 seasons.

Conradt made the announcement that she was stepping down in 2007 after the selection show for the women's NCAA tournament. It was a long shot that her team would receive a bid, just like it was the year before, and to Conradt that was unacceptable. Before the selection show, Conradt told her players that she would be resigning as head coach and at the press conference tears filled their eyes. "It's appropriate at this point and time that there be a change," Conradt said. "It's not acceptable that Texas not be in the NCAA Tournament two years in a row. I've had a wonderful time representing this university. It's not an easy decision. I just feel as if it's time for a change."[6] Conradt didn't miss a tournament for two years in a row and she would not accept that level of performance for the program that she built. As an athletic director she knew the ins and outs of the business, and was not a coach that had to be shown the door, after all she had set the expectation for the program, her program. "I loved coaching, love the university," Conradt said. "If things had been going good, I probably would have been here until I was 90. But things need to be better. This is a bottom-line business. It's about winning."[7]

Her career record speaks for itself. "No one can take away what Jody Conradt has done," her assistant coach Clarissa Davis said. "She set the standard that was emulated by everyone. Everyone looked at what she did with our team in 1986 and changed how they recruited, how they trained, how they thought, and how they played. Jody Conradt changed the game forever."[8] Famed Connecticut women's basketball coach, Geno Auriemma remembers coaching against Conradt early in his career and planning his program after hers. "She was way ahead of the curve," Auriemma said. "She had it all figured out before anybody else did."[9]

Conradt has certainly been a pioneer for basketball, but she has been a pioneer for advancement of women as well. In addition to her numerous awards, an endowment was created in her name at the University of Texas by the College of Liberal Arts and Center for Women's and Gender Studies (CWGS). "Understanding the challenges and opportunities that motivate young women to compete and succeed in every field requires both academic research and the presence of strong role models as examples for our students," said CWGS Director Susan Sage Heinzelman. "No one represents women's potential for excellence and leadership better than former coach Jody Conradt."[10]

"It is both gratifying and humbling to be associated with this Excellence Fund, which will advance, enrich, and educate women students," said Conradt. "One of the most rewarding aspects of coaching and athletics administration was witnessing the maturation, confidence-building, and empowerment of undergraduate women. Developing leaders is central to our university mission. The academic programs offered by the College of Liberal Arts and the Center for Women and Gender Studies prepare young women for such roles."[11] Conradt always said that her favorite part of her job was working with young people. She has been an inspiration and hero to many, hopefully future generations strive to make the impact that she has made. Conradt continues to serve in a part-time role for the women's athletic department in public relations and fundraising.

Notes

1. Travis Richmond, "Conradt steps down from women's AD post, returns to coaching full-time," *The Daily Texan*, August 6, 2001.

2. Ibid.

3. Ibid.

4. Ibid.

5. Ibid.

6. Chip Brown, "After 31 seasons, Conradt resigns at Texas." *The Dallas Morning News*, March 12, 2007.

7. Ibid.

8. Ibid.

9. Pam Schmid "Back among elite; Texas had slipped some since its glory days of the '80s, but coach Jody Conradt has the Longhorns contending for another national title" *Star Tribune*, April 6, 2003.

10. The University of Texas at Austin, "Jody Conradt Fund to Support Female College Students," College of Liberal Arts, December 2, 2009 http://www.utexas.edu/news/2009/12/02/jody_conradt_fund/, (accessed March 23, 2010).

11. Ibid.

Kay Yow

Coaching to Win in Life

by Stacy Martin-Tenney

Courtesy of NC State Athletics.

Kay Yow coached at North Carolina State for 34 seasons of her 38-year career. Reynolds Coliseum served as the classroom where she taught young women the game of basketball and some of life's hardest lessons. Yow won an Olympic gold medal for coaching women's basketball in the 1988 Seoul Games, while she battled cancer. She coached her team to a 17-0 winning streak during the 2006–07 season while she battled cancer. She showed up to practice every day and sat on every game bench, while she battled cancer. Kay Yow taught her players perseverance. Not only did she teach the brand of perseverance one displays on a basketball court but she also inspired the kind of perseverance that one needs to battle some of life's greatest challenges.

Yow fell in love with the game of basketball at a very early age and it was a love affair that lasted her lifetime. Her mother, Cora Elizabeth Yow, played basketball for a mill team in their hometown of Gibsonville, North Carolina. She taught her three daughters how to play the game and she taught them not to lose. Kay Yow became enamored with the game—she played her sisters until she wore them out, and then she went down the road to play with her brother and the neighborhood boys. This never-ending love story had just begun. She went on to play in high school and quickly garnered the scoring records for her high school. Yow grew up during the time that girls played six-on-six basketball as opposed to the more physically demanding boys' game where they played five-on-five. Her talents on the court helped prove to skeptical physical education experts that girls were more than capable of playing basketball; they could compete at the same level as the boys.

She went to college at Eastern Carolina University to earn her teaching degree so that she could work as a librarian or teacher. There were still limits on the careers open to women in 1964. Yow came back to the game that she loved when she took a girls' basketball coaching job at Allen Jay High School in High Point, North Carolina so that she would be hired as an English teacher. The boys' basketball coach and athletic director offered their support for practices and games, but soon Yow was flying solo and felt as though she had truly found her calling. "Really, it was like love at first sight," she said in 2004.[1] She went 22-3 her first season and had continued success for the next three years before returning to her native Gibsonville to coach for a season there.

Yow was offered the job at Elon College where she established a winning program for the next four years. She amassed a 57-19 win-loss record over her four years at Elon and had the privilege of coaching her younger sisters, Susan and Debbie, on the 1974 team that won the state title. The Yow sisters were all destined for success in women's athletics from that point forward. Susan became the women's basketball coach at Belmont Abbey College in North Carolina and Debbie became the athletic director of the University of Maryland. Kay Yow was hired by NC State in 1975 as the women's athletic coordinator, softball coach, and volleyball coach, and was tasked with establishing the women's basketball program for the Wolfpack. Her 34-year career had just begun, but in her first season she coached the women's basketball team to a victory against their fierce rivals, University of North Carolina, during the first televised women's basketball game in North Carolina. A short two seasons later she led the team to the first regular season ACC women's basketball title in the league's first official season of women's basketball. Yow's career continued to flourish at NC State and she coached national teams to World University Games, Goodwill Games, and World Championship gold medals.

The defining moment of her coaching career came when she was diagnosed with breast cancer in 1987. Yow underwent a radical mastectomy procedure to remove the cancerous tissue from her breast and 20 lymph nodes. Yow continued to coach and she coached the US women's basketball team to an Olympic gold medal the very next year. Yow was determined not to let anything beat her and continued to coach the game that she loved. The cancer went into remission and Yow's career swelled with success. She developed the Wolfpack basketball program to one of the top programs in the country and cemented her place in history as one of only six coaches in women's collegiate basketball to attain 700+ wins, and later 900+ wins. Through her 34 seasons at NC State, her teams have come and gone but she has remained a guiding force on the court and at the University. Women's collegiate basketball has historically struggled with game attendance from fans, but Kay Yow brought them in packs. During her bout with cancer, they would fill Reynolds Coliseum in pink t-shirts supporting not only her but her cause—the fight against breast cancer. Her players would lace up their high tops with pink laces, and not only listen to the play she was calling, but to the grace, dignity, and class in which she delivered it, all while battling cancer. The humanity was what everyone could relate to, they felt as though she was there for them and they were going to show up for her. Fans, neighbors, and strangers would stop Kay Yow on the street and thank her for her story and inspiration.

She impacted her players, her fans, other coaches, the school, and, most importantly, the other women fighting for their lives against the same awful disease. Yow kept going. Basketball wasn't a treatment for the disease but it was good medicine for the soul. She was determined to be there even at her worst when she could only sit on the bench. Her players would never give up because they only had to look over at the bench and know that Coach Yow showed up that day. "She's just been a great friend to so many people; obviously left her footprints all over the place with the kids she has taught and molded," Tennessee coach Pat Summitt told ESPN. "And she is a woman that had fought such a hard fight, but it was always about everyone else, never about Kay."[2]

While it was never about Kay, she managed to make quite a few impacts on the game of basketball that could only reflect positively on her leadership and coaching prowess. Eighty-five of her players were named to the ACC Honor Roll for registering a 3.0 GPA or better for a full academic year. She set the standard in North Carolina women's basketball and for the Atlantic Coast Conference when the school became a founding member. To recognize her for numerous accolades in coaching basketball, she was inducted into the Naismith Hall of Fame, named coach of the year by several associations including John and Nellie Wooden, *USA Today*, *Sports Illustrated*, and the WBCA. She has received several honors for her tremendously courageous bout with breast cancer, the Bob Bradley Spirit Award, and the North Carolina governor presented the state's highest sports honor, the Laurel Wreath Award. All this while the cancer returned and she radically changed her lifestyle, eating habits, and every routine except practice. She defeated it again, but was forced to take a hiatus for a 16-game stretch during the 2006–07 season.

After successfully defeating the second bout of cancer, the school dedicated the court to her at Reynolds Coliseum, it is now and forever will be "Kay Yow Court." Through her tumultuous fight with the disease, she clung to her faith and to her team; that was her catharsis. In a 2007 interview, Kay said, "I have to go through it. I accept that, and I'm not panicked about it because the Lord is in control. But it just would be so saddening if I had to go through it and I couldn't help people. But then I see I'm helping others in a greater way than I ever have. That's the amazing thing, you know?" She was the amazing person who smiled through it all. "In December 2007, the Kay Yow/WBCA Cancer Fund in partnership with The V Foundation was established as a charitable organization committed to finding an answer in the fight against women's cancers."[3]

Only two seasons later, the cancer would return once more and this time the fight took everything she had. Yow made the impossible decision to step down for the remainder of the 2008–09 season because she felt that she didn't have the energy to devote that the team deserved. "The ability of any patient with stage four breast cancer to continue at her chosen occupation depends on symptoms from the disease itself, symptoms that can result from the treatments, and the physical and psychological demands of the job," said Dr. Mark Graham, Yow's longtime oncologist. "Back in late 2006 and early 2007, and again now, the balance of all these factors has not allowed Coach Yow to coach up to her high standards."[4]

On January 24, 2009, Kay Yow succumbed to breast cancer, the disease that riddled her body but could not break her winning spirit. She imparted perseverance, hope, and faith to the Wolfpack community and the basketball community. Rutgers University women's basketball coach, Vivian Stringer, reached out to Yow when she was diagnosed with breast cancer herself. "She taught all of us how to handle personal battles with a great deal of grace and acceptance and by believing that God would see us through. She rarely complained, as most of us would or ever wonder why this had happened to her. When I myself was diagnosed with breast cancer, Kay was one of the handful of people I told. I asked her why me? Kay was the person I could best identify with and knew would understand. And she did."

Yow coached basketball while battling cancer. Yow raised money for women's cancer research while battling cancer. Yow was awarded numerous accolades for her career achievements while battling cancer. Yow made a difference in the lives of 34 seasons worth of women's basketball players at North Carolina State University while battling cancer for more than two decades. "I need to make a difference in the lives of other people," she said in 2002. "If I'm not doing that, I've missed the whole point of my gift of life."[5] Cancer may have taken Kay Yow's life, but she won the battle.

Notes

1. ESPN.com News Services, "Kay Yow dies at 66;" ESPN.com, January 30, 2009, http://sports.espn.go.com/ncw/news/story?id=3857041, (accessed March 30, 2010).

2. Ibid.

3. NC State University, "Coach Yow Passes Peacefully Saturday Morning," Featured Stories: Outside the Classroom, January 2009, http://www.ncsu.edu/featured-stories/outside-the-classroom/jan-2009/yow-memorial/index.php, (accessed March 30, 2010).

4. NC State University, "Yow to Step Down for Remainder of Season," Featured Stories Outside the Classroom, January 2009, http://www.ncsu.edu/featured-stories/outside-the-classroom/jan-2009/kay-yow/index.php, (accessed March 30, 2010).

5. Ned Barnett, Rachel Carter and Edward G. Robinson III, "Kay Yow: An inspiration to all who play," *Charlotte Observer*, January 24, 2009.

Ron Hunter

Coaching to Win in Life

by Stacy Martin-Tenney

Basketball coaches and coaches of every sport aim to teach their athletes not only the game but the life skills that will reach far beyond
any court or playing field. Ron Hunter has done exactly that and continues to pursue his humanitarian mission with the same fervor and
passion with which he coaches the game of basketball. Ron Hunter
was the first basketball coach to coach an entire collegiate basketball game barefoot in order to raise awareness for Samaritan's Feet,
an organization with a goal of raising 10 million pairs of shoes in 10
years for impoverished people around the world. His quiet walk barefoot down the hardwood has echoed a loud statement for worldwide
outreach.

Manny Ohonme, founder of the Charlotte, North Carolina based
Samaritan's Feet, thought that the game of basketball would be the
best way to spread his message of hope and generate simple acts of
kindness and love. After all, it was a stranger from America that first
gave him red and white canvas shoes to play basketball when he was
just a young boy in Nigeria. Manny's talent on the court earned him
a scholarship to the University of North Dakota, where he earned
his degree and launched his business and a life far from his family
still living in poverty in Nigeria. When he returned to his homeland
for his father's funeral, he stopped by the playground and watched
the young boys play ball in their bare feet and remembered how one
pair of shoes took him on a completely different path in life. He was
determined to make a difference.

Four years later he was halfway to his goal of raising 10 million pairs of shoes. Manny had been raising money and collecting
new shoe donations from individuals and had even begun selling
shoes. Someone could buy a pair of sneakers for $29.99 and one pair
would be donated to the cause. Samaritan's Feet needed a big statement that would be noticed and galvanize donations. Todd Melloh,
the director of marketing for Samaritan's Feet, reached out to his
good friend Ron Hunter, the basketball coach at Indiana University

Purdue University at Indianapolis (IUPUI), and asked him to coach a game barefoot for the cause.

Hunter agreed to the challenge and set a personal goal of raising 40,000 pairs of shoes in honor of the 40th anniversary of the death of Dr. Martin Luther King. Hunter's personal hero was Dr. King and truly believed that his sacrifice then allowed him to be a Division I head coach today. Before he stepped onto the court that night he completed interviews with the media to help get the word out and made time for a pedicure. In a game that is sometimes defined by the brand of shoes that the superstar players are wearing, a coach wearing no shoes at all was certainly a statement. Hunter had already raised 30,000 pairs of shoes prior to tip off that night, but

Ron Hunter (right) shakes hands with former head coach Greg Gary of Centenary.

then Converse stepped up and made a donation of 15,000 pairs of shoes. "When she said 15,000, I'll be honest with you, people couldn't see me, but I was crying," Hunter admitted.[1] Hunter's team won the game that night, and when all the shoes were counted, his bare feet had raised a total of 110,000 pairs of shoes that night, but it was the moral and humanitarian victories that Hunter was proudest of that night.

"Even if we didn't get the 40,000. If I got the 10 shoes . . . that's going to make their lives different. That they won't have diseases, that they can walk to school, that they won't be ridiculed, that they'll smile, that they'll be able to be a better person in wherever their community might be. Then I think we're doing the right thing."[2] Coaches are always looking to the next game, and Hunter is no exception. He wanted to do more and so did his players. "My team came to me. I didn't ask them. They said, 'Coach, we want to help you with this mission. We want to go to Africa. We want to deliver the shoes to the children ourselves,'" he said proudly.[3]

Unfortunately, the trip to Africa had to be cancelled due to threats the U.S. State Department received about travel to Nigeria. Hunter and Samaritan's Feet traveled to Peru instead. They arrived in Lima, and rode a bus daily into remote mountain villages, where shacks were built into the sand dunes with leftover materials thrown to the side of the road. The ride in was filled with laughter each day while the ride out of the mountains was consumed with silence. The thoughts from the day and the constant prayer requests from the villagers beleaguered their minds. "The hardest part was leaving every day," sophomore Adrian Moss said after returning to Indianapolis. "We'd give out 300 pairs of shoes, and 500 more people would be in line. You'd leave thinking, we made them happy for one day but they're still there."[4] The players and coaches did not simply deliver shoes; they immersed themselves in the lives of these Peruvians.

Hunter asked his players and coaches to wash the bruised, battered feet of the villagers before they placed shoes and socks on their feet. At first their reaction was dismay, but soon realized that this was Hunter's way of symbolizing the biblical story of Jesus washing his disciple's feet. "Then I realized when you washed the feet, that's when you got to interact with the kids," assistant coach Matt Crenshaw said. "You got to talk with them. By the end of the first day, every single one of us washed feet. By the end of the trip, we didn't even think about it."[5] What they did think about at the end of the trip was how many more there were to help and how their own closets back home were too full with unworn sneakers. They thought about the little girl who prayed for one good meal each day, which was a far cry from the strips of restaurants and fast food on every corner waiting for them at home.

"I took my players completely out of their comfort zone, to places they didn't know, to do things they didn't understand and they were incredible," Hunter said. "I wish every coach in America could experience this with his players. I know there are coaches who win national championships, who go to Final Fours. If you told me I had to exchange this experience with my players for a Final Four, I'd say keep your Final Four. This will stay with me far longer."[6] It will stay with his players far longer than their college ball win loss record and hopefully they will pay forward this invaluable lesson that they received from their coach.

The lasting impact Ron Hunter and team made far outweighs the 15,000 pairs of shoes they delivered in Peru. These players and coaches were not just being cheered for scoring on the court, but how they scored in the game of life. Their efforts have not gone unnoticed by media, other sports teams, and their communities. The stories are pouring in. "I've heard from people involved in soccer, football, hockey," said Hunter, ticking off sports with his fingers. "Here's the really crazy part . . . everyone has different twists they want to add. I heard from a swim team that wants to put their shoes on for a meet! I'm telling you, this whole year has been really unbelievable and overwhelming."[7] Hunter asked the National Association of Basketball Coaches to support his efforts to raise one million pairs of shoes by coaching barefoot on January 17, National Barefoot Day, and over 300 coaches at all levels of the sport kicked off their shoes for the cause. Youth coaches were coaching barefoot and sending Hunter boxes and boxes of sneakers from their own community. Georgetown University Athletics Department donated over 500 boxes of athletic shoes to Samaritan's Feet in support of Coach Hunter. Indiana Governor Mitch Daniels declared January 16 "Barefoot Day" in the state and supported the cause himself by going barefoot that day.

One of the challenges of their success is managing and storing all of the shoes donated. Coach Hunter's home and workplaces have become regular storage units for the shoes until they can all be organized by gender, size, and type to ease the volunteers' process for fitting the children with shoes. "Throughout this whole process, people in Indiana have shown that their level of generosity is as high as their love for basketball," said Manny Ohonme.[8] Leaders in the community have actually made warehouse space available to ease some of the storage burden on the coach. In the future, they hope to encourage more modern means of donating to Samaritan's Feet through five-dollar online donations or texting campaigns while still persuading individuals to act and give a simple gift that will mean so much to a child without any shoes.

"When I left Peru, I knew that I had to continue to do this," Hunter said. "The tears on the kids' faces that I saw that we couldn't help were enough to say that I will do this for the rest of my lifetime."[9] Hunter's decision to become the first coach to go barefoot got national attention. He recently was selected an ABC News Person of the Year. There is no doubt that with the passion Ron Hunter brings to the Samaritan's Feet cause that the nearly 300 million impoverished children worldwide who have never owned a pair of shoes will soon be shooting hoops in their new sneakers after a few more barefoot coach basketball games.

Notes

1. ABC News, "Coach and Relief Organization Collected Shoes for Children in Africa," January 25, 2008, http://www.samaritansfeet.org/news/coach-and-relief-or ganization-collected-shoes-for-children-in-africa, (accessed March 21, 2010).

2. Ibid.

3. Ibid.

4. Dana O'Neil, "IUPUI hands out shoes in Peru, receives 'love and attention' in return." ESPN.com, August 12, 2008, http://sports.espn.go.com/ncb/columns/story? columnist=oneil_dana&id=3523918, (accessed March 21, 2010).

5. Ibid.

6. Ibid.

7. Kyle Whelliston, "Coaches lose shoes for a good cause," Special to ESPN.com, January 15, 2009, http://www.samaritansfeet.org/news/espn-highlights-coach-hunter -and-samaritan-s-feet, (accessed March 21, 2010).

8. Ibid.

9. Associated Press, "Several hoops coaches to go barefoot for charity," *USA Today*, January 9, 2009.

Joe Ehrmann

Coaching to Win in Life

by Jessica Bartter Duffaut

It is no secret that sport can offer its youthful participants valuable life lessons in teamwork, determination, accountability, and respect. But Joe Ehrmann is determined to use football to teach his youthful participants the meaning of love and manhood—not the uber-machismo idea of manhood, but the respectful characteristics of being a good husband, father, and man through healthy relationships. In addition to the perplexing idea of using football to teach love, Ehrmann's audience is high school boys, typically, far off from the days of marriage and fatherhood. But from personal experience, Ehrmann knows it is never too early for such valuable lessons.

Courtesy of Joe Ehrmann.

At the all-boys Gilman School in Baltimore, Maryland, Ehrmann asks the football players on the team where he has served as assistant coach since 1995, "What is our job as coaches?" They respond in unison, "To love us!" Then he asks, "What is your job?" to which the boys quickly and loudly reply, "To love each other!"[1] Ehrmann's football experience was a bit different.

Ehrmann started playing football at a young age in Buffalo, New York. He excelled at Riverside High School, starting for both the offense and defense for four years en route to a standout football career at Syracuse University from 1969 to 1972. He also lettered in lacrosse at Syracuse. His college football accolades include starting for the Orangemen defensive line, earning All-American honors and being named to the University's All-Century team in 1999.

Ehrmann's dominance continued in the NFL where he thrived with the Baltimore Colts after being their first-round draft pick (10th overall) in 1973. Ehrmann's impact on the Colts was almost immediate and he was described "as a leader of their celebrated sack pack of the mid-1970s," who "ate quarterbacks for lunch" by HBO's *Real Sports with Bryant Gumble*.[2] Ehrmann earned a spot on the All Pro team in 1976 before heading to the Detroit Lions in 1981. After two years with the Lions, he spent three seasons with the United States Football League (USFL) amassing 13 years as a professional football player. His success largely came from the constant pathological teachings of his father who insisted real men don't cry, love, or show other feelings, and that real men should dominate and control people and circumstances around them. Thus, Ehrmann used football to drive his opponents into the ground and best prove his manhood.

That attitude changed in Ehrmann when he was forced to watch his younger brother and best friend, Billy, die of cancer during the 1978 season. Billy was just 18 years old. It was only then that Ehrmann could no longer hold back his emotions his father taught him to resist. He let the tears come and they almost didn't stop. Ehrmann went through a period of self-evaluation and reemerged with a new sense of what would from now on be most important to him in life. His revelation caused him to breakdown the façade of tough guy masculinity prevalent on the field and in the locker room that he was accustomed to and, instead, acknowledge what he still believes today are the two things of utmost importance: "relationships and having a cause beyond yourself.[3]

Ehrmann decided, "The only measurement, the only standard at the end of someone's life looking back isn't about power, prestige, possession. It's one thing. What kind of father were you? What kind of husband were you? What kind of friend were you?"[4] Ehrmann didn't just talk the talk. He had long been involved in charity work like most professional athletes, but after Billy's death, Ehrmann dedicated more time and resources to all he could accomplish off the field. When he was approached to help found the Ronald McDonald House of Baltimore after the inaugural charity was opened in Philadelphia, Ehrmann couldn't help but imagine how helpful such an organization could have been for him and his parents clutched to the side of Billy's hospital bed the previous year. Ehrmann was onboard with its mission and determined to resurrect the House in honor of his brother. The Baltimore Ronald McDonald House was established in 1982 an Ehrmann has remained a constant source of support ever since.

Also following Billy's passing, Ehrmann met with the Colts' unofficial team chaplain and truly discovered the Bible for the first time. Ehrmann found a spiritual path that he followed to the Dallas Theological Seminary where he took classes in the off seasons. In 1985, he was ordained specializing in urban ministry from the Westminster Theological Seminary in Philadelphia.

As Ehrmann has reiterated over the years, his life's mission became centered around the relationships he established, particularly with his family. And his extended family included his longtime supporters and adopted hometown of Baltimore, Maryland. So, in 1986, he, together with his wife Paula, a psychotherapist, established The Door, an inner-city community center to address poverty, racism, and social justice. Soon thereafter, they co-founded Building Men and Women for Others (BMWO), an organization that addresses issues of masculinity and femininity and the healthy development of boys into men and girls into womanhood. They also launched a racial-reconciliation project called Mission Baltimore. Most recently, the Ehrmann's have added Coach for America to their organizational repertoire. Coach for America seeks to redefine and reframe the social responsibility of sports, coaches, players, and parents. Joe provides keynote speeches, workshops, and seminars "combining Joe's life experience as a coach, elite athlete, and educator with Paula's 25 years as a psychotherapist."[5] The two "designed and implemented a life-coaching program that is radically different from traditional coaching models . . . provid[ing] individuals and groups with the skills they need to achieve personal and professional goals, improve relationships, and increase productivity."[6]

The Ehrmann's have long advocated for children meanwhile raising four of their own. Daughter Alison is Executive Director of Digital Marketing for *Time* while Esther played basketball at Drexel University and is currently a kindergarten teacher and coach. Son

Barney is an All-American lacrosse player at Georgetown and younger brother Joey plays football at Wake Forest. Joe Ehrmann has dedicated himself to his faith and was a pastor at the 4,000-member Grace Fellowship Church in Maryland. He is a highly demanded and effective public speaker who finds motivation in motivating others.

In 2007, the Father's Day Council and American Diabetes Association recognized Ehrmann as Father of the Year. While his four children would attest to that, the award more importantly acknowledges his parenting of the Baltimore community. His message is one of inclusiveness and encouragement that struggles to reestablish an important sense of community in each of us. Joe Ehrmann encourages others to find their community and their purpose, because, as he said, "Winning in *life* is everything."[7]

Notes

1. Jeffrey Marx, *Season of Life* (New York: Simon & Schuster, 2003), 3.

2. YouTube, "A Different Way—Joe Ehrmann," Real Sports with Bryant Gumble, http://www.youtube.com/watch?v=yQRRGIaZjNs, (accessed March 19, 2010).

3. Jeffrey Marx, "He turns boys into men," *Parade Magazine*, August 29, 2004.

4. Joe Ehrmann, email to author, March 26, 2010.

5. Coach for America, "What we do," Building Men and Women for Others, http://www.buildingmenandwomen.org/about/index.html, (accessed March 19, 2010).

6. Ibid.

7. Coach for America, "Home," http://www.buildingmenandwomen.org/index2.html, (accessed March 19, 2010).

Glenn Johnson

Coaching to Win in Life

by Jessica Bartter Duffaut

When the great Grambling Coach Eddie Robinson died in 2007, many believed an era in football that stresses life's victories off the field and textbooks over playbooks, died as well. But one need look no further than South Side Chicago at Dunbar Vocational Career Academy for a shining star that glimmers with the teachings of Coach Robinson and the success of making boys into responsible, invested men. At Dunbar, another man who simply goes by "Coach" can be found fathering, disciplining, and teaching his players—and oh yes, coaching a little football too. His name is Glenn Johnson.

Glenn Johnson is a retired Chicago Public School teacher. He was named Chicago's Teacher of the Year in 1987 by the Blum-Kovler Foundation. By any standard, he has had a wonderful career as an educator, administrator, and high school football coach capped off in 2009 with an induction into the Illinois High School Football Coaches Hall of Fame. But Coach Johnson is still hard at work well into his 60s. Most who know Johnson figure he will never retire. Former colleague Tom Kowalski, said "Football, particularly chasing perfect offensive sets, is his passion in life. Sure he likes a good movie, is a budding historian, and will listen to his collection of old Motown songs on his iPod, but it is just to pass time until he can be back on the football field trying to orchestrate the perfect running game."[1]

Six days a week, he can be found in Dunbar's dark, dingy locker room. In the center of this dank basement setting is a large area with spray painted dots on a dirty cement floor where Johnson's football players bounce around following different patterns working on their quickness and agility. Strength training is done in a caged room off to the side where a universal machine from the 1980s supplements a variety of free weights, most donated from William Fremd High School, an affluent suburban high school whose coaches, Mike Donatucci and Eric Wenkowski, were kind enough to think of Dunbar and Johnson when they were redesigning and restocking their own weight room. Johnson's elongated office sits right outside the varsity locker room—a large, separate area that doubles as a study hall, nap area, and equipment room. Johnson teaches his athletes to respect the locker room because he tries to model the small things that one of his heroes and mentors, Eddie Robinson, taught the football team at Grambling State.

Coach Johnson may not know his win-loss record but he is no stranger to victory. With league, city, and state championships under his belt in different sports at different schools, Johnson is more concerned with the person he builds than the wins he accumulates. He first started changing lives in Chicago at Carver High School where he established the football program in 1971. He moved to South Shore High in 1976 and coached the girls track team to a state championship in 1981 before returning to the gridiron at Dunbar in 1988. That is 39 years of coaching—22 with the Mighty Men of Dunbar. It is obvious his tenure is long with one glimpse into his messy office. Johnson has turned it into somewhat of a shrine to all the lives he's touched, because, as he would argue, they've touched him. Around the office hang pictures of many former Dunbar athletes who went on to lead successful lives. The biggest space is reserved for Rausell "Rocky" Harvey, who broke Illinois High School State records in 1997 rushing for over 2,500 yards, averaging 15.3 yards per carry and scoring over 40 touchdowns. Harvey, who later went on to star at the University of Illinois will tell you that the only person who could stop him in his junior and senior years was Coach, who routinely took him out of games when a victory was in hand, sometimes as early as the first quarter. His office walls also include letters hanging from restaurants and hotels the team has visited that talk about how wonderful it was to host his team. It is these precious items covering his walls that make him feel more successful than any of his trophies and plaques.

Kowalski worked alongside Johnson for five years beginning in 2002—the same year the Mighty Men won the City Championship. Kowalski remarked, "What amazed me most about working with Coach was the daily stream of former players who stopped in to see him. Often, they came back to show off—a new job or promotion at work, a newborn baby, or a brand new college degree. All the conversations were essentially the same: 'Thanks, Coach for keeping me off the streets and treating me like a man.' Mind you,"

Kowalski said, "this wasn't just one player; this was an everyday occurrence for five straight years."[2]

For years Coach Johnson has pulled together a football team by trying to out-recruit the six prominent street gangs on whose turf Dunbar sits. Many of his student-athletes come from the notoriously violent Englewood neighborhood and have to take multiple buses in order to get to school each day. Dunbar sometimes is little more than a safe haven for students to get a couple of warm meals. Johnson even had to wake one of his players off a bench one summer morning for practice after the youngster was forced to live on the streets. Once Johnson gets them on the field, he focuses on building their character and encouraging them to plan for college. He even opens the school on Saturdays to serve his players with a safe alternative to the streets.

The Dunbar Academy only sends about half of their general student body to college, many to Chicago City Colleges where they pursue an associate's degree. Kowalski said, "Many others join the armed forces while some find themselves on the street, looking for jobs in a sluggish economy. But football players at Dunbar generally go to college thanks to Johnson's lessons and encouragement. Some go off to school to continue their athletic careers; many go simply to study because Johnson has ingrained education as a vital component of their life."[3]

Johnson built Dunbar into quite the powerhouse in the 1990s but the better his team got, the more he searched for tougher opponents. He would routinely take his teams to Memphis or Dayton or anywhere else to have the Mighty Men compete against the best in the land. And often they prevailed. Johnson recognized the value in having his team travel for a number of reasons. The trips helped his teams bond; the new locales were often the first out-of-state trips for many of his adolescents; the new cities presented educational opportunities; and the new sights expanded his players' horizons. Kowalski said, "Whenever a Dunbar team visits a place they have never been before, Johnson arranges a lesson for the boys. They attended museums in Memphis, learned the history of Dayton, and now know that Geneseo, Illinois was a stop along the Underground Railroad. Football, to Coach Johnson, is about much more than a game."[4]

Just like the disciples of Eddie Robinson, former players have sent their sons to play for their beloved former coach, Johnson. In

2000, Johnson's starting quarterback, Keith Roberson, was commuting one hour and 15 minutes on a train and two buses daily just to play for Johnson who had coached his father at Carver High in 1974.

Kowalski said, "Glenn Johnson is so much more than a football coach—even if he will never admit it. 'Coach'—the only name he really responds to—is a hero. A true to life, real American hero."[5]

Notes

1. Tom Kowalski, interview with author, March 25, 2010.
2. Ibid.
3. Ibid.
4. Ibid.
5. Ibid.

3

PLAYING TO WIN IN LIFE

by Richard Lapchick

There are athletes who, by their example, show others what is possible. They take people without hope and help them find it. They seek out people without promise and work with them to achieve it. In *Playing to Win in Life*, we talk about the stories of 10 athletes who did just that.

Derrick Brooks, the great former Tampa Bay linebacker, worked with young people and helped to fund their educations. In one instance, he took a group of 20 high school students to South Africa.

Justin Allen was a basketball player at Arizona State University who hoped to play in the NBA. That dream was dashed when he was diagnosed with Hodgkin's disease. After extensive hospitalization and therapy, he made it back to the court where he inspired his teammates and fellow students.

Felipe Lopez was the top high school basketball player in the country. Everyone predicted a distinguished NBA career. Recruited by every major program, Felipe was also perhaps the greatest Latino basketball player in the United States. He chose to stay at home and attend St. John's University in order to be near the Dominican community which idolized him. He said that he stayed to give them hope.

Warrick Dunn, one of the NFL's superstars for the last decade, used his own resources to acquire new homes for single mothers and their families. He made down payments and purchased furniture for these homes in the Tampa Bay area.

Priest Holmes, the former Kansas City All-Pro player, not only led his team on the field but also created examples for them by his extensive involvement in the Kansas City and Baltimore communities. He helped with programs for low-income neighborhood children to prepare to go to college, to be able to escape poverty and the violence of the cities. This was only the beginning of a lifelong career in support of children in his community.

Amber Burgess was a student at Columbine High School when 12 fellow students and her beloved coach, Dave Sanders, were gunned down on that terrible day. This superstar softball player and gifted student was chosen to be the spokesperson for all students at the national ceremony commemorating the lives of those lost in the shooting. Amber became a great softball player at the University of Nebraska before becoming a professional softball player. However, it was her courage and spirit at Columbine that inspired many other young people to keep their hopes alive.

Pamela Malcolm was a highly-touted high school senior for her basketball skills when she was in a car accident that took away her ability to walk, not to mention her ability to play collegiate basketball. But this star earned an athletic scholarship nonetheless.

Johnnie Williams' athleticism helped him heal grave injuries that left him paralyzed in the war in Iraq. Johnnie's passion for life is now evident in his commitment to wheelchair competitions ranging from weightlifting to skiing to trap-shooting.

Jacob Madonia was a carefree college junior when he was told the cyst he had removed from his foot was actually a malignant tumor. After setting his sights on beating his Synovial Sarcoma cancer, he added that to his long list of victories. His sights are now focused on the 2012 Olympics.

Breeanna McMahon was a senior and team captain of the Freedom High soccer team when she was injured during a team fundraiser. One leg had to be amputated and the other had to be rebuilt but that did not prevent her from standing on the field to kick-off the game Senior Night.

These 10 heroes used their game to give other people hope in the battle for life and happiness.

Derrick Brooks

Playing to Win in Life

by Jenny Yehlen

Professional athletes are role models, whether they choose to be or not. This is not necessarily something they elect to become, but is rather occasioned by the popularity of the professional sports industry and the media outlets that take advantage of that popularity. Professional athletes are in the limelight constantly and people of all ages look up to and admire them. Fans, especially kids with very impressionable minds, want to play like Mike, dress like Kobe, and rap like Shaq.

These days, with the smothering media coverage that exists, all aspects of an athlete's life are public. There are so many athletes in professional sports who are good, upstanding citizens, with big hearts, good values and morals, and who choose to make a positive difference in society with the power that they hold through being an athlete. The problem is that these aren't the athletes and the instances that get media exposure. In general, people yearn for conflict and drama in the news and in the world of sports. That is what catches a fan's attention and is often what draws people to the wide world of sports. Yes, the philanthropic activities of professional athletes are reported, but not to the extent that the rebellious, trash-talking, fight-starting, name-calling, money-seeking activities are. Lawsuits, drug abuse, spousal abuse, and physical violence are just a few of the typical topics that are covered in sports news. If all of the benefits, foundations, charities, and programs that professional athletes are involved in were talked about and reported as much as all the negative activities, maybe professional athletes would be seen in a little better and more realistic light.

Derrick Brooks, formerly of the Tampa Bay Buccaneers, was a professional athlete who more kids should emulate. His performances, both on and off the field, are very commendable. He is arguably one of the best defensive players to play the game and he has also been named as No. 1 on *The Sporting News*'s list of 99 Good Guys in pro sports.[1]

Brooks grew up in Pensacola, Florida, not having much in his childhood, but he was happy. He was a very smart kid, but he didn't always take education as seriously as he does today. It took learning a tough lesson from his stepfather in elementary school for him to see the importance and seriousness of education. From then on, being a good student was a top priority for him. He graduated from high school with a 3.94 GPA and he received both undergraduate and graduate degrees from Florida State. The importance of education is what he preaches to all of the youth with whom he works and talks.

The All-Pro linebacker has been considered the best in the NFL. He was drafted by the Bucs in 1995, along with Warren Sapp. Brooks was worth every penny, and then some. He was an excellent open-field tackler and an amazing playmaker, which led him to 11 Pro Bowl appearances. He was the NFL's Defensive Player of the Year in 2002, the same year he helped lead the Bucs to their first Super Bowl Championship. His last season with the Bucs was in 2008, completing his 14-year career in the NFL. Shortly after that season, Brooks was chosen as the top outside linebacker on *USA Today's* All-Decade Team for the 2000s. He is respected by not only his teammates, but also by players he competed against. This, along with his commitment, dedication, drive, and love for the game, made him a very good captain, a leader among his teammates, and a very easy person to follow. Prior to the 2005 season, Brooks had played in 160 consecutive games and started in 144 of them which demonstrates his durability as well as his skill. He became the franchise's most prolific tackler and ranked among the best in the league consistently.

In 1996, shortly after Brooks was drafted by the Bucs, he created a charity called the "Brooks Bunch," which is an organization that works with Boys and Girls Club members, mostly in the economically disadvantaged areas of Tampa. The goals of the program are to provide the kids with a role model and mentor, to emphasize the importance of education, and to give them opportunities to see the world that they would not otherwise be exposed to.

Giving money to a charity or organization to help kids is a very noble thing to do, but money does not fix all problems. That's why Brooks chooses to be much more hands-on with the youth he works with. He sits down and really gets to know the kids, the parents and their situations, and he makes a personal effort to make some kind of positive difference in their lives. The program is designed not only to help kids in their present situation, but to help prepare them for the future. This means instilling values, beliefs, morals, and certain behaviors that will make the kids better people over the course of their lives. Taking on these goals takes time and energy, both of which Brooks is willing to give, a rarity for such a superstar athlete. Brooks tells the kids to be respectful, get good grades, and get involved.

A major part of his program includes out-of-town educational field trips that have included tours to Washington D.C., the Western United States (which involved a stop at the Grand Canyon), a trip to colleges and universities in New York, Chicago, Atlanta, and Tallahassee, and two trips to Africa. Prior to the trips, the kids have classes to learn about the place or places they will be visiting. There was a special selection process for the trip to Africa, because only 20 kids could go. After attending sessions to learn about the culture and history of Africa, the kids had to write essays explaining what they learned and why they should get to go on the trip. A 2.5 GPA was also a prerequisite.

This trip was the experience of a lifetime for these kids. The following is a list of just a few of the activities that the tour included: eating crocodile and ostrich around a campfire at a safari base camp, watching a mother elephant charge at their car, taking a gondola to the top of Table Mountain, meeting with local high school students, traveling to Soweto to see where Nelson Mandela lived, and then traveling to Robben Island to see where he was imprisoned for 26 years, and watching tribal African dances performed by the natives. Each year the trips seem to be getting harder to top. It's going to be hard to go above and beyond a two-week tour in Africa, but knowing Derrick Brooks, he'll find some way to outdo himself. Both professionally and personally, he just keeps getting better and better.

The Derrick Brooks Celebrity Golf Classic is the biggest fundraiser for Derrick Brooks Charities Inc., which supports all of the programs, events, and opportunities that Brooks promotes. The tournament will celebrate its 10th Anniversary in 2010. Some of the other activities include the game-day ticket program, and teaming up with the Bucs to raise money for Hurricane Ivan relief efforts, specifically for his hometown of Pensacola. The Golf Classic always includes several pro football players showcasing their golf skills and has been a huge success.

The work of Derrick Brooks does not go unnoticed. His giving nature and devotion to helping kids is very well-known and talked about amongst the NFL franchises. He was recognized in 2000 when he received the highest charitable award annually presented by the NFL, the prestigious Walter Payton Man of the Year Award. Brooks has been a spokesman for United Way in several different capacities. Also, in 2002, Brooks was named to the NFLPA Diversity Committee to work with NFLPA executive director Gene Upshaw on the issue of diversity in the NFL.

Brooks is a man who remembers where he came from and who helped him get to where he is today. He was an All-American at Florida State University while earning two degrees. In March of 2003, Florida Governor, Jeb Bush, appointed Brooks to FSU's board of trustees. As demonstrated in all other aspects of Brooks' life, he is a doer, not a talker. He wants to be a part of making big decisions for the University and a part of great improvment.

Another testament of Brooks' dedication to education is his recent venture of becoming a founder of a charter high school in the state of Florida. The Brooks-DeBartolo Collegiate High School opened in 2007 with a mission to provide a rigorous and relevant academic environment. Additionally, Brooks has also joined the boards of the Florida Department of Education Foundation, Brooks-DeBartolo Charities, Inc, St. Leo's University, and the Governor's Council on Physical Fitness.

When Brooks isn't out making a difference in the lives of other kids and families, he is spending time with his four children, and his wife, Carol. Derrick Brooks is a very special athlete and a very special person. Although he is no longer playing football, he will continue to make a positive difference through his charities and his work in the community. Brooks will perpetually be a good role model and society would be a much better place if kids had more role models like Brooks to admire and to emulate.

Note

1. Paul Attner, "Lighting up young lives", *Sporting News*, July 31, 2000.

Justin Allen

Playing to Win in Life

by Brian Wright, with Austin Moss II

He was Malta High School's leading scorer with 2,143 points, with senior season averages of 26.7 points, 15 rebounds, and 4.7 blocks. With statistics like these Justin Allen stepped onto the campus of Arizona State University with hopes of taking his talents to the NBA. At ASU, Allen was revered by his teammates, coaches, and faculty. He was famous for his easy going and lovable spirit. His sense of humor was apparent when describing his most memorable moment in his freshman season. "That's the game," he said, "when Eddie House and I combined for 64 points."[1] Allen scored only three points that game.

To Allen, the basketball team at Arizona State was his family and the gym was his home away from home. Heading into his sophomore season, Allen was given a statistic that impacted his life more than any free throw, field goal percentage, or any other basketball percentage he could have ever imagined. On September 14, 2000 he was diagnosed with Stage II Hodgkin's disease and given an 80 percent chance to live.

Allen's diagnosis of Hodgkin's was as big a surprise to him as it was to everyone around him. He actually could feel the tumor but thought it was just a pulled abdominal muscle. Allen, the athletic program, and the entire University were in shock. Allen began treatment immediately to stop the spread of the cancer to other organs and lymph nodes in his body. He underwent six months of treatments including radiation and chemotherapy to kill cancer cells and shrink the tumor. Allen was forced to redshirt the 2000–01 season while undergoing treatments that left him sick and bedridden for 11 to 12 hours a day. His weight dropped from 215 pounds to 190 pounds.

Despite the extensive treatments, Allen remained dedicated to school and his teammates. He was frequently visited by coaches and players while in the hospital. As a sign of unity and compassion the entire basketball team decided to shave their heads when Allen's therapy caused him to lose his hair. Allen's courage through his recovery motivated everyone around him. When members of the Arizona State basketball team would begin to slack off, all it would take was for one person to remind everyone how much Allen wanted to be out there with them and the practice environment would change dramatically.

While balancing school and therapy, Allen attended most Arizona State basketball practices and found relief in shooting on the sidelines while encouraging his teammates. Allen was back on the court in May of 2001. He wanted no pity or special treatment from any of his teammates. He challenged them not to go lightly on him because he would be playing as hard as he could with them. Allen is competitive and courageous. At a time when many people would feel burdened and discouraged Allen thought of his sickness as just another obstacle that he had to overcome. Allen knew that obstacles appear in life, and that they are just obstacles, not barriers barring you from continuing on with your life. Allen remained positive that he would overcome his health challenges and continue living his life to the fullest.

Though exhausted from the therapy, Allen managed to earn a 3.23 grade point average the season of his diagnosis, and graduated with an overall grade point average of 3.46. Allen would go on to serve as a key reserve for the Arizona State Basketball team the next few seasons. He earned his bachelor's degree in Justice Studies and was the recipient of the Jimmy V Foundation's Comeback award in 2003. In a May 2003 interview with Sundevils.com, Allen commented on his bout with cancer saying, "It made me grow up a lot quicker and it made me realize there was more to life than what I was doing. It really puts things in perspective. You think cancer is something that happens to other people, but when it happens to you it's a wake up call and it really puts things in perspective."[2] Allen's new outlook helped him overcome his illness and has helped guide him as he continues to fulfill his life.

Since his playing days at Arizona State, Allen has played professional basketball in Australia and Japan. Allen has also taught history and coached high school basketball in Arizona. "You've got to live your life every single day," said Allen.[3] This is exactly what Allen is doing now with wife, Eddy, and son, Elijah by taking advantage of every moment and personifying Jimmy Valvano's memorable quote, "Don't give up, don't ever give up."

Entering college, Justin Allen imagined a season where Arizona State would win the Pac-10 Conference title and the National Championship. Looking back he understands he won a much more important challenge in the game of life.

Notes

1. Arizona State Sun Devils,"Justin Allen's Battle Against Cancer Helps Another Student," Official site of Arizona State Sun Devils, September 29, 2005, http://thesun devils.collegesports.com/sports/m-baskbl/spec-rel/032502aaa.html, (accessed March 25, 2002).

2. Ed Odeven, "Life altering experience came early for Oita's Allen," *Japan Times*, April 13, 2007, Sports, Hoop Scoop.

3. Ibid.

Felipe Lopez

Playing to Win in Life

by Brian Wright

New York City basketball is a legend in its own right with storied heroes and folklore that have been passed down from generation to generation. There is something special about the basketball played there and the players and fans who take part in it. Throughout the celebrated lifetime of New York City basketball there have been many legends, but few have lived the life of Felipe Lopez—one of the greatest basketball players in New York City high school basketball history. His name is frequently mentioned alongside such NYC basketball greats as Bob Cousy, Kareem Abdul-Jabbar, Pearl Washington, Chris Mullin, Kenny Anderson, and Stephon Marbury. A tremendous talent with an enormous heart, Lopez set a new standard for what a basketball legend in NYC would have to accomplish and how one could impact the community through one's status as a basketball celebrity. Through his performance on and off the court, Lopez became a role model for the Latino community and a trailblazer in encouraging their participation in the game of basketball.

Lopez was born in Santo Domingo of the Dominican Republic. As a young child he grew up playing baseball, the most popular sport in his native land. Though he enjoyed baseball, it never really captivated him the way that basketball did. As a young child playing in a pick-up baseball game Lopez was hit in the face by a ball and decided that day that basketball was the right sport for him. Though choosing between baseball and basketball was an important issue he faced at the time, Lopez was also confronted with an unfavorable economic situation for himself and his family which was much more important. Due to this economic status of Lopez's family in the Dominican Republic, they were forced to leave the country in search of better opportunities for their family. Lopez stayed behind but would return to his family during the summer of his eighth grade year of school. At age 13, Lopez's arrival in the South Bronx borough of New York City was definitely a change of environment and change of pace for him. He was faced with many cultural challenges including a language barrier, since at the time Lopez spoke very little English. Lopez adapted very quickly and began to use basketball to learn the culture of inner-city New York. While playing at a local basketball court with some friends, Lopez learned exactly what he didn't want to become involved in. Lopez saw a drug transaction transpiring that must have gone wrong because the two drug dealers began to fire gunshots at each other. This scared Lopez and sent him to the gym to work on developing his basketball skills.

Lopez found a famous gym where many other great New York City players have practiced and made it his home away from home. This was the famed Gauchos gym in the South Bronx. This was a safe haven for Lopez and countless other teammates and friends while growing up in South Bronx. Lopez's budding talent and potential could be spotted at first glance when entering Gauchos gym. Gym owner Lou d'Almeida found himself buzzing and raving about Lopez's talent as well. From the time spent with Lopez in the gym, d'Almeida knew that Lopez was a special kid and a phenomenal athlete. By this time Lopez had grown to over 6-foot-5 and his status around the city was growing larger. Lopez attended Rice High School, a local private school and he began to flourish there as well. Lopez's athleticism and raw talent on the court left college coaches and the media on the edge of their seat while filling high school gyms and stadiums to capacity. Lopez never seemed to disappoint the crowds who were eager to see him get out on a fast break and slam down a monstrous dunk. Lopez played three successful seasons at Rice High School and then the hype began about what college he would attend or whether he would go straight to the NBA.

As a young teenager Lopez understood but didn't know the nationwide and eventual international effect that he was having not only on high school basketball, but within the context of his Latino heritage as well. Lopez was a trailblazer who opened the doors for many Latinos in the city of New York, as well as around the country, to compete and become regarded as among the best basketball players in the United States. Though he didn't know the full extent of his celebrity at the time, Lopez had become a role model athlete in the Latino community.

In his senior year of high school, Lopez was frequently compared to NBA greats such as Michael Jordan and Charles Barkley, and graced the cover of *Sports Illustrated*, a feat few high school athletes have the privilege of doing. Throughout all of the media attention and hoopla, Lopez never lost sight of his humble background or his commitment to using his newfound celebrity status in basketball to improve his community. Lopez had lived in poor and underserved environments. When asked about this, Lopez told *Sports Illustrated*, "I have so many good ideas in my head, I want to change the unhappy world around me. So I must use creativity in the classroom and on the court to bring hope."[1] This was a profound statement for such a young person who carried the weight of people's mammoth athletic aspirations for him on his shoulders, as well as carrying the torch for the Latino community. It showed his understanding of the bigger picture in society, and how he could use sport to impact society in a positive way.

Lopez would go on to set records as a senior in New York City high school basketball as well as leading his team at Rice High to the City Championship. He was named the National High School Basketball Player of the Year. While excelling on the court, Lopez was able to achieve equivalent success in the classroom, graduating from Rich High School with a 3.5 grade point average. With his vast success came options as his senior year concluded. Lopez was offered a $500,000 contract to forgo his collegiate eligibility and play professional basketball in Spain. Lopez also had scholarship offers to almost every college and university with a basketball team in the United States.

After much contemplation and counsel with his family, Lopez chose to remain in New York and attend St. John's University. He made this decision based not only on the academic and athletic standards of the University, but for cultural reasons as well. Lopez wanted to stay in New York because of his respect for his heritage and the huge Latino population there. He wanted to be in a large Latino community so the youth and other members of the community had the chance to see him play and so that he could be a positive role model for those community members. Lopez also wanted to remain close to his family members. Attending St. John's University was the best decision for him to accomplish all these things.

Lopez achieved a great deal of success as a collegiate athlete at St. John's and left the University with a career average of 17.6 points, 6 rebounds, and 2.5 assists per game. Athletically, the hype and media attention that surrounded Lopez while in high school were tough expectations to fulfill, and in some people's perceptions, he never had the career his talent initially promised. Lopez was drafted 24th in the first round of the 1998 NBA draft. He was traded on draft night and played his rookie season with the Vancouver Grizzlies. During his rookie campaign Lopez showed flashes of brilliance and ended the season averaging 9.3 points and 3.3 rebounds. Injuries would ultimately limit Lopez's development and slow down a career that most people who saw him play felt would be a great one. For the next several years, Lopez would bounce around the NBA landing briefly with several different teams. Although Lopez's basketball career took a different path then many people expected, he is still one of the biggest legends in New York City basketball history, especially in the Latino community. In the later years of his career in the NBA, Lopez served as a community relations ambassador for the NBA and brought basketball and other life lessons and training to the various Hispanic countries around the world. He conducted basketball camps and clinics and promoted education, leadership, character building, healthy living, and HIV/AIDS awareness and prevention.

Felipe Lopez's family instilled morals and values in him when he was a child so that he developed a commitment to improving the lives of his family and others in the community. He has been an ambassador and pioneer for Latinos on and off the court. He is a role model citizen and uses his status as a basketball celebrity in a positive way to help others achieve a better life. Felipe Lopez is a legend not only on the basketball court, but also as a social activist in the community.

Note

1. Tim Crothers, "Felipe Lopez" *Sports Illustrated*, December 20, 1993.

Warrick Dunn

Playing to Win in Life

by Jenny Yehlen

Warrick Dunn had a very busy and very successful year in 1997. He graduated from Florida State University with a degree in information studies and he was chosen in the first round (12th pick overall) of the NFL draft by the Tampa Bay Buccaneers. In his rookie season, he started in 10 of 16 games, and he led the Bucs in both receptions and rushing. Thanks to his stellar performance, he was given Pro Bowl honors and was also named NFL Rookie of the Year by *Football News*, *Pro Football Weekly*, and *Sports Illustrated*. He was also honored by being selected as Offensive Rookie of the Year by the Associated Press, *Football Digest*, and *College and Pro Football Newsweekly*.

As if his football commitments didn't keep him busy enough in his first year of being a professional athlete, he also found the time to create a program called "Homes for the Holidays." Seeking out philanthropic causes are usually not on the top of the priority list for rookie pro athletes, but Dunn has proven that he is not like most of his peers. He wasted no time in figuring out how he could use the power that he holds as an athlete in the professional world of sports to give back to his community and help those that are less fortunate than him.

The program is very special to Dunn because he can relate to the people he is helping. The purpose of the program is to assist single mothers in owning their first home by providing the down payment on a house and then furnishing the house with everything that a first-time homeowner would need, such as furniture, food, linens, lawn mower, gardening supplies, washer, dryer, dishes, pots and pans, and more. It is a very stabilizing factor to be a homeowner, but it is also very hard to become a first time homeowner, especially for a single mother. It is very disheartening for women who work day and night to provide for their kids, yet never feel like they are getting anywhere. Dunn's program gives women that little extra boost needed to get them into their first home and it rewards them for working so hard to take care of their families.

Homes for the Holidays works with other non-profit organizations that run first-time homeownership programs, such as Habitat for Humanity, United Way's IDA program, and Community Redevelopment programs. Once a year these non-profit organizations nominate single mothers as recipients of the program. The women must have completed the mandatory course work and be properly prepared to be homeowners.

This is an important cause to Dunn because his mom was a single parent and the sole provider of his family. Dunn grew up in Baton Rouge, Louisiana and was the oldest of the six children. Dunn's mother, Betty Smothers, did everything she could to make ends meet, which meant finding extra jobs to earn extra cash wherever and whenever she could outside of her police officer duties. Warrick will admit that he didn't have many material things growing up but, more importantly, he had the love of his friends, family, and coaches. Ms. Smothers also taught her son how to give of himself and to be generous to those in need. She obviously taught him well, because he is doing just that with the establishment of the Homes for the Holidays Program, and eventually, the creation of the Warrick Dunn Foundation.

A horrible tragedy occurred in 1993 when Ms. Smothers was shot and killed in the line of duty. Dunn was just a senior in high school. He became the glue that held the family together. Ms. Smothers was never able to achieve the dream of owning her own home before she died, so Dunn's program enables other single, working women to achieve that dream. Dunn wants to help women out who are working hard to provide for their families. Ms. Smothers is surely looking down on her son and boasting with pride at the wonderful man he has become.

The Homes for the Holidays campaign has been so successful and so inspirational that there have been other NFL players who have tried to duplicate the program in their own respective cities. Kurt Warner, former quarterback for the St. Louis Rams, New York Giants, and Arizona Cardinals and his wife Brenda, established the program in 2002 when they provided two single mothers with new homes of their own. Warner also extended the program to his hometown of Des Moines, Iowa in 2004. A fellow Rams teammate, cornerback Jason Sehorn, helped place six single mothers and their families in to their first homes from 2000 to 2002, when he played for the New York Giants. There has been a handbook of the program created so that it is easy for other NFL players to implement this program. There are single mothers struggling all over the country that could benefit from this program immensely. The idea is to make it easy for athletes to adapt this program to their own communities.

As of May 2009, this program has helped a total of 86 single parents and 233 children find permanent homes of their own. And those numbers are going to continue to grow, not only in the three cities in which Dunn operates his program, but in other locations where the program has been instituted by other athletes. Dunn created the Warrick Dunn Foundation in 2002 when he was traded to Atlanta and he expanded the program in his new team's city. With that expansion the program then helped women in Baton Rouge, Louisiana, Tampa, Florida and Atlanta, Georgia.

Dunn has received some very prestigious awards. He was honored with an "Oprah's Angel" by Oprah Winfrey herself in the spring of 2002. He has received several other special honors for his philanthropic ventures. He was the Atlanta Falcons Man of the Year in 2003, was named to the *Sporting News* "75 Good Guys in Sports" in 1999, 2000, 2003 and 2004, and he was on the list of *Sports Illustrated*'s 101 Most Influential Minorities in Sports in 2003. In January of 2009, Dunn was presented with the Bart Starr Award, which honors the NFL Hall of Famer and his commitment to be a positive role model to his family, teammates, and community. NFL players vote and determine the winner of this award each year. "Just to be mentioned in the same breath as Bart Starr is an incredible honor," said Dunn. "I've won a lot of awards, but this is one I'll really cherish because of what it stands for."[1]

Along with being named NFL Rookie of the Year in 1997 and being given Pro Bowl honors in that same year, Dunn was also a Pro Bowler in 2000 and he was inducted in to the Florida State University Hall of Fame in 2002. During Dunn's tenure at Florida State, he became the first FSU running back to record three 1,000-yard rushing seasons and he ended his career as the Seminole's career leader in rushing yards with a total of 3,959 yards.

Recently, Dunn has been showing his support for the United States. In March of 2005, he traveled to Kuwait, Afghanistan, and Iraq with linebacker Larry Izzo of the New England Patriots. They went on a week-long United Service Organizations (USO) Tour helping to dedicate a new USO building called the Pat Tillman Center, at Bagram Airbase near Kabal, Afghanistan. Just a year earlier, he traveled with teammate Keith Brooking, Baltimore tight end Todd Heap, and then-NFL Commissioner Paul Tagliabue on a trip to Germany to visit members of the United States Armed Forces.

Dunn played five seasons with the Tampa Bay Buccaneers and was then traded to the Atlanta Falcons, where he played for six years. After the 2007 season, Dunn was let go from the Falcons. Owner, Arther Blank said this was a very difficult decision and that, "In my mind, Warrick will always be a part of the Falcons family."[2] Dunn returned to play for the Bucs for one more season in 2008 and then chose to retire and explore a new position within professional football: ownership. Dunn joined six other minority owners in this venture. Just as majority owner, Blank, had foreshadowed, Dunn reunited with his Falcon family.

All of Warrick Dunn's experiences show the extent he will go to help out those who are in need. He is truly a special man, both on the playing field and off. He published a book in 2008 called *Running For My Life: My Journey In The Game Of Football And Beyond*, which gives a little insight as to how his life experiences shaped him to be the great man that he is today. Dunn will continue to be a positive role model for many years to come and he hopes that in the future, we will see variations of the Homes for the Holidays program all over the country.

Notes

1. "Warrick Dunn Wins Prestigious 2009 Bart Starr Award," *U.S. Newswire*, January 31, 2009, http://www.highbeam.com/doc/1P2-19825344.html, (accessed February 27, 2010).

2. Charles Odum, "Falcons Release Veteran RB Warrick Dunn," *AP Online*, March 3, 2008, http://www.highbeam.com/doc/1A1-D8V65VF80.html, (accessed February 15, 2010).

Priest Holmes

Playing in Life to Win

by Brian Wright

With an amazing stat line of over 7,500 rushing yards and over 80 touchdowns as a professional football player, Priest Holmes has had an extraordinary professional career on the football field. He has been one of the most successful running backs of the past decade as a member of the Baltimore Ravens and Kansas City Chiefs. His success on the field can be largely attributed to his tremendously intensive work ethic and his desire to perform to the best of his ability every time he steps onto the football field.

Along with being a great football player Holmes has also been a dedicated and committed citizen participating in numerous charitable events and community service projects in the Kansas City and San Antonio areas. Growing up as a child in Fort Smith, Arkansas and later in San Antonio, Holmes was raised to always think about improving the community in which he lived as well as focusing on success in academics and sports. It was from this initial guidance instilled in him as a young child that has made him a man of high moral and social values and standards. This led to Holmes' deep passion and commitment to make a difference within the community and help others growing up in situations less fortunate than his.

As a youth, Holmes was a standout on the field as well as in the classroom. Holmes participated in numerous social clubs and teams outside of football and was a star member of the Marshall High School chess club in San Antonio, Texas. Priest was always an analytical and serious thinker and even used his chess strategies to help him on the football field. This idea paid off and, due to his stellar production as a high school student-athlete, Holmes earned the Offensive Player of the Year award from the *San Antonio Light* newspaper, as well as being awarded a full scholarship to attend the prestigious University of Texas. As a highly-touted recruit, Holmes lived up to the expectations of many who surrounded the University of Texas football team and received "Fabulous Freshman" honorable mention team honors in 1992 from *USA Today*. Holmes continued his success on the field throughout his collegiate career, ultimately preparing for the National Football League (NFL) draft at the end of his senior year.

Despite his lightning quick speed and proven ability to have an impact on the football field, Holmes was overlooked by NFL scouts and went undrafted in 1996. Holmes was unwavering in his desire to play in the NFL and tried out for the Baltimore Ravens during training camp of the 1996 season. Holmes played well and impressed the coaching staff enough to be on the opening day roster. Holmes' commitment to hard work and excellence quickly made him a star on the field. In just his second season in the NFL, Holmes rushed for over 1,000 yards and scored seven rushing touchdowns. This initial success launched Holmes' All-Pro career. He helped the Baltimore Ravens earn an NFL Championship trophy and achieved many personal accolades along the way. In 2001 Holmes joined the Kansas City Chiefs and was named the NFL's leading rusher that year as well as a Pro Bowl selection honoring the season's best offensive and defensive performers. Performing at the All-Pro level in the NFL takes hard work and dedication to train on the field as well as the time spent off the field learning plays and studying film. Though Holmes was committed to performing at the All-Pro level and spending time developing his athletic skills and physique, he always made time to work in the community to make society a better place for our youth.

As a player continuing to grow up himself in Baltimore, Holmes wanted to make an impact in the community as quickly as possible. He frequently heard reports of acts of violence and crime that had plagued the youth and families within this region. According to data released by the FBI, the city of Baltimore reported over 18,630 violent crimes within city boundaries.[1] Alarmed by such statistics, Holmes knew that with his celebrity status as an athlete, his positive influence could impact the minds of the at-risk youth in the area and help reduce the city's crime rate.

Holmes decided that one of his first projects would be the Maryland Department of Education's Program GEAR UP—Gaining Early Awareness and Readiness for Undergraduate Programs. This program was designed by the Maryland Department of Education to prepare students from low-income neighborhoods for college. This was an extremely important program to Holmes due to his firm belief in the importance of education.

While in Baltimore, Holmes also partnered with others striving to make improvements and contributions to the community. Holmes signed on as an official sponsor and contributor to the scholarship fund of Dr. Ben Carson, the Head of Pediatric Neurosurgery at John's Hopkins Children's Hospital. As a sponsor and contributor, Holmes attended local area schools and gave motivational speeches to young people about the importance of staying in school and aspiring to attend college. Following his mission to increase the awareness of the importance of education in the Baltimore community, Holmes became a sponsor and eventual keynote speaker for the Ronald McDonald Corporation Ray Kroc Youth Achievement Awards. The recipients of the Ray Kroc Achievement awards were given scholarships to attend college from the Ronald McDonald Corporation.

Holmes' commitment to the community in which he lived and worked continued in Kansas City after he decided to continue his football career with the Kansas City Chiefs. Holmes spends countless hours and dollars in the inner city of Kansas City helping young student-athletes realize their potential on the field and in the classroom. Addressing a lack of funds for athletics in the inner city of Kansas City, Holmes created the Sports Dental Safety for Kids Project. Through his charitable foundation TeamPriest in collaboration with Chili's Restaurants and the Samuel U. Rodger's Health Center's dental staff, Holmes provided top-of-the-line custom made mouth guards for each student-athlete playing a sport that required a mouthpiece for protection in the Kansas City area. Holmes discovered through research done by the Sports Dental Safety for Kids Project that these mouth guards were very useful in preventing serious injuries including major dental problems and concussions. This project is ongoing for Holmes and his TeamPriest organization, and each year every student-athlete who participates in the various sports requiring mouthpieces in Kansas City receives a custom mouth guard.

TeamPriest's programs are not just geared toward student-athletes in the community of Kansas City. Stemming from Holmes's passion for chess as a teenager he started a chess club within the youth community in the inner city of Kansas City.

In 2007, Priest retired from football and has turned his attention to his hometown of San Antonio and trying to impact the lives of the youth there. Priest in conjunction with the San Antonio Spurs have formed the Priest Holmes-Spurs Student Incentive Program.

This initiative is designed to reward students with tickets to San Antonio Spurs home games for academic achievements and participation in extracurricular activities. Holmes and the Spurs' investment in this intiative required a $40,000 contribution but its impact on community goes well beyond its financial value. These young children have a role model to look up to in Priest Holmes. Holmes has also created a celebrity weekend in June in San Antonio to benefit local charities that seek to improve the well-being of children and families in San Antonio.[2] Holmes understands the role he can play in improving lives of these young children and continues to work daily to make a positive change.

Holmes' contributions to Baltimore, Kansas City, and San Antonio are varied and widespread, but the ultimate goal of each has always and will always remain the same: to positively help young people. His efforts always focus on teaching the importance of education and helping youth strive to reach their full potential on the athletic field as well as in the classroom.

Throughout his amateur and professional careers, Holmes has been a role model as an athlete and as a citizen. He lives his life with the passion and commitment to better society. When asked why he does so much work in the community, Holmes responded "For me it is just a way to give back, I think it's part of being a professional; and it's about taking advantage of your opportunity. As a professional athlete you're definitely going to touch lives, and most likely it's going to be a child's life and you really want to touch that life in a special way."[3] This is the winning spirit that sport is all about. It is not the numbers of wins and losses one attains as a player or coach, or the statistics that one compiles during the game. It is the way one can change society for the better. This is Priest Holmes' message.

Holmes has received numerous community leader and civic awards over the span of his professional career, but the title of one award he has received stands out as a perfect description of what he has meant to the communities with which he has been involved. That award is the Glen S. Pop Warner Award given to the individual who the award committee thinks has most effectively inspired the youth of today to become great achievers of tomorrow. This is what Holmes has done, not through scoring 20 touchdowns in one season or leading the NFL in rushing, but by touching the lives of America's youth. Priest Holmes is truly a hero for the ages.

Notes

1. Journal City Council of Baltimore. December 5, 2005, www.baltimorecity council.com/Council_Journal/05-12-05~23rd.pdf, (accessed March 30, 2010).

2. Natalia Montemayor, "Priest Holmes rallies local students, promotes education," *La Prensa*, November 2, 2008.

3. NFL Players, Inc. Interview. NFLPlayers.com, http://www.nflplayers.com/ players/player.aspx?id=25151&section=media, (accessed December 12, 2005).

Amber Burgess

Playing to Win in Life

by Jenny Yehlen

It started like any other day of school for most students in Littleton, Colorado—rushing to class, frantically searching for the homework assignment that is due first period, asking mom for lunch money, envisioning the impending summer break, and saying hi to friends in the hall before class. Yet, this sunny spring day of April 20, 1999 at Columbine High School ended in tragedy when two students turned on their own, murdering 13 and wounding 21 more in the most devastating high school shooting in U.S. history.

Investigations later discovered the shooters, driven by hate, were targeting athletes and minority group members. A likely target during the shootings at Columbine, Amber Burgess, a softball player, happened to be out of town at her grandmother's funeral during the tragic shootings that took the lives of her coach and mentor, Dave Sanders, and her classmates.

A top scholar-athlete and leader at the school, Burgess was asked to address the 70,000 people attending the Columbine High School Memorial Service alongside then-Vice President Al Gore. Since the tragedy, Burgess has dedicated her life toward making a difference in the lives of others and honoring the lives of her fallen coach and fellow students.

While most high school seniors were dreaming about graduation and contemplating college life, Burgess' senior year was stained with tragedy. Although that pain can never be forgotten, Burgess learned to harness it into her community outreach and uses it to benefit others.

A top athlete in the state of Colorado, Burgess was a member of the USA Junior World Softball team. With the Junior National team, she traveled to Taipei, Taiwan to compete and during her senior year, Burgess earned a spot on the U.S. National Blue Team. Burgess was a finalist for the Fred Steinmark Athlete of the Year Award for excellence in athletics and academics given by the Denver *Rocky Mountain News*.

Burgess' statewide and nationally known talent earned her a softball scholarship to the University of Nebraska where she started college in the fall of 1999. Burgess was a leader on and off the field and was truly committed to community service. She was chosen as captain of the team after only one season, a sign of the high regard in which she was held by her teammates. As a freshman, Burgess immediately became involved in the Husker Outreach Program. She was an active member of the Student-Athlete Advisory Committee, a monthly volunteer for Meals on Wheels, a weekly volunteer for the Team Spirit hospital visitation program, and was nominated for the NCAA Foundation Leadership Conference.

She lives every day to the fullest, and despite being directly affected by the tragedy at Columbine, she was described as one of the most positive and enthusiastic student-athletes among the 700 who were part of Nebraska's program during her collegiate career. Burgess strives to make an impact on the national level with programming ideas and concerns and has been a keynote speaker at a "Stop the Violence" conference.

Burgess' freshman year at Nebraska started with impressive statistics on the field and her senior year ended in the same fashion. She was selected to the Academic All-Big 12 Team three times. The senior catcher and communication studies major was named to the 2003 Verizon Academic All-District VII team selected by the College Sports Information Directors of America. The three-time co-captain was considered one of the top defensive catchers in Nebraska history. She graduated with three of the top 10 single-season putout marks in school history. During her senior year, Nebraska opponents stole just 19 bases on her as she caught opposing runners attempting to steal 18 times. Burgess played in over 250 games at the University of Nebraska, which ranked fourth on the all-time list at the time.

After graduating, Burgess was interested in continuing her softball career. Professional softball had failed in the United States before, and unless she was training for the Olympics, opportunities were scarce. Then, in 2004, the National Pro Fastpitch league was developed. The Denver-based league consisted of six teams which played 60 games each during the June through August season. Though it is a professional sports league, it is different than many would imagine. There are no million-dollar contracts and billion-dollar stadiums, no arrogant attitudes representing what sport is not, and no steroids or dress code violations. The National Pro Fastpitch league was hoping for less than half a million dollars to sustain itself in its first year and was not planning to profit. Burgess was ecstatic to be making just over $5,000 for the 60-game season and to showcase softball to the hundreds of thousands of youth and high school softball players across the country. Burgess played for the love of the game, the true spirit of sport, and it showed on the field.

Despite the loss of a role model and friend in high school, Amber Burgess persevered, determined not to let her two violent classmates instill fear into her life. She maintained good grades and was the starting catcher for one of the top softball programs in the country, a feat sure to make Coach Sanders smile.

It wasn't until after Burgess' playing career ended that she realized there had been something missing ever since that dreadful day in 1999. A tragedy like Columbine would change anyone's perspective and outlook on life. Burgess admits that she lost her killer instinct on the field. Burgess still had a successful and meaningful collegiate and post-collegiate career, as described, but she admits, "Before that day, if I'd strike out, I'd be furious. After that day, I'd say, 'Hey, I struck out, but I'm alive.' I totally lost my competitive nature. Totally lost it."[1]

Ten years after Columbine, Amber Burgess Wade is a wife and a mother and a proud firefighter in the city of Lincoln, Nebraska. She is one of 15 women on the 300-person force and she admits that it is wonderful to have something new to be passionate about. Even after softball, Burgess continues to be a positive role model and reaches out to her community through her role as a firefighter. She says she is feeling like her old self again, and we can all be thankful for that.

Note

1. Kevin Simpson, "10 Years Later, Columbine Remembers," *The Denver Post.* April 19, 2009.

Pamela Malcolm

Playing to Win in Life

by Jenny Yehlen

There are innumerable challenges that go along with being a collegiate athlete, most of which center around balancing academics and athletics. There is the expectation to attend class, complete all assignments, and get good grades, while at the same time giving 110 percent in the weight room, learning a full playbook, vying for a starting spot, and performing up to a coach's and teammates' expectations. Pam Malcolm was looking forward to being a student-athlete and experiencing all of the above, but unfortunately, she never got her chance.

In the spring of 2002, basketball player Pam Malcolm was a highly-touted high school senior, ranked 86th in the nation by *Street & Smith*'s recruiting list and was also a McDonald's All-American nominee. The Colchester, Connecticut native from Bacon Academy, who was a leading shot-blocker in Connecticut high school history, had signed a letter of intent to play basketball for Coach Mary Burke at Bryant University. She had high hopes of continuing that stellar play throughout her collegiate career and achieving great things as a Bryant Bulldog.

Malcolm's life was turned upside down two weeks later when she was in a car accident, which left her with a broken neck, a torn anterior cruciate ligament, and a punctured leg. The driver of the car walked away from the horrific accident, but Malcolm was not so lucky. Dreams of a standout career at Bryant were shattered and replaced with hopes of walking again.

Malcolm could have given up on basketball, given up on her scholarship, and given up on Bryant University, but that would have been too easy for her, and that wasn't the path she wanted to take. Coach Burke visited the young star in the hospital shortly after the accident and assured her that she did not have to worry about losing her scholarship because of her injury. Burke made a commitment to Malcolm and she was going to stand by her word. Malcolm would do the same.

After six months of agonizing rehabilitation, Malcolm was able to arrive on the Bryant University campus to begin her collegiate career. She was confined to a wheelchair for almost two years, but still managed to be a contributing member of the basketball team, without ever stepping foot on the game court. She showed up to 6 a.m. practices, traveled with the team, smiled in team pictures, and encouraged and motivated her teammates from the sideline. She was a proud member of the 10-member scholarship roster and served as a wonderful source of inspiration when cheering her team on to victory. The Bryant Bulldogs women's basketball team had much to celebrate during the years that Malcolm was a part of the program.

Malcolm's hard work and dedication to her own workout regimen and physical therapy schedule paid off two years after the accident when she was able to trade in her wheelchair for a pair of crutches. Unless there is a medical breakthrough, Malcolm will need crutches for the rest of her life, but she is optimistic that she will lead a normal life. "Her ultimate goal is to keep improving, hoping one day science will erase the struggle to perform everyday tasks."[1]

Another reward for her dedication to her teammates and basketball team came on senior night for the Bryant Bulldogs. She started and participated in the one and only game of her collegiate career and she scored two points. Fellow Bulldog student-athletes lined the sidelines, fans, friends, family and high school coaches were in the crowd. She started the game standing underneath the hoop and when her teammate passed her the ball, she kissed it right off the glass for two points and an unforgettable memory. The entire gym gave her a standing ovation, recognizing her strength, spirit, and inspirational attitude. She came out of the game right after her moment of glory, but her team would go on to beat Merrimack that night. It was surely an evening that Malcolm will not soon forget.

Pamela Malcolm graduated from Bryant University in May of 2006, after only three and a half years on campus. Her hope is to move on to a career in social work where she would no doubt continue to be an inspiration to those in the next chapter of her life.

Note

1. Brett Orzechowski, "For Malcolm, Bryant keeps the dream alive," *New Haven Register*, January 29, 2006.

Johnnie Williams

Playing to Win in Life

by Jenny Yehlen

Johnnie Williams has been an athlete all of his life, but he has never trained like he does now. Williams was a football player growing up in Brandon, Florida. He was an average teenager growing up, until one decision made him extraordinary. After graduation, he decided that joining the Army was the best thing for him to do, both personally and professionally. With the support of his family, he entered the Army in 2001, was sent abroad to Germany, and in 2003 was deployed to Iraq to fight for his country.

Like many men and women that enter into armed combat for the United States, Williams' life would never be the same again. Four months into his tour of duty, Williams' Humvee was was hit by a truck and he was thrown from the vehicle, resulting in a broken pelvis, two broken bones in his back, a torn artery, and a torn stomach. When he awoke, after a week of lying unconscious, he was told he would never walk again. "I kind of felt like my life was over,"[1] Williams said. He returned to his hometown, but seriously contemplated whether life was worth living after all he had been through and his current predicament.

Being young and fit, Williams was able to bounce back from his injuries rather quickly, but he was still left in a wheelchair. Within a year after his devastating accident, he decided to train to compete in the National Veteran Wheelchair Games, which is a multi-event sports and rehabilitation program for military service veterans who use wheelchairs for sports competition due to spinal cord injuries, amputations, or certain neurological problems. The event attracts more than 500 athletes each year and continues to grow. The National Veterans Wheelchair Games is the largest annual wheelchair sports event in the world and it is an extremely inspiring event both to watch and participate in. In his first outing at the Games, Williams won three gold medals in weightlifting, discus, and shot-put events, and a silver medal in javelin.

Williams had found something to make life worth living. He hit a point where he could either give up on life or move on and make the best of it. He chose the latter, and is making every minute count. With this new attitude, Williams said, "Live life to the fullest because you never know if you'll live to see tomorrow."[2] This is a message that everyone should take to heart—not just those fighting in a war or living with a disability—to never take for granted the precious time we are given.

Williams is part of a growing number of veterans participating in disabled sporting events. In addition to the National Veterans Wheelchair Games, many of the disable veterans also participate in the Paralympic Games. The first Paralympic Games were held in 1960 in Rome, the same city the Olympics were held that year. These "parallel" games have only grown in number of participants and popularity since their start.

The feats that Johnnie Williams and his fellow disabled athletes achieve are nothing short of amazing. They battle both the physical and mental aspects of being physically handicapped, and, in Williams' case, deal with the aftermath of fighting in a war. Williams trained hard until he could bench 360 pounds and has proven himself to be a multi-faceted athlete. He was looking to extend his talents to skiing and trap-shooting. There is no doubt that with his new outlook on life, anything Johnnie Williams puts his mind to, he will achieve.

Notes

1. Andrea Adelson, "Paralympic Games will soon see influx of war veterans," *The Orlando Sentinel*, March 18, 2007.

2. Courtney Hickson, "Veterans Go For Gold in Wheelchair Games," *Army News Service*, June 21, 2004, http://www.militaryinfo.com/news_story.cfm?textnewsid=1049, (accessed on March 15, 2010).

Jacob Madonia

Playing to Win in Life

by Jessica Bartter Duffaut

When doctors told Jacob Madonia they found a baseball-sized tumor in his foot, he was determined to beat it.

The football and track star grew up in Rome, New York with his parents, Donald and Judy, and sisters, Leona and Dana. While attending the Rome Free Academy for high school, Madonia made the varsity football and track and field teams as a sophomore. He captained the track squad for three years helping to lead the Black Knights to the New York state team title in 2005. He was named an All-Central New York and All-League honoree. The shot put and discus star won three league and sectional titles before graduating in 2005. Madonia also earned All-League honors as a football lineman.

Madonia's track and field skills—best suited him with the University at Buffalo, The State University of New York. His high school coach had played under the Buffalo coach, so Madonia recognized the program as one he could excel in. He was deemed the outdoor team's "Top Newcomer" and scored eighth place finishes in the shot put and discus as a freshman at the Mid-American Conference (MAC) Championships.

A drive to train pushed Madonia, and he returned his sophomore year to have an even better season. He was named "Most Improved" of both the indoor and outdoor teams after finishing third in shot put at the MAC Indoor Championships and sixth in the MAC Outdoor Championships. He was invited to compete at the Intercollegiate Association of Amateur Athletes of America (IC4A) Championships, a "super-conference" meet where he finished 19th. But perhaps most importantly to Madonia was his selection to the Academic All-MAC honor roll for the indoor and outdoor seasons.

While redshirting his junior season, Madonia visited the doctor in April of 2008 to have what appeared to be a cyst removed from his left foot. A week later, doctors told him the cyst was actually a baseball-sized malignant tumor and that he had a rare type of cancer of the soft tissue called Synovial Sarcoma. Madonia began chemotherapy almost immediately. His chemotherapy was in-patient which meant he was in the hospital for a week undergoing chemo, followed by two weeks out of the hospital. The resolute athlete continued to train as much as possible while out of the hospital despite losing 20 pounds from the treatments.

After three rounds of his chemotherapy, in June of 2008, Madonia was forced to undergo a second surgery. While this one was more successful in removing all the cancerous tissue, it came at the price of Madonia's middle toe. Doctors allowed Madonia to recover from the surgery for approximately 12 weeks before placing him on a radiation schedule. Five days a week for nearly two months, Madonia underwent radiation treatments in attempt to shrink the remaining cancerous tumor cells.

Between April and November of 2008, Madonia underwent two surgeries, chemotherapy and radiation, but returned to collegiate competition in January 2009. Throughout his entire treatment, Madonia made every practice when he wasn't hospitalized, whether it was in a wheelchair, on crutches or, eventually, on his own two feet. Madonia was considering redshirting again for the 2008–09 season. Instead, the indomitable athlete decided over the Christmas break that we would return for the 2009 season. Upon returning to competition Madonia won his first shot put throw at 55'2"—just one foot under the best throw he'd ever had. His determination to continue training throughout his therapy proved to be advantageous.

Although Madonia was no longer a junior, his third season still showed the improvement he had hoped for. With an outdoor shot put mark of 55'1"—a throw that earned him second place at the MAC Championships and a spot in the NCAA East Regionals, Madonia was certainly back. Again, Madonia earned All-Academic honors for the indoor and outdoor seasons. His valiant efforts on and off the field and his victorious throws earned him the Coaches' Award for the 2008–09 outdoor season.

Despite his medical turmoil, Madonia had no trouble completing his psychology degree in four years. With one remaining year of athletic eligibility, Madonia competed the 2009–10 season as a graduate student. Madonia, the captain of his team, is also working toward his master's in exercise physiology.

In Buffalo's second meet of the 2009–10 season, Madonia qualified for the IC4A Championships. In his third meet, Madonia provisionally qualified for the NCAA Championships with a throw of 58'5". On February 27, 2010, Madonia's determination was rewarded as he was crowned champion of his conference by winning the shot put event at the Mid-American Conference Championships—the same competition he had placed eighth in as a freshman. As of March 1, 2010, Madonia received a ranking of 31st in the nation—a feat for any athlete, particularly one who almost lost the ability to compete at all.

Madonia is on track to graduate with his master's degree in December, 2010 though he won't be ready to give up his throwing career. As he steadily improves his distances, Madonia's long-standing goal to represent his country at the Olympics is a dream he is ready to pursue wholeheartedly. But it is not only his own athletic performance that Madonia is concerned with. When asked what he plans to do with his exercise physiology degree, Madonia said, "I know I want to work with people on either improving athletic performance or improving their health. I am very interested in athlete performance, but I also find myself drawn to the clinical side such as rehab. There are a lot of areas that I still want to explore."[1]

Also important to Madonia is his goal to help start a fund for pediatric cancer patients in Buffalo, New York. Jacob Madonia was fortunate to receive the help and attention he deserved that likely saved his life. He said, "So many people in my life have been affected by cancer since my diagnosis and I would really like to take a more active role in helping to fight cancer."[2]

Just seeing the brave face and attitude with which he fought his own cancer is surely powerful motivation for many around him. Fight on, Jake!

Notes

1. Jacob Madonia, interview with the author, February 28, 2010.
2. Ibid.

Breanna McMahon

Playing to Win in Life

by Jessica Bartter Duffaut

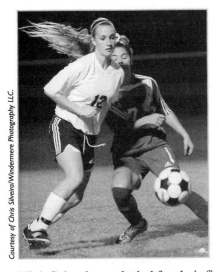

Courtesy of Chris Silveira/Windermere Photography LLC.

Most high school seniors lead their team from the field, vying for college scholarships and hoping for district championships to cap off their high school careers. Bree McMahon planned to do just that but this "soccer-holic"—as described by her mother, Kathleen—had already earned a college scholarship to play at Brevard College in North Carolina. Her senior season of 2009–10 was going to be icing on the cake as her Freedom High School squad tried for their first ever post-season appearance. They saw early success and the Patriots enjoyed their best season in history, earning their first trip to the playoffs after going 13-7-1 during the regular season. And senior captain Bree McMahon did all she could to lead and inspire her teammates through this tremendous season. Unfortunately, Bree was forced to do so from the bench, unable to lace up her cleats and run on the field like every season before.

In September 2009, Bree McMahon was having fun with her club soccer teammates washing cars to raise funds for their club costs, when a teammate moving one of the cars slipped on the pedals and accelerated instead of breaking. Seventeen-year-old McMahon was pinned between a brick wall and the vehicle. Her legs were crushed. Her survival was questionable. McMahon was rushed to Orlando Regional Medical Center where doctors performed two surgeries over 18 hours. McMahon's condition worsened and doctors were forced to amputate her left leg in order to save her life. Once McMahon was stabilized, doctors spent hours reconstructing her right leg. The next week was spent carefully monitoring her right leg and her health in preparation for a second amputation if needed. Upon waking up from a drug induced coma six days later and learning her left leg had been amputated, McMahon interrupted the doctor delivering the news to ask "When can I run?"[1] Her next response was to have her parents tell her friend and teammate behind the wheel that fateful day that, "I'm not mad at her."[2]

This beautiful, spirited, life-loving teenager was an instant headline grabber. Local and national news shows and papers vied for the opportunity to speak to the 17-year-old hero. Just two weeks into her ordeal, while lying in her hospital bed with one leg gone and one almost entirely immovable, she said, "Watch me come back from this. And I will come back from this."[3] McMahon didn't remember life without soccer and didn't want to consider it. She started playing when she was five years old. Her dad, David McMahon, coached her first team with the Catholic Youth League. She played for that league until she was 12 and could join her school and club teams. In middle school, she even played on a competitive Under-13 boys' team as the only female member when there were no competitive girls' teams accessible. The winning team voted McMahon their "Tough as Nails" award recipient. At the time of her accident she was playing three seasons of soccer, year-round. Soccer was McMahon's life.

McMahon spent four weeks in the hospital and underwent six more surgeries before she was allowed to return home. She didn't waste time wallowing in self-pity or hiding in embarrassment. McMahon instantly forgave her friend and teammate who caused the accident and didn't fear returning to her old life of school, soccer, cell phones, and friends. She already had her homecoming dress for the dance in November 2009 and she was determined to attend with her boyfriend as planned. The day after she was released from the hospital in a wheelchair, McMahon went to Freedom High's soccer practice. McMahon didn't just want to go home; she wanted to go where she felt most at home: on the soccer field, surrounded by teammates and friends.

McMahon's friends and family want to console and comfort her. People she's never met want to tell her she is their hero. Professional athletes Mia Hamm and Ryan Longwell have called, texted, and sent care packages to McMahon—who inspires *them*. But McMahon doesn't have time for all that attention. She is too busy rehabbing herself and helping others. After her own release from the hospital, McMahon returned to visit a boy who was diagnosed with bone cancer and faced 30 weeks of chemotherapy. She went to a nearby high school's junior varsity baseball game to support an athlete making his pitching debut with his prosthesis after losing his leg in a boating accident more than a year and a half prior. She befriended a fellow former high school athlete who became paralyzed after a routine gymnastic move. They swapped physical therapy woes and hospital stories. The list of those McMahon touches will no doubt continuously grow for this inspiring young athlete.

Senior Night for this teen was just as special as one would expect. Like the other seniors, she trained extremely hard and put in the extra practice time needed to get herself on the field come game time. But McMahon's tireless efforts came in a sports-medicine facility with her physical therapist. McMahon's devotion to her rehab paid dividends to her right reconstructed leg as well as her left leg in learning to manipulate her prosthetic. On January 13, 2010, McMahon took the field for the sacred Senior Night ceremony. With her family by her side, she pushed up out of her wheelchair and carefully balanced on her two wobbly legs, weak with fear that she might fall. She grasped two crutches and slowly—but gracefully—walked across the field. The stands were gleaming with bright smiles and tear-soaked cheeks as McMahon did what so many of us take for granted every second of everyday: walking. McMahon stood proud as Freedom High School retired her No. 12 jersey and presented the McMahon family with a check for $12,000. Money had been raised at every game, all season and was greatly needed and appreciated to help cover the costs of McMahon extensive medical treatment. The bills will continue as surgery and therapy are expected in the long-term.

By April 2010, McMahon had undergone 12 surgeries but expected her number to reach 16 or more, including a planned tendon transfer surgery that will give flexion back to her ankle, as well as a skin graph procedure. Also in the spring of 2010, she was fitted with a new bionic prosthetic leg that is controlled by a computer chip. McMahon is well on her way to "coming back."

Officials let McMahon ceremoniously kick-off the game that Senior Night but McMahon is determined it won't be her last on-field kick. At the time of her accident, she had two athletic scholarships on the table and at least two more planned official visits to colleges vying for McMahon to don their jersey. After careful consideration to schools in Georgia, North Carolina, and South Carolina, McMahon chose Brevard College who is proud to uphold their scholarship offer. Brevard's academic program also intrigued this National Honor Society member. McMahon will be a freshman at Brevard in the fall of 2010. She has already planned her return to the field by her sophomore season, hoping to be better than before. Kathleen McMahon said, "Bree's goals never changed or wavered. She wanted to play soccer in college and she will."[4] No matter the extent of her return to the game she loves, she will no doubt inspire a new team to accomplish great things in her presence. Teammates must simply glance to the bench when in need of a boost. McMahon's special smile and expert enthusiasm are sure to bring victory to her new team.

For a high school senior at the top of her game, dreaming of playing soccer in college and imagining her senior prom and upcoming graduation, this life-altering injury would be overwhelming. But for Bree McMahon, it was just another speed bump on the road to great success; a speed bump she is elegantly coasting over. Upon the retirement of her high school jersey, Mike Bianchi, reporter for the *Orlando Sentinel* said, "Her No. 12 uniform was retired . . . for posterity purposes. Too bad, they can't preserve her class and courage for future generations, too."[5] Fortunately, despite it all, Bree McMahon has managed to preserve her class and courage all along on her own.

Notes

1. Kathleen McMahon, email to author, April 1, 2010.
2. Mike Bianchi, "Teen soccer player who lost her leg: 'Watch me come back from this,'" *Orlando Sentinel*, October 13, 2009.
3. Ibid.
4. Kathleen McMahon, email to author, April 1, 2010.
5. Mike Bianchi, "Bree McMahon takes the walk of a lifetime," *Orlando Sentinel*, January 13, 2010.

4

TRANSCENDING SPORT TO HELP SOCIETY

by Richard Lapchick

This section brings together a group of athletes and coaches who were dominant in their sport. Most are hall of fame players or coaches who were not only spectacular in their game but also went on to use that game to create a platform to make a better world.

Dot Richardson, while arguably the greatest softball player of her generation, simultaneously became a doctor. Her Olympic gold medals are perched next to her medical degree, catapulting Dot Richardson to be a role model for a generation of young girls to believe in what many had previously thought impossible.

Kareem Abdul-Jabbar is arguably the greatest big man ever to play basketball. Jabbar's teams were unrivaled in high school, college, and in the pros. Jabbar took his intellect and applied it off the court as the writer of four books, an actor, and a coach who took his game to a Native American reservation to coach a high school team.

"Tiny" Archibald, whose stature gave him his nickname, was anything but tiny in becoming an NBA superstar and a community activist in the New York Metropolitan area helping at-risk young people.

Dave Bing, an NBA superstar after a brilliant collegiate career at Syracuse, went on to show African-Americans that they can become entrepreneurs and leaders in industry.

Alan Page was one of the greatest players in Minnesota Vikings history. He earned his law degree while playing in the NFL. As a public servant, he was elected to the Minnesota Supreme Court as its first African-American member.

Bill Bradley took his academic and athletic talents from Missouri to become a college great at Princeton, a Rhodes Scholar, an NBA standout, a United States Senator, and a presidential candidate.

"Dr. J," aka Julius Erving, made basketball into an art form in the NBA. Transforming the game, Erving became its ambassador and a major sports executive for the Orlando Magic.

Jackie Joyner-Kersee, believed by many to be the greatest athlete of her generation, never forgot her roots in St. Louis where she built programs to assist impoverished youth.

Lawrence Burton, a legendary NFL player as well as an Olympic athlete in track and field, became even better known at Boys Town in Nebraska where he devoted his life to helping young people.

After Julie Foudy graduated from Stanford University she was accepted into their medical school. But this soccer phenom chose a different path and went on to captain the U.S. Women's Soccer team for 13 years while advocating for the rights of women and children.

Dean and Diane Alford founded and run the Miracle League which produces specially-constructed baseball complexes for children with physical and mental disabilities. Their dream-producing organization started as one field in 2000 and has grown, in just 10 years, to more than 100 rubberized fields with another 100 on their way.

Mallory Holtman and Liz Wallace, two softball players from Central Washington University, reignited hope in many sports fans that sportsmanship still exists when they helped an opposing player around the bases to complete her own run and solidify their loss in the game.

Travis Roy, whose college hockey career lasted 11 seconds, has devoted the 15 years since his career-ending injury to helping others with spinal cord injuries.

Then there were the coaches who transcended the game.

Coaches Derrick DeWitt and Dave Frantz changed the course of a community's vision of itself by giving an opportunity to Jake Porter, a mentally challenged player on Frantz's team, to score a touchdown on the game's final play.

Dean Smith became the winningest coach in college basketball history at the University of North Carolina. Smith also became the leading activist against alcohol abuse and took important stands on racial issues in sport and in society.

Joe Paterno, the coaching giant at Penn State who put together an astonishing career record of more than 394 victories led his team at the age of 83 to a 11 and 2 record and a bowl game victory in 2009.

Paterno is among Penn State's most generous philanthropists as well as a man who has helped young people in his charge to become leaders among men.

Pat Summitt, the winningest coach in the history of women's college basketball, spent her years at Tennessee helping young girls become women and leaders, not only in sport but also in society.

Tom Osborne was an outstanding football coach at the University of Nebraska for more than two decades when he retired with three National Championships and 65 Academic All-Americans. He went on to become a United States Congressman and then ran for Governor in the State of Nebraska where his popularity was enormous before returning to Nebraska as Athletic Director.

Geno Auriemma led the University of Connecticut women's basketball team to one of the most extraordinary records in college sport with five National Championships. He is also known for his philanthropy and service to the community.

Floyd Keith, a former college football coach, now coaches society from his leadership role at the Black Coaches and Administrators organization.

Captain Ed Nicholson runs Project Healing Waters. Originally founded at Walter Reed Medical Center, the program has expanded to more than 70 locations providing basic fly fishing, fly casting, and fly tying instruction for active military personnel and veterans.

All these individuals, so great in their athletic careers, were even greater as leaders!

Dr. Dorothy "Dot" Richardson

Transcending Sport to Help Society

by Brian Wright

Ben Carson, the Head of Neurosurgery at Johns Hopkins University chronicled his life in the book *Gifted Hands*. If there was another person who could write a book with that title, it would be Dot Richardson. She is this title personified.

As a child, Richardson was a talented baseball player and desired to join a Little League team like her brother. But she quickly learned Little League baseball was reserved for boys. After being pleasantly shocked by the skill level of 10-year-old Richardson, one enterprising coach finally offered her a chance to play on his Little League All-Star team—as long as Dot would promise to cut off her hair and dutifully answer to the name "Bob." Disappointed, the Richardson family politely declined."[1] Richardson was eventually discovered and welcomed by a fast-pitch softball coach who asked Richardson to join her team. Richardson soon found herself amongst a team of girls older and more experienced than herself. Seemingly unconcerned, she remained on the team and used the time to develop her skills. Richardson ultimately developed into an All-American softball player in college, establishing and breaking numerous softball records. She was named the NCAA Player of the Decade for the 1980s and is still one of the driving forces in the advancement of softball.

In 1979, Richardson had the honor of representing her country in the Pan American Games. This team won the gold medal. Richardson went on to win four other gold medals in the Pan American Games over her career. Richardson also helped lead the United States women's softball teams to four World Championships. Richardson is a monumental figure in the sport of softball. In 1993, Richardson decided that she would take a break from softball and embark on a different dream and a totally new way to use her "gifted hands."— she enrolled in medical school.

The amazing athletic awards and accomplishments that Richardson had received thus far in life did not diminish her desire to help others. During her residency in 1996 at the University of Southern California Medical Center, the Olympic Committee decided to include softball as an Olympic Sport. Richardson, with her experience and love for the game, pondered a return to the sport to represent her country. She knew that scheduling conflicts between softball and her residency would occur. Richardson decided an opportunity to compete for her country on the highest level of competition was too great of an honor to miss and began training for the Olympic team. Following strenuous and rigorous hours of work at the medical center to complete her orthopedic residency, Richardson attended workouts at the campus softball field of her alma mater, UCLA. Knowing her time at the field was limited by her responsibilities at the hospital, Richardson decided that she would bring the game closer to her. She built a batting cage in her apartment and used it on the days she couldn't make it to the field. Richardson spoke with the heads of the Medical Program at USC and they granted her a one-year leave of absence from her five-year residency to pursue her athletic goals in the Olympics.

As the Olympic Games began, the United States team was considered by many to be the favorite, which was largely because Richardson joined the team. Fittingly, Richardson was the first person to hit a homerun in Olympic history. This initial success continued throughout the tournament and Richardson hit the game-winning homerun to win the gold medal in the 1996 Olympic Games.

In 1999, Richardson started the Dot Richardson Softball Association (DRSA). DRSA is an instructional, non-profit organization offering educational opportunities to softball coaches and athletes. The Coaches Educational Series is a six-part program that offers instruction on basic and advanced skills, coaching principles, health and safety issues, communication skills, and conditioning and nutrition issues.

Richardson returned to the Olympics in 2000 where, with her help, the United States, again won the gold medal. With two gold medals on her long list of achievements, Richardson returned to medicine to pursue her life-long passion. In 2001, Richardson discovered a way to balance her career as a doctor with her passion for athletics. She became the medical director at the National Training Center in Clermont, Florida. The 300-acre sports, health, fitness, and education campus is unique in that it unites athletic facilities with a hospital, medical office buildings, a community college, and a four-year university. Physicians, medical specialists, nurses, athletic trainers, physical therapists, exercise physiologists, exercise specialists, personal trainers, coaches, and instructors are all on staff to create this world-class training facility. The National Training Center currently boasts an aquatic center, track & field complex, cross-country course, multi-purpose athletic fields, softball and baseball fields, and the plans for expansion are extensive. While Richardson no longer trains for the Olympics, she is able to help others on their road to Olympic glory.

In 2004, Richardson would take part in the Olympics in a totally different manner as an NBC Olympic commentator focused on providing an athlete's perspective on women's fast pitch softball. In addition to her new role as expert Olympic analyst, Richardson became the first "Girls-Explore" Doll and author of a children's inspirational book titled *Go For It!* The dolls and children's book are designed to inspire young girls between the ages of 8–12 years old to pursue and their goals by looking back at the accomplishments of other successful women. Other women featured in the "Girls-Explore" line are Ameila Earhart, Harriett Tubman, Bessie Coleman, and Babe Didrikson Zaharias. For Richardson to be the first doll/book released speaks volumes to Richardson's impact on her sport and in the lives of young girls across the country.[2] In 2007 Richardson continued to innovate the sport of fast pitch softball with the development of the PFX Tour. The PFX Tour is a grassroots development intiative bringing the sport's best softball players together with aspiring amateurs for clinics, skill showcase sessions, pro-am skill challenges, and meet and greets for the families and young players.

Richardson's courage, competitiveness, and determination to achieve excellence defined her Olympic appearances. While success in the Olympics usually leads to endorsements on Wheaties boxes and other lucrative opportunities, Richardson chose another route. She decided it was time for her to fulfill her life's goal to inspire youth around the world to achieve their goals and believe nothing is impossible.

Notes

1. Richard Lapchick et al. *100 Trailblazers: Great Women Athletes Who Opened Doors for Future Generations*, (Morgantown, Fitness Information Technology, 2009), 400.

2. "Olympic Gold Medalist—Doctor Now TV Commentator, Children's Book Author and Doll; Softball Icon Dot Richardson First Girls-Explore(TM) Doll," *PR Newswire*, August 10, 2004, http://www.highbeam.com/doc/1G1-120395675.html, (accessed February 27, 2010).

Kareem Abdul-Jabbar

Transcending Sport to Help Society

by Jenny Yehlen

When Kareem Abdul-Jabbar was born as Ferdinand Lewis Alcindor Jr., there was no doubt that he was going to be a big man and accomplish big things. At birth, has was a 12-pound, 11-ounce baby boy who was 22 1/2 inches long. Lewis grew up as an only child in a Catholic home in a middle-class section of Harlem. He was a quiet child, but because of his size he hardly went unnoticed.

At age nine, Abdul-Jabbar stood 5-foot-8 and was bigger than all but one boy at the Catholic school he attended in Pennsylvania. Even though he was one of the biggest guys in the crowd, he was not one of the toughest. Abdul-Jabbar also stuck out at school because he received all A's in his classes and he was well spoken, which contributed to his being harassed by the other kids at school. Abdul-Jabbar took his first shot at a basketball hoop when he was nine years old. The sport felt very natural to him and thus became the outlet Abdul-Jabbar used to get away from everyone and everything that was going on in his life. Basketball became his comfort zone.

Abdul-Jabbar continued to grow and develop both physically and as a basketball player throughout his pre-teen and early teen years. As an eighth grader he stood 6-foot-8 and was able to dunk a basketball. He pushed himself to get better and he constantly challenged himself.

By age 14, Abdul-Jabbar was standing at 6-foot-11 and the star of his varsity high school team at Power Memorial High School in New York City. His basketball domination began at the high school level and would continue throughout his career. The overall record of Abdul-Jabbar's high school team was 95-6, which included a 71-game winning streak. He was also a four-year letter winner (1962–65), three-time All-City selection (1963–65) and three-time All-American selection (1963–65) at Power Memorial High School. These were only stepping stones for accomplishments to come.

His stellar high school play earned him the opportunity to play at UCLA for one of the greatest coaches in basketball history, the incomparable John Wooden. The team Abdul-Jabbar played on would also go down in history as one of the greatest ever. Unfortunately, in those days, freshmen were ineligible to play on the varsity team. The freshmen had their own team called the Brubabes, and that year, they beat the two-time defending national champions and preseason No.1 varsity team 75-60. The Brubabes went 21-0 that season and Abdul-Jabbar averaged 33 points and 21 rebounds. The next year, in his first varsity appearance, Abdul-Jabbar set a UCLA record by scoring 56 points. He broke his own record later in the season by scoring 61 points.

The three years that Abdul-Jabbar spent at UCLA can only be described as complete domination. There was no championship title or individual accomplishment that he didn't achieve. He led the Bruins to a three-year record of 88-2 and to three straight national championships (1967–69). He also accrued several accolades for himself. With those three national championships, he became the first player to be a three-time NCAA Tournament Most Valuable Player (1967–69). Abdul-Jabbar was also *The Sporting College News'* and national Player of the Year in 1967 and 1969, the Naismith Award Winner in 1969, and a three-time All-American selection (1967–69). He left the school as the leading scorer in UCLA history and the sixth highest scorer in major college history with 2,325 averaging 26.4 points per game.

While attending classes and playing basketball at UCLA, Abdul-Jabbar began studying the Muslim movement and the teachings of the Koran. A few years after he graduated from college, Abdul-Jabbar changed his name from Ferdinand Lewis Alcindor Jr. The Muslim leader who served as his mentor renamed him Kareem Abdul-Jabbar, which means "noble, powerful servant."

In 1969, Abdul-Jabbar was drafted by the Milwaukee Bucks who had the worst record in their conference. Abdul-Jabbar established himself instantly as a force to be reckoned with. He was a different kind of big man than the league was used to seeing. Typically, the center position tried to exploit force and strength but Abdul-Jabbar was a long, lanky, finesse player, who used his agility down low. His patented skyhook shot was virtually unstoppable and it has yet to be replicated by another player. He earned Rookie of the Year honors in his first season with the Bucks. He also led the team to 56 wins, a 29-game improvement from the previous season. During his second year with the team, the Bucks won 66 regular season games and continued on to win the world championship. Abdul-Jabbar won the first of his six MVP titles this same year.

Abdul-Jabbar was traded to the Los Angeles Lakers prior to the 1975–76 season. Abdul-Jabbar helped lead the Lakers to five world championships (1980–82, 1985, 1987 & 1988). Abdul-Jabbar retired from professional basketball in 1989 at the age of 42. He was the first player to play 20 years in the NBA. The impressive list of highlights that Abdul-Jabbar accrued over his 20-year career has yet to be surpassed by any NBA player. At the end of his career, Abdul-Jabbar was at the top of nine NBA statistical categories, including points scored (38,387), seasons played (20), playoff scoring (5,762), MVP awards (6), minutes played (57,446), games played (1,560), field goals made and attempted (15,837 of 28,307), and blocked shots (3,189). Furthermore, he played in 18 NBA All-Star games (1970–1977, 1979–1989), was an NBA MVP (1971–72, 1974, 1976, 1977, 1980), an NBA Finals MVP (1971, 1985), and was selected to the NBA First Team (1971–1974, 1976–1977, 1980–81, 1984, 1986), and to the NBA All-Defensive First Team (1974–75, 1979–81).

In 1993, Abdul-Jabbar was the first basketball player ever to receive the National Sports Award, presented by President Bill Clinton, and he was inducted into the "Presidential Hall of Fame" along with four other athletes. His induction into the Basketball Hall of Fame soon followed in 1995.

He has spent the majority of his time since retiring from playing basketball coaching and writing. His love and passion for the game will never end, so now he focuses on passing on his knowledge to the next generation. Abdul-Jabbar does many public speaking events retelling inspirational stories that led to his success or speaking of his inspirational writings and the messages that they convey. He worked on the Fort Apache Indian Reservation as an assistant coach, creating hope for and teaching basketball skills to Native American basketball players. He believes that people in his position, with time and money to share, should do so. Abdul-Jabbar's Skyhook Foundation focuses on academic and athletic excellence through discipline, leadership, teamwork, sportsmanship, and conflict resolution, and helps youth realize their potential through education and athletics. He has also helped to fight hunger and illiteracy. He has written several books (*Giant Steps*; *Kareem; A Season on the Reservation*; *Black Profiles in Courage*; and *Brothers in Arms*) and appeared in movies.

He has also coached for the Los Angeles Clippers, worked as a consultant for the Indiana Pacers, and coached the USBL's Oklahoma Storm. In 2004, he was hired by the New York Knicks, and most recently, he has been employed by the Lakers. Abdul-Jabbar is currently fighting chronic myeloid leukemia, but he doesn't believe it will stop him from leading a normal life. He is also working on a documentary exploring the Harlem Rens and their experience in New York after WWI. Basketball is in his blood and he will continue giving back through the sport for as long as he can. Kareem Abdul-Jabbar was, and still is a very much admired basketball player, but he is as much admired as a person.

Nate "Tiny" Archibald

Transcending Sport to Help Society

by Jenny Yehlen

Professional athletes have been getting bigger, taller, and stronger since the beginning of professional sports. Seven-footers in the NBA are now commonplace, and there are even 7-foot-tall women playing in the WNBA. Size and strength are a big part of the game, but there are ways to play big without being big and to exploit strengths that aren't necessarily physical. NBA Hall of Famer, Nate Archibald, also known as "Tiny" Archibald, is a perfect example of the undersized player who had to work twice as hard to accomplish the same things that bigger, stronger competitors achieved.

Growing up in the Bronx, Archibald was a very shy, reserved child. And his basketball skills did not become apparent until later in his teen years. He was actually cut from the basketball team in his sophomore year and he came very close to dropping out of DeWitt Clinton High School. Fortunately, for himself, and for all those who were "Tiny" Archibald fans during his career, he did not drop out of school and he did not give up on his aspirations to play basketball. He came back the next year and made the basketball team as a junior. From then on, he continued to improve and he earned All-City accolades in both his junior and senior years. In spite of being a quiet person, he was also the captain of the team his senior year, which says a lot about him as a player and his ability to lead. If this story sounds familiar, it's because Michael Jordan had a similar experience early in his early basketball career, and he obviously went on to have a successful career.

The 6-foot-1, 160-pound point guard was very deceiving and he could do a lot more on the court than was apparent from his size. Spectators often doubted his ability. Despite his size, he was a dominating player at every level in which he played. It was always only a matter of time before he disproved those who had doubted him.

Archibald attended Arizona Western Junior College and maintained his aspirations to play in the NBA. After his first year, he transferred to the University of Texas at El Paso, where he had the opportunity to play for Don Haskins, the coach who put his own name in coaching history when he started five black players to win the 1966 National Championship game. Archibald played for UTEP from 1967 to 1970 and averaged more than 20 points per game as a junior and as a senior. He was also an Honorable Mention All-American and was named Most Valuable Player of the Western Athletic Conference (WAC) his senior year. Years later, he was selected to the WAC 20-year All-Star Team as well.

The Cincinnati Royals, coached by Hall of Famer Bob Cousy, took a chance on Archibald in 1970 when he was chosen in the second round of the NBA Draft. There were many skeptics, as there had been throughout Archibald's career, but just as he had done in the past, he proved himself on the court. He far surpassed everyone's expectations that first year in the league.

Archibald was a quick and crafty penetrator who seemed to go to the basket at will. He was also a very impressive outside shooter with deep range and he possessed phenomenal passing skills as well. He was a triple threat player who was always ready to shoot, penetrate, or pass. A defender couldn't play off of him and protect the drive because he could shoot the three. At the same time, if the defender played Archibald too tight, he would drive right around to the basket. And to really make things tough for defenses, nobody else's player could help because he would inevitably find the open man. Needless to say, his arsenal of offensive weapons made him a very difficult player to guard. When the Royals moved to Kansas City/Omaha in 1972, and became known as the Kings, Archibald received the nickname of "Nate the Skate" because of his smooth moves on the court. In the first season as the Kansas City Kings, "Nate the Skate" averaged 34 points per game, along with 11.4 assists. He became the only player in NBA history to lead the league in both of those categories in the same season.

Archibald's NBA career lasted 14 years. During that time, he played for Cincinnati (1970–72), Kansas City/Omaha (1972–76), New York Nets (1976–77), Buffalo (1977–78, injured, did not play), Boston (1978–83), and Milwaukee (1983–84). He was a slasher and a penetrator, and when he went to the hoop, almost inevitably, he either scored or was fouled. Consequently, he led the league three times in free throws made, and twice for free throws attempted. Archibald was an All-NBA First Team selection three times in 1973, 1975, and

1976, an All-NBA Second Team selection in 1972 and 1981, a six-time All-Star Game selection, and MVP of the 1981 All-Star Game. A high point of his career was when he helped lead the Boston Celtics to an NBA Championship in 1981 along with three consecutive years of having the best NBA record from 1980 to 1982. Archibald was inducted into the Naismith Memorial Basketball Hall of Fame in 1991 and named one of the 50 Greatest Players in NBA History in 1996.

Archibald retired from the NBA in 1984 and moved back to New York. He proceeded to run basketball schools for underprivileged kids and to work as the athletic director at the Harlem Amory homeless shelter until it closed in 1991. While he was working these jobs, Archibald earned a master's degree in Adult Education and Human Resources Development from Fordham University in 1990. He proceeded to earn his Professional Degree in Supervisions and Administration in 1994 and is currently working on his doctorate in education.

In more recent years, Archibald accepted a coaching position in the National Basketball Developmental League (NBDL). He became the head coach of the Fayetteville Patriots halfway through the NBDL's inaugural season in 2001. Archibald loves coaching and sharing his knowledge of the game with others. His passion for the game is obvious, which is why it was such a hard decision for him to step down from his coaching position less than a year after he was appointed.

In January of 2002, Archibald was offered a position with the NBA's Community Relations Team. It was a hard decision to make, but difficult as it would be to leave the sidelines as a coach, he could not turn down this unique opportunity with the NBA. He knew this position would allow him to combine his two loves of basketball and community service. However, Archibald did grace the sidelines again when he was hired as the head coach of the Long Beach Jam, an American Basketball Association team. The passion that Nate "Tiny" Archibald has for coaching and giving back to the community, will surely drive him to be very successful in whatever his next venture may be.

Dave Bing

Transcending Sport to Help Society

by Jenny Yehlen

Dave Bing knew he wanted to own his own business at a very early age, even before he had thoughts of playing in the NBA. His interest in entrepreneurship started when he went to work with his dad who was a contractor. Helping his dad on construction sites helped Bing develop a strong work ethic that would guide him throughout his life, both as an athlete and as a businessman.

Bing had to overcome some obstacles early in his life to become a successful athlete. At the age of five he was playing with two sticks that were nailed together. As he was running around, he tripped and one of the nails struck Bing's left eye. Surgery saved his eye, but Bing was told by doctors that his vision would be permanently impaired. He was told by others that he was too small to play basketball. It was his high school basketball coach who helped him realize his potential to earn a scholarship to play Division I college basketball.

Bing graduated from Syracuse University in 1966 as an All-American and educated for his future business ventures with degrees in economics and marketing. He was the second overall pick in the NBA draft, and he began his pro career with the Detroit Pistons. He averaged 20 points per game that first year and earned NBA Rookie of the Year honors for the 1966–67 season. The very next year he led the NBA in scoring with 27.1 points per game.

Tragedy struck prior to the 1971–72 season when Bing was poked in the eye during an exhibition game by a member of the Los Angeles Lakers. He had surgery for a detached retina and spent three months recuperating. Bing was back on the court in late December despite doctors telling him that returning to the court could continue to worsen his eyesight. Bing's peripheral vision—which basketball players rely heavily upon—was also impaired by the injury. One of Bing's many strengths on the court was driving to the basket, drawing defenders to him, and finding the open man and dishing off the ball. Thus, it was very impressive that Bing continued to be an assist leader after his injury.

After nine seasons with the Pistons, Bing received the opportunity to play for the Washington Bullets in front of his hometown crowd. He spent two seasons with the Bullets and one last season with the Boston Celtics before retiring from the game in 1978.

Some athletes find the transition out of professional sports very difficult. This was absolutely not true in Bing's case. From the time he entered the NBA, he was preparing for his post-basketball career, when he would get his chance to fulfill his dream of starting his own business. During the off-season, when most professional athletes take the time to relax, rehab, and prepare for the next season, Bing chose to go out and get a job. He worked at a bank, for the Chrysler Corporation, and for a small steel company over the course of his NBA career. When he retired, he was offered a job with Paragon Steel, but he chose to go into their management-trainee program and after only two years, he created Bing Steel.

It was a bit of a struggle at first, partially complicated by his image as an athlete. Stereotypes of black athletes made his transition harder. He had to create a new name and image for himself as a serious businessman with serious potential in the business world. Within two years, Bing Steel began to generate profits and, by 1990, sales had grown to $61 million. Bing expanded his corporation and collectively, the different companies belonged to the Bing Group.

Bing's steel start-up proved his business success and prowess as a businessman. But Bing has had other post-basketball successes as well that are manifest in his developing sense of social responsibility in metropolitan Detroit. The city has been plagued by serious unemployment for many years, and Bing took it upon himself to help the unemployed find and keep jobs. The problem was the people he wanted to hire weren't very qualified for the jobs that were available. Instead of simply passing over these candidates, Bing chose to help the candidates become more qualified. In 1999, the Bing Group teamed up with its biggest client, Ford, and built a $4 million dollar training facility in Detroit. Some of the trainees who came to the facility didn't work out as Bing had hoped, but the majority developed the skills they needed to work in Bing's manufacturing facility.

At one point, Bing's company was the fifth largest African-American-owned business in America and Bing worked hard to break down the racial prejudices that still exist in corporate America. Although Bing has begun the process of selling his steel manufacturing company, he will continue to be an advocate for social change in Detroit, only now he will be advocating from a political office. Leading up to his political career, Bing sat on several boards, such as the Michigan Minority Business Development Council and the National Association of Black Automotive Suppliers. In addition to those memberships, he also served several different charitable organizations, many of which worked to improve education for children in Detroit. Bing is truly a respected entrepreneur, philanthropist and leader in the community of Detroit, and as of May 2009, Bing added leading political figure to his list of accomplishments. Bing was voted in to the Detroit mayoral office in May to take over for a scandalous mayor. This first election was to see him finish out 2009 as an interim position, but again in August, he was voted by the people of Detroit to be their mayor for the next four years.

Bing has been inducted in to the Naismith Basketball Hall of Fame, he's had his jersey officially retired by the Pistons, his company has been voted Company of the Year by *Black Enterprise* magazine, and he has improved the Detroit community through employment opportunities, giving to charities, and education programs for children. With all that Dave Bing has achieved in his life and for all those people that he has helped, there will still never be a point when Bing will feel like he's done enough. Now, more than ever, he is going to work hard to turn around the city of Detroit. He faces a large budget deficit, rising unemployment rates, and criticism that he may not be the man for the job, but he knows what he's up against. "I've been here long enough to know what our problems are and what our issues are, and it's not going to be easy,"[1] Bing said. Bing continues to make big strides for social change, economic improvement, and the betterment of the Detroit community.

Note

1. Corey Williams, "NBA great Bing says running Detroit won't be easy." *AP Online*. May 6, 2009, http://www.highbeam.com/doc/1A1-D980NCVO0.html, (accessed February 27, 2010).

Alan Page

Transcending Sport to Help Society

by Jenny Yehlen

Being a professional athlete is intense and all-consuming and most athletes have little time for anything other than playing their sport. Alan Page managed to be a standout professional football player, while simultaneously earning his law degree. This was no easy task since attending law school demands a level of engagement that is probably equal to participating in professional sports. Page graduated from the University of Minnesota Law School in 1978 and he didn't retire from professional football until 1981. Although Page accomplished some amazing feats in his football career, education has always been the most important aspect of his life. Valuing education is what Page emphasizes to the youth of his community.

Page began his professional football career with the Minnesota Vikings in 1967 after being an All-American defensive end at Notre Dame. He was converted to a defensive tackle when he joined the Vikings and became a starter in the fourth game of the season. Those first three games were the only games in his 238-game career in which he didn't start. Page was the first defensive player to be NFL MVP in 1971. He was Defensive Player of the Year in 1971 and '73. He received All-Pro honors six times and he won four NFL/NFC title games. For his performance on the field, he was eventually inducted in to the NFL Hall of Fame in 1988.

Page concluded his NFL career with the Chicago Bears in 1981 but his legacy is even greater today. He practiced private law and later became Minnesota's assistant attorney general, a position he held until 1993 when he was elected to the State Supreme Court. Page was the first African-American to be elected to that court, and was re-elected in 1998 and 2004. If he chooses to run again, 2010 would be the start of his final term. Despite Page's legal responsibilities, he has always found the time to emphasize the importance of education to the community.

In a speech given at Kent State University, Page spoke of improving society through educating our youth, taking responsibility for our actions, and ridding society of prejudice and bias. Page noted,

"If we're going to solve society's problems, we're going to have to provide education opportunities and equal opportunities for all children and people."[1]

Page's drive to get involved with the educational system came from a situation that occurred during his football career. He and a few teammates were asked to study their new playbook, and it became very apparent to him that several of them were struggling to read the text. It amazed him that his fellow professional teammates made it through high school and college without being able to read very well. Page was appalled not only at his teammate's inability to read but at the educational systems that failed students and he decided to make a commitment to improve such systems. This inspired Page and his wife to become co-founders of The Page Educational Foundation in 1988.

In his induction speech at the NFL Hall of Fame, he chose to focus on the establishment of the Page Education Foundation and promote the benefits of educating our youth. At that ceremony, Page focused as much on education as sports. "At the very best," he said, "athletic achievement might open a door that discrimination once held shut. But the doors slam quickly on the unprepared and the undereducated."[2]

The basic purpose of The Page Education Foundation is to encourage Minnesota's youth of color to continue their educations beyond high school. The program offers a variety of resources ranging from mentoring and service-to-children projects to partial scholarships for college. After a scholarship applicant has been granted some kind of financial aid, the only requirement is the student volunteer in the community with elementary school students. The direct financial benefits that college students are receiving are a very important part of the program, but the goal of the program is more long-term. It is attempting to reach children at a very critical age and instill in them the importance of education. The children in the program are not simply trying to become more book-smart; the program also aims to develop the children's character and make them good people and good citizens.

In the Foundation's first year, there were ten scholarship recipients and in 2009, there were 560 scholarships awarded, showing the growth of this wonderful foundation. Many recipients, who come from low-income families and are often first-generation college students, would not have gone to college without the help of the Foundation. In total, Page Scholars have served over 275,000 hours of community service.

Page said that he was very fortunate to have parents who taught him the importance of education at a very young age and he recognizes that many children today are not as fortunate. Several factors may cause parents not to stress education, such as poverty, discrimination, low literacy, or an inability to speak English at all. The Foundation wants to create a sense of hope within young children of color by providing opportunities for them.

In November of 2000, Page was recognized by the Minneapolis community where he currently resides by having a Twin Cities Landmark named after him to remind future generations of the impact he has had in the community. The Mixed Blood Theater celebrated its 25th year of existence by renaming the theater the Alan Page Auditorium. The Mayor of Minneapolis declared the day to be Alan Page Day.

Page has always taken his accomplishments in stride. He has achieved so much in his life, yet he still strives to do good deeds and help others every day. Some may find this sort of ambition and drive wearing, but it is that drive that gets him out of bed every day. He loves having that purpose to push him to be the best he can be all the time. He still hopes to teach one day but is unsure if he'll ever get the opportunity.

Page also occasionally attends local schools to hold hearings and then answer questions from students to give them some insight into the judicial system. He also helped establish the Kodak/Alan Page Challenge, a nationwide essay contest which encourages urban youth to recognize the value of education.

In May of 2003, Page joined a very elite group of people when he was honored by Scholarship America with one of its prestigious President's Awards. The President's Award is given to an individual who has demonstrated outstanding support to education primarily through the support of scholarship programs and programs designed to improve educational access and encourage educational achievement. He received the award for establishing the Alan Page Foundation and the Page Scholars Program. Scholarship America is the nation's largest private sector scholarship and educational support organization. Page joined Tom Brokaw of NBC News, Roger Enrico of PepsiCo, and former Senate Majority leader, Robert Dole, just to name a few fellow award recipients.

The work that Alan Page has done throughout the years in providing educational opportunities for children of color has made him a well-respected, well-known leader in the Twin Cities community. His strong educational beliefs, along with his athletic prowess, have made Alan Page a true hero in sports and education.

Notes

1. Brian Lavrich, "Football hall of famer Alan Page emphasizes education in Kent State U. speech," *University Wire*, February 23, 2001, http://www.highbeam.com/doc/1P1-42280766.html, (accessed February 23, 2010).

2. "Page, Alan Cedric," *West's Encyclopedia of American Law*, 2005, http://www.highbeam.com/doc/1G2-3437703229.html, (accessed February 26, 2010).

Bill Bradley

Transcending Sport to Help Society

by Brian Wright

Growing up in the small town of Crystal City, Missouri, Bill Bradley had large dreams. Bradley developed a love of learning and the skills to participate in competitive sports while very young. At the age of nine, he picked up a basketball and became passionate about learning how to play the sport. As the years progressed, Bradley's basketball skills did as well. As a varsity high school basketball player, Bradley was a local star averaging over 27 points per game, and finished high school with over 3,000 points. Bradley was honored as a two-time *Parade* All-American selection during his high school career. As a student, Bradley was very diligent in balancing athletic and educational requirements. He maintained a very high grade point average and was considered by his teachers to be a superior student. At 6-foot-5, Bradley had swiftly become one of the most sought-after high school players in the country. He received more than 70 scholarship offers to very prestigious and well-known basketball institutions, such as the University of Kentucky. So Bradley surprised many people when he chose to attend Princeton University where he paid for his own education since the school did not award athletic scholarships.

Bradley was able to adjust to collegiate life very quickly. He became a leader on the court and among the general Princeton student body. On the basketball court, Bradley led the men's varsity basketball team in scoring each of his three years. He compiled over 2,500 total points, averaging over 30 points per game. Bradley led the Princeton Tigers to three consecutive Ivy League basketball championships as well as an unexpected trip to the NCAA Final Four in 1965. Bradley was named the 1965 Collegiate Basketball Player of the Year, an honor not typically awarded to student-athletes at Ivy League institutions. Bradley was awarded the James E. Sullivan Award which honors the United States' top amateur athlete. Bradley also had the honor to captain the 1964 gold-medal winning United States Olympic team.

With such time and effort spent in developing and polishing

his basketball skills, some assumed Bradley would have less time and energy for anything else. But Bradley was an exceptional student, which was recognized by the Rhodes Selection Committee when they awarded him a Rhodes scholarship to continue his studies at Oxford. Bradley was one of only 32 Rhodes Scholarship winners from the United States. After graduating from Oxford, Bradley chose to pursue his childhood desire to play basketball professionally.

Bradley soon found himself in Italy, playing professional basketball with the Olimpia Milano team and competing for the European Cup. Bradley made a large impact on the success of the team which won the European Cup and in the process he caught the eye of NBA scouts. The New York Knicks, intrigued the most by Bradley, signed him to a contract. Bradley played the game with such intelligence and was considered by many to be a model for playing with the proper fundamentals. While playing for the Knicks, Bradley was a key contributor, averaging 12.1 points per game and was a great compliment to other Knicks players. Bradley contributed to two different NBA Championship teams with the Knicks in 1970 and 1973. He played 10 full seasons in the NBA before he retired and pursued new and different goals.

Bradley wanted to positively affect social change and believed the easiest way to do so was through politics. In 1978, Bradley ran and won his first post as the Senator from New Jersey, replacing four-term incumbent Senator Clifford P. Case. Though entering as a new member, Bradley took a strong stance on issues of education, child poverty, gun control, and health care reform. Bradley also supported a campaign to stop racial profiling by federal and state police officials. Bradley's commitment to public service and social justice earned him the respect of the voters in New Jersey.

Bradley established an annual event where he would walk along the streets of Jersey City and meet people within the community which he coined the "Labor Day talk-to-citizens stroll." Aware of the ever-growing problems within society, Bradley felt that he could better change the state of this country by becoming president. Bradley made his run at office in the 2000 presidential primaries when he challenged front-runner and Vice President Al Gore for the party's nomination. Bradley's campaign was based on his commitment to solve the social problems that had motivated him to run for public office. He campaigned to end poverty, particularly among children.

He also remained committed to ending the gun violence that had killed so many children. Education for all was also a major point of interest for Bradley. This was due in a large part to his experience as a student and how important a role it played on shaping and developing his life. Though he was unsuccessful in winning the democratic nomination, he pointed out some glaring social problems that needed attention and change.

While Bradley no longer holds a political office, his commitment to improving education around the United States stays strong. As a board member of DonorsChoose.Org, Bradley is helping millions of students across America get the resources they need to help prepare them for life and give them the best education possible. DonorsChoose.Org is an online resource that brings students and teachers together with willing donors that help teachers accomplish their goals of properly educating the students.[1] While Bradley's method has shifted from legislation to philanthropy, his goal of improving our communities through a commitment to education has remained constant and through this organization he is doing so one classroom at a time.

Bill Bradley is truly one of a kind; he is the only professional athlete in American history who combined a superb record as a sportsman with a career as a political reader who aspired and nearly achieved his party's endorsement as a presidential candidate. He introduced the Student-Athlete Right-To-Know Act that, for the first time, allowed high school recruits to know the graduation rates of the colleges recruiting them. The Bradley Bill, an important piece of legislation which he sponsored and which carries his name did more to help integrate the peoples of the former Soviet Union and the Warsaw Pact countries into the world community of nations than any other initiative undertaken by the American government. But whether dealing with education, social justice, or poverty in Kiev and Minsk or in Jersey City and Patterson, Bill Bradley's commitment to helping underserved populations is legendary. He is a man among men; a hero among heroes.

Notes

1. "Actors Claire Danes and Zac Efron, Senator Bill Bradley Use National Philanthropy Day To Announce DonorsChoose.org Opening in all 50 States," *PR Newswire*, November 15, 2007, http://www.highbeam.com/doc/1G1-171404717.html, (accessed March 1, 2010).

Julius Erving

Transcending Sport to Help Society

by Jessica Bartter Duffaut

Legend has it the game of basketball started with peach baskets nailed to the gym wall, a soccer ball, and a court half the size of current National Basketball Association (NBA) regulations. It took only 13 rules to explain the new game in 1891 when Dr. James Naismith, a Canadian-born American minister, invented "basket ball" to give young men more activity during the brutal winter months in New England. Obviously, the game has evolved year after year, with new generations of players and coaches inventing new moves and strategies hoping to outshine their predecessors. It may be hard for younger generations, particularly athletes, to imagine, but basketball did not always receive the interest and acclaim it is accustomed to now. The history of the NBA in the 1950s and 1960s involved a few diehard fans, minimal television coverage, and mediocre salaries for players. That is until Julius Erving emerged on the hardwood floor with his commanding hands that handled the ball like no one before him.

There would be others to follow, Michael Jordan, Larry Bird, Magic Johnson among them, but Julius Erving set a new standard for excellence on the basketball court. Fans—white and black alike—respected Erving for his humanity and celebrated him for his game. Erving put up the numbers in high school, college, and his early career in the American Basketball Association (ABA), but went somewhat unnoticed until his time in the NBA. Erving first picked up a basketball when he was eight and quickly appreciated the challenge it presented. Erving started his career at Roosevelt High School in New York in 1964 at just 5-foot-9. A friend and teammate nicknamed him the "Doctor" after he nicknamed his teammate the "Professor." When he became a professional athlete, teammates shortened it to "Dr. J," which is what he is affectionately known as now. In his junior and senior high school years, Erving made All-Conference, was named Outstanding Player, and caught the interest of the University of Massachusetts as he grew to be 6-foot-3. In his very first collegiate game, Erving scored 27 points and had 28 rebounds, a school record at the time.[1]

Although he only stayed at UMass for two years, Erving left a huge mark. He started in all 52 games and finished with 1,370 points, the best in school history, even compared to the totals posted by many four-year players. He broke or tied 14 school records ranging from rebounds to minutes per game. His talent was certainly worthy of an invitation to the first Olympic development basketball camp, but still Erving was overlooked after his sophomore year. When an invitee was injured, Erving arrived as the replacement. Although it was a last-minute decision, Erving proved he was the right choice. The team toured Eastern Europe and the Soviet Union and Erving emerged as the best player despite almost missing the opportunity entirely.

After his successful stint with the Olympic development team, Erving turned pro with the Virginia Squires of the American Basketball Association in 1971. His first professional game with the Squires remains his most exciting event in what became a 16-year-long professional career. He had 20 points and 19 rebounds that night.[2] Erving knew the fast pace of his team coupled with their creative style was sure to change the game of basketball and please fans of all ages. Erving is credited with adding style to what was once a running game with physical giants who could dominate the basket.

Erving continued to grow until he was 25, but at 6-foot-7, he did not play his size.[3] Erving proved athleticism was a prerequisite for basketball. The graceful way he flew through the air like an agile six footer doing skills only previously performed by the giant seven footer amazed fans and filled arenas with spectators intent on seeing his basketball genius.

Erving played two seasons for the Squires before spending three with the New York Nets, also of the ABA. During those three seasons he was named to the ABA All-Star First Team each year, earned ABA MVP honors, and two ABA Championships in 1974 and 1976. Erving led the ABA in scoring in 1973 with an average of 31.9 points per game and in 1974 with 27.4.

In spite of stars like Erving, the ABA had been struggling for years and reached an agreement at the conclusion of the 1976 season to dissolve and merge with the NBA. While many players from disbanded teams were picked up individually by NBA teams, the Denver Nuggets, Indiana Pacers, San Antonio Spurs, and Erving's New York Nets were absorbed into the league as teams. Shortly after the merger, Erving was traded to the Philadelphia 76ers. Erving stayed with the 76ers from 1976 until 1987, leading his team with his play and his off-the-court presence. In 1981, at the age of 31, he was named MVP of the NBA. Erving appeared in the NBA All-Star game every year from 1977 to 1987. He was the game's MVP twice. He was named to the All-NBA First Team in 1978 and every year from 1980 to 1983 as well as the All-NBA Second Team in 1977 and 1984. In 1983, Erving led the 76ers to an NBA Championship.

While the aforementioned are all great accomplishments for an athlete, it was more important for Erving that he be respected as a person by his teammates and the fans. The character and persona that Erving presented made it difficult for anyone to think otherwise. As Erving redefined the forward position, he defined the role of the professional athlete as well. He showed that he was a leader on and off the court, committed to his community with a dedicated attitude and strong work ethic. While his athleticism was unmatched, he served as a valuable role model for aspiring and current professional athletes.

Erving retired as a professional athlete in 1987 at the age of 37. He was ready for new challenges in life and was determined to never fully devote his life to just one thing again. "I never want to be, totally consumed by any one endeavor, other than my family life," he said.[4] Erving has been involved in many business endeavors, both in and unrelated to sports. He has been one of the owners of the Coca-Cola Bottling Company in Philadelphia, Garden State Cable in New Jersey, and Queen City Broadcasting in New York. He has served several companies including Spaulding Sporting Goods, Converse Shoes, Dr. Scholl's, Shearing Plow, and Jiffy Lube as a spokesman, consultant or member of the advisory staff. Erving served NBC as a commentator, the Orlando Magic as executive vice president, NBA International as director, and the marketing and management firm JDREGI as president. Erving also enjoys giving motivational speeches sharing the countless lessons he learned as a professional athlete.

In life, Erving has a knack for seeing the whole picture. It was evident on the court that he could see more than his defenders. The values instilled in him as a boy from his mother were everlasting and helped him to think big. She stressed the importance of education and being a good person, something she thought was really not a difficult thing to do with the right mindset. Erving grasped her love and advice and developed into an intelligent and confident man ready to conquer anything. Erving's attitude helped him see the world and open his life to academics, family, and other important aspects that helped him grow emotionally and spiritually. Even when basketball became the center of Erving's life, he wondered what other areas in his life he could expand. Julius Erving emerged from the NBA as more than a great athlete, but also as a fine human being helping others succeed in and out of the world of sports.

Notes

1. Academy of Achievement, "Julius Erving Interview: The Great and Wondrous Dr. J," Las Vegas, Nevada, June 26, 1992, http://www.achievement.org/autodoc/page/erv0int-1, (accessed February 25, 2010).

2. Ibid.

3. Ibid.

4. Ibid.

Jackie Joyner-Kersee

Transcending Sport to Help Society

by Stacy Martin-Tenney

Jackie Joyner-Kersee pictured with Richard Lapchick at the National Consortium for Academics and Sports' 2003 Giant Steps Awards Banquet and Hall of Fame Induction Ceremony.

Jackie Joyner-Kersee has always had "a kind of grace"[1] as an athlete because while she is a tough competitor she has always demonstrated poise and charm on and off the track. Her race in life has been filled with obstacle after obstacle, but she breezed past each one with her head held high as if each was just another hurdle on the track. Her maternal grandmother, Evelyn Joyner, named her Jacqueline after former first lady of the United States, Jacqueline Kennedy Onassis, a woman known for her elegance. Evelyn knew that Joyner-Kersee would also be a first lady.

Joyner-Kersee quickly secured the title of "Greatest Woman Athlete of the Twentieth Century"[2] assuring her place as the first lady of track and field for quite some time. She competed in the heptathlon, a two-day event comprised of the 100-meter hurdles, high jump, shot put, and 200 meters on the first day, and the long jump, javelin, and 800 meters on the second. It's not simply that she was the first female to become so decorated in track and field, for as time passes her records will be passed on to future generations of runners. Rather, Joyner-Kersee will remain in our memories because of the way she conducted herself with such class.

Joyner-Kersee grew up in East St. Louis, Illinois, and spent most of her time at the Mary Brown Community Center that offered sports to young people as well as story time and painting. Joyner-

Kersee's neighborhood was plagued with violence and drug abuse, so the community center was as much a safe haven as it was an opportunity for personal growth. Al and Mary, Joyner-Kersee's parents, had married young and were barely out of childhood themselves when they gave birth to Jackie. Mary Joyner was extremely conscientious about her daughter's future and so she pushed her in the classroom and on the athletic fields, to break the cycle of babies having babies that seems so compelling in a poor community. Her daughter was to know greatness, not poverty. Joyner-Kersee's trek to the top would start when she joined the track club at age nine without any financial resources. She sold candles to her elementary classmates to raise money for track meet travel expenses. She ran in a pair of shoes until the rubber wore out or they fell off. She didn't need shoes to race past her competition. She was a good student as well. Joyner-Kersee had it all from a young age.

Evelyn Joyner doted on Joyner-Kersee by playing dress up with her and painting her tiny fingernails so they would match her own. Joyner-Kersee felt like the first lady when her grandmother was around. She was the adult who always made her feel special as a child. Evelyn planned a trip from Chicago to visit her darling granddaughter, and Joyner-Kersee could rarely contain her excitement anytime her grandmother planned a visit. The trip was only a few days away, when the family received a call that Evelyn would be visiting the angels instead. Joyner-Kersee's step-grandfather was a destructive alcoholic. He had come home drunk from the bar and shot her grandmother while she was sleeping with a 12-gauge shotgun. Joyner-Kersee had it all, except her loving grandmother. She never drank or used any recreational drugs because she saw how their use often leads to violence. She is proud of the fact that her family never became victims of violence because they continued to expect great things from one another and encouraged one another's hopes and dreams, just as Evelyn encouraged Joyner-Kersee to be the first lady of whatever her heart desired.

Joyner-Kersee became a talented high school athlete in track and field as well as basketball. She was so successful that she was offered a scholarship to UCLA, consistently one of the top track and field programs in the country. She was so talented that she is one of the few athletes who could handle the demands of two sports and her coursework. Her mother asked her to come home for Christmas her freshman year, but she declined and promised to come home in the spring. Unfortunately, she would return home sooner than that. Joyner-Kersee's mother died suddenly from meningitis just a short time after the Christmas invitation she declined. Joyner-Kersee went home to attend her mother's funeral. Her three siblings were terribly grief stricken. As the eldest child Joyner-Kersee had to remain strong. She held her head high above the abyss of emotion drowning everyone else. Returning to school, she remained strong for nearly a year but the wave of grief found her in Los Angeles the next Christmas when Joyner-Kersee realized that she wouldn't be getting a call to come home that year. The tears flowed and she momentarily lost the resilience that she so elegantly displayed on the athletic fields. Her indestructible façade may have cracked, but it would not crumble. She endured the almost insurmountable pain, and continued on the path her mother had set her on all those years ago. She continued her education to set an example for her family, showing them life will go on and they will not become victims of tragedy.

It is often said that when a door closes, there is an open window. However, one can get seriously scraped climbing through. Joyner-Kersee saw her open window as an open lane on the track, but in 1982 she developed a condition known as exercise induced asthma. As a woman who characterized herself as invincible she was shaken to the core when told that she has limitations. Jackie Joyner-Kersee denied that she had a disease, but today she admits that she was scared to acknowledge it. She went so far as to hide her inhaler from people, even when her breath escaped her and she needed to use it. Eventually, she couldn't deny its existence any longer; she didn't take her inhaler with her to practice one day and ended up in an emergency room feeling suffocated and losing control. When she woke up, she awakened with an awareness of her disease and realized that her medication was life-sustaining. However, her athlete persona had to realize that a new routine and workouts were part of that medication, and that she was not weak and vulnerable because of it.

Once again, doors seemed to be closing on her and her escape to the field or track from life's anxiety seemed to be slipping away. Someone special stepped in and helped her manage her disease as well as her track and field career. Bob Kersee was the assistant coach at UCLA and had experienced the loss of his mother as well. He offered his support to Joyner-Kersee and then helped her gain control of her asthma. He encouraged her to continue in track and field as the same fierce competitor that she had always been, and helped her realize that the asthma was not a limitation, just something to contend with and be treated for. His compassion and reinforcement were invaluable to Joyner-Kersee and they became good friends. Four years later, they became husband and wife. Bob has the same fire in him that Joyner-Kersee does when it comes to competition. He is her biggest critic and her biggest fan on the track. He will scream at her on the track and cook her dinner the same evening. They truly complement each other and their relationship has proven successful in life and in sport.

Joyner-Kersee became a household name because of her remarkable athletic achievements. Her willpower to compete with asthma enhanced her prestige. Her collegiate athletic career started her on the path to success when she set the NCAA record for the heptathlon twice. She continued to play basketball for UCLA during this time as well and was recognized as the UCLA All-University Athlete for three years. In 1984, Joyner-Kersee won the silver medal at the Olympics and finished fifth in the long jump. She won numerous heptathlon titles after that at the World Championships and Goodwill Games. She graduated from college, married Bob, and then in 1988, she struck gold. She set the world record in the heptathlon at the U.S. Olympic Trials and won the long jump. She traveled to the Olympics and won a gold medal for both the heptathlon and the long jump events. She beat her own world record in the heptathlon and set an Olympic record in the long jump. In 1992, she won gold once more in the Olympic heptathlon and stole silver in the long jump. Four years later, Joyner-Kersee won a bronze medal in the long jump after she had pulled a muscle and had to withdraw from the heptathlon. In fact, she did not lose a heptathlon for over 12 years from 1984 until the 1996 Olympic Trials.

Her success in track and field built the pedestal on which she so gracefully speaks from today. She was a star female athlete during a time when girls who competed in sports were commonly referred to as tomboys. She challenged that perception by exuding what she calls "a kind of grace." She describes her definition of grace in her autobiography which appropriately is titled *A Kind of Grace*. She continues to promote women in athletics and encourages young girls to follow in her footsteps.

Her career came full circle around the track and finished at her starting line in East St. Louis. The community center that she enjoyed so much as a child had closed while she was traveling the world for track meets and publicity appearances. She took a percentage of all of her endorsements and raised $40,000 to reopen the center for the children of East St. Louis and give them some of the same opportunities that had placed her in such an advantageous position. It wasn't enough, but Joyner-Kersee would not be deterred. She explored other ways to finance a brand new 37-acre facility that will boast both indoor and outdoor tracks, basketball courts, and state-of-the-art computer rooms. She is determined to create opportunities for children who are facing the same tough decisions and turbulent lifestyles that she did when she was their age. One such experience that she provided was a trip to New York City for the Macy's Thanksgiving Day Parade for 100 children through her Jackie Joyner-Kersee Community Foundation. The inspiration that she received at the Mary Brown Center when she was nine was so profound that all of her efforts are focused on her foundation today.

She also speaks out about asthma as her next great opponent. She says that she approaches fighting the disease as if it is one of her competitors and her treatment is the training she needs to be competitive. According to Letterlough of the *Philadelphia Tribune*, African-Americans "only represent 12 percent of our population, [but] they comprise 26 percent of the deaths related to asthma."[3] Joyner-Kersee was fortunate enough to have the proper medical treatment for her disease, but she realizes that so many do not have the availability of sound medical care that is needed to manage the disease properly. She knows that African-Americans are more likely to simply attempt to live with asthma, and she wants to use her status to draw attention to how tragedy can happen without treatment and how one can live a full and complete life with it.

She also speaks about the importance of goal setting and violence prevention. She challenges her audience to think about what could happen at their school even though they have not experienced a violent act as of yet, and how they could prevent it. The loss of her grandmother had a profound influence on her life. She now wants to provide a positive influence for today's youth. She had goals and dreams that carried her out of an impoverished neighborhood and that brought her back to that same town with a renewed purpose. She emphasizes that having goals is a real antidote to violence. Her audience may have come to hear Jackie Joyner-Kersee, the world's greatest female athlete, but they left hearing a message that challenged them to be serious about their future.

Joyner-Kersee has experienced the power that sport can have, and she has done everything she can to utilize that power. She has even entered the business of sports, first and foremost through her endorsement money that she has funneled into the Jackie Joyner-Kersee Community Foundation. She ventured outside her sport to become certified as a sports agent with the National Football League Players Association from 1998 to 2001, a role that only five females had filled at the time. Her company Elite International Sports Marketing Inc. is designed to help athletes prepare for a career in athletics as well as what they can do after their career is complete. She has been extraordinarily successful in the heptathlon in track and field, and she is becoming an exceptional leader in the heptathlon of life. In 2009, the NCAA recognized her as one of the recipients of the Silver Anniversary Award bestowed upon six former student athletes on the 25th anniversary of the end of their collegiate athletic career. Joyner-Kersee's accomplishments as a professional athlete, in her career, and through her charitable and civic organizations certainly shine brightly.

Notes

1. Jackie Joyner-Kersee with Sonja Steptoe, *A Kind of Grace*, (New York: Time Warner, 1997).

2. Joy Duckett Cain, "The Jackie nobody knows. (Jackie Joyner-Kersee)" *Essence*. August 1, 1989.

3. Michael Letterlough, "Breathing Easy; Olympic gold-medalist Jackie Joyner-Kersee talks about her battle with asthma." *The Philadelphia Tribune*. April 3, 2005.

Lawrence Burton

Transcending Sport to Help Society

by Jenny Yehlen

Lawrence Burton was a football player, and a pretty good one at that. He was probably the fastest guy in the sport when he played at Purdue University in the early 1970s. His speed was very impressive on the football field, and he was also able to transfer those skills to the track. He started running track at Purdue and eight months later he qualified for the 1972 Olympic Games, which was an amazing accomplishment. Even when he continued on in the NFL, there was no one who could match his speed.

One would think that the fastest guy in college football would have been a track athlete but he wasn't until he went to college. He used his lightning speed on the football field of Mary N. Smith High School, in Eastern Shore, Virginia. That speed earned the 6-foot-1, 175-pound flanker back a scholarship to Purdue. There were other top programs knocking on Burton's door, but he chose to attend Purdue because the players who chaperoned him on his official visit told him that they had to study on Saturday night instead of bringing him to a bunch of crazy college parties. Typically, the fun and craziness of an official visit is what attracts football recruits. The recruits want a feel of the college atmosphere and a chance to hang out with potential teammates. Burton was not a typical recruit and he continued to be atypical, in a good way, throughout his college career. He was something bigger, something better. He also had something bigger to be preparing for, with the birth of his son and marriage that both took place in 1970, before he went off to college. Burton continued to prove his special qualities as he grew up and moved on with his life.

When Burton arrived at Purdue, academics and football were his top priorities (besides his wife and child), but he wanted to run for the track team as well. When he asked the track coach his freshman year if he could join, he was told it was too late. Burton was persistent, he came back the next year and the coach agreed to let him join the team. Burton was a natural, and people started turning their heads when this new guy started beating guys he should not have been beating. He set the world record for the 60-yard dash that year and went on to qualify for the 200-meter dash in the 1972 Olympic Games in Munich, Germany. He came in fourth at the Olympics. Burton has said of his experience in the Olympics, "It impacted my life. It told me I had to work harder. If I would have won the gold then maybe I would have got stuck on myself. The message it sent me was that I had accomplished a great deal, but I still had a lot to do. It was a great message."[1]

After his stint at the Olympics, it was right back to football training camp at Purdue. He proceeded to have successful junior and senior seasons. Burton graduated with his bachelor's degree in sociology and earned the NCAA Postgraduate Scholarship in 1975. Burton caught the eyes of the New Orleans Saints and he was their number one pick in the 1975 NFL Draft. Burton played three seasons with the New Orleans Saints and two full seasons with the San Diego Chargers. In 1980, during his third season with the Chargers, and his sixth season overall, Burton was having a good training camp, he was performing well, but he made a personal decision that it was time to retire. His decision had nothing to do with football. He simply felt it was time to pursue some of his other goals. Although this was a sudden decision to outsiders, and many people were shocked, it was something Burton and his wife, Ida, had been discussing. She was very supportive and she knew of her husband's dreams and aspirations.

During the off-seasons of his years in the NFL, Burton worked with kids in a program through the New Orleans Police Department. He really enjoyed the work of helping children that were in need. As his football career wore on, he found himself thinking about the children more and more, and wondering who was helping them during his season when he couldn't be there. He found himself realizing that there was more out there than football and started to feel the strong desire to do more to help at-risk kids.

He didn't have any plans set in stone when he officially retired. His idea was to work with Ida to start a foundation or home to help socially troubled youth get counseled back into their mainstream environment. One of his friends informed him of Boys Town, the well-known program in Omaha, Nebraska. This was a program that had been started by Father Edward J. Flanagan in 1917, and had been helping young people ever since.

Very much intrigued, Burton and his wife traveled to Boys

Town to learn about the program and then bring that knowledge back to New Orleans to start their own organization. At the end of their visit, the two were offered jobs as family teachers and they gladly accepted. The program was exactly what they wanted to be involved with, and it didn't matter that they didn't create their own foundation. All that mattered was that they would be helping children.

Burton moved his wife and family to Boys Town, but it was much different than how it had been portrayed in the movie with Spencer Tracy. The movie was set early in the program's existence when Father Flanagan, who died in 1948, was still heading up the program. Needless to say, the problems kids were facing in 1975 were very different than the problems kids faced in the 1920s and 1930s. Burton entered the program when it was still adjusting to youth of a new generation.

After 13 years of housing troubled kids in Boys Town, being a good role model, and acting as a father figure, Burton got the opportunity to start his own version of Boys Town in Long Beach, California, and he jumped at it. When he left Omaha to start the new chapter, the kids gave him an engraved clock that said, "Lawrence Burton An Inspiration." To Burton, that was more meaningful to him than a Heisman Trophy or a gold medal would have been. It was tough leaving the program in Omaha, and it was hard for some of the kids to see him go. One kid had said, "This man took time to be with me. What's better than that? You look at Michael Jordan, and he's fine. He does a lot for kids, but I don't think he'd give up his career to be with kids. Lawrence did."[2] It was also very fulfilling for Burton to hear the kids telling him what a difference he had made and how much he would be missed. He moved his wife and his youngest daughter out to California to start anew.

Along with his new Boys Town program, Burton also became the program director for the Price Family Campus and Coordinator of the Emergency Residential Care Center, in Long Beach, which houses homeless, runaway, and abused or neglected kids ages 11 to 17 providing them with basic living and survival skills. The average stay is only 30 days.

He was the recipient of the *Sports Illustrated* Civic Leader Award for his work at Boys Town in 1993. Burton earned his master's degree in human development and family living from the University of Kansas. Burton has sat on several boards and committees in his local area of Long Beach, each one serving for the betterment of youth and society. He is a member of the Long Beach Area Chamber of Commerce, the NAACP, and the Western States Youth Services Network; a board member of the California Child, Youth, and Family Coalition; on the Los Angeles Coordinating Council; a mentor for Long Beach Polytechnic High School; on the men's society of the First AME Church in Los Angeles, and is a spokesperson and ambassador for the NFL.

Burton ran the Long Beach Boys Town until 2008, but is continuing to devote his life to others. His new venture includes helping deaf and developmentally challenged adults in California through the Willie Ross Foundation, of which he is the executive director.

Lawrence Burton was very lucky to find his passion to help others and have the opportunity to be driven by that passion. He was fortunate to have a loving family to support his dreams, and he is now able to return the favor. Burton has two grandsons that play football for Venice High School, one of whom is bound for the University of Florida in the fall of 2010. His grandsons inherited not only their grandfather's athletic ability, but also his good nature and big heart. Lawrence Burton was an amazing athlete but proved to be an amazing person with his decision to leave professional football and devote his life to helping at-risk children.

Notes

1. Chris Anderson, "Answering to a Higher Calling," *Herald Tribune*, Oct. 30, 2009.
2. Ibid.

Julie Foudy

Transcending Sport to Help Society

by Stacy Martin-Tenney

Julie Foudy played on the United States Women's National Soccer Team for 18 years and served as captain for 13 of those 18 years. During her career the team won two Olympic gold medals and two World Cup Championships. Foudy's success extended beyond the soccer field as she led the fight to prevent any changes to Title IX and preserve the equality it brought to sports for women when she served on the Presidential Commission in 2002. Her leadership has inspired the Julie Foudy Sports Leadership Academy for young girls so that she can help them find their voice as sports helped Foudy find her own.

Foudy was very young when she made the national team and faced the pressure of performing on the field and making sacrifices off the field to advance her athletic career. Things like high school graduation and proms came secondarily to breaking into the starting roster and playing in an international tournament. Foudy's parents encouraged her to make her own decisions about soccer. She still feels sad about missing graduation but realizes that it was an important choice. Leaders make difficult choices everyday and more importantly learn to accept the consequences of those decisions.

It was only the first of many decisions she would make during her lengthy career. Foudy started playing on the national team in the very early years when the team was mainly listed on paper and only played together during matches. Then, the sport started to grow and the team bonded. They were only earning $10 a day for playing, and the first Women's World Cup took place in 1991 without many people realizing what it meant to the sport, even Julie's parents. Foudy said, "I think the great thing about the '91 team is that they're a group of women that were completely committed to the game, but at the same time there was always laughter ringing in the halls, the bus, everywhere—which is something we talk a lot about now. Everything we did was fun."[1]

By the mid 1990s the team entered into its first real contract battle with the federation and, as usual, Foudy was at the helm as the veteran. She spoke up for the team and fought for a fair living. The team was traveling quite a bit staying in terrible hotels and unable to maintain a regular income. Foudy admits it wasn't much of a contract, but after sharpening her negotiating skills and expanding her prowess as a leader, she was ready for the second round. The game had grown in popularity and the fans were engaged so it seemed that the Federation would be receptive to a better contract, after all they were not asking for millions, just to be compensated fairly since they were playing full time. A frustrating moment in the negotiations aligned with a fortuitous meeting. Foudy was brought into a round table that Spalding had organized and met with another trailblazer in women's sports, Billie Jean King. Foudy sought out King's advice on the problems she was having with the Federation. Foudy explained, "We're trying to get them to change the system, but they wouldn't." Foudy remembers King saying, "Well, that's your problem. They're not going to want to change, because it just costs them money. You've got to do it yourself."[2] Leadership is hard work, and sometimes it is hard work done alone. Foudy had the spark she needed to continue the negotiations and knew that she was seeking something more, not for herself but for the future of the game.

"It was like an epiphany. So with every contract negotiation after that, Billie Jean would always be in my ear saying, 'What's right for the next generation? What are you doing for them? It's not about what you're getting out of it, you gotta set the precedent for the next group coming through to make sure you leave it in a better place.'"[3]

Julie Foudy left women's professional soccer in a better place than she found it, but it was soccer that inspired Foudy to strive for continuous improvement. She was the President of the Women's Sports Foundation from 2000 to 2002 and continued to serve on the Board of Directors for seven more years. Foudy continues to advocate on their behalf for athlete's rights and Title IX. She is very accomplished, but her most impressive feat is establishing the Julie Foudy Sports Leadership Academy (JFSLA).

The Academy is the next evolution of Foudy's successful soccer day camps, but it delivers the best of both worlds. "The JFSLA is a five-night, six-day residential Academy for girls ages 12-18. The Academy focuses on two overlapping components—sports and leadership. The aim of the JFSLA is to expose students to Julie's great passion: the concept of not just being a leader on the field but a leader in life."[4] Foudy wanted to impart her leadership lessons through the game that taught them to her.

Julie Foudy brings in soccer stars from the Olympic gold medal and World Cup teams, professional players from the former WUSA, and some of the best collegiate players and coaches in the country to coach the adolescent girls attending the academy. She teaches them the basics through fundamental drills and technique training and then tests their skills in small field games and match play. The soccer fields double as classrooms for the leadership curriculum. Foudy has learned through experience how sports and leadership walk hand in hand, so she reinforces leadership lessons through soccer drills and skills like team communication through the founding leadership themes.

"Students will participate in hands-on activities and do team-building exercises that focus on the following themes: how to develop the confidence to lead, the different roles and styles of leaders, how to be a positive leader on your team, and how to be a leader in your community—which includes a service learning component that each student can take to her own community."[5] Foudy was a student of the real world and firsthand experiences, so she brings in guest speakers and other motivational instructors to lead sessions for the girls. The Academy curriculum focuses on five themes of leadership: self, team, school, community, and life. The themes will help prepare the girls to be well-rounded leaders in every arena. The Academy emphasizes interactive learning and promotes their philosophy, "Live. Lead. Pass it on!" The Academy also helps students develop their own plan of action for a leadership project to work on in their own community.

Alana Lynch, of Trumbull, Connecticut, attended the Julie Foudy Sports Leadership Academy for two years. After returning to her community, the eighth grader organized a community soccer club equipment drive and re-sold the used equipment at a discount to the recreational league parents. Alana loves playing soccer and wanted to bring the game to others who could not afford to play before her equipment consignment. The proceeds from her service project benefitted TOPSoccer, an outreach program for soccer that benefits mentally and physically disabled youth. TOPSoccer was planning to start a program in Alana's hometown later that year and this funding was a pleasant surprise. Alana knows that it will be difficult to have the Olympic soccer career that Foudy enjoyed, stating, "I would like to but it's one in a couple of million,"[6] but she knows that she can make a difference and be a leader in her community today.

Julie Foudy has created a vehicle in which she can continue to give back to the soccer community, yet she can continue to lead others in creating better communities and paying it forward. She sums up the Academy's impact best in her letter to the students, "We have always believed that you do not need a gold medal or a captain's arm band to lead. Leadership is personal, not positional. We can ALL make a positive difference in this world. The choice is yours; as we say at the Academy, CHOOSE TO MATTER! And equally important, as I learned while playing for the Women's National Team . . . LOVE what you do! Laughter permitted."[7]

Notes

1. HBO Sports, "Dare to Dream: The story of the U.S. Women's Soccer team," Interview with Julie Foudy, http://www.hbo.com/sports/daretodream/bios/julie_foudy .html, (accessed March 30, 2010).

2. Ibid.

3. Ibid.

4. Julie Foudy Sports Leadership Academy, "Academy Philosophy," http://www.ju liefoudyleadership.com/Academy_Details/academy_philosophy.htm, (accessed March 30, 2010).

5. Ibid.

6. Susan Silvers, "Girl kicks in for charitable cause," February 14, 2009, http:// www.juliefoudyleadership.com/Alumni_in_Action_/2008.htm, (accessed March 30, 2010).

7. Julie Foudy, "Letter from Julie," Julie Foudy Sports Leadership Academy, http://www.juliefoudyleadership.com/Academy_Details/Letter_from_Julie.htm , (accessed March 30, 2010).

Mallory Holtman
and Elizabeth Wallace

Transcending Sport to Help Society

by Jessica Bartter Duffaut

Courtesy of the National Consortium for Academics and Sports.

Mallory Holtman (left) and Liz Wallace

With smiles on their faces, and a stranger's arm around each of their shoulders, Mallory Holtman and Elizabeth Wallace wondered how peculiar they looked to the small crowd of spectators at their April 26, 2008 doubleheader. It was Senior Day at Central Washington University and Mallory Holtman ended her college softball career with a bang—not with a grand slam or even a homerun, but with a single act of sportsmanship that shook up the nation.

Senior first baseman Mallory Holtman topped Central Washington University's all-time career list of homeruns and even had more homeruns than anyone in the history of the Great Northwest Athletic Conference. But it was her trip around the bases on that April day while completing a three-run homerun for the opponents that is the most memorable to her. It was the second game of a doubleheader at Central's Gary & Bobbi Frederick Field. Central Washington had already lost the first and needed to clinch the second game if they were to have a chance at the playoffs. Instead, Holtman and Wallace sealed their team's fate by assisting an injured opponent around the bases in the top of the second inning enabling her three-run homerun to count en route to their own 4-2 loss.

It all started very innocently. Western Oregon had runners on first and second when Sara Tucholsky came up to bat. Tucholsky wasn't a particularly strong hitter. In her previous 34 at bats, she had just three hits. But this game was important and with one strike on her, Tucholsky knocked the next pitch out of the park. The ball cleared the centerfield fence for the first homerun of her career—high school or college. As she rounded the bags, thinking to herself that it was about time for her to hit a homer, her excitement carried her right over first base without tagging the bag. Just before reaching second base, she realized her mistake and turned back toward first to tag-up. Unfortunately, her right leg did not pivot correctly, and her Anterior Cruciate Ligament (ACL) tore. Tucholsky shrieked in pain and collapsed to the ground. The cheers and excitement that followed her ball clearing the fence quickly hushed over the field. The runners who had been on first and second slowly touched the home plate and looked to their teammate with concern as she dragged herself back to first base, crawling in shear agony. Western Oregon Coach Pam Knox looked to her player in great pain and then to the umpire and asked what could be done. She knew no one on their team could touch Tucholsky, players or training staff, or she would be called out. According to the umpire, if a runner was put in for Tucholsky, her three-run homerun would have become a two-run single. Coach Knox was determined not to take away Tucholsky's first and only homerun.

Holtman knew the rules as well and instinctively asked the umpire if she could not only touch Tucholsky but actually carry her around the remaining bases. The umpire, looking a bit perplexed at Holtman's request, told her yes, indeed, she and her teammates would be permitted to help Tucholsky, despite his surprise that they would want to. So, together, Holtman and Wallace approached Tucholsky, asking if she would like their assistance. Tucholsky's instant gratitude said it all.

With smiles on their faces, and an arm around each of their shoulders, Holtman and Wallace carried Tucholsky to second, bent down to tap her left foot on the base and then carried her to third and did the same. The three joked under their breath at how ridiculous they must have looked to their fans—different jerseys, different schools—working together to help one team score a run. Imagine their surprise when they brought Tucholsky to the home plate to a crowd of her Western Oregon teammates and found them with tears running down their cheeks. Holtman and Wallace left the homerun hitter with her teammates who, only now, could touch and assist her. As Holtman and Wallace turned to face their teammates, they were shocked to see the stands also full of emotion and more visible tears.

Tucholsky and Western Oregon went on to win that game 4-2 and soon after clinched the school's first ever conference championship in softball history. Tucholsky's career, however, ended with that tap on the home plate, though her stardom was just beginning. The courageous sportsmanship of Holtman and Wallace became an instant Internet sensation and quickly appeared on local, national, and cable news stations everywhere—not just as a sports-related story but as an inspiring story of character and selflessness. The wildfire-like spread shocked the three women who were just playing the game they loved with passion and integrity.

Holtman recalls the decision to carry Tucholsky as anything but that. It wasn't a decision she had to make or an idea that she contemplated. It came naturally because it just seemed like "the right thing to do."[1]

Elizabeth Wallace, who started playing baseball at five and softball at eight years old, graduated college in December 2009 summa cum laude with a Bachelor of Arts degree in Education with endorsements in Elementary Education and Teaching English as a Second Language (TESL). She fulfilled her student teaching requirement in a fifth grade classroom in Bremerton, Washington before moving to just outside Missoula, Montana where she currently substitute teaches. She plans to head southwest to California soon with her husband's next naval assignment. Ideally, she will find another fifth grade classroom to impart her wisdom upon, just as her mom did for 19 years after teaching special education for 10. Apparently, even heroes have their own heroes.

Mallory Holtman and Sara Tucholsky both graduated in 2008 but their lives are forever intertwined. Because of the great attention given to their initial meeting on the field, Holtman and Tucholsky started the Sportsmanship Defined Foundation, an organization "to help and give back to all of those who have helped them achieve their goals and have allowed them to create a non-profit foundation to help those in need, just as they were supported and encouraged during their lives."[2] Speaking to youth and adults about sportsmanship and right vs. wrong has become second nature to Holtman and Tucholsky. They are highly sought after motivational speakers because their message is an important and powerful one.

Holtman has also remained close to her alma mater and can still be found in Central Washington's dugout as an assistant coach. She plans to complete her master's degree in Athletic Administration in June 2010 and hopes to be a head coach one day soon.

In recognition of their sportsmanship, Holtman, Wallace, and Tucholsky won the "Best Moment in Sports Award" at the 2008 ESPY's among many other awards. Perhaps their most prized gift is the bond they have now sealed.

Wallace is teaching now because, as she said, "I want to make the world a better place. I want to leave a lasting impression and I can't think of a better way to do that than to teach, inspire, and help the younger generation. I may never be the next great American author, or a scientist that cures cancer or the next president of the United States, but I do have the opportunity to teach someone who may be and can impart a love of learning and understanding of the world that can lead to their great feats. As a teacher I also have the ability to positively affect people's lives on a daily basis. That's invaluable to me."[3]

Mallory and Liz already imparted an "invaluable" sportsmanship lesson on our nation. Hopefully it is one that will long be remembered on fields, courts, and arenas for generations to come. They proved when playing with passion and integrity, skill and sportsmanship will come naturally.

Notes

1. Mallory Holtman & Sara Tucholsky, Sportsmanship Defined, Our Story, http://www.sportsmanshipdefined.org/story.html, (accessed March 5, 2010).

2. Our Mission, Sportsmanship Defined Foundation, http://www.sportsman shipdefined.org/index.html, (accessed February 22, 2010).

3. Elizabeth Wallace, interview with the author, February 22, 2010.

Travis Roy

Transcending Sport to Help Society

by Stacy Martin-Tenney

Courtesy of the National Consortium for Academics and Sports.

Travis Roy's life changed in an instant. Eleven seconds into his collegiate hockey debut, he crashed head first into the boards when checking another player and cracked his fourth vertebrae. Darkness filled his world and when his body flailed onto the ice, he knew that he was not getting up from the ice. The life that he knew as a virile, agile 20-year-old hockey player was no more, and it was replaced with the life as a quadriplegic. Roy is now confined to a 300-pound wheelchair that he controls by blowing or sipping air into a tube. He has some control of his right shoulder and so he can raise his arm to greet you, but cannot control his right hand or feel it. Roy had plans, goals, and dreams of playing hockey in the National Hockey League and on the Olympic team. Those plans changed in an instant, but Roy has adapted and feverishly pursues helping other spinal cord injury survivors through the Travis Roy Foundation. Travis Roy, a motivational speaker, helps others see that challenges sometimes choose you in life.

Travis Roy's accident happened in his first game as a Boston University Terrier in 1995 and he looks back with bittersweet lenses. "I don't remember those 11 seconds," he said, recalling the events of October 20, his college debut against North Dakota, in the delirious moments just after BU's 1995 NCAA championship banner had been raised. "I know I went to hit the player . . . I sort of deflected off of him . . . I didn't get him square . . . my head hit the boards . . . I remember a very, very, very brief blackout . . . then I realized I was flying through the air and I flopped to the ground. If you see the tape, you can see there's no control of my body as you see me fall to the ice."[1] He remembers looking into his dad's eyes and knowing that he was not getting up from this fall. He remembers thanking his coach Jack Parker for letting him start on the ice that day, a hockey dream come true to play in college. It was only for 11 seconds though, and there are so many times that Roy thinks about what could have happened differently in that eleventh second. It is difficult for any athlete to walk away from their chosen sport, it is impossible for any athlete to be forced away from their sport, and it is unthinkable that any athlete would not even be able to walk after competing in their sport. Travis Roy has faced the unthinkable, but it was and continues to be a very difficult path.

Roy was in the Boston University Medical Center for three and a half months after the accident in what he refers to as a vegetation state. He doesn't remember any of it. From Boston, he was moved to the Shepherd Spinal Center in Atlanta, a special spinal cord injury recovery center. Shepherd helped Roy form his abilities today. He learned how to navigate his wheelchair, forward, backward, left and right. "I was finally able to get into a wheelchair, and that was a very exciting thing. I was able to do something on my own . . . I mean, it took a lot to get used to with this chair, but it's great."[2] He learned how to clutch something between the wheelchair arm and his right arm. He learned to paint with a mouth brush, "and I painted an American flag, and I got to say I was pretty inspired at that."[3] Shepherd plans outings for their patients so that they rejoin the outside world. Travis joined the Roy family at a TGI Fridays restaurant, but he was not filled with joy of independence; instead tears overcame him as he realized that he couldn't feed himself. The independence that spinal cord injury patients lose is draining on them and their family members and the Travis Roy Foundation aims to help patients maintain or regain as much of their independence as possible because Roy has faced this unbearable weight himself and understands how degrading it can be.

The Travis Roy Foundation also believes in providing hope to spinal cord injury patients because that is the guiding principle for Travis. It was a very sobering moment when the doctors showed him his scans and the shreds of spinal cord that remained. Murmurs filled his room in the months following the accident that he would come back; he would recover with positive thinking. While Travis believes that he will walk again, he realizes that it will require medical breakthroughs, most likely in stem cell research that has had its own controversial challenges to overcome. After his accident, Travis Roy described his injury and X-rays. "Some of those miracle stories . . . the way I see it, their spinal cord is barely affected. You are paralyzed, but once the swelling goes down, some people do get their full body back. But I pretty much . . . I came close to severing my spinal cord. So there's not much there," he said matter-of-factly. "There's only a few strands that go down to the rest of my body. It was pretty frustrating to see that," he said, "because there's little hope medically that I can ever come back."[4] Travis has come a long way from that moment after the accident, because he delivers a message of hope and positive thinking to audiences throughout New England. He believes in himself and he believes in the research. "It's a story I believe in," Roy said. "The experiences I've had and the choices I've made."[5]

His life after the accident has given him impressive life experiences like carrying the Olympic torch on its way to Atlanta. When he speaks to young kids, he recounts the struggle but emphasizes the lessons he has learned. "It has taken a while," he said, "but I am realizing how lucky I am today. I still have my family, my friends, and my pride. I'm asking you to think, stay positive, and take advantage of the things you can do, rather than dwell on what you cannot do."[6] There are days that Roy admits he wants to cash it all in because he is frustrated with all that he cannot do, but it is the hope that researchers will find a way to regenerate spinal cord cells and cure paralysis that keeps him going. He believes so deeply that he will walk again that he refuses to get rid of his tennis racket, his golf clubs, his bike, and most certainly refuses to give away his skates. "There'll be a medical breakthrough," he writes. "It'll be a little while, but I will use those things again. My faith in that helps keep me going."[7]

Roy was lucky in a way. His accident happened in a televised NCAA hockey game. He has an extensive insurance policy that the NCAA purchased to cover his care and because of his sport-related spinal injury a sort of celebrity recognition has opened other doors. Other quadriplegics are not so lucky. That is why he feels so passionately about providing support through the Foundation. The Foundation supports research and grants money to individuals to afford the expensive adaptive equipment to spinal cord injury survivors. "It is amazing the effect a new wheelchair, a voice-activated computer, or an automatic door opener has on someone with a spinal cord injury. It gives that person a little bit more independence, which enables them to live a fuller life," Roy said.[8] Travis knows those effects all too well. The Foundation has helped individuals like Larry, a C5–6 quadriplegic, who has trouble entering his house without a ramp and struggles with taking a shower. The Foundation awarded Larry a grant for $3,600 to make modifications to his home, which will help his family as much as it helps him. Michael was injured in a minor league football accident and cannot safely enter or exit the family van because his face barely clears the doorway. The foundation awarded his family a $6,000 grant to make modifications to their vehicle. These simple tasks of transportation, bathing, and entering one's home are acts we all take for granted every day, but Travis Roy protects the well being of people like Larry and Michael. The Foundation aims to offer independence and hope. "I've been amazed at the success it's had," Roy said of the Foundation. "It's been a really unique experience. It's done really good things. People that can't afford wheelchairs and modifications to get through their houses . . . all the things that have made my life easier and given me a chance to be successful, I want to return that."[9]

Travis Roy has certainly returned the love that he received when people opened their piggy banks up for him all those years ago by opening up his piggy bank for those less fortunate than him. That is why he remains in the public eye and continues to be an advocate for stem cell and spinal cord research, despite his desire to stay out of the spotlight. "I don't need to see my name or my face out there again. This story is dead. The next story you'll do about me is when there's a cure and I walk again. There's something positive in every situation," Roy said. "It's just that sometimes you have to look pretty hard to find it. Sometimes we choose our goals or challenges, and sometimes the challenges choose us."[10]

Notes

1. Michael Madden, "I am still the same Travis Roy' Former BU hockey player talks of life after paralyzing accident," *The Boston Globe*, March 15, 1996.

2. Ibid.

3. Ibid.

4. Ibid.

5. Rachel Lenzi, "It's Roy as in joy, of living," *Portland Press Herald*, July 11, 2004.

6. Bob Clark, "The power of love; Travis Roy's book is an inspiration; 'Eleven Seconds' by Travis Roy with E.M. Swift (Warner Books)." *The Boston Herald*. January 5, 1998.

7. Ibid.

8. Travis Roy, "TRAVIS ROY FOUNDATION AWARDS 4th QUARTER INDIVIDUAL GRANTS" travisroyfoundation.org, (accessed March 1, 2010).

9. Kristen Walsh, "Positive attitude essential, skaters told Young hockey players hear from Travis Roy," *The Patriot Ledger*, September 25, 2006.

10. Ibid.

Dean and Diane Alford

Transcending Sport to Help Society

by Stacy Martin-Tenney

A quote from a famous baseball movie, "If you build it, they will come," seems to fit the Miracle League and the *Field of Dreams* they build for disabled youth in communities across the country. The first Miracle League field was created in 2000 in Conyers, Georgia after a local businessman, C. Dean Alford, envisioned a baseball field suited to the needs of disabled children. Dean was inspired by a Rockdale County youth baseball coach, Ed Bagwell, who invited a wheelchair-bound child named Michael out onto the field to play with his friends. That simple act motivated a community to create a league for all of the disabled children who wanted to play baseball. They appropriately called it the Miracle League.

The Miracle League has a mantra: "Every child deserves a chance to play baseball."[1] They wanted to provide the disabled children with the same opportunities as the able-bodied children, to wear uniforms, play on a team, catch a ball in the field and, of course, round the bases on their way to a homerun. The rules are simple and every game ends with each team and each player winning. They accomplish this positive experience for the kids by making sure that during their modified two inning games every player bats once and scores a run in each inning. The most fundamental rule for every child is that they are safe on base at all times. The league had some difficulties though trying to play on the regular baseball fields because of the challenge the dirt posed on the way to the bases and the obstacles created by the bases themselves for wheelchairs and crutches. Volunteers in the community can join the Miracle League as an official "buddy" of a player to help them through the tasks they might need assistance with, but most players prefer to do as much as they can on their own. It's funny how a little friendly competition breeds self-confidence and independence.

Playing on the regular little league fields, brought on another amazing surprise. The able-bodied athletes playing on the next field over began watching the Miracle League games and started volunteering to be "buddies" for the Miracle players. "It's the pride they have in playing on a sports team," Dean said. "It is so amazing the way the program has taken off. The able-bodied players from other teams always come over to work with us, and it's a win for everyone who participates. Whoever would have thought that removing physical obstacles would open up so many possibilities?"[2] Dean was so impressed by the community response and the growth of the league itself, which had grown to 35 players on four teams by 1998, that he began to passionately pursue fund-raising to create a "field of dreams" for these children. Dean was no stranger to evangelizing causes for those less fortunate having been a state representative for Georgia. He was a local Rotary Club member and galvanized the community leaders in the Rockdale County and Conyers Rotary Clubs to raise nearly $1 million in funding.

Dean built an entire four-field little league complex with one artificial field for the handicapped children. He built it and they came. The field was completed in 2000, and the number of children participating had nearly doubled. Three of the fields are grass and one is artificial turf, but all of them are outfitted with wheelchair accessible dugouts, water fountains, restrooms, and stadium lights. Dean shares his passion for the Miracle League with his sister Diane Alford. Diane serves as the National Executive Director for the Miracle League and is constantly inspired by young kids realizing their dreams. "It's an experience that neither the children nor their parents ever thought they'd get to enjoy," said Diane Alford. "This concept is really transforming the lives of these children," she said. "They are beginning to feel empowered. It's like, 'Well, hey, if I can play baseball, what else can I do?'"[3]

The Alford siblings soon realized that this feeling should be contagious and they set a goal to build a Miracle League field in other communities. After the field in Conyers, a second park was built in Myrtle Beach, South Carolina two years later. "That's when I realized this league would be taken across our great country," said Diane, "The goal is for 500 fields, and then 800 fields, until it's natural to have one in any community."[4] After leading the effort to build the Miracle League complex in Georgia, Dean promised more, "through endowments we can help sponsor other fields and provide construction and fundraising support to touch other children's lives the way we have over the past two years."[5] Diane said, "Right now, we're serving about 10,000 children, but when we realize our long-term goal, we'll be serving roughly 1.3 million children."[6] As of 2010, the Miracle League had 200 member organizations, and had built over 100 rubberized fields and broken ground on another 100.

Diane is doing everything she possibly can to help as many children as she can, including working 60 hours a week without any payment. She spends a great deal of time encouraging volunteers, parents, and communities to donate and get involved. Alford reaches out through media and builds relationships with corporations all in an effort to raise awareness for their cause. She believes in the miracle of restoring a child's confidence through the game of baseball. She also believes that she can break through the social stigma that some people feel around handicapped individuals. "For so long we did not know how to respond to children and adults with disabilities, so in return, we just didn't respond," she said. "The appropriate response is the same you give to your families—that is, love, compassion, a hug a day, and a kiss a day."[7]

The Miracle League provides love and compassion for these baseball players. It gives 11-year-old Tyler Baker a chance to play the game he loved but had never played because of his wheelchair. "I think it's really neat to play baseball. I'm really excited," said Baker. The Miracle League hopes to build more Miracle fields in communities around the country and the world until there is a field of dreams in every community.

Notes

1. The Miracle League, "History," http://www.miracleleague.com/history.html, (accessed March 23, 2010).

2. Pamela Keene, "Building a Dream: Creating miracles for children with disabilities," *Georgia Magazine*, April 2009, http://georgiamagazine.com/archives_view .asp?mon=4&yr=2009&ID=2131, (accessed March 23, 2010).

3. Greg Grasa, "Miracle Workers; Reifen Rubber Co. of Manheim uses recycled tires to make blocks for Miracle League baseball fields, which are specially suited for children with disabilities," *Lancaster New Era*, October 25, 2004.

4. Melanie Hughes, "A league of their own," *The Morning Call*, February 22, 2006.

5. "First-Ever Baseball Complex For Children With Disabilities Opens Near Atlanta," *PR Newswire*, April 26, 2000. http://www.highbeam.com/doc/1G1-61696836 .html, (accessed February 15, 2010).

6. Greg Grasa, "Miracle Workers; Reifen Rubber Co. of Manheim uses recycled tires to make blocks for Miracle League baseball fields, which are specially suited for children with disabilities," *Lancaster New Era*, October 25, 2004.

7. Elizabeth Lund, "'Miracle' on the ballfield," *The Christian Science Monitor*, June 30, 2004.

Jake Porter, Dave Frantz, and Derek DeWitt

Transcending Sport to Help Society

by Brian Wright, with Austin Moss II

The Boston Celtics captured the hearts and imagination of the public by winning 13 straight National Basketball Association World Championships. UCLA did it with their 88-game winning streak under head basketball coach John Wooden. Most recently, the great teams of Michael Jordan and company in Chicago won 72 of 82 regular season games, and the New England Patriots won 18 straight regular season and playoff games during the 2007 season. These athletic teams have one thing in common: they were beloved for winning. Yet the story of coaches Dave Frantz and Derek DeWitt who enabled Jake Porter to score a touchdown in the waning seconds of a game for Northwestern High in McDermott, Ohio inspires those who hear it as much as even the most diehard fans of the Celtics, Bruins, Bulls, or Patriots.

At an early age, Jake Porter was diagnosed with Chromosomal Fragile-X, also known as Fragile-X syndrome. Fragile-X syndrome is a genetic condition that is identified by a weakness or break in the structure of X chromosomes. The result can be mental retardation or autism. It is the second leading cause of mental retardation and Down syndrome, and is responsible for one out of every 10 cases of autism. Fragile-X syndrome is found in one in 3,000 men and one in 4,000 women. One in 250 women carries the gene without knowing so.

Porter moved to McDermott, Ohio at the age of 13. McDermott is in Scioto County, which is one of the few counties in which the school system integrates mentally challenged children beginning in elementary school. Porter was immediately accepted by his peers in school, and was a popular student and active participant in extracurricular activities. Porter was involved with the boy's football, basketball, and track teams. While he didn't play in actual games, Porter never missed a football practice. Athletics, teamwork, and the opportunity to socialize with his fellow classmates made it all worthwhile for him.

In the final game of his senior season, Porter's head football coach at Northwestern High, Dave Frantz, called the opposing coach from Waverly High to discuss letting Porter play in the game. Frantz and Waverly High's Coach Derek DeWitt agreed that if the game resulted in a lopsided score that Porter would get a chance to play. Heading into the game Northwestern High was a tremendous underdog and was felt by many to have little or no chance to beat Waverly.

True to form, Northwestern High trailed 42-0 with just five seconds remaining in the game. At this time Frantz decided it was time for Porter to play. Porter ran onto the field and entered the huddle for the instructions on the next play. The play called was "84-iso." It was designed for Porter to get the ball and run to the left side of the offensive line. The line set, the receivers set and the ball was snapped. The quarterback turned and handed the ball to Porter in the backfield and he took a couple of unsure steps. As he stopped and looked towards his team for direction he saw that the teammates and opposing players were pointing downfield towards the end zone. Porter began to run and didn't look back until reaching the end zone 50 yards away.

The reaction was overwhelming. People shouted and cheered while others could not help but shed a tear for this child's amazing delight and joy. Porter celebrated with his teammates in the end zone as if they had won the game. Had they? Well that depends on where you look. The score may not reflect a win for Northwestern but ask anyone in the stadium who was there that night and they will tell you that there was no loser. Porter won an ESPY award presented by ESPN in 2003 for his courage displayed on and off the field.

Coach Dave Frantz now serves as Northwest High School's Athletic Director and in 2008 was named the Southeast District Athletic Director of the Year.[1] He also was the recipient of the Sportsmanship, Ethics, and Integrity award from the Ohio Interscholastic Athletic Administrators Association. Coach Frantz's legacy will forever remain as the Coach who chose to do something special and gave a young athlete an opportunity to compete in a sport where most would not accept him. Coach Derek DeWitt, who is now the first African-American Head Coach of Chicago's Waukegan High, gave up a shutout to honor the dedication of an opposing player and the humanity of an opposing coach.[2] With his courageous and positive spirit, Jake Porter showed us all that sports can have an impact beyond wins and losses. Porter made it clear that through courage, a positive attitude, and passion, anything is possible. Without ever making the game winning shot, or scoring the final touchdown to win the game, Porter has shown us all what it really means to be a winner.

Notes

1. Ohio Interscholastic Athletic Administrators Association, "Fall Conference Awards Winners," The OIAA, http://www.theoiaaa.com/DistrictDefault.aspx, (accessed March 1, 2010).

2. Jeff Bonato, "Waukegan Coach A Winner On and Off the Field," *Lake County News Sun*, February 19, 2009, Sports Section.

Dean Smith

Transcending Sport to Help Society

by Joslyn Dalton

If coaches are defined as legendary for the records they set, the influence they have on their players, and their involvement in the community, then Dean Smith most certainly fits that definition. With 879 victories in 36 seasons as the head coach of the University of North Carolina, he is one of the winningest coaches in the history of NCAA men's basketball. Smith's winning percentage (.776) is impressive, and his consistency is remarkable. He accumulated at least 20 victories in 27 straight seasons; a period in which his team achieved 23 consecutive NCAA Tournament berths. Smith's Tar Heels advanced 13 times to the Sweet 16 and 11 to the Final Four. After winning the NCAA's National Invitation Tournament in 1971, Smith won the NCAA National Championship in 1982 and again in 1993. Prior to the 1997–98 season, Smith announced his retirement.

A master motivator and game tactician, Smith is known as the innovator of the four-corner offense, the run-and-jump defense, and the foul-line huddle. Smith cultivated a basketball program that valued academics, graduating an astounding 96.6 percent of his players. While at UNC, he coached 26 All-Americans, 25 NBA first-round draft picks, and 13 future Olympians. Some of his past players include: Vince Carter, Billy Cunningham, Brad Daugherty, Antawn Jamison, Bob McAdoo, Sam Perkins, Rasheed Wallace, and James Worthy. Michael Jordan also played for Smith. As a freshman, Jordan's late game jump shot clinched the Tar Heels' 1982 national championship victory. Regardless of the individual success of some of his players, Smith remains unbiased. "It's not just the great ones I remember," he said in his autobiography, *A Coach's Life.* "I remember each of them, and not just as ballplayers."[1]

In honor of his dedication to the game, the University of North Carolina named its basketball arena the Dean E. Smith Center, commonly referred to by fans and media as the "Dean Dome." He has been inducted into the Basketball Hall of Fame, National Collegiate Basketball Hall of Fame, and FIBA Hall of Fame. Named the

National Coach of the Year four times, he also is an eight-time recipient of the Atlantic Coast Conference Coach of the Year award. *Sports Illustrated* called him their Sportsman of the Year in 1997 and he has been honored with the Mentor Award for Lifetime Achievement by the University of North Carolina.

Following his example, many of Smith's former players have become well known coaches in their own right. After playing for Smith, Roy Williams spent 10 years as a North Carolina assistant coach before becoming the head coach at Smith's alma mater, the University of Kansas. In 2003, Williams made the difficult decision to leave the Jayhawks' program in order to rejoin the Tar Heels. In just his second season as UNC's head coach, Williams won the 2005 NCAA National Championship title. In addition to Williams, Larry Brown also played for Smith. Brown coached several collegiate and NBA teams during his career. Most notably, he guided the Detroit Pistons to an NBA title in 2004.

Earlier in his career, Smith received the honor of coaching the 1976 U.S. Olympic basketball team. During this period, he decided to change his approach from the way he had led in college. "I'll bench a guy for maybe some little thing, just to teach him something in college," he said. "But in the Olympics, if it's going to cost the game, no way."[2] His tactics proved valuable and his team left Montreal with the gold medal. Outside of his Olympic experience, Smith never left UNC for the NBA although the offers were made. "I'm a college guy. I love college, the faculty, the student body, young people to teach," Smith said.[3]

Smith's exposure to the game started young. His father, Alfred, was a successful football, basketball, and track coach at the high school level. Under the guidance of his father, Smith played positions that required leadership such as quarterback, catcher, and point guard. His talent allowed him to play freshman football as well as varsity basketball and varsity baseball for the University of Kansas. Enrolled on an academic scholarship, he pursued a degree in mathematics and joined a fraternity. Smith rarely played during his time in Lawrence and spent most of his time on the bench. Rather than sulk over his lack of playing time, Smith used this opportunity to carefully watch his coach, Phog Allen, who had been coached by basketball's inventor, James Naismith.

After graduating, Smith stayed at Kansas for one season as an assistant coach to Allen before entering the U.S. Air Force, where he coached his base's football team. In 1955, Smith returned to the States. He became an assistant coach for Bob Spear at the Air Force Academy before joining Frank McGuire at the University of North Carolina in 1958. A year later, McGuire was forced to depart UNC due to speculations surrounding recruiting violations. At 30 years old, Smith became his replacement as the team was placed on NCAA probation. Throughout Smith's 36-year coaching career, his team never had an NCAA violation.

The magnitude of Smith's influence stretches off the court and beyond the classroom. Chapel Hill, North Carolina was a segregated city when he first arrived in 1958. While still an assistant coach, Smith caused a stir when he went with a black member of his church to a restaurant that was not open to serving African-Americans. Ten years later, the Tar Heels basketball team returned home from a tough loss at Wake Forest to find the image of their head coach dangling from a tree. Two weeks later, another effigy hung after a loss to North Carolina State. The scare tactics did not silence Smith from civil rights activism. Instead, Smith wanted to change the segregation he saw within his own athletic department.

Nigerian Edwin Okoroma joined North Carolina's soccer team in 1963 as the school's first black student-athlete. Encouraged by his assistant pastor, Smith was persuaded to recruit an African-American player. After observing his own father become the initial high school coach to win a state title with the first black player in Kansas tournament history, Smith knew the task would be difficult. Walk-on Willie Cooper joined the Tar Heels for the 1964–65 season as a member on the freshman basketball squad before transferring schools. It was not until 1966 that North Carolina had their first African-American scholarship athlete.

Smith diligently searched for someone skilled on the court. Yet at the same time, he needed someone smart enough to meet the rigid academic standards of the classroom. He finally found what he was looking for in valedictorian Charlie Scott. With the Tar Heels, Scott led UNC to the NCAA Final Four in 1968 and again in 1969. Although widely regarded as the best player in the Atlantic Coast Conference, Scott was overlooked for Player of the Year honors in both his junior and senior years. "That was the only time in college that I felt things were done in a prejudicial manner," he said.[4]

In addition to helping desegregate Chapel Hill in the early '60s, Coach Smith has addressed other social issues in his lifetime. He took a political stance for a nuclear freeze in the '80s and became a well known advocate against the death penalty. Considering the welfare of student-athletes, Smith has spoken out against gambling on college sports. He also has joined forces to denounce the advertisement of alcoholic beverages at sporting events. Furthermore, Smith has stated that he thinks college athletes should be paid by the NCAA. "From 1952 until 1973 the NCAA gave athletes $15 a month. Today, that would be about $250," he said. "Why not bring that back, especially when you see the enormous size of the TV contract?"[5]

As a head coach, Dean Smith has revolutionized the game of basketball. However, it is his efforts off the court and in the community that separate him from other coaching legends. Idolized by his players, the measure of Smith's impact can best be seen by the respect he has earned from opposing teams. According to Jay Bilas, a former Duke standout, "If basketball had a Mount Rushmore, Dean Smith's face would be on it."[6]

Notes

1. Mike Puma, "He's the Dean of College Hoops," Special to ESPN.com, January 5, 2007, http://sports.espn.go.com/espn/classic/bio/news/story?page=Smith_Dean, (accessed March 15, 2010).

2. Nick Charles, "Top Tar Heel," CNNSI.com, November 21, 1999, http://sports illustrated.cnn.com/thenetwork/news/1999/11/19/oneonone_deansmith/index.html, (accessed March 10, 2010).

3. Ibid.

4. Richard Lapchick, "Scott and Smith gave new look to Tobacco Road," Special to ESPN.com, February 28, 2008, http://sports.espn.go.com/espn/print?id=3268786 &type=Columnist&imagesPrint=off, (accessed March 19, 2010).

5. Rick Reilly, "A Man of Substance,"CNNSI.com, March 17, 2003, http://sports illustrated.cnn.com/si_online/news/2003/03/18/life_of_reilly_0317/, (accessed March 10, 2010).

6. Mike Puma, "He's the Dean of College Hoops," Special to ESPN.com, January 5, 2007, http://sports.espn.go.com/espn/classic/bio/news/story?page=Smith_Dean, (accessed March 15, 2010).

Joe Paterno

Transcending Sport to Help Society

by Joslyn Dalton

Known for his resilient work ethic and love for competition, Joe Paterno is a passionate leader in one of America's most popular sports. Among Division I college coaches, Paterno became football's winningest coach in 2001. His continued dedication to the Nittany Lions of Pennsylvania State University is unmatched. Spanning 13 U.S. presidencies, Paterno is also the sport's oldest coach. Born in 1926, 83-year-old Paterno is not distracted by the implication of his age. "I hate to see people get old when they're not. They get talked into being old . . . They put 83 in front of my name; it doesn't bother me."[1] Although wiser, his enthusiasm for the game, vibrant coaching personality, and old school outlook has yet to go out of style.

Paterno's loyalty is reflected in his numbers. In over 60 seasons as an assistant and head coach, he has missed just three games out of 682. He began his Penn State tenure in 1950 as an assistant coach to Rip Engle, his own college coach while playing quarterback for Brown University. With the onset of Engle's retirement in 1966, Paterno took the reigns as the head coach. In his next 44 seasons, Paterno would rewrite the record books. His career record of 394 wins, 129 losses and three ties as head coach has helped turn Penn State into one of the nation's most successful programs.

Paterno's Nittany Lions have captured two National Championships, one in 1982 and another in 1986. He has coached five undefeated teams. He has had 23 teams finish in the Top 10 and 35 teams finish ranked in the Top 25. During Paterno's career, he has enjoyed 36 bowl appearances and 24 post-season victories, both records among college coaches. A symbol of football dominance in the East, the Lamert-Meadowlands Trophy has been awarded to Penn State 24 times under Paterno's guidance. He has developed 77 first-team All-Americans and 350 of his former players have received professional contracts from the NFL, 31 as first-round draft picks. Although individual talent has graced Beaver Stadium, the value Paterno places on team is evident in that he still refuses to put last names on the backs of his players' jerseys.

Off the field, Paterno's approach to his student-athletes remains grounded in academics. "I think kids ought to come to college to come to college, and play football as an extracurricular activity," he has said.[2] Expecting excellence in the classroom, Penn State achieved an 85 percent Graduation Success Rate, the highest graduation rate in college football in 2009. The University has produced 15 Hall of Fame Scholar-Athletes, and *ESPN The Magazine* has granted 34 players first-team Academic All-American status. To help further their education beyond an undergraduate degree, 18 Nittany Lions have been award with NCAA Postgraduate Scholarships. Paterno is quick to point out that his wife has had an imperative role in helping his young men in the classroom. "My wife, she tutors kids for me. We take them over to the house. You'd be amazed how many kids who played pro football sat in my kitchen every morning at 7 o'clock."[3]

Paterno's own experience with athletics and academics molds his coaching style and philosophy. Raised in Brooklyn, New York by Italian parents, his football success sprouted in high school. Playing for the best Catholic school team in the city, Paterno's only loss during his senior year came at the hands of St. Cecelia, a team coached by the renowned Vince Lombardi. Paterno earned an athletic scholarship to Brown where he also enjoyed playing two years of basketball. Following in the footsteps of his admired father, Paterno planned on attending law school upon the completion of his undergraduate degree and athletic eligibility. He was accepted into the Boston University law school before his football coach invited him to Penn State as an assistant coach.

Paterno's career change proved to be advantageous. His cultivation of a winning program that graduates its players is widely respected. In 2010, the Maxwell Football Club renamed their top college coaching honor the Joseph V. Paterno College Coach of the Year Award. In 2007, he was honored with an induction into the National Football Foundation and College Football Hall of Fame, which has also recognized him as the first active coach to be selected for the "Distinguished American" award. In 2004, he was chosen by his peers, media members, Heisman Trophy winners, and members of the College Football Hall of Fame as the second-best college football coach of all-time. A five-time National Coach of the Year,

Paterno was the 1998 winner of the Eddie Robinson Coach of the Year Award, which recognizes college coaches who are role models to student-athletes. In 1986, *Sports Illustrated* acknowledged him as their Sportsman of the Year.

As active members of the community, Paterno and his wife enjoy volunteering with the Special Olympics Summer Games. Giving both of his time and money, Paterno has the reputation of being one of the most charitable coaches in history. "Football coaches are getting paid too much. We've lost what should be our mission. I think our mission is to take a bunch of young kids and make sure football is a meaningful experience for them that helps them 10, 15, 20 years from now."[4] Taking advantage of a salary that has increased drastically over his tenure, the Paterno family has contributed in excess of $4 million to the University they call home.

Over the years, Joe Paterno has embodied the very characteristics he expects his young men to develop. Preaching the importance of family, education, loyalty, and service, he has built a football program on values and principles. When asked about retirement, the decorated coach responded by saying, "It's important you get up and have something that makes you hustle. I've been fortunate. I've got a heck of a good job. I've got a hell of a good wife."[5]

Notes

1. Steve Greenberg, "Sporting News Conversation: Joe Paterno," SportingNews .com, February 9, 2010, http://www.sportingnews.com/college-football/article/2010 -02-09/sporting-news-conversation-joe-paterno, (accessed March 10, 2010).

2. Ibid.

3. Ibid.

4. Ibid.

5. Ibid.

Pat Summitt

Transcending Sport to Help Society

by Joslyn Dalton

In the world of college basketball, one coach stands alone. The University of Tennessee's Patricia Head Summitt became the first coach in college basketball—man or woman—to sink 1,000 wins with a victory over Georgia on February 5, 2009. Her longevity and success has been incomparable. She is the only coach to have two Division I basketball courts named in her honor, and at the start of her 36th season, she held an overall record of 1,005-193 (.839) in route to building one of the best programs in the country.

Courtesy of University of Tennessee Athletics.

Throughout Summitt's life, success has consistently followed her. As the daughter of Richard and Hazel Albright Head, she was born in Henrietta, Tennessee in 1952. Much was expected of Summitt and her four siblings. Her father was a no-nonsense disciplinarian, and he insisted that hard work be the backbone of his family. He demanded that his children become strong students in the classroom, and he always had a lengthy list of farm chores waiting when they returned home from school. Summitt never missed a school day from kindergarten through high school. With her chores finished and schoolwork complete, her escape became playing basketball with her three brothers.

After attending Cheatham County High School, Summitt went on to play basketball and volleyball for the University of Tennessee at Martin. In 1973, a year before graduating college, Summitt made her first U.S. national team and earned silver at the World University Games in the Soviet Union. During her senior season at Tennessee-Martin, she suffered a season-ending knee injury. Summitt was determined to not let the setback derail her hopes of making the 1976 Olympic team.

Upon her graduation, the University of Tennessee, Knoxville offered Summitt a graduate teaching assistantship. She also was awarded an assistant coaching position for the women's basketball team. Summitt was prepared to attend class, assistant coach and take advantage of the athletic training services UT had to offer so she could rehabilitate her knee. A few weeks prior to arriving on campus, Summitt was informed that the program's head coach had decided to take a sabbatical. At 22 years old, Summit assumed the head coaching spot with no previous coaching experience. She was virtually the same age as the seniors on the team. "I was absolutely overwhelmed and scared to death," she said, reflecting back.[1]

In her first season as head coach, Summitt's responsibilities were stretched. She still managed to lead her team to a winning record, while working on her master's degree, teaching classes, and recuperating her knee. That summer, she was granted a spot on the silver medalist U.S. World Championship Team and the gold medalist Pan American Games Team. By 1976, Summitt reached her goal of making the Olympic Team. She served as co-captain and led her team to a silver medal.

Balancing her own playing career with coaching, Summitt's first two years for the Lady Volunteers became the only time she would fail to win at least 20 games in a single season. In the years that followed, Summitt's coaching success rapidly bloomed.

Entering her 36th season as head coach at Tennessee in the 2009–10 season, Summitt has won a combined total of 27 Southeastern Conference tournaments and regular season championships. In 28 consecutive NCAA Tournament appearances, she has garnered a multitude of wins. John Wooden, the legendary coach from UCLA, is the only coach to have surpassed Summitt's national championship total. He won 10 titles in 29 years, while Summitt has accumulated eight in her first 35 seasons.

Summitt's early titles came in 1987, '89 and '91. She then won a string of national championships in '96, '97 and '98. Most notably, her 1998 team posted a perfect season with a 39-0 record. Between 1999 and 2006, Summitt's teams advanced to the Final Four five times. They captured three runner-up finishes and finished third twice. Following a championship drought, Tennessee took command once again with back-to-back national championship titles in 2007 and 2008.

Summitt's demands on the court are consistent with her expectations in the classroom. Entering the 2009–10 season, 100 percent of all student-athletes who completed their eligibility under Summitt have earned their degrees. Her student-athletes include 12 Olympians, 19 Kodak All-Americans, 72 All-SEC performers, 10 first-round WNBA draft picks, and 30 WNBA players.

Summitt's success permeates into her international coaching record. In 1977, she was asked to coach the first U.S. Junior National Team which in two years brought home two gold medals. In 1979, she took the U.S. National Team to the William R. Jones Cup Games, the World Championships, and the Pan American Games. Summitt's guidance captured two gold medals and one silver. Having missed the 1980 Moscow Olympics due to the United States' boycott, Summitt steered the 1984 U.S. Women's Olympic basketball team to its first gold medal.

Summitt's tenure has earned her a multitude of honors and awards. Prior to her 36th season with the Lady Vols, she has been named the NCAA and SEC Coach of the Year seven times. In 2009, *The Sporting News* named her one of the "50 Greatest Coaches of All-Time" while recognizing her as the only woman to make the cut. Summitt is a past recipient of the WNBA Inspiring Coach Award, the John R. Wooden Legends of Coaching Lifetime Achievement Award, the Joe Lapchick Character Award, and the Dick Enberg Award.

Summitt has been inducted into the Basketball Hall of Fame, the Women's Basketball Hall of Fame, and the Women's Sports Foundation Hall of Fame. A five-time Naismith College Coach of the Year, she was awarded the Naismith Coach of the Century in 2000. Her star player, Chamique Holdsclaw, was chosen as the Naismith Player of the Century.

Summitt is a decorated figure for women's sports. In 1997, she was honored by then-First Lady Hillary Clinton at a White House luncheon as one of the "25 Most Influential Working Mothers" according to *Working Mother* magazine. Summitt's son, Ross Tyler, was born in 1990. With her 1,000th victory, Summitt became the first women's basketball coach to earn a contract worth over one million dollars. The University of Tennessee offered her a contract extension through 2014 which includes a one million dollar longevity bonus if she completes her 40th season with the Lady Volunteers.

In addition to coaching, Summitt has ventured into a number of other areas. She has served as the Associate Athletic Director at Tennessee, the Vice-President of USA BASKETBALL and a WNBA consultant. She is highly recognized for her abilities as a motivational speaker, commencement speaker, color commentator and author. Summitt has written two successful books, *Reach for the Summitt* and *Raise the Roof.* Utilizing the platform provided by her success, she is an active philanthropist and has acted as a spokesperson for the Verizon Wireless HopeLine program, the United Way, the Juvenile Diabetes Foundation, and Race for the Cure. Additionally, Summitt is active with Big Brothers/Big Sisters and served as the Tennessee chair of the American Heart Association.

In all, Summitt has coached more than 150 young women. Regardless of her own achievements, she is quick to point out that those surrounding her have had a tremendous impact on her success. "My parents taught me a long time ago that you win in life with people. And that's important, because if you hang with winners, you stand a great chance of being a winner."[2] Pat Summitt will be remembered as one of the greatest role models in the history of women's sports not only for her personal success, but also for the company she keeps.

Notes

1. Tennessee (W) Official Website, "Player Bio: Pat Summitt," The Official Site of the University of Tennessee Women's Athletic Department http://www.utladyvols .com/sports/w-baskbl/mtt/summitt_pat00.html, (accessed March 4, 2010).

2. Ibid.

Tom Osborne

Transcending Sport to Help Society

by Richard Lapchick

Tom Osborne may have had it easy at the University of Nebraska with the luxury of a fully-funded program that provided excellent compensation for his staff, wonderful facilities, and a recruiting budget that would make most coaches envious. But don't be fooled. Osborne worked every bit as hard as any coach anywhere during his 36 years in Nebraska athletics, including his 25-year reign as head coach. He wanted to ensure that Lincoln, Nebraska served as a wholesome and safe environment for young boys who wanted to become men amidst the cornfields of America's heartland.

In Osborne's case, he saw firsthand how easy it was for a Division I-A program to build broad bodies with little concern for developing inquiring minds. In the 1960s, Osborne, then a graduate assistant coach, became Nebraska's first academic counselor and began his work to balance academics and athletics. Thirty years later, 82 percent of his student-athletes who completed their eligibility graduated. This is especially significant considering only 49 percent of football players graduated at that time nationwide. Today, Nebraska graduates 94 percent of all student-athletes who complete their eligibility, a figure that leads the Big 12 Conference—something they have done for seven straight years.[1] As of October 2008, the University of Nebraska led the nation with Academic All-Americans in all sports with 269 since 1962. Of those, 65 were football players.

Osborne did not forget his athletes who left for the NFL before they finished their degrees either. Instead, he made every effort possible to convince them to come back to complete what they started. Six former Cornhuskers returned to graduate in 1994 alone. And Osborne's legacy lives on as seven former football players returned in 2004–05 despite the fact that Osborne resigned his coaching position seven years earlier.

Osborne enjoyed success for decades and Nebraska won its third national championship in four years in 1997 but he decided to move on and focus his efforts elsewhere. He was the first defending national champion coach not to return the following season. In his

25 years as head coach, the Nebraska football team never won less than nine games in a single season. The Huskers went to a bowl game every year and won 13 conference titles. Osborne posted a 255-49-3 record equivalent to a .836 winning percentage, the best for active Division I-A coaches at the time of his retirement and sixth best all time. Osborne's teams outscored their opponents 11,317 to 4,345. Since he first started with the team as an offensive coordinator in 1962, the Huskers have sold out every game, an NCAA record as of November 9, 2005.

But Osborne wanted to do more than just build great athletes in Lincoln. Osborne admitted that most of his time spent coaching was actually off the field assisting players with personal, family, cultural, academic, and spiritual issues that in turn affected their performance on the gridiron. Osborne recognized that to be a good coach meant more than instruction on the field or in the weight room. He was committed to coaching his players in life as well.

In addition, Osborne was committed to coaching youth in life before they even considered becoming a Husker. Osborne and his wife, Nancy, established an endowment in 1991 that provides scholarships to students who have gone through his Husker TeamMates Program, which matches Huskers football players as mentors with at-risk junior high school students. Sensitizing and educating his student-athletes, Osborne is helping save lives in the community long after his retirement. The TeamMates Program has since become a state-wide mentoring program that pairs adult volunteers with middle school students for one-on-one mentoring. Nebraska athletics has the nation's most expansive school outreach program, reaching over 150,000 young people in 2007–08 with messages about making responsible choices about school and drugs.

Osborne is a fourth-generation Nebraskan and developed TeamMates to invest in the future of his home state. He and his wife noted the lack of adult interaction children were receiving and decided to step in to help children reach their full potential.

Born and raised in Nebraska, Osborne had been a standout athlete in football, basketball, and track and field at Hastings High School, about 100 miles west of Lincoln. Osborne attended Hastings College before being drafted in the 18th round by the San Francisco 49ers. He was later traded to the Washington Redskins where he spent two seasons. Osborne didn't see his professional career going much farther in the NFL, so he returned home and enrolled at the University of Nebraska to pursue a master's degree and PhD in educational psychology. Thus, began a relationship with the Huskers that spanned four decades.

Although Osborne was 60 years old when he left Nebraska football, retirement did not suit him for long. Just three years later, Osborne found a new job, one just as demanding and, just as rewarding. In January of 2000, Osborne announced his plans to run as Republican Congressman for the 3rd District of Nebraska. At that time, four of the six Republicans who had announced their candidacy the previous fall dropped out. Despite his lack of political experience, Osborne's reputation in a state where Saturdays are dedicated to football helped to defeat his opponents before the campaign even began. Osborne's reputation enabled him to transcend traditional party politics and he won a landslide victory with 82 percent of the votes.

Osborne had never shied away from speaking out politically when it involved the NCAA, the College Football Association, or the Big 12 or Big Eight Conferences. So, when at the age of 63, Osborne discovered a new venue to work on behalf of the American people and continue to improve the state of Nebraska, it seemed quite fitting that he use his new platform for that purpose. Osborne's success in the political realm has led to his third term representing Nebraska's 3rd Congressional District. The Nebraskan native is most concerned with keeping Nebraska's talented young people in the state and boosting economic development. Osborne pays particular attention to the abuse of methamphetamine by Nebraskan young people and he developed a media presentation entitled "Methamphetamine: One of Rural America's Greatest Challenges." While in office, Osborne also prepared a Rural Economic Development Handbook, an Entrepreneurship Handbook, and a Youth Entrepreneurship Brochure.

An athlete at heart, Congressman Osborne led the fight for two measures regarding sports that were signed into legislation. The Anabolic Steroid Control Act lists anabolic steroids or steroid precursors as controlled substances, thereby prohibiting their over-the-counter sale. The Sports Agent Responsibility and Trust Act (SPARTA) protects student-athletes from deceptive and exploitative sports agents.

In 2006, Osborne ran for Governor of Nebraska in the Republican primary. Although he gained 45 percent of the votes, Governor Dave Heineman won with 49 percent.

Osborne returned to academia in the fall of 2007 to teach leadership and business ethics as a senior lecturer for Nebraska's College of Business Administration. Taking residence back on campus, the University's athletic department heavily relied on his expertise. By October 16, 2007, Osborne was named Nebraska's "interim" athletic director. It was decided over the next two months that he would remain as the official athletic director until at least July of 2010.

"I've spent the majority of my life working with the athletic department at the university and I want to do what I can at this point to continue in the pursuit of excellence that has been previously established," he said.[2]

As part of the award ceremony that honored Coaches Tom Osborne and Willie Stewart in 1994 at the Center for the Study of Sport and Society's 10th anniversary celebration, the Center launched its Sport and Society Hall of Fame to honor people from the world of sport who make a truly distinctive contribution to society, one that extends far beyond the game itself. Muhammad Ali was rightly the sole initial inductee.

Ali watched, awaiting his turn to be inducted. Moved by the entire evening, Ali reflected on Osborne and Stewart: "That's what coaching should be all about." Coming from "The Greatest," this was perhaps the highest accolade of all.

Notes

1. NU Media Relations, "NU Leads Big 12 in Exhausted Eligibility Grad Rate for Seventh Straight Year," November 19, 2009, The Official Web Site of Nebraska Athletics, http://www.huskers.com/ViewArticle.dbml?SPSID=368149&SPID=45821&DB_OEM_ID=100&ATCLID=204836469, (accessed March 25, 2010).

2. Nebraska Official Website, "Bio:Tom Osborne," The Official Web Site of Nebraska Athletics, http://www.huskers.com/ViewArticle.dbml?DB_OEM_ID=100&ATCLID=919755, (accessed March 25, 2010).

Geno Auriemma

Transcending Sport to Help Society

by Joslyn Dalton

When Title IX passed in 1972, the University of Connecticut initially struggled to adequately support their women's athletic programs. By the mid-1980s, under pressure from female athletes and the public, UConn's administration decided to put additional resources toward their women's teams. They specifically prioritized the sports with the best revenue potential. Women's basketball became a prime target even though the Huskies had experienced only one winning season in an 11-year history. To revitalize the program, Connecticut turned to a newcomer in the coaching ranks, Geno Auriemma.

Auriemma was born in Montella, Italy and immigrated to the U.S. with his parents at the age of seven. A graduate from West Chester State in Pennsylvania, he was only 31 years old when he accepted the head coaching job at UConn in 1985. Initially, his bold confidence and big ideas seemed out of place for someone with such a thin résumé.

Before his arrival to Connecticut, Auriemma worked as an assistant girls and boys high school basketball coach. Collegiately, he was the women's assistant at St. Joseph's University from 1978 to 1979 and served as the primary assistant women's coach at the University of Virginia from 1981 to 1985.

In 24 seasons with UConn, Auriemma has redefined the game of women's basketball. His program is the standard by which all others are measured. His only losing season was his first, and at the conclusion of the 2008–09 season, Auriemma had won over 85 percent of his games, the best among active Division I coaches. After 23 seasons, his overall record is 696-122. In just 716 games, he became the fastest coach to pass the 600-win mark.

Clearly consistent, Auriemma's success is highlighted by three perfect seasons. In 1994–95, 2001–02, and 2008–09, the Huskies went undefeated en route to three NCAA National Titles. UConn captured three additional national championships in 1999–2000, 2002–03, and 2003–04 to bring their total to six under Auriemma. In his 23 seasons the Huskies have won 17 Big East regular season titles and 15 Big East tournament titles while reaching the Final Four a total of 10 times. Auriemma is the first coach in women's basketball history to have consecutively reached the Final Four five times.

Combined with a 39-0 finish in 2001–02, UConn won its first 31 games during the 2002–03 season to set the Division I women's basketball record for consecutive victories at 70 wins. Eventually, the Huskies lost to Villanova in the Big East tournament to end the streak, which had included 18 victories over ranked opponents.

Well-coached and stacked with talent, Auriemma's 2008–09 team went through the season with a perfect 39-0 record. Their dominance continued into the 2009–10 season. The Huskies broke their own NCAA record for most consecutive victories. Entering the 2010 NCAA tournament, UConn had won 72 straight games. Throughout this streak, the Huskies have won every game by double digits. The legendary John Wooden of UCLA is the only coach to achieve a longer string of victories. Wooden amassed 88 wins from 1971 to 1974.

Auriemma's recruiting tactic has been to take high school All-Americans and turn them into unselfish contributors. His players have also worked diligently in the classroom. Auriemma has compiled a 100 percent graduation rate from every freshman that has completed her eligibility under him. Overall, his prevailing success on the court has translated into a combined total of 24 National Coach of the Year honors. He was inducted into the Naismith Memorial Basketball Hall of Fame and the Women Basketball Hall of Fame in 2006. In what was one of the greatest tributes to his career, Auriemma was named the head coach of the U.S. National Team, which will compete in London at the 2012 Olympic Games.

As the Huskies' success continues to add up on the court, some have wondered if UConn's dominance actually hurts the sport. From

1999 to 2010, UConn earned an outstanding record of 371-28. Rutgers coach Vivian Stringer brought her team within 10 points of UConn during the 2008–09 season. "It's not their fault, but it's not a great thing for the sport," she said. "How can anybody enjoy a game that is really not much of a competition?"[1]

ESPN analyst Doris Burke responded, "Did anyone ask John Wooden when he was in midst of the 88-game streak, 'Is this good for men's college basketball?' It didn't happen. If they are beating (you) on a nightly basis, then get better."[2]

Although Auriemma does not apologize for his team's dominance, he is concerned with the continued lack of support women's sports programs receive from administrators. "They don't put enough money into the program," he said. "They fulfill their obligation by having a women's program. They go, 'Look, graduate the kids, keep them out of trouble. I've got my hands full with the men's basketball program and the men's football program. So don't bother me.'"[3]

Auriemma believes things won't change unless women's basketball coaches are held accountable not only for wins and loses but also for implementing a style of play that will attract people to the game. "If you just have a program and nobody is minding the store, it's not going to happen. Nobody's going to care," he added. "Every men's program in America is trying to make the NCAA Tournament. You can't say the same for every women's program."[4]

Gender is not the only diversity issue Auriemma has raised. When his team faced Stanford during the NCAA Final Four in 2009, he boldly addressed the media about his concerns surrounding the perceptions being placed on Stanford. "People (in) the sports world like to make judgments on people by how they look," he said. "It's grossly unfair. White kids are always looked upon as being soft. Stanford's got a tremendous amount of players who for whatever reason, because they don't look like Tina Charles or Maya Moore, the perception out there is going to be, well, they must be soft."[5]

Charles and Moore, both African-American players, are arguably the two most accomplished players in UConn's history. Auriemma added, "I watched (Stanford) play and nobody goes harder to the boards. Nobody takes more charges. Nobody runs the floor as hard. Those kids are as tough as any of the kids in the country."[6]

A committed advocate for women's basketball, Auriemma's legacy on the court has carried into the community. He currently lives in Manchester, Connecticut with his wife, Kathy, and their three children. Coach Auriemma was recently named the newly elected President of the Women's Basketball Coaches Association. In this capacity, he joined forces with the V Foundation for Cancer Research, founded in 1993 by ESPN and former North Carolina State coach Jim Valvano. As a co-founder for Geno's Cancer Team, Auriemma and his wife encourage philanthropic acts at all levels of Connecticut schools. In a similar role, Auriemma has been the chair of Why-Me of New England, a fund-raising organization for breast cancer research. He also has served as the State of Connecticut honorary chair for the American Heart Association and co-chair for the Connecticut Arthritis Foundation.

UConn's athletic department could have hardly known where it would be two decades after hiring Coach Geno Auriemma. He has turned a women's basketball program once cast aside and overlooked into a national powerhouse. When asked about the future, Auriemma addressed his Huskies' second record-setting streak. "It's going to end," he said. "I don't want it to end because we got a kid injured. I don't want it to end because somebody got in foul trouble. I want it to end with our best on the floor (in) the last three minutes and somebody beats us," he added. "I'll be the first to shake their hand."[7]

Notes

1. Richard Deitsch, "UConn's march into history raises question: Are Huskies too good?" CNNSI.com, March 9, 2010, http://sportsillustrated.cnn.com/2010/writers/rich ard_deitsch/03/08/uconn.win.streak/index.html, (accessed March 20, 2010).

2. Ibid.

3. Jeff Jacobs, "Geno Auriemma Channels His Inner Brandi Chastain," Currant.com, March 22, 2010, http://blogs.courant.com/uconn_womens_basketball/ 2010/03/geno-auriemma-channels-his-inn.html, (accessed March 22, 2010).

4. Ibid.

5. Jonathan Abrams, "Auriemma Says Perceptions of Stanford Based on Race," NYTimes.com, April 4, 2009, http://thequad.blogs.nytimes.com/2009/04/04/auriem ma-says-perceptions-of-stanford-based-on-race/, (accessed March 20, 2010).

6. Ibid.

7. Kenneth Best, "Women's Basketball Sets Record with 71st Consecutive Win," UConn Today, March 9, 2010, http://today.uconn.edu/?p=11016, (accessed March 20, 2010).

Floyd Keith

Transcending Sport to Help Society

by Richard Lapchick

I have known Floyd Keith from his days as head football coach at the University of Rhode Island. I learned about his history and appreciated that his simply being an African-American head coach was a breakthrough. I always thought of him as a coach, a member of a noble profession. I was out of touch for a while until he called me and said he was a candidate to become the Executive Director of the Black Coaches Association.

I had been in awe of the BCA when the likes of John Thompson, John Chaney, and Nolan Richardson had fought so dramatically for African-American coaches and student-athletes in the 1980s and early 1990s. But it had lost its way and its influence by the time Floyd Keith called. I had a sense he could start a much needed resurgence. Indeed he has.

He spoke to my graduate students in the DeVos Sports Business Management Program at the University of Central Florida in the fall of 2006. Floyd stunned many of them when he said, "If you are black, you have a greater chance at becoming an Army general than a head football coach in Division I-A. The Army is 26 percent black and 8.3 percent of the generals are black. In Division I-A schools, 51 percent of the football players are black, but only four percent of head coaches are black."

He is part of the reason that we went from five to 15 coaches of color in the Football Bowl Subdivision (FBS) since he spoke at UCF in 2006. In fact, it was still at five when we attended the funeral of legendary Grambling football coach, Eddie Robinson in April 2007. It has changed that fast. Floyd Keith, Executive Director of what is now called the Black Coaches and Administrators (BCA), continues to fight for more opportunities. He is passionate about monitoring the hiring practices of colleges for people of color and trying to raise awareness in the disparity between the number of African-American football players and African-American football coaches. He is largely responsible for the creation of the Hiring Report Cards. There have been five in football and they opened the hiring process to the point where in 2008 and 2009 African-American coaches were not only interviewed but hired in record numbers. The BCA's *Women's Basketball Hiring Report Card* helped launch a jump from a low point of eight coaches of color in the 2008 report to 25 in the 2010 report.

In 2001 when he took over the BCA it had become virtually irrelevant. It was broke and broken due to financial mismanagement and poor leadership. He immediately went to end the broke part. Keith raised more than one million dollars annually and increased the number of BCA corporate sponsors from one in 2001 to more than 25. The organization has grown from 172 paid memberships in 2001 to more than 2,800 paid memberships.

It is no surprise that Keith is often attacked by those who do not like outspoken drum majors for social justice. He is not welcomed in all circles nor is he immune from racial attacks via e-mail or phone. Keith and the organization are often accused of raising racial issues where there are none. But the thing that is a far more troublesome sting is the unequal hiring practices that have led to the lack of opportunities for African-Americans in head coaching and key administrative positions. Keith is the only African-American to have ever been the coach of a Division I football program in New England, where he was coach at the University of Rhode Island from 1993 to 1999. In 1995 he was named Coach of the Year for New England Division I/IAA when he led Rhode Island to the Atlantic 10 New England Division championship, their best effort since 1985. The head coach for Howard University from 1979 to 1982, Keith has held assistant head coaching positions at Indiana University, Arizona, Colorado, and Miami of Ohio. He was a two-year starter at Ohio Northern University until he suffered a career-ending injury during his sophomore year. Keith has centered his life around football and knows the business he now finds himself taking on. His discipline and people skills, especially that of a strong leader, have helped project him to the forefront of these issues in college sport.

One more skill has helped him in the transition to fighting for social justice instead of wins on the field. He told my students that his grandfather helped him plot his course for his role in the BCA when he said that if you are ever looking for an answer as to why, all one needs to do is look for and follow the money trail. With that early lesson, Keith is always seeking new strategies. He is willing to push forward into the federal courts to remedy the hiring situation by citing Title VII of the Civil Rights Act of 1964. The Act prohibits discrimination in employment. If a case is pursued, it could threaten the funds received by colleges and universities from the federal government. He pushed back against the NCAA as he fought for the Eddie Robinson Rule, modeled after the NFL's Rooney Rule.

"I have become more convinced we will see some sort of legal action take place that will alter the current discourse in the equitable hiring of intercollegiate head football coaches within the next 10 years. If the colleges lose money in court, like they did in Title IX cases, they will take note for sure," Keith said.[1]

Keith has gained access to a wide audience through various outlets including speaking on campuses and in Congress. He is always quoted in the media when these issues come up. You often see him on TV and hear him on the radio. He is a regular in TV documentaries on hiring practices.

Keith won the National Consortium for Academics and Sports' Giant Steps Award in 2007. Keith also has been recognized by *Sports Illustrated* as one of "The 101 Most Influential Minorities in Sports" and *Black Enterprise* as one of the "50 Most Powerful Blacks in Sport." He was named the All-American Football Foundation 2004 Executive Director of the Year and the 2005 Johnny Vaught Outstanding Head Coach Award. In 2003, Keith was inducted into the Ohio Northern University Athletic Hall of Fame.

Along the way, Keith has sought partnerships, especially with the NCAA. He was closely allied with the late NCAA President Myles Brand. The BCA and the NCAA launched coaching academies for minority coaching candidates to help advance their careers. Brand supported the BCA's *Hiring Report Card*, and created the first vice presidency position for diversity and inclusion by appointing Charlotte Westerhaus to the position.

Keith collaborated with the NCAA by developing the BCA's Achieving Coaching Excellence Program for women and men basketball coaches, also known as A.C.E. The program was made possible through a matching grant from the NCAA's Committee on Women's Athletics and the Office of Diversity and Inclusion. It is designed to help further advance the careers of minority men's and women's basketball coaches.

Many of the football and men's and women's basketball coaches hired in the last three years have gone through these programs. They not only develop skills but also professional networks. On a personal level, Keith speaks lovingly about his wife, Dr. Nicole Keith, and their four children. Nicole joined him when he accepted the NCAS Giant Steps Award. They are a strong professional team and address audiences about balancing professional and personal lives. I speak to Floyd every Saturday morning. When I ask him about his weekend, it is always filled with family events. He is madly in love with Nicole and is as devoted a father as I know. I am the godfather of their son.

While there are many important leaders fighting for equal opportunities for people of color, I think Floyd Keith is one of the most influential, especially in sports. His work with the BCA will help other African-Americans to be future pioneers in sport. When I wrote a book about 100 African-American pioneers in sport, I closed with an epilogue on Floyd Keith as the torchbearer of the dream of so many.

Note

1. Richard Lapchick, interview with Floyd Keith, September 20, 2006.

Ed Nicholson

Transcending Sport to Help Society

by Jessica Bartter Duffaut

Ed Nicholson is not a physician or psychiatrist or superhero, but that hasn't stopped him from helping to save thousands of lives. He spent 30 years defending his country with the U.S. Navy. Now this retired Navy captain is saving more lives on the home front. He is saving military personnel; he is saving families; he is saving mothers and fathers.

   Nicholson is a passionate man with a deep devotion to his country and a deep-rooted love for the outdoors. Growing up in Wadsworth, Ohio, Nicholson's favorite pastime was to amble through the fields and woods with his basset hound by his side and a rifle or shotgun in his hand. He could often be found enjoying the fresh air and nature's beauty without a care in the world. So when his uncle first introduced him to fly fishing in North Carolina, it seemed like a natural fit for Nicholson.

   Nicholson left the woods of Ohio for the University of North Carolina from which he graduated in 1964. He then joined the Navy for what he thought would be two years of obligatory service after receiving a commission as an Ensign. It wasn't long after he set out to sea that Nicholson found his love for the Navy and serving his country. He served on seven different ships culminating in commands of a destroyer and frigate. Nicholson did a tour in Vietnam serving as a Riverine Advisor in the Mekong Delta. In addition to Nicholson's sea-going assignments, he completed post-graduate school in Monterey, and earned his master's degree in Strategic Studies at the Naval War College. He also commanded two ordnance-related shore installations before retiring as Captain in 1994.

While at sea, Nicholson was exposed to a different side of nature, but his shore duty assignments allowed him to rekindle his "affair with fly rods, shotguns, bird dogs, and time spent in the field."[1] As did his civilian life while he worked for Applied Ordnance Technologies in Southern Maryland the 10 years post-naval retirement.

In 2004, Nicholson underwent cancer surgery at the Walter Reed Army Medical Center in Washington, D.C. He had been planning for his retirement to be consumed with days of hunting and fishing after his recovery. But while he was recuperating at Walter Reed, his emotions were inundated with the flurry of injured and disabled military personnel returning from war; many of them young and seemingly lost, fearful of their future in a wheelchair or with a prosthetic. The missing limbs were obvious to Nicholson but the emotional and social rehabilitation concerned him. Some suffered from post-traumatic stress disorder, depression, and suicidal ideation after returning home from war. He could only imagine how they would cope with and adjust to their new lives.

Nicholson wanted to reach out to the "wounded warriors," as he calls them, and thought what better way to brighten their lives than to spend a day together fishing or hunting. He thought of the tranquility he found on a lake or river while fly fishing and decided to share his skill in hopes it would serve others as a form of therapeutic rehabilitation. Nicholson approached the local Trout Unlimited chapter in D.C. who expressed great interest in Nicholson's idea. He met John Colburn who had already been trying to organize fly tying classes at Walter Reed. Together, they approached Occupational Therapist Colonel Bill Howard with their idea of fly fishing as a complement to the rehabilitation of the wounded. Howard instantly recognized its unlimited potential in treating his patients' physical, emotional, and mental ailments.

Nicholson and Colburn started hosting fly tying lessons along with fly casting and fly fishing instructions. Their classes allowed patients to escape the dreary walls of a hospital room and step away from their therapy sessions. After initial fly tying and fly fishing classes, and with an improvement in weather, Nicholson and his volunteers took his students outside on the lawn of Walter Reed to practice casting. They taught the newly disabled as well as the physically able, and, most importantly, they taught those in dire need of a distraction, boost of confidence, and sense of normalcy.

Nicholson recognized fly fishing provided ample relaxation time to help our veterans heal their livelihood. He wanted to make sure it would become a regular thing for participants, something they could rely on, so Nicholson soon cast aside his retirement plans and drew up new plans in his mind to help wounded warriors of all services at Walter Reed. Although, the concept of the program and the work began in 2005, Project Healing Waters Fly Fishing, Inc. wasn't founded until early 2007. It was founded to carry on Nicholson's new mission in life.

While Nicholson's use of fly fishing may sound simple, its impact has been exponential. In addition to typical physical and occupational therapy exercises, participants are using fly fishing to rehab an injured hand or become accustom to their new prosthetic. The greatest benefits, though, are not always visible. Nicholson uses fly fishing to heal the heart and mind. Fly fishing requires a particular finesse, expertise, and patience. It requires a certain level of compassion as well since the fly fishers gently release every catch back into the lively waters. Mastering such qualities "recapture what the horror of war has taken away."[2] After witnessing the tremendous turnaround of countless patients who grew more independent and formed more positive outlooks on life, Nicholson and the Project Healing Waters Board of Trustees decided to increase the program's reach beyond Walter Reed. In 2007, they voted to bring the program to veterans' hospitals and other military hospitals around the country. They reached out to Trout Unlimited and the Federation of Fly Fishers to provide volunteers who would serve as teachers and hosts to the participants. The Walter Reed model proved to be a viable one as Project Healing Waters has since expanded to over 90 programs across the country and in Canada providing peaceful, stress-free, all-expense paid programs and hundreds of fishing trips to thousands of disabled active duty military personnel and veterans. Nicholson said, "We just don't take people fishing. We work with a staff to help them in their physical and emotional rehabilitation."[3] Together, they are casting away the pain.

Many service men and women describe their return home as a difficult transition. Even when surrounded by loved ones, their family members may not understand war like their fellow service members can. Their daily lives change drastically and they often struggle to reemerge into the routines of their family and friends. Project Healing Waters' national trustee Carole Katz said, "Many veterans have difficulty resuming their former lives. Their families, friends, or employers are eager for them to take up where they left off as though nothing had happened. For some of them, this is impossible whether because of post-traumatic stress disorder or something else." She said, "Those with PTSD or other mental disabilities may benefit from learning a new sport, the excitement of a catch, getting outdoors for some physical activity, or the camaraderie of fly fishing."[4]

Program participant turned volunteer, and now Heartland Regional Coordinator, Rick Trowbridge, was first introduced to Project Healing Waters when he was at Ft. Leonard Wood Army Hospital in Missouri. He was suffering neurological damage to his right side and fighting anger and depression after returning home from his second tour of duty in Iraq. He says it took only two fly fishing trips for his life to make a complete 180 degree spin. "It did so much for me personally, for my outlook and attitude, and my hand problems," he said, "I began volunteering. I know of two soldiers who were contemplating suicide who, when we took them fishing, said they could start to see a future."[5] Trowbridge is one of several program alum who have stayed connected either on a volunteer or employee basis in order to pay forward the tremendous impact Project Healing Waters has had on them.

Fellow fly fisher and country music artist Sam Tate had a powerful exchange with an army vet one day while out fishing in Montana. He was so moved by his interaction, he wrote a song about it. His experience and the words of the song he entitled "The River Just Knows" lined up tremendously with the mission of Project Healing Waters so he approached the organization with his demo. Nicholson and Katz were deeply touched by the power of his lyrics. They quickly laid the track to a slideshow of their wounded warriors fishing and posted it on their website. Nicholson says people often tell him when their days get tough, listening to this song helps put things in perspective. He's heard it hundreds of times, but "still find[s] the message very compelling." In 2009, country artist Rodney Atkins recorded the theme song of Project Healing Waters and released it on his CD entitled "It's America." The chorus goes as follows:

> "The river don't talk,
>
> The river don't care
>
> Where you've been
>
> Or what you've done
>
> Or why it is you're standing there.
>
> It just rolls on by,
>
> Whispering to your soul,
>
> 'It's gonna be alright.'
>
> The river just knows."

Ed Nicholson, who now resides in Port Tobacco, Maryland, has selflessly devoted his retirement to "serve the deserving past and present members of our armed forces who have made great sacrifices in the service of our nation."[6] Like the river, he just knows.

Notes

1. Ed Nicholson Biography, email to author, April 2, 2010.

2. Outside the Lines Video, "Project Healing Waters," *ESPN*, February 13, 2009, http://espn.go.com/video/clip?id=3905245&categoryid=null, (accessed April 7, 2010).

3. Project Healing Waters, "ESPN Video," Newsroom & Media, ProjectHealing-Waters.org, http://www.projecthealingwaters.org/html/videos/ESPNVideo.html, (accessed April 7, 2010).

4. Deborah Weisberg, "Rod-building, fly-fishing program for vets launches Pittsburgh chapter," *Pittsburgh Post-Gazette*, December 21, 2008.

5. Ibid.

6. Project Healing Waters, "About Us," ProjectHealingWaters.org, http://www.projecthealingwaters.org/html/501c.html, (accessed April 7, 2010).

5

HURDLERS OVERCOMING OBSTACLES

by Richard Lapchick

In the introduction to *150 Heroes*, I wrote about how Taylor Ellis brought me a book that he read as a young man that inspired him to expand his horizons. It told the stories of seven athletes who overcame great obstacles in their lives. This section, *Hurdlers Overcoming Obstacles*, captures the lives of 17 individuals who showed the world that they were able to smash whatever obstacles were before them.

Bob Love was an all-NBA player and superstar with the Chicago Bulls before anyone knew Michael Jordan. A life-long stuttering problem, hidden from the public during his NBA career, made his post-NBA career almost impossible until someone reached out to offer him help. Love has become the spokesperson for the Bulls in the Chicago community.

Someone read the life story of Mark Brodie and said this is the only story in the book that may be hard for a child to read. Mark Brodie was targeted for stardom as a high school basketball player. Because of his lack of attention to academics, he bounced around from college to college, became a drug addict and a male prostitute. After hitting rock bottom, Mark went back to school under the auspices of the National Consortium for Academics and Sports degree completion program. He not only finished his undergraduate degree but got two masters degrees and a PhD.

President Clinton greeted Dwight Collins in the White House because this extraordinary young man led by his example as a deaf athlete. He inspired his teammates at the University of Central Florida on the football team about what the human spirit could enable one to achieve.

Samantha Eyman became an outstanding softball player in spite of having only one fully-developed arm and hand. She did not allow what she lacked to inhibit what she could accomplish.

Dave Clark, in spite of two bouts with polio as a young man and as an adult, has accomplished great things as a baseball player and coach in professional baseball.

Eddie Lee Ivery used his great skills as a football player to become a superstar at Georgia Tech and later to play in the National Football League. Then he succumbed to the temptations of drug abuse. Hearing about the opportunity to return to finish his degree through the Consortium at Georgia Tech, he did so and reclaimed his life and took control of his destiny.

Loretta Claiborne did not allow challenges to get in the way of becoming a great athlete. Her life became an inspiration for hundreds of young people and a movie was eventually made about her saga.

The amputation of a limb did not hold back Sam Paneno, a football player at the University of California, Davis, from pursuing his life's dreams.

Kathryn Waldo did not let cystic fibrosis stop her ice hockey career as a star player at Northeastern University where she kept getting back on the ice.

Born without hands and with malformed feet, Shane Wood refused to use prosthetics. Regardless, he played sports to build his character and confidence.

Adam Bender, an eight-year old, also refused to wear the prosthesis his mother tried to fit him with. Nonetheless, Bender has excelled at soccer, baseball, flag football, and wrestling. More importantly, he has excelled at life with his motto, "Let us play!"

After being born without a fibula, Katie Holloway was off and running once she was fitted with a prosthesis at 18 months old. She blazed a brave path when she earned a Division I basketball scholarship and currently represents the United States on the Sitting Volleyball Team.

After surviving on the streets with his drug-abusing mother who exposed him to prostitution at an early age, Maurice Torres also earned a basketball scholarship. He was determined to show his siblings that success could be theirs while he was the first in his family to go to college.

Kyle Maynard wanted to be just like his father who played football and wrestled. His parents were hesitant at first since their son was born without hands or feet, but before long, Maynard proved the wrestling mat was where he belonged.

Martel Van Zant couldn't hear the plays from his coach or the words of his teammates at Oklahoma State but he could feel the emotion in the stands has fans from both teams stomped their feet for this exceptional football player.

Charlie Wilks, a 14-year-old high school football player brings new meaning to the football term "blind side" and inspires teammates and opponents in the process.

Aaron "Wheelz" Fotheringham is an 18-year-old wheelchair athlete who was the first to do a back flip on skating ramps in his wheelchair. He has revolutionized the freestyle of extreme sports in what he calls "hardcore sitting."

Looking at the lives of these 17 individuals makes it more than understandable why Taylor Ellis found heart and inspiration from the stories of the seven athletes he read about more than 40 years ago. The 17 athletes portrayed here in *Hurdlers Overcoming Obstacles* will give hope to anyone who reads about these extraordinary people.

Bob Love

Hurdlers Overcoming Obstacles

by Jenny Yehlen

Bob "Butterbean" Love is widely known as one of the greatest players ever to sport a Chicago Bulls jersey. Love is currently employed as the Community Relations Director for the Chicago Bulls and is a well-known public speaker. While he has become an inspiration to everyone who hears him speak, it was not so long ago that he was in desperate need of some inspiration of his own.

Being one of 14 brothers and sisters growing up in a small town in Louisiana, Love's family didn't have much, so he didn't have a real basketball hoop to shoot at when he was younger. He used to shoot at a coat hanger hoop nailed to his grandmother's door. His love for the game became apparent at a very young age and he dreamt of becoming a professional basketball player. In addition to the economic obstacles that he faced, Love developed a severe stuttering problem at a young age that he struggled with for most of his life.

His insecurities about his speaking ability kept him very quiet in school. Love's alternative to excelling in school was to excel in athletics—becoming an amazing high school athlete. He was the quarterback of the football team and he found his words much easier on the football field than he did in the classroom or in a social setting. Love grew to be 6-foot-8 by the time he was 18. He was recruited to play college football at Southern University in Louisiana where he had a very successful career. Love found success on the basketball court as well, receiving All-American honors his sophomore, junior, and senior seasons. He was also the first black athlete to make the All-South team, and he became the first player from Southern University to make the pros. In 1965, Love was drafted to the NBA which, at that time, consisted of only nine teams, as opposed to the 30 NBA teams that currently exist. He was drafted by the Cincinnati Royals in the fourth round, and was first traded to the Milwaukee Bucks and then to the Chicago Bulls.

Love played for the Bulls from 1969 to 1976, during which time he became a three-time NBA all-star, led the Bulls in scoring for seven straight seasons, and scored enough points to be the second-leading scorer in Bulls history, accumulating 12,623 points. He ranks only behind Michael Jordan on the all-time Bull's scoring list. Even as an NBA star, Love was hindered by his speech impediment. Although he grew up, he did not outgrow his stuttering problem since no one had really taken the time to sit down and help Love with his speech. The media would pass him up for interviews because they said they didn't have the time, so he never got as much recognition as he deserved. Also, he was overlooked for endorsement opportunities because many of them involved speaking. Love was obviously a very dominant player in the league, but he never got to take full advantage of his superstar status.

Love's career was cut short by a back injury that forced him to retire in 1977. He was told by doctors that he might never walk properly again. Love had always depended on his physical skill and ability as an athlete. It was hard for him to accept that his body was letting him down. His physical health wouldn't be the only thing that would let him down. It was at this point that Love's life took a turn for the worst. To add insult to injury, one night he came home to find that his wife had left him, and she had taken the furniture from their home, his rings, and almost everything else of any value. She told him she didn't want to be married to a stutterer and cripple. Love hit rock bottom and stayed there for quite some time.

It took Love almost seven years to find a permanent job after his departure from the NBA. He found it hard to sell himself to any personnel director. He didn't have any work experience other than playing basketball, and his stuttering problem made employers believe he lacked confidence and competence. Communication is a key to success in the workforce, no matter where one works and the people interviewing Love felt his stutter would hinder him from communicating effectively.

Finally, in December of 1984, an old NBA friend of Love's hired him to work as a busboy at Nordstrom's cafe in Seattle for $4.45 an hour. Each day he had to endure the embarrassment of someone recognizing him as a former NBA star and questioning what he was doing working at a café. Eventually, he moved up to washing dishes and then to preparing sandwiches. One of the store's owners, John Nordstrom, told Love that the company was willing to pay for a speech therapist if he was interested so that they could promote him.

In 1986, Love began working with a speech therapist, named Hamilton. Love could tell Hamilton genuinely cared about him and improving his speech. Love worked with Hamilton two hours a day, three days a week, for a year. Essentially, he had to learn to speak all over again. He showed the same dedication to learning how to speak that he had demonstrated as a basketball player, and in June 1987, he gave a public speech at a high school awards banquet. It was a very emotional experience that brought tears to his eyes when he was finished. Armed with newfound confidence, he continued improving his speaking abilities. Love's boss kept his promise and promoted him to manager in charge of health and sanitation for 150 store restaurants nationwide. He held this position for about two years, until he was promoted to corporate spokesperson at Nordstrom's.

In 1991, Bulls Owner Jerry Reinsdorf expressed interest in having Love return to the Bulls organization as the team's goodwill ambassador to the Chicago community. Love's goal had been to somehow get back into the sports industry, so he was ecstatic about this opportunity. Love gladly took the position with the Bulls and he was so proud to be able to represent his former team. Love has been the Director of Community Relations ever since. In the years since Love took this position, he became only the second Chicago Bull in history to have his jersey retired at Chicago Stadium. The number 10 jersey hangs proudly from the rafters of the stadium. Also, he found a new love of his life and remarried. He is the subject of a book that was written about him, and he has become an effective motivational speaker.

Love makes over 400 appearances every year and speaks to thousands of teenagers and adults on behalf of the Bulls organization. He visits schools and other non-profit organizations telling the story of his life. He shares how he got to the position he is in today by overcoming many obstacles, working hard, and never giving up. His presentations also focus on the importance of dreams and how to hold on to them. He emphasizes education as well. In a presentation to a group of sixth graders in 2004, Love said, "Put education first, then the sky will be the limit. Listen to your teachers and have your work done."[1] Love's story of perseverance can serve as inspiration not only to athletes, but to all people who are facing adversity.

Because of Love's popularity within the Chicago community, he was approached and encouraged by community leaders to run for the office of city alderman. This just shows that Love's arm reaches far beyond the basketball court. It is not his basketball skills and accomplishments that are making him successful, but the person he has become and the relationships he has created within his community. He truly loves what he does both for the Chicago Bulls organization and for the Chicago community. In a 2009 speech to the Aurora University Black Student Association, Love said, "I'm a living example of dreams coming true. I'm enjoying myself more now than when I was in the NBA. I'm making a difference in people's lives."[2] Bob Love's genuine love for the people of Chicago has made him very effective and tremendously admired by everyone he reaches.

Notes

1. Michael Puente, "Love goes beyond the court Chicago Bulls great stresses education, tells kids 'the sky will be the limit'," *Daily Herald* (Arlington Heights, IL), November 20, 2004.

2. Mike Knapp, "Bulls great's journey speaks for itself," *The Beacon News* (Aurora, IL), April 19, 2009.

Mark Brodie

Hurdlers Overcoming Obstacles

by Richard Lapchick

Mark Brodie is a child of the 1960s and a teenager and young adult of the 1970 and '80s. His story should not have been anything special. Brodie was raised in Queens Village, New York in a large Catholic family with a hardworking father, a devoted mother, and six very energetic siblings.

The reason's Brodie's story goes from what should have been "the boy next door" to the "disaster that waited beside the road," lies in the problems that always accompany a family where alcoholism and dysfunction are present. Brodie's family was strong but his father fought a losing battle with alcoholism and died when Brodie was only 17. His mother, who was Brodie's hero, tried to keep her family afloat with a mentally retarded daughter and a host of other problems. Brodie was a middle child and his prowess in sports enabled him to escape the turbulence at home. When he reached high school he had grown to 6-foot-4 and became one of the city's best basketball players by his junior and senior years at Bishop Reilly High School. After making Street and Smith's All-American team and other All-City and All-Queens teams, Brodie was heavily recruited nationally.

He chose Florida State over Hawaii and USC. Brodie later said that "I wanted to go away because I felt that being away from all the problems at home would make life easier on my mom. I also was under the illusion that I would go pro within two years and that college was only a stepping ground for me. I was dazzled by recruiters of the 1970s with their flashy cars, flashy rhetoric, and promises of gold and never paid attention to the wonderful offers that a free education would grant me." Brodie would learn that lesson later when he returned to school as a regular student.

Brodie enrolled at Florida State and played for legendary coach Hugh Durham. Brodie was very thin and didn't play much as a freshman but was getting better just as he flunked out of school. From there he enrolled in a junior college and, though he was ineligible for half the year, helped the team to a national No. 1 ranking at one time. After leaving junior college, he was recruited again and was settling on Jacksonville University when he decided to go back home and enroll at St. John's University. He attempted to be a walk-on with Lou Carnesecca. He was sure he would make the SJU Redmen but he arrived out of shape and out of focus. Sadly, he was cut by Carnesecca. Brodie said, "It was all timing . . . I wasn't used to being a walk-on and just figured I could show up and they would want me. The only problem was SJU wasn't going to wait for me to get in shape . . . It is too bad . . . after a scrimmage at Madison Square Garden I started to feel my game coming back but Carnesecca let me go the next week. I always wonder if it would have been different had I succeeded at St. John's but this boy did not come back a conquering hero."

After SJU, Brodie was lucky to get a scholarship to play in Canada for Steve Konchalski at St. Francis Xavier University, where he blossomed into what he would have been in the States. With a 24-second clock, Brodie flourished. He was All-Canadian and broke or held seven school records in the two years he played there, but again he flunked out of school and was left without a team. His problems really started when he went to Europe and played professionally. This was where his small drug habit became an addiction and the tailspin that brought Brodie to the brink of disaster.

After developing a cocaine and valium addiction in Amsterdam, Brodie came home to the United States and returned to Queens Village. He worked during the day as a dispatcher for a cab company and at night as a prostitute to feed his drug habit. He was too ashamed to face his old friends and felt that he was a failure.

After a summer working in the Hamptons as a lifeguard, he had an epiphany of sorts. He was working as a prostitute when Len Bias died of a cocaine overdose. He said to his "client" that he "used to be a ball player," and when the woman said "you are nothing but a whore," Brodie decided to change his life. He moved to Florida, but after a few months was back into drugs and prostitution. When he overdosed and was waiting for medical attention, he came across an article about the National Consortium for Academics and Sports and how it helped former athletes go back to school. "I immediately straightened out, left the hospital and wrote a letter to the NCAS Director, Richard Lapchick. When Lapchick contacted me, my life changed to where I am today. It may seem unbelievable but I am a professor at Auburn University with two BA degrees, two MA degrees, and am finishing my PhD. The NCAS program allowed me to enter school again at Virginia Commonwealth University where Dr. Richard Sander was my mentor and helped guide me back to reality and success. I kept talking to Dr. Lapchick who kept me afloat."[1]

School was terrifying at first for Brodie because he had never been a real student before. He was only an athlete. After finding his way as a scholar under the tutelage of Dr. George Longest, Brodie graduated with honor grades in history and English from VCU and went on to graduate school at Clemson University, Bowling Green State University, and then to Auburn University where he worked on his dissertation under the tutelage of Dr. Jon Bolton.

Though he feels he has found his niche as a college professor, Brodie still remembers where he came from. "My biggest thrill at 40-something years old is when I have a student-athlete in one of my classes. I feel like I am looking in the mirror at myself 20 years ago and realize how much I want to tell them, how much I miss it, and how lucky they are. I want to make them realize what they have in their hands . . . success!"

Brodie noted "Many people, especially my mentor and friend Richard Lapchick, my mom and family, and many people who know my story, tell me I am a hero. I am no such thing. I am just extremely lucky to have friends and a mother who sacrificed everything for her children . . . especially the one (me) who really needed help. When I receive my doctorate, it will belong to her and my late brother Bill (the real scholar in my family), my family and to Richard Lapchick and the people at the National Consortium for Academics and Sports. I am eternally grateful."

"Sometimes when I feel life or academia is becoming too serious I always think to myself I may not be the only professor that is concerned with students and my chosen field of study. But I am one of the few who can dunk a basketball or sink a clutch basket in front of 10,000 people. I have had more than my 15 minutes of fame and that is why I love teaching and advising youngsters pursuing their dreams." Brodie said that, like Shakespeare's Falstaff, he "has heard the chimes at midnight . . . but has survived the darkest alleys and deepest demons to finally understand himself and the world he now inherits."

Mark Brodie wants to continue teaching and working with athletes. His dream is to advise athletes and work in compliance with a major university sports program. He is certainly more than qualified. Brodie said, "I have worked with many of Auburn's nationally-ranked football players and in Carnell "Cadillac" Williams to Will Herring and Antarrious Williams, I have found youngsters who are not only gentlemen and super athletes but dedicated students and great young men who have benefited from the fine example set by Coach Tommy Tuberville and the Auburn athlete enrichment program." Mark Brodie has arrived after a very long and difficult journey.

Brodie finished his PhD in 2007 and since has been teaching at Auburn University. He hopes to find work in athletic student services/compliance and continue to teach and work with student-athletes. He has taught and advised more than 100 student-athletes at Auburn. "They put them in my classes. I can't help my affinity for them." He hopes that having five academic degrees and a published dissertation will make him very attractive in the open market. Brodie said he "has finally beaten the dragon that waits by the side of the road" and now just wants to give back, financially and personally to those, especially his mom and me, he says, who helped him recover the boy from the New York playgrounds . . . he was very good. I know Mark's mom was a stalwart for him but, otherwise, he really did it all on his own once he found himself.

Note

1. All of the quotes in this article are from Mark Brodie, interview with author, March 26, 2010.

Dwight Collins

Hurdlers Overcoming Obstacles

by Jessica Bartter Duffaut

If you can't hear the play from the coach, can't read the lips of your teammates, and miss the cheers of the crowd, what kind of football player would you be? If your name is Dwight Collins, the answer would be exceptional.

Collins was not born deaf, but before he could learn to talk, he contracted meningitis at the age of 11 months; resulting in the loss of his hearing. A fighter from a young age, this did not deter Collins from success. Collins' parents encouraged his assimilation into the hearing world by putting him in public schools and forcing him to get summer jobs like most other teenagers. As a sixth grader, Collins found his love for football and began dreaming of stardom in the NFL.

Collins earned great attention on the field as a high school player for Barbe High School in Lake Charles, Louisiana. During his senior year, Collins amassed more than 2,000 yards rushing and scored 27 touchdowns. College scouts lined-up to watch Collins play in the hope that he would continue his stardom at their institution. Upon learning he was deaf, most scouts ceased their efforts to recruit Collins.

A few schools saw past what others thought as a barrier—his deafness—and only saw the talent and spirit embodied in Collins' play. Collins considered athletic scholarship offers from Gallaudet University, McNeese State University, and the University of Central Florida. Gallaudet is the only university in the world in which all programs and services accommodate deaf and hard of hearing students. McNeese State was located in his hometown of Lake Charles. But the University of Central Florida won Collins over by also sharing his academic commitment by promising to provide an interpreter on and off the field. Collins also believed Central Florida had the strongest football program, and he was ready for the challenge.

Note takers and interpreters assisted Collins in his classes, helping him to maintain a 3.80 grade point average. In an ultimate demonstration of support, running backs coach Alan Gooch enrolled in

American Sign Language classes to better communicate with Collins, and signed plays to him from the sideline. Gooch took the crash course after Central Florida signed Collins, so that on the first day the young athlete showed up to the field, Collins would have someone with whom to communicate. In 1997, Gooch was named the Assistant Coach of the Year by the American Football Coaches Association for his work with Collins, earning a $5,000 scholarship for the school.

Collins' inspiration is felt throughout the communities in which he has lived. In high school, a seven-year-old deaf boy's parents frequently made the two-and-a-half-hour drive to Lake Charles to inspire their son with Collins' attitude. Collins was able to challenge the boy's belief that he could not participate in sports and other activities with hearing people. By watching Collins, the young boy learned to believe in himself and follow his dreams of playing sports because Collins was proof that it is possible to beat the odds.

President Clinton welcomed Collins to the Oval Office during in his senior year at Central Florida. The President commented that Collins "gave hope to many people who had none before." Coming from the President of the United States, this is indeed lofty praise.

Samantha Eyman

Hurdlers Overcoming Obstacles

by Jessica Bartter Duffaut

Not many individuals would be glad to be born with only one hand, but that is the case with Samantha Eyman. Eyman's quick foot speed, great throwing arm and fierce competitiveness made her a standout outfielder for the Saint Xavier University's softball team. Her skill level alone was enough to get her noticed on the field, but her lack of a left hand made her abilities even more notable.

Eyman was born without a left hand, and remarkably would not wish it any other way. She looks at not having a left hand as a gift and believes with two hands she would not have accomplished the things she has with one, since it has pushed her to work that much harder. Eyman does have a left elbow and most of the forearm. When she was born, doctors made a thumb-like extremity out of her hip bone to make her arm more maneuverable. Because of it, she is able to tie her own shoes and much more.

Watching her two older brothers play in youth baseball leagues made Eyman an early fan. At their home in Palos Hills, Illinois, Eyman often joined her dad, a former Marine Corps baseball player, and brothers in their backyard practice sessions. At the age of five, she convinced her parents to take her to T-ball registration and she hasn't looked back since. Just a year later, Eyman debuted in the fastpitch softball world. Before Eyman began concentrating on softball, she had played volleyball, basketball, and ran track, but never explored soccer because, she said, it never interested her since hands are unnecessary; it was not challenging enough for her.

When Eyman was eight, she fulfilled a dream that many only fantasize about. She met her idol, Jim Abbott. Abbott, a former professional baseball player for 10 years, pitched for the California Angels, New York Yankees, Chicago White Sox, and Milwaukee Brewers despite the fact that he was born without a right hand. Similarly to Abbott's style of play, Eyman would wear her glove on her right hand and, after catching the ball, would cradle the glove in her left arm, then pull out the ball with her right hand to throw it. -

Abbott taught her his quick ball exchange and now she teaches it to other kids.

In addition to her talent, Eyman's charismatic personality and spirit were a great attribute to her team. As a freshman, Eyman played in 44 games, posting a .943 fielding percentage in the outfield. Her sophomore season, Eyman started in 55 games, earned a .236 batting average and scored 30 runs, the second highest on the team. This effort earned Eyman the Most Improved Player honors in 2003, but she didn't stop there. Eyman continued to make strides, and in just her junior season at Saint Xavier University, she was named team captain.

Eyman utilized her time at Saint Xavier to volunteer her expertise each summer at the University's softball clinics where she offered valuable advice on working hard and never giving up. She understands that parents of children with disabilities like hers may not know what to do. She wants to be there for them and show both the parent and the child the possibilities. Eyman majored in elementary education, and graduated from Saint Xavier in 2005.

Eyman led with both inspiring words and actions as a student-athlete and has motivated a number of other athletes, some with similar disabilities, to achieve their goals. Eyman's inspirational attitude enables her to touch the heart of everyone she meets; athletes and non-athletes; young and old; male and female; regardless of whether they have one hand or two.

In 2008, Eyman and husband Dan Zintak welcomed son James John into the world. At 16 months old, James was diagnosed with Chronic Granulomatous Disease (CGD). CGD affects the immune system and James had to undergo a bone marrow transplant among countless other procedures in 2010. While Samantha is a hero to so many, her son James is her hero. Samantha and Dan devote all their time and love to James, no doubt enjoying every precious smile he flashes them. Just like Samantha's smile does, James' smile can light up a room.

David Clark

Hurdlers Overcoming Obstacles

by Jessica Bartter Duffaut

His parents were told he would be lucky to live and if he did, he would have very little muscular movement. Experts said he would never walk and that he would be confined to a wheelchair for the rest of his life. Luckily, David Clark was too young to remember his life-threatening bout with polio when he was just 10 months old. His first memories, rather, are of physical activity encouraged by his parents despite doctors' predictions. When he was just three years old, Clark

Courtesy of David Clark.

recalls that his daily routine consisted of sit-ups, push-ups, stretching exercises, and chin-ups on a bar his father put up in the doorway. Clark did not know he should not have been able to do such physical activity, but he did know rather quickly that he could do whatever he set his mind to.

Clark's lifetime achievements make him a hero in the minds of many, but in his mind, there are no heroes greater than his own parents. Clark's mother and father never treated him differently and offered nothing but encouragement. In the 1950s, many kids who suffered from polio were forced to go to special schools, but Clark's parents placed him in Gregg School, a regular elementary school. For that, he is indebted to them.

Clark started school wearing leg braces and using crutches, far from the confines of a wheelchair. He faced ridicule from some of his classmates, but his physical education teacher, Bill Schnetzler, treated Clark like every other student in the class. In third grade, after Schnetzler explained the activities for the day, Clark turned and walked away, thinking he had to sit this one out. Schnetzler stopped him in his tracks and demanded he try before giving up. The students had to climb up a rope tied to the ceiling, and to his own surprise, Clark was the first student in the class to get to the top. When he got down, he was rewarded with an ice cream bar. While the ice cream bar lasted only a few moments, the lesson Schnetzler taught him about never doubting oneself lasted Clark a lifetime.

Throughout school, Clark pushed himself athletically and found a love for baseball and ice hockey. In 1970, he graduated from East High School and enrolled in Corning Community College in New York. There he played goalie on the ice hockey team before transferring to Ithaca College. In 1971, Clark got his first big break in baseball and was signed o the Pittsburgh Pirates' farm team in Hunnewell, Missouri. Clark excelled as a pitcher but his hitting suffered. It took him 11 seconds to get to first base on crutches, compared to the average of four seconds it took most players. But in 1973, the designated hitter rule was instated and Clark's career was saved. Clark balanced his athletic career with his studies, and in 1974 he graduated with a bachelor's degree in physical education.

Clark's played all over the country for teams in Florida, Indiana, Texas, New Jersey, Connecticut, and Delaware before traveling overseas to play in Sweden. In the 1970s, American teams were paying Clark $40 a week, $5 a day for meals and covering some other expenses. Sweden offered Clark a four-year $100,000 contract to play and manage—an offer he could not pass up.

Sweden was rewarding for Clark, both athletically and personally. Athletically, Clark managed two different Swedish Elite League teams, the Rattvik Butchers and the Leksand Lumberjacks, over an eight-year period, winning three Elite League titles with Leksand. Additionally, Clark served as the pitching coach for the Swedish Junior National Team over the eight-year span. Additionally, he met his wife, Camilla, whom he married in 1995.

The fullness with which Clark lives his life and the appreciation he shows for each day makes his journey look easy. But Clark had to push himself very hard for the success he enjoyed and he earned every bit of it. In the off seasons, Clark would work out four hours a day during which he ran five miles on crutches. Despite the crutches, Clark typically ran a 13-minute mile for five consecutive miles. The physical strain eventually caught up with him and in 1988 when he was 35 years old, Clark was diagnosed with post-polio syndrome. His muscles that had to work twice as hard to compensate for his polio damaged muscles were extremely fatigued from years and years of being overworked.

Though his playing days were over, Clark remains close to baseball and hockey. 2010 marked his fourth year working as a scout for the Baltimore Orioles and his first year as a color commentator for the Florida Everblades of the East Coast Hockey League, his local hockey club. Clark also recently signed on with Major League Baseball International to serve as a roving coach overseas. He has previously worked as a scout for the Atlanta Braves, Florida Marlins, San Diego Padres, New York Yankees, and Chicago White Sox; as coach and owner of the Indianapolis Clowns barnstorming baseball team; as head coach of the Corning Community College baseball team for six seasons; as assistant coach at Otterbein (Ohio) University for one season; and in Atlanta as the baseball supervisor of sports information at the 1996 Summer Olympic Games. Wherever Clark has worked, his determination and courage have made him an inspiration to everyone around him.

This same determination has been displayed at Clark's baseball camps. Clark has owned and operated several baseball camps over the years, most recently working with the Minnesota Twins farm club in Florida, the Ft. Myers Miracle, to supply a camp for disabled youth. The team supplies the facility, the players supply inspiration, and Clark supplies the know-how to bring it all together for physically and mentally handicapped athletes to compete, learn, and enjoy the game of baseball.

Clark believes that people with limitations are not always given equal opportunities and are the recipients of prejudice and discrimination. Clark is a pioneer for the physically disabled in the baseball world. He was often ostracized, sometimes by his own teammates, but he kept his mouth shut and did his job on the field, eventually earning the respect of his teammates and his opponents.

Clark no longer has the physical agility he once had, but he is still very able. As the years have progressed, it seems his activities have increased, against all odds for someone with post-polio. In 2008, *Diamond in the Rough: The Dave Clark Story* was released. He travels extensively for speaking engagements and book signings telling his incredible story to men, women, and children so that they too can realize what they can accomplish if they only try. Clark's message when he speaks is that everyone can dream. He has nothing negative to say about his life, noting that he has been blessed with great opportunities and a wonderful family. Coupled with the high demands of his work and travel, Clark is the busy father of two. Clark and his wife Camilla are the proud parents of 10-year-old daughter Elicia and nine-week-old Trey, born December 30, 2009.

David Clark's entire life story has been one of overcoming the odds. Standing 5-foot-2 and weighing only 130 pounds, Clark hardly resembled your typical professional athlete, but he pushed himself to the limit every day in order to prove that he belonged. Richard Lapchick acknowledged it is Clark's courage, valor, and strength that "helped him overcome polio and post-polio to show people in the world of sports what actually can be done when one commits to something. His career as a player, coach, and teacher has inspired thousands of other people who have fewer challenges to excel. More importantly, his achievements have encouraged others who have had physical challenges to realize that they can be overcome." Clark has taught so many about life, living, and loving.

Eddie Lee Ivery

Hurdlers Overcoming Obstacles

by Jessica Bartter Duffaut

The National Consortium for Academics and Sports was created in 1985 in response to the need to "keep the student in the student-athlete." The mission to create a better society by focusing on educational attainment and using the power and appeal of sport to positively affect social change was first put to work with the Degree Completion Program (DCP). Innovative for its time, DCP allowed student-athletes to stay in school with tuition assistance beyond their athletic eligibility, as well as allowing former student-athletes to return to school to complete their degrees.

For many high school students, an athletic scholarship is their only means to earn a college education. Regardless of whether or not they make the grade, family incomes cannot always support the cost of college tuition. So when the next level, professional sports, comes calling and flashing dollar bills, many student-athletes take the bait and leave their college without completing their degrees.

One such former student-athlete is Eddie Lee Ivery. Ivery was raised by his mother and grandmother. Both were on public assistance and neither had even an elementary school education. But that didn't prevent Ivery's mother from putting pressure on him to get a college education. Even when the scholarship offers came pouring in, Ivery's mother sat him down and reinforced what a blessing it was for him to have the opportunity to get a college degree. In fact, Ivery received 90 scholarship offers from all over the country. Most likely, it was Ivery's record breaking 1,710 yards rushed his senior season that garnered such attention. While scholarships came in from coast to coast, Ivery decided to stay in his home state of Georgia. And Georgia Tech was happy to have him since he was dubbed the greatest football player ever to come from the state of Georgia.[1]

At Georgia Tech, Ivery continued to accomplish great things on the football field. He scored 22 touchdowns for 158 points, set a NCAA single-game rushing record of 356 yards, a single-season rushing record of 1,562 yards, and a single-season all-purpose yards record of 1,879. His all-purpose record of 1978 still stands as of 2009.

Ivery's single-game rushing record was set in just 26 carries during a game where the field had to be cleared of snow twice and Ivery was feeling under the weather. Had the 20-mile per hour winds and 20 degree temperature with a wind-chill factor of zero been a little more accommodating, perhaps Ivery would have rushed for more than 356 yards in Tech's 42-21 win over Air Force. He went on to break seven Georgia Tech rushing records before he was drafted in the National Football League's first round by the Green Bay Packers in 1979.[2]

Despite his success on the field, Ivery's professional career was filled with turmoil from injuries, drugs, alcohol, and family problems off the field. After eight seasons, Ivery left the NFL but the fast-paced life didn't leave Ivery. For 15 years he was hooked on alcohol and cocaine and his life spiraled out of control. There were car accidents, jobs losses, arrests, bankruptcy, and eventually divorce. He struggled with his addiction until his wife finally walked out and took their two children with her. Losing his family was a rude awakening for Ivery. In an attempt to get his life back on track, Ivery went back to Georgia Tech to complete his degree and was one of the early professional athletes to graduate through the National Consortium for Academics and Sports' Degree Completion Program. He earned his bachelor's degree in management in 1992. When Ivery walked across that stage to receive his diploma, it had been more than 16 years since he first enrolled at Georgia Tech.

Despite several stints in rehab, Ivery still struggled with an addiction problem until he checked-in for the last time in 1998. This time his rehabilitation program was successful, and Ivery was able to revive his relationship with his two children. He often flew to Florida to visit his daughter Tauvia at Florida A&M University. He watched his son, Eddie Jr., receive acclaim playing football and Eddie Sr. crossed his fingers that his son would follow him to Georgia Tech. Eddie Jr., who rushed for 1,430 yards and 14 touchdowns as a senior at Chamberlain High School in Tampa, was a member of the National Honor Society with a 4.16 grade point average, and he did commit to Georgia Tech in 2002. Perhaps making up for lost time, father and son were together at last because the senior Ivery was also back at his alma mater assisting Georgia Tech Athletics as an assistant strength and conditioning coach while his son competed for the football team. Eddie Jr. struggled with knee injuries for a few years before officially cutting his career shy of the four years. Ivery Sr.

also served as an assistant player development coach at Georgia Tech and after seven years with the Yellow Jackets, he returned to the high school arena. In 2008, Ivery began his second stint as a football assistant at his other alma mater, Thomson High School. Simultaneously, Ivery is working at the McDuffie Achievement Center as the parent involvement coordinator for the county school system. Ivery reflects on his own experiences to help guide adolescents—and sometimes their parents—to success, personally and professionally, academically and athletically.

Ivery said, "The satisfaction that I get out of life now is when I go out and inspire, motivate, and encourage a kid to reach his full potential; not just on the field, but also the off-the-field decisions he's going to have to make in life. It's the most satisfying feeling that you can get when you see a kid's life change because of the encouragement and motivation that you have given to him."[3] Although Eddie Lee Ivery is ashamed of some of the decisions he made in his life, he has learned to make the most of them and uses them to teach, and thus, help the students and athletes with whom he now works.

Notes

1. Gene Asher, "True Gridiron Grit: Tech's Eddie Lee Ivery overcame injury and personal problems to triumph on and off the field," *Georgia Trend Online*, January 2003, http://www.georgiatrend.com/features-sports-leisure/eddie-lee-ivery.shtml, (accessed June 29, 2005).

2. ACC Football, "*2009 ACC Football Legends: Eddie Lee Ivery, Georgia Tech: Ivery honored for record-setting career as a Yellow Jacket*," TheACC.com, http://www.theacc.com/sports/m-footbl/spec-rel/090809aah.html, January 26, 2010.

3. Ibid.

Loretta Claiborne

Hurdlers Overcoming Obstacles

by Brian Wright, with Austin Moss II

The power of sport is evident in the fact that 40 million American youth play organized sports. Sports can help kids make friends, build self-esteem, stay active, and feel a part of something. They can also be a fun and engaging way for kids to learn the important lessons of camaraderie, leadership, character development, sportsmanship, and responsibility. Despite the positives associated with youth participation in sports, studies have found that 75 percent of those who play organized sports will quit by the time they are 14 years old. It has also been stated in research that if a female is not active in sports by the age of 10, there is only a 10 percent chance she will be participating at age 25. Loretta Claiborne is one of the few who broke the mold as her athletic involvement did not begin until she was 17, only to be followed by stardom as an athlete and as an individual.

Claiborne, born legally blind and mildly mentally disabled, was raised in a single-parent home in the projects of York, Pennsylvania with her six brothers and sisters. Unable to walk or talk until she was four, Claiborne was behind in what society declares as natural child development. After receiving corrective laser eye surgery and beginning school, Claiborne could not escape the teasing and torment she faced from her fellow classmates. She was constantly on the receiving end of ridicule from her peers at school and in her neighborhood. The relentless teasing isolated Claiborne, causing her to feel lonely, sad, and angry. To compound her obstacles, school officials recommended she be removed and institutionalized. Luckily, her mother refused. Though down, Claiborne never counted herself out, and in 1970 she found her passion in running and in the Special Olympics.

The little girl who could not walk until she was four developed into a world class runner and Special Olympics Medalist. She was introduced to the Special Olympics organization by social worker and friend Janet McFarland. Today, Claiborne has competed in more than 25 marathons across the United States, and she has won numerous medals and awards in the Special Olympics. After years of feeling out of place and angry about being treated differently than others, Claiborne felt she found a place to belong, thanks to sports. Claiborne was the first Special Olympic athlete to compete in the Boston Marathon, and she placed in the top 100 female runners both times she ran. She also ranked in the top 25 runners in the Pittsburgh Marathon. Claiborne found an outlet for her pain through running, and in the process discovered several other sports. Claiborne won 10 medals in seven different Special Olympic events and continues to train in figure skating, soccer, alpine skiing, basketball, golf, softball, aquatics, and bowling. She even has a black belt in karate and she broke the women's record for her age group in the 5,000 meter event.[1]

Vice President George Bush honored Claiborne with the Spirit of Special Olympics Award in 1981 and Special Olympics, Inc. honored her as Athlete of the Year in 1990. A year later, she was named Special Olympics Athlete of the Quarter Century by *Runner's World* magazine. She has been inducted into numerous halls of fame including the National Girls and Women in Sports Hall of Fame. In 1996, Claiborne was honored at ESPN's ESPY Awards Show with the Arthur Ashe Courage Award. Each year, the Arthur Ashe Courage Award is presented to the person or persons whose courage and conviction transcend sport. Fellow honorees of past years include Howard Cosell (1995), Muhammad Ali (1997), Dean Smith (1998), and Billie Jean King (1999). A movie was produced by Walt Disney Productions and aired on ABC-TV depicting the story of Claiborne's inspiring journey, and portraying her witty and compassionate personality.

Claiborne's achievements continued off the athletic field as well. She speaks four languages, including American Sign Language and has received honorary doctorate degrees from Quinnipiac College and Villanova University. It is believed she was the first Special Olympic athlete to receive such honors. Claiborne has worked tirelessly challenging government policies regarding individuals with mental disabilities. She has appeared on ESPN, Lifetime Television, Nickelodeon, *CBS This Morning, ABC's Wide World of Sports*, and *The Oprah Winfrey Show*. Claiborne's efforts have expanded beyond the borders of the United States as well. She accompanied Arnold Schwarzenegger to light the Flame of Hope in 2001 in Capetown, South Africa for a campaign to increase the number of South African athletes involved in the Special Olympics. The campaign was co-chaired by Nelson Mandela, former South African president and leader of the anti-apartheid movement, and Timothy Shriver, former President, Chairman, and CEO of Special Olympics. Claiborne also attended the Global Athlete Congress planning session in Dublin, Ireland to assist in the strategizing for the 2003 World Games.

Claiborne's accomplishments have earned her worldwide acclaim and recognition but what separates her from other athletes is her incomparable humility. Claiborne even turned down an invitation from President Bill Clinton to go running because she had to fulfill a promise she made to a friend who was performing at an event. If you ask Claiborne, she will tell you that her biggest accomplishment is positively impacting the lives of youth around the world. Claiborne has spoken before the United States Congress as well as to hundreds of other organizations, reaching over 100,000 people. The message Claiborne relays to audiences is simple but powerful: focus on one's abilities, not disabilities. In 2005, she launched the U.S. version of her biographical children's book, *In Her Stride*.[2]

In 2009, the Smithsonian's National Portrait Gallery unveiled an historic painting, created by David Lenz, of the Special Olympics founder Eunice Kennedy Shriver.[3] Shriver became the first person other than a President or First Lady to be featured on a portrait commissioned by the Gallery. Shriver was accompanied on the painting by four Special Olympians, including Loretta Claiborne. Claiborne was known to be a good friend of Shriver and was asked to give the welcome address at the funeral service of Eunice Kennedy Shriver in late 2009.[4]

Claiborne's life journey has taken her places she could never even imagined and taught us to focus on what one can accomplish in life, not what others try to predetermine. Friends Lynn and Sigmund Morawski described Claiborne best as "an undiscovered treasure until Special Olympics opened her world to possibility. She is an unexpected find of incredible talent, worth, and inspiration."[5]

Notes

1. Loretta Claiborne, "Loretta's Story," www.lorettaclaiborne.com/bio.htm, (accessed December 7, 2005).

2. Loretta Claiborne Achievements. "Loretta Claiborne Awards and Recognition."

Loretta Claiborne. http://www.lorettaclaiborne.com/achievements.htm (accessed March 1, 2010).

3. Face to Face, "Eunice Kennedy Shriver," National Portrait Gallery, http://face 2face.si.edu/my_weblog/2009/08/eunice-kennedy-shriver-19212009.html (accessed March 1, 2010).

4. NECN, "Loretta Claiborne: The Queen of Humanity is gone," Comcast, http://www.necn.com/Boston/New-England/2009/08/14/Loretta-Claiborne-The-Queen/1250 261003.html, (accessed March 1, 2010).

5. Sigmund Morawski, email to author, September 28, 2007.

Sam Paneno

Hurdlers Overcoming Obstacles

by Brian Wright, with Austin Moss II

Jesse Jackson noted in one of his most famous speeches that, "If they can conceive it and believe it, they can achieve it. They must know it is not their aptitude but their attitude that will determine their altitude."[1] Sam Paneno personifies this quote. As an incoming transfer to the University of California, Davis football team, Sam Paneno was deemed an immediate impact player on the team and on the season overall. As the starting running back, he showed glimpses of greatness in his first game. This had the UC Davis campus and football team buzzing about the upcoming season.

In his second game of the season against Western Oregon, Paneno displayed the athletic ability and skill that had coaches and media raving about him. The game with Western Oregon remained close and regulation ended in a tie. Behind Paneno's 100 yards rushing and two touchdowns, the UC Davis Aggies went into the overtime period confident that they could win the game. The Aggie players and coaching staff knew the importance of winning this game and how it could propel the team into a very promising season. The score read 33-33 as the overtime opening whistle blew. The crowd was inspired and the two teams were ready. The Aggies won the coin toss and elected to receive the ball. Paneno stood ready on the sideline for his chance to continue the game and his success on the field which would hopefully lead his team to victory.

In the first play from scrimmage in overtime Paneno got the ball and made a move to free himself from the defense and find a hole in the defensive line to run through. Paneno found a running lane which was eventually closed, and he was tackled on what the coaching staff and spectators considered to be a routine play. As the pile of defenders cleared, Paneno was left lying on the ground holding his leg in excruciating pain. Team officials came to his aid and found he had injured his knee on the play. The trainers saw that his knee was dislocated but it didn't seem like an atypical football injury.

What initially appeared to be a common knee injury would soon take a turn for the worst. Paneno discovered that his knee dislocation would be a life-threatening and a life-changing injury. He was rushed to the hospital and doctors proceeded to work on his dislocated knee. What doctors did not expect, and what added an extreme level of uncertainty about surgery was the severely damaged artery behind Paneno's knee. This is very uncommon in most knee injuries. The damaged artery caused an interruption in the normal blood flow between Paneno's leg and foot. As doctors realized the severity of this injury, they knew that the damage done to the muscles and nerves of Paneno's lower leg were probably irreparable. The doctors' immediate thoughts were to amputate the leg. Knowing Paneno's commitment and passion for sports they explored alternative procedures to repair his leg but amputation began to look like the only option. After numerous failed surgery attempts to save Paneno's leg, there were no choices left.

For most athletes in their prime, this diagnosis and the resulting surgery would have been permanently devastating and in some cases would have led to depression and lack of hope for the life they had ahead of them. Paneno, however, had the courage to put the surgery in perspective and remained positive about his future. "I have no bitter feelings. I got a chance to play football for a long time. A lot of people don't get that opportunity."[2]

This is not to say that Paneno wasn't saddened by the fact that his football playing career was over. He certainly was. But he had the courage and the desire to embrace the positives rather than dwell on the negatives. This courageous attitude Paneno displayed is what being a courageous athlete is about, and many times what is missing among athletes today. Paneno spent much of his recovery time in the hospital after the surgery reminiscing about the positive experiences and relationships he had due to his involvement in sports. Paneno realized that he had an important message to deliver to each and every individual he would now meet. The message was of how sports impacted his life in a positive way, and how it could positively affect others who participate in sports. Upon being released from the hospital, Paneno rejoined his teammates on the football field without any feelings of sorrow or remorse. His teammates and the Aggies' coaching staff could see his extreme gratitude for all the experiences he had while participating as a student-athlete.

While facing the toughest loss of his young life, Paneno realized that a greater good could come out of his situation. He knew that through his experiences he could be a pioneer in helping adults and children cope with a similar condition to his own. He also realized that even without playing collegiate or professional football that he could still have a positive impact on others. Paneno's ideas of service to others became a plan of action as he mentored many recent amputees and their families on how to cope with the lifestyle changes and the attitude it takes to overcome this adversity.

Paneno is now a lawyer at the Alliance for Children's Rights, which is a nonprofit dedicated to protecting those who may not have a voice.[3] He earned his law degree from UC Davis. Paneno defends the rights and futures of abused and impoverished children throughout the Los Angeles area. He enjoys this work particularly because it lets him speak for those who would otherwise go unheard. Paneno was hired away from a private firm where he was making twice as much money, but he jumped at the opportunity because of a commitment he felt to the kids.[4] The commitment is enhanced by the duty he feels he has to his younger brother, Rocky, who was in an accident shortly after Sam's injury and was left paralyzed. They have inspired each other to push on and live life as best they can. Sam continues to pursue recreational interests such as rock climbing and surfing, and Rocky has recently graduated from USC.

Paneno was the co-winner of the inaugural NCAA inspiration award, thanks in part to his perseverance and work with foster kids. Tandem Properties has established the Sam Paneno Football Scholarship at UC Davis, which is given to a player who has overcome extreme and adverse circumstances.[5]

Paneno's amazing spirit and courage has influenced his coaches, teammates, family, friends, and everyone else who hears his remarkable story. Paneno personifies what we define as strength, courage, determination, and the will to succeed. Whether Paneno has ever heard Jesse Jackson speak about "people's attitude determining their altitude" is not known, but he lives it. Every day of his life he doesn't just think about helping somebody in need, he does it. Paneno's positive attitude has led him to great success off the field and has allowed him to have a positive impact on society. Sam Paneno has used his life experiences in sports to make things better in the world. Hopefully as his life's story and message spreads, his impact on society will continue to grow.

Notes

1. Brainy Quote, "Jesse Jackson Quotes," http://www.brainyquote.com/quotes/authors/j/jessejacks128747.html, (accessed March 6, 2010).

2. Pat Lafontaine, *Companions in Courage: Triumphant Tales of Heroic Athletes*, (New York: Warner Brothers Inc., 2001), 140.

3. Jerry Crowe, "Sam Paneno gives back more than he lost," *Los Angeles Times*, April 9, 2009, Sports Section, Crows Nest.

4. Ibid.

5. Football Scholarship, "Sam Paneno Football Scholarship" Tandem Inc. http://www.tandemproperties.com/main.aspx?p=14, (accessed March 1, 2010).

Kathryn Waldo

Hurdlers Overcoming Obstacles

by Jessica Bartter Duffaut

Forced to skate at top speeds, stop suddenly on ice, and start quickly on thin blades, with large sticks in tow, and wearing up to a quarter of one's body weight in extra pounds of equipment makes ice hockey a difficult sport. Furthermore, it has a harsh reputation built by hard plays, rough conditions, and tough players.

It may not be the sport of choice for most parents when looking for physical activity for their three-year old child suffering from cystic fibrosis, but for Maureen and Joe Waldo, this very decision back in 1979 may have been the smartest they ever made. In fact, it quite possibly saved their daughter much pain and themselves much heartache, and perhaps even extended their daughter's life, who lived to be an unanticipated 33 years old.

At only two months old, Maureen and Joe Waldo brought their newborn to the doctor with concerns over lingering congestion in her chest. The diagnosis was devastating: cystic fibrosis—a genetic disease in which a defective gene causes the body to produce an abnormally thick, sticky mucus that clogs the lungs and leads to life-threatening lung infections. These thick secretions also obstruct the pancreas, preventing digestive enzymes from reaching the intestines to help break down and absorb food. Specifically for the Waldos, the prognosis was that their baby girl, Kathryn, would only live to the age of 18-20 in the best of circumstances.[1]

Refusing to be innocent bystanders, Kathryn Waldo's parents encouraged their daughter to exercise; they even forced her to do so at times. They believed, despite doctors recommendations to the contrary, that deep breaths of fresh air were the best medicine for their daughter's condition. Moreover, during coughing bouts as a child, Joe Waldo ordered his daughter to sprint around the block in hopes it would help open her lungs and ease her breathing. Her parents even encouraged her older brother David to include her when he played football, baseball, and basketball. Then, at the young age of three, Kathryn followed her brother onto the ice rink where their father was a coach.[2]

Kathryn Waldo's hockey skills earned her a spot on a boy's team where she played for years until high school. Waldo's hockey opportunities were still limited to the boy's team where she became the first girl to make the high school team. She went on to become the first female captain of the team as well. In a fast paced sport like hockey, lung capacity is important for stamina. Though Waldo's lung capacity was only 60 percent of that of a healthy individual her age, Waldo insisted the cold air in the rink opened her airways and eased her breathing. She said, "Nothing's better for me than hockey. The skating makes you work really hard, and then you take in the cold air from the ice. It opens your lungs up and keeps things moving in your body."[3]

Waldo also stayed active year-round by playing softball. This physical activity seemed to help Waldo's health. Doctors had warned she would constantly be in and out of hospitals, yet by the age of 18, she had only been hospitalized twice. In addition to the sports, Waldo had a strict regimen that helped her maintain her health. A hot shower in the morning helped open her lungs, followed by a five to eight minute nebulizer treatment to break up the mucus in her lungs. Cystic fibrosis also affects the digestive system, which caused her to eat four times as much food as a healthy person her size and forced her to take pills each time she ate or drank so that her body could absorb the nutrients properly.

Waldo proved that not much could hold her back and that she was one-of-a-kind by earning a hockey scholarship to Northeastern University. Waldo stood out in the rink, but for different reasons than you may think. In her freshman year, Waldo led her team in scoring and was named Most Valuable Player (MVP). After her freshman season, shoulder surgery was followed by a lung infection that landed Waldo in the hospital where she missed the beginning of her sophomore season. Yet, Waldo returned later in the season and dressed for 27 games en route to helping her team win the conference championship. Though she missed much of her junior season due to another illness, she returned her senior year for another successful season. In 2000, Waldo graduated with a degree in education.

After waiting a year for a donor and spending seven months in a hospital on a ventilator waiting for the transplant surgery, Waldo had a double lung transplant in 2002. Though her lungs were weak, her heart was resilient and it wasn't long before she found herself back on the ice. But the anti-rejection drugs took a toll on her kidneys and she had to be on dialysis for a year and a half before she died on December 9, 2009 of lung and kidney failure.

The tiny 5-foot-2, 115-pound Waldo was considered a "powerhouse" by teammate Emily Sweeney. Another teammate, Jessica Wagner, said, "She was little in stature but bigger than life, someone you never forget. She never let on or talked about her illness, and players new to the team never really knew until we'd visit her at Children's Hospital when she would be getting treatment for her lungs. To not just play but to be a star was amazing, truly amazing."[4]

The Waldos were ahead of the curve on treating their daughter's illness. While it was avoided in the past, medical professionals now actually *recommend* exercise for individuals suffering from cystic fibrosis. In part, as a result, the life expectancy for cystic fibrosis patients has increased to 30 years. The Waldos may have rewritten history for their daughter enabling her to do so for many others by defying the odds and inspiring through leadership and example. Kathryn Waldo is not remembered for her frail lungs, but for her strong heart.

Notes

1. Pat LaFontaine, *Companions in Courage: Triumphant Tales of Heroic Athletes*, (Time Warner Trade Publishing, 2000), 99.

2. Ibid., 100.

3. Ibid.

4. Marvin Pave, "Kathryn Waldo, 33; her grit and skates propelled NU team," *The Boston Globe*, December 16, 2009.

Shane Wood

Hurdlers Overcoming Obstacles

by Stacy Martin-Tenney

Necessity is said to be the mother of invention. It was necessary for Shane Wood to be able to play baseball, so Jake Harrison invented a leather baseball glove that resembled a lacrosse stick for him. Wood was a typical teenager with an unusual adaptation. He was born without hands and with malformed feet. Wood demonstrated a resilient and determined attitude at an early age. His mother fought with him to wear the prosthetic hands that were created for him. Dana Perry lost that battle when, at just thirteen months old, Wood decided that he wanted no part of artificial limbs. He simply used them to take the devices off his arms and that was the end of that problem. Dana resigned herself to allowing Wood to use his natural hands, "a type of tough, calloused hands."[1] Wood could do almost anything with his hands and just as a young child learns the finer points of dexterity, Wood learned to grasp his own unique version of it.

He never thought of himself as disabled, incapable, or defeated. He identifies himself as a normal person who as a child was capable of playing sports and interacting with others all on his own. Once Wood made his wish to be like everyone else known, his mom made sure that she treated him as such. If he truly did not want help, there would be none forthcoming. Some might look at this omission of assistance as cruel treatment to a child with adaptive challenges, but Dana knew that it would only strengthen her son's will and independent nature. She would have been the toughest little league coach around, because there were no excuses and the word "can't" was not a part of her or her son's vernacular. Wood has never even said that word to his mother, with one minor exception. He will regularly say it in reference to what he is able to do with his artificial hand. The commonly accepted treatment of disabled people is to coddle them and assist them with tasks they cannot perform on their own. Wood defied the thought of such treatment. Instead he pushed himself to new limits everyday and his mother's demands that he overcome the challenges that are placed before him.

When Wood was six he began playing soccer just like the other kids his age in a youth soccer league. Soccer is a physically taxing sport even for someone who doesn't have misshapen feet. Wood was certainly not disadvantaged though as he actually seems to use his adaptation to a competitive advantage. He quickly excelled at soccer; in fact by the time he was 13 he had perfected his scoring abilities. His team won the city championship and he was the leading scorer. His ability to run fast for a sustained period suited another sport as he became one of the fastest sprinters at Brownwood Junior High and competed in the mile run as well.

Wood thrived in middle school, and he began to explore new challenges. He tried out for the football team, which instills fear in the hearts of some mothers with completely healthy, young boys. Dana only encouraged her son's newest endeavor with love and support. Wood was so skilled at the sport, and demonstrated such endurance and enthusiasm, he was able to play both offensive and defensive tackle. He starred in the classroom as well with a B+ average, and was a talented musician, playing the trombone in the band. He was actively involved in the student council. In the little bit of spare time he found, he learned how to bowl, fish, ski, and roller skate. Wood was a child with a seemingly infinite source of energy. He also regularly participated in his church's youth group. The activities listed would rarely be associated with a child who has disabilities, but Wood refuses to think of himself as disabled.

The only activity that seemed beyond reach to him was playing baseball. He had accomplished countless ventures with what he had been given, but limitations were disconcerting to Wood. He attempted to play baseball but it seemed like an insurmountable task without a way to grasp a baseball while catching or throwing. Wood has inspired many people with his ability to smash barriers; Jake Harrison was one of those people. He is a saddle maker by trade, and motivated by Wood's determination, he constructed a glove that would enable Wood to play baseball. His final design made it possible for Wood to throw a baseball with remarkable accuracy and play center field like a pro. He could even field ground balls with the lacrosse like scoop design. The Texas Rangers learned of Wood's talents on the baseball field when he was 13 and were so inspired by him that they granted him the honor of throwing out the first pitch on opening day of the 1991 season.

Wood's popularity grew at school and his excitement mounted as the day approached. He was going to meet Nolan Ryan, one of the greatest players of all time. He played for the "Little League" Rangers, but on April 8, 1991 he was going to be one of the Texas Rangers, attending team practice and the team dinner. It was all a little overwhelming, even for Wood who could overcome anything. Then the stakes were raised. President George H.W. Bush was going to join Wood on the pitcher's mound for the honor. A young man with a very outgoing nature became shy and quiet when asked about the opportunity to share the spotlight with someone so important. He wouldn't have traded that opportunity for anything, but he said that meeting Nolan Ryan was the highlight of his life.

Sports fostered Wood's strength and his character, and a well-known sports figure served as the ultimate reward for the young man's valiant efforts. The cooperation with his teammates and the self-confidence he gained through his own skill has surely set him on a path destined for success in whatever field he chooses in life. Shane Wood demonstrated tenacity and vigor so gracefully that it inspired a community, a professional baseball team, as well as a president. His courageous efforts should instill a belief in us that playing sports can open up doors even if they seem to shut us out. It just might take a little ingenuity.

Note

1. Victor Inzunza, "On Opening Day 1991 . . . A boy, a president," *Fort Worth Star-Telegram*, April 8, 1991.

Adam Bender

Hurdlers Overcoming Obstacles

by Stacy Martin-Tenney

2009 National STUDENT-Athlete Giant Steps Award Winner

Adam Bender
Barrier Breaker

When Adam Bender was born, he had a malignant tumor surrounding his entire leg and over the next year, the tumor did not respond to chemotherapy. His parents, Michelle and Chris, faced the unthinkable—possibly losing their infant son to cancer. In an effort to save him, they made the incredibly difficult decision to let the doctors amputate his leg at the pelvis before this one-year old even had a chance to use it. Adam is unlike the other 98 percent of amputees since he does not have a stump of muscle and bone left; the doctors took everything to prevent any chance of cells metastasizing. Many parents and children might have merely tried to survive this struggle. Not Adam. Not the Bender family. They excelled.

Michelle Bender had her doubts and even prayed that Adam's leg was still there under his little cover when she walked into recovery after the amputation. Adam quieted those thoughts. "I felt something hit me in the forehead," Michelle said. "I was laying in this chair, and I thought, 'What the heck?' I sat up and I looked, and that little turkey was standing at the crib on one leg and he had thrown his pacifier at me—and laughed. And that's the moment, I remember that I thought, 'He's going to make it. He's going to be okay.'"[1]

Adam was going to be more than okay and he was going to be more than a boy with one leg. At age three, he challenged his parents to let him play sports like his older brother Steven. "Soccer was first," Chris Bender said. "I think it just fit him fairly well. As a 3- to 4-year old, you're playing on a fairly small field. And so he didn't have trouble covering a lot of ground. He learned to swing through on his crutches and kick a ball."[2] Adam convinced his mom to remove his prosthesis so it did not inhibit his play and he was off scoring goals and not paying any attention to the other kids on the field.

Yes, Adam had to overcome physical challenges to play sports. However, some of the more difficult challenges were the hurtful words by parents in the local sports leagues who were threatened by Adam's playing time and success on the field. At this young age, Adam had to overcome both the physical obstacles that were ever-present, plus he had to deal with the criticism and politics of youth sports. Not only did he cope, but he spoke out about why physically challenged children should be allowed and even encouraged to pursue their dreams of playing sports. "I hope that when others see me play, they will be aware that a physical challenge can be overcome when you have the desire and you believe in yourself. My wish is that all children, no matter what their ability, who want to play sports be given the chance. With the help of my family, I want to start an organization that will help kids with physical challenges be able to participate in sports. In my own words 'Let us play!'"[3] Adam was just eight years old when he spoke these words. He expanded his sports interest beyond soccer to baseball, flag football, and even wrestling.

Michelle and Chris refuse to shelter Adam no matter how foreign that concept is for parents. "I was a little hesitant when we first brought him up here for baseball," Michelle said. "I thought his spirit might be crushed if he got out every time. Then I thought, 'Who am I to micromanage his feelings?' He's going to have to learn how to deal with this stuff. The more I shelter him, the more he'll think, 'I'm fragile.' I don't think I'll ever tell him he can't do something."[4] Michelle has faced Adam's strong will before. For example, when he wanted to play baseball and a coach said that it would be better for Adam to play in the league for children with disabilities. "I don't want to play in the Miracle League," Adam told his mother. "I'm too good for that. They'll never get me out. Those kids in wheelchairs can't catch me."[5] So with her strength of will she called the local baseball league and told them that Adam would be playing baseball in their league. With support from his parents and a couple of great coaches, Adam played baseball.

"The first time I saw Adam Bender, I watched Adam try to field a ground ball," said Bruce Rector, one of Adam's coaches, "and he fell like a ton of bricks. He fell as hard as a kid could fall, and my initial reaction was to step forward to try to help him. And then I looked over and I saw his mom and dad, and they weren't rushing over. I could tell they were paying attention to him, making sure he was okay, but sure enough, Adam rolled over in his own way, he got up, back on one leg, dusted himself off and was ready to go. And that told me a lot about not just Adam Bender, but the Bender family. He's a very unique kid, and a special kid with a special heart, that's been raised in a way that was unique for a kid with his challenge in a way that's going to propel him to a lot of success in life."[6]

There is no such thing as impossible for Adam. He is the kind of kid who is defined by his positive thinking and the attitude that anything can be accomplished. He finds a thrill in contrarianism and proving people wrong if they say he cannot do something. Coaches have sought after him to play for their team because he will find a way to win and that is a positive attitude that can't always be coached. Other coaches have even put him in positions like wide receiver with double coverage at Adam's request. He is not a kid that wants protection although he expects it from his line since he plays quarterback for his flag football team. In fact, during baseball season he jumps in front of the players running toward home plate defending his team against a run whether it leaves him with a concussion or a few bruises.

Adam's determination is not just present on the playing fields, although that is where he prefers to spend most of his time. At the sight of the rusted wheelchair stuffed into the corner of the Bender garage, his face filled with anger. Michelle pleaded with him that it was just in case he hurt his leg, but Adam would not stand for it. A few hours later, the wheelchair was gone. He humored his mother for a while longer when it came to his awkward prosthesis. "I'm never ashamed of my child, but you think, 'Okay, the world is not always that accepting,'" Michelle said. "So you want to present your child as the most normal child you can. So we did this prosthetic thing, put the prosthesis on him, and he walked with it just to please Mom. Put it on him for pictures and all that . . . But he was miserable, and I'm thinking, 'Who am I doing this for, me or him?' I realized it was for me and he didn't want to wear it."[7] Adam has learned a valuable lesson that will arm him for the normal peer conflicts in adolescence, teenage years, and even adulthood—sometimes you can't care about what other people think and you have to be brave enough to follow your own path.

Normalcy might be defined a little differently for Adam, but he does many of the same things that his older brother and younger sister do including listening and ignoring his parents. His presence in the "normal" youth sports leagues is both comforting to him and helps define normal for the other kids on his team. They now understand from firsthand experience that people with disabilities can do things just like they can, they celebrate homeruns, sulk about being thrown out at first, and laugh in the dugout just like everyone else. Adam seems to strive for normal in so many ways to prove others wrong. These very efforts have proven him to be extraordinary.

This eight-year old's story started to inspire many others near and far, including Nick Swisher, a Major League Baseball player. He flew in Adam and his family to catch a ceremonial first pitch at a Chicago White Sox game after reading a story written about Adam that his friend sent him. It wasn't too long after that game when Garth Brooks, the country music star, requested Adam's presence at a charity gala. He had even become a YouTube sensation. All of these youthful celebrity appearances still did not go to his ego, probably because it is so far from how he defines himself as an average kid.

The lesson Adam Bender has taught all of us is that circumstance does not matter, and that we should all play the game with a vigorous passion. Adam takes the field with the same determined game time expression no matter what sport he plays. Success is the same for him or another young boy, throwing a touchdown or a few, beating the throw to first base, or wrestling in the state finals of a youth tournament. "The energy and zeal that he has on a daily basis will carry him wherever he needs to go," Chris said. "I worry about him less than either of my other two kids. I do, and that's strange, but I'm not as worried about him. I don't see that demeanor leaving him. I just don't think it will."[8]

Notes

1. Jeremy Schaap, "Kentucky boy embodies the power of one," November 11, 2008, ESPN: E60, http://sports.espn.go.com/espn/e60/news/story?id=3695819&lpos=spotlight&lid=tab2pos1.

2. Ibid.

3. Adam Bender, "Adam Bender—Let Us Play!" http://site.adambender.net/ (accessed February 28, 2010).

4. Mike Fields, "Kid can do it all on one leg," June 1, 2008, Kentucky.com Lexington Herald-Leader, http://www.kentucky.com/601/story/584471.html, (accessed March 21, 2010).

5. Jeremy Schaap, "Kentucky boy embodies the power of one," November 11, 2008, ESPN: E60, http://sports.espn.go.com/espn/e60/news/story?id=3695819&lpos=spotlight&lid=tab2pos1.

6. Ibid.

7. Ibid.

8. Ibid.

Katie Holloway

Hurdlers Overcoming Obstacles

by Jessica Bartter Duffaut

Katie Holloway once said, "No one should feel sorry for me. This isn't a disability, it's just a challenge. And challenge is just something that makes you stronger."[1]

She was just 12 years old when she spoke those words of wisdom well beyond her years. She was referring to the fact that she was born with fibular hemimelia, which basically means without the fibula in her right leg. While the fibula is not weight bearing, it is one of the two bones in the lower leg and provides an important connection to the ankle joint and attachment for leg muscles. Holloway's condition was not diagnosed until she was 10 months old. While her parents were faced with the most difficult decision they ever had to make, Holloway believes they made the best possible one—amputation. It was either amputate her foot or perform a series of bone stretching surgeries in attempt to salvage the leg, so at 20 months old, doctors amputated her right foot and ankle. Almost immediately following her surgery, Holloway was fitted for her first prosthesis and she began walking within the first five minutes.

Given the opportunity, Katie Holloway made a run for it. Such determination would become a theme in Holloway's life. Despite a slightly late start on two feet, she was on the basketball court by the age of four. As a middle schooler, the 5-foot-11-inch athlete played a sport every season, going from volleyball to basketball to softball—both on school and club teams. What was her favorite of the three? Well, that depended upon the season, because Holloway was content being active no matter what the activity.

In high school, her basketball skills allowed the shy Holloway to shine. She led her Lake Stevens High School in Washington State to a district championship and state playoffs as a junior in 2003. Success breeds attention and her play garnered just that of college recruiters across the country. It's nearly impossible to tell Holloway plays with a prosthetic without being told, but when told, a few recruiters quickly turned away. Division I basketball players with one leg is virtually unheard of and the fear of the unknown proved too heavy for some big-name programs. But Holloway persevered. She had set her goal of playing college basketball at the age of 14, and she was not one to let others decide her fate. In fact, when Holloway is told she can't do something or won't succeed, "it's things like that that make [her] want to work harder." Holloway added, the negativity "fuels me more, to go better, to go faster."[2]

And succeed she did with a Division I basketball scholarship to play at California State University at Northridge (CSUN). CSUN coaches couldn't care less about their new recruit's prosthetic leg because the 6-foot-4 post player had talent well beyond most with two legs. As a freshman in the 2004–05 season, she was named to the All-Big West Freshman Team. The next two years brought more conference accolades as the sophomore was named Big West Sixth Woman of the Year.

Getting her education paid for at a Southern California school while playing the game she loved may sound glamorous, but Holloway was facing new surroundings that forced her to establish her abilities and explain her leg all over again. Holloway had only showed her leg devoid of her prosthetic to her family and very closest of friends. College presented a new challenge as she shared living quarters with classmates and hotel rooms on the road with teammates. One incident even involved her cutting off the leg of a Barbie doll just below the right knee to help explain herself. No matter the antic Holloway used, it was her level of play on the court that transitioned the focus from her leg to her basketball skills where they belonged, which in turn, allowed Holloway to open up about her leg on her own terms.

The CSUN volleyball coach and former Olympian, Jeff Stork, suggested sitting volleyball to Holloway in 2006. Sitting volleyball

Courtesy of B.J. Hoeptner Evans, USA Volleyball.

is played by able-bodied and disabled athletes alike on a net that sits three-feet high while players sit on the ground. It has been a part of the Paralympics since 1980. After Holloway's initial hesitation to Stork's suggestion, she agreed to take the free flight to Atlanta to try out for the national team. She was named to Team USA on April 27, 2006 and her first competition with the team could not have been on a much bigger stage: the 2006 World Championships in the Netherlands in June. Holloway had always loved volleyball and sitting volleyball presented her with a new challenge as well as an opportunity to represent her country internationally. There was one big problem though; to compete with Team USA in sitting volleyball, she had to play without her prosthetic. In fact, the team even hid her leg from her during a training camp, part of an initiation and a way to force her to get comfortable without it. Eventually she found comfort without her prosthetic and learned to feel more secure with herself. She said, "My life turned into a 180. I was open about my leg, I could share it. I was finally at ease about sharing it with other people."[3]

For the first time, Holloway was suddenly surrounded by other women just like herself. She acquired a new comfort level with her prosthesis and could soon be found wearing shorts and sandals, and getting pedicures on both feet. The experience pushed Holloway to see the bigger picture. She was no longer afraid to be looked at as an example, "I hope that people can see me and know that they can do it, that they're capable to do anything they put their minds to." She said, "If you're not physically able, that you're mentally able to do anything."[4]

Victory soon followed her new outlook as Team USA placed fifth at the 2006 World Championships. She returned to CSUN after that summer for her junior year of basketball before traveling to China for the 2007 Sitting Volleyball Invitational in Shanghai. This time, Team USA left the international competition with a silver medal, a vast improvement from their recent fifth place finish and a promising sign as the 2008 Paralympics were approaching. First though, Holloway returned to CSUN for her senior year and her best basketball season yet. She averaged 14.5 points per game and 7.2 rebounds per game, led the Big West Conference in field goal percentage (.554), and was named second-team All-Big West for the 2007–08 season. All of Holloway's hard work was paying dividends and she was receiving the recognition she deserved. She even appeared in *Sports Illustrated*'s Faces in the Crowd feature in the June 9, 2008 issue just after graduating from CSUN with her degree in sociology.

Holloway spent the summer of 2008 training with Team USA in preparation for their September arrival in Beijing for the Paralympic Games. From the moment she stepped off the plane, Holloway described the experience as "awesome."[5] Holloway set aside time to explore China with her teammates climbing the Great Wall and exploring the Forbidden City. She enjoyed every minute and even found excitement in the cafeteria of Olympic Village, "because it was always full of athletes in all shapes and forms." She added, "I was very inspired to see all these people with disabilities doing something amazing with their lives."[6]

"Amazing" is also a fitting description for Team USA's performance in Beijing. First up, they faced Lithuania. In their last preliminary round match, Team USA faced Latvia and swept the games three straight sets with dominant scores: 25-12, 25-17 and 25-11. They met the tournament favorites, the Netherlands, in the semifinals but managed to stun them in a grueling five-game, two-hour match. The finals, and gold medal match, brought Team USA face-to-face with the host nation, China. The Americans were guaranteed a medal but would have to settle for silver as they lost 0-3 to the returning gold medalists. It should be noted that Holloway was the leading scorer for Team USA, totaling 63 points on 38 kills, 17 blocks, and eight aces. She played in 15 of the team's 17 sets, starting all five matches. In addition, she was the team leader in points in four out of the five matches, including a 23-point effort in a semifinal win over the Netherlands, where Holloway led the team with 23 points and a hitting percentage of .274 in the match.

The über-competitor struggled momentarily with the silver because, of course, it wasn't gold. But the reception she and her teammates received upon returning to the United States helped Holloway grapple with her achievements. Nonetheless, she committed herself to winning the gold next time around and even moved to Oklahoma City to train full-time with the team. They are currently preparing for the 2010 Sitting Volleyball World Championships to be held at the University of Central Oklahoma in Edmond, Oklahoma. No matter the color, Holloway is determined to walk away from the 2012 Paralympics with another medal earned by their best play. No regrets on the court is her main goal. And so far, no regrets in life for Katie Holloway as she has lived it to the fullest, challenging those who doubted her and proving her naysayers wrong. Perhaps that alone is even better than any medal she could win.

Katie Holloway won't just relish in her accomplishments though, she wants to use her experiences and knowledge to help others cope with amputation and enjoy all that adaptive sports have to offer. She plans to attend graduate school at the Oklahoma State University in the fall of 2010 and eventually return to the Children's Hospital in Seattle, Washington where her amputation was performed. Her goal is to create a program there for families whose children are about to undergo limb amputation surgery that would educate parents on the realities of growing up with a prosthetic and answer questions their doctors cannot. Equally important, Holloway's program would focus on the patient, educating the children on day-to-day activities with a prosthetic and using their interests to build a personalized program for adaptation back into their daily lives. The adjustment will be difficult for her patients, but the expertise that Holloway can offer will ease the pain. She said, "Ultimately, the program would provide hope and assurance to young families in a stressful situation,"[7] something she still wishes she could have done when her parents faced that exigent decision 24 years ago.

Notes

1. Mark Reiman, "Katie Holloway," *Incredible People Magazine*, April 17, 1999, http://www.incrediblepeople.com/people(1999-04-17).htm, (accessed March 7, 2010)

2. YouTube, NorthrideAthletics, "WBB: Katie Holloway Fox Sports Feature," July 16, 2009, http://www.youtube.com/watch?v=gpNT6MCyazU&feature=related, (accessed March 9, 2010).

3. YouTube, NorthridgeAthletics, "WBB: Katie Holloway YES Feature," July 24, 2009, http://www.youtube.com/watch?v=lkRFeBkOiq8&feature=related, (accessed March 9, 2010).

4. Ibid.

5. CSUN Athletics, "Holloway's Olympic journey ends with silver lining," September 24, 2008, http://gomatadors.cstv.com/sports/w-baskbl/spec-rel/092408aaa.html, (accessed March 9, 2010).

6. Ibid.

7. Katie Holloway, e-mail to author, March 16, 2010.

Maurice Torres

Hurdlers Overcoming Obstacles

by Stacy Martin-Tenney

Maurice Torres had every reason not to be a collegiate basketball player. He faced unthinkable situations at only four years old, and survived multiple foster homes and orphanages throughout much of his youth. By the grace of a Baptist minister, he was given a second chance in a loving home and flourished into a successful student-athlete. While Torres is mindful of his past, he does not discuss it much and certainly has not let it impact his future.

Torres was one of five children born to a mother addicted to drugs and who earned her wage through prostitution. The younger siblings were left in the care of relatives safe from the perils of street life, but Maurice slept in dark alleyways with his mother when he was only a boy "We lived on the street sometimes," he said. When they had money, she rented an apartment for them to stay in, but that only promoted the prostitution. He remembers sitting outside the door while one man entered and sounds that a toddler did not understand filled the apartment for an hour before the man left and another one entered. "I'd be told to stay in one room and she'd bring a man into another. He'd stay for an hour, then leave. Soon, someone else would show up, and it would start again."[1] This existence only lasted about a year.

Sometimes his grandmother would try to care for the children in her senior citizen apartment residence, but she would have to keep them hidden. While their grandmother provided a much safer environment than the violence of the street that was the alternative, it was deemed a harmful situation for the children, and the Division of Youth and Family Services were called in to take them. A child being ripped away from his mother is a painful thing to imagine, and it left a deep scar on Maurice Torres' memory at the age of five. Big men yanked him out of his grandmother's apartment and his mother trailed after them screaming for her child. These men were cops taking Torres and his siblings away from the life they knew to an orphanage where they would at least have a roof over their heads and square meals. Torres did not understand what was happening to his family. "I remember I was frightened. Scared. I didn't know what was going on." He also remembered his mother's desperate plea. "The last thing I heard my mother say the day we were taken away is that she wanted us together," he said.[2]

Her cry motivated young Torres to strive to keep his brothers and sisters together. He bore the burden of looking out for them at age five. The Newark Division of Youth and Family Services protects children, but as with any system, it is inhibited by its resources and splitting brothers and sisters up is unfortunately common practice to accommodate the group home or foster parents capabilities. The family was initially split up and sent to different homes, but little Maurice fought for his mother's final cry and continued to petition the social workers to reunite his family. Soon, they were able to move three of the five into a Newark family's foster home. One sister was actually adopted and another sister was sent to live in another foster home, but three of them could be together. Life is tough in the foster system, and while the foster parents try to do the best they can, sometimes just providing for basic needs in a stable environment is all the kids need. "Our foster mother took good care of the three of us," said Torres. "Always made sure we had clean clothes and enough to eat."[3] Eventually, the Torres family was split up again. Maurice was sent to a group home.

He found happiness on the basketball court, showing off his moves to anyone that came by the group home. Reverend Brian Davis, a Baptist minister, was one of the frequent visitors providing food for the group home. He noticed Torres on the basketball court. "He told me that, when he came to visit, I would show off on the playground. He said he thinks I was marketing myself."[4] Davis was certainly sold on Torres. He reunited Maurice with his brother Andre and sister Shanta so they could live together once more. Davis already had four children, two adopted, but was more than welcoming to the Torres children when he brought them home in 1995. Maurice refers to Brian Davis as his father, although Davis' adoption of the three children was not final until 2004. Just one year later, Maurice was off playing basketball for Montclair State University in New Jersey, the first person to go to college in his family.

Maurice arrived on campus and immediately made an impact on the basketball court. In his first start for the Red Hawks, he scored 26 points and collected eight rebounds in a win against Staten Island.

His athletic career was impressive with an average of more than 12 points and four rebounds per game. He left his mark in school history with three school records for his tremendous three-point shot. Torres owns the best three-point field goal percentage for an individual game (.750), tied the school record for the most three pointers made in a game (8), and owns the single season record for the most three-point field goals (57). As a senior, Torres came off the bench to score 15 points in a half. "Mo's contributions to our team and program extend beyond basketball," said Montclair State head coach Ted Fiore. "His leadership and work ethic never go unnoticed and those qualities serve as an inspiration to his teammates and our staff."[5] Time management is one of the most daunting tasks any collegiate student-athlete undertakes. In his limited free time, Torres found a way to give back. He tutored middle school kids, volunteered for Habitat for Humanity, and served as the Student Athlete Advisory Committee President at Montclair State. Torres is a role model. He even participated in a project supported by the Center for Non-Violence and Prevention Programs at Montclair State University called the "Real Men of MSU" which produced a calendar of men who were willing to support women and speak out against violence against women. "Maurice is a great young man. His accomplishments are impressive, especially in light of his difficult early years," said Director of Athletics Holly Gera. "Maurice works hard, on and off the court, and we are extremely proud that he wears a Montclair State University uniform. It is our privilege to know him."[6]

Maurice Torres' early years might have been spent in a dark alley, but his future is bright because he has planned it that way. Torres has been honored for his accomplishments and story of personal courage both by Montclair State University Foundation when he received a Student Carpe Diem Award for his "Seize the Day" spirit and, of course, by the NCAS as a Courageous Student-Athlete. "Maurice is a young man of great character. He is always willing to give of himself to benefit others," said Tara Rienecker, Coordinator of Student Development for Athletes at Montclair. "This quality has transcended in his home life, to the basketball court, with his fellow student-athletes, and in the community. I am extremely excited he has been chosen to receive this prestigious award."[7] Maurice has been an exemplary student in finance and has participated in internships with Prudential Financial. He is not sure what his future holds, but he knows that this is just the beginning of a bright one. "Can't talk about endings because I think my life has just begun," he said.[8]

Notes

1. Deborah Cohen, "Student making the most of his shot," NJ.com Family & Kids, February 11, 2008, http://blog.nj.com/njv_bob_braun/2008/02/student_making_the_most_of_his.html, (accessed March 23, 2010).

2. Ibid.

3. Ibid.

4. Ibid.

5. New Jersey Athletic Conference, "Montclair State's Torres presented with the NCAS courageous athlete award," Men's Basketball, July 17, 2008, http://www.njacsports.com/news/2008/7/17/MSU's%20Torres%20Named%20Couragous%20Athlete.aspx, (accessed March 23, 2010).

6. Montclair State University, "Montclair State's Maurice Torres Named Recipient of Courageous Athlete Award by NCAS," January 25, 2008, https://www.montclair.edu/news/article.php?ArticleID=1851&ChannelID=10, (accessed March 23, 2010).

7. Ibid.

8. Deborah Cohen, "Student making the most of his shot," NJ.com Family & Kids, February 11, 2008, http://blog.nj.com/njv_bob_braun/2008/02/student_making_the_most_of_his.html, (accessed March 23, 2010).

Kyle Maynard

Hurdlers Overcoming Obstacles

by Stacy Martin-Tenney

"Kyle [Maynard] is one of the most amazing athletes that has ever lived," said Cliff Ramos, his high school wrestling coach.[1] Most people would not expect, nor believe, that quote to be attributed to a young man born a congenital amputee, but when they hear Kyle Maynard's story, they begin to understand Ramos' words. They soon become believers in Kyle Maynard's mantra of "No Excuses," also the title of his book chronicling his journey. Maynard wanted to be a championship athlete, but he also wanted to have a normal life despite the limitations that his amputations might pose.

Maynard was the first born child of parents Scott and Anita Maynard. The doctors don't know why Kyle faced congenital amputation, a condition that results from fibrous bands pinching off developing extremities by constricting the membrane. "I suppose at first we just focused a lot on his face. He was my blond-haired, blue-eyed angel," Anita said. "He was our first, so that was tough as it is. But you know, everything was a learning experience. For all of us."[2] Kyle quickly proved that he was only limited physically, and for whatever he lacked in physical ability, he would more than overcome with drive and his mental concentration. As a toddler he learned how to grip things with his biceps by watching other children use their thumb and finger. Soon, he was able to draw with crayons, and even refined his art skills after his mother instructed him that he should stay inside the lines. "He was tough. I remember as a little boy he would scribble all over the place," recalls Anita. "Until one day I told him you had to stay between the lines, and that was the

last time he ever colored outside the lines again."[3] It seemed like
Kyle only needed to be challenged to overcome something.

Maynard can use a cell phone, eat French fries, open medicine
packages, and type 50 words a minute. He was even an adoring and
irritating older brother to his three younger sisters. "I've never
thought of myself as being any different from anybody else," said
Maynard. "I didn't know anything different. When you're born a
certain way, things are normal to you. I was your normal two-year
old coloring outside the lines, but I progressed like any kid. People
were always trying to adapt things to fit me when I was younger, but
it never seemed to work. I knew I had limitations, but there wasn't
anything that was going to stop me or get in my way."[4]

"I looked up to my dad so much growing up. He was a wrestler and football player. He pushed me to do things and I wanted to
be just like him. My mother helped me socially. She always made
sure I was surrounded by a lot of friends and a well-dressed, well-
mannered kid."[5] When Kyle was in middle school he pressed his
parents to let him play football just like his dad had in school, and
he played, but he ended up with two broken feet. "I always told Kyle,
'Don't assume you can't do something,' but even so, football was
hard on him," said Scott. He decided to steer his aspiring son to his
other sport, wrestling. "In the end, wrestling was perfect, because
his opponents couldn't run from him."[6] Kyle found himself on the
wrestling mats, because it gave him confidence in his abilities. "I
don't know where I'd be without wrestling," Kyle said. "I love to
compete. I love to get physical. I love dominating someone like that.
I love to win. It's such a huge part of who I am."[7] As with any new
task, it was challenging to learn the skills and challenging to face
defeat when everyday he experiences new challenges. The first year
he lost 35 matches straight. Frustration set in. "I was getting worried," he said. "Because losing in combat like that is very tough on
the ego."[8]

He realized that he would have to create some of his own moves
to grapple with opponents. Through a lot of practicing with his father and Chuck Ramos, his dedicated high school wrestling coach,
Maynard became a wrestler. Not just any wrestler, but a hall of fame
wrestler. His speed and strength to weight ratio are credited for his
success on the mats, but he also delivers fierce moves like his sig-

nature "jawbreaker" where he holds his opponent's head in a vise grip between his two arms. Opponents began to tap on the mats in submission. Some appeared to tap out for other reasons, but they still tapped out which meant a win for Maynard. "I guess I freaked them out," said Maynard.[9] By his senior year, he helped his team to second place during the state championships, and had tallied a 35-16 win/loss record in individual matches. He was inducted into the Georgia State Wrestling Hall of Fame and presented with the Medal of Courage from the National Wrestling Hall of Fame. He was presented the ESPY award for Best Athlete with a Disability. He was not offered any scholarships to wrestle in college, but he did earn a spot on the University of Georgia club wrestling team. "Of course, we were proud of him for that," Anita said. "But we're just proud of him, period. Of the fact that he taught himself to eat on his own as a kid, and that now he's off in college and totally self-sufficient. He might inspire others now, but he's inspired us his whole life."[10]

He was just like any other college student with piles of laundry and ramen noodles littering his dorm room. He talks about girls, favorite songs, and comedians, and other aimless topics with his friends. Kyle puts others at ease about his disability through humor. The captain of the club team, Chris McDaniel, picked up a pair of long sweats lying on the mat and shouted to Kyle. "Hey, Kyle," McDaniel said, "These your warm-up pants?" Maynard shook his head "Ah, no, Chris. A bit too much leg room."[11] Maynard is so eager to be seen as "normal" in every way shape and form, that he will force you into thinking of him that way, whether you were ready to or not. "I really feel like I'm average," Maynard said. "But people seem to think otherwise. So, I'm reaching out."[12]

Unfortunately, the stares still happen when Maynard takes the mat in the collegiate club matches. Kyle took a loss against a three-time state champion, who pins other wrestlers in under a minute, and was so disappointed. That wrestler commented after the match, "That guy was tough . . . I knew I couldn't let him get my legs, or I'd be through. I'm very happy."[13] Kyle began to focus on the next match and how to improve, because to him there are "no excuses" for his performance.

Maynard wrote his book *No Excuses* while attending the University of Georgia so that he could share his inspirational stories with others. He has taken his circumstances in life, what some would consider a disability or handicap, and turned it into something positive in every arena he enters, school, wrestling, and the daily activities that we all take for granted. His story is one full of hope and promise and leaves his audience with a changed mindset about their own circumstances. If he can do it, then they can do it. After all, it only takes willpower and Kyle's motto is, "It's not what I can do but what I will do." There will be obstacles, but it only takes perseverance to overcome those obstacles. "There have been some major high points in my life, but there have been some major low points too—like losing the first 35 matches in a row when I started wrestling in sixth grade or playing football, and as the guys got bigger, finding myself on the bench more and more," Maynard continued. "It was hard to keep going, but I finally found my niche and fell in love with wrestling. I am at home on the wrestling mat."[14] Kyle seems to be at home speaking to wounded veterans, young athletes, or corporate gatherings. His story transcends across every walk of life. He continues to seek out new challenges and succeeds at more of them than someone with two legs, two arms, and twice his age.

Kyle left school temporarily to promote his book and pursue his motivational speaking career, but he also began to pursue his next challenge, mixed martial arts. Kyle was denied a license to fight by the Georgia Athletic and Entertainment Commission despite his training in jiu-jitsu and submission wrestling. "Kyle is very good," Paul Creighton, his trainer, a former UFC fighter himself said. "He submits a lot of guys. People wonder 'How does he do submissions?' Well, I can tell you, he's very proficient and he's very strong. He's a bull."[15] After being denied by Georgia, Maynard decided to fight in Alabama where mixed martial arts is not regulated. "It's the biggest misconception to think I can't strike," Maynard said. "It cracks me up how many people think that. I'm not going to be an Ernesto Hoost kickboxer, but I can strike."[16] Kyle made history again when he stepped into the cage at the Auburn Fight Night in Auburn, Alabama against a fully-able opponent. Maynard lost his debut fight, but he won yet another battle proving that he is capable of fighting or doing anything else he sets his mind to. "I wanted to win so bad, but it was still one of the best moments of my life."[17] A movie titled *A Fighting Chance* is being filmed to chronicle Maynard's story especially as it relates to him making history as the first quadruple amputee to enter a cage fight.

Maynard is not content making history or pushing himself past his limits, he wants to train others to be physically fit. He owns his own business, No Excuses CrossFit, in Suwanee, Georgia. Cross Fit is a specialty fitness center that does not focus on specialized training. "CrossFit started as a maverick gym in Santa Cruz, having become the principal strength and conditioning program for elite police forces, military special operations teams, champion martial artists, and Olympic athletes worldwide. It also does a great job of getting the average everyday Joe into spectacular shape."[18] Maynard is the President and Owner of No Excuses Cross Fit and continues to push himself and the athletes to new levels of fitness. He also owns a three-floor townhouse and continues to travel for speaking engagements. At age 23, he had accomplished more than most, and the only question is what will he do for his next challenge?

No matter what it is, his positive attitude and enthusiasm for life are sure to carry him through it. His passion and pursuit of excellence is catching. He credits his parents for his success. "My parents have been a huge driving force in my success," said Maynard. "I can't imagine being put in the situation they were put in when I was born. But my mom said she looked at my face the first time she saw me and knew things would be all right."[19] Things turned out more than all right for Kyle Maynard and most certainly will continue to turn out that way, because he will make it happen.

Notes

1. The Connecticut Forum, "Kyle Maynard," The Connecticut Forum, http://www.ctforum.org/popups/bio.asp?event_bio_image_id=3397, (accessed March 23, 2010).

2. Marco R. della Cava, "Wrestler's world is never limited by his disability," *USA Today*, November 18, 2004.

3. Ibid.

4. Bryan Bloodworth, "Ultimate determination No excuses in life for this wrestler," *The Pantagraph*, July 16, 2006.

5. Ibid.

6. Marco R. della Cava, "Wrestler's world is never limited by his disability," *USA Today*, November 18, 2004.

7. Ibid.

8. Ibid.

9. Ibid.

10. Ibid.

11. Ibid.

12. Ibid.

13. Ibid.

14. Bryan Bloodworth, "Ultimate determination No excuses in life for this wrestler," *The Pantagraph*, July 16, 2006.

15. Mike Chiappetta, "Amazing Maynard lives the MMA dream," Special to ESPN.com, April 24, 2009, http://sports.espn.go.com/extra/mma/news/story?id=40 93672, (accessed March 23, 2010).

16. Ibid.

17. "Amputee Kyle's fighting fit," *The Mirror* (London, England), April 30, 2009.

18. No Excuses CrossFit, "What is CrossFit?" December 10, 2009, http://www.noexcusescrossfit.com/?cat=38, (accessed March 23, 2010).

19. Bryan Bloodworth, "Ultimate determination No excuses in life for this wrestler," *The Pantagraph*, July 16, 2006.

Martel Van Zant

Hurdlers Overcoming Obstacles

by Stacy Martin-Tenney

Martel Van Zant was born deaf. He was born without eardrums, which doctors believe was a result of his mother suffering from chicken pox while she was pregnant. He strives to prove himself as an athlete, to define himself without his disability. "I'm a deaf athlete, but I don't want to be called a 'deaf athlete,'" he said through his interpreter Allie Lee. "I'm an athlete first."[1] Van Zant became one of the top high school football players in Texas and went on to play Division I-A football at Oklahoma State with the assistance of an interpreter. Yet he continues to fight misperceptions of his disability.

"A lot of people, they focus on that deaf side and they tell me 'Good job' and 'Congratulations' and that 'You're doing well for a deaf person,'" Van Zant said with the help of Lee. "You know, I understand that, because that's what a lot of the public sees and that's fine."[2] He wants to move past his disability quickly and he wants others to move past it too. His family never treated him like a deaf person, in fact they enrolled him in regular school after the second grade and he excelled. The only thing he struggled with was the treatment he received from others who thought that he was less intelligent than them. "I felt like I was just as equal as anyone else, just as capable," Van Zant said. "You know, people don't really think that I'm dumb, but some people tend to think that because I'm deaf I might lack a little bit in experience and intelligence. My family didn't treat me as a deaf person."[3]

Martel found a way to level the field through playing sports. Not only did he level it, he raised the bar for others. He was a standout athlete in soccer, basketball, and track before he even tried out for the football team in eighth grade. When he finished his career as a cornerback at Lee High School in Tyler, Texas, he had 21 interceptions. His performance should have made him a national recruit and did land him on the state's top 100-prospect list. It seems like his disability intimidated some of those top powerhouse football schools, but Oklahoma State, Texas A&M, TCU, SMU, Colorado, and Arizona called on Van Zant. Les Miles was the current OSU Coach at the time, and he had a deaf brother, so he was able to communicate with Martel through signing. "Some of the other schools, they were a little tentative on recruiting because it was their first experience with a deaf athlete or they just didn't know how to go about working with a deaf athlete," Van Zant said.[4]

Van Zant selected Oklahoma State, but Miles soon stepped onto the coaching carousel and became the head coach at Louisiana State University. Joe DeForest was Van Zant's secondary coach and knew he was an extremely talented player. Coach DeForest knew there were challenges ahead and a lot for Martel to prove on the playing field to the coaches and players. "Of course there's hesitation, but [it disappears quickly] once you realize that the kid has so much awareness and he wants so much to be good," DeForest said.[5] There would still be a communication barrier that Van Zant and Coach DeForest would need to overcome so that the plays could be called.

A heating and air conditioning technician by the name of Allie Lee heard of Van Zant signing with his Cowboys. Lee had been an OSU fan his whole life and immediately offered his services to the school when Van Zant joined the team. "It's like they say, 'It's kind of a dream job,'" Lee said. "There would be no other way for me to come in and work with this team like this."[6] His commitment is astounding, driving from Oklahoma City to Stillwater, a 132-mile round trip daily. Lee is by Van Zant's side during classes, team meetings, practices and, of course, games.

Calling plays in to Van Zant during the game required a lot of practice early on for Lee. He knew the basics of the game as a casual fan, but it was different in the heat of the moment during game time. Van Zant, Lee, and DeForest created a symbiotic relationship. "He had to understand football, football terms and the speed of the game and how quick you teach," DeForest said of Lee. "There's some slang involved in football and that's something we had to work through."[7] Based on the slang terms and the need for speed when calling plays on the field, Lee improvised and created slang signs for zone defense or cover two. During Van Zant's freshman year, there were some tense moments of learning. Lee confused kickoff return with punt coverage during practice one day. "It was a big learning experience for me," Lee said.[8] "I've learned a lot coaching Martel because it makes me kind of condense my thoughts and learn how to communicate with him in a non-slang way and really be precise with what I say to him," DeForest said.[9]

Martel still needed to communicate with his teammates. A benefit in our instant communication society is that everyone has a cell phone and can send text messages to communicate. So Van Zant uses text messaging to communicate with his roommates and many other teammates. Most of them had an interest in learning sign language, some have signed up for the American Sign Language class the university offers, while others just ask Van Zant to teach them the basics and some slang. "Now we can understand kind of more of what he's saying," Linebacker Roderick Johnson said after taking the university class. "But we don't understand fully what he's saying. We know a couple of signs that we can signal to him jokingly."[10] The team has figured out ways of communicating the things they need to on the field rather than yelling "ball" or a change in the play, they have found other ways to signal to Martel. "It's really cool the guys have made the effort to come up with signals to help Martel with a check or a change," Lee said. "It also helps them because he's teaching them to be more visual."[11]

Building that relationship with his coach and fellow players has surely helped him bridge the communication gaps on and off the field. It has built confidence in his play. Despite his learning curve, Martel Van Zant continued to excel on the football field. Roderick Johnson said, "Early on in his career it caused a little bit of confusion . . . [Now] he's perfect. He hardly makes any mistakes."[12] In 2006, the first full year of starting at corner, he finished fourth on the team in tackles, including 45 solo stops. He received an award from the Football Writers Association of America for courage.

Van Zant finished his collegiate career as a standout player and unfortunately suffered a dislocated ankle tendon late in the 2007 season. Maybe that was why he was not invited to the 2008 scouting combine for the NFL in Indianapolis. Maybe it was because he was deaf. Either way, Martel Van Zant is fearless and is certainly not afraid to prove himself to anyone. There have been two other deaf players in the NFL, former Cardinal Bonnie Sloan and ex-Bronco Kenny Walker. He and Allie Lee traveled to the combine anyway. "I'm just trying to let teams know I'm here and that my ankle is going to be all right," Van Zant said. "This, obviously, is all new to me, but teams are asking questions and I'm just trying to let them get to know me."[13] Van Zant wanted to prove that the communication barriers have long since been broken and that he and Lee are a team in sync. "If a team drafts Martel, they're also getting Allie," said Kelli Masters, Van Zant's agent.[14] Van Zant does not want to retrain another interpreter. Van Zant said, "Having to teach an interpreter and learning everything in the NFL would be really tough on me."[15] Alice Van Zant feels blessed to have Lee be an advocate for her son, "Having Allie Lee is basically like having a member of the family with him. Because he has Martel's best interests at heart and we love him for that. Everything about him is sincere. Some people are in it for whatever reasons, you know, fame or whatever. But he is very sincere."[16] Initial reviews from scouts were good. "Teams are talking to him and, hopefully, they're realizing, 'Hey, this guy is an athlete and he's no different than anybody else,'" Masters said.[17]

Tennessee called him out to practice, but Van Zant had lost considerable speed with his ankle injury and just wasn't ready yet. His opportunity to play came in the Arena Football League instead and it was still thrilling news for Van Zant when he was selected by the Manchester Wolves in 2009. "I made the team!" he texted, sending joy through a Blackberry. "I'm so grateful for the opportunity. I know I have the skills and the dedication. I'm ready for this."[18] Assistant head coach, Brian Hug, knew sign language because both of his parents were deaf. "I knew sign language before I knew how to speak," said Hug. "When we talked about bringing Martel in, I knew it would take work. But I also knew it would be worth it."[19]

Martel Van Zant has overcome a great deal to become a triumphant football player. He has inspired stadiums full of people to cheer him on even though he cannot really hear them. "I can't hear it, but yeah, I can feel it pounding," said Van Zant. "It's hard to explain. It's more like when you feel excitement. I feel every beat in my chest. It's so great."[20] He feels the vibration and sees the excitement of the crowd. Yet, they cheer louder for him than any other player. Many of the fans reach out to him through letters because of some hardship their children are going through or to simply tell him how motivating his story is to them. Van Zant strives to leave his disability behind every day, but for moments such as these, he relishes it because he is helping someone else. "All these kids that look up to me as a role model," Van Zant said. "I've received letters from all these kids, and when I went to the state fair the other night, I met some deaf kids out there who recognized me from TV. I think it's pretty cool."[21] Alice Van Zant is as proud as any other mother of all her son has accomplished. "He's always successful because he's overcome so much," Alice said. "Some people in similar circumstances are afraid. But watching Martel do it, it's like, 'why not me?'"[22] Martel plans to continue playing as long as he can, and would love to make an NFL team, but said that if he doesn't then he plans on coaching others. No matter his undertaking, Martel Van Zant's contribution will certainly be deafening.

Notes

1. Cory McCartney, "Loud and clear," SI.com, November 10, 2006, http://sportsil lustrated.cnn.com/2006/writers/the_bonus/11/08/van.zant/, (accessed March 23, 2010).

2. Ibid.

3. Ibid.

4. Ibid.

5. Ibid.

6. Ibid.

7. Ibid.

8. Ibid.

9. Ibid.

10. Ibid.

11. Mike Baldwin, "Part of the family: Interpreter Allie Lee has become the right-hand man for Oklahoma State cornerback Martel Van Zant," *The Daily Oklahoman*, October 1, 2006.

12. Cory McCartney, "Loud and clear," SI.com, November 10, 2006, http://sports illustrated.cnn.com/2006/writers/the_bonus/11/08/van.zant/, (accessed March 23, 2010).

13. Pat Yasinskas, "For Van Zant, it's more than just the injury issue," ESPN.com, February 21, 2008, http://sports.espn.go.com/nfl/draft08/columns/story?columnist=ya sinskas_pat&id=3257497, (accessed March 23, 2010).

14. Ibid.

15. Cory McCartney, "Loud and clear," SI.com, November 10, 2006, http://sports illustrated.cnn.com/2006/writers/the_bonus/11/08/van.zant/, (accessed March 23, 2010).

16. Ibid., McCartney.

17. Pat Yasinskas, "For Van Zant, it's more than just the injury issue," ESPN.com, February 21, 2008, http://sports.espn.go.com/nfl/draft08/columns/story?columnist=ya sinskas_pat&id=3257497, (accessed March 23, 2010).

18. Lesley Visser, "However it's delivered, good news for cornerback Van Zant," http://www.cbssports.com/cbssports/story/11540408

19. Ibid.

20. Stan Grossfield, "Deafness is no obstacle for Arena Football player," *The Boston Globe*, June 2, 2009.

21. Cory McCartney, "Loud and clear," SI.com, November 10, 2006, http://sports illustrated.cnn.com/2006/writers/the_bonus/11/08/van.zant/, (accessed March 23, 2010).

22. Jeffrey Rake , "Cowboys' Van Zant inspires on and off the football field," *The Topeka Capital-Journal*, October 18, 2007.

Charlie Wilks

Hurdlers Overcoming Obstacles

by Jessica Bartter Duffaut

Growing up in Emporia, Kansas, there wasn't much for Charlie Wilks to do other than play football. Wilks brings new meaning to the term "blind side" in football. He said, "I play football with the four senses I have left to me. One quality sets me apart; I can't see."[1]

Oftentimes, Wilks is asked "How do you do it?" His answer is simple and involves something many of us take for granted and do very passively: listening. "I'm listening to the quarterback say 'down, set, hike.' Then the middle linebacker, he'll yell 'go.'"[2]

Charlie Wilks was born June 5, 1995 with sight. At about five years old, his mother noticed his sight seemed to be deteriorating. Doctors discovered Wilks had a brain tumor. The tumor expanded to the size of an orange, crushing his optical nerve, thus detaching the connection from his brain to his eyes.

He underwent three surgeries to remove the tumor, while his sight continued to deteriorate and he was suffering a seemingly constant migraine. After the surgeries were complete, the tumor was gone, but so was Wilks' vision. However, his vision for the future, figuratively, was as strong as ever. During his treatment in the hospital, Wilks established a friendly rapport with a young man who had been in a skiing accident and suffered severe brain trauma. On Charlie's last day of therapy, as he was leaving the hospital, he went out of his way to tell his new friend to never give up. He was just six years old.

Wilks grew up very closely with his grandfather, Al Reynolds, who played in the very first Super Bowl with the Kansas City Chiefs. Reynolds had an eight-year career in the NFL and shared his passion for football with his grandson. They would watch games together, Charlie listening intently and learning with every hike of the ball. And Reynolds had loads of stories of "the good ol' days" to recite to his grandson.

Charlie even remembers seeing football before he lost his sight. Just like many other kids, he thought, "Hey, those people are hitting each other. I want to do it."[3] Charlie asked his mom if he could play football. Understandably, her hesitation came from concern for his safety. But she was determined to give her son a normal life. Besides, Charlie took the liberty of asking the coaches of the seventh grade team if he could try out. Their welcoming response gave his mom little choice. Like every other kid on his team, Charlie earned his spot. He was deemed a defensive lineman of his middle school team. His coaches recognized his competitiveness and passion for the game instantly. And they couldn't argue with his size. At 14 years old, Wilks was 5-foot-10 and 185 pounds. His nickname on the field is "The Beast." While it may not sound endearing, Wilks is proud of his nickname because of all the work he has had to put in to earn it. Some opponents would never know Wilks cannot see them unless they are told. And those who do know often hold back, afraid to rough up the blind kid. Until, that is, he hits them once. One hit is all it takes for them to realize The Beast is for real. He suggests his opponents show him no mercy because he hits hard and has no plans to show mercy for anyone else.

Wilks tried out for and made the freshman team at his high school in 2009. He played nose guard for the Emporia High squad. Charlie admits, "There have been times when I've tackled my own teammates on accident."[4] And he won't deny that his hearing is so keen he can't help but overhear the play from the opponents huddle every now and then. Just like any other team, Charlie's team's success comes from the way they work together. Teammates help line him up for each play and guide him back to the huddle when needed. They may tap him on the leg or call to him for assistance. And he helps them right back, trying to break up the plays, and block the center, all in hopes of sacking the quarterback—a feat Charlie can proudly say he has accomplished.

Wilks uses a special device to read and write. His sense of humor is vibrant and his attitude is brilliant. While he won't hesitate to crack a blind joke, he acknowledges the value in someone like him stepping on the field. "It's not every day," he said, "that a sighted person can look at a blind person and say 'they're doing it, so he can do it.'"[5]

Charlie's talent is not limited to the football field. He is musically gifted and plays the guitar, saxophone, and keyboard. He is also learning Braille music. He enjoys track and field and was a long distance runner in the eighth grade. As a freshman in high school, his events included shot put and long jump. Wilks also has a passion for hunting and, with his grandfather's help, was able to get two deer in his first two years of hunting. The ever-outdoorsman, Wilks also loves to fish and once caught a 28-pound king salmon in Alaska. Wilks is only a freshman in high school but has already planned to double major in engineering and music in college.[6]

Remarkably, Wilks is not scared of much, but he admits, "I think my biggest fear would be getting my sight back. Once you go blind, you start imagining the world as this perfect place. Getting your sight back and seeing how imperfect it is, crushes some blind people. To be honest, getting my sight back would be like another low point in my life."[7] I wish we could all have the perfect world Charlie sees.

Wilks doesn't just play football for the love of the game. He recognizes his ability to show others their own abilities. He said, "I want people to remember that disabilities aren't things that get in your way. If you use them right, disabilities can be your greatest ability. It's like if you imagine a disability as a crutch, don't use the disability as a crutch, you should use the disability as a leg and start running."[8] Charlie Wilks was just 14 when he spoke these words well beyond his years in wisdom. He is obviously off and running. Let's try to keep up.

Notes

1. Charlie Wilks, E:60 "Blindside" Video, ESPN.com, November 10, 2009.
2. Ibid.
3. Ibid.
4. Ibid.
5. Ibid.
6. Jennifer Cunningham, email to author, April 8, 2010.
7. Ibid.
8. Ben Houser, "Blind football player listens, learns," ESPN.com E:60, November 10, 2009.

Aaron Fotheringham

Hurdlers Overcoming Obstacles

by Jessica Bartter Duffaut

Courtesy of Hardcore Sitting, LLC.

Don't call it wheelchair skating. That's not what Aaron Fotheringham does. He named it "hardcore sitting" and now calls it Wheelchair Moto X. And he can do that because he pretty much invented it.

Aaron "Wheelz" Fotheringham is an 18-year-old extreme sport athlete. Because he was born with spina bifida, he is confined to a wheelchair. Spina bifida is a neural tube defect that happens in the first month of pregnancy when the spinal column doesn't close completely which can cause fluid on the brain, partial paralysis, bladder and bowel control difficulties, learning disabilities, depression and other issues. While spina bifida affects each patient differently, it has left Fotheringham unable to walk. When he was just three years old, doctors suggested his parents buy him a wheelchair. But the wheelchair sat in the corner of his room for years while Aaron preferred braces and crutches to get around. He was fond of his wheelchair only when his friends or siblings went bike riding and the chair helped him keep up. At eight years old, after his third painful hip operation, Fotheringham starting using the wheelchair full time. But that hasn't stopped him from dropping in on skate ramps daily.

Fotheringham is surrounded by skateboards and bikes but his apparatus stands out. Fotheringham is in a "tricked out" wheelchair. And he isn't at a special skate park; it's just your run of the mill ramps. His custom wheelchair is built "with welded braces, joints and crossbeams to take a pounding, a scrape bar, shock absorbers and independent four-wheel suspension, and soldered spokes on modified 26-inch downhill mountain bike wheels."[1] This chair enables Fotheringham to replicate what he sees done by the BMX riders and skateboarders around him. He does similar stationary spins and can grind the edge with the wheels of his chair. Don't forget to add power-sliding, carving, handplants, wheelers, and rollouts to his list of tricks. Fotheringham is revolutionary, too. Without being able to watch and learn from other "hardcore sitters," Fotheringham literally jumped at the chance to invent his own moves and tricks. While attending an action sports summer camp, Fotheringham practiced a back flip into a bin of foam 50 or 60 times before attempting it on the regular ramp. He tried at least 15 more before landing it successfully. On July 13, 2006, at age 14, Aaron Fotheringham was the first person to land a back flip in a wheelchair. The feat was captured on a video camera and made Fotheringham an international Internet sensation, but it did not come without some bruises and scratches.

On October 25, 2008, Guinness World Records came to Aaron Fotheringham hoping to put him and his back flip in the record books. They traveled to his hometown of Las Vegas, Nevada to witness Fotheringham's invention. He had successfully landed the back flip dozens of times since his first in 2006, and had the video footage to prove it, but Guinness World Records made it official. His unofficial record for consecutive back flips is six in a row. Completing a single flip takes great precision and monitoring of his speed. Unlike skateboards or bikers, Fotheringham cannot gain speed by pedaling or kicking after he drops down the ramp. If Fotheringham were to reach down and try to speed up his wheels, he would actually cause the opposite effect to his chair. But the wrong speed can cause a catastrophic under- or over-rotation of his wheelchair during the flip. He also doesn't have the liberty of flexing his body in the air to manipulate his jump or speed. In addition, unlike skaters or bikers, Fotheringham is strapped into his chair, adding to the nastiness of his spill when he doesn't land the back flip or any other trick. But Aaron doesn't let bad landings stop him. "Sometimes he makes it, sometimes he overshoots and gets a little roughed up," but Fotheringham "gets right back up and goes for it again."[2] And thankfully, he wears a dirt bike helmet and elbow pads.

Fotheringham has come a long way. It all started with encouragement from his older brother, Brian. Brian and Aaron are two of the six adopted children in their family to Steve and Kaylene Fotheringham. When Aaron was eight, he accompanied Brian and their father to the skate park. Brian would bike and Aaron would watch. After a few weeks of this routine, Brian suggested Aaron drop in a quarter pipe for himself, rather than watch Brian from outside the park's fence. Aaron was a bit nervous but glad to be included in his older brother's activities so he didn't hesitate long. As one might expect, Aaron fell almost instantly. But as anyone who knows Aaron might expect, he got right back up and tried it again. Aaron was hooked and within a year, he started competing. He has added a few BMX freestyle competition titles to his list of accomplishments including an appearance in the 2005 Vegas AmJam BMX finals. For Aaron, the championships are "secondary to the joy of riding and hanging out with friends at the skate parks."3

Courtesy of Hardcore Sitting, LLC.

Fotheringham can be found at his hometown skate park in Las Vegas almost every day that he isn't on the road. This teenager is in high demand around the world and is often traveling for appearances and performances. With the assistance of his mother, he has traveled the world inspiring others, some in wheelchairs, most not. Fotheringham has been requested at many summer camps for disabled children serving as a coach and mentor. Most kids consider him a friend. Fotheringham finds great joy in "showing young kids with disabilities that a wheelchair can be a toy, not a restriction."4

To ensure wheelchairs maximize their functionality, Fotheringham has taken great pride in participating in their construction. Since he was 12, he has been sponsored by and worked with Colours in Motion, Inc., a wheelchair manufacturer that specializes in sport chairs and chairs for children. Together, they have been conceptualizing, building, and test-running countless prototypes. Before Aaron can find something that needs tweaking, he usually wrecks the chair first. Imagine the toll his body takes, if the chair he's strapped to needs replacing every year. He is "currently learning how to build wheelchairs so they hold up to what [he's] doing," and plans to "build Wheelchair Moto X chairs for other people" in the future.[5]

Fotheringham took part in the adaptive sports demo of X Games XIV and XV in 2009 and 2010. The X Games are a biannual (summer and winter) event competition covered by ESPN that features extreme action sports. In 2010, Fotheringham was requested at the Vancouver Paralympics to perform his trademark back flip in the Winter Games' opening ceremony. Of the experience, he said, "It was a lot of stress, but it was like a dream come true!"

When asked what is important for people to know about him, Aaron said, "If there's anything I could say, it is that I am not *in* a wheelchair, I'm *on* it."[6] Aaron Fotheringham may not win an X Games competition or a world championship but his success is measured differently. Fotheringham is successfully changing "the world's perception of people in wheelchairs."[7] Most importantly, he has fun doing it!

Notes

1. Ken Ritter, "Teen takes wheelchair to the extreme: He's known for his 'hard core sitting,' back flips, stunts," *The Dessert News*, March 5, 2007.

2. Karina Hamalainen, "Wheelchair wheelies: a Las Vegas teen breaks skate-park records—in a wheelchair," *Science World*, April 6, 2009.

3. Aaron "Wheelz" Fotheringham, "Bio," AaronFotheringham.com, http://www.aaronfotheringham.com/bio/, (accessed April 5, 2010).

4. Ibid.

5. Aaron Fotheringham, email to author, April 12, 2010.

6. Ibid.

7. Aaron "Wheelz" Fotheringham, "Bio," AaronFotheringham.com, http://www.aaronfotheringham.com/bio/, (accessed April 5, 2010).

6

CREATING A BETTER WORLD

by Richard Lapchick

There are individuals whose names may not resonate in a huge way in the world of sport but whose lives are filled with acts that help create a better world. This section includes 14 such people who dedicated a significant part of their lives to *Creating a Better World*.

Dirceu Hurtado inspired his fellow students when he returned from a life-threatening brain aneurysm to rejoin his teammates on the soccer team at Fairleigh Dickinson.

Destiny Woodbury had her family ripped apart as a six-year old. Determined to keep them together, she virtually became the mother of her younger siblings. Confronted with high crime and drugs among her peers, she chose to enroll in after-school programs to stay safe. She developed into such a great athlete that she was representing the University of Rhode Island in track and field when she won her award. Despite a childhood marked by poverty, her mother's drug addiction, and her father's absence, Destiny Woodbury grew up and became an outstanding athlete and woman.

Stacy Sines was a collegiate swimmer who had an aneurysm in the wall between the upper chambers of her heart. While waiting to get permission to return to the pool, she helped others who had medical problems and became their hero. Stacy has become known for her character and compassion as much as her swimming abilities.

Jennifer McClain followed so many athletes before her who defied the odds by refusing to let a birth defect define her life. Born with spina bifida, she endured seven intensive surgeries in her first 22 years. While at Quinnipiac College, she was on the volleyball team and was a dean's list student.

In his teenage years Lawrence Wright did not know if he would end up in jail, dead, or on an NFL team. By the time he was 18, he decided to move in the direction that would help him at the University of Florida to succeed academically and athletically. By the time he did succeed, he created the "Right Trak" program to help bring others along with him academically and socially.

Dr. Lonise Bias suffered the tragic death of her two children, both outstanding basketball players, and has committed to spend the rest of her life crusading against drugs and violence. The death of Len Bias in 1986, the number one draft choice of the Boston Celtics, made America realize that cocaine was not a recreational drug but a lethal one. Dr. Bias has driven that home to audiences for over two decades since her tragic loss.

Alfreda Harris, a legendary figure in Boston, has helped young girls become women through sport. Say her name in Boston and you see inspired faces react to the greatness that she has been able to achieve for other people.

After Maggie Maloy was a victim of a horrible assault followed by a terrible accident, her body seemed to crumble. Yet she was able to come back to school and compete in cross country. She enrolled at Defiance College, almost as a statement that she was defying all of the odds and would succeed. Her courage overcoming all of the physical problems has inspired many others around the nation to overcome their hardships.

Jodi Norton, a diver who proved her greatness as a high school All-American, had critical health issues and injuries that could have ended her career. But she persevered and became a champion diver at Columbia University. Diagnosed in 1994 with Lupus, Jodi hasn't let that stop her. She created the L.I.F.E. Foundation which supports other people who have Lupus to be able to continue their college education.

Bob Hurley Sr. has had an extraordinary record as a high school basketball coach in New Jersey. Hurley has taken children from the inner-cities and insisted they become students while becoming fine athletes. Discipline and academics became part of the successful formula that helped so many people overcome the odds on his teams and go on to college and productive lives.

Tanya Hughes-Jones became the NCAA's Woman of the Year in 1994 after a great career as a high jumper. She became America's top high jumper in 1992 and 1993 and represented the United States in the Barcelona Olympics when she was only 22. Of particular note is the role model status that she created for other athletes around her as an Academic All-American, as someone who became successful in the business world and as a mother. She recently joined the ministry with her husband.

Michele Leary suffered a heart attack as a junior swimming for UMass, Amherst in 1988. She has used her own medical experiences to drive her career as a physician now caring for the needs of others.

Danny Wuerffel, a Heisman Trophy winner from the University of Florida, also found his calling in the ministry and established Desire Street Ministries working to better impoverished neighborhoods through spiritual and community development.

Dick Hoyt has allowed his son to compete in over 1,000 races despite the fact that he was born a spastic quadriplegic with cerebral palsy, Dick has pushed, pulled and towed his son across every finish line. They have competed in triathlons, marathons, 5Ks, and everything in between. Team Hoyt has been going strong for over 30 years with no sign of slowing down, despite the fact that Dick is approaching 70 years old.

Each selfless athlete in this chapter has taken the lessons they've learned in competitions to build their best game plan to better the lives of others.

Dirceu Hurtado

Creating a Better World

by Jessica Bartter Duffaut

Described by his coach as "magical"[1] on the field for his soccer prowess, Dirceu Hurtado is more like a miracle off the field. A standout soccer player in high school, this Peruvian native set the state record in New Jersey with 73 goals scored in his three-year varsity career, during which he also earned All-Conference, All-County, and All-State honors every year. Highly recruited for obvious reasons, Hurtado committed to Fairleigh Dickinson University (FDU) in Teaneck, New Jersey because they shared his commitment to academics and agreed to let him take off his freshman soccer season to focus solely on his grades.

After a full year of making the adjustments most college freshman face, and working hard in the classroom, Hurtado was looking forward to starting his soccer career as a Knight at Fairleigh Dickinson. But his career almost ended before it began. While home alone on June 3, 1999, Hurtado suffered such a severe headache that he called 911. When the rescue crew arrived, they found Hurtado unconscious and rushed him to the hospital. There he underwent surgery to relieve the pressure on his brain that an aneurysm left when a blood vessel burst. For one long agonizing month, Hurtado's parents sat by his side in the hospital while his condition left him in a coma. His father left his job to care for their eldest son but was reassured by the support Hurtado's team pledged. His coach, Seth Roland, guaranteed his scholarship regardless of whether or not he played and his teammates organized a fundraiser to assist with the medical bills. Though doctors tried to warn his parents that Hurtado may not survive, to no one's surprise, he awoke from his coma.[2]

Upon waking up, he recognized those of whom were there in support, his coach, teammates, roommates, and family, but had trouble talking to them and couldn't move his right side. After undergoing another surgery to drain fluid from his lungs caused by pneumonia, Hurtado faced months of therapy learning how to walk, talk, and write again. This former soccer star's coordination was problematic, to say the least. His father, a former member of the Peruvian National Soccer Team, thought soccer would be Hurtado's best therapy. But what had brought him so much joy for years, was painful and frustrating. The realization that what used to come naturally now needed so much work was crushing to Hurtado's spirit. Hurtado recalled, "I couldn't talk too much. I saw everybody. I wanted to talk to them. I wanted to walk and I just kept falling and falling. I was like a little kid."[3]

For one long agonizing year, Hurtado steadily improved his daily functions and his coordination. Had it not been for his family and friends, soccer may have been a thing of the past. Fortunately for his teammates, Hurtado returned as strong as ever. In Fairleigh Dickinson University's season opener in 2000, Hurtado made his debut, scoring a goal on his team's way to a 3-1 victory. His magic continued as he scored two goals in each of the next two games. Early on, he led the Northeast Conference (NEC) in goals and was tied for the lead in assists, proving his ability on the field, but more importantly, his desire to persevere.[4]

With Hurtado healthy, the FDU Knights began rewriting history on the field. The 2000 season saw NEC regular-season and tournament titles. Hurtado's team was headed to the post-season for the first time since 1989, after 11 NCAA Tournament appearances from 1963 to 1989.

The Knights got a taste of victory and success that drove them to improve the next season. They also had to succumb to another dose of tragedy as Coach Roland's wife died of brain cancer shortly after Hurtado's recovery. The Knights drew on their loss as a source of motivation.

The inspiration of Marjorie Roland's memory and spirit helped lead the Knights to their second straight regular-season league title in 2001. In the conference tournament, FDU played the University of Maryland, Baltimore for the crown. The game became the longest in NEC Men's Soccer Tournament history as the "epic physical battle"[5] lasted 142 minutes. With deep-rooted motivation on their side, the Knights were victorious, clinching the NEC tournament and a spot in the NCAA Tournament.

The epic battle of the conference tournament led to several more epic battles in NCAA play. In the first round, FDU faced Boston College and after a scoreless regulation, finally scored in the third overtime to end Boston College's season. The second round brought No.

12 Princeton to FDU. Though FDU had lost to Princeton earlier in the season, the Knights refused a repeat outcome and beat the higher-ranked squad 2-1. The FDU victory sent the team to the Sweet 16 where they faced the favored Seton Hall, another team to which the Knights had suffered an earlier season loss. Winning 1-0 secured the Knights a spot in what was called "The David against Goliath quarterfinal showdown"[6] against the University of North Carolina, Chapel Hill. After FDU lost their lead in the 77th minute, they were awarded a penalty kick with 31 seconds left in regulation. Hurtado was chosen for the important kick, one that would no doubt seal the fate of the game. Drew Brown, Director of Athletic Communications of FDU said, "Cool as ice, he buried it in the back of the net to send the game into overtime."[7] Eventually, in the third overtime, the Knights lost and ended their storied season. Yet, their success against the eventual-champions did not go unnoticed and the FDU squad finished 11th in the final national poll for 2001.

Hurtado was an offensive force to be reckoned with, and never thought twice when distributing the ball among his teammates. The metal plate in his head did make Hurtado hesitate when heading the ball. He had to learn how to head the ball correctly so as to not affect the protective plate, and he learned to be wary of jumping in the air and challenging opponents—a battle he never forfeited before.

Hurtado completed his first collegiate season with first team All-Conference and Mid-Atlantic Region accolades, was named Most Valuable Player of the Northeast Conference Championships and Rookie of the Year by the conference. He led his team with 43 points, 17 goals—five of which were game-winning—and nine assists. His scoring average of 2.05 per game was 15th in the nation in 2000. With no doubt about his resolve, Hurtado was named Comeback Player of the Year by the New Jersey Sports Writers Association and was awarded the Eastern College Athletic Conference's Award of Valor. In 2001, he finished second on the team with 27 points on 10 goals—four of which were game-winning—and seven assists. In 2004, Hurtado graduated from FDU with a bachelor's degree in individualized studies.

Hurtado's return from a life-threatening brain aneurysm inspired fellow student-athletes, particularly his little brother, Victor Giovanny, who followed in his big brother's footsteps to FDU soccer. Hurtado's teammates appreciated his presence as they felt they played their best with him on the field as he pushed everyone to the top of their game. His coach was continually amazed by his magic feet and spectacular moves and his parents couldn't have been more proud. However, it is what Hurtado has accomplished off the field that has made him a true inspiration as a human being, a student, an athlete, a teammate, a brother, a son, and a friend.

Notes

1. Gregory Schutta, "Heads Up!" *The Record*, September 21, 2000.

2. Ibid.

3. Ibid.

4. Ibid.

5. Drew Brown, "Getting their kicks while heading to the ball: Soccer team enjoys 'Cinderella' season," FDU Magazine Online, Spring 2002, www.fdu.edu/news pubs/magazine/02sp/soccer.html, (accessed January 28, 2010).

6. Ibid.

7. Ibid.

Destiny Woodbury

Creating a Better World

by Jessica Bartter Duffaut

As she and her younger brother and sister were being taken from their mother by the Department of Children, Youth, and Families, the bright six-year old held on to the hope that they would once again be a happy family. Even at that young age, Destiny Woodbury was a mother to her siblings, and viewed her own mother more as a big sister figure who was fun to be with—when she was around. Forced into a lifestyle demanding maturity, Woodbury graciously accepted the responsibility without hesitation. Upon returning home from school each day, Woodbury fed her toddler brother with baby cereal, the only food in the house, and gave her infant sister a bottle of milk. She took it upon herself to ensure that she and her siblings were fed and cleansed; not a typical lifestyle for a six-year old, but certainly one that Woodbury was good at. Woodbury picked up on the fact that her mother was using the family's food money to buy drugs and other substances for herself, some days forcing her three young children to go without any food at all.

Remarkably, Woodbury acknowledged that her family was living in poverty because of the daily choices her mother was making. Woodbury decided she could make a better choice for herself and her siblings, and asked her grandmother if they could move in with her because of the lack of food and care they were receiving from their mother. Woodbury's grandmother, Ella Mae, was shocked to learn that her daughter was still addicted to drugs and knew the circumstances must be rough for a six-year old to want to move out. Perhaps Woodbury derived her courage from her grandmother, because in exceptionally courageous fashion Ella Mae called a social worker in on her own daughter. The social worker contacted the Department of Children, Youth and Families and within two days of Destiny's request, she and her siblings were removed from their mother's home.

Between Woodbury and her two siblings, there were three different fathers, none of whom offered support. Ella Mae, who was working nights, was faced with the decision to raise her grandchildren or continue working. In Ella Mae's mind there was no question of what to do, and she quickly quit her job. In addition to the new challenge of raising three young children, Ella Mae was faced with supporting the family off her nominal savings and a monthly $820 check from the state. After two years of making ends meet, Ella Mae was awakened by fire fighters, and gas and electric company employees, who informed her that the building she called home was being condemned. After a few days in a hotel, Ella Mae and her grandchildren moved to a shelter, where they stayed for two and a half months. After living with Ella Mae's sister and her five children for a brief period things began to look up when Ella Mae got an apartment—the same apartment where she resides today, establishing a stable home environment for her grandchildren.

Woodbury and her brother and sister saw their mother occasionally throughout the years, usually around birthdays and holidays. At times she appeared to have cleaned up her act, looking healthy with a new place to live, and in turn, rekindling Woodbury's dream to have her back in their lives. But Woodbury's dream was dashed as her mother lost her battle with drug addiction and overdosed in July 1998, the summer before Woodbury entered high school. Though she would never see her mother again, Woodbury was determined to fulfill the rest of her dreams.[1]

Woodbury knew her future would be determined by the choices she made then, so she enrolled in several after school programs, choosing to stay off the streets and away from drugs. Woodbury was active in Unified Sistas, Youth Talking 2 Youth, Teen Institute, Children's Crusade, and America's Promise, and joined the cross country, and indoor and outdoor track and field teams. In high school, Woodbury discovered two of her passions—running and chemistry, both of which helped her achieve her dream of attending college. Woodbury's grandmother had not made it past the eighth grade and her mother never graduated from high school, so Woodbury wanted to be the first in her family to attend college and, in the process, show her brother and sister that they were capable of the same success. Woodbury worked hard for years, not only for herself but to inspire her siblings and even challenge them to do better. Both her brother and her sister learned from their fearless leader and earned such good grades that they received the opportunity to attend private high schools.

Woodbury attended the University of Rhode Island (URI) and worked hard to represent URI as an athlete and to succeed as a student. As a sophomore she anchored URI's 4×400-meter relay squad to indoor and outdoor Atlantic-10 Conference Championships as well as an indoor New England Championship. Woodbury and her teammates set indoor and outdoor school and Atlantic-10 records. She broke records in the 400 meters and 4×400 relay indoor events and records in the 400 meters, 4×400 relay, 4×100 relay, and the sprint medley relay events of outdoor track. As of 2010, all still stand except one.[2] Woodbury also worked hard to maintain her grades and was—and still is—committed to the community. She even made a presentation to the school board in her former community when they threatened to cut funding for her high school's cross country team. By impressively telling her story and the impact sports had on her life, the cross country team was saved.

As a member of URI's Student-Athlete Advisory Committee, Woodbury represented her fellow student-athletes at the NCAA Leadership Conference in 2004. Her leadership skills continued to flourish and over the holidays, Woodbury organized her team's sponsorship of three different families. She was instrumental in organizing the families' needs and the food and gift drives with her teammates.

Woodbury graduated in 2007 with a bachelor of science and a bachelor of arts in Chemistry, as well as a bachelor of arts in Secondary Education and a minor in Leadership. She was named to the Atlantic-10 Conference Commissioners Honor Roll twice. She won the Victor J. Baxt Scholarship and earned a summer internship at the chemistry lab of Teknor Apex.

Just before graduation, Woodbury attended a job fair on campus. She was interested in teaching in a low-income area and wanted a job that she could juggle with her continued athletic training. Teach for America presented the perfect opportunity. Teach for America seeks to "eliminate educational inequity by enlisting our nation's most promising future leaders in the effort."[3] They recruit "outstanding recent college graduates from all backgrounds and career interests to commit to teach for two years in urban and rural public schools."[4] Woodbury found her calling and was accepted at a school in Houston, Texas in the summer of 2007 and taught eighth grade until 2009. Woodbury has fallen in love with teaching and has remained at the school beyond her Teach for America requirements in order to teach sixth grade. The effervescent role model to her students also never stopped setting an example for her siblings. Her younger sister, Jasmin, is currently a nursing student at the University of Rhode Island.[5]

Being a student-athlete seems easy in comparison to Woodbury's daily functions today. The hands-on teacher leaves work and heads to the track for her own athletic training as she hopes to qualify for the 2012 London Olympics. With the absence of a cafeteria and dorm, Woodbury juggles the real world—her job, cooking, cleaning, mortgage payment, and other bills—with her running. But she wouldn't have it any other way.[6]

Despite a childhood marked with poverty, scarred by drug abuse, and the absence of a father, Destiny Woodbury faced life squarely and triumphed over the adversities she faced. Every time she accomplishes a goal or a dream, she wonders how it can help those around her, especially her family. This courageous student-athlete has lived through fearful times and seen fearful sights, but in the end, has emerged fearless.

Notes

1. Atlantic 10 Conference Outdoor Track and Field, "Destiny Woodbury Named Recipient Of 2005 Giant Steps Award," Atlantic 10 Conference, http://www.atlantic 10.com/sports/c-otrack/spec-rel/041205aaa.html, (accessed January 27, 2010).

2. Destiny Woodbury, interview with the author, February 25, 2010.

3. Teach for America: What We Do, "Our Mission and Approach," Teach for America, http://www.teachforamerica.org/mission/mission_and_approach.htm, (accessed January 27, 2010).

4. Ibid.

5. Destiny Woodbury, interview with the author, February 17, 2010.

6. Ibid.

Stacy Sines

Creating a Better World

by Jessica Bartter Duffaut

Stacy Sines, some would say, has a heart of gold. Medical professionals were forced to disagree when they found an aneurysm in the wall between the upper chambers of her heart. This was not the first time Stacy had faced physical adversity, and it would not be the last. But it was the most serious and challenging thus far.

Sines began her collegiate swimming career in 1999 at Washington College in Chestertown, Maryland. During her freshman year, Sines was hospitalized for two weeks with a pulmonary embolism, a blood clot on her lung. It was revealed that Sines suffered from Factor V Lieden, a condition that causes blood clots to form quickly.

Sines was crushed when she was told by her doctor that she could no longer train, and that she would most likely miss the remainder of her freshman season. Determined to contribute to her team, Sines hunted for a second opinion, where she received permission to train, but in moderation. It was a matter of days before Sines was training at full capacity and amazingly, in just four weeks she competed in her first Centennial Conference Championship where she swam five personal bests, earning five medals.

Sines' renewed appreciation for life and swimming carried her to success as a sophomore. Though she was constantly monitoring her physical condition, her sophomore season would later prove to be her only healthy one. She returned to the Conference Championships and took the crown, earning her a spot at the NCAA Division III Championships, where she place 2nd in the 200-yard freestyle and 14th in the 500-yard freestyle, earning All-American honors.

A shoulder injury slowed Sines her junior year, but did not stop her. An ultrasound on her injury revealed an aneurysm in her heart. Her coach broke the news to her and ordered her out of the pool. Reluctantly, Sines sat on the bench, but soon earned medical clearance once again, getting back into the pool within just 10 days. Not missing a beat, Sines returned to the Conference Championships for the third straight year and won two individual events and one relay, earning three gold medals. Sines placed 14th at the NCAA Division III Championships in the 200-yard freestyle. Sines was now a two-time All-American.

All the accolades Sines enjoyed her junior season came amidst the mental agony of her health. Sines, her family, and her trusted team of medical professionals were constantly performing tests to determine her best medical options. A transesophageal echocardiogram allowed doctors to view the internal structures of the heart and its major vessels. Cardiologists discovered Sines had abnormal holes in the wall between the heart's upper chambers, an atrial septal defect (ASD), which increases flow to the right ventricle and lungs, potentially causing significant stress on the blood vessels. ASD, combined with Sines' Factor V Leiden, put her condition on high alert. After much debate, Sines was convinced open heart surgery was the best for her situation, a decision she noted as the most mentally taxing part of the ordeal. The procedure was performed in late July of 2002, followed by three weeks of cardiac rehabilitation.

Although Sines was eager to swim competitively, she knew she had to wait for medical clearance. But that didn't stop her from jumping in to help others as she went to work as a lifeguard within weeks of the surgery. She even found the time and energy to teach swimming to young children.

A young boy named Michael, one of Sines' swimming students, particularly touched her heart. Michael was battling a brain tumor. Familiar with hospital visits and medical costs, Sines wanted to raise money for Michael's family to help with their medical expenses. Her idea, "Bike for Mike," showed her compassion and competitiveness. Sines moved a stationary bike from the fitness center to the dining hall on the Washington College campus. She sent an email to the entire campus informing them of her great intentions. Her determination enabled Sines to bike for eight hours and one minute straight, helping her to raise almost $700 for Mike. Sines later choreographed another fundraiser for a fellow swimmer who was confined to a wheelchair after a diving accident.

In 2004, Sines graduated from Washington College with a degree in Business Management and has since worked in the real estate world as both an educator and at a title company as a project manager. Most recently, Sines took her extensive knowledge of the mortgage licensing process to Resource Real Estate Services in Owings Mills, Maryland where she is the Director of Marketing and Advertising. More importantly, she is the proud mother of a four-year-old daughter born in June 2006.

While her heart may be healthier now than it was when she was a child, she no longer has time to swim competitively. Nonetheless, on her lunch break, Sines can often be found doing laps at her local pool. Ultimately, Sines hopes to return to school to become a cardio-radiologist in order to help diagnose heart conditions like her own. Sines was fortunate that doctors caught her condition when they did and she wants to pay it forward. Perhaps during her surgery, the instruments used were made of gold, because her heart shines even brighter now than it did before. Stacy Sines' character and compassion are rare to find, but easy to admire.

Jennifer McClain

Creating a Better World

by Jessica Bartter Duffaut

Jim Abbot didn't let his lack of a right hand stop him from becoming an exceptional pitcher who earned a college athletic scholarship, spent 10 years in the major leagues, and was a member of the 1988 U.S. Olympic Team that was the first to win gold for American baseball. Shaun White didn't allow his heart birth defect to prevent him from dominating the X-Games at 16 years old and reach the pinnacle of success as an athlete—two Olympic gold medals as a snowboarder.

Jennifer "Tex" McClain is another of so many athletes who defied the odds as she refused to let a birth defect define her life. McClain was born with spina bifida, the most common permanently disabling birth defect. Though the effects are different for each spina bifida patient, the results can be debilitating for all. Spina bifida is a developmental birth defect caused by the incomplete closure of the neural tube when the spinal column doesn't close completely. It can cause varying levels of physical and mental issues. McClain's condition required her to have extensive surgery to remove meningocele, a cystic protrusion from her lower vertebrae and spinal cord area. McClain was just one day old when she underwent this life-saving surgery. During her first 22 years of life, McClain underwent seven more intensive surgeries to strengthen her spine.

At an early age, doctors warned McClain that she would have severe motor skill damage that would prevent her from being able to run or jump. McClain thought she would see for herself rather than accept their opinion and took up volleyball, a sport that requires both running and jumping. McClain found that not only did she thoroughly enjoy volleyball, she was also very good at it. After a successful and highlighted high school season, she earned an athletic scholarship to Quinnipiac College in Connecticut.

The Spring, Texas, native, who bears the nickname of her home state (Tex), was named captain during her sophomore, junior, and senior seasons and led the team from her position as setter. In volleyball, the setter is similar to the quarterback of a football team. It is the setter's responsibility to call and run the plays, dishing out assist after assist, for her teammates to attack. In control of her offense at all times, McClain set several school records at Quinnipiac College. More than 15 years after she graduated, McClain still ranked in the top 10 in games played per season and career, hitting percentage, assists per game, career service aces, service aces per game, total digs, solo blocks, block assists, and total blocks. She was an all-around presence on the court. McClain still topped the career and season assist lists as well. While she led the Braves on the court, McClain pushed herself hard in the classroom and earned a 3.33 grade point average. The international business major also earned the Eastern College Athletic Conference's Award of Valor in 1999, the same year she graduated.

McClain also found time to give back to her community. She visited recreation centers and middle schools to introduce the sport of volleyball and to teach children the fundamentals. McClain also reaches out to the spina bifida community as a motivational speaker and guidance counselor. She particularly enjoys helping young children born with spina bifida realize that they can accomplish many things despite doctors warnings or recommendations. She is a living example that the illness will not define you if you don't let it, and that her abilities as an individual, an athlete, a student, and an inspiration are what define Jennifer McClain.

Lawrence Wright

Creating a Better World

by Jessica Bartter Duffaut

Six feet under or in a six-by-six jail cell was where Lawrence Wright was headed. However, at the age of 18 he made a choice that many adolescents don't know they have. He charted a new path for himself, headed for higher education, college football stardom, and a career in the National Football League.

After losing his spot on the University of Miami's football squad because he failed the NCAA's required entrance exam, Wright decided his life needed to change. He enrolled in the Valley Forge Military Academy, a boarding school in Wayne, Pennsylvania, where he spent months learning discipline and the value of education. Valley Forge stresses academic excellence, character development, personal motivation, physical development, and leadership. Upon completion, Wright emerged with a new outlook and appreciation for all that was ahead of him in life and a new sense of individual responsibility that drove him to pursue a college degree. He signed with the University of Florida hoping to lead their football squad to their first national championship.

As Wright's life began moving in the right direction as a college student-athlete, he realized that a little mentoring in his hometown could go a long way and possibly save more lives like his. He began to focus on how he could best be a mentor, not something most self-described "thug from the 'hood'—a thief, a bully, a 'straight F' student"[1] and fatherless teenagers are cut out to be, but Wright was determined, and he had help.

In 1994, Wright, along with friends Arthur King and Marlin Barnes, founded a program called "Right Trak" in their hometown of Miami, Florida. It was marketed as a summer football camp to get kids ages eight to 15 interested. Once they showed up, Wright was determined to teach them much more than football fundamentals. Wright wanted to teach the children, many of whom were fatherless like him, self-discipline and self-esteem by helping them with their studies, going on field trips, and just hanging out. Wright and the Right Trak mentors were hard on the kids as well, teaching them proper study habits and demanding to see their report cards. Wright worked hard too. He wrote out the business plan, developed a budget, raised the funds necessary, and set-up non-profit status for Right Trak.

Wright preached what he understood having faced many hard times himself. Tragedy struck Wright's young life that now has him living for much more than himself. One of his best friends and Right Trak co-founder, Arthur King, an Austin Peay University football player, died in his sleep of a heart attack in 1994. Within the next two years, Wright also lost best friend and Right Trak co-founder Marlin Barnes, a University of Miami linebacker who was murdered in his dorm room, and Jean Francois, the father of Wright's godson, who committed suicide.

Right Trak may have saved Wright who felt lost after losing three friends when he turned to the children to absorb life from their vibrant outlooks. On the football field, Wright performed in memory of his friends. At practice he donned a jersey with number 156, the combined numbers of King and Barnes and during the games, his undershirt shined with the pictures of King and Barnes and the message "4 Ever #1 Life Goes On."[2]

Wright excelled on the field, achieving his goal to bring home the first national championship to the University of Florida. As a junior, this strong safety led the team with 109 tackles and 25 "big plays." In 1996, as a senior, Wright utilized his newly developed leadership skills and led the team to its fourth straight Southeastern Conference Championship and the Gators' first national championship. That year, Wright won the Jim Thorpe Award, given to the best defensive back in college football. In April of 1997, the Cincinnati Bengals signed Lawrence Wright as a free safety, kicking off his rookie season as a professional football player.

Wright, a first-team All-SEC and third-team All-American selection, was named to the Southeastern Conference's All-Decade team for the 1990s in 2001. While the list of honors and accolades goes on, Wright was most proud of his selection to the College Football Association's Scholar-Athlete Team. As a 10-year-old who suffered with dyslexia, Wright was unable to read. Dyslexia is a learning disability that affects one's ability to acquire and process language which typically causes trouble in reading, spelling, and writing.

Wright overcame this obstacle and was a regular on the Southeastern Conference Honor Roll.

In 1996, Wright was named a "community hero" and was honored to help carry the Olympic torch to Atlanta for the Summer Olympics. By that time, Right Trak had already assisted more than 40 at-risk youth in his hometown. He had help from doctors, lawyers, artists, the physically disabled, and professional athletes who he called upon to lecture the kids. Wright, who was a building construction major, designed the architectural plans for an all-inclusive community center to serve the athletic and academic needs of Right Trak full-time.

After three years with the Bengals in the NFL, Wright spent one year with the XFL. Then Wright returned to his community work. He created the World of Production with his wife, Richelle. They instituted Tools 4 Life, a mentoring program that taught young male and female athletes important lessons about character, image, and principles. Wright used the lessons he learned playing football to design the fundamental principles of the program. World of Production, now called Lawrence Wright & Partners, is an umbrella company that manages a variety of Wright's companies that all pertain to creating a difference.

Lawrence Wright & Partners was "created with problem solving in mind" and "defines itself as a total design build developing entity that comprises itself in to several aspects of global development." The company "emphasizes a need to saturate the world at-large with developmental projects, programs, and resources that will produce a more enhanced way of life for each society embraced by its touch for betterment."[3]

In 2010, the company teamed with Jesus People Ministries (JPM) to build a 200,000 square foot JPM Centre in Miami, Florida. The Centre hopes to instill justice, potential, and motivation "through providing for at-risk youth in need of transitional housing, affordable housing for the elderly, youth enrichment programs, and tutorial services along with performing arts and performing arts training."[4]

Lawrence Wright's life is a story of perseverance and fortitude that proves everyone deserves a second chance. Brought up in an environment that would have served as his excuse for failure, Wright persevered and ultimately triumphed.

Notes

1. Mike Bianchi, "Lean on Lawrence: Lawrence Wright of the University of Florida helps at-risk children in Liberty City where he grew up," *The Sporting News*, December 2, 1996.

2. Ibid.

3. Lawrence Wright & Partners, "100 Years of Experience," Lawrence Wright & Partners, http://lawrencewrightandpartners.com/, (accessed January 27, 2010).

4. Jesus Ministries, "JPM Centre's Million Project," http://www.jpmcentre.org/, (accessed March 10, 2010).

Dr. Lonise Bias

Creating a Better World

by Brian Wright

According to data compiled by the National Household Survey on Drug Use and Health, 46 percent of Americans 12 or older report illicit drug use at least once in their lifetime. It is alarming numbers such as this one that have shaped and directed Dr. Lonise Bias' life. As a parent, Bias lost two children to drugs and violence. From these tragedies, Bias now works to save millions of lives by educating youth, as well as adults of the consequences of drugs and violence. Bias describes her life as helping youth to realize their self-worth, their potential, as well as their ability to be warriors in the fight against substance abuse.

Bias' first tragedy occurred at what should have been a time of great celebration. Her son Lenny was an All-American standout basketball player at the University of Maryland at College Park. Lenny was considered by many to be one of the most talented players ever to play basketball at the University of Maryland, as well as in the Atlantic Coast Conference. He was selected second overall by the Boston Celtics in the 1986 NBA draft. Two days following the draft, Lenny was found dead in his dormitory room on the campus of the University of Maryland. The cause of death was cardiac arrest due to a cocaine overdose. Her son's death was a wake-up call for Bias, who suddenly realized that there is something terribly wrong in a society in which those who are the most successful face such intense pressures that they cannot handle and often fall victim to their own successes.

Bias' second tragedy came four years later when her younger son, Jay Bias, was murdered. A promising student-athlete, Jay exhibited similar athletic and academic talent displayed by his older brother Len. Jay and friends, taking a break for lunch at a local shopping mall were approached by a man in a jewelry store who accused Jay of flirting with his girlfriend. As Jay denied the accusation and decided to leave the shopping mall and return to work, his car was approached by the perpetrator's car, and seconds later gunshots were fired, killing Jay Bias.

The two tragedies that hit the Bias family are not isolated events. Tragedies like this happen every day and everywhere. A dynamic public speaker, Bias now lectures on the effects of drugs and violence in the community. Bias is known for passionately and powerfully expressing her beliefs, because she can sympathize with victims and explain the tragedies she has had to face in her life as a parent. While some social activists leave parents out of the discussion, Bias does not. She feels that educating parents is a key part in solving the problem that plagues our communities. Bias feels "It is the duty of every adult to look out for not only their children, but the children of their neighbors as well."[1] It was because of this belief that Dr. Lonise Bias founded The Abundant Life Resources A More Excellent Way, LLC (TALRAMEW). TALRAMEW is a community centered resource that focuses on helping youth, families, and the community navigate the challenges of daily living.[2] Dr. Bias delivers inspiring messages of hope to families and communities that don't immediately see hope in their day to day lives. As a society, we must confront drugs and violence in the community. Courageous and inspirational people such as Dr. Lonise Bias prepare us for that confrontation.

Notes

1. Bannerman Menson, Ayittey "Parents Must Act To Save Children, Lonise Bias Says Speaker: 1959 Principles Won't Work on '93 Kids" *St. Louis Dispatch*, August 2, 1993.

2. Bias Consulting, LLC, "About Us," http://lonisebias.org/AboutUs.html, (accessed March 3, 2010).

Alfreda J. Harris

Creating a Better World

by Brian Wright

Too often, the goal of completing one's education while transitioning from amateur to professional athletes is sadly neglected. Those who promote the image of a student-athlete often forget that the individual is, in fact, a student as well as an athlete. One person who is definitely not guilty of this is Alfreda J. Harris. Harris has been a long-time promoter of the importance of academics for youth, whether or not they are athletes. She has played an active role in the betterment of society by focusing on developing and mentoring young people across all socio-economic classes, races, ethnicities, and varying beliefs about the importance of attaining higher education. Throughout her life of service to youth and the community, Harris has instilled strong values and goals in the young people with whom she has worked. She has made a positive impact and contribution to their lives.

As head basketball coach at Roxbury Community College and the University of Massachusetts, Boston, Harris promoted her philosophy of performance in the classroom, as well as on the court to all of her players. Known for her "no-nonsense" attitude with regards to performance in the classroom, Harris gained the respect and love of her student-athletes that continues to this day. While compiling an outstanding 136-20 career record with these two institutions, she was able to develop extremely successful and educated athletes and professionals. Harris' guidance propelled many to outstanding careers. She always explained to her players that while basketball was important to their success at the University, excelling only in sport meant winning only half of the game. When asked about the role of sports in education by staff of the Center for the Study of Sport in Society, Harris responded, "Basketball is a tool to get an education, but athletics without academics is a losing proposition." This quote epitomizes Harris' beliefs and shows her conviction about the importance of academics.

Harris continued to make a difference in the lives of young people through her work as the Founder and Administrative Coordinator of the John A. Shelbourne Recreational Center. Here Harris found ways to inspire youth in the local inner-city community. Harris also helps to prepare them for successful athletic and academic collegiate careers. At the Recreational Center, Harris teaches young men and women what they need to attain a full athletic or academic scholarship and what they need to do to be successful at institutions of higher education.

Harris was also the founder of one of Boston's oldest and most respected youth basketball leagues, the Women's/Men's Boston Neighborhood Basketball League (BNBL) as well as the Boston Shoot-Out Basketball Tournament. This league was used to promote positive interaction among the youth of Boston and also to provide an arena for these youth to display their talents while remaining off of the streets and away from trouble.

Harris has held many positions serving the community of Boston while touching the lives of the youth. She served as the Project Director for Harvard School of Public Health's "Play Across Boston" campaign, as well as a Project Director for Northeastern University's Center for the Study of Sport in Society. In 1993, Harris was appointed to the Boston Public School Committee charged with seeking innovative ways to improve the education process for all of Boston's youth. Harris has been an integral figure in the Boston educational system as well as in the development of youth through sports and still serves as the elected Vice Chair of the Boston School Committee.

The countless hours Harris spends working with youth teaching important life lessons has played a major role in her life's mission to improve the education levels of the youth in Boston. She has been a visionary in her outreach programs and has touched countless lives of youth growing up in the City of Boston. She genuinely cares about the development of young people regardless of their race, gender, religion or economic status and strives daily to improve upon their awareness of their potential on the playing field as well as in the classroom. In June 2007, Harris was honored by the John A Shelburne Recreation Center, and the the entire local community when the gymnasium of the recreation center named after her. Harris' desire to teach local youth not only about sports but about life started right there on that court in Boston and now, deservingly so, it bears her name. Now retired from the recreation center, Harris' legacy is strong, and her mission remains intact—to make better citizens and a better community through the development of the youth in the Boston Community.[1]

Harris is loved by all who know her in the Boston community for her devotion to her players and students. Those she touches never forget her and the impact she had on their lives. Many of the young men and women who were touched by Harris have also taken up the challenge of improving public education in the communities in which they live and work. Some members of the Boston community refer to Harris as the "Godmother of Hoops,"[2] but if you ask any of her players, or anyone who has come in contact with Alfreda Harris they will tell you she is not only the Godmother of Hoops, but also the Godmother of Hope.

Notes

1. Joe Fitzgerald. "Leader's legacy lives on at rec center," *The Boston Herald*, June 30, 2007.

2. Mike May, "First Annual SGMA Heroes State Winners Announced," Sporting Goods Manufacturers Association's (SGMA), 1995, http://www.sgma.com/press/1994/press990463577-29903.html, (accessed December 5, 2005).

Maggie Maloy

Creating a Better World

by Brian Wright, with Austin Moss II

Every two minutes a woman in the United States is raped. Few teenagers at the age of 15 can imagine the pain and mental anguish of being a victim of rape. Maggie Maloy can. While participating in her morning cross country high school practice on September 16, 1994, Maloy was abducted, brutally beaten, raped twice, and shot five times. Her abductor shot her as she lay on her stomach covering her head with her hands. She was struck twice in the back, once in the armpit, and once in the head as a second grazed the top of her head. Leaving her for dead, he fled the scene. With a collapsed lung and a paralyzed right arm, Maloy remained on the ground until she was found by police. Despite all the distress and pain, Maggie found strength in the hope of returning to her sport and competing at the highest level.

Defying all odds and expectations set by her doctors, Maloy was back in school within six weeks of the incident. By the spring of 1995, she was running on the track. After graduating from Galion High School in Ohio in 1997, Maloy enrolled at Defiance College. As a collegiate student-athlete, Maloy competed with three of the five bullets still permanently lodged in her body—two in her right lung, and one in her sinus cavity. This was not a deterrent for Maloy. She offered no excuses, and competed successfully for almost three years at Defiance.

Maloy had just finished her third indoor-track season, when disaster struck again. On February 13, 2000, while driving her car, an icy road caused Maloy to lose control and collide with a van. The accident left her pelvic bone broken in three separate places. This left Maloy essentially immobile from the waist down and she had to learn to walk again. Lucky to be alive, Maloy did not lose the desire to compete at Defiance because of the accident and knew from her past experiences that she had the power to overcome adversity in her life.

For three grueling months Maloy spent countless hours in rehabilitation with doctors and therapists. The payoff was priceless. Maloy was back on the track for the fall of her senior year. She was able to compete in cross country, and indoor and outdoor track. She was selected as the captain of the team and received All-Conference honors for her accomplishments on the track. Maloy also helped lead the Defiance College cross country team to its first conference title in the school's history.

Maloy still holds three top-10 records for Defiance's outdoor track team. Maloy is sixth in the 800-meter run with a time of 2:31.8; second in the 1,500-meter run with a time of 5:02.2; and second in the 3,000-meter run with a time of 11:58.6. Maloy set each one of these records in 2001 after learning to walk all over again.

In the spring of 2001, Maloy graduated with her bachelor's degree in Communication. In January, 2002, she and Sam Paneno were the first student-athletes to be honored by the NCAA as recipients of their Inspiration Award.

Since Maloy's graduation, she has continued to deliver her message in hopes of creating a better world. In November 2006, Maloy started the advocate program for the city of Bucyrus, Ohio. In this position, she works alongside the city prosecutor assisting young people who are victims of domestic violence in the healing process and helps to place their lives on the path of recovery.[1] In August 2007, Maloy enrolled in the Paralegal Program at Capital Law School in Columbus, Ohio. She earned her paralegal certificate and graduated in August 2008.

Most recently, Maloy was co-author of *You're Not Alone: The Journey from Abduction to Empowerment*, a survival guide for abduction victims released by the U.S. Department Office of Juvenile Justice and Delinquency Prevention. This book provides information to help abduction victims readjust to their 'new normal' way of life once they have been returned home (after being abducted).[2] Maloy continues to work for the Advocate Program and spread her inspiration through public speaking across the country. "Right now, I'm just trying to enjoy life and experience God by giving sermons", said Maloy.[3] Maloy has answered the call that God has placed on her life and hopes to pursue studies in seminary school in the near future. In addition to her current activities, Maloy remains an avid runner and has a newfound passion for cycling. Her lifetime dream would be to cycle across the United States with a Christian cycling tour.

The courage Maloy has shown in overcoming her physical and emotional hardships has inspired many others around the world to work to overcome their own hardships. Maggie Maloy is a true inspiration for her courage and determination in achieving her life's goals despite its many challenges.

Notes

1. "OJJDP News @ a Glance". Office of Juvenile Justice and Delinquency Programs. http://www.ncjrs.gov/html/ojjdp/news_at_glance/223021/on_1.html

2. "OJJDP Publication Abstract". Office of Juvenile Justice and Delinquency Programs. http://ojjdp.ncjrs.gov/publications/PubAbstract.asp?pubi=244130

3. Maggie Maloy, interview with author, March 18, 2010.

Jodi Norton

Creating a Better World

by Brian Wright, with Austin Moss II

Most student-athletes suffer a variety of minor aches, pains, and muscle soreness as they compete in their various sports. Jodi Norton was no exception. She was an All-American high school athlete who stood out on her high school team as well as on Team Orlando, an elite diving team. Norton balanced training four hours a day with her studies so she disregarded her fatigue, soreness, and occasional dizziness as ordinary side effects of strenuous physical exercise.

Norton's hard work earned her a scholarship to the University of Arizona to compete on their diving team. In her first year of participation as a student-athlete at the University, Norton found that the frequency and intensity of pain she experienced was a little different than most others on her team. She was often sick with skin rashes and severe joint pain that forced her to miss some of her diving practices. Norton decided to leave the team to focus on getting the medical attention she needed, but unfortunately her condition was misdiagnosed.

Norton had an interest in medicine and transferred to Columbia University to study pre-med. Yet, Norton's excruciating pain continued to cause her to miss classes and diving practice. When the pain did not cease, Norton was admitted to the emergency room three months after transferring to Columbia. In the E.R., she finally heard a definitive explanation for the pain she had suffered from for years.

Norton was diagnosed with lupus, a very serious, incurable, chronic autoimmune disorder characterized by periodic episodes of inflammation of and damage to the joints, tendons, other connective tissues, and organs, including the heart, lungs, blood vessels, brain, kidneys, and skin. Norton's personality and courage did not let her just give in to her disease. She decided to research it to become as familiar with her condition as possible. Though she was experiencing the effects of lupus on her body, Norton continued to compete. Her school and participation in athletics were frequently interrupted by trips to the emergency room for meningitis, pericarditis, swelling of tissue around the brain, and battles with Lyme disease. Lyme disease is an infection caused by a bacterium that is carried by ticks and is transmitted to humans through tick bites. The disease affected Jodi's entire immune system and caused her to experience headaches, muscle and joint pain, and severe fatigue. The effects of lupus and Lyme disease were daunting and seemed nearly impossible to overcome. Nonetheless, Norton remained a strong competitor on the diving team and persevered in spite of her obstacles. Her courage and desire were always on display as she battled her disease and continued to practice and compete.

At the 1995–96 Eastern College Athletic Conference (ECAC) Diving Championship, Norton managed to compete despite having a broken hand. At the end of the first day she had to be rushed to the emergency room for intravenous medication for swollen tissue around her brain. Remarkably, Norton returned the following day and was able to compete and amazingly finished 10th overall. She attributed her success to the fact that she would visualize the competition when she could not compete for health reasons. "I would visualize everything, so when I got up on the board, I was confident."[1] This was Norton's final competition and to perform so well under all the adversity she faced was a testament to her courage and desire to succeed.

During her spare time, Norton sits with medical students to share her experiences and also visits young children who have recently undergone chemotherapy. Jodi graduated from Columbia University with a 3.8 grade point average and then enrolled in Bryn Mawr College's Post-Baccalaureate Premedical Program.

While pursuing her own career in medicine, Norton and fellow student-athlete Adina Gravit established an organization called Lupus Inspiration Foundation for Excellence (LIFE). The co-founders started LIFE as student-athletes and the organization continues to be managed by student-athletes throughout the U.S. on a volunteer basis. LIFE promotes awareness of lupus and seeks to help college students with lupus earn their degrees. LIFE recognizes the obstacles students with lupus face while in college and assists them by providing them with scholarships. Scholarships are awarded to students based on merit and to those who have shown courage and perseverance to overcome lupus.

Norton is extremely proud of the organization's success. "We have given out 43 LIFE scholarships to students across the nation, and we are the only organization that gives scholarships to students with lupus," said Norton.[2] It is important to know how competitive the field is for this prestigious scholarship. Last year only eight scholarships were awarded out of about 100 applicants. That is less than a 10 percent chance to receive such a life-changing and significant honor. Norton is currently working with the organization on publishing a book that will contain general information about lupus, the LIFE organization, and the essays, degrees, and schools of the first 50 scholarship recipients.

Norton continues to work tirelessly with the LIFE organization, while also giving inspirational speeches to various groups across the country. Every day she is striving to promote more awareness for the least recognized and funded disease that affects Americans. "I think a lot of people are unaware how common lupus is," said Norton.[3] "Ninety percent of the people diagnosed with Lupus are women, and ninety percent of the women experience symptoms during childbearing (college) years."[4] Norton also emphasized the fact that the highest incidences occur in Native Americans and African-Americans. According to the Lupus Foundation of America, more than 16,000 new cases of lupus around the country are reported each year and 6,000 victims die from the chronic disease.[5] These are very important statistics that Norton feels Americans, more specifically women and minorities, need to know.

Jodi Norton continues to battle with lupus while she pursues a PhD in medicine. She became the 14th lupus patient in Chicago to receive a bone marrow transplant, however, she is still in search of an exact match to help strengthen her immune system.

Jodi Norton is a courageous, inspirational, and skilled leader. Norton realizes that we all face adversities and how she handled hers is a model of how we all should deal with and overcome the obstacles of life.

Notes

1. Amy Callahan, "Jodi Norton: Adversity Doesn't Keep Diver from Soaring," Columbia University, October 10, 1997, http://www.columbia.edu/cu/record/archives/vol23/vol23_iss6/16.html, (accessed December 4, 2005).

2. Jodi Norton, interview with author, March 5, 2010.

3. Ibid.

4. Ibid.

5. Lupus Foundation of America, "About Lupus," New Jersey Chapter, http://www.lupus.org/webmodules/webarticlesnet/templates/newjersey_lupus.aspx?articleid=996&zoneid= 228, (accessed March 5, 2010).

Robert Hurley Sr.

Creating a Better World

by Stacy Martin-Tenney

It is not how he says it but what he says that makes the difference to his players. He may yell and, yes, even curse to get their attention, but he drives the point home. Robert Hurley, Sr., is a man who has devoted his life to a small Catholic school in Jersey City that is home to a majority of underprivileged students of color mostly from single parent homes. Adversity is an understatement when describing the situation that the students and the school face. St. Anthony High School is a private school in the inner city seen as a safe haven by parents who work extra jobs to pay the $3,250 tuition that might give their children a better life than that which they could provide alone. Hurley is a man who accepted that responsibility and challenge and strives daily to teach kids the fundamentals of life through basketball. Bob Hurley has coached basketball at St. Anthony for the last 33 years and has won 90 percent of his games and 22 state titles.

Hurley knows what the typical fate of a child growing up in the inner city. He witnesses it firsthand every day. Hurley has been a probation officer for Hudson County in New Jersey for as long as he has been a basketball coach. He knows most of these kids will join a gang, end up in jail, or buried in an early grave, but he also knows that some of them have a chance to grow up and go beyond the streets of Jersey City. That's why he has devoted so much time and passion into St. Anthony and his basketball team.

Every student at St. Anthony's is in some way an underdog. Many have always been taught that they had no chance. So when Bob Hurley walks into the gym and takes a chance on them, they listen even if he shouts. The team borrows gyms to practice in and home games really have not been possible. The only practice facility frequented by the St. Anthony Friars has been a local establishment called the White Eagle Hall that gets used more by its bingo patrons than the team. The floor is 29 feet too short, but to compensate the basketball goal is propped up on radiators making it two inches too high. The remaining 65 feet of the floor are menacing. It defends the offensive players better than the defense sometimes due to its jutting nail heads and water logged spots from leaks that absorb the ball from a player's dribble instead of returning it to his hand. After their grueling practices, the boys pay for their practice time by setting up the 200 chairs and 63 tables for bingo. The Eagle, as it is affectionately called, builds mental toughness. The players come from broken homes and dangerous streets and have never been given a thing, not even a gym. Hurley exploits these factors to instill a winning attitude in his players. He coaches his basketball team by telling them before every game that their next opponent is the best team they have ever played. He conveys the message that the team is going to have to fight and play hard for a win. Thus, his players know how to fight and how to struggle, and Coach Hurley taught them to know how to win.

Hurley is an old school coach, the one that kicks an athlete out of practice for just looking at him wrong so that he can create and maintain a disciplined atmosphere. He can just look at his team and deliver a stare that melts their hardened exterior. As a coach, he challenges his athletes to practice every day with intensity and desire. If they don't, they go home. Hurley's eldest son, Bobby Hurley Jr., knows the intensity and the look all too well. Bobby was often kicked out of his dad's practices and mostly for no reason at all. But, the coach knows that kicking someone out, especially his own flesh and blood, serves his purpose. He wants to demonstrate seriousness in practice and prove that no one is safe from his wrath. Bobby had come to terms with his father's intense methods long before and knew when he had become an example for the team. One reporter over the years captured Bobby's thoughts on his dad with this quote: "We don't have a lot of what other teams take for granted, but we have my dad, and he's the reason St. Anthony is where it is today. You have to come to every practice ready to play because he never loses his intensity."[1] Bobby's younger brother, Danny, grew up in the house of Hurley, too. At times Dan grappled with the pressure to fill his brother's shoes and carry the family crest of basketball. Bobby was an All-American at Duke and Dan played at Seton Hall. Bobby began a career in the NBA, only to have it cut short by a horrific car accident. Their father's influence on them certainly molded them into the successful athletes and human beings that they are today. Besides, they say imitation is the highest form of flattery and both sons chose to follow the footsteps of their father into coaching. Both have thriving teams and are complemented, like their father has been, for being a good person that takes a genuine interest in helping young men succeed. What made Bob Hurley unique in today's sports world was his expectation of perfection and his never-give-up attitude.

Hurley is the coach that yells when the team is leading at the half because they missed their foul shots. Winning isn't enough for him. That's why he will scream at the team for an hour after a game for not playing as hard as their opponent even when his team won. It's been recounted that after a game one night Hurley asked his team to name the coach for the opposing team. When he called on certain players for the answer, the only sound was silence. He asked about another school's coach who happened to be a New Jersey legend like Hurley. Again there was silence. He immediately launched into a tirade regarding their attitudes being bigger than their knowledge of the game, because knowing the game meant knowing who was in it and its history and it was about having respect for those that came before you.

He called them out for acting too cool and told them to go back to their miserable existence as part of the group. But then he followed it with a challenge to step away from the Jersey City streets and the group that resided on its corners. Hurley left the gym that night naming every coach in New Jersey since he played in 1965, all the while wondering if he got through the generational gap. His coaching style has always been in another era, but he realized the disconnection between not only himself and his players, but between his players and the way things should be. They care about having car keys now, not the SAT scores that can get them into college, and he told them as much to prompt a value change. Failure isn't acceptable and there are no excuses. He expects his teams to end their season in the final game of New Jersey's state championship, the Tournament of Champions. Most of all he expects his players to go to college. Anything else is a disappointment.

Basketball may be his means, but providing opportunity for the students at St. Anthony is the end goal. In Hurley's 33 years of coaching, all of his players have graduated from St. Anthony and gone on to college. Hurley will scream and shout during practice, but if his players can tolerate it, then he is abidingly loyal to them off the court. He has taken an interest in each player and encourages them to improve their test scores. It is an underprivileged private Catholic school in the inner city that is on the brink of disaster or closing almost every year, but he has the full support of the nuns that run the school to get his players academic help so they can go beyond the streets of Jersey City and onto a basketball court on a college campus.

His 2003–2004 team struggled academically and failed to qualify for a Division I institution. It is a failure that the coach is greatly embarrassed by. Hurley has stayed at St. Anthony High for 33 years because he knows he is making a lasting impression on the youth of Jersey City. The attachment he forms with his players goes beyond the walls of the gymnasium and the lines on the court.

The Rivers family received quite a lot of Hurley's care and consideration. Willie and Mamie Rivers worked multiple jobs and raised 14 children. Their son, David, was a star athlete for Hurley and went on to play basketball for Notre Dame and then the Los Angeles Lakers. David's younger brother Jermaine had a bright future under Hurley's leadership until he was plagued by frequent headaches. The doctors discovered a massive and inoperable brain tumor. Time was slipping away for Jermaine. Hurley organized a fundraiser for the family and sent Jermaine to South Bend, Indiana to see his brother one last time. Jermaine passed away just a year and a half after his diagnosis at age seventeen. The Rivers made a connection with Hurley that outlasted any basketball game, so when David's nephew, Hank, started getting into trouble with a gang, Hurley stepped in. Hurley was aware of Hank's history with grand theft, guns, and drugs as he was in and out of the Hudson County Courts since age fourteen. Hank was on the verge of a lengthy sentence that would usher him into adulthood. Hurley stepped into the courtroom and testified that he would save this kid from the streets and turn Hank's life around. Hurley was publicly known for his ability to reach kids on the basketball court and professionally he is known for being tough as a probation officer. If anyone could turn him around, it was Hurley.

He allowed Hank to practice with the St. Anthony team during the spring semester of his sophomore year after his plea was granted by the judge, but he was not permitted to join the team until he proved that he would be serious about his studies and change his behavior in the community. Hurley kept Hank off the streets and from his usual routine and influences by spending one-on-one time with him after practice to work on the 6-foot-8 player's post moves. Hurley taught Hank fundamentals for the court and off the court. He often spoke to Hank about changing his value system and his choice of so-called friends. He explained that Hank didn't have to be confined to Jersey City or even New Jersey's borders. The observation of what life could be like for a semester was motivation enough for Hank Rivers to make a change. Hank exchanged his gang colors for St. Anthony's colors, traded his gang members for his teammates, and spent time on homework rather than street corners. Hank's choices led to success on the court as well and he was the starting center for the St. Anthony Friars that year. When he was a senior he became ineligible for high school basketball because he had already turned 19. Some coaches would have walked away because Hank couldn't help the team anymore. Hurley doesn't give up, though. He sent Hank to New York to play AAU basketball until graduation so he could develop his skills. Hurley knew that Hank's ticket out of town was basketball. He followed through once more and got Hank a scholarship to Southeast Community College in Nebraska, where row houses were replaced by rows of corn. Hank is now playing for Stephen F. Austin University in Texas and misses Hurley screaming at him to push him past what he thought his breaking point was. Now Hank pushes himself.

Hurley dares his athletes to be the best and does so by setting expectations for them above and beyond what any of them thought possible. He provides a structure for them that won't allow them to fail. That's why Hurley is legendary. He has been inducted into the New Jersey Sports Hall of Fame and named as a Sporting Goods Manufacturers Association Hero. He was named Sportsman of the Year by the Mercier Club of Montclair in 1992. He is likened to a miracle worker in *The Miracle of St. Anthony*, a book chronicling the storybook history of the school and its basketball teams. Hurley's heroic deeds and miracles occur in the lives of Jersey City youth, whether it's his children or the community's children. Robert Hurley Jr. has screamed at his kids over the city noise for the past 33 years, so that they would hear something more than gunshots and sirens in their futures. He was rewarded in 2010 when he became only the third high school coach who was ever inducted into the Basketball Hall of Fame.

Note

1. Tim Crothers, "The Friars are kings of the road," *Sports Illustrated*, December 18, 1989.

Tanya Y. Hughes-Jones

Creating a Better World

by Jessica Bartter Duffaut

The epitome of a student-athlete, Tanya Hughes-Jones constantly challenged herself to do better in the classroom and on the track, and she shone brightly in both. At the University of Arizona, Hughes-Jones stood out as an athlete, as a student and as a fine young woman. While majoring in interdisciplinary studies, earning four NCAA outdoor track championships, and training for the Olympics, Hughes-Jones earned a 3.44 grade point average. Her hard work did not go unrewarded as she was recognized as a GTE Academic All-American. But it was not her grades alone that helped her be an inspiration to so many. Hughes-Jones was chair of the University of Arizona's NCAA Student-Athlete Advisory Committee and served as a spokesman for the University's NCAA Choices Alcohol Awareness Program.

Hughes-Jones' responsibilities as a spokesperson for social change were greatly increased when she represented the United States in the 1992 Barcelona Olympics. She was only 20, the youngest on the U.S. women's track team that year. Though she didn't come home with a medal, Hughes-Jones was the only American athlete to make the high jump finals. Hughes-Jones was also a member of the 1993 World University Games Team where she captured the gold medal in the high jump.

In 1992 and 1993, the *United States Track & Field News* rated Hughes-Jones as the best high jumper. In 1992, she was named NCAA Female Track Athlete of the Year and in 1994, she earned the highest honors for a collegiate athlete by being named NCAA Woman of the Year after being selected from a pool of 389 nominees. The criteria for this award include academic achievement, athletic excellence, and community leadership.

At the 1994 US Olympic Festival in St. Louis, Missouri, she won a gold medal with a jump of 6 feet, 1 1/2 inches. Hughes-Jones graduated from the University of Arizona in 1994 and went on to pursue her master's degree.

Hughes-Jones' civic leadership continued after college as she served as keynote speaker for the 1995 Project TEAMWORK Human

Rights Squad Forum. Project TEAMWORK trains young people with diversity and conflict resolution skills, providing them with alternative strategies to handle the conflicts they face and avoid the violence that often stems from conflicts between individuals from different cultures, religions, races, and ethnicities. After each Project TEAMWORK presentation, Human Rights Squads are formed at the school to serve as an active vehicle for students to promote the value of diversity, learn conflict resolution skills, and foster life-long community service participation. At the end of the school year, the Human Rights Squad Forum brings together all chapters of the various Human Rights Squads where they are provided with a venue to demonstrate their knowledge and understanding of the Project TEAMWORK principles. Tanya Hughes-Jones' insights about diversity and conflict resolution were invaluable to the participating youth in 1995.

Hughes-Jones worked for the IBM Corporation before she joined her husband, Michael Jones, in the ministry. Michael Jones was also a highly-touted college athlete who played football at the University of Colorado before a short stint in the NFL. He had a successful business career with Pepsi Cola and started his own insurance agency before accepting his call to go into the ministry. In 1998, with their first child, one-month-old Jocelyn, Tanya and Michael moved to Richmond, Virginia, so that Michael could attend seminary school for his master's of divinity. In the same year, Tanya earned her license as a minister. Together in 2005, they launched the Village of Faith Ministries with a vision to "Reach families with a simple gospel message that will help them change the world."[1] Within its inaugural year, the Ministry had 400 members and had launched the Celebrate Life Broadcast, which airs every Sunday morning. Tanya and Michael expanded their Ministry to two locations, serving over 1,300 members.

Hughes-Jones became a role model for other student-athletes by achieving Academic All-American status, and by becoming successful in the business world, church life, and as a wife and mother. Tanya is committed to "changing the world—one family at a time."[2] Her success thus far is immeasurable.

Notes

1. Village of Faith Ministries, "Our Story," http://www.myvofm.org/our-story, (accessed March 5, 2010).

2. Village of Faith Ministries, "Pastor Tanya Y. Jones, http://www.myvofm.org/pastor-tanya-y-jones, (accessed March 5, 2010).

Michele Leary

Creating a Better World

by Jessica Bartter Duffaut

Some people choose to become doctors to help people; others do it for the money. Some follow the footsteps of a parent; others want to discover the cure for Alzheimer's. It was Michele Leary's own health scare that originally turned her off of the medical profession, but eventually made her realize her life's purpose and moved her to pursue her own career path as a physician. Today, Leary is treating patients, diagnosing illnesses, and reading lab reports. About 20 years ago, Leary was on the other end of the medical spectrum, as a patient in the emergency room.

Leary competed for the swim team at the University of Massachusetts, Amherst, from 1985 to 1990. The peaceful early mornings and calm waters had attracted her to the pool in high school where Leary first started swimming. Swimming, to her, "is as natural as breathing."[1] While she thought her chances were slim, her love for the sport led this weary freshman to UMass, Amherst swim tryouts. Leary was a self-described "slow swimmer" but her potential impressed Coach Bob Newcomb enough to earn her a spot as a walk-on.

Leary's love for swimming continued to grow at UMass, Amherst as she fervently trained in the pool and studied in the classroom. After early success as a freshman, Leary took a year off to treat a nagging shoulder injury from her high school javelin career. Shoulder surgery forced her to redshirt her second year during the 1986–87 season. Without skipping a beat, Leary retuned for her sophomore season and began making a career out of breaking records.

Ready for her junior year of competition, Leary's season was abruptly cut short. On October 28, 1988, Leary began feeling dizzy and experienced pain and tingling in her left arm and pressure in her chest. Her family had a history of coronary artery spasms. Even so, it was a surprise to everyone, including Leary and the medical professionals, that a 21-year-old healthy college athlete could suffer a myocardial infarction (MI), more commonly referred to as a heart attack.

Doctors told Leary she needed eight weeks to recover and that she would have to stay out of the pool until January 2, 1989. Leary followed her doctors' orders but was back in the pool on January 3. Leary swam in her first meet on January 6. Coaches and teammates were shocked by Leary's speedy recovery and were even more impressed with the success she had in the pool after two months off and minimal training. During the half season that she was actually able to compete, Leary broke New England records in the 50-, 100- and 200-meter freestyle, records that had been standing for over seven years.

As a senior, Leary returned to break all her own records again. She finished her fifth year with 12 record-breaking competitions, seven of which were individual records. At the start of the 2006–07 season, four of Leary's records remained—the 50-, 100-, and 200-yard freestyle, and the 100-yard butterfly. Her name could also be found in the top ten of the record books for the 400-yard individual medley and 200-yard butterfly events.

Leary attributed her impressive performances to a common motivator; "When people tell you that you can't do something, it makes you want to do it even more." Leary carried that attitude into her professional life when she began pursuing medical school. Despite the fact that she was well past the average age of first year medical students and that she was a female in a predominately male profession, Leary enrolled in Touro University College of Osteopathic Medicine in 2001, 11 years after she graduated from UMass, Amherst.

The challenges she faced as a student-athlete, balancing strenuous competition with demanding academics, prepared her for the demands she faces today. Leary and her husband, Gary Searer, welcomed their first daughter, Arden, to the world on June 2, 2004, just before Leary's third year of medical school. Leary believes it is her participation in sports that enabled her to "juggle the demands of a husband, a baby, and medical school" because sports gave her strength and endurance and taught her persistence.

Leary credits her speedy recovery from her myocardial infarction to her persistence and tries to teach its value to those she meets. As an active contributor to her community, Leary comes into contact with many young boys and girls who doubt themselves much like she did in her early swimming career. By sharing her story of determination, patience, and perseverance, Leary is able to motivate many children who say "I can't" to say "I'll try." Her tale of triumph often inspires the "I'll try" to become "I did it!" Leary has volunteered her time and offered her story to participants in the Oakland City At-risk Girls-only Science Day, Oakland inner-city youth and master's swimming programs. She spent many years instructing the swimmers on stroke and turn techniques, but they all learned more about life from the inspirational Leary.

For four years Leary studied symptoms, diseases, drugs, and treatments because she is one of the medical students who enrolled with the intention to one day help people as a doctor. Today, that is a reality. Leary is board certified in Family Medicine and is near completion of her residency in Downey, California. Never one to shy away from challenges, Michele and Gary welcomed their second daughter, Iona, in early 2009 in the midst of Leary's demanding residency program. The Chief Resident took one year off to relish in motherhood with her newborn and is planning a fellowship in neuromusculoskeletal medicine/osteopathic manipulative medicine (OMM) in 2010–11.

Leary describes both her young girls as "water-bugs." Perhaps they will follow in their mother's strokes to swimming success. In 2007, Michele Leary was inducted into the University of Massachusetts at Amherst Athletic Hall of Fame for the important marks she left on UMass swimming. Though years into her marriage, it took the Hall of Fame induction for Gary to realize what a big deal his wife really was. Before visiting UMass for the ceremony, he "just didn't understand" the extensiveness of Michele's awards and success. Little did he know, he married a swimming superstar!

Leary has faced many challenges with success and plans on accomplishing much more in the coming years, most importantly, raising a loving family. Reflecting nearly two decades ago, Leary credits the support she received from her teammates and Coach Newcomb with her ability to survive a heart attack mentally and physically, at such a young age. While she certainly learned a great deal about herself and about life, Michele Leary doesn't think of herself as a hero. "All I did was go back and forth a few 100,000 times in a pool." But what she doesn't realize is that with every stroke and every flip turn she defied the odds and inspired so many to realize what life is really about and all that can be accomplished with persistence.

Note

1. All information and quotes are from an interview with the author on February 24, 2010.

Danny Wuerffel

Creating a Better World

by Joslyn Dalton

As a college athlete, Danny Wuerffel is best known as the 1996 national championship quarterback for the University of Florida. His talent on the gridiron also allowed him to collect a plethora of awards during the 1996 season which included winning the Heisman Trophy, Draddy Award, and Walter Camp Award, all three of which reflect upmost prestige. With 32 national, conference, and school records to his credit, Wuerffel earned legendary status as one of the greatest college football players of all time.

In keeping the student in student-athlete, Wuerffel excelled outside of the pocket. He had the rare distinction of being an All-American football star, as well as two-time academic All-American. During his senior year as a Gator, he was named the NCAA Academic All-American of the Year. He accumulated a career grade point average of 3.74 while earning his bachelor's degree in public relations.

In 1997, the New Orleans Saints drafted Wuerffel. After three years with the franchise, he moved into the NFL's European League where he found success in being a part of the World Bowl Championship team. He was selected by the European media as the league's most valuable player. Upon moving back to the U.S., he played one season each with the Green Bay Packers, the Chicago Bears, and the Washington Redskins.

Regardless of the national spotlight Wuerffel gained as a result of his success, his priorities remained unfazed. "The world just pounds the message into your brain that if you make enough money and if you're successful in your field, that's all you need," he said.[1] But Wuerffel's upbringing taught him that there was much more to life than trophies that rust and recognition that fades. "I believe we were made to find fulfillment in our relationship with God. When we look for it in other places, we come up empty," he shared.[2]

Born in 1974 and raised by his father who was an U.S. Air Force chaplain and his mother who was actively involved in the church, Wuerffel said that he grew up not questioning if God exists but to what extent. With the world at his fingertips during his college career, he challenged himself to remain in pursuit of more than fame and fortune. He began to study the Bible for himself and make his faith his own rather than relying on what he had been taught from his parents. "It's a humbling experience to realize what your own nature is. To look at yourself and see selfishness and pride and the attitude that you can just do your own thing," he said.[3] In spite of the distraction of everyone around him in awe of his talent and promise, Wuerffel strived to submit to his savior, determined to live his life in a way that would bring honor to God. "My desire is to acknowledge Him in all my ways—in my marriage, in my family, in football—whatever I'm doing," he said.[4] True to his life's mission, Wuerffel has used his platform to give back to all the communities that he has lived and played sports in.

In 2004, Wuerffel retired from football in order to focus his time and effort in one of America's toughest and poorest neighborhoods, the Upper Ninth Ward in New Orleans. He learned about Desire Street Ministries during his career with the Saints. He was so passionate about the faith-based, non-profit organization that he moved his family back to the city in order to work full-time with the ministry. For over 15 years, Desire Street Ministries has dedicated its ministry to the improvement and support of local leaders in the development of impoverished neighborhoods. Wuerffel currently serves as its Executive Director, as well as the Director for Desire Street Academy (DSA), an Upper Ninth Ward school for junior and senior African-American males from underserved neighborhoods. While the students of DSA are welcome to study both academics and athletics, the Academy teaches Christian spiritual growth while focusing on extensively preparing students for college or trade school education.

In the aftermath of Hurricane Katrina, which affected New Orleans in 2005, Desire Street Ministries and DSA were forced to relocate, after being completely destroyed, until the rebuilding process could take place. Desire Street took an interest in helping to rebuild New Orleans as a whole and not just their organization by becoming involved in a variety of other community programs.

—Wuerffel has been able to find peace among the chaos caused by the hurricane. While he used to worry about throwing an interception or losing a football game, the storm reminded him how valuable it is to set his sights on something more. "God is doing a new thing as a result of this storm . . . Sometimes it's just hard to see it while it's happening," he said.[5]

Wuerffel's involvement with community service also stretches back to his Florida roots. He serves as the University of Florida Fellowship of Christian Athletes (FCA) President as well as the FCA President for Fort Walton Beach High School, the place he graduated as valedictorian and led his football team to the state championship title. He also is active on the Board of Directors for Professional Athletes Outreach. Along with his wife, Jessica, he is a national spokesperson for Caps for Kids. Wuerffel became a presidential appointee to the White House Council for Service and Civic Partnership as a result of his dedication to community outreach. As a popular public speaker, Wuerffel has also written a book, *Danny Wuerffel's Tales from the Gator Swamp: Reflections of Faith and Football*, and is working on a second book.

The notoriety that Wuerffel experienced throughout his playing days could have easily made him selfish. Yet Danny Wuerffel has never lost track of what he is about—serving others. Although he was a dedicated football star and disciplined student, it is the authenticity of his devoted faith that has cultivated his lifestyle of servant leadership.

Notes

1. "Danny Wuerffel: The Quarterback with a Servant's Heart," CBN, http://www.cbn.com/700club/guests/bios/danny_wuerffel010506.aspx, (accessed April 13, 2010).

2. Ibid.

3. Ibid.

4. Ibid.

5. Ibid.

Dick Hoyt

Creating a Better World

by Stacy Martin-Tenney

Dick Hoyt took up running because his son, Rick, asked him to participate in a charity run for a lacrosse player paralyzed by a car accident. Rick was born a spastic quadriplegic with cerebral palsy due to oxygen deprivation from the umbilical cord that wrapped around his neck during delivery. He has never been able to run and has lived his life in a wheelchair. Dick Hoyt knew that his son was more than the vegetable the doctors said Rick was. Dick feverishly pursued inclusion activities for Rick. Rick wanted his dad to push his wheelchair in the race to prove that life did not stop with paralysis. The duo, or Team Hoyt as they are known, has since completed over 1,010 races including 234 triathlons, 212 10Ks, 89 half marathons, and 67 marathons. Rick certainly inspired their endeavors from his wheelchair over the last 33 years, but it was Dick's passionate pursuit of his son's dreams that pushed them across thousands of finish lines.

When Rick was born, his parents, Dick and Judy Hoyt, furiously refused the doctor's wishes to institutionalize him. They stared into his wide eyes and knew that there was light in them and so they brought him home. Dick and Judy had two more sons, Russ and Rob, which made Rick the big brother. The three boys played street hockey together when they were young and it was normal for Rick to be in a wheelchair. Russ fondly remembers, "We'd go out and play street hockey and Rick would be the goalie, and that's how he actually lost the two front teeth. The blood was dripping down his chin, but we won, so there was a smile on his face."[1] Rob commented years later, "Growing up with a person with a severe disability, at an early age you just take it for granted. 'What? You don't have a kid in a wheelchair in your house?'"[2] Dick and Judy knew that Rick could understand them as they taught him the alphabet and basic words, and sought out a way for him to communicate with them.

Engineers at Tufts University created an interactive computer that allowed Rick to express himself. Rick could select letters by a simple tap on his wheelchair headrest. A sports fan at heart, Rick selected "Go Bruins!"[3] as his first words, proving that he understood the world around him. The Bruins were in the Stanley Cup finals that year. The Hoyts finally convinced administrators to accept Rick into public school, at age 13.

Rick heard of the benefit run for the paralyzed lacrosse player while attending a basketball game. Rick typed a message on his special computer, "Dad, we have to do something for him. I want to show him that life goes on even though he is paralyzed."[4] He persuaded his dad to push his wheelchair in the five mile race, despite Dick's lack of long distance running experience. Dick had served as a Lieutenant Colonel in the Air National Guard for many years, so he was in athletic shape, but pushing a wheelchair in a five mile race without much training would not be easy for anyone. Team Hoyt finished next to last. Dick took one look at Rick's smile and knew it was all worth the effort and the beginning of a powerful bond between father and son. In a *60 Minutes* interview, Dick Hoyt recounted the experience and what Rick said to him after they crossed that finish line, "'Dad when I'm running it feels like my disability disappears'. And that was a very powerful message to me because he just—think about it—this is somebody who cannot talk, use their arms or legs and now, by running, the disability disappears."

Dick built up his mileage to marathon distance and Rick's wheelchair was adapted for his comfort through the long rides and so that it was more ergonomic for Dick to push while he ran all of those miles. People looked at them strangely when the Hoyts started lining up for these races and race organizers did not even approach them at first. Then they raced. People continued to stare, but runners were staring as Dick ran past them pushing a wheelchair with his son Rick sitting in it. Team Hoyt's times are competitive, not elite, but certainly competitive. Their best time in the marathon is 2:40:47 while their best half marathon is a little more than half of that time at 1:21:12.

Their favorite race is the Boston Marathon, which they have competed in for 27 years. The 2009 Boston Marathon was their 1,000th race. Team Hoyt posted on their website that "Rick always says if it comes down to doing one race a year he would like it to be the Boston Marathon: his favorite race. Dick Hoyt hopes that he is able to push Rick in the Boston Marathon when he is 70 years old (2011)! Neither Dick or Rick are ready to retire yet."[5]

The course record for the open men's division in the Boston Marathon is 2:05:52, achieved by Robert Kiprono Cheruiyot from Kenya in 2010. Just imagine, Dick Hoyt would only be 35 minutes behind him on their best day and he is pushing Rick in his chair. They are an impressive team and an awe-inspiring story at marathon and half-marathon races. Other participants crowd into the speaker series just to listen to their story and frequently wait for autographs and just a moment to share how the Hoyts have inspired them.

Rich Lomas is one such individual. His son Sammy was born with a rare condition related to the deletion of part of chromosome 22 and is only the eighth person in the world to be diagnosed. His condition confines him to a wheelchair, too. Rich is a fantastic runner and spent the summer training to push Sammy in the wheelchair during the Falmouth 7.1 mile road race that occurs every summer. Rick and Dick Hoyt compete in that race frequently and Rich and Sammy lined up right next to them at the start and finished not too far behind them. Running road races is not easy and it requires a lot of training and a lot of pounding on the pavement. Dick is in fantastic shape because of his commitment to his son. The feeling Rick enjoys from running is not the only reason to be grateful for their countless competitions. In 2003, Dick suffered a heart attack, and it was the running fitness that saved his life.

Running thousands of miles is not the only Hoyt hobby. They swim and bike those miles too. They have completed over 234 triathlons, including six Ironman Triathlons and seven Ironman 70.3 Triathlons. Ironman races are comprised of three components, a 2.4 mile swim, 112 mile bike ride, and 26.2 mile run, and thus are incredibly difficult for the ordinary competitor. Dick and Rick are anything but average, they are extraordinary. Just like for the runs, they outfitted a boat that Rick could ride in while Dick strapped a bungee harness to his back and pulled the boat through the water as he swam. During the transition areas, Dick must carry Rick from the boat to the bike and transfer him from the bike to the running chair. No other competitor lifts weights during the transition area, but what is one more challenge for this incredible father and his son? And for the bike, a custom bicycle was developed so Rick could lead the way as Dick cycled those grueling distances. In triathlons, the run is last, and so they return to their roots and Dick pushes Rick across the finish line yet again. "Also adding to their list of achievements, Dick and Rick biked and ran across the U.S. in 1992, completing a full 3,735 miles in 45 days," said the Hoyt website.[6]

All of these accomplishments would not have been possible if Dick had given up on his son as the doctors had advised. Instead of giving up, he ran towards a finish line with an incredible passion and pursuit of Rick's achievement. Rick graduated from Boston College with a degree in special education. He taught for a year, but then turned his attention to computers and now works for Boston College developing the "Eagle Eyes" computer system; it helps him communicate through eye and head movements.

Rick was once asked, if he could give his father one thing, what would it be? Rick responded, "The thing I'd most like is for my dad to sit in the chair and I would push him for once."[7] Rick would do anything for his father, but his father is quick to credit Rick for their achievements. "It was Rick who was the motivation," Dick Hoyt said, "He asked me to race."[8] Nothing is impossible with unconditional love and a little determination; Dick Hoyt proves that every mile he runs.

Notes

1. CBS Broadcasting, Inc., "Hoyt Brothers Cheer On Family For Their 25th Run," WBZ Boston, April 3, 2006, http://wbztv.com/bostonmarathon/Boston.Marathon.Dick .2.577742.html, (accessed April 2, 2010).

2. Ibid.

3. "Two dads, two sons—a lot of love," *The Herald Tribune*, Section C1, August 18, 2009, http://www.heraldtribune.com/article/20090818/COLUMNIST/908181012 /-1/NEWSSITEMAP?p=all&tc=pgall, (accessed April 2, 2010).

4. Associated Press, "Father, paralyzed son ready for final Ironman race," *ESPN .com*, October 23, 2006, http://sports.espn.go.com/oly/news/story?id=2631338, (accessed April 2, 2010).

5. Teamhoyt.com, "About Team Hoyt: The Beginning of Team Hoyt," http:// www .teamhoyt.com/about/index.html, (accessed April 2, 2010).

6. Ibid.

7. Ibid.

8. Associated Press, "Father, paralyzed son ready for final Ironman race," *ESPN .com*, October 23, 2006, http://sports.espn.go.com/oly/news/story?id=2631338, (accessed April 2, 2010).

7

FIGHTING RACISM

by Richard Lapchick

A significant part of the work of the National Consortium for Academics and Sports has been to create programs that help combat racism in our country. Perhaps the problem that plagued us more than any other, racism has been a blemish on our society as well as in sport. There have been other individuals in sport, some noted in the *Barrier Breakers* section such as Jackie Robinson, who have taken on enormous roles in that struggle. In this section we present the lives of nine individuals whose names most people do not know but whose lives surely represent *Fighting Racism.*

Wally Triplett and Dennis Hoggard were the inspiration of the Penn State football teams of 1946 and 1947 who chose not to play rather than play without their full squad during an era of segregation and heated race relations, especially in sports.

Dionte Hall was a 14-year-old boy who was followed into a fast-food restaurant one afternoon by a group of white teenagers who taunted him with racial epithets and then put a noose around his neck. Hall quietly let the courts take the case while helping to educate his community on the history of lynching and its meaning.

Michael Watson, a college basketball player, was attacked by two white men in suburban Maryland. The incident was recorded on video tape, yet the all-white jury acquitted the two attackers.

Darryl Williams, who was an aspiring NFL player, was gunned down by three white teenagers during the half-time of his first varsity game during the busing controversy in 1970s Boston. A quadriplegic, Williams became an inspirational speaker against racism until his untimely death in 2010.

Richard Green and David Lazerson, an African-American and a Hasidic Jew, created a basketball program in the Crown Heights section of Brooklyn to combat the growing fear that was rapidly developing between the African-American and Hasidic communities which lived side-by-side in Crown Heights.

Tommie Smith and John Carlos electrified the world of sport with their defiant black-gloved clenched fists on the victory stand in the Mexico City Olympics in 1968. Vilified by the media at first, they have become iconic symbols of standing up against racism.

The lives of these men are testimony as to what the individual can do to take on issues as gigantic as racism in our country.

The 1946 and 1947 Penn State Football Team

Fighting Racism

Special Contribution by Diana Kenepp

The story of "that team" actually began during the 1944–45 academic year. It was a time before the Civil Rights Movement when segregation was the norm and racial intolerance was pervasive in American Society. An outstanding high school athlete from suburban Philadelphia, Wallace Triplett III, received a recruiting letter and scholarship offer—a sight unseen—from the University of Miami, a segregated institution. Discovering that Triplett was black, the offer was rescinded. So in the fall of 1945, Triplett arrived by bus at The Pennsylvania State University with an envelope that contained a senatorial scholarship awarded for academic achievement. After registering at a local hotel, he met with Coach Bob Higgins to inquire about joining the football team.

Triplett became Penn State's first African-American to make the varsity squad and start in a game. Three others had preceded him on freshman teams prior to World War II when first year students couldn't compete on the varsity squads.

By 1946 many of the military veterans returned to school and rejoined the football team. Dennis Hoggard was one of those veterans. Penn State now had two black players whose presence necessitated a momentous decision the team would make midway through the season. A game was scheduled for late November with the University of Miami. Penn State was notified that the team was welcome but they could not bring their black players. A team meeting was called to discuss the issue. Although some teammates were unhappy about not going, they agreed unanimously to play "All or none." Thus, the game was cancelled. This statement against racial injustice was heard around the country and it would not be the last time the team would take a stand. Their decision influenced Penn State's boxing team to decline an invitation to the Sugar Bowl tournament because blacks were barred from participation. The boxing team had no African-Americans at the time.

The following year, 1947, would be a highly successful year for "that team." It began with a win over Washington State, played in Hershey Stadium. The game was promoted as The Chocolate Bowl by the sponsor, Hershey Chocolate Company. The men of '47 continued their winning streak. When the team arrived in Annapolis for a game against Navy, they encountered an environment of taunts and jeers. At the hotel where the team was to be housed, "that team" experienced firsthand racial injustice. As the players were given room assignments and keys it became apparent that Triplett and Hoggard were being ignored. When the coaches inquired, they were told that there were no more rooms. It was too difficult to move the entire team so Triplett and Hoggard had to be taken to a hotel that accommodated blacks. It would not be the last time "that team" found itself with housing difficulties due to segregation.

The 1947 team set school rushing and defensive records. Their NCAA defensive records for fewest rushing yards allowed per game (17), per rush (0.64), and fewest total yards allowed in a game (minus 47) were intact after a half century. They also had six shutout games in their undefeated season and won the school's first Lambert Trophy.

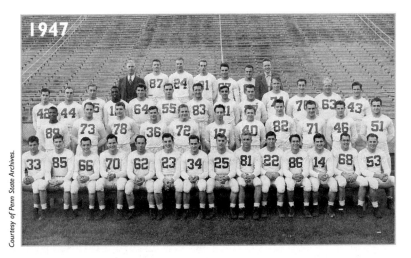

Toward the end of the season speculation that they would be invited to a bowl was rumored in the press. However, of the four bowls existing in 1947, the Rose Bowl was predetermined, and the Orange Bowl and Sugar Bowl would not allow blacks to participate. The Cotton Bowl would be the only possibility. Coach Higgins called a team meeting to discuss the ramifications if an invitation was extended. Captain Steve Suhey told the team that a meeting wasn't necessary because they had made their statement the previous year: We play all or none. We are Penn State.

After negotiations and discussions, the Cotton Bowl officials told Penn State they would receive an invitation if the Southwest Conference Champion would agree to play them. "So with SMU's blessing," Cotton Bowl officials set up the game. That didn't please everyone and some intolerant zealots referred to the game decisively as "The Chocolate Bowl."[1] However, Dallas was a segregated city and no hotel accommodations were available. The team had to stay at a nearby Naval Air Station so players could be housed together.

The game ended in a 13-13 tie. However "that team" was victorious in breaking a color barrier and making statements against racial injustice.

Note

1. Louis Prato, *The Penn State Football Encyclopedia* (Champaign, IL: Sports Publishing, Inc. 1998), 195.

Dionte Hall

Fighting Racism

by Jenny Yehlen

Hate crimes, racist jokes, and racial stereotyping prove that racism is still very evident in today's society. Although segregation was eliminated on the law books, there are instances like what happened to Dionte Hall to prove how much work still needs to be done to alter attitudes towards race relations and to curb racist behavior.

Dionte Hall, a 14-year-old junior varsity basketball player from Largo High School in St. Petersburg, Florida, was walking through the parking lot of a fast-food restaurant with two of his friends on January 14, 2004. Suddenly, he heard shouts from across the parking lot, so he turned around to see what was going on. He turned only to see someone waving a rope, tied in a noose, in the air. As the young man, who was 19-years-old, was waving the noose in the air, he yelled racial slurs. Hall and his friends did not react to the racist gesture and they entered the Wendy's Restaurant.

The group of friends was sitting innocently, eating their food, when the same boy from outside came up behind Hall and actually slipped the noose around his neck. The boy had been bet $10 by one of his friends to walk over to Hall and put the noose around his neck. He continued to whisper derogatory comments in Hall's ear as well. In spite of the rage festering inside of him, Hall chose to remain calm in this horrible situation. He didn't retaliate in a violent way, which would be the instinctive reaction by most people being harassed. He didn't try to get into a fight and he didn't even want to sue the boy for his actions. He remained very calm. Hall wanted to retaliate in the most positive way he could, and he succeeded in doing that. He demonstrated a maturity that was truly beyond his years.

Hall handled the matter by returning to school and talking about the incident with his basketball coach, who immediately took him to the school resource officer. Charges were brought up against the 19-year-old boy who committed the horrible prank along with a couple of his friends who were involved in the incident. The "attacker," who actually committed the crime, was charged with a misdemeanor battery and not a hate crime.

Because Hall handled the situation in such an exemplary manner, the local police department presented him with a proclamation and a letter of commendation. The letter stated "Dionte restrained himself from physical and verbal retaliation. He practiced the teachings of Dr. Martin Luther King Jr., through nonviolence."[1]

Whether or not he knew it at the time, his ability to resist retaliating was the best possible stand he could take against hate crimes and discrimination, and for that he has been commended. We can only hope that others follow in Hall's footsteps and fight racism and discrimination in a strong, yet peaceful way.

This incident has changed Hall's life forever. He refuses to simply move on with his life like nothing ever happened. The incident has motivated him to make a difference and he has been active in working to change laws pertaining to minors and hate crimes. Hall wrote to then-President Bush and he and his parents have held news conferences on the issues urging people to support the new law.

Hall and his family want aggressive prosecution for individuals who commit hate crimes and additional legislation that might hold parents responsible for instilling beliefs in children that might result in violence against others because of their race, ethnicity, sexual orientation, or religious beliefs. Hall's parents obviously instilled positive values in the mind of their son and today Dionte Hall and his family are continuing to fight for tolerance, understanding, and social justice.

Note

1. Shannon Tan, "Teen who faced noose, slur commended for courage," *St. Petersburg Times*, February 18, 2004.

Michael Watson

Fighting Racism

by Richard Lapchick

The story of college basketball player Michael Watson offers a telling example as to why many African-Americans have so little faith in the American judicial system. The story could easily have taken place in Mississippi in the 1960s, but actually took place in Maryland in 1995. On the Wednesday afternoon before Thanksgiving, Michael Watson sat in a state court in Frederick, Maryland, waiting for his share of American justice.

His former teammates at Mount St. Mary's were practicing for the opening game of the 1995–96 season. Seven months earlier Watson, then a graduate student, had helped lead the small school to victory as Mount St. Mary's beat Rider College to win the Northeast Conference Championship and advanced to the NCAA Tournament. Watson had scored 15 points, garnered 11 rebounds, and hit six straight free throws in the last minute to slam the door on Rider's attempt to get to the "big dance" for the third year in a row.

Those spectacular basketball moments had helped Watson forget more painful ones. Around 1 a.m. on October 30, 1994, Watson and his date pulled up to a Thurmont, Maryland, convenience store to get some food after a college party. Inside the store, three white men assaulted Watson. The back injuries Watson suffered kept him off the basketball court for several weeks while he underwent physical therapy. The back pain recurs occasionally, but far less often than the mental agony.

About 12 hours earlier, a busload of hooded and robed members of the Ku Klux Klan had marched at the State House in Annapolis. They shouted "white power" while one carried a poster of the face of assassinated civil rights leader Dr. Martin Luther King circled by a target. The caption read, "Our dream came true." Klan members were outnumbered more than ten to one by protesters who shouted them down, and tensions grew in the state capitol.

Did those tensions travel across the state into Thurmont, near the home of the leader of the Maryland Klan? According to Watson, one of the three men who attacked him shouted, "You don't belong here. This is Klan country. You're a nigger, boy." At the trial, the assailants denied the remarks, but they could not deny what the store's videotape had captured. It clearly showed the three men assaulting Watson, shoving and hitting him while he held up his hands to ward off their blows.

A shocked Mount St. Mary's President, George R. Houston Jr., wrote a letter to the college community. In it he said, "We have all available resources, and we expect a fair, thorough, and prompt investigation."[1]

The investigation produced the videotape and witnesses who only testified for Watson. While no one could verify the racist remarks, witnesses corroborated Watson's version that seemed indisputable given the evidence on the videotape.

Through the help of various local friends, counselors, and nationally prominent activists, Watson began to recover from the emotional scars of the attack. He did not seek publicity. There were no television cameras in the court, no Chris Dardens or Marcia Clarks for the prosecution, and no F. Lee Baileys or Johnny Cochrans for the defense. There were no Mark Fuhrmans or Stacey Koons on the Thurmont Police. The case was an easy one for him to win from all possible perspectives.

While waiting for the slow wheels of justice to turn, Watson focused on basketball as his source of emotional rehabilitation. "There was no sense of race on our team. We were all so focused on winning. We worked together with a special solidarity. Our team was a safe haven for me and while we were together, I was able to forget what had happened outside the walls of Mount St. Mary's. My white teammates gave me the perspective that those three attackers did not represent all white people. However, when I was away from my teammates, the pain always came back."[2] Watching his attackers go to prison was going to be his final step toward recovery. Watson was poised to celebrate a heartfelt Thanksgiving. Dino Flores, the prosecutor, was confident that the case would be a cut-and-dried victory for the prosecution. When jury selection began on Monday the first ominous portent appeared. An all-white jury was chosen. Still confident, prosecutor Flores took his case to them.

The witnesses in the store verified what was seen on the videotape. A defense lawyer called Watson a racist and claimed that he provoked the attack against the three white men. Raised to respect everyone regardless of color, Watson cringed in disbelief at what he was hearing.

Nevertheless, when the jury went out on Wednesday, Watson and prosecutor Flores felt confident. Watson said, "I was 90 percent certain of a favorable outcome. The evidence was clear and the judge had ruled favorably on most of Flores' motions. The 10 percent of doubt came only from what I knew about the fate of blacks in the justice system. But I was sure."[3] Two hours later the jury returned with "not guilty" verdicts on the charges of assault and on the charge of committing a hate crime.

The verdict, read to an incredulous Michael Watson, lent a hollow ring to the end of Mount St. Mary President Houston's letter to the community: "It is imperative that all government officials, community and church leaders join us in making it inescapably clear that this country has 'zero tolerance' for racist actions such as these."[4]

Watson said, "I just sat there for several minutes. The accused were gone before I totally realized what happened. There is nothing I can do but carry the scars throughout my life while these guys went out, free to celebrate or do whatever the pleased."[5]

Thurmont, Maryland is seven miles from Camp David, where President Clinton prepared for Thanksgiving. Without any national publicity, the president, like most Americans, did not know who Michael Watson was or why he could not join in his fellow countrymen in their Thanksgiving celebrations.

I was sickened when I watched the videotape of the attack. Surely the verdict should have been just as clear as it should have been in the first Rodney King Trial when videotape clearly showed King being badly beaten by the police. I wrote a column for *The Sporting News* to bring this case to national attention and begin the healing process for Michael Watson. Though the national media picked up the article, Watson never got another day in court. I was inundated with more hate mail than at any time since the end of the apartheid era, and even received two telephone death threats after the article was published. The one good thing we both got was the beginning of a rich friendship that I treasure. The case unfortunately demonstrated the depth of racism in America and how hard it is for blacks to obtain justice without status and public attention to force a second look. We indeed have a long road yet to travel.

The NCAS gave Watson a Giant Steps Award in 1996. He graduated and had a successful career in corporate America but always felt he could do more. He recently told me that, "My life journey over the last 14 years has had a tremendous impact on my life. From my ordeal, I have a new profound outlook on life.

"Over the last two years, I have attended Biblical Theological Seminary pursing a Doctrine of Ministry. This has been an uplifting life experience for me to have an opportunity to minister to people about the relationship with Jesus Christ and mankind in a spiritual way. I have a different outlook of people today because of my ordeal. I tend to look at people in a different light, because of what God has done for me.

"My goal and aspirations are to become a pastor of inner-city Baptist church, located along the east coast where there is need for a Missional church. It is not only my concern with local church body, but also with the local community. I think that the education that I'm receiving is both fundamental and essential for pastoring people.

"I'm a product of the inner city. I know that I will be more equipped and an example to the local community members to allow them to see what God has done for me and how he's delivered me as a testimony to others."[6]

Michael Watson ultimately became a stronger person as a result of what he calls his "ordeal" and now will spend the rest of his life serving people. I know that his church members and the community the church serves will be much richer with Pastor Watson.

Notes

1. Richard Lapchick, *Splitting the Difference*, (Maryland: Madison Books, 2001), 285.

2. Ibid.

3. Ibid., 286.

4. Ibid.

5. Ibid.

6. Michael Watson, interview with author, March 22, 2010.

Darryl Williams

Fighting Racism

by Brian Wright

A hero is often someone with exceptional courage, nobility, and strength. Fictional heroes are generally indestructible, possessing incredible physical strength and using that strength to right the world's wrongs. In real life, however, they are very different. Darryl Williams was a real world hero.

As a 15-year-old high school student in 1979, Williams was an exceptional student and athlete. As an athlete, Williams participated in basketball and football. Like most 15 year olds, Williams thought little about race relations, violence, and how those issues pertained to his life. Issues of making the next big catch for his high school football team, or coming up with a key defensive stop in the fourth quarter of his basketball game seemed much more relevant.

One split second of racist violence inspired by hate quickly changed his life forever. At the end of the first half of a high school football game, Williams excited his teammates and the crowd by making a seemingly impossible catch. With his spirits high, Williams would never have guessed that his feelings of triumph would soon turn to pain and agony. As the third quarter of the game began, Williams stood on the sidelines waiting to enter the game. He never did. As he waited, three young, white males had taken position on a nearby building waiting to take their shot to kill Williams. Shots of gunfire rang throughout the football field as Williams was stuck by the sniper's bullets. His career was over; Williams would never be able to play football again. Doctors' examinations found that he was paralyzed from the neck down. Williams, a 15-year-old high school student-athlete, was devastated.

Williams lay in the hospital wondering "why." Why had this happened? What had he done to anybody to make them feel like they had to take his life and his livelihood? After years of strenuous thought as to "why" this had happened, Williams found that he did not understand why and never would. He did understand though that it was a racially motivated hate crime just as many crimes before that had plagued this country. This hatred in many instances would have sparked retaliation or an equivalent hatred in his heart for an entire race or group of people. But Williams chose to love and motivate rather than to hate. He made a conscious decision to dedicate his life to helping people denounce racism and to work to promote tolerance, respect, and understanding.

"I made peace with my situation long ago," Williams said. "I understand where hostility and ignorance come from and I'm able to rise above it. Ultimately it has a lot to do with knowing that other people look to me for inspiration. They get inspiration and strength from me and that makes me feel honored."[1]

After losing the use of his arms and legs, and after hearing countless broken promises of medical and financial support after the shooting, Williams said, "A lot of people perceive me as a white-person hater, because my injury was at the hands of a white person. I can't fault the whole race for that because there are bad people in the white race; there are bad people in the black race as well. You don't hate a whole race of people for one other person."[2] Williams worked for decades to fight racism and promote racial understanding through public speaking where he used his own experiences to inspire others while speaking from his wheelchair. His ability to forgive, as well as his passion for improving society, led him down a path of service to his community and for the entire human race.

On March 28, 2010, Darryl Williams passed away suddenly. It was a shocking loss to those who loved his passion and perseverance and the man he had become. It is believed that he died of respiratory failure in his sleep. He was 46 years old.

Of Williams, Richard Lapchick said, "What greater sign of hope of the black community's forgiveness for all the wrongs done to them over the centuries, than the attitude of Darryl Williams." Upon his death, Lapchick reflected, "He was a real hero and was the most serious reason I decided to go into sports." Williams' remarkable display of forgiveness, courage, strength, as well as self-empowerment is a model for all humans to live by and will truly be missed.

In 2004, Williams said "It's discouraging that we are not making as much progress as I would have hoped in 25 years, especially in the area of racial intolerance. I take personal offense to it because I had my fun and did my thing, but not at the expense of harming anyone else. And I have to deal with this situation that I have, and I see these people without any regard for human life, let alone any respect for themselves. They are wasting their life, their time. If there's anyone who can attest to how valuable time is, and a person's physicality, it's me."[3]

His powerful words ring an eerie tone now that he is not here to lead us, but it's not too late to make Darryl Williams proud.

Notes

1. Dan Shaughnessy, "To the end, a man felled by hatred rose above it," *The Boston Globe*, March 29, 2010.

2. Dan Shaughnessy, "Paralysis can't stop this man," *The Boston Globe*, February 6, 2001.

3. Dan Shaughnessy, "He chose to be a better man, not a bitter man," *The Boston Globe*, September 28, 2004.

Richard Green
and Dr. David Lazerson

Fighting Racism

by Brian Wright, with Austin Moss II

The racial tension occurring in the Crown Heights section of Brooklyn, New York in 1991 seemed to be insurmountable for local residents to overcome. This downward spiral of negative sentiment was directly correlated to a fatal car accident that had occurred in the neighborhood. While walking down the street on a warm summer afternoon, a seven-year-old African-American child, Gavin Cato, was struck and killed by a car that had lost control and jumped the curb. The driver of the vehicle was identified as Yosef Lifsh, a Hasidic Jewish resident of the Crown Heights community. Stemming from the accident, emotions and tempers flared between members of the African-American and Jewish residents of Crown Heights. The hostile emotions that materialized led to a racial uproar and riots between the two communities. Many in the African-American community considered the death of young Cato a homicide rather than an accident. In an apparent act of retaliation to young Cato's death, a 29-year old visiting Australian rabbinical student was stabbed to death. Hatred and anger now engulfed both communities which seemed ready to wage war. Leaders from both communities preached war against one another and an eventual chaos seemed unavoidable. How could the eventual war and violence be prevented? Many individuals in the community felt hopeless, believing there was nothing that could be done to prevent the ensuing violence. Contrary to this common feeling of despondency, two local social activists, Richard Green and Dr. David Lazerson (or Dr. "Laz" as he is endearingly known by members of the Crown Heights community) knew that violence and war would lead to the eventual demise of Crown Heights.

As many men and women gathered in the community to promote violence, irrational behavior, and hatred, Green constantly combated these discussions with words of wisdom and peace. As his peace message began to spread, Green became the target of many negative comments and racial slurs from members even within his own community. Green was undaunted in his commitment and his message began to resonate among many former proponents of violence. As Green worked to instill awareness about peace within the African-American community, Lazerson simultaneously worked on the minds of young Hasidic Jews. Lazerson, a serious intellectual with a passion for community relations, understood the importance of spreading a message of peace and understanding rather than one of violence and retaliation. Green and Lazerson knew that a peaceful resolution of the existing tensions required a sense of cooperation and shared purpose where opposing sides could express their thoughts, feelings, and concerns without fear of violence. In order to accomplish this, the two men arranged meetings between young members of the Hasidic and African-American communities to discuss the differences they were having in a safe and peaceful environment. Through these meetings members of both communities where able to express their feelings, experiences, and concerns through a non-violent, open discussion forum approach. Green and Lazerson also arranged meetings with Mayor David Dinkins to discuss methods to obtain peace and solutions to other issues surrounding the youth in Crown Heights at the time.

It was Green's feeling that for the African-American community to be angry at the Jewish community for all of their misfortunes was unfair and a mistake. He felt that the African-American community should instead be angry with the lack of resources and services throughout the community as a whole.

Green and Lazerson sought creative new ideas to bring together the youth of the two warring communities, so they created an environment that would prompt discussion and ease fears. They concluded that sports would be the best medium and that it had the potential to have a very positive effect on improving race relations within the community. Green and Lazerson introduced it to members attending the meetings. The young members of the group agreed on the impact sports could have on improving the current situation of the neighborhood and found playing sports a great way to learn about and interact with one another. Green and Lazerson had assessed how sports transcended all cultures, genders, and races as well as tearing down all barriers of hatred and bigotry. They knew that participating together in sports would shed a new light on why and how things were done differently in each community, and open the doors for a new open-minded approach to communication. The teams they created at random, with African-Americans and Hasidic Jews on each, started playing weekly football and basketball games together. Soon suspicious behavior was replaced by teamwork and trust. The two groups struggled together and they began to see similarities in their struggles off the court as well. Crown Heights was transformed into an atmosphere filled with compassion and hopefulness.

While Green and Lazerson saw sports as an important ingredient for positive social change within the community, their ideas for improving racial cohesiveness and creating awareness between the two ethnic groups were not limited to involvement in sports. Green established the Crown Heights Youth Collective which provided counseling, tutoring, job-training, as well as art, music and dance groups for youth in the Crown Heights community. This Youth Collective would eventually merge with the Crown Heights Jewish Community Relations Council to become what is known today as Project CURE (Communication Understanding Respect Education). Green and Lazerson would continue to launch creative and innovative social and racial awareness projects as they started their own bi-racial rap group which held "CURE" concerts to promote positive social interaction between the two communities. Project CURE's vision and message had grown so much within New York City that members of Project CURE participated in an exhibition basketball game during the halftime of a New York Knicks game at Madison Square Garden. This provided Green and Lazerson with national exposure to promote their cause and their vision for race relations in this small city of Crown Heights. Through the work of these two great men, Project CURE has improved the lives of countless young men and women growing up in the Crown Heights area and in other parts of New York, and even throughout the rest of the world.

Dr. Lazerson now resides in North Miami where he teaches psychology at Florida International University and teaches special education in the Broward County school system.[1] Even though Dr. Lazerson's residential location has changed, he still continues to show his love and affection for humanity. At the Quest Center, a school for disabled children, Dr. Laz has formed the Sing and Sing Choir that performs pre-rehearsed hand signals and sign language while he sings and plays guitar.[2] There is no doubt that Dr. Laz's faith and love has brought joy to the lives of many disabled children. He continues to be honored for his work in race relations, contributions in the field of special education, and community service. In 2007, two colleges honored Dr. Lazerson as he was named a Distinguished Alumni Recipient from the University at Buffalo and Buffalo State College.[3]

Richard Green continues to be an active leader in the Crown Heights community. He still serves as Chief Executive of the Crown Heights Youth Collective, in which he advocates to youth in the community and works towards bridging the gap.[4] Nearly 20 years have passed since the death of seven-year-old Gavin Cato, and Richard Green continues to carry the torch for peace. Significant progress has been made with the race relations between Hasidic Jews and African-Americans in Crown Heights. However, Green and other community leaders are continuously searching for new ways to heal old wounds as they focus their efforts towards achieving a united community free of hate and crime.

Richard Green is a leader and a visionary who seized the opportunity to make a positive social change in the way people acted within the community of Crown Heights, as well as around the world. Dr. David Lazerson is also a visionary, with the belief that sports and other forums for communication can help transcend any barrier that the youth of Crown Heights faced in social differences and community relations. The two men understood that in order to prevent the detrimental dynamics from forming within the Crown Heights region, individuals were going to have to be open to embracing diversity and social differences. As they realized the positive effects that sports and other social programs could have on the community they also realized that it is creative programs like these that will help eliminate bigotry, racism, stereotypes, and violence around the United States and the rest of the world. Richard Green and Dr. David Lazerson are social heroes not only in their home of New York City but also social heroes and role models to all of society.

Notes

1. Fred Tasker, "Movie tells how peace emerged from riots," *The Miami Herald*, June 10, 2004, Tropical Life.

2. Crown Heights Info, "Dr. Laz: Hero to the disabled," Crown Heights, http://www.crownheights.info/index.php?itemid=10430, (accessed March 2, 2010).

3. Dr. Laz, "Awards," Dr. Laz Awards and Grants, http://www.drlaz.com/grants.html, (accessed March 3, 2010).

4. Cryil J. Barker, "Richard Green: race relations basics in Crown Heights." *New York Amsterdam News*, May 29, 2008.

Tommie Smith and John Carlos

Fighting Racism

Special Contribution by Horacio Ruiz

Tommie Smith stands on the winner's podium, his country's national anthem booming through Mexico City's Olympic Stadium and his country's flag raised the highest. There is an Olympic gold medal dangling from Smith's neck—his reward for winning the 200-meter race in world-record time—but the medal is hardly the object of the moment's attention. Smith has his right fist raised, clenched in a black glove, with his head bowed down and eyes shut.

John Carlos stands a few feet below Smith on the winner's podium, the winner of a bronze medal in the same event. He is Smith's fellow countryman and his pose mirrors Smith's. He bows his head and lifts his left fist in the air, clenched in a black glove. He does not open his eyes. Neither man looks as the American flag is raised into the air. In that moment, Smith and Carlos create a lasting image for black power in the United States, demonstrating the impact two individuals can create in protest. Many interpretations have been made of the protest. At its broadest it is applied to international human rights and to a more specific point, the treatment of African-American people in the United States. Those moments during the playing of the national anthem of the United States would change the lives of Smith and Carlos forever—and the American sports scene.

Ten days prior to the beginning of the 1968 Olympics in Mexico City, a group of students protesting against the Mexican government was surrounded by the Mexican army and fired at in the Plaza of Three Cultures. An estimated 270 students died and more than 1,000 were wounded in what would be called the Tlatelolco Massacre. The preceding months had seen the assassinations of presidential hopeful Robert F. Kennedy and civil rights leader Dr. Martin Luther King Jr. In 1967, before the assassinations of two of the most prominent leaders in the United States and the Tlatelolco Massacre of 1968, sociologist and civil rights activist Harry Edwards had asked a group of black American Olympians to boycott the Mexico City Games. Edwards was well aware that the Mexico City Games would be the first to be televised live to an American audience—creating the perfect platform for a protest. Edwards created the Olympic Project for Human Rights with the intention of bringing to light the social injustices faced by African-Americans on the world's premiere sporting platform. As the Olympics approached, however, the boycott seemed less likely to occur as the majority of African-American athletes did not agree on a boycott being the best form of protest. Instead, each athlete was left to create his or her own form of protest.

A closer look at the protest of Smith and Carlos reveals intricate symbolism. Both Smith and Carlos went to the podium shoeless and wearing black socks to represent black poverty in the United States. Smith wore a black scarf to represent black pride. Carlos put a string of black beads around his neck to represent those who had been lynched. Smith would later explain that his right fist represented black power in America and Carlos' left fist represented unity in black America. Both fists together, represented an arch of unity and power. All three athletes on the podium, including Australian silver-medalist Peter Norman, wore Olympic Project for Human Rights badges on their jackets. Norman, knowing that Smith and Carlos would stage their protest, had asked if there was anything he could do. They handed him the human rights badge, and he became forever unified with them not just because of his place on the podium, but because of his show of solidarity. Smith and Carlos would reunite as pallbearers at Norman's funeral nearly four decades later.

Although the conservative Australian media pushed for Norman to be sanctioned, Julius Patching, Norman's team manager, refused to take any action against him. Smith and Carlos would become victims of a much more powerful political machine. Both were removed from the Olympic Village and banned from the Olympics by International Olympic Committee president Avery Brundage. "The basic principle of the Olympic Games is that politics plays no part whatsoever in them," read an IOC statement. "U.S. athletes violated this universally accepted principle . . . to advertise domestic political views."[1]

Smith and Carlos returned home to San Jose—heroes to some and enemies to many others. They were subjected to death threats and hate mail, schoolyard insults, and bricks smashing through their windows. For many years, they were relegated to the fringe of the track and field community, forced to alter their school schedule so that they had to take night classes, and had difficulty finding jobs. Neither man got a meaningful job in the United Sates until Smith was hired as a coach at Oberlin College by sports activist and Oberlin athletics director Jack Scott. Despite the life-altering consequences, neither regrets his actions.

"I knew it was going to be big," Carlos told the *Orlando Sentinel* years after his stand on the podium. "I was prepared to face the repercussions. What I wasn't prepared for at all was how it would touch everything. I had only been thinking about me being John Carlos, not me being a young married man with a kid. It was hard for us. We still feel it today."[2]

It seemed as if Smith was primed to protest for black Americans and to be a symbol of the social movements of the 1960s. In his autobiography, *Silent Gesture*, he remembered growing up in a family of sharecroppers working to harvest cotton or grapes, only to see the major portion of their crop handed over to white landowners. But a particular event is etched into Smith's memory: watching his father pulling their family wagon filled with 10 children to the side of a road so that a lone white man could pass. It was an early lesson in Smith's life about his place in society.

Today, Smith is a faculty member at Santa Monica College, where he also is the head men's cross country and track and field coach. Carlos is working as the track and field coach and as an in-school suspension supervisor at Palm Springs High in Palm Springs, California.

Thirty-seven years and one day after their protest, San Jose State—Smith's and Carlos' alma mater—unveiled a statue of their famous pose in the 1968 Olympics. Back in 1968, San Jose State was the one place the two runners were well-received, as students cheered them on and ex-president Robert Clark called them "honorable young men."

"It's an honor for us, but we also realize this isn't all about us anymore," Smith said at the ceremony. "The history of what happened will live on long after we're gone, and I'm just glad a part of it will live at San Jose State."[3]

Notes

1. Jennifer Rosenberg, History of the Olympics, About.com, http://history1900s.about.com/od/fadsfashion/a/olympics1968.htm, (accessed June 14, 2010).

2. Rick Maese, "Strike a pose: Smith, Carlos sent powerful message at '68 Olympics," *Orlando Sentinel*, July 27, 2004.

3. "Statue honors Olympics sprinters' civil rights protest," *Jet Magazine*, November 7, 2005.

8

CREATING A NEW GAME
PLAN FOR COLLEGE SPORT

by Richard Lapchick

I have written two books on ethical issues in college sport, one published in 1986 and one in 2006. It struck me how many of the problems in college sport that existed in 1986 persist to this day. There are a group of leaders, some directly involved in college sport, others in higher education, and others who work from the outside. All have worked hard over the years to bring improvements to the lives of our student-athletes and integrity to the games they play. Those are some of the people we showcase in *Creating a New Game Plan for College Sport.*

Joe Crowley was the president of the University of Nevada, Reno for more than two decades. During that time, he also served as president of the NCAA and was a major change agent in that role on the issue of race and sport in college.

Clarence Underwood and C.M. Newton were both prominent athletic directors at Michigan State and the University of Kentucky, respectively. Underwood was one of the small number of African-American athletics directors in Division IA and has worked throughout his career to make sport be more equitable for women and people of color.

C.M. Newton, a prominent coach, was the first to play five African-Americans at the same time in college basketball. As athletic director at Kentucky, he made courageous decisions such as eliminating the alcohol sponsorships of Kentucky athletics at a cost of nearly $400,000 a year to the University.

Sister Rose Ann Fleming leads the academic advising program at Xavier University in Cincinnati. Dedicated to her student-athletes,

Sister Fleming makes sure that every Xavier student-athlete succeeded in the classroom.

Judy Sweet was a pioneer for women. Serving as athletics director of the University of California, San Diego, Judy was a vocal advocate for the implementation of Title IX. She became the first woman to first serve as president of the NCAA and later joined the NCAA as one of its top leaders while remaining a strong advocate for women and girls in sport.

Dick Schultz, a former athletic director, became the executive director of the NCAA and began to address some of the "old school policies" in college sport that had led to so many athletics departments breaking the rules and creating a student-athlete population where graduation rates were very low in the revenue sports.

There were two men who worked for reform from the outside including Creed Black, a giant in the publishing industry, who started the Knight Commission on Intercollegiate Athletics in the 1990s. The Knight Commission pushed the NCAA to get presidents more involved in the overseeing college athletics on their campus. Richard Astro, then the Dean of Arts and Sciences at Northeastern University in Boston, financed the start of the Center of the Study of Sport in Society. Sport and Society had many pioneering programs teaching conflict resolution, working on the issue of men's violence against women, and getting students to balance academics and athletics. Richard agreed to have Sport and Society help launch a national movement with the National Consortium for Academics and Sports in 1985. After positions as Provost at the University of Central Florida and Drexel University, Richard Astro joined the Consortium as its Chief Academic Officer. The Consortium, of course, implemented the degree completion program and the community service program, both of which have had such an extraordinary impact on college sport in America.

Myles Brand was a champion for student-athletes, Title IX, and civil rights in sports as he led the NCAA. His 2009 passing came after he had righted many injustices in college sports, but we must continue to follow his lead and make sports live up to its ideals.

These men and women have been there for decades insisting that sport at the intercollegiate level live up to its ideals.

Dr. Joseph Crowley

Creating a New Game Plan for College Sport

by Richard Lapchick and Stacy Martin-Tenney

Joe Crowley is best known for his presidency at the University of Nevada at Reno, as he served the institution for a record setting 23 years from 1978 to 2001. When he stepped down, he had served his university longer than any other president among the nation's leading universities. He also outlasted every chief executive in the state of Nevada. Concurrent with his presidency at Nevada, Crowley completed a term as the president of the NCAA from 1993 to 1995, a feat only accomplished by one other man.

Joe Crowley played an historical role in the history of race and sport when a dramatic confrontation was unfolding between the Black Coaches Association and the NCAA. Crowley, as the NCAA president, stepped in to mediate the controversy between the university presidents and the Black Coaches Association, thereby avoiding congressional intervention. Both parties now credit Crowley with resolving a conflict that could have possibly led to a significantly bigger confrontation including a walk-out of coaches.

His fervor for the advancement of women's athletics and his unconditional support of Title IX set the University on pace to be one of the most progressive institutions for female athletes. Crowley treasures the expansion of women's athletics at Nevada where there are 12 varsity sports for women. His support of intercollegiate athletics at the University of Nevada secured him the Jake Lawlor Award after his presidency in 2005. Crowley created opportunity all across the campus during his tenure. He was a catalyst for the remarkable growth and development of the University and the quality of its student body. When he took on the role of President, he set out to integrate the University and the City of Reno. The disconnection between the two had widened greatly. He established the UNR Foundation in 1987 to recapture the University's heritage as a land-grant institution in accordance with the intent of the Morrill Land Grant Act of 1862. The isolation of academia and the city didn't melt over night, but slowly advisory boards were formed with a renewed focus on the school's founding charter.

Dr. Crowley began his educational career in his home state of Iowa and received his bachelor's degree from the University of Iowa. He went on to attain his master's from Fresno State University and his doctorate from the University of Washington. For his service to his beloved University of Nevada, it bestowed an honorary doctorate degree upon him. Although his commitment to higher education has been demonstrated throughout his presidency, Crowley's first impression was made in the classroom. He started teaching political science at the University of Nevada in 1966 and steadily made his presence known. He was the chair of the Faculty Senate, and then later he served as department chair of political science before he was asked to serve as Interim President. A year later, it was clear that Crowley deserved the position permanently.

History intertwines nicely with one of Crowley's favorite subjects to teach: politics. After retiring as president, he began to teach a course entitled "American Constitutional and Cultural History" at UNR. He also found time to lobby for higher education during the 2001 legislative session. His expertise was requested at San Jose State University in 2003 as that University searched for a new president. Crowley graciously came out of retirement and helped the school determine what its needs were and what characteristics they desired in a president. While at San Jose he conducted sessions that educated the students and faculty about the academic presidency, a subject about which he has a wealth of knowledge and experience as is evidenced by the four books he has published on the subject. After San Jose, Crowley began a new book chronicling the history of the NCAA as it approaches its centennial celebration in 2006. *In the Arena: The NCAA's First Century* commemorates the 100th anniversary. He then accepted the position of Interim President at UNR. Everyone wanted him because he leads so well.

Joe Crowley's commitment to education has extended far beyond a classroom, an athletic program, and a campus. During his career he has served on the board for the National Association of State Universities and Land Grant Colleges and he served for a decade on the board for Collegiate Women Sports Awards. He serves on the Board of Directors and on the Planning & Development Committee for the National Consortium for Academics and Sports. Both Fresno State and Iowa conferred distinguished alumnus awards upon him for his exemplary service in education. His most prized accomplishment occurred when his name was ascribed to the newly constructed student union in 2007 on the University of Nevada at Reno campus. The union was constructed with formal and informal learning environments and social components in order to serve as a cornerstone on campus, much like the man whose name accompanies it. The dedication suggestion came from the students to honor Joe Crowley and his lasting contributions to their school and its campus. He was also named to the Nevada Advisory Board for the Grant Sawyer Center for Justice Studies, an organization called upon to provide guidance based on their area of expertise in either academic, legal, or public institutions. Crowley is certainly a significant figure in the Nevada community that can offer a wealth of knowledge.

After his interim presidency, Crowley headed back to his roots in the classroom to teach college sophomores in a Western Traditions course outlining the American Constitution and History. Crowley established a capstone course for seniors in journalism that examines the interaction between media and politics. He is also writing and, with his wife, Joy, doting on their children and grandchildren, all of whom live close by. He is still active with the NCAA and the NCAS among other organizations locally and in Nevada.

In our modern world, Joe Crowley is, above all, an educator. In that regard, he serves as a model of what a university president should be!

Clarence Underwood

Creating a New Game Plan for College Sport

by Stacy Martin-Tenney

Clarence Underwood is very much like "the man who is actually in the arena"[1] as described by Theodore Roosevelt in his poem "In the Arena." Underwood has lived "himself in a worthy cause."[2] He dared to better the lives of children in any way he could. The arena that Underwood chose for his worthy cause was education, and more specifically the education and development of student-athletes, "who strives valiantly" as a group themselves. Underwood's endeavors on sports fields began at a young age, but he never gave up the fight because he knew that making a positive difference in a young person's life would shape that person's future for years to come.

Underwood grew up in Gadsden, Alabama on the baseball and football fields in town. As an exceptional student-athlete, he also found time to compete in track and field. After graduation, this honorable young man went on to represent his country in the 82nd Airborne Division of the United States Army at Fort Bragg, North Carolina. In his youth he also joined Dr. Martin Luther King's efforts to help African-American adults finish their education and register to vote. Underwood's commitment to education and heightening awareness for others prompted his own return to the educational arena. He enrolled at Michigan State University (MSU), and a long relationship between MSU and Underwood began.

He received his bachelor's degree in physical education in 1961 from MSU. Underwood finishes what he starts and has maintained that philosophy throughout his career, no matter what the arena. This pattern and his deep ties to Michigan State might have started when Underwood furthered his education at MSU and received a master's degree in physical education and counseling in 1965. After a brief stretch as an educator in the public school system of East Lansing, Michigan, Underwood felt a void from being away from Michigan State. He soon took a position as the University's Assistant Athletic Ticket Manager, and happily became a member of the MSU staff.

He quickly moved up the ranks to Assistant Director of Athletics in 1972, a duty he fulfilled for a decade. His attachment to student-athletes was just beginning to blossom as were the programs that he implemented during this time. The pivotal difference Underwood made was a commitment to a student-athlete's academic career. He was charged with implementing academic support services that would be tailored to a student-athlete's needs. This devotion to a student-athlete's education was groundbreaking for the time. Athletes were being abused by the system and exploited for their athletic talents by universities without regard to what their lives would be like after sports. The National Academic Athletic Association recognized his concern about this problem when his peers elected him president. Overhauling a system and the values of the athletic department was an enormous undertaking in itself, but Underwood also organized all issues pertaining to eligibility, financial aid, rules interpretations, managing the staff, and athletic certification.

Underwood never wanted to be a part of eliminating opportunities for education, especially for underrepresented groups. A large part of his career has been allocated to improving Title IX compliance and increasing gender equality at MSU. The length of his career mirrors the fight for women's equality, but in the 1970s the fight was just beginning. Again, Underwood took those brave steps into unknown territory and he developed Michigan State's first Title IX proposal to demonstrate their compliance to the new federal law. In 1983, another opportunity in the athletic world presented itself. Underwood had a chance to enter a larger, more powerful arena, the Big Ten Conference. He was appointed as the deputy commissioner of the conference. During his tenure he created the Big Ten SCORE program for inner-city children to learn that Success Comes Out of Reading Everyday. He was a proponent of the Big Ten Advisory Commission designed to draw attention to minority/equity issues. His familiarity with establishing standards for student-athletes in the classroom, as well as on the field of play at Michigan State, proved beneficial as he helped establish superior standards in academic advising conference wide. His people skills, always shining brilliantly, assisted him as he worked with every athletic director from the member institutions and as the administrator for men's sports.

Underwood's intimate knowledge of the rules that he gained during his Big Ten interlude would prove invaluable to Michigan State as they attempted to create a compliance program. The University requested that he return home to become the Assistant Athletics Director for Compliance. He is credited with the execution of MSU's first official compliance program. Underwood was passed over in 1992 for the athletic director position. The school chose its first female athletic director, Merrily Dean Baker, instead. He was thought of as the man for the job since he was so accomplished and educated, as well as the fact that he had been a Michigan State guy for most of his professional life. Trustee support, the former AD and football coach, and students were not enough influence, though. Baker soon realized Underwood's potential contributions, and promoted him in 1994 to Senior Associate Athletics Director. He was the department's official responsible for student-athlete welfare, a cause dear to his heart. He challenged the system to do more for these student-athletes as he created cultural programs that dealt with controversial and ethical issues they might face.

After two athletics directors were terminated at MSU, Underwood was named as the Interim Athletic Director in 1999. By the end of the year, his appointment to Athletic Director was approved. Underwood set his own term at three years. That was all he believed he needed to put the program back in order and fulfill important expectations.

Underwood was well known for his people skills and communication abilities, so unifying the people in the department was an obvious place to start. He set expectations for his coaches regarding their treatment of their athletes. It was to never be dehumanizing or abusive, and coaches had to take an interest in each of their athletes on and off the field. They were now accountable, but it didn't take the form of a malicious threat. Underwood hosted family events like Christmas ice-skating, a welcome back tailgate, even a backyard barbecue at his house so everyone in the department could start to mend the fences between sports. Underwood knows that he had to befriend and care for his coaches so that he could make the University's athletic programs successful once again.

Next, he drastically overhauled the athletic facilities on campus: added a new basketball complex, reinstalled natural grass in Spartan Stadium, reconstructed the track and field complex, renovated Jenison Field House and Ralph Young Field, and added new artificial turf for women's field hockey. His investment paid off in one of the most successful periods in Spartan history. Men's basketball won an NCAA Championship, football won the Citrus Bowl, hockey won a CCHA Tournament title, and at least 15 sports sent at least one athlete to an NCAA Championship.

Clarence Underwood describes the Women's Athletics Varsity Letter Celebration as the most enlightening and joyous event of his tenure at Michigan State. It was organized in celebration of the anniversary of Title IX and in response to the years of correspondence with former female student-athletes from Michigan State. The AIAW, which formerly governed women's athletics and institutions, lacked the authority to grant these student-athletes varsity letters like their male counterparts. It was fitting that a man who had struggled for so long to provide an equal playing field for women's athletics awarded women who represented over 50 years in Spartan athletic history for exceptional performances. Underwood is a man "who knows the great enthusiasms."[3]

Underwood certainly knows the truth behind the first few lines of the poem, "It is not the critic who counts; not the man who points out how the strong man stumbles, or where the doer of deeds could have done them better."[4] He has faced his own critics and challenges over his 27-year professional career. He was a man concerned with the job and accomplishing things for others; he never looked for credit for himself. Clarence Underwood demonstrated the essence of leadership in the arena of college athletics with dignity and class. Underwood retired as the Michigan State University Athletic Director in 2002 and since has spent his time traveling the state to motivate students.

Notes

1. Theodore Roosevelt, "The Man in the Arena." Chapultepec, Inc., posted June 2, 2004, http://www.theodore-roosevelt.com/trsorbonnespeech.html, (accessed November 11, 2005).

2. Ibid.

3. Ibid.

4. Ibid.

Charles Martin "C.M." Newton

Creating a New Game Plan for College Sport

by Stacy Martin-Tenney

Charles Martin "C.M." Newton is credited with changing the game of basketball. His career truly came full circle upon his retirement as Director of Athletics at the University of Kentucky in 2000. The knowledge and experiences he has acquired through his career encompass all realms of athletics, basketball in particular. He gained an intimate knowledge of the game as a student-athlete at the University of Kentucky and further applied that knowledge during his tenure as the head coach at Transylvania University, the University of Alabama, and Vanderbilt University and as an athletics officer at Andrews Air Force Base. His commitment to the rules was fostered throughout the years as assistant commissioner of the Southeastern Conference and during the time he served as the chairman of the rules committee for the NCAA. Although Newton's commitment to the game of basketball is impressive, the truly remarkable aspect of his career is his propensity to act with integrity in any situation he faced.

Newton exemplified the characteristics of a genuine athlete from an early age. In high school he was a star on Ft. Lauderdale High School's football, basketball, and baseball teams, achieving all-state honors in each sport. His versatility as an athlete was attractive to a number of schools with prestigious athletic programs, but he ultimately chose the University of Kentucky to launch his collegiate career in athletics. While attending school, Newton pitched for the Wildcats' NCAA tournament baseball teams and was a letterman on Adolph Rupp's storied National Championship basketball team in 1951. He even found time to win a couple of campus intramural football championships as quarterback. After the championship, Newton signed a contract with the New York Yankees and pitched in the minor leagues for two years.

Newton participated in the Air Force ROTC program while he was at Kentucky. When he graduated with a degree in physical education in 1953, he was commissioned as an athletics officer at Andrews Air Force Base in Washington, D.C. In 1956, he briefly returned to professional baseball, until another offer arose that seemed like the right thing to do. Newton had been offered the Chair of the Physical Education Department and the head basketball-coaching job at Transylvania University in Lexington. After careful consideration for the well-being of his young family, he decided that it was the best move he could make. His professional athletic career came to a close.

Newton has thought of his experience at "Transy," as he affectionately calls it, as one of his happiest.[1] He integrated the Transylvania basketball team with an African-American basketball player in 1965, an infrequent scene in those days, but he knew it was the right thing to do. After 12 years of coaching and teaching, he was recruited once again by a legendary coach for the head basketball coaching position at the University of Alabama.

Coach Paul "Bear" Bryant, who was the football coach at the University of Kentucky while Newton played for Coach Rupp, was now the football coach at Alabama and leading the search for someone to turn around the basketball program there. Having received Rupp's recommendation, Bryant hired Newton. Newton created a successful program after a couple of challenging years. His team's numerous accolades include three SEC Championships, and two NCAA and four National Invitation Tournament appearances. The most lasting and heroic change that Newton made at Alabama was recruiting their first African-American scholarship player, Wendell Hudson from Birmingham, to integrate the basketball program. Thankfully, Bryant supported Newton and Hudson publicly, which eased some of the angst surrounding their bravery in a region seriously plagued by segregation. Newton recognized the weight his decision carried and it virtually opened doors for other African-Americans around the SEC to participate. Newton became the first college basketball coach to play five African-Americans all at once. Once again, Newton simply did what was right. Newton was awarded SEC Coach of the Year three times during his tenure at Alabama.

He left Alabama and coaching in 1980 in search of new challenges. He saw an opportunity to gain experience in administration and accepted a position as assistant commissioner of the SEC. He had always demonstrated an affinity for the rules of the game as a coach and a player, and had begun to examine the game on a larger scale when he started serving on the NCAA Rules Committee in

1979. He continued to serve on the committee until 1985 and during that time the committee implemented two rules that effectively brought basketball into the modern era, the shot clock and the three point shot. The game would never be the same. Once again, Newton left his mark.

He had hopes of becoming the commissioner of the SEC, but was lured back into coaching by Vanderbilt University. Vanderbilt was an institution determined to do things right, a philosophy close to Newton's heart, and so their offer was irresistible. He was challenged once more to rebuild a program, and succeeded again to the tune of two more NCAA tournament appearances and two more SEC Coach of the Year awards. A joyful time in his house was undermined by a troubling time down the road at his former home, the University of Kentucky. Kentucky's basketball program was beleaguered by NCAA violations with likely sanctions following close behind. After the 1988–89 season at Vanderbilt, Newton accepted his greatest challenge yet.

Newton was hired at the University of Kentucky as the Director of Athletics with the challenge to reform an entire athletics program weighed down by NCAA sanctions. The basketball program was under fire and desperately needed to be rescued. This longtime coach knew what to do: find someone to do things right. He convinced Rick Pitino to turn the program around. Pitino soon confirmed that Newton's decision was right. He had an overall record at Kentucky of 219-50 and three NCAA Final Four appearances, along with an NCAA Championship in his eight-year tenure. Newton credits Pitino as the catalyst for the rest of his success at Kentucky, because basketball was just the beginning.

Newton set out to make changes in every realm within his reach. He crossed lines of social reform yet again by hiring Bernadette Mattox to rebuild the women's basketball program. Mattox was the University of Kentucky's first African-American women's basketball coach. She had a positive effect on the program and took the team to their first NCAA appearance in eight years. He was again faced with an opening for the men's basketball coach when Pitino went to the Celtics, Newton broke new ground once more at Kentucky. He hired Orlando "Tubby" Smith to be the school's first African-American head coach. When questioned about his courageous choice, he simply responded that Tubby was the best man for the job, giving no weight to any inquisition regarding race. Tubby proved Newton's decision as his predecessor did by winning two NCAA championships for the Wildcats in 1996 and 1998. A unique opportunity greeted Newton at the 1998 NCAA Championship, as he was also the Chairman of the NCAA Men's Basketball Tournament Committee, so he was fortunate enough to present the championship trophy to Tubby Smith and his Wildcats. Newton also revived Kentucky's football program and made it competitive once again by hiring Hal Mumme as head coach.

That choice proved controversial after the fact and after Newton's retirement because, unfortunately, Kentucky returned to the NCAA sanctions list, this time for football violations. One blemish can sometimes taint a previously untarnished record. However, Newton takes it in stride and accepts responsibility for the violations despite the fact that it was actually men he had hired in football operations whose misguided actions warranted sanctions.

Newton has obviously displayed a commitment to providing opportunities for those who are sometimes overlooked. Non-revenue sports are another group that fight for anything they can get. They are typically the programs cut due to the pressing need to comply with Title IX, so opportunities are limited for non-revenue sports. Newton added three sports to Kentucky's athletic program, women's and men's soccer and softball. It has proven difficult for universities to add programs due to the financial obligations that accompany them. Rarely does a department add a men's program due to Title IX compliance. But Newton knew it was right and that Kentucky should invest in their student-athletes. In fact, several of Kentucky's non-revenue sports have attained national distinction under Newton's watch.

The visible improvements to the University of Kentucky's campus are an important part of Newton's legacy. He changed the face of the campus through expansions to the baseball and football stadium and construction of a new soccer and softball complex, tennis stadium, and Nutter field house, a building as important to the community as the track and field and football teams. The building that Newton expresses the most pride about is a three million dollar facility to house the Center for Academic and Tutorial Services (CATS), an academic center for Kentucky's student-athletes. The center opened in 1981 as the first in the nation, but Newton demonstrated that academics are a priority through the construction of the new facility in 1998. He has also been devoted to former Kentucky student-athletes finishing their degrees and has created the Cawood Ledford Scholarship Fund, named for the longtime "Voice" of the Wildcats, to fund their education. He knew that funding education was the right thing to do with the money, and encouraged all former student-athletes to come back and earn their degrees. Since Newton made this decision, Kentucky has always provided funding for finishing degrees and leads the country with one of the most extensive degree completion programs.

In a time when athletic department budgets are overstretched and some are folding completely, requiring financial support from academia, the University of Kentucky Alumni Association under Newton's leadership has accepted fiscal responsibility for the University's William T. Young Library. They have pledged $3.2 million annually to retire the construction bonds for the library. Newton is undeniably a leader in the sports world, but he has demonstratively reminded people that he was an educator through his loyalty to CATS, scholarships for student-athlete degree completion, and funding a facility on campus where no sports will be played. Commercialism has crept into athletics funding for some time now and the illusive dollars are hard to resist.

After a drunk-driving incident involving a Kentucky student-athlete ended in a horrific accident and the student-athlete's death, Newton made an unheard of stand against the alcohol sponsors for athletics and refused to renew Anheuser-Busch, Miller Brewing, and Maker's Mark advertising contracts that provided more than $400,000 yearly. He placed a higher importance on every student's life—not just student-athletes' lives—than funding traced to a possibly destructive influence on college students. He has made moral and ethical choices as an athlete, a coach, and as an administrator.

Newton served in numerous associations and on several boards and committees while he was a coach and an administrator. While he was serving as Kentucky's Director of Athletics, he found the time to support the game of basketball on an international level. He was actively involved with USA Basketball (formerly ABAUSA), the governing body for basketball internationally. He became their vice president in 1988, and four years later he took on the role of president until 1996. He was responsible for the change from amateur athletes representing the Olympic team to the selection of NBA players and the original "Dream Team." He continued a dramatic effort to expand women's basketball internationally. His powerful impact on the game of basketball has not gone unnoticed. In 1997, the Naismith Basketball Hall of Fame awarded Newton with its highest distinction, the John Bunn Award. In 1999, the Atlanta Tip-off Club recognized his contributions with the Naismith Award.

Newton has distinguished himself in both the world of sport and education as a leader and proponent of change. His actions speak to the character that he embodies—kind, determined, and committed to being respectful and ingenuous character. His contributions to the game of basketball have ushered the game into the modern era and his contributions to society have crossed racial boundaries that have separated the human race for too long. He has set a precedent for academic excellence and commitment at all of the universities he served, and he has made dramatic and lasting changes at the University of Kentucky. C.M. Newton has truly come full circle in his career and has taken the time to teach everyone else what he has learned along the way.

Note

1. Tony Neely, "Recognizable Class," *Kentucky Alumnus*, Summer 2000, Volume 71, Number 2.

Sister Rose Ann Fleming

Creating a New Game Plan for College Sport

by Stacy Martin-Tenney

When athletes arrive on campus, they soon find out who is actually calling the plays, and it is not their coach. Sister Rose Ann Fleming wields tremendous power on Xavier University's campus. While teaching English and fiction at Xavier in 1985, she was approached about becoming a full-time academic advisor for Xavier's student-athletes. She had been working with several of the basketball players and had been quite successful. Xavier was a small institution of 6,600 students at that time and had no one in place to handle the special needs of student-athletes. She was not a stranger to academia, as she was currently pursuing a degree in business when the school asked her to take on this new role. Over the years Sister Fleming has earned several degrees including a law degree and master's degrees in English, business administration, and theology, as well as a doctorate in education administration. Before she arrived at Xavier she served as President of the Summit Country Day School in Cincinnati and President of Trinity College in Washington, D.C., for eight years each. Xavier placed great importance on academics and wanted to convey that in her position with student-athletes, so Sister Fleming worked from academic affairs, not in the athletic department.

Some might say that it would be hard to establish relationships and networks with the coaches and athletes from such a position, but it wasn't an obstacle to her. She knew that her task of getting athletes degrees was of great importance and so it carried with it tremendous power. New coaches may be surprised to find her walking in and stopping practice, but it became a familiar scene. Xavier's men's basketball coach during the 2009–10 season, Chris Mack said, "Sometimes, she'll schedule an appointment or an academic meeting right in the middle of practice. I'll say, 'Sister, we have practice at 4.' She'll say, 'No, this is important.'"[1] Former athletes would tell stories about a nun pulling them out of practice or chasing them down after a game to find out why they had slipped up in the classroom. At least once she has shown up to an NCAA tournament game with books in hand to discuss a basketball player's class work. She demonstrated that athletic success doesn't waive a student-athlete's academic responsibilities. It definitely is not a common sight and it definitely is not common practice on most college campuses. Sister Fleming set a standard of excellence and required accountability from her athletes early on. So, now if she calls, they answer. Missing class is definitely not an option for student-athletes at Xavier. Professors at other institutions may let the occasional absence slide for athletes after they had a late night at the game or an early practice. However, there are no excuses for missing class, according to Sister Fleming. Even though her frame is small, her presence is as strong as her tallest athlete. She has also been known to call an athlete that missed class, while patiently allowing the phone to ring 100 or more times to wake them up. She has even shown up at their door ready to escort them to class when they choose sleep over attending school.

Sister Fleming embodies another characteristic commonly attributed to nuns—discipline. Her athletes know her rules: don't miss a class, do your own assignments, study hard, maintain a 2.0 GPA, take a minimum of 12 credit hours, find a career and pursue it. Sister Fleming knows that she is preparing these student-athletes to be successful in life, not just in sports. She has plenty of time to emphasize these rules and even make them habits during her study hall sessions. She mandates that every freshman attend study hall for two hours Sunday through Thursday at the library.

After such strict expectations and rules imposed upon them, one might think the student-athletes would find it hard to work with Sister Fleming, or at least be a little resentful, but that is hardly the case. A visit to Sister Fleming's office would quickly dispel that notion. Her walls are lined with photos capturing the friendships that she has formed with her student-athletes over the years. She is loved, admired, and most definitely respected by all of her students. Some have likened her to a concerned and loving grandmother figure who conveys her eagerness for her students to do their best. She has built relationships with them, which is why they comply with her requests so willingly.

Working closely with the coaches over the years has helped her reach student-athletes. She knows that it doesn't work to punish someone who is doing her or his best. It is imperative that the student finds value in accomplishing the task. She has taken a motivational approach to encourage the behavior she desires from her student-athletes instead of an approach based on punishment. Although she is not opposed to the concept; most coaches give her the ability to bench a player for not meeting their academic obligations if she feels it is necessary. She is always fair and firm in her approach, treating all players equally no matter what their status on the team. Motivation and punishment are strategies that can be found in some coach's playbooks as well.

Now that she has established the system and the expectations, the student-athletes actually do some of the enforcing. When recruits visit the campus the emphasis on academics quickly becomes apparent. Sister Fleming credits the coaches for not just recruiting the best athlete, but an athlete who is also serious about academics. The Xavier athletes even start to screen the new recruits by stressing the significance of keeping the streak alive. Someone on the street would probably assume they were talking about winning basketball games, but it's more important than that. They are referring to the fact that since 1985, Sister Fleming has ensured that every basketball player who exhausts his athletic eligibility at Xavier earns a degree. Talented athletes have succumbed to their teammate's pressure of finishing their degrees instead of entering the draft and a chance at millions. Xavier University's graduation rate has consistently ranked among the best of NCAA Division I institutions. One might even credit Sister Fleming with a national championship in academics. Xavier's athletes regularly achieve a higher graduation rate than the rest of the student population. Sister Fleming has instilled academic values in these student-athletes and knows that she is helping them to become better people.

She has been a pioneer in integrating the worlds of academics and athletics. When she started there wasn't a game plan in place. There was only the knowledge that someone needed to be responsible for helping athletes become student-athletes. The time demands and energy required by student-athletes can be extremely overwhelming, especially for freshman. She knows that the life of a student-athlete is more difficult than the typical student so she guides them through the system. There were very few NCAA guidelines twenty years ago when she started in this field. She is now a powerful force behind them. As an exemplary leader in academics and sport, Sister Rose Ann Fleming has received numerous awards for her tireless efforts. Her alma mater recognized her lifelong service to education through the Alumni Career Achievement Award in 2004. Xavier's former Head Basketball Coach, Skip Prosser, didn't believe in MVP awards for his team and has never awarded one. But he wanted to distinguish Sister Fleming's efforts to help student-athletes graduate. She wasn't the player with the most points, but she was definitely credited with numerous assists for student-athletes and the highest grade point average, so she earned the MVP award. In 2000, she was honored by Xavier for her abundant accomplishments and contributions to the school when she was inducted into the Xavier University Athletic Hall of Fame. Sister Fleming is a testament to the fact that one need not be an athlete to make an important mark on the world of collegiate athletics.

The difference she makes can be heard in the voices of the student-athletes themselves. Terrell Holloway, a sophomore guard for Xavier said, "She's probably been the most important person to me here at Xavier University to make sure I get the proper education. She basically runs the program."[2] Fellow sophomore guard Brad Redford echoed those sentiments, "I know when my family gets to talk to her, they love talking to her and she is so excited about what I'm doing and the rest of the guys are doing."[3] Sister Fleming continues to succeed in her mission to help student athletes earn their degree even at 77 years old and after 25 years as the lead athletic academic advisor. "While they give so much of their lives to Xavier in terms of their sports, we too in return can make sure they have an opportunity to earn their degree. That has been a constant interest of mine to make sure that each athlete ends up with a degree that they've worked for,"[4] Fleming said.

Notes

1. John Branch, "At Xavier, Nun Works Out Players' Academic Side," *The New York Times*, March 15, 2010.

2. Ray Crawford, *"Hoops Heaven: Sister Rose Ann Fleming Combines Faith and Basketball,"* *FOX Sports Ohio*, February 28, 2010, http://www.foxsportsohio.com/pages/landing?Hoops-Heaven-Sister-Rose-Ann-Fleming-Com=1&blockID=171800&feedID=, (accessed March 22, 2010).

3. Ibid.

4. Ibid.

Judy Sweet

Creating a New Game Plan for College Sport

by Stacy Martin-Tenney

Judy Sweet is not a stranger to change. In fact, for most of her life she has been a proponent of change in sports. She pioneered the landscape of college athletics and helped transform it from a barren scene to one full of opportunity and promise. The idea of diversity is commonplace today, but when Judy Sweet was growing up in Milwaukee, Wisconsin in the 1960s it was radical. Her first groundbreaking move in sports was walking on to the sandlot to play a game with her brothers and cousins. She quickly proved herself and enjoyed plenty of opportunities to play sports, as long as she didn't stray outside the confines of the neighborhood. The sandlot was only the first of many changes she would make throughout her career and it was a valuable lesson to push the barriers of what was allowed. Judy Sweet has broken many barriers in her quest to cultivate women's participation onto the sporting landscape.

Sweet's journey has not been without struggle and opposition. Change is hard to accept for most and many take a great deal of comfort in doing things the way they have always been done. She left the sandlot and went on to high school and college only to be stifled once more by intramural programs instituted for educational and recreational purposes. Organization and competition elements familiar to boy's sports were absent from the girl's activities. Sweet missed the proverbial boat for women's sports when Title IX passed in 1972, banning the unequal opportunity that Sweet had experienced in her playing career. She had graduated with honors from the University of Wisconsin three years before. Sweet had majored in physical education and mathematics, which led her to take a position at Tulane University as a physical education teacher. Her humble and quiet start soon flourished and she moved across the country to Arizona. The Painted Desert's majestic scene surely inspired her to paint her own landscape.

Sweet began teaching at the University of Arizona and simultaneously pursued a master's degree in education. As usual she graduated with honors. Sweet stayed on at the University for one more year and began her career in athletic administration. A taste for change persuaded her to move closer to the ocean. She arrived in San Diego and taught at a local high school for one year before she began her long career at the University of California, San Diego. She joined the faculty as both a teacher and a coach. Her attachment to student-athletes and her

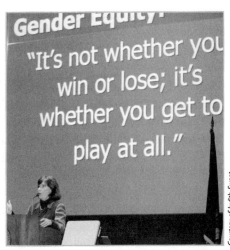

Courtesy of Judith Sweet

mission to safeguard their welfare began. After only a year she became an associate athletic director. As previously demonstrated, Sweet is a woman who quickly excels at any task she undertakes, so just over a year later she was promoted to the director of athletics at UC San Diego. Sweet had made her first sweeping stroke of change to the inhospitable sporting landscape on a grand scale.

Control of both men's and women's athletic programs is atypical for a woman in the new millennium but it was non-existent in 1975, until Judy Sweet took a brave step into a constantly changing, yet rigidly resistant, environment for women. She became the first female athletic director of a combined intercollegiate athletic program in the nation. Athletic directors predictably were promoted from coaching a major male sport such as football, basketball, or baseball at that time. In fact, some even served dual roles as the head football coach and athletic director. Sweet broke the mold. She faced opposition from her peers. Some were hesitant to accept her at all. The coaches whom she had befriended to shape student-athlete talents just two years before became antagonistic when she cut their budgets so she could create a more equitable environment between the men's and women's athletic programs. Every landscape has its own unique color scheme and the sports realm is no different. Color was added to Sweet's landscape by letters with "the most colorful" negative language that expressed resentment and biases for her newly acquired position. Sweet soon realized "the hurdles that had to be overcome."[1]

Pioneers have climbed mountains to pursue their dreams, and

Sweet learned on the sandlot how to overcome such barriers. During her 24 years of service at UC San Diego she experienced unrivaled success, and started establishing new landmarks in the expanding environment for women's athletics. Her athletic department supported 23 varsity sports and brought 25 NCAA Championships home to San Diego. UC San Diego teams were National Runners-up 32 times in her 24 years. In 1997–1998, UC—San Diego won the Division III Sears Director's Cup for program excellence; this marked the first time that an athletic department directed by a woman had been awarded the Cup. Additionally, it was the first time an athletic department without a football program had won the award. Sweet did not only keep her department in the forefront of success, she continued to foster her education and earned a master's of business administration with distinction from National University in San Diego.

Sweet committed herself to improving student-athlete welfare throughout her career without regard to gender, although she had a distinctive viewpoint as a female to guard opportunities for future female athletes. Her perspective has been sought out by 20 different NCAA committees over the years and her contribution has broadened her impact on college sports. She started out as the NCAA Division III Vice President in 1986 and then served as the first female Secretary-Treasurer of the NCAA from 1989–1991. During that time she also served as the Chair of the Budget Committee. She made history yet another time when she took on the role of NCAA President from 1991 to 1993. She was the first female president of the Association during a time when the position was voluntary and not contracted. She blazed a new trail across the sports landscape and created more opportunity for her female counterparts. Sweet's commitment to student-athletes has never been contingent on contracts of service. She truly cares about providing the best experience possible for student-athletes in any way she can. She has also served on the NCAA Council and Executive Committee, as well as the Review and Planning Committee. For seven years she served as Chair of the Special Advisory Committee to Review Recommendations Regarding Distribution of Revenues, a committee formed in response to the billion dollar television contract with CBS.

Exhibiting leadership is second nature to Sweet. She has made ethical choices and implemented policy that benefited student-athletes. More importantly, she motivates others to join her cause. Sweet excels quickly at any endeavor she pursues. She has been recognized for her exemplary leadership with a variety of awards throughout her career. Sweet was National President of the Athletic and Recreation Federation of College Women from 1968 to 1969. Later in 1984 she was named Outstanding Young Woman of America. Just a few years later in 1990 she was the *Los Angeles Times'* selection for Top Southern California College Sports Executive of the 1980s. Southern California is an arena historically filled with fierce sports competitors in the administration as well as on the playing fields. The Times' selection speaks volumes about her extraordinary leadership at UC San Diego.

Her commitment to excellence transcended decades and the 1990s were no exception. Just like wines have very good years, 1992 was Judy Sweet's year. She was named the Administrator of the Year by the National Association of Collegiate Athletic Administrators. The W.S. Bailey Award was conferred on Sweet by the Touchdown Club of Auburn-Opelika to distinguish her from the nation's athletic administrators. Women's Sports Advocates of Wisconsin, Sweet's native state, inducted her into their Lifetime Achievement Hall of Fame. She has convincingly demonstrated her abilities.

One year later she was named Woman of the Year in District 38 by the California State Senate. Twelve calendar pages after that honor she forged through new territory once more by offering her service and experience to the United States Olympic Committee Task Force on Minorities. Sweet dedicated her time to that committee for the following two years. Her wealth of knowledge and firsthand experience on the front lines of the gender equity fight was invaluable to the minority task force. In 1998, Judy Sweet was the recipient of The Honda Award for Outstanding Achievement in Women's Collegiate Athletics. Sweet served on the Board of Directors for the National Association of College Directors of Athletics (NACDA). Sweet stepped down from her longtime position of Director of Athletics at UC San Diego in 1999 to return to a faculty position there.

Sweet's expertise was requested by the NCAA once more in 2001 to hold one of their premier positions as Vice President for Championships. Sweet would oversee planning and organization for all of the 88 NCAA Championships except Division I men's and women's basketball, football, and baseball. Cedric Dempsey, the NCAA President at that time, was quoted by Wallace Renfroe in a *NCAA News* release as saying "Her depth of knowledge of college sports and administrative experience in running a broad range of events will ensure that NCAA Championships continue to be great experiences for student-athletes."[2] Sweet understands how valuable the experience of a championship is for student-athletes and wants to ensure that it is unforgettable as well.

Sweet joined the NCAA national office team and quickly took on additional responsibilities as the Senior Women's Administrator, a role designed to reflect a position typical to member institutions' athletic departments. The position has its roots in a role that was established in 1981 to look out for women's issues in athletic departments of universities, and the role had expanded in responsibilities by 1990 at those institutions, but lacked reflection in the national office. Sweet was once again the first woman to take the job and has left a lasting impression on sports that will benefit her successors. The position may have originated with the idea of guaranteed female involvement at the top of the NCAA governance, but it has evolved into a position with appropriate responsibility and accountability in all facets of the organization that has the added benefit of a female perspective. She never made the fact that she was a woman an issue but instead used it as a competitive advantage. She has been described as "a quiet, effective fighter for opportunities" by Dale Neuberger, the former president of the Indiana Sports Corp[3]. Her focus on gender equity encompasses suggestions that come from both men and women.

Judy Sweet constantly seeks out new challenges and so she accepted the promotion to Senior Vice President for Championships and Education Services in 2003 in addition to maintaining her role as the Senior Women's Administrator. Her new role in education is to implement leadership programs. Leadership is a concept that Sweet knows inside and out. Myles Brand, former NCAA president, described Sweet as the "conscience of college sports" and regularly consulted with Sweet for her indispensable knowledge.[4] She was one of the four senior vice presidents who reported directly to Brand, and the only woman. Sweet gained so much status and prestige with the NCAA that she was the only living and active college sports icon to have her name grace the title of a meeting room at the NCAA Headquarters while she held her position. Sweet retired from the NCAA in 2006.

Judy Sweet's leadership is impressive and resilient, and she worked every day to instill the same drive and values in student-athletes. Her final alteration to the sporting landscape is the most irreversible and ongoing in affecting student-athletes lives by creating an equitable environment that provides a positive experience for both young men and women. Her hope is for them to become the leaders of tomorrow, when the sun sets on her majestic landscape.

Notes

1. Mark Montieth, "Clearing the path" *The Indianapolis Star*, October 30, 2005.

2. Wallace I. Renfroe, "Judy Sweet, Long-time Athletics Leader and Administrator, Joins NCAA Staff as Vice-President for Championships." *The NCAA News*, November 1, 2000.

3. Mark Montieth, "Clearing the path" *The Indianapolis Star*, October 30, 2005.

4. Ibid.

Creed Black

Creating a New Game Plan for College Sport

by Stacy Martin-Tenney

Creed Black was the quintessential newspaper man, always in search of the truth in the story. He started working at the *Sun-Democrat* in his hometown of Paducah, Kentucky at age seventeen and literally, a storied career was born. During the post World War II occupation period in Europe, he worked on the *Stars & Stripes* newspaper. He then decided to pursue formal training in journalism at the Medill School of Journalism at Northwestern University in Chicago. He enhanced his experience during his college years by editing the *Daily Northwestern*, and working the copy desk at both *The Chicago Herald-American* and *The Chicago Sun-Times*. Black graduated with highest honors from Medill with a distinction in political science, a subject that no doubt interested him enough to engage in a political science master's program at the University of Chicago.

Black was clearly a highly educated man with vast experience in journalism, an asset to any newspaper. He served as an editorial writer and executive editor of the *Nashville Tennessean* and as vice president and executive editor of *The Savannah Morning News and Evening Press*. He quickly climbed the ranks among editors and traveled across the country still holding steadfast to truthful stories. He also served as vice president and executive editor of *The Wilmington Morning News* and *Evening Journal*, and he fulfilled his duties as managing editor and executive editor at *The Chicago Daily News*. His success was notable and he was called upon to act as Assistant Secretary for Legislation of the Department of Health, Education and Welfare for eighteen months in Washington, D.C. *The Philadelphia Inquirer* quickly appealed to Black following his period of public service to accept their offer of vice president and editor. He not only accepted the offer, he went on to win Pennsylvania's most prestigious awards for both column and editorial writing. Black returned to his home state of Kentucky in 1977 when he was named chairman and publisher of The Lexington Herald-Leader Co.

Creed Black has been known for promoting integrity in journalism throughout his career. But it is in moments of great adversity when our values and ideals are challenged, and it is through that adversity that the character of great men is revealed. Creed Black was still the publisher of The Lexington-Herald Leader Co. in the early 1980s when the University of Kentucky's student-athletes were suspected of being bought by alumni. They really were hardly inconspicuous about how well they were living compared to the rest of the state, one of the poorest in the Union at the time. Driving expensive sports cars to the race track and parading to the twenty dollar window, it was just a matter of time before it could be proven. The question was: would someone actually publish the truth if it came out? The Commonwealth of Kentucky lived and died with the successes and failures of the University of Kentucky's athletic programs, the attachment ran so deep that any laceration to the Wildcats' reputation would clearly bleed deep blue. In 1985, two reporters finally exposed convincing proof that implicated both the basketball players and coaches of the University of Kentucky in a scandal that shook the entire state. The players had been on the take for years and the coaches were facilitating it.

Creed Black was faced the most poignant question of his journalism career. To publish or not to publish? The story was verified and true to his nature, he published the truth and stood by his reporters and editor who broke the story. Black's newspaper faced tremendous pressure as it was subjected to circulation and advertising boycotts publicly denouncing the paper printing the story. Marketing and circulation revenues are as important to a paper for its very survival. But this was only the beginning of Black's adversity. The public had already convicted and condemned him and his staff, so the executioners came out of medieval times to deliver their sentences. A bomb threat evacuated the building, rifle shots cleared the pressroom and delivery men were chased down the streets by angry subscribers with axes. The public was outraged at such an attempt to malign the athletic department at the University of Kentucky. When no one else believed in him or the veracity of the *Herald's* story and his world was caving in around him, Creed Black held steadfast to his morals, values, and integrity. He never wavered in his battle against corruption. In fact he wrote a piece saying that he could understand the uproar as he was a native of Kentucky as well, but he did not condone the tumultuous actions of the public.

Creed was a man who understood the value of education, and

so as turbulent as the situation had been, he still knew it was an experience that carried with it a tremendous opportunity. He demonstrated so eloquently that subscribers of a newspaper do not read the stories because the paper pampers them with what they want to hear, but they subscribe for the facts and the truth delivered in a strong, objective manner that allows them to decide what they want to believe. In 1985, especially after all the paper encountered, one would typically assume that the newspaper's relationship with the public was beyond repair. In actuality, the newspaper became a case study for publishers everywhere. Their Sunday circulation went up 60 percent, and their daily circulation had increased by 30 percent without an evening paper. It is quite obvious why the Kentucky Journalism Hall of Fame inducted Creed Black in 1986.

The incident in Lexington and the unlikely, positive economic impact that resulted from it provoked study by executives of Knight-Ridder, Inc., a newspaper empire partly created by the Knight brothers, James and John. The Knights also created one of the largest private foundations in the country, the Knight Foundation, an organization dedicated to supporting the arts, journalism, and higher education. Undoubtedly impressed by Black's dedication to journalism and fidelity, the two brothers requested Black to be president of the Knight Foundation in February of 1988. Black's uncompromising nature and sincere devotion to the integrity of education made him the man for the job.

The Knight Foundation soon established an independent commission to examine and to offer reformatory advice to collegiate athletics. Black wasn't a stranger to confronting corruption in athletics and knew that the problem had to be confronted with solutions not just exposed on page one of the country's newspapers.

The commission was formed to investigate the extent to which corruption and scandalous behavior of collegiate athletics has tainted institutions of higher learning and threatened their academic integrity. It recognized that intercollegiate athletics are suitably placed at universities when they are implemented in an appropriate manner and operated properly. The commission felt strongly that the downward spiral of intercollegiate athletics was in large part due to the heavy influence of commercialism involved in the game today. Black saw firsthand what kind of impact a story about intercollegiate athletics corruption can have on a community. He realized that because of the high visibility associated with intercollegiate athletics, the scandals and violations attributed to an athletic team would most likely be attributed to the nature of the academic groups at the institution as well. Essentially, what someone knew about an institution's sports teams would be what they knew about the institution. Black and the Knight Commission set out to strengthen the focus on academics at Division I-A schools by placing some perspective on the role that intercollegiate athletics should play at a university. Black was careful to consider the hostility such an investigation would elicit, and so he cautioned the public that the commission's goal was to attack the flagrant problems by returning authority to the presidents and faculties of institutions because they are the individuals who can earnestly guard the intellectual and academic integrity of universities. So, the Knight Commission convened a panel of the presidents of universities from the major athletic conferences who could speak to the problems that they themselves knew all too well.

Black resigned from his presidency of the Knight Foundation in 1998, although he still serves on the Board of Trustees. His work with the foundation helped it grow from a small organization to one of the largest private foundations in the country. The foundation grants approximately 23 million dollars annually to fund higher education journalism and arts programs as well as teachers and students. His leadership on the Knight Foundation's commission on intercollegiate athletics provoked "A Call to Action" by American universities and the NCAA when the report was published. Presidents were becoming more involved in the operations of athletics departments and the welfare of the student-athlete. Many new forms of legislation have been proposed and passed to change the face of intercollegiate athletics. Although, there are still scandals and violations, it is not the only print on page one of the country's newspapers today. Creed Black tackled corruption through discussion and publication of difficult issues in academics and sports that others were either too fearful of or too complacent in accepting the status quo.

He has received numerous awards throughout his career that have recognized him for his enduring commitment to integrity in education and journalism. He was welcomed into the National Conference of Editorial Writers as a life member in 1989. He received an honorary Doctor of Laws Degree from Davidson College in 1991 and an honorary Doctor of Humane Letters from Centre College in

Kentucky in 1996. His alma mater of Northwestern thought that his illustrious service deserved a place in the Medill School's Hall of Achievement in 1997, where he became a charter inductee. He has always been a leader for each of his employers, and he has also led associations when he served as president of the National Conference of Editorial Writers, the American Society of Newspaper Editors and the Southern Newspaper Publishers Association. One of the most prominent awards an author can receive is the Pulitzer Prize. One of the most notable honors an editor can receive is the request to serve as a Pulitzer juror. Creed Black's knowledge and breadth of experience certainly qualifies him for such an honor, his character and commitment to truth and justice certainly secured him the honor six times. Black still receives requests to speak at numerous institutions, especially journalism schools. Each time he conveys the importance of writing a story with objectivity and veracity, and not succumbing to pressures and prejudices.

Notes

1. Mark Montieth, "Clearing the path" *The Indianapolis Star*, October 30, 2005.

2. Wallace I. Renfroe, "Judy Sweet, Long-time Athletics Leader and Administrator, Joins NCAA Staff as Vice-President for Championships." *The NCAA News*, November 1, 2000.

3. Mark Montieth, "Clearing the path" *The Indianapolis Star*, October 30, 2005.

4. Ibid.

Richard Astro

Creating a New Game Plan for College Sport

by Richard Lapchick

When you read the biography of Richard Astro, it conveys a tapestry of a distinguished academic career; a scholar of American literature with book and article credits on the likes of Steinbeck, Hemingway, and Malamud; a successful 35 years in higher education administration as the Provost of Drexel University, M.C.P. Hahnemann Medical University, and the University of Central Florida; a Dean at Northeastern University and a department chair at Oregon State; and the Chief Academic Officer of the National Consortium for Academics and Sports.

The reflection in the mirror would seem to be of a scholar absorbed in scholarly work; a man whose academic life was the dominant theme in everything he did. There is no doubt that his many years in higher education have led to distinction and great achievement academically. But Richard Astro said that when everything is said and done, his greatest achievement has been helping to found Northeastern University's Center for the Study of Sport in Society. Astro knew that there were problems in sport. Being an academic, he may have been thinking of studying those problems with possible proposals for solutions when he started to bring me and Bob Lipsyte of the *New York Times* together to brainstorm what Northeastern might do. The name that had been talked about was the "Center for the Study of Sport and Society." After a rich series of discussions between people from the world of sport and some of the academicians in Boston, particularly at Northeastern, I was approached to become the first director of the Center.

Astro knew there was something there and the combination of my life as an activist and his life as an academic resulted in the creation of the Center that became a combination think-tank but much more, an active agent for social change. Astro had the courage in tight budgetary times to have Northeastern put up the initial funding. That $200,000 initial investment would grow 20 years later to a Center that had a budget 10 times that size as well as the creation of the National Consortium for Academics and Sports (NCAS). Tom

Sanders and I brought forth the NCAS as an idea to Astro to expand the work of the Center with degree completion and community service across the country. At the time, I might have expected Richard Astro to say, "No, this is ours. This is Northeastern's," in the way I have seen happen so many times in higher education. But Astro, a man with a vision, said, "Let's spread the programs around." The National Consortium was conceived and grew exponentially over the next 25 years. It now comprises more than 240 universities and colleges which agree to bring back any athlete who went to their school on a scholarship in a revenue sport with tuition paid in exchange for the students performing service in the communities where the schools are located. This organization has grown into one that is so important to college sport in America. More than 30,000 athletes who had not finished their degrees have returned. They have worked with over 18 million young people in the community service program on issues like conflict resolution, men's violence against women, and academic balance with sports. Astro's willingness to start organizations, even if he wasn't so directly involved in the implementation, was critical to the success of Northeastern's Center and the NCAS.

But it was in the first few months of the Center's existence when we started our initial program with the New England Patriots that Astro's genius pushed us into the birthing canal. If the course that we taught with New England was successful, the Center might live past its first year. If the players weren't interested, then the Center would be forever small or would fail in a short period of time. So the "Bridge Course" was conceived to get those first 13 New England Patriots back into school to begin finishing their degrees. Richard Astro and Pete Eastman teamed up to be the front and back ends of the course. Astro assigned Eastman, the Chairman of the Speech and Communications Department, to engage the players in ways to improve their communication with the outside world, thus increasing their popularity and potential with commercial endorsements. I was more skeptical once we left the hands-on approach to hear Astro talk about Steinbeck and Hemmingway and to tell pro athletes that there was some comparison between *The Old Man and the Sea* and themselves. The Patriots ate it up, as did the Bruins and the Red Sox after them.

The rest, as they say, is history. The Center's early successes, fueled by his vision and his application, launched the Center and the Consortium into what they are today. Among the 13 New England Patriots in the original class were Keith Lee, Robert Weathers, and Lin Dawson. Robert is the Associate Director of the Consortium 25 years later. Keith, as the Chief Operating Officer of the Consortium, is responsible for all the day-to-day operations. Lin Dawson has been very active with the NCAS and served as its COO at one point. I am still the President of the Consortium. Three people together after all these years; how happy we were when Richard Astro joined us as the Chief Academic Officer of the Consortium in 2002, coming full circle and no longer being the theoretician but an active, day-to-day implementer of the vision he helped create.

Dick Schultz

Creating a New Game Plan for College Sport

by Stacy Martin-Tenney

Dick Schultz has managed to excel in athletics at so many different levels from high school, college, professional, and finally to the Olympic level. He has also worked in many different capacities as an athlete, an educator, a coach, and an administrator. Schultz started out as an athlete. He attended Central Iowa College where he received All-Conference honors in baseball, football, and basketball. Schultz performed well enough in his college career to move on to the professional level where he managed a baseball team in an era when pro athletes were not making the kind of money that they do today. Off-season jobs were common. Schultz found himself working at the high school level as a teacher, coach, and athletic director. Schultz also honed his entrepreneurial skills and started his own construction business.

Schultz pursued his master's degree at the University of Iowa. He also coached freshmen teams in both baseball and basketball at Iowa. After Schultz finished the degree, he was promoted to the head baseball coaching position and the assistant basketball coach. He also became the head basketball coach in 1970, a position which he held until 1974. Schultz became the special assistant to the president at Iowa. Two years later he became athletics director at Cornell University which was followed by six years as AD at the University of Virginia before being appointed as the executive director of the NCAA in 1987.

When Schultz assumed the leadership position of the NCAA, the staff warmed to him quickly. It is rare that a leader is so forthcoming and generous with responsibility. He was accommodating as a manager and he attempted to flatten out the organizational structure so that his staff could take on more tasks. Schultz empowered his staff long before it became a trend in organizational dynamics. He valued their creative and analytical skills. He only wanted to help them do their jobs better because he knew that it would reflect positively on him. Schultz changed the relationship between the National Collegiate Athletic Association and its member institutions. Formerly, the two were separated and the governance structure of the association seemed bureaucratic and dictatorial. But Dick changed all of that with "The State of the Association Address" from the Executive Director at the annual NCAA convention. Providing information and sharing responsibility became the theme for Schultz's tenure at the NCAA. His leadership translated into a change in hiring practices as well. The Association provided such a wealth of experience so that NCAA staff members moved to positions at universities or conference offices after a few years to expand the understanding of the NCAA by those offices.

Strengthening the role of the membership was an integral piece of Schultz's tenure at the NCAA. The reform movement that he was so well-known for encapsulated legislation that targeted the academic part of a student-athlete's collegiate experience as well as a distribution of revenues from the NCAA's mammoth television contract. He made the NCAA more accessible to its member institutions. In turn, he encouraged the university presidents and chancellors to take a more active role in the Association as well.

Schultz was a strong proponent of gender equity and initiated a study to look into its affects. The tide of college athletics was beginning to turn and the athletics directors at institutions were no longer the only ones responsible for the student-athlete's welfare. Schultz put responsibility back in the hands of capable people. Another part of his reform movement was to place sanctions on those institutions that violated the NCAA principles and bylaws. While NCAA chief, an internal investigation alleged that he might have been aware of a scandal while he was AD at Virginia. The specific violation was that booster club members had allegedly provided money to athletes as no-interest loans, along with graduate assistants receiving unwarranted compensation. The university received minor penalties. Schultz resigned from the NCAA because he didn't want to embarrass the Association and the work it was doing to restore the integrity of intercollegiate athletics.

During Schultz's last four years with the NCAA he also served on the executive committee of the USOC. The experience prepared him for the position of executive director of the USOC, which he assumed in 1995. His knowledge and experience in athletics was sought out by the USOC search committee and he was persuaded to accept the position of Executive Director after several phone calls. The

NCAA supplied letters stating that Schultz was not guilty of collusion in the Virginia incident. Schultz employed many of the same management techniques that he utilized at the NCAA, like a flatter organizational structure and giving responsibility back to the employees. He also set out to provide the organization with a strategic vision that encompassed a global focus, an imperative factor for an effective Olympic Committee.

Schultz has certainly faced some difficult challenges throughout his career and he has faced each one with strength, integrity, and determination. The Salt Lake Olympic Organizing committee, which is separate from the USOC, had its own alleged scandal of giving bribes to IOC members to secure the Salt Lake bid. Schultz cooperated with the investigation committee fully and condemned the conflict of interest. Members of the Salt Lake Organizing Committee were removed from their positions and a USOC member charged with accepting bribes was also dismissed. Schultz acted with integrity and attempted to restore the dignity of the Olympic Games. Dick Schultz crossed the finish line with his head held high.

Myles Brand

Creating a New Game Plan for College Sport

by Richard Lapchick

With the passing of Dr. Myles Brand, America lost a champion for student-athletes, Title IX, and civil rights in sports. I have been working on these issues for three decades and no one did more than Myles Brand to make college sport live up to its ideals in those areas. No one was ready when he passed away in 2009. Like many others, I felt like I lost a hero and a friend.

Myles Brand was the philosopher who will be remembered not only for his eloquence, but for his insistence on fighting for justice in sport, especially regarding graduation rates, gender equity and diversity, and inclusion. It is why the NCAS gave him a Giant Steps Award. Ironically, he died in the same week that so many well-known figures displayed not eloquence but arrogance as newspapers were filled with the stories of the bad behavior of Congressman Joe Wilson, Serena Williams, Roger Federer, and Kanye West.

I have been involved in studies of and efforts to try to improve graduation rates since the late 1980s. There was little movement until Brand, who became NCAA President in 2002, marshaled the Academic Progress Rate which created penalties in the form of lost scholarships for poor academic performance, as well as positive incentives for good results. Before this was passed a school could literally go for decades without graduating a single student-athlete and not be subject to NCAA penalties. Dr. Brand helped get this passed because, as a former university president at Oregon and Indiana, he almost automatically had the trust of the increasingly influential college presidents. By reaching out to them, he earned the trust of many athletics directors. He needed both.

While the graduations rates increased substantially, I continued to point out the huge gaps between the rates of African-American and white students. This troubled Brand a great deal. A few years ago he urged me to do a study on the graduation rates of African-American student-athletes. He was right that they were improving significantly. In the last study released in April 2009, I noted that, "I have been studying graduation rates for more than 20 years. The low rates for African-American student-athletes have always been my biggest concern. The improvement shown in this study is impressive. The increases in the Graduation Success Rates (GSR) for African-American student-athletes in the revenue sports were five percentage points in men's basketball to 54 percent and women's basketball to 76 percent, respectively, and four percentage points to 58 percent in Division I-A football in the three years since the initial study. That is substantial and is very good news for college sport."

I was on the Board of the Black Coaches Association (now the Black Coaches and Administrators) when Brand took the NCAA reigns. A few months later he came to the BCA Executive Board meeting. Prior to his arrival, the Board prepared responses to what they assumed would be resistance to the BCA's agenda. When he left the meeting, we were all gratified that he had spoken in accord with the entire agenda. We knew we had an ally. Did we ever.

He created the Office of Diversity and Inclusion with a Vice President in the person of Charlotte Westerhaus at the helm. He got the NCAA to invest resources in programs to help promote opportunities for people of color and for women as coaches and administrators.

I believe he was as frustrated as all BCA members were by the lack of progress for African-Americans as head coaches, especially in, but hardly limited to, football. BCA Executive Director Floyd Keith, Myles Brand, and I all testified before Congress in 2008 about the issue. Floyd and I urged the adoption of what we called the "Eddie Robinson Rule," which was close to the NFL's Rooney Rule to get minorities into the interview process for major head coaching jobs. Eddie Robinson, the legendary Grambling State coach who was the winningest coach of all-time when he retired, was never asked to even interview for a Division I job in his 57 years in the game. Floyd and I had strongly supported this for years, but Myles thought the NCAA membership would not go along. It was really our only area of real disagreement on the issue. Although we disagreed, I never doubted that Myles wanted the same results and thought the Robinson Rule wouldn't work. We had that much faith in his integrity. In his speech to the NCAA in 2008, he said, "The lack of African-American head football coaches, frankly, is an embarrassment to all of intercollegiate athletics. The talent pool exists and it contains men who are ready and able to successfully lead these teams. But we are yet to see more than eight head coaches among the 119 teams in the Football Bowl Subdivision. And as bad as that is, it is worse in the Football Championship Subdivision and in Divisions II and III. Recognition of this problem has grown recently, and good leadership is emerging especially among the Division I athletic directors and others. But proof of change is in the actual appointments to these positions, and that has not yet occurred."[1]

He must have been smiling down from above when the 2010 football hiring season ended with a record 15 coaches of color hired to lead their schools in 2011.

I met with Brand and Bernard Franklin, NCAA senior vice-president for governance, membership, education, and research services in 2004 while the NCAA debated what to do about the persistently controversial issue of the use of Native American names and mascots for sports teams. I shared my view that they should be banned outright as long as they were offensive to some Native Americans. In February 2005, the NCAA banned the use of American Indian mascots by sports teams during its postseason tournaments only, but that was a big start and a huge controversy that reigned for years. Drs. Brand and Franklin never backed down and fought hard against members who fought the change. I felt it was a critically important public stand.

When conservative public forces outside of sport began to join resisters inside sport to try to weaken the effects of Title IX in 2005, Myles jumped right into the fray. This time he even took on the President of the United States. The Department of Education in the Bush Administration tried to move an online survey to gauge women's interest in whether certain sports should be adopted, kept, or dropped. Brand stood up for justice again and told the schools not to use the surveys. Brand beat Bush and Title IX stayed strong.

Beyond the public figure was an adoring husband of Peg Brand, an IU Professor of Philosophy and Gender Studies. I asked him in the summer of 2008 if he was going to get much vacation time and he told me "probably not but I will really enjoy co-teaching a course with Peg. I can't imagine anything more enjoyable."

I am the president of the National Consortium for Academics and Sport (NCAS). We gave our Giant Steps Award to Myles Brand in 2006 because we felt he had taken on the hard issues as NCAA President including poor graduation rates, the gap in those rates between African-American and white student-athletes, the failure of some institutions of higher education to comply with Title IX issues, and the fact that our college programs were not giving adequate opportunities for people of color to gain key decision-making positions in college sport.

I was not surprised when Brand accepted the award by acknowledging two of his heroes: Jackie Robinson and Birch Bayh. Robinson, of course, broke the color barrier in sports and Bayh was a champion of Title IX of the Education Amendments Act of 1972 which gave women equal opportunities in sports and academics in public education.

There is no doubt that Myles Brand became one of my heroes who fought and won the good fight to right injustices. I was blessed to call him a friend.

Note

1. Myles Brand, State of the Association Address, January 12, 2008.

9

CREATING THE ENVIRONMENT

by Richard Lapchick

Problems existed not only in college sport but at the high school, Olympic, and professional sport levels. In the section *Creating the Environment*, the work of six men stood out.

Gene Upshaw and Paul Tagliabue led efforts in the National Football League and the Players Association to have the league serve its communities more effectively.

David Stern not only spirited the growth and development of the NBA but helped spread the NBA's message of service in communities where teams play and players live.

Billy Payne helped bring the Olympic Games to Atlanta in 1996 and used the Olympics as a platform to showcase not only the talents of individuals but what a community like Atlanta could do to serve the Olympic movement while benefiting its citizens.

H. Ross Perot, one of America's wealthiest men and later a presidential candidate, helped the State of Texas to create "No Pass, No Play" legislation. It was the first of its kind in the country and demanded that students had to maintain a "C" average in order to participate in sport in Texas.

Clinton Albury, a coach at Kilian High School in Dade County, Florida, demanded that his football players succeed academically even without state mandates. Albury assumed the leadership of a football team whose players' academic performance met the state's standards, but not Albury's. He challenged them to perform in the classroom and converted his already winning team into a group of scholar-athletes.

Rich DeVos, the co-founder of the Amway Corporation and one of America's wealthiest individuals, became owner of the Orlando

Magic in the 1990s. His team served as a model for all in sport in terms of sports organization that constantly gave back to the community. Rich DeVos also made the donation that made the DeVos Sport Business Management Program at the University of Central Florida a reality; he created the Institute for Diversity in Ethics and Sport at UCF and then endowed the National Consortium for Academics and Sports with gifts to these organizations totaling $9 million.

Lewis Katz and Raymond Chambers invested in the New Jersey Nets and together have donated their portion of the profits to the inner-city schools and children in the surrounding communities, the same communities where they started their humble beginnings.

Mike Ilitch dreamt of playing professional baseball as a young boy but grew up to own professional baseball and hockey teams instead. Ilitch utilized his business acumen to build his sports teams as both winners and contributors to the community. Similarly, Jerry Reinsdorf, owner of MLB's Chicago White Sox and the NBA's Chicago Bulls, has been instrumental in advocating for the greater good of sport while leading from two different leagues.

Thomas Sanders first led by example as a player and later as an executive for the NBA. His appreciation for and understanding of the sport of basketball and the NBA allowed him to positively shape hundreds of citizens who were also professional athletes.

These men used their influence to make sport at the high school, Olympic, and professional levels be all it could be.

Paul Tagliabue & Gene Upshaw

Creating the Environment

by Jenny Yehlen

"There is no 'I' in team" is a common saying used by anyone trying to motivate a group of people, or a team to work together in harmony to achieve a common goal. As a mock response to that saying, some may reply, "But there is a 'me' in team," implying that the individual performance overrides team accomplishments. For some reason, the team and the individual seem to be on opposite ends of the spectrum when it comes to professional sports, and it is extremely difficult to find that happy medium that satisfies the individual athlete, yet it is in the best interest of the team.

This is exactly the task that Paul Tagliabue, the NFL Commissioner from 1989 to 2006, and Gene Upshaw, the former executive director of the NFL Players Association from 1987 to 2008, undertook. Over 18 years, the two worked together to create the incredibly successful entity that the NFL is today. Tagliabue stepped down from his commissioner position in 2006 and sadly, Gene Upshaw passed away in 2008 from pancreatic cancer. Fortunately, their legacy lives on through their predecessors and the relationship they worked to build for many years.

Although Tagliabue worked with all of the NFL teams and treated them all fairly, he will admit he was partial to a couple of teams as a kid. He was a fan of the New York Giants because they were so close to home. He also rooted for the Cleveland Browns because they had Italian-Americans on the team and Tagliabue was of Italian heritage. Of course these interests remain as part of his past and had no bearing on decisions he made for the teams in the League. Tagliabue was an athlete himself growing up in Jersey City, New Jersey. While he was not a standout football player, he was a stellar hoops star. His basketball skills and impressive grades earned him a scholarship to Georgetown University where he majored in government. He graduated from Georgetown in 1962 as senior class president, basketball team captain, Rhodes Scholar finalist, and dean's list honoree. He immediately received a public service scholarship to attend the New York University School of Law.

Tagliabue's first job was with a big-time firm in Washington, D.C., that just happened to serve as the primary outside counsel for the NFL. Tagliabue had been working with and learning about the NFL since he started practicing law in 1965. That made him a logical candidate to follow Pete Rozelle as the commissioner of the League. There were some big shoes to fill as the head of the NFL when Rozelle decided to step down from his position after 29 years. Rozelle was in charge from 1960 to 1989. Obviously, a lot of change occurred during those three decades. Economically, socially, and athletically, there was a lot to deal with not only in the world of sport, but in the world in general. It only made sense for Tagliabue to step in since he had served as Rozelle's chief legal counsel for over 20 years and he knew what was going on with the teams. Because of this connection, the transition from the third commissioner to the fourth was very smooth.

Gene Upshaw had been serving as executive director to the NFLPA for two years by the time Tagliabue became NFL Commissioner. Just as Tagliabue had been involved with the NFL prior to being appointed as Commissioner, Upshaw had been involved with the dealings of the NFLPA long before he took the head position as well. He was no newcomer to the workings of the Players Association.

Upshaw had been a part of the first AFL/NFL combined draft in 1967, after being named as a NAIA All-American at Texas A&I University (now known as Texas A&M—Kingsville). He was drafted in the first round by the Oakland Raiders and played in the NFL for 16 years until 1981. During his playing time, he also served as an NFLPA player representative and officer for 13 years. He was an All-Pro offensive guard and was elected into the Professional Football Hall of Fame in 1987, the first year he was eligible. Upshaw was voted as the Lineman of the Year in the AFC in 1973 and 1974 and received the honors of Lineman of the Year in the NFL in 1977. Upshaw is the only NFL player in history to play in three Super Bowls in three different decades.

Upshaw was the captain of the offensive team for eight of his years. During his 15-year tenure with the Raiders, they made 11 playoff appearances, won eight division titles, one AFL Championship, two AFC titles, and two Super Bowl Championships. He is still revered as one of the greats, being named to the AFL-NFL 25-year All-Star Team and to the NFL 75th Anniversary All-Time Team.

Upshaw was a leader which accounts for his success as head of the NFLPA for so many years. Upshaw became known as a strong labor leader in America and molded the NFLPA to be at the top of its class as a players association.

The relationship between the League and the players was not in good shape when Tagliabue took office in 1989. There was no collective bargaining agreement because the strike in 1987 had resulted in no contracts and the players union was filing a suit against the League.

At the top of Tagliabue's priority list when he was appointed as Commissioner was to develop a good relationship with Upshaw and the players association. Tagliabue realized that instead of competing and fighting with the players, the league should be communicating and compromising in order to make the NFL successful. Upshaw understood these sentiments and agreed with the philosophy. Eventually, Tagliabue and Upshaw became known more as business partners as opposed to enemies working with conflicting interests. Upshaw did receive some criticism for this since the players union and the League had tended not to agree on things in the past, but Upshaw did what he believed was right and in the best interest of both the players and the league.

While Tagliabue and Upshaw worked together as partners and created a stronger relationship between the two associations, there were no strikes or work stoppages in the NFL. Every other professional league had a stoppage of play in that time period. This is a big improvement after two strikes took place in the NFL in 1982 and 1987, prior to Tagliabue's arrival. Tagliabue and Upshaw orchestrated two big changes, which saw the owners agree to free agency, and in turn, the players agreed to a salary cap. The Collective Bargaining Agreement (CBA) has been extended four times since Tagliabue's initial negotiations with Upshaw.

Tagliabue retired in July of 2006, after completing one final TV deal and long-term contracts with players. He stayed on with the NFL as a senior executive and consultant through 2008. In regards to his own tenure, Tagliabue said, "Building a strong relationship with the NFL Players Association is the thing I'm most proud of."[1] He also shared that it had been a privilege to spend so much time working with the NFL and that it was not an easy decision to step down, but it seemed like the right one. When Upshaw passed two years later, Tagliabue spoke about his friend and colleague, saying, "Few people in the history of the National Football League have played the game as well as Gene and then had another career in football with so much positive impact on the structure and competitiveness of the entire league as Gene,"[2]

Because of their unique relationship, Tagliabue and Upshaw were able to get the players and the league heavily involved in service activities in the communities where they played. They were generous with time and money as was epitomized by their combined efforts in the fall of 2005 in response to the tragedy of Hurricane Katrina. Through their combined efforts more than $15 million was donated to the relief organizations, demonstrating the power of sport to help society. Upshaw and Tagliabue showed that management and labor can work together for the larger good and the hope is that mentality continues in their absence. They are what real leadership in professional sport is all about.

Notes

1. Associated Press, "NFL commissioner Tagliabue to retire in July; Decision 'right for me, right for the league'," *Telegraph Herald*, March 21, 2006.

2. Dave Goldberg, "NFLPA head Gene Upshaw dies of cancer at age 63," *AP Online*, August 21, 2008, http://www.highbeam.com/doc/1A1-D92MRFR80.html, (accessed February 27, 2010).

David Stern

Creating the Environment

by Jenny Yehlen

Individual athletes have to take care of themselves and are responsible for their own actions, but there is a hierarchy of power and responsibility that exists high above the position of the athletes. There are coaches who have some say over their individual players and above them is the team organization that has many layers of executive leadership. At the top of the organizational structure are the president, CEO, owner, general manager, etc. Even higher up the ladder are officials of all professional leagues who are responsible for the teams, the coaches, and the players. At the head of the league offices is the commissioner of the league, who has the responsibility of managing the entire league. Pleasing everyone all the time is an art form that is yet to be perfected, especially for a league commissioner who has to deal the difficult task of overseeing contracts, salary caps, league rules, and punishments for breaking rules.

In the NBA, the commissioner is David Stern, a role he has held since February 1, 1984. This is not what Stern dreamed of doing when he was boy, especially since he was only seven years old when the NBA was originally constituted. His interest in basketball when he was young was limited to being a Knicks fan and playing basketball on the local courts in Chelsea, New York.

Wanting to stay close to home so he could continue to work at Stern's Deli, the family business that he had jumpstarted, Stern chose to attend Rutgers University. He graduated from Rutgers as a Dean's list student and as a Henry Rutgers Scholar in 1963. He immediately went to law school at Columbia University from which he graduated in 1966. His first connection with the NBA was joining the firm Proksauer and Rose, which represented the NBA; he served as outside counsel. Stern left the firm in 1978 and joined the NBA family by becoming general counsel. He was soon appointed the executive vice president of the league in 1980. Four years later he was elected as the fourth commissioner of the NBA.

Prior to Stern's selection as commissioner, the NBA was not doing very well. The league was close to bankruptcy, fans were drifting away, drug abuse was a major issue among the players, and management-labor wars were rampant.

Since Stern became commissioner, league revenues have increased over 500 percent. An increase in popularity led to the addition of seven expansion teams. Stern has even crossed the gender barrier with the founding of the Women's National Basketball Association (WNBA). Stern worked to create The National Basketball Developmental League (NBDL) and to negotiate some very lucrative television contracts. He has worked hard to make the NBA more global. In addition to the expansion teams, Stern opened international offices in Barcelona, Hong Kong, London, Melbourne, Mexico City, Singapore, Taiwan, Tokyo, and Toronto. The NBA now broadcasts games in over 200 countries in more than 40 different languages.

Player rosters have become more and more diversified in recent years. In 2005, there were a total of 82 international players from 36 countries in the NBA. These numbers keep growing, along with the NBA's global market. Stern wanted to reach people around the world so basketball fans from China could watch Yao Ming, fans from Germany could watch Dirk Nowitzki, the French could cheer on Tony Parker, and Canadians could root for Steve Nash. Exhibition games are played internationally which helps the NBA reach out to youth around the world.

The League gives a great deal domestically to children in particular. Stern thought it would be a good idea and great connection to expand these efforts across the globe. Basketball Without Borders summer camps was created to give kids the opportunity to play basketball. This program is about more than simply providing courts, equipment, and the opportunity to play. NBA players and other counselors teach the children the rules of the game and some X's and O's of offense and defense. More importantly the kids also learn about leadership, teamwork, cultural differences, the importance of education, and living a drug-free lifestyle. Thus far, this program has reached kids in Turkey, Greece, and over 20 African countries.

With the leadership of David Stern, the NBA and its players and organizations are involved in numerous community service programs. He knows what a substantial impact NBA players can have in the community. A few of the other programs that the NBA is involved with are the Read to Achieve Program, child abuse prevention, alcohol abuse prevention, volunteerism, hunger relief, and the Special Olympics.

The NBA and the WNBA have also had the best record for hiring women and people of color in all of sport. Both have had the top grades throughout the 18-year history of the *Racial and Gender Report Card*. The NBA, under David Stern's leadership was also the first pro sport to have Diversity Management Training implemented throughout the league.

Over Stern's 25 years as the commissioner he has had to deal with a lot of changes: ballooning player salaries, shifting target markets, and the change in a basketball game from being purely a sporting event to more of an entertainment event. Stern's job is never dull. There are always new issues to be addressed and problems to be solved. There is never a way to please everyone, but Stern's job is to do what he believes is best for the league. David Stern has been making good decisions for over 25 years, and NBA fans around the world should be grateful for his strong and insightful leadership.

Billy Payne

Creating the Environment

by Jessica Bartter Duffaut

Kids often have lofty dreams of representing their country in the sport they love and standing on the Olympic platform, beaming with pride and a gold medal while singing their national anthem and holding back the tears. On the contrary, Billy Payne's Olympic dreams did not start until he was almost 40 years old. Payne's dream was different. He did not want to run the 4 × 100-meter relay, swim the 200-meter freestyle, or even play basketball with the American Dream Team. Although all three would have been an honor for this former football star, Payne's dream was to bring the summer Olympics to Atlanta, Georgia.

Payne was born and raised in Georgia and felt a need to give back to the communities that had brought him so many good memories. The good football memories started in high school at Dykes High where he led his team as quarterback to the 1964 North Georgia Championship. Payne knew his destiny would take him to the University of Georgia where his father had been a star and later officiated southeastern conference games. Payne followed his father's footsteps and played lineman for the offense and defense at Georgia. While playing for coach Vince Dooley, the Bulldogs lost only four games and played in three major bowl games during Payne's three years on the team. Payne was team captain and earned All-Southeastern Conference honors as a defensive end.

Since football is not an Olympic sport, Payne's only chance of playing beyond college was in the National Football League (NFL). Payne decided his skills would be better utilized as a lawyer. After graduating from law school in the top 20 percent of his class in 1973, Payne was employed at a law firm in Atlanta. He specialized in real estate law but after two years, when the real estate market began to do poorly, Payne and a friend started their own law firm.

In 1987, Payne dedicated a new sanctuary for a church in Dunwoody, Georgia after he chaired a three-year, $2.5 million fundraising effort project. The sense of collective joy that emerged from the crowd inspired Payne to do something else for the community so that he could experience that joy once again. Up before the sun the next day, Payne explored idea after idea until he was still left with nothing. Payne looked through the ideas he had already rejected and realized the common denominator among all of them involved sports and community. Like a light bulb, the word Olympics flashed in his brain. This was the beginning of a nine-year project that Payne brought to fruition. The journey was met with doubt, criticism, and personal debt but Payne fought back with sheer competitiveness, determination, and personal sacrifice.

Payne thought the Olympics would bring a similar sense of collective joy to the City of Atlanta, but on a larger scale. Payne believed the international event could reshape the Atlanta community by crossing color barriers, improving economic status, and fixing neighborhood disparities. Payne planned to leverage change in the city by sharing economic benefits with disadvantaged neighborhoods and building a sense of community. With such goals, it is hard to imagine the city did not support Payne's dream right away. Instead, many laughed at or ignored him. He first approached the Chamber of Commerce to ask them to bankroll his plans but they did not even think his request was worthy of a response. Payne received similar reactions from the local community, business establishments, and government.

Unfamiliar with failure, Payne refused to give up. He turned to wealthy friends who could easily write six-figure checks to create a pool of seed money for the Games. Despite the fact that he had two children at home nearing the age of college, which meant large bills for tuition, Payne quit his law practice and mortgaged some of his real estate properties, putting himself $1.5 million in debt, an amount he added to the seed money. Payne's friends, now known as the Atlanta Nine, were the only ones who believed his plan could work. Payne volunteered himself for three years traveling and soliciting to have the 1996 Summer Olympics in Atlanta. Eventually Payne garnered support and positive recognition for his efforts. One key supporter was Mayor Andrew Young who was a civil rights leader, three-term congressman, and former United Nations Ambassador. Payne recognized the symbolism of a white organizer and a black mayor working together to bring a shared dream to life. Initially, Mayor Young's international credibility helped Payne's efforts with the International Olympic Committee; then Payne's southern charm kicked in. After three years of living off savings and loans, Payne began earning a salary as the chief executive officer of the Atlanta Committee for the Olympic Games (ACOG). With the official support of his city behind him, Payne persevered. Now that Atlanta was in the race, many believed the odds were stacked against the city—or any other city in the United States for that matter—because the 1996 Summer Olympics marked the 100th anniversary of the modern Olympics. Athens, Greece, was thought to be a shoe-in for the centennial games. Known as a fierce competitor, this did not deter Payne. On September 19, 1990, Payne's hard work and sacrifice was rewarded. It was announced in Tokyo that Atlanta had been selected over Athens by a vote of 51-35.

Though both Payne and the city were ecstatic, the work done to bring the Olympic Games to Atlanta had really just begun. Many thought Payne, the lawyer, would walk away as if just getting them to come to Atlanta was enough. But Payne planned to see his dream through and had no intention of stepping down as CEO of the Atlanta Committee for the Olympic Games. Instead, Payne made room for the experts and worked alongside them to establish a $1.7 billion budget and then oversaw the spending of it. He was also charged with overseeing some 90,000 employees, volunteers, and concessionaires. The Games were played in 31 different athletic venues around the Atlanta area, 10 of which were built specifically for the Olympics. Some of the construction caused controversy, particularly in the poor, predominately black neighborhood of Summerhill where the new Olympic Stadium was constructed. Thirty years before, the city of Atlanta built a baseball stadium in the same neighborhood and now residents feared that once again, they would be excluded from the economic benefits of the stadium. However, Payne envisioned the Olympics in Atlanta to do just the opposite. He and the ACOG consulted a neighborhood committee regarding jobs, traffic patterns, and parking to ensure that the stadium could reap compensation for the community. The stadium was a $209 million gift from the ACOG to the community after it was used for the Olympics.[1]

In another effort to better race relations in the Atlanta area, Payne suggested golf be added as an Olympic sport, and that the Augusta National Golf Club would serve as host. An avid golfer himself, Payne was quite aware of Augusta's history of discrimination and hoped that raising the issue would help eliminate the lack of racial equality there. Though this idea was not passed, he knows it would have been the right thing to do for the exact reasons that it received opposition.

After years of seven-day work weeks and 14-hour days that started in the office at 5 a.m., Payne finally saw his dream come to life when on July 19, 1996, the summer Olympics opened in Atlanta. Atlanta welcomed over 2.5 million spectators to watch more than 10,000 athletes from 179 nations compete in 271 events in 26 different sports. The 1996 games were successful for American athletes, who took home 36 more medals than any visiting country— earning 44 gold, 32 silver and 25 bronze medals. The Games were also a success for the city of Atlanta which is now more internationally recognized and has experienced a higher tourism rate since 1996. Atlanta was only the third American city to host the summer games, and the first to win the bid on its first try.

After a short recovery period, Payne had to return to work to pay off the numerous debts his passion for the Olympics had built for him. Though he toyed with the idea of a new career in sports with the Atlanta Falcons, the University of Georgia, or numerous other sport company positions he was offered, Payne took a position in the corporate world and later became a partner at an investment banking firm in 2000.

After Payne made a strong bid to include golf an Olympic sport and use Augusta National as the 1996 Olympic venue, the Augusta National Golf Club, home of The Masters Tournament, invited Payne to be a member. After joining the infamously-exclusive membership, Payne was asked to chair the Club in 2006. Payne became the first native Georgian to serve Augusta as chairman. Although Payne was unsuccessful in introducing golf as an Olympic sport in 1996, he was successful in starting the movement, and in 2009 in was announced that golf will make its Olympic debut at the 2016 Games in Rio de Janeiro, Brazil.

Since 1996, Payne estimates he has made more than 3,000 speeches describing his experiences in spearheading the Olympic effort. He is still called upon for advice by representatives from other

Olympic hopeful cities, but the best advice Billy Payne could offer is how to believe in yourself when no one else does and how to stick by your dreams. You never know just how much you can accomplish until you try.

Note

1. John Meyer, "Man with the plan after nine years, finish line in sight for Billy Payne's grand vision of Atlanta Olympics," *Rocky Mountain News*, May 5, 1996.

Dr. Clinton Albury and H. Ross Perot

Creating the Environment

by Jessica Bartter Duffaut

Balancing academics and athletics is often a difficult task for high school student-athletes. While athletics are the fun part of a being a student-athlete, emphasis on education needs to be reinforced from parents, coaches, teachers, and even teammates to help teenagers juggle the demands of both. In 1982, Texas governor Bill Clements was concerned the education system was not doing its part to emphasize academics in their state's athletic departments and decided to take a stand. He called on Ross Perot for assistance to evaluate the state of Texas' public education and offer recommendations on how to make improvements.

Ross Perot was a billionaire, born and raised in Texas, who often spoke out against the U.S. Government when he believed it had failed its people. Clements had seen success with Perot three years prior when he asked for his assistance in developing policies that reduced illegal drug use in Texas. Perot's early political involvements led him to later run for President of the United States in 1992 and 1996.

Perot accepted Clements' new challenge wholeheartedly and put a lot of effort into a study examining the current state of the education system and other systems with proven track records. Perot even spent an additional $2 million of his own money so that he and his committee could travel to cities all over the state and hold public hearings and news conferences to gather as much information as possible. Some of the generalized recommendations they received were the equalization of spending among rich and poor districts, tying teacher salaries to their job performance, and putting more of an emphasis on academics rather than athletics in high school. In accordance with this last recommendation, Governor Clements and Perot instituted a major legislative change with the "No Pass, No Play" rule. No Pass, No Play was a public education policy introduced to Texas schools that required students to have passing grades in order to be eligible for competition with their school's extracurricular activities, including sports teams. The specifics of the rule required competency testing and certification for teachers and barred student-athletes from participating in sports for six weeks if they failed a class. The rule impacted student-athletes by threatening a consequence that none wanted to face. It also prevented high schools from placing too much emphasis on sports.

Surprisingly, public opinion began to support No Pass, No Play. A poll conducted by the Public Policy Laboratory at Texas A&M University showed that 76 percent of Texas residents favored the new law. Nationally, a Gallup poll indicated that 90 percent of adults favored restricting those with less than a C average.

Perhaps the group that got the biggest surprise was Texas coaches. Educators said No Pass, No Play worked *because* of the academic efforts of the coaches. Goree Johnson, the Roosevelt basketball coach in Dallas, emphasized the coach's influence. He held up the start of practice until 4:00 p.m. so his players could work with teachers after school. His staff also made weekly grade checks and assigned mandatory early-morning tutoring for athletes found to be behind academically. Johnson did not lose a single player. Also in Dallas, Spruce basketball coach Val Rhodes reported a change in players' attitudes toward grades. More than half of his team began appearing in his office at 7:30 in the morning to study. Teachers knew they could contact Rhodes about potential problems and arranged conferences with parents, Rhodes, and students. The link between academics and athletics was being forged.

The results in Dallas were evident. The city's rate of ineligibility for varsity football players dropped from 16 percent in 1985 to 7.2 percent in 1986. Basketball saw a similar drop from 17.8 percent to 11.8 percent. An analysis by Theodore L. Goudge and Byron D. Augustin in *Texas Coach*, March 1987, showed how the percentage of ineligible athletes was directly related to the size of the school: the larger the school, the higher the percentage of athletes with academic problems.

The Texas landmark legislation was a stimulus to coaches across the country, one of the best examples of whom is Clinton Albury, who took over as football coach of Dade County's Killian High School in 1984. He discovered that his team's grade point average was 1.3. Horrified, he instituted a mandatory study hall. There was only a D average eligibility standard, but Albury brought in honor students to tutor his athletes. In specialized study halls, they taught math and English three days a week, science and history the other two. By the 1986 season, the team's GPA had risen to 2.45. No one failed a course. At the end of the season, 23 players signed with colleges and universities for athletic scholarships. That was believed to be the highest number of signed players in Dade County history. Dade is football country. All were Prop 48 eligible.

Were Killian's teachers merely marking them at an easier standard? Apparently not, since all 23 did well enough as college freshmen to stay eligible. It was a testament to Albury, who later moved into a full-time academic position at Killian so he could offer the program to all student-athletes.

But the most startling case was that of Killian student-athlete Paul Moore. He was the type of player that many would say could never be eligible under a 2.0 (C average) system. He would, according to the argument, be victimized by society's good intentions. In fact, Moore was reading on a first or second grade level in 1984. Then Coach Albury got him into a program for learning-disabled students. He graduated in June 1987 with an 11th grade reading level and a 2.3 GPA in core courses. He exceeded 700 on his SATs. He was eligible under Prop 48 at Florida State in 1987–88, but was redshirted. He was a running back for the 1989 Sugar Bowl team.

In 1994, Albury left Killian High School when asked by the new principal at South Miami High School to join his staff. The principal invited Albury because of the success his athletic academic program had at Killian for 17 years. Nine years later, when Killian High School got a new principal, Albury was asked to return as dean of Academic Discipline and Student Development. The new principal was well aware of Albury's academic impact on athletes and gave him full reign to resurrect the athletic academic program. Albury created an Athletic Academic Advisor position and together they ran the Basic Athletic Learning Links (BALL) Program. BALL was mandatory for all athletes, whether or not they were in season. BALL was divided into two programs. If the student-athlete was earning a C– or D in a core class he/she was assigned to Program I to receive tutoring from honor students. If a student-athlete was received D's or F's on their report card, he/she was assigned to Program II and placed with a teacher for an hour after school each day. Within the first semester that Albury implemented his new program, 21 percent of the athletes assigned to mandatory study halls improved their grades to a C or higher. By the second semester, this figure reached 47 percent.

After his program lost support, Albury moved to Miami Springs Middle School where he is was the eighth grade administrator. While his new position dealt mainly with discipline, Albury utilized his time with students to provide the academic advisement he is known for.

H. Ross Perot and Clinton Albury worked hard to put the emphasis back on the student in the student-athlete. Independently, they each proved that with proper guidelines, encouragement, and support, high school students can excel in both athletics and academics.

Richard DeVos

Creating the Environment

by Stacy Martin-Tenney

Richard DeVos has dedicated his life to encouraging other people to give from their hearts to the fullest extent. His heart has always been overflowing with generosity and encouragement. Unfortunately, DeVos' heart began to fail physically when he was 70 years old. DeVos approached this challenge with the same ferocious faith and irrepressible determination that he did his business and philanthropic efforts. Even when faced with death, he continued in his race to make the world a better place. The only hope the doctors gave him was a heart transplant. His donations to society have come back to him a billion times over throughout the years, and a new heart came his way too, just in time.

DeVos is among the strong and resilient people of the world. The recovery from such an operation was not an insurmountable feat for him, but he will caution others to be prepared for the tough road to recovery. His caution is not meant to discourage others, but help them strengthen their souls. DeVos had a history of heart problems over a 10-year period before the transplant, so finding a heart for him when the supply was so limited was a daunting task. A 70-year-old man in failing health with additional complicating factors would be written off by doctors as a tragic tale, but DeVos has an air of magic about him. The doctors worked overtime to find him a heart that would match his generous soul. When they were stifled in the U.S., they crossed the ocean to find DeVos a heart. They located a doctor in London who believed in DeVos' will to live. So, DeVos moved to London. His spirit was undaunted and he relied on his faith to carry him through.

One day a young woman waiting for a heart and lung transplant received the greatest gift she would ever know from a stranger. A car accident in the Czech Republic claimed a victim's life, but he donated his heart and lungs to the seriously ill young woman. Her disease necessitated a concurrent heart and lung transplant, which left her healthy heart available for someone else. Richard DeVos was that someone. One life was lost, but two hearts were found. It is very fitting that DeVos' donor remained alive and healthy. Since his miraculous and marvelous recovery, DeVos has devoted his new life to persuading others to donate their hearts to others, both figuratively and literally, as organ donations seem to have flattened out.

DeVos is a compassionate and brilliant man who has been able to combine both qualities into a sound business. He graduated from Grand Rapids Christian High School with a diploma in one hand and a business plan in the other. He developed his plan further at Calvin College in Grand Rapids with his longtime business partner and high school classmate, Jay Van Andel. They embarked on several direct sales ventures and even formed their own corporation in 1949 called the Ja-Ri Corporation. They found that they enjoyed the entrepreneurial lifestyle, especially the countless hours and sleepless nights that afforded them their own business path.

Ten years after the Ja-Ri Corporation formed, DeVos and Van Andel had tailored their business acumen and polished the principles of their business to form the Amway Corporation. Amway set out to fulfill the American dream the American way. The two men set out to form a multilevel marketing company that recruited people to do direct sales and then rewarded them in accordance with their efforts. The company was founded on sound ethical and moral principles like helping people help themselves and helping neighbors, businesses, and families. These two men felt so strongly about their employees conducting business with hope, freedom, family, and reward in mind, that they carved this code into stone outside Amway headquarters. It has developed into a successful, multibillion-dollar international business with operations in over 80 countries around the world. In 2000, Amway became a subsidiary of Alticor, Inc., a $6.2 billion business, with sister companies Quixtar Inc., and Access Business Groups, LLC. The DeVos and Van Andel families still serve on that board and Dick DeVos and Steve Van Andel assumed their respective father's responsibilities in the company.

DeVos built his business on sales, but he would reference his heart instead. He has always believed in an individual's ability to accomplish noteworthy achievements, so he encouraged his employees to do just that. The word "encourage" has its roots in the French word for heart—"cour."[1] DeVos has built an empire on encouraging and enriching people's lives whether they are his consumers or his employees. He would say that he is in the business of hope. It is hope that keeps the heart striving for more, and it is hope that warms the heart when it is cast out into the cold. DeVos knows how tough rejection is, both as a salesman and a heart transplant patient. Facing rejection after the transplant is usually a daunting task for the patient because they have been sick for so long and their hope for survival is wrapped up in one organ. DeVos characterizes the post transplant rejection fears he faced as mild in comparison to someone's first sales pitch rejection, because he just has to maintain his anti-rejection medication regimen with a few pills. If science could encapsulate DeVos' hope for the world and genuine encouragement, then people could overcome life's rejections. Unfortunately, the pill doesn't exist, but DeVos' book titled *Hope from My Heart* does. He illustrates how positive reinforcement and patience are the medicine to overcome rejections in life. The first time a salesman knocks on a door, he is filled with fear of rejection. But, one day soon a knock will turn into a sale and faith will be restored.

DeVos has always lifted others' spirits, especially in tough situations. There have been countless stories through the years of his one-on-one pep talks and full-scale speeches about the importance of encouragement and the power of perseverance. He gave a commencement address to a class containing an extraordinary number of high achievers, but he spoke to the hearts of the young adults without honor cords and tassels, assuring them that they were still destined for greatness. Another unique aspect of DeVos is his personal involvement in other people's lives when they are discouraged. He has even gone for a ride with an Amway pilot the day after the pilot crashed one of the company's helicopters into Lake Michigan, to exhibit his faith in the young man's abilities. DeVos' heart is full of compassion, integrity, and passion. One of those passions is the game of basketball.

In 1991, the DeVos family capitalized on another business opportunity and purchased the NBA's Orlando Magic. DeVos' four children have been very involved in his business endeavors and the Magic were no different. He wanted to establish a family atmosphere in the competitive and adversarial environment of sports, so he assigned the responsibility of the team to his daughter Cheri's husband, Bob Vander Weide. His presence is very much a part of the organization though, as he frequently visits the locker room to cheer on the players and encourage them in life outside the arena. His attachment to the organization runs deep and it reflects the principles that he holds so close to his heart. The team has been a model citizen of the NBA with its extensive philanthropic activities and respectful behavior. The Orlando Magic Youth Foundation, the giving arm of the team, has impacted an estimated one million children's lives. DeVos is a brilliant businessman with the foresight to realize that the model and message that the team conveyed would carry extraordinary weight in society. He envisioned a team that, by example, would create a special environment in the world of professional sports.

The sports business is still a business though, and a business must be profitable and successful to support the community service values that DeVos embraced. Success came relatively quickly for the DeVos family's newest endeavor. In the Magic's sixth season after their inception, they advanced to the NBA finals. DeVos initiated the team's campaign slogan himself for the Finals that year by simply asking, "Why not us, why not now?"[2] Many quickly recognized that DeVos' investment could be profitable for the long-term. They were on their way to greatness. Unfortunately, the team lost the championship series that season, but DeVos only saw it as another opportunity for encouragement. The team came back strong the next year and was considered a title contender once more if they could win against the Chicago Bulls and a Michael Jordan comeback. Denied once more, DeVos continued to preach the virtue of perseverance. Over the course of DeVos' ownership the team has won an Eastern Conference Title and two Atlantic Division Championships. They have had winning seasons 11 of DeVos' 13 years and have advanced to the playoffs eight times. DeVos incorporated the sound business principles that had catapulted him into one of the most successful businessmen in America when he purchased the Magic, putting his heart into a young basketball franchise.

The Magic play their games in the TD Waterhouse Arena, which is a relic of the former design style for basketball arenas. Early in the new millennium the team started advertising their need for a new arena to compete with the rest of the league and the latest trend of luxury corporate boxes. The Magic needed to turn a profit and they needed a facility where their fans would be comfortable. TD Waterhouse was not it. DeVos is truly the nobleman of owners because the Magic is a class organization and he has personally donated enormous amounts of money to causes in and around Central Florida. However, all the public heard was a billionaire asking for money.

His battle was strictly a business decision. He needed to do what was right for the team as well as the town and began shopping the team around for buyers. All of them wanted to move the team out of Orlando. DeVos remained the owner and reaffirmed that this was central Florida's team. Most owners would have sold, but DeVos knew what the team means to the town, and he put Amway's name on the arena when the TD Waterhouse sponsorship deal expired. The DeVos family ushered in a new season in Magic basketball when the team celebrated its second Eastern Conference Championship in franchise history during the 2008–09 season and will open a brand new arena in their hometown of Orlando for the 2010–11 season, assuring their commitment to the community.

You can learn an immense amount about how to conduct business from Richard DeVos, and especially how to conduct it ethically in the sports business where the culture values winning above all else. DeVos and his wife Helen have established the Richard and Helen DeVos Foundation to support organizations that share their beliefs. One of the beliefs they value most is education. They have given to many educational institutions throughout the years. In Richard DeVos fashion, he found a beautiful way to blend philanthropy and business by creating a graduate sport business management program at the University of Central Florida that would encompass his values of diversity, ethical decision-making, and commitment to community. The program was created from funding received by the DeVos Foundation and the gift was matched by the state of Florida. It provides a unique learning environment that is unparalleled across the nation due to its relationship with the Orlando Magic that provides firsthand practical application. Richard DeVos has given these students hope and has encouraged the dreams in their hearts. He is always striving to make a difference in this world. What better way than to educate future leaders in the sports industry? Richard DeVos may have started out just leading by example in the sports industry, but has now created the standard for excellence, simply by donating his heart to others.

Notes

1 Pat Williams, *How to be Like Rich DeVos*. (Deerfield Beach, Florida: Health Communications, Inc., 2004), 109.

2. Shaun Powell, "Two owners who are the envy of the NBA (Leslie Alexander; Rich DeVos)" *The Sporting News*, June 19, 1995.

Lewis Katz
and Raymond Chambers

Creating the Environment

by Jenny Yehlen

Buying a professional sports organization costs a great deal of money. But that cost can usually be turned in to a very lucrative profit—the driving force behind most investments. Most owners of professional sports teams try to make money, and lots of it. There is a significant amount of money floating around the NBA, not only amongst the players, but within management, ownership, and the league itself. Many people might argue that it is wrong for athletes—and sports in general—to be making so much money when there is so much need in our society and in the world. This wouldn't be as much of a problem if all sports team owners had the same mindset as Raymond Chambers and Lewis Katz. The majority of wealth belongs to only a few, but when those few choose to distribute the wealth to those less fortunate, good things happen.

Raymond Chambers and Lewis Katz have worked hard to be a part of that wealthy group of owners. They are great businessmen. Chambers and Katz were actually the chief financial backers in the sale of the New Jersey Nets, but, collectively, a group bought the team for $150 million in 1998. There are a group of 17 investors who have put money into the Nets organization and Katz tends to lead the group. Although the duo of Chambers and Katz work to make the organization profitable, just as they did in their prior business ventures, they don't want the money for themselves. Chambers and Katz have donated their 38 percent share of the profits to improving conditions in several New Jersey cities, including Newark, Trenton, Paterson, Camden, and Jersey City.

Another aspect of this heartwarming story is that both Katz and Chambers were born and raised in New Jersey. Katz grew up in Camden, New Jersey and graduated from Camden High School. Like many sports team owners, Katz began his career in the business world far away from the sports industry. He was raised by a single mother and attended Temple University on a scholarship. His summer job was selling dog food, which wasn't the most glamorous of jobs but it paid the bills. After Temple, he graduated first in his class from Dickinson Law School and established his own law firm of Katz, Ettin, Levine & Weber, P.A. He also has held the position of chairman and CEO of Kinney System Holding Corporation, which is a major parking company, prior to being a team owner. As Katz's hard work made him increasingly successful, he gave more and more back to those in need. Katz's success allowed him to dive into a totally different arena of business and to become the philanthropist that he truly was at heart.

Raymond Chambers, although he has the same big heart that Katz has, is quite a bit different from his philanthropic partner. He tries to stay out of the media as much as possible. Katz is more the spokesperson for the effort that he and Chambers take on in giving back through sports. Although this was the first venture in sports for both Chambers and Katz, they both have a good grasp of how to go about being effective in giving back to the community. They concluded that the very visible, public image of sports and athletes was a great pipeline to use for their cause. There needed to be role models showcasing the good that can be done, and that is exactly what Katz and Chambers are doing. Chambers, however, chooses to be more private about the issue and doesn't want public attention or acclaim for the good he is doing. He would rather the attention be focused on the people in need, perhaps prompting others to donate their time and resources.

Chambers, who also worked his way up from humble beginnings, was the son of a steel warehouse manager. He grew up in Newark and put himself through college at Rutgers University by playing keyboard in a band called the Ray-tones. He began his career as an accountant before he began investing on his own. The best business decision he made was creating a partnership with Wesray Capital Corporation. This was the corporation that established him financially, and allowed him step down from his management position in the late 1980s. He then turned to philanthropy.

Both Chambers and Katz, being part of an ownership group, pledged their shares of the profits to the inner-city schools and the children living in New Jersey cities. The money actually went to a trust called the Community Youth Organization, of which Katz was the co-chairman. Education was the main focal point of the Community Youth Organization. Specifically, the money went towards minority education, scholarships, and mentoring. The Boys and Girls Club of Camden and Newark, the two owner's hometowns, have been vastly improved as well. In addition to helping the kids of New Jersey, Katz is also very committed to the Jewish community. He has played a part in acquiring land and the construction of a new Jewish Community Campus both in Atlantic City and Cherry Hill, New Jersey. Chambers was also a vital contributor and fundraiser for the $190 million performing arts center project in Newark.

The new ownership took control of the New Jersey Nets in 1998. Their mission was not only to give back to the community through their financial donations, but also to get the Nets players more involved in community relations. Each player was expected to "adopt" a city in New Jersey and act as a mentor to the kids and members of that community. The owners realized that to many professional athletes this obligation may seem ludicrous and totally outside the scope of their responsibilities. The answer that Chambers and Katz have came up with to this opposition was simply not to bring those kinds of players to the Nets Organization. They were looking to hire athletes who shared their view about the power athletics has to shape young lives and to accept that vision. There were many players in the NBA who didn't fit that mold, but Chambers and Katz were committed to finding those who did. Lewis and Katz succeeded in discovering several players who were committed to their organizational philosophy and very willing to help out, and that is what they will be remembered for. Katz and Chambers and their ownership group created a strong partnership with the Yankees organization in 1999. YankeeNets LLC was created largely due to television broadcasting rights. The New Jersey Devils also were sold to YankeeNetsLCC in 1999. This partnership did not ultimately flourish, and in 2004, agreements were made to break up the holding group and separate the Yankees, Nets, and Devils. The Nets ended up being sold in 2004 to a group led by real estate developer, Bruce Ratner.

What Chambers and Katz chose to do is indeed very admirable, and what is even more commendable is that they are always looking for new ventures to take on and different ways to help others. There are so many people in need in the world and there certainly should be more people like Raymond Chambers and Lewis Katz.

Mike Ilitch

Creating the Environment

by Brian Wright, with Austin Moss II

In today's sports world mostly dominated by the glamour and fame of professional athletes, we tend to overlook many people working behind the scenes for the betterment of the sport. One such person is Mike Ilitch, owner of the National Hockey League's Detroit Red Wings and Major League Baseball's Detroit Tigers. Many critics and analysts spend their time assessing the success of the owner of a franchise by the team's wins and losses, or the amount of money spent to sign players, or even the cost of tickets and concessions. Ilitch's contribution to the world of sports has made much more of an impact than just that short list of quantifiable items. As a young child, Ilitch dreamed of playing in Major League Baseball. He knew the opportunity to become a professional baseball player was a long shot, but he had set his mind on it and was determined. Little did he know at the time that he would become a member of an even more exclusive sports group as an owner of a professional sports franchise.

The path to success was not always smooth for Ilitch when he pursued a professional career in baseball. As a young man Ilitch was selected to join the Tiger organization as a player on one of its minor league teams. Playing shortstop, Ilitch was considered to be a great athlete who had a good eye and a strong bat. Though he had a more than respectable minor league career, Ilitch was never called up by the Tigers.

This setback, which seemed a major obstacle at the time, would have a positive impact on his life for years to come. As his dreams of playing in the majors ended, Ilitch began to explore other alternatives to make a good living for himself and his family. Ilitch spent time deciding what he could be good at and what there was a market for and determined that his niche was in the restaurant business. As time progressed, his desire to open a restaurant of his own did as well. Ilitch decided that his main product would be pizza. With the entrepreneurial desire of owning his own pizza parlor, Ilitch did not have the financing or experience to immediately take on his own store. He decided to approach a local businessman, an owner of a

Detroit area night club, to pitch his pizza parlor. Ilitch presented the idea well enough to convince the man to give him an opportunity and began selling pizza out of the back room of the nightclub. Much to the surprise of everyone except Ilitch, the business began to boom and the demand for his pizza was rising.

As Ilitch's customer base grew, he knew he had established a successful business and wanted to find a way to expand it. Thus, Ilitch began looking for financing to move the business into its own establishment. After selling pizza door-to-door and taking out a small $15,000 loan, Ilitch and his wife Marian had made enough money to purchase their first store. In 1959, the pizza that was sold out of the backroom of a local night club was renamed Little Caesars, which was Marian's pet name for Mike. Today Little Caesars is one of the largest take-out pizza restaurants throughout the United States and Canada. Ilitch took a simple dream and grew it into one of the nation's largest take-out pizza chains. Considered by many to be one of the top businessmen in the world, Ilitch has never become complacent.

In 1982, his passion for sports led him to the doorstep of the Detroit Red Wings of the National Hockey League. The owners at the time, the Norris family, had placed the Red Wings on the market for $8 million. Though the Red Wings were then one of the worst teams in the NHL, Ilitch knew their potential, given their long tenure and successful history in Detroit. As he reminisced on the drastic growth of Little Caesars, Ilitch realized what was possible when an organization is committed to putting a quality product out there for the public. Ilitch's determination to turn the organization around led to a quick change in performance on the ice. The team rapidly developed into one of the best teams in the NHL. Under Ilitch's reign, the Red Wings won 13 Division Championships, six Western Conference Championships, four President's Trophies, and four Stanley Cup titles. The support from the city of Detroit also increased under Ilitch's direction, achieving 367 consecutive sellouts at Joe Louis Arena. In 2004, *Forbes* magazine listed the Detroit Red Wings as the most valuable franchise in the NHL at $256 million. *ESPN Magazine* also ranked the Detroit Red Wings as the eighth rated sports franchise in all of professional sports, as well as honoring Ilitch as the number one professional sports franchise owner in all of professional sports. It is awards and accolades such as these that display

Ilitch's passion for success and his commitment to the organizations he operates.

Ilitch genuinely cared about the welfare of his players more than the record of the team. Truly committed to the education of the players, the Red Wings offered to pay 100 percent of the tuition for those players who wanted to complete their education. In 1991, more than 25 percent of the players enrolled in college courses thanks to Ilitch's commitment.

Although owning one of the largest pizza chains as well as one of the most prominent professional hockey teams was a task in itself, Ilitch felt that he could also assist the community of Detroit by purchasing and improving the Detroit Tigers of Major League Baseball. Ten years after purchasing the Detroit Red Wings Ilitch purchased sole ownership of the Detroit Tigers from Tom Monoghan. Although the Tigers have not achieved as much "on-the-field" success as the Red Wings, they are still regarded by most to be a well-run and potentially successful organization.

Ilitch's success in the Detroit community was not just achieved at the restaurant and professional sport levels. As a competing member of amateur athletics in his youth, Ilitch knew the role it played in his life, and the role it could play in positively affecting the lives of others. He wanted to somehow incorporate amateur athletics into the organizations he owned and add positive social value to the communities within the Detroit area. He decided to implement an amateur AAA Hockey Program under the Little Caesars company umbrella. In this amateur hockey program there is the Little Caesars Amateur Hockey League as well as the Little Caesars Amateur Hockey Club. The league began with less than 30 travel teams for 450 boys. Today, the league consists of more than 900 travel and house teams with 16,000 youth hockey players competing in over 100 rinks in the Detroit metro area. 2010 marked its 31st season.[1] Ilitch's amateur hockey program has also produced more than 240 hockey players who have played, or currently play in, collegiate and professional hockey leagues. For Ilitch, achieving positive social influence in the community through amateur athletics was another way to reach the lives of youth and influence them to become positive contributing members of society. Ilitch's ability to see the "big picture" concerning our communities and develop a plan to positively change these communities is evidence of his creative and innovative leadership ability.

Ilitch is not only giving back to people in the Detroit community, he is also making an impact on the national level. In 2006, Ilitch felt the urge deep within his heart to start the Little Caesars Veterans Program after he had a memorable encounter with a paraplegic war veteran.[2] The program was created to provide honorably discharged veterans an opportunity to work after they complete their service and transition into civilian life. The program gives veterans the opportunity to utilize their leadership, teamwork skills, and dedication to run a business. Ilitch has a deep connection and passion for this program because he knows what it felt like to sit and say, "What now?" after his career ending baseball injury. The creation of this program is a true testament of the passion Ilitch has to assist others.

Today, Ilitch finds himself among few others who have achieved a great deal of success in the world of sports franchise owners. Ilitch has been as he has been inducted into the Hockey Hall of Fame in Toronto, Canada, as well as the Michigan Sports Hall of Fame. He has also received numerous awards and accolades as a businessman and pioneer for positive social change in the sports industry. Mike Ilitch believes in the power of sports to impact the lives of others as it had positively impacted his youth, and he has employed his belief to work for the betterment of society.

Notes

1. The Official Site of the Little Caesars Amateur Hockey League, "LCAHL History & Background," http://lcahl.pucksystems2.com/page/show/110-lcahl-history-and-background, (accessed March 6, 2010).

2. Little Caesars Veterans Program, "Veterans Program Information," Little Caesars, http://franchise.littlecaesars.com/VeteransProgram/tabid/76/Default.aspx, (accessed March 1, 2010).

Thomas "Satch" Sanders

Creating the Environment

by Jessica Bartter Duffaut

The life of a professional athlete is more than guts, glory, and glamour. The transition from high school and college to the pros is never predictable and often uncontrollable. Rookies are pulled in several different directions by their agents, their families, their coaches, their teammates, and their own personal beliefs, which are often challenged by the pressures of a new life in the fast lane of groupies, alcohol, drugs, and money. Professional athletes go from the practice gym to the airport to a hotel to an arena, only to be off on an airplane to another city for the same routine over and over again. In the National Basketball Association (NBA) teams play about 90 preseason and regular season games with a potential 28 more in the playoffs. This is equivalent to three or four high school or college seasons. The subsequent wear and tear on the athlete's body, coupled with the emotional pressures, can end the career of a great athlete too soon.

Thomas "Satch" Sanders was one member of the NBA whose hard work and durability enabled him to perform at the highest level game after game for years. In fact, during Sanders' 13-year career as a professional basketball player he played in 450 consecutive games.

After a great career at New York University, Sanders was a highly-valued player in the 1960 NBA draft where he was the Boston Celtics' first pick and the eighth overall pick. Sanders spent all 13 years of his professional career with the Celtics where his defensive skills earned acclaim. While he was a force for the offense too, averaging 9.6 points per game for his career, it was his smart and talented play on the defensive end of the court that earned him recognition. Sanders played in 916 games, the sixth highest in Celtics history, totaling 22,164 minutes. He had 5,798 rebounds, 1,026 assists, and 8,766 points. The 6-foot-6-inch center helped lead the Celtics to eight championships before retiring in 1973.

Like all athletes at the end of their careers, Sanders was faced with a difficult transition into the working world. In 1973, Sanders took the head coaching position of Harvard University's men's basketball program. He inherited a team with great potential that had failed to capitalize on its talent and hoped Sanders would turn them around. Sanders utilized the tried and proven coaching strategy of legendary Coach Red Auerbach, who focused on defense. Auerbach believed that most players enter the league with sufficient offensive skills and that it is their defense that requires the most attention. Sanders was known for his dedication as a defender so the strategy seemed like the perfect fit. Sanders also relied heavily on scouting reports and opponent films to develop a powerful offense, tough defense, and a winning game strategy for his team. Before even stepping on the court, Sanders accomplished great feats. He was the first African-American to be named head coach at Harvard and the first African-American to coach basketball in the entire Ivy League.

Sanders' time with the Harvard Crimson was the perfect stepping stone to a coaching career in the NBA. And why not go where he was loved the most? Why not go where his number 16 jersey hung from the rafters? The fan-favorite returned to the green and white of the Celtics as their coach during the 1977–78 season, and for part of 1978–79. But the fates doomed Sanders' coaching career as injuries and unfortunate trades hurt the team. Satch left the Celtics before the end of his second campaign.

Sanders joined Richard Lapchick shortly after the founding of Northeastern University's Center for the Study of Sport in Society in 1984 as Associate Director. He helped conceive the degree completion and community service programs which became the cornerstones of the National Consortium for Academics and Sports, an organization he helped create with Lapchick and Richard Astro in 1985. Now the NCAS is made up of more than 230 member institutions which have helped bring back more than 30,000 former student-athletes to finish their degrees. These athletes have worked with more than 18 million young people on conflict resolution, staying in school, violence prevention, saying no to drugs and alcohol, reading, and much more. Sanders helped lay the foundation for what has become a large and impressive enterprise.

As a Celtic player in the late 1960s, Sanders was paid about $8,000 a season—a fraction compared to today's average NBA salary that exceeds $5 million.[1] Sanders spent his off-season working as a sporting goods department store manager and a copywriter, as well as selling securities and in the real estate mortgage industry. While Sanders' transition into the working world was eased by the fact that during his day in the NBA, players usually had summer jobs anyway, he understood the transition for other athletes is not as simple. In today's league where players make millions of dollars with their playing contract, endorsements, and sponsor deals, the majority leave the league just a few years later at a young age still, and many without a college degree.

Sanders recognized that the transition *into* the league is equally difficult, particularly for the young draft picks who abandon their college careers and education. Interested in working with NBA players, Sanders joined the league offices of the NBA in 1987. He took on the challenging role of vice president and director of player programs. Sanders' job entailed designing programs for current and former professional basketball players, focusing on rookies and veterans. The programs taught players how to cope with the special pressures associated with that status. Sanders oversaw an off-season player program that offered internships, classes, and educational advancement opportunities so players might avoid the financial troubles that often comes hand in hand with temporary seven figure salaries. Sanders' programs also involved post-career counseling, educational development, employment opportunities, anti-drug and alcohol education, media training, and non-profit foundation development.

Sanders wanted players to think of the skills they would need after life on the court before it was too late. Through the NBA player programs, Sanders presented players with all the proper tools. During his 18 years in this department Sanders was able to develop relevant and interesting programs because he brought a wealth of experience to the job.

As a player, Sanders was once confronted in a club in Boston by a belligerent man. Jealousy drove the man to threaten Sanders and flash a gun that was concealed in his pants. Sanders was faced with the options of fighting back, surrendering, or walking away. To no one's surprise—except to the belligerent individual—Sanders sat down and turned his back to the man antagonizing him. In the process he made himself a bigger target for insults and verbal abuse, but dodged the inevitable violent and potentially dangerous attack. The man drew attention to himself which allowed management to take heed and escort him out. Sanders learned that, to an extent, it was possible to control his environment and he later passed on this valuable lesson to countless players.

In contrast, Sanders learned the difficulties in controlling one's surrounding environment in the face of racism. After accepting the Harvard coaching position, he purchased a home in an upscale suburb of Boston. Some neighbors and community members made Sanders feel unwelcome by yelling obscenities outside his house late at night and dumping trash on his lawn. Though Sanders was scarred by the experience, he learned from it and was able to use it and other experiences to work effectively with hundreds of NBA players.

Many of the players with whom Sanders worked moved on from basketball to successful careers in a variety of different fields. And while some may have been successful without Sanders' guidance, the fact is that the increased number of players who have successful post-basketball careers since Sanders assumed his position in the League office is proof that his impact on NBA players has been very substantial. From the time when he first donned a Celtic uniform in 1960, he has utilized his searing intelligence and his personal warmth and charm to help his fellow players. The NBA is a much better organization because Satch Sanders was been a part of it for so many decades.

Note

1. S.F. Heron, "The average salaries of NBA players," Helium, http://www.helium.com/items/923616-the-average-salaries-of-nba-players, (accessed February 25, 2010).

Jerry Reinsdorf

Creating the Environment

by Joslyn Dalton

As a young boy growing up in Brooklyn, New York, Jerry Reinsdorf was an avid Dodgers fan. "Everybody in Brooklyn lived and died with the Dodgers," he said.[1] Even though he was passionate about sports, Reinsdorf's career goal throughout his time at George Washington University was to transform himself into the best tax lawyer possible. In 1957, he moved to Chicago to pursue his post-graduate education. He earned a law degree from Northwestern University. Upon graduation, the 24-year old served as a lawyer for the Internal Revenue Service. Even though in this position he often found himself working in the sports industry, he did not seriously consider the possibility of pursuing a career path in such. "At that point, I just wanted to be the best tax lawyer I could possibly be. I had a four-year commitment to the IRS, and I wanted to serve it out and get into private practice," he said.[2]

Like an athlete who desires to make the pros, Reinsdorf whole-heartedly pursued the business world. His talent as a lawyer and ability to out-think those around him created the opportunity to quickly advance up the corporate ladder. By 1964, he left the government and began to work for a large Chicago firm. Three years later, he ventured into a smaller firm where he began to put together pools of capital for real estate investment. As the founder of the Balcor Company, Reinsdorf achieved great success and personal wealth. In 1982, he sold Balcor for $102 million to a division of American Express. Financial stability allowed him to branch into more diverse ventures. Sometime around 1975, Reinsdorf came across an ad in the *Wall Street Journal* that caught his attention: "Somebody (was) looking for investors to buy a baseball team. I got back to him, and I agreed to invest $500,000," Reinsdorf remembers.[3]

After dabbling with the idea of being a minority partner for a variety of teams, he reached a conclusion that changed the direction of his career. "I remember thinking to myself. 'Why do I want to be a minority partner with no say, in a team that did not even play in the city that I lived?'"[4] Reinsdorf's financial security enabled him to consider majority ownership. In 1981 he made the leap and purchased the Chicago White Sox baseball franchise. In 1985 he bought the Chicago Bulls basketball franchise.

Upon taking over, Reinsdorf quickly improved both teams. As an owner, Reinsdorf considered his role to be that of a CEO. "It's your job to identify what positions have to be filled, and go out and get good people to do those jobs who can do them better than you can do them, and make sure they talk to each other," he reflected.[5] In searching for the best people for the job, Reinsdorf helped facilitate diversity in sports management. Most notably, in 2006, his baseball club became the first franchise to win the World Series with a Latino manager, Ozzie Guillen, and the only African-American general manager in Major League Baseball (MLB), Ken Williams. Furthermore, Reinsdorf served as co-chairman of baseball's Equal Opportunity Committee. In 1998, the MLB purchased more than $260 million in goods and services from minority and women-owned businesses stemming from the League's relationship with the Diverse Business Partners (DBP) Program. This number has jumped to over $700 million as of 2010. Reinsdorf's White Sox annually rank among baseball's leaders in the DBP Program.

Reinsdorf's ability to surround himself with the right people for the job has been demonstrated through his seven World Championship titles, one from the White Sox and six from the Chicago Bulls. Throughout 24 seasons as chairman of the White Sox, Reinsdorf's team captured the American League division championships three times, including an AL Central title in 2000. The Sox also won division titles in 1983 and 1993 before winning the World Series in 2006, the first time for the franchise in 88 years. Purchasing the Bulls at a time when the team was hemorrhaging money, Reinsdorf turned the franchise around quickly. During the 1990s, his Bulls became a dynasty winning six league championships during an eight-year span. The success of the Sox and Bulls caused the value of the teams to skyrocket and to gain prominence in the sports industry.

With his teams a success on the field and the court, Reinsdorf embarked on two development projects. He spearheaded the United Center project which became the home arena for the Bulls in 1994. He also had a significant role in the development of U.S. Cellular Field, the home of the White Sox, which opened its gates in 1991.

Throughout it all, Reinsdorf has not lost his focus on the community. When asked what the World Series win for the White Sox meant to him in 2006, he revealed how sport has the ability to affect society. "The thing that made it the most gratifying was the impact it had on the community. I was excited when we won, but I had no idea of the aftermath—what was going to occur afterwards," he said. "To give back to the community was the most gratifying and exciting."[6]

Under Reinsdorf, the goal of community initiatives for both the Sox and Bulls is to improve the quality of life for Chicagoans of all races and genders. Both of his sport franchises have established a history of service by contributing time, materials, and resources while donating millions of dollars to causes in Chicago's community. CharitaBulls and various White Sox charities share the mission of enhancing the lives of Chicago's youth. The Sox charities have made multimillion dollar donations to the Chicago Park District while also providing annual ongoing support to programs such as Special Olympics and the Inner City Little League. In addition to rebuilding all of the city's baseball diamonds and backstops during the 1990s, White Sox Charities made a one million dollar contribution to build four ball fields—one for baseball, one for girls' softball, one for Little League baseball, and one Miracle Field. The Miracle Field, which is a field specifically designed for children with special needs, is the third field of its kind built in the last year in the Chicago area with funds from Chicago White Sox charities.

As for the Bulls, in 1987—just two years after buying the team—Reinsdorf founded the non-profit organization CharitaBulls to aid in the team's civic tasks, especially where children are concerned by actively creating and supporting educational, recreational, and social programs. "Children look up to athletes. I know there's a responsibility for athletes to give back. Our major stress in our civic actives is education," he said.[7] During the 1990s, CharitaBulls donated $4.5 million to construct the James Jordan Boys and Girls Club and Family Life Center, in memory of James Jordan, the father of Bulls' great Michael Jordan. Many large donations have helped round out the financial contribution Reinsdorf has made to his community of Chicago.

Reinsdorf's contributions as well as the success of his teams have granted him a variety of honors. He is a recipient of the Order of Lincoln Award, Chicago Park District's Chicagoan of the Year Award, the 1992 PUSH Bridgebuilder Award, the National Italian-American Friendship Award, Northwestern University's Award of Merit, the U.S. Air Force American Spirit Award, the Guardian of Children Award and in 2009, he was awarded the Sports Lawyers Award of Excellence. Organizations such as Keshet, the Interfaith Organizing Project, American Academy of Achievement, Cystic Fibrosis Foundation, the Trial Lawyers Club of Chicago, and the Chicago Historical Society have accredited Reinsdorf's efforts. He has been awarded a place in the Chicago Jewish Sporting Hall of Fame, the National Jewish Sporting Hall of Fame, and the Chicago Sports Hall of Fame. In 2008, he was appointed as a Trustee of the National Baseball Hall of Fame and Museum.

In spite of all the recognition, Reinsdorf remains modest. "You know, awards don't mean anything to me. Believe me; I would turn them down if I thought I wouldn't hurt people's feelings. I have no interest in the recognition," he said.[8] This view only solidifies how selfless he has been throughout his years of giving. With so much to boast about, Jerry Reinsdorf remains not only a hero, but a humble hero at that.

Notes

1. Stephen Hicks, "Interview with Jerry Reinsdorf," The Center for Ethics and Entrepreneurship, July 20, 2009, http://www.ethicsandentrepreneurship.org/20090720/interview-with-jerry-reinsdorf/, (accessed April 12, 2010).

2. Ibid.
3. Ibid.
4. Ibid.
5. Ibid.
6. Ibid, Hicks.
7. Ibid.
8. Ibid.

10

COMING TO AMERICA

by Richard Lapchick

America has long been viewed as a haven and a refuge for oppressed peoples. Whether America is viewed in a favorable or unfavorable light at any given moment in its history, we always find individuals oppressed in their own country who come to America for freedom.

Coming to America is about four men and one woman who escaped the horrors of their own countries. They came to the United States where they became successful athletes.

Gilbert Tuhabonye came here after most of his family and friends were murdered in Burundi. His own body was covered with burns.

Mohammad Rafiq's parents made a dangerous escape from Afghanistan to provide him and his siblings with an opportunity to achieve the American dream.

Sevin Sucurovic left Bosnia with his family to escape the ethnic cleansing that was ravaging the former Yugoslavia.

MaCharia Yuot, one of the Sudanese Lost Boys, came to the United States to obtain freedom from the civil war which was claiming millions of lives in Sudan.

Shamila Kohestani stood her ground against the Taliban in Afghanistan to fight for the rights of women.

Tuhabonye graduated from Abilene Christian, where he was an All-American cross country runner and won an NCAA Division II title. Yuot became a soccer player at West Catholic High School in Philadelphia and later enrolled in Widener University where he ran cross country. Rafiq won a basketball scholarship at Idaho State University. Sucurovic was a football player at the University of Kentucky. Kohestani earned a soccer scholarship to Drew University in New Jersey. All survived a personal horror to tell America the stories of the conflicts in their homelands.

Gilbert Tuhabonye

Coming to America

by Jessica Bartter Duffaut

Courtesy of Holly Reed Photography.

Many of us became aware of the Tutsi-Hutu conflict through our knowledge of global politics or interest in international news. Many have seen the movies *Hotel Rwanda* and *Sometimes in April*. However, few know that the origins of the conflict can be traced to the neighboring country of Burundi where Gilbert Tuhabonye survived a horrible massacre and witnessed the murder of his classmates, friends, and teachers.

Tuhabonye was raised in Burundi, a hilly and mountainous, landlocked central African country that borders Rwanda. Tribal warfare has devastated the country for decades, leaving the fertile land mostly underdeveloped. Sparse resources and political turmoil have left Burundi as one of the poorest countries in Africa and the world. The enormity of the conflict between the Tutsi minority with the Hutu majority contradicts the small size of the country.

As a seventh grader, Tuhabonye began developing his cross country skills by running five miles each way to and from school every day. As a junior in high school, Tuhabonye's pastime began to put him in the spotlight. His athletic skills stood out in the 400- and 800-meter events.

But at the age of 18, while attending high school biology class, Tuhabonye was subjected to torture and death, memories he still sees in his nightmares. The incident was instigated on October 21, 1993, when some members of the Tutsi tribe assassinated Burundi's first democratically-elected president to hold office, who also happened to be the first member of the Hutu tribe. Tuhabonye's boarding school, where Tutsis and Hutus peacefully lived and attended school together, quickly became a target for retribution to the Hutu soldiers determined to kill Tutsi tribesmen. Without warning, Tuhabonye, his classmates, teachers, and other high school staff were surrounded. Classmates and friends were suddenly separated by tribe and made to feel like enemies. The Tutsis were stripped naked and beaten. Tuhabonye was struck in the chest with a heavy stick that caused him to cough up blood for two weeks. The tortured and beaten Tutsis were rounded up and led to an off campus building, sprayed with gasoline, and then locked inside the building that was lit on fire by Hutu soldiers. As the students pounded on the door and screamed for mercy, Tuhabonye alternated between fighting to stay alive and begging for death to take him. At last, he buried himself beneath the burning bodies of his classmates. Those bodies formed a human shield and saved his life.

After eight hours of enduring the stench of burning flesh, the sounds of agony and the sight of death, fear for his own life led Tuhabonye to a brave escape. After the fire died down, he grabbed the nearby skeleton of a dead friend and used it to break a window.

After escaping the grim site of live cremation, Tuhabonye was forced to run from Hutus who spotted him fleeing. Since Tuhabonye was burning from his daring break out, the Hutus decided to leave him and let him die in the grass. But Tuhabonye survived the severe burns on his arms, legs, and back, and was finally found by Tutsis in the field two days later. At the hospital where he was taken for treatment, Tuhabonye was forced to sleep on the floor because no beds were available.

Word spread quickly of Tuhabonye's survival and with so many perishing that day he was dubbed a spiritual being for having made it out alive. The Tutsis hailed him as a god, while the Hutus feared him as the devil. Tuhabonye later came in contact with a Hutu soldier involved in the massacre. The soldier dropped to his knees in front of Tuhabonye and begged to be killed. Despite his traumatic experiences, Tuhabonye has forgiveness in his heart. He told the soldier to "get up, I forgive you"[1] and even offered to talk about it.

It took Tuhabonye a long time to fully recover, but the scars on his body will never allow him to forget. About a year after the incident, Tuhabonye began jogging again and eventually returned to running competitively. In April of 1996, the International Olympic Committee awarded Tuhabonye a grant enabling him to move to the United States. Living in La Grange, Georgia, Tuhabonye trained for the 1996 Summer Olympic Games in Atlanta. Though he failed to make the Burundi team, he did carry the Olympic torch. An ironic celebration with fire, Tuhabonye wondered if it was in God's plan for him all along.

Tuhabonye later enrolled at Abilene Christian University in Texas to continue his education while pursuing his athletic dreams. In 1998, Tuhabonye was an All-American cross country runner and won the NCAA Division II indoor title for the 800 meters. Today, he coaches other runners who find his story and talent helpful and inspirational. His popular and award-winning training group, Gilbert's Gazelles, focuses on both individual and group training, combining his "joy of running, a love for life, and state-of-the-art coaching techniques in a educational and inspiring format that has grown into one of the most popular training programs in Central Texas."[2]

Amazingly, Gilbert Tuhabonye continues to speak forgiveness and faith, and like many other athletes he relies on sport to overcome his obstacles. Tuhabonye has successfully tried to use sport to show the world that there is more to Burundi than murder and mayhem. Visible individuals like Tuhabonye, the epitome of hope and humanity, open our eyes to an unfamiliar and horrifying world of genocide and help teach us the art of forgiveness.

Notes

1. Ian O'Connor, "Burundi's Tuhabonye works on his running a long way from war-torn home," *Knight Ridder Tribune*, July 25, 1996.

2. Gilbert's Gazelles, "Run With the Lion," http://www.gilbertsgazelles.com/index.php, (accessed on March 11, 2010).

Mohammad "Mamo" Rafiq

Coming to America

by Jessica Bartter Duffaut

Mohammad "Mamo" Rafiq, pictured with his mother Fatima at the NCAS' 2006 Giant Steps Awards Banquet and Hall of Fame Induction Ceremony.

As an Afghanistan-born Muslim, Mohammad Rafiq stood out as a minority student on the campus of the predominantly white Idaho State University in Pocatello, a small city in southeastern part of the state. Rather than shy away from talking about his culture and beliefs, he took it upon himself to educate non-Muslims about the religion that is so important to him and his family. Rafiq embraces his differences and celebrates the United States for the freedom it provides to individuals of all faiths.

Rafiq's home country is extremely different: 99 percent of Afghanis are either Sunni or Shi'a Muslims. But Rafiq calls the United States home now. In 1979, the Soviet Union invaded Afghanistan. Shortly thereafter, Rafiq's father was arrested for working with an American company in Kabul. When his father was finally released, Rafiq's parents wasted no time in escaping their war-torn country. His parents, two older siblings, and two uncles headed for the border between Afghanistan and Pakistan in the dark of the night. The border was patrolled by Soviet troops, and his family was forced to hide in a cave while soldiers battled right outside the entrance. Rafiq was just a baby when they fled and his cries had to be muffled in a blanket to avoid capture. His family did not bring any food with them and were forced to sleep in the cave, but they successfully crossed the border into Pakistan the next day.

Rafiq and his family lived in Pakistan as refugees for eight months until their applications for asylum and their church sponsorship were approved in the United States. Rafiq's first American experience was in Seattle, Washington. His family later joined other family members in Thorton, Colorado, before settling in Yuba City, California. By this time, Rafiq was in the third grade and began playing basketball with his older brother at the local park.

Rafiq worked hard at the sport that he loved and in 2000 earned a full athletic scholarship to play basketball at Idaho State University, an NCAA Division I program. Rafiq felt a sense of accomplishment as his parents gleamed with pride in the realization that their American dream for him would be fulfilled. Rafiq's parents did not have the opportunity for higher education in Afghanistan and though they could not help their three children with their homework in the United States, they taught them the importance of becoming educated. Rafiq, the youngest of three, had just ensured his right to a college degree, becoming their third and last child to do so.

At Idaho State, Rafiq made the athletic honor roll in 2001 and 2002. Life at Idaho State was exciting and successful until tragedy struck our nation, hitting Rafiq too close to home. It was the fall of his sophomore year when 19 Islamic terrorists simultaneously hijacked four U.S. domestic commercial airliners, crashing two into the World Trade Center, one into the Pentagon, and the fourth into a rural field in Pennsylvania, during a day commonly known now as 9-11. The attacks of 9-11 caused 2,986 deaths and changed the lives of millions. Americans were rightfully angry but many misdirected their anger toward Middle Easterners living in this country. Incidents of harassment and hate crimes against those who appeared Middle Eastern or Muslim became increasingly common. Nine people were murdered as a result of this backlash. Many were Sikh, mistaken for Muslim. Many American Muslims say they have experienced increased discrimination and suspicion since 9-11. Many are also frustrated that their religion is often viewed as extremist, even violent.

As a proud Muslim and a proud American, Rafiq felt a strong sense of responsibility to teach his team at Idaho State that being Muslim is not about suicide missions and hatred. After discussing the incident with his teammates and coaches, one coach decided to contact the National Collegiate Athletic Association (NCAA) where they determined that Mohammad Rafiq was the only Afghani Division I men's basketball player in the United States. Rafiq agreed to do an interview with ESPN's SportsCenter because he wanted to be a positive role model for the Muslim and NCAA student-athlete communities. Later in 2002, he was selected to represent all of Idaho State's student-athletes at the NCAA Foundation leadership conference.

Unfortunately, Rafiq was needed elsewhere and was unable to attend the conference. Following the events of September 11, 2001, Rafiq's father was hired by the United States Department of Defense to work as an interpreter in Afghanistan, requiring him to be out of the country 11 months of the year. Simultaneously, Rafiq's mother, Fatima, developed health issues that required tender care and attention.

Devoted to his family, Rafiq withdrew from Idaho State University and forfeited his scholarship to move back to California and provide his mother with the necessary assistance. Rafiq's mother only speaks Dari, so he escorted her to psychotherapy appointments where he translated for her. Rafiq also served as her translator through her diagnosis, treatment, and surgery for breast cancer. Sadly, Rafiq's father passed away in his home country while working for his adopted country. Rafiq did not let the circumstances prevent him from finishing his education. While he was living with and caring for his mother in Yuba City, he enrolled at the University of California at Davis, approximately 55 miles away. Rafiq also joined the UC Davis basketball team. Rafiq commuted over 100 miles a day to practice and class and then back home to attend medical appointments with his mother.

Rafiq juggled his responsibilities well, but after one year as a student-athlete at UC Davis, Rafiq was forced to quit because of medical issues of his own. He experienced hip and back pain that was so excruciating it kept him up at night and made walking very difficult. His condition perplexed the athletic trainers and eight different specialists until finally he was diagnosed with a genetic deformity in his hip bones. Normal activity and years of basketball had resulted in bone-on-bone contact, tearing most of the cartilage in his hips. The specialist warned Rafiq that without special surgery, he would most like need two hip replacements by the age of 35.

In what should have been his final semester in March of 2004, Rafiq went in for the recommended surgery on just one of the hips. Doctors surgically dislocated his right hip and inserted metal screws. Because he was in a wheelchair for six weeks, on crutches for the following six weeks, and then had difficulty walking for a month, Rafiq was forced to withdraw from UC Davis. Rafiq scheduled surgery on his left hip in December, 2004, but was better prepared for the necessary recovery time. He planned to attend UC Davis in the winter part-time and return full-time in the spring to avoid the mobility issues he faced with the first surgery. Rafiq's careful planning enabled him to juggle five different jobs and maintain a grade point average above 3.0. Rafiq's family responsibilities also grew as he wed Junie Noriega, and just six days before his second surgery the couple welcomed their first born, Mateen, into the world. Rafiq graduated in 2005 with a degree in history. Deservedly so, he was awarded the 2005 NCAA Ethnic Minority Postgraduate Scholarship for Careers in Athletics.

Because he cherished his time spent at Idaho State, Rafiq returned there to earn his master's degree in physical education with an athletic administration emphasis. Rafiq feels a strong sense of commitment to Idaho State because of the opportunity it provided him, not only with the athletic scholarship and the chance to earn a college degree, but also the support they offered during the many difficult and trying times he faced in his college basketball career and his personal life. While earning his master's degree, Rafiq served the men's basketball team as a graduate assistant coach as well as the graduate assistant academic advisor. Rafiq was responsible for the student-athlete's study hall and for welcoming recruits to campus. He had become the face of the team. Rafiq also volunteered with the women's squad.

After graduating in 2007 with a 3.9 GPA, the Olympic Committee of Afghanistan approached Rafiq requesting that he coach their national team. Since then, Rafiq has proudly led the group of Afghani-Americans, all of whom live in the United States, across the U.S. and internationally for competitions. Rafiq himself has scheduled several of their competitions and tours against American colleges for exposure and practice. Team members are scattered from California to Virginia and New York to North Carolina, but Rafiq manages to unite them in the name of his birth country. He describes the job as "a tremendous honor and an enormous challenge."[1] It has also been rewarding. In 2010, the Afghanistan National Basketball team won the first team gold medal in the history of the country at the 11ᵗʰ South Asian Games in Dhaka, Bangladesh. Coach Rafiq has much to be proud of.

Mohammad and Junie are now the proud parents of two after daughter Amani joined big brother Mateen four years later. The Rafiq family is living in California with Fatima, who dotes on her grandchildren. Rafiq is a basketball player, Afghani, husband, father, Muslim, coach, and American. It is his diverse background and experiences that have enabled him to respond to challenges with a sense of humor and determination while recognizing the importance of things and prioritizing his many responsibilities. His devotion and appreciation for his culture and family have enabled him to embrace those who show a similar passion to the people and things they value most, despite the fact that they may differ from him. Mohammad Rafiq has faced the personal adversities in his life with maturity, motivation, and an optimistic attitude in hopes that he will make a positive lasting impact on future generations. He already has.

Note

1. Mohammad Rafiq, email to author, March 23, 2010.

Sevin Sucurovic

Coming to America

by Jessica Bartter Duffaut

At just nine years old, a day in the life of Sevin "Sevy" Sucurovic consisted of constant ringing in his ears from surrounding gunfire, antagonizing fear that his father might not return home from the front lines of war, and a five-mile walk each way to and from school in the poverty-stricken, economically-disadvantaged country of Bosnia.

Yet, like so many children, Sucurovic dreamt of a professional career in sports, as either an athlete or an executive, and even hoped to go to college one day and be the first in his family to earn a secondary degree. Though his dreams have been met by challenge after challenge and hurdle after hurdle, it would take much more to stop this would-be courageous student-athlete or bring his spirit down.

The breakout of the Bosnian War in the early 1990s created havoc, particularly in the life of young Bosnians. In addition to the unrelenting concern for his solider father, Sucurovic said the "best years of my childhood were spent just struggling to survive instead of learning about life and pursuing my dreams." Sucurovic recalled "sleeping dressed in four pairs of pants and three or four jackets during the war all in order to have some clothes to change into later if we needed to leave our house quickly because of danger."[1]

While most would let their dreams die, Sucurovic didn't, and even turned to sports as an outlet. Kicking around the soccer ball served as an escape from the reality of a war-torn home. Sucurovic said that even the "path to school was unsafe and I was constantly wondering if a grenade would strike at any moment killing me and everyone around me." Such morose thoughts could have had a detrimental effect on such a young child, but Sucurovic's knowledge and experience with the most morbid of upbringings has served to develop an uplifting and optimistic attitude in the young man that he is today—in part because Sucurovic found sport and learned early on of its impact on society and individuals like himself.

While the Bosnian War was documented from 1992 to 1995 when the Dayton Accords was signed, Sucurovic recalls the war starting earlier and lasting longer, beyond the cease-fire agreement. Five long years, in his memory, of the bloody war left Bosnia, Sucurovic's home, in a desultory state. No jobs were available and even today the country's unemployment rate hovers around 40 percent.[1] The death toll from the war is estimated at nearly 100,000 people, and the United Nations agencies recorded approximately 1,325,000 refugees and exiles.

In 1996, Sucurovic's father wanted to pursue a better life for his family outside of Bosnia and believed the best opportunities for his wife and two boys would be in the United States. However, in order to defect, they had to have a family member already living in the U.S. who would sponsor them. Fortunately, for the Sucurovics, they had relatives in Boston, Massachusetts. Unfortunately, the necessary paperwork took nearly two years to complete.

Finally, on February 17, 1998, the Sucurovic family left what had been their only home with nothing but three suitcases, $2,000, and high hopes. Two days later, Sucurovic first set his eyes and feet on American culture and soil at the age of 16. Success didn't come overnight, but the Sucurovic family was accustomed to working hard. Sucurovic's father was forced to work two—sometimes three—jobs while his mother worked two of her own. Even Sucurovic himself worked at a nearby grocery store while attending high school. Despite their best efforts, the high cost of living in Boston forced the Sucurovics to relocate again, just six months later, to Lexington, Kentucky. Having friends in Lexington reassured them during this difficult decision, but after moving during the war, this relocation would be a relatively easy one. However, it was a new beginning once again.

Retreating to his comfort zone with a soccer ball, Sucurovic's love for the game quickly came into play. Though he was one of the better athletes on the field during high school soccer team tryouts, his inability to speak English was a big enough turn-off to the coach that Sucurovic did not make the team. Instead, during a regular P.E. class at this newest school, he was spotted kicking a ball by coach Simpson, the football coach. Simpson was thoroughly impressed. Though Sucurovic did not know what football was and had never seen a game played, he greeted the football coach's interest with curiosity for a new learning experience, particularly because soccer was now out of the question. Sucurovic made the junior varsity team with little training and, after guidance from coach Simpson, was quickly competing for the varsity kicking spot.

Sucurovic's luck abruptly ran out when leaving football practice one day in the fall of 1998. It had been a typical high school training session except that Sucurovic, the junior kicker, was outperforming the senior and returning starter kicker on varsity that day. While walking across the school parking lot on his way home, Sucurovic was struck from behind by a car whose driver was supposedly blinded by the sun. X-rays revealed fractures in the C2 and C3 bones, the second and third vertebrae in his neck. The accident and injuries that could have left him paralyzed and should have required surgery did not break his spirit. Since the surgery would have stopped him from ever again playing football, he opted not to have the surgery and to let time heal his neck, which kept him out of football for his entire junior season. Ironically, the driver of the vehicle happened to be the varsity kicker who Sucurovic had just beaten out on the field.

All this happened within the first year of Sucurovic being in this country, yet he continued to pursue his dreams. He returned for his senior year during the 1999–2000 season and earned the recognition he deserved. Sucurovic made the All-City Team and earned Academic All-State Honorable Mention despite the fact that he was still learning to read and write fluently in English. Sucurovic enrolled at the University of Kentucky and even secured a walk-on spot on the Wildcats football squad. After two years as a "forgotten walk-on," Sucurovic earned playing time in his third year and went on to earn a scholarship in his fourth and fifth years. Sucurovic graduated as the fourth all-time leader for a single season punting average in Kentucky's history and even led the SEC in punting average his senior season.

From Kentucky, Sucurovic earned a bachelor's degree in education while majoring in kinesiology with a minor in business. Sucurovic contemplated trying out for the National Football League (NFL) and trained for a couple of months before pursuing graduate school. The conscientious student, who was still perfecting his English, then enrolled at the University of Central Florida's DeVos Sport Business Management Program to receive master's degrees in sport business management and business administration in 2005. Upon graduation, less than 10 years after moving to the United States, with three degrees in hand, Sucurovic took a job with a professional soccer club in the Netherlands. He is currently the international manager of Cambuur Soccer Schools, recruiting young talent into the game that he loves. If he is unable to secure professional athletic careers for the players he comes in contact with, he tries to guide them to collegiate careers in the United States where they can earn an education. In 2008, Sucurovic started his own sport consulting and marketing agency, Pro Soccer Schools, LLC.

Sucurovic is paying it forward. He acknowledges that "if there weren't so many people in my life who supported me, I wouldn't be where I am today. I am fortunate that people around me took an interest in my success. Mentors played a huge role in my development." Sucurovic credits his family for playing a huge role in encouraging him to pursue his dreams, but recognizes that many other young soccer players don't have the same support. Instead, he strives to be the building block from which they can construct their success and foster their dreams.

Sucurovic's life experiences have brought many questions to his mind like, "How did I survive that whole long bloody war without any injuries just to come to the United States in pursuit of a better life and be hit by a car? Why did I have to come to the United States to achieve equal opportunity? Why couldn't I, nor generations before me, have a childhood that American kids have enjoyed for years?"[2] Sucurovic's curiosity for life has pushed him through his education and pursuit of happiness. Though Sucurovic has not learned the answers to all these questions and may never do so, his most important lesson has come from sports. He believes sport has changed his life and he has witnessed firsthand the positive impact it can have on a community and society. He has seen it can bring individuals from so many walks of life together to act as one, with common goals and common dreams. Most importantly, Sevy Sucurovic is living his American dream. He said, "The U.S. has been good to my family and I, but it all came from hard work. My family and I did not and still do not wait for things to happen for us. Sport has taught me to make no excuses. And nobody gave us anything for free."[3] It is all deserved, Sevy.

Notes

1. The World Factbook, Central Intelligence Agency, Country Comparison: Unemployment Rate, https://www.cia.gov/library/publications/the-world-factbook/rank order/2129rank.html, accessed February 22, 2010.

2. Sevin Sucurovic, interview with the author on February 11, 2010.

3. Ibid.

MaCharia Yuot

Coming to America

by Jessica Bartter Duffaut

Fighting starvation, exhaustion, dehydration, the sub-Saharan sun, wild animals, and militia gunfire describes just one day of MaCharia Yuot's three-year journey to freedom. A native of the Dinka tribe of Southern Sudan, Yuot was forced to flee his homeland and his family because of civil war that raged from 1983 until 2005. At the innocent age of nine, Yuot left his parents and three sisters because government troops were reportedly killing adults, enslaving girls, and kidnapping boys. The boys who were kidnapped were used as cannon fodder or were forced to walk through minefields risking their lives to lead their violent captors to safety. In an attempt to avoid their impending capture, Yuot and more than 26,000 young boys fled their villages. Finding safety in numbers, Yuot began his journey with dozens of other boys and young men. Together they walked about 500 miles without a steady supply of food, water, or shelter. Yuot recalls, "walk[ing] at night and sle[eping] during the day because it was too hot to walk then and there was no shade. Water was rationed. You couldn't drink unless you really needed it, and the same with food."[1] Traveling at night was also strategically done to avoid capture and enslavement.

Thousands lost their lives along the way, succumbing to fatigue, animal predators, gunfire, disease, and malnutrition. Yuot persevered—500 miles and two months later he was one of the lucky ones who survived the arduous journey. From the story of Peter Pan, international aid workers named the survivors the "Lost Boys of Sudan" when they crossed Sudan's eastern border into Ethiopia.

After approximately three years in Ethiopia, the country's government changed, leaving the Lost Boys unwelcome and on foot once again. The orphans were forced away in 1991 by more gunfire. The journey proved to be a deadly one once more. As they were chased by government tanks and armed militia from Ethiopia, the boys frantically tried to cross the River Gilo and many were consumed by the river—either by drowning, or killed by crocodiles and hippopotamuses. They traveled another 400 miles along the Sudanese and

Ethiopian border, eventually crossing into Kenya about a year later. They were received into a refugee camp called Kakuma where survivors finally settled, and where Yuot received much of his schooling and even played soccer. It is estimated that only about 10,000 boys, less than half of their original number, survived the past four years and still incomplete journey.

The story of the Lost Boys could not be ignored, therefore, the United States committed to provide asylum to about 3,800 of the orphans in 1999. With the help of the Office of the United Nations High Commissioner for Refugees, the U.S. Department of State began transferring these youth to the U.S. for resettlement processing into 38 different states. Yuot was sponsored by the Lutheran Church and resettled in Philadelphia, Pennsylvania. Because he arrived during winter in the mid-Atlantic United States from the sub-Saharan desert of Africa, the weather did not help Yuot's plight. However, he was welcomed into a home with several other Lost Boys and enrolled in the West Catholic High School as a junior. Yuot joined the soccer team. The athletic skills he brought with him from Africa helped him adjust to life in America.

In his senior year in 2002, Yuot began running competitively at the encouragement of friends who recognized his talent. Yuot was not a stranger to long distance running and excelled on the cross country team. Despite it being his first year running competitively in the sport, Yuot finished third in the 3,200 meters at the Catholic League Championships. The championships were held at Widener University in Chester, Pennsylvania. That was the first encounter Widener's track and field coach, Vince Touey, had with Yuot, but Touey quickly recognized Yuot's potential as a collegiate athlete. After Coach Touey approached him, Yuot was excited with the prospect that he could attend college and continue his new love for running.

While in Kenya, Yuot had studied Swahili, Arabic, and English, in addition to his native Dinka language. Yet, at the time of his high school graduation, Yuot was not fluent enough in English to enter college. Yuot studied English intensely at the Language Company's Pennsylvania Language Institute for several months. The Institute is located on the campus of Widener University, enabling Yuot to practice with the student-athletes after each day's class. Yuot's intense studying paid off and after acing the Test of English as a Foreign Language, Yuot enrolled in Widener University in the spring semester of 2003. That semester, despite missing the fall cross country competitions, Yuot finished second in the Middle Atlantic Conference Championships in the 5,000 meter event in outdoor track and field. He ran it in 15 minutes and 0.12 seconds, missing the win and the national qualifying time by a mere five seconds.

In his first cross country season the next fall, Yuot finished third in his first race, and then won every race thereafter, including the Middle Atlantic Conference cross country title when he ran five miles in 26 minutes and 19 seconds, beating the next closest opponent by 23 seconds. His domination in the sport and leadership on the team were pleasant surprises to Coach Touey. By winning the MAC title, Yuot secured his spot at the NCAA Division III Cross Country Championships where he was the runner up in 2003. He also won the Middle Atlantic Conference cross country title in 2004. Later that academic year, Yuot took home the MAC Championship titles in the 1,500-meter run for indoor track, as well as the 5,000-meter run and the steeplechase events in outdoor track. These accomplishments earned Yuot the right to call himself the first Widener University student-athlete to receive All-American honors in cross country, indoor track and field, and outdoor track and field.

During his senior year, Yuot set out to do the impossible. At the Division III National Track and Field Championships, he entered the 10,000-meter run on Thursday, the 3,000-meter steeplechase on Friday, and the 5,000-meter race on Saturday. Just competing in the three back-to-back races was a huge undertaking, but no stranger to pain, Yuot was determined to walk away with all three titles. It started with a victory in the 10,000-meter in 30 minutes and 26.99 seconds, followed by the 3,000-meter steeplechase that he won with a Widener-record time of 9 minutes and 3.88 seconds. The third and final day proved to be the toughest, not because of the distance but because the conditions were near 90 degrees. Nonetheless, Yuot captured the 5,000 meters in 14 minutes and 48.96 seconds becoming "the first track and field athlete in Division III history to win three NCAA championships in as many days."[2]

About his unprecedented competition, Yuot said, "I just wanted to leave a mark that would be remembered. I wanted to show the next generation of runners that winning three distance events can be done. I wanted to show that if I can do it, somebody in the future can do it."[3]

He was named NCAA Division III Men's Track and Field Athlete of the Year in 2006 and would become a 13-time All-American and six-time NCAA Division III National Champion before graduating in 2007 with a degree in social work.

Yuot hopes to continue his success on the Olympic stage. In November 2007, Yuot competed in the Olympic trials for the marathon and finished a respectable 33rd. He continues to train for the next Olympics as running has become an integral part of his life. Yout is a member of Team USA Minnesota. In 2008, he placed seventh in the USA 10K Championships, 10th at the USA 8K Championships, and 13th at the USA 15K Championships.[4]

Yuot was blessed, he believes, in 2007 when he received his American citizenship. "I think coming to America and becoming a citizen was [a] great moment. It was very exciting for me because it has so much meaning and can lead to great success. It was a blessing to me because of the amazing experiences I've had in America: my success in school, my success outside the classroom makes me proud, and having friends as well as mentors in life here makes achieving the goals I have easier while staying focused."[5]

With American citizenship, Yuot was able to receive his American passport. And with the help of ESPN for an E:60 special featuring Yuot, he was able to return to Sudan for the first time in nearly 20 years. He was able to find his mother and sisters, but was not able to reunite with his father who had died shortly after Yuot first left Sudan. The emotional reunion was filled with happiness and sorrow as Yuot struggled to understand the lack of change in Sudan despite the great fortune that he himself has encountered since making a new life in the States.

Regardless of Yuot's personal struggles, it is evident that he is an accomplished and dedicated athlete and student of life. The violence and death that has devastated the Sudanese has amounted to what is arguably one of the most brutal wars of the past century. Civilians have been targeted over and over, either by deadly raids or forced famine. According to the estimates by the U.S. State Department, the combination of war, famine, and disease in southern Sudan have killed over two million people and displaced another four million such as Yuot and his family. Though relief workers from the United Nations and Red Cross scrambled in the 1990s to provide the Lost Boys shelter, food, and medical attention, their sheer number made it overwhelming. So did their needs resulting from the long-term effects of hunger, disease, and dehydration. Many refugees remain at Kakuma surviving on food rations and a gallon of water a day for cleaning, cooking, and drinking provided by aid organizations.

Having lost everything, MaCharia Yuot appreciates that he has a good place to stay, good friends, a good education, and a passion for running. Yuot believes, "The more you struggle in life, the better you are as an athlete, a brother, a husband or wife. Quitting is a habit. I won't quit."[6]

Notes

1. Frank Litsky, "After Walking Hundreds of Miles for Survival, a Refugee Turns to Running," *The New York Times*, October 29, 2007, http://www.nytimes.com/2007/10/29/sports/othersports/29sudan.html?ei=5088&en=a7b344ca75c2b8c0&ex=1351310400&pagewanted=all.

2. Joseph Santoliquito, "'Lost Boy' Yuot runs to Div. III glory," *Special to ESPN.com*, June 6, 2006, http://sports.espn.go.com/ncaa/news/story?id=2466635, accessed February 24, 2010.

3 Interview via e-mail with author, February 23, 2010.

4. Adam Jacobs, "Macharia Yuot, Josh Moen Join Team USA Minnesota, *The Final Sprint*, August 27, 2008, http://www.thefinalsprint.com/2008/08/macharia-yuot-josh-moen-join-team-usa-minnesota/#more-7391.

5. David Cohen, "Who is Macharia Yuot?" The American Distance Project, July 22, 2008, http://distanceproject.wordpress.com/2008/07/22/who-is-macharia-yuot/.

6. Interview via e-mail with author, February 23, 2010.

Shamila Kohestani

Coming to America

by Stacy Martin-Tenney

Shamila Kohestani was born during war in Afghanistan and has grown up knowing nothing but war. When Kohestani was 8 years old, the Taliban assumed rule of Afghanistan implementing severe restrictions on Afghan women, while reigning terror on society. Kohestani could have succumbed to the pressures, but her fighting spirit carried her onto a soccer field where she realized her own dreams of playing soccer and the dream of other Afghan women looking for opportunity. Her heroism instills bravery and promise in the hearts of many of her countrywomen.

Shamila's experience as a young girl greatly influenced her choices as an adult. She was only nine years old when Taliban soldiers burst into the Kohestani home with machine guns and destroyed televisions and radios before setting fire to family keepsakes. Later, at age 14, a soldier questioned her for improperly wearing a burqa. She defied the Taliban, an action that sentenced many women to death. "I was outside, wearing a burqa, but because I had just started to wear it, I did not have enough practice to keep all my body covered," Kohestani said. "[He] asked me why I had not covered the front part of my body. He beat me. But I threw the burqa off and escaped."[1] Determined and willful, she continued to pursue her dreams of education and playing sports. "I asked myself, how long will I have to stay at home [for school], not go outside and not get [a real] education?" Kohestani recalls. "Then I was convinced that the situation will not remain as it is and maybe one day I will go to school, play soccer, and do whatever I like."[2]

During Taliban rule, Kohestani and her six sisters were not allowed to attend school. Their family sought out underground schools and traded books with other families, acts that could have earned them severe punishment. Women were banned from the workplace and schools. Before Taliban rule, it was estimated that more than half of the student population at Kabul University was female. These same women now could not leave their home without being covered head to toe in a burqa and in the company of a man from their household. Despite the supervision, they were not allowed to speak in public. Martin Luther King Jr. once said, "The ultimate tragedy is not the oppression and cruelty by the bad people but the silence over that by the good people."[3] Kohestani would not be silent. In 2001, the United States overthrew the Taliban in Kabul during the aftermath of the September 11th attacks on the United States.

With the newfound freedom of their fledgling democracy, Kohestani started playing soccer with her brother, once more defying the customs of the male-dominated society. Afghan girls had been sheltered from so many things and sports had historically been one of those, so it was an ostentatious sight to see a young Afghan girl kicking a soccer ball. "I wasn't a girlie girl," Kohestani said. "I didn't want to stay in the house and play with dolls."[4] In 2002, she was able to attend public school again, but had missed so many of the fundamentals of learning during her formative years. She was still missing a formal outlet for her soccer skills.

Two years later, Awista Ayub, an Afghani-American woman who immigrated to Connecticut with her family at a young age, felt passionately about providing positive experiences through sports for young Afghan women. She had experienced firsthand the possibilities that sports participation had afforded her in the United States, having played women's ice hockey at the University of Rochester. "These girls had dreams of becoming something and had passion in life, and it was cut short for a while," said Ayub.[5] Ayub brought eight young women, one of whom was Kohestani, to the United States for a soccer clinic through her Afghan Youth Sports Exchange program. Shortly, after that trip she organized a five-day clinic in Kabul with 250 Afghan girls and again Kohestani stood out among her fellow athletes on the soccer field.

Kohestani gathered a group of young women together to play soccer regularly. The sight of women kicking soccer balls was still repulsive to many—if not all—of the men, and women faced terrible discrimination. Yasamin Rasoul pioneered the development of this women's soccer group with Kohestani and she described the challenges they faced: "The men made fun of us, called us bad, bad names. They were throwing rocks at us sometimes. It was hard, but when you want something, you have to fight for it."[6]

Kohestani has always demonstrated a fighting spirit. She was recognized in 2006 in the United States for her efforts in promoting women's sports in Afghanistan at the ESPY awards when she accepted the Arthur Ashe Courage Award on behalf of all Afghan women soccer athletes. On that same trip, Kohestani attended the Julie Foudy Sports Leadership Academy and met a coach that provided her with the opportunity of a lifetime. "She wasn't an amazing soccer player, but the energy and the joy that she brought to the field for every practice—I have to say that stayed with me," said Carolyn Conforti-Browse, a counselor at the academy and a teacher and coach at Blair Academy.[7] Carolyn was inspired to ask the Blair headmaster for a scholarship so that Kohestani could attend the academy for a year of post-graduate study. Julie Foudy, former captain of the U.S. women's squad, offered to pay for Kohestani's travel back to the U.S.

In the meantime, Kohestani, Afghanistan's team captain, delivered an unbelievable performance for the women's soccer team in a Pakistan tournament, scoring six of the team's 11 total goals. "The captain was the star of our team," said Saboor Walizada, the team's coach.[8] Kohestani has been glorified as a national female sports hero by other young Afghan women. She plays soccer in the same stadium where the Taliban had executed women that defined their rule.

Kohestani traveled to Blair Academy, where she would study, hoping to be able to attend college the following year, but she had a lot of studies she had to make up from the time where she had been banned from learning. Kohestani was voracious for information and took in any and every opportunity to learn. She listened to music that fellow students recommended and looked up words they said in the dictionary so she could understand. The burden placed on her with class work, private tutors, a demanding course load, pressures of friends, and sports are enough to stress any 20-year old, but she didn't feel pressured, she felt privileged. "I have an opportunity that nobody else has, and I am going to take advantage of it," Kohestani said. "I think I am the luckiest girl in Afghanistan."[9] Kohestani returned to Afghanistan at the end of the school year, but only temporarily.

Drew University in Madison, New Jersey, offered Kohestani a scholarship to continue her education and soccer career. She walked onto campus looking like an average 20-year-old freshman, wearing jeans, running shoes, and pink nail polish. Initially she was isolated and quiet on the soccer field, but soon blossomed into the outspoken, engaged team player that she was in her native land. Ann Mularz, a senior goalkeeper, remembers the first time Kohestani scored on her. Kohestani pumped her fist and yelled "Goal!" Mularz loved the trash talk from the freshman. Mularz said of Kohestani, "She doesn't give up, or put her head down. If she messes something up, she just comes back and said, 'Next time.'"[10] Kohestani has not only endured terrible experiences, but she has flourished into a leader on the soccer field and for a country. Drew University soccer coach Racine says it best, "(Shamila) is not only an amazing story. She's an amazing person."[11]

Shamila may have left the harsh reality of Afghanistan and the challenges she faced as a female athlete, but she has not left her culture. She prays toward Mecca for 15 minutes, five times daily. She even fasts during Ramadan from sunrise to sunset, despite a difficult, draining soccer-training schedule. Even something as powerful as thirst is no match for the willpower of Kohestani. She pushes through and continues to share her experiences. "When I first came here, people would ask, 'What did you do for fun in Afghanistan?'" Kohestani said. "I'd say, 'What do you mean fun? What is fun? I spent all my life in war.'" She tells American kids, "You need to appreciate everything you have, because everywhere there are people who are starving, people who have nothing. Here there is so much."[12]

The Afghan women and the world need to appreciate everything that Shamila has done for sport and for equality. "Some people think I'm the baddest girl ever because I played soccer. They are still saying very nasty things," Kohestani said.[13]

Kohestani plans to return to Kabul after graduation, and continue her pursuit for women's rights. The deeply ingrained traditional attitudes will be challenging to overcome, and it will not be as swift as she is on the pitch, but she will not be deterred. "In a soccer game, Shamila is always less than 100 meters away from the goal, and she has a soft, green field under her feet," said Fatema Hussaini, a law student at Kabul University and a women's rights activist. "But in the game of gaining freedom, she and other Afghan women might be 100 years away from the goal," Hussaini adds, "and the field is full of difficult barriers."[14] Barriers don't stop this determined young lady; she has a powerful corner kick.

Notes

1. Omid Marzban, "Afghanistan: Once Whipped By Taliban, Girl Makes Mark As Soccer Star: September 13, 2007," Radio Free Europe/Radio Liberty, http://www.rferl.org/content/article/1078658.html, (accessed March 22, 2010).

2. Ibid.

3. Joe Drape, "Shamila's Goal," *New York Times Upfront*, April 14, 2008.

4. Wayne Coffey, "Drew University soccer star Shamila Kohestani leaves Taliban behind," *New York Daily News*, October 18, 2008.

5. Joe Drape, "Soccer as an Escape to Hope for Afghan Teenager," New York Times.com, February 11, 2008, http://www.nytimes.com/2008/02/11/sports/soccer/11blair.html, (accessed March 22, 2010).

6. Omid Marzban, "Afghanistan: Once Whipped By Taliban, Girl Makes Mark As Soccer Star: September 13, 2007," Radio Free Europe/Radio Liberty, http://www.rferl.org/content/article/1078658.html, (accessed March 22, 2010).

7. Joe Drape, "Soccer as an Escape to Hope for Afghan Teenager," New York Times.com, February 11, 2008, http://www.nytimes.com/2008/02/11/sports/soccer/11blair.html, (accessed March 22, 2010).

8. Wayne Coffey, "Drew University soccer star Shamila Kohestani leaves Taliban behind," *New York Daily News*, October 18, 2008.

9. Ibid.

10. Ibid.

11. Ibid.

12. Omid Marzban, "Afghanistan: Once Whipped By Taliban, Girl Makes Mark As Soccer Star: September 13, 2007," Radio Free Europe/Radio Liberty, http://www.rferl.org/content/article/1078658.html, (accessed March 22, 2010).

13. Wayne Coffey, "Drew University soccer star Shamila Kohestani leaves Taliban behind," *New York Daily News*, October 18, 2008.

14. Omid Marzban, "Afghanistan: Once Whipped By Taliban, Girl Makes Mark As Soccer Star: September 13, 2007," Radio Free Europe/Radio Liberty, http://www.rferl.org/content/article/1078658.html, (accessed March 22, 2010).

II

LEGENDS LIVE ON

by Richard Lapchick

We are often asked what we want to be remembered for. Many of us, no matter how many good things we do and what life path we choose, would live on in the memories of our families and friends. But then there are some whose life contributions are so great that the memory of what they did while they graced the planet will continue to live on and bring inspiration to future generations. Such are the stories of the nine lives portrayed in *Legends Live On*.

Jerry Richardson, an African-American man, led a group of Native American girls who happened to play basketball to great success on the court on their reservation. What Richardson and the girls did for others on their reservation helped many youngsters overcome the high rate of alcoholism and the high dropout rate from school. Still a young man, Richardson was killed in a car crash.

Coach Perry Reese Jr., also an African-American, went to an Amish community where he was the only person of color. Initially resisted, he eventually won the hearts of everyone in the community who all came together to mourn his loss.

Derrick Thomas and Reggie White, two of football's greatest players, were both taken from us early in their lives. But it was not until after they made extraordinary contributions in their communities where they devoted so much of their time to helping others.

Ewing Kauffman was the owner of the Kansas City Royals. His philanthropy enabled thousands of people and dozens of organizations to do work to better our society.

Coach Dave Sanders led student-athletes at Columbine High School to success on the playing field. The beloved coach gave his life on the tragic day of the shootings at Columbine trying to save more students until he was finally stopped by the two shooters.

Ralph Wiley, one of America's most thoughtful writers who mentored most of today's successful African-American sports journalists, died of heart failure when he was just 52 years old.

Jason Ray, the charismatic mascot of the University of North Carolina's Tar Heels, gave life to countless others upon his death because being an organ donor was so important to him.

Finally, Jon "Blazeman" Blais had his Ironman career cut short by Lou Gehrig's disease, but he used every last bit of his strength to start ALS awareness raising efforts that have continued in his honor.

The legacies of these men will always be remembered by those they touched and those who have heard and read about them.

Jerry Richardson

Legends Live On

by Joslyn Dalton

On August 31, 1996, the University of Central Florida's (UCF) football program achieved their first Division IA victory in a come-from-behind thriller over William and Mary. The final score was 39-33. The conquest marked the program's ascendency from Division III to the premier level of college football. For UCF's athletic community, this triumph should have been one to rejoice. However, the elation of the moment soon turned to sorrow as word was received that head women's basketball coach, Jerry Richardson, had been killed that night when his vehicle was struck by a stolen car traveling close to 100 mph. At 40 years old, Richardson's life came to a tragic and untimely end.

His death proved to be a significant loss for both the program and the community. Richardson had spent his first three seasons rebuilding the Knights underperforming women's program. In his fourth year as coach, he had led his team to a birth in the NCAA Division I Tournament, a milestone for the school. Richardson's coaching philosophy had been developed through his own experience as a basketball player and also during his time coaching on a Navajo reservation. In only a short amount of time as a basketball coach, Richardson had succeeded in developing his athletes into successful, confident young women.

As a talented young athlete growing up in Texas, Richardson had hopes of playing collegiate basketball. However, when it didn't work out, he enrolled at Northwestern University on a track scholarship. Upon graduation, he continued his education and received his master's degree from Louisiana Tech.

In 1982, following graduate school, Richardson accepted a mid-semester job as an English teacher at Three Nations High School on the Navajo Nation Reservation in Shiprock, New Mexico. At first, the small, impoverished Navajo community was skeptical of Richardson's presence. Most of the students had never seen a black man, and they didn't know what to make of him. In the midst of his new surroundings, Richardson reached for the familiar. He jumped at the opportunity to coach of the girls basketball team, viewing it as a way to reconnect to his favorite childhood sport.

Initially, Richardson's bold and aggressive style clashed with the often shy demeanor of his young athletes. Having faced racial prejudice his entire life, Richardson once again saw it as an obstacle to overcome. "They fought me. They fought success. They fought the system," he said.[1] Over time he developed trust with his players as they warmed up to his coaching style. Richardson taught his players how a positive attitude could make any goal obtainable. Familiarity soon bred success on the court. Under his tutelage, Richardson led the Lady Chieftains to a remarkable four State Championships.

With his basketball team a success on the court, Richardson began to see improvements elsewhere in the reservation. In a community beset by poverty and alcoholism, it was common to have the school's dropout rate hover around 50 percent. However, Richardson understood the significance of preparing his players for life beyond the basketball court. "The trophies gather dust, the kids don't," he said. "They keep moving."[2] Under his leadership, 80 percent of Richardson's athletes went on to continue their education in college. Soon, others on the reservation began to take notice. Parents discovered a newfound sense of pride in their daughters. The community's unemployment rates decreased and alcoholism became less prevalent. Astonishingly, the team's success attracted enough attention and funds that the school was able to build a new basketball gymnasium, which became the finest building in all of Shiprock.

Richardson's success became nationally recognized. He traveled to Orlando, Florida, in 1991 as a recipient of the National Consortium for Academics in Sports' Giant Steps Award. While attending the awards banquet, Richardson was introduced to Richard Astro, who happened to be in charge of hiring a new UCF women's basketball coach. Astro arranged to visit Richardson in Shiprock to see his team in action. When he made the trip, Astro was impressed with what he saw. The entire town was there, rallying behind their coach and his players. In the varsity game, Astro watched the Lady Chieftains dismantle their opponent who consisted of taller and more talented girls.

The fans were in a veritable frenzy throughout and those sitting next to Astro told him that this was commonplace. Following the game, Astro and Richardson met and talked well into the night. After years on the reservation, Richardson disclosed that he felt he was ready for new challenges and he was confident his assistants could maintain the quality of the program he had created. After arriving back in Florida the next day, Astro called Richardson to offer him the position.

Arriving in Orlando in 1992, Richardson inherited a program badly in need of restructuring. In his first year with the UCF Knights, the program moved into the Trans-American Athletic conference (now known as the Atlantic Sun Conference). By his fourth season, Richardson started to see the fruits of his labor. His team won the Conference Championship, which helped capture the attention of a growing fan base. The win also gave UCF its first birth into the NCAA Division I Tournament. Following a first round loss, Richardson quickly turned his attention to the following season. Unfortunately, he would not live to coach another game.

The news of his unexpected death shocked and greatly saddened the surrounding community. Wayne Allen, the head women's basketball coach at Florida Atlantic at that time noted, "It puts a whole different perspective on the season," Allen said a few months after Richardson's accident. "It seems as though you are here one day and the next day you're gone."[3]

During his time with the school, Richardson had become a strong force on campus and in the surrounding Orlando community. Although he managed a hectic basketball schedule, he balanced his time with philanthropic activities. At the time of his death, he had enthusiastically served on the Board of the Coalition for the Homeless.

When filmmaker Rick Derby heard about Richardson's life story, Derby wanted to provide a captivating glimpse into Richardson's Navajo experience. After 12 years in the making, Derby's film aired nationally on PBS in December 2002. "I wanted to find out how this male, black coach taught a team of Navajo teenage girls not to play basketball, but to cope with and overcome the intense and debilitating feelings of victimization and self-defeat," Derby said.[4] The film ended up winning HBO's 2002 Documentary Feature Prize for "its powerful storytelling, compelling characters, and its presentation of a rarely seen set of unique cross-cultural relationships."[5]

Jerry Richardson was in many ways a quiet and introspective man, yet he was an excellent coach and the impact of his life spoke volumes. More important than teaching his athletes how to win on the court, Richardson taught them how to win in life. Today, his achievements continue to inspire others and to those who knew him, his legacy lives on.

Notes

1. Press Release, "OPB Presents 'Rocks with Wings,' A Film about Winning, Losing and Everything in Between," http://pressroom.opb.org/programs/rocks-wings/, (accessed March 28, 2010).

2. Richard Crepeau, Sport and Society Broadcast for Friday September 6, 1996, http://www.h-net.org/~arete/archives/threads/crepeau/90696.html, (accessed March 28, 2010).

3. Sharon Robb, "FAU Coach Mourns for a Colleague,"Sunsentinel.com, November 26, 1996, http://articles.sun-sentinel.com/1996-11-26/news/9611250498_1_men-s-soccer-team-jerry-richardson-wayne-allen, (accessed March 26, 2010).

4. Press Release, "OPB Presents 'Rocks with Wings,' A Film about Winning, Losing and Everything in Between," http://pressroom.opb.org/programs/rocks-wings/, (accessed March 28, 2010).

5. Ibid.

Perry Reese Jr.

Legends Live On

by Joslyn Dalton

In the heart of Ohio rests an Amish settlement that for years existed closed off from the world. With no traffic lights or fast-food restaurants, the town of Berlin, Ohio, was unwelcoming to outsiders. The community, held together by the commonality of religious belief, found escape through the sport of basketball offered at Berlin's local high school.

When Charlie Huggins moved to town as Hiland High's new boys' basketball coach in 1982, excitement stirred the otherwise uneventful town. Huggins himself was not of concern to the people. His résumé boasted two Ohio state basketball championships. It was the assistant coach he brought with him, Perry Reese Jr., who stimulated fear in the people of Berlin who were not accustomed to the color of his skin or his religion. A year after adding Reese to the coaching staff, Huggins decided to quit. Leaving high recommendation to the school board, Huggins wanted Reese to take over the responsibility of head coach.

In 1979, Reese began his coaching career at Guernesy Catholic High School in Cambridge, Ohio. During the summer months, Reese developed a relationship with Huggins while assisting him during basketball camps. Eager for the opportunity to join Huggins in Berlin, Reese, who was African-American, quickly found himself as a foreigner in an all-white community. Reese endured racism and rejection. Instilled in the upbringing of the Amish was the oppressed history of their ancestry. Children of Berlin were taught that during the Reformation in Europe more than 400 years ago, the Amish were burned at the stake by Catholics.

Threatening phone calls and difficulty in finding a place to live did not scare Reese out of town. Skepticism further grew toward Reese once the community discovered he failed to complete his college education. Unqualified to teach at Hiland High, Reese worked at Berlin Wood Products. The opportunity to work outside of the school proved helpful for Reese. Through his work ethic and dedication to his job, Reese's coworkers slowly came to appreciate him.

Over time, they called him the original "Black Amishman."[1]

The success of Reese's basketball teams made it easier for him to feel accepted into the surrounding community. In his first 52 games with the Hiland Hawks, Reese accumulated 49 wins. During his 16-year coaching span in Berlin, 11 of Reese's teams were named Sectional Champions and 11 teams won the Inter Valley Conference Championship. On five separate occasions, Reese's teams made it to the final four of the Ohio State Championship tournament, taking the title in 1992. In total, he won 78 percent of the games he coached while at Hiland.

Reese's coaching success became noted outside Berlin. In 1990 and 1999, the Associated Press named Reese Coach of the Year. In addition to basketball, Reese coached volleyball and track during his tenure with Hiland High.

The manner in which Reese dealt with ridicule and handled success was a testament to the humility and discipline he possessed. Those surrounding him started to consider Reese's values as not much different from their own. His respectful and unselfish demeanor was impressive. His influence on his players was profound. Reese required that his teams pray before and after each game. He made certain his young men respected their families, a significant Amish virtue.

As an example to the players he coached, Reese finished his degree from Muskingum College in New Concord, Ohio. At Hiland, he earned a position teaching history and current events. His open door policy made him popular with the students. He was viewed not only as a coach and educator but also as a confidant. Reese became a trusted friend and role model to the entire community. His students treasured their conversations with him on topics such as race, religion, relationships, and other troubles.

During the 1999–2000 basketball season, Reese began to experience memory loss and head pain. It was later discovered that he had an inoperable brain tumor and was given only months to live. The town that had learned to tear down barriers and embrace change was now forced to face the slow fade of the "Black Amishman" they had grown to love. On November 22, 2000, Perry Reese Jr. died at the age of 48, leaving behind a community stricken with grief. More than 800 people, some who were former players now living in Atlanta, Chicago, South Carolina, and even Germany, came back to Berlin honor the impact Reese left on their lives. Six ministers and three counselors walked the halls of Hiland High to comfort students, teachers, and staff during the weeks following his death.

Reese's final mission during his lifetime was to establish a college scholarship fund for students in need. Since his passing, the Perry Reese Jr. Memorial Scholarship Fund continues to grow in available assistance for inspiring young graduates of Hiland High.

In 2004, another event was created to celebrate Reese. The "Classic in the Country" became an annual festival held over the weekend of the Martin Luther King holiday.[2] Commemorating the diversity of both Dr. King and Mr. Reese, the Classic basketball tournament continues to bring together the best female players and teams from around the country. The tournament is played in the 1,800-seat Perry Reese Center, which was built in 1999 with community donations. The venue includes a scoreboard and backboard similar to what the NBA arenas use. The legacy of Reese and the draw of the "Classic in the Country" has helped catapult Berlin into a more industrialized town.

In early 2001, author Gary Smith told Reese's story in *Sports Illustrated*. Smith's article, "Higher Education," was chosen as one of the magazine's "Stories of the Decade." Jerry Bruckheimer, producer of the sports-oriented *Remember the Titans* and *Glory Road*, has since purchased the rights to Smith's article. As of early 2010, Smith commented that he had last heard the movie was on "prolonged hold."[3]

Utilizing the influence of sport, Reese's life and continued legacy bridged the gap between two different racial and religious worlds. In building a winning basketball program, Reese was able to teach a town to embrace change. In the simplicity of living out his life, Reese undeniably reached the lives of all who knew him. Once considered an outsider, Perry Reese Jr., gently became the heartbeat of a community which remains hard at work continuing the legacy of their original "Black Amishman."

Notes

1. Gary Smith, "Higher Education," *Sports Illustrated*, March 5, 2001.

2. Matt Flojancic, "Ohio: Classic in the Country Unites Community," http://www.maxpreps.com/news/XweVSBsitkyJUN3RKX8IAQ/ohio-classic-in-the-country-unites-community.htm, (accessed March 3, 2010).

3. Roger Metzger, "Commentary: Proposed Perry Reese movie still stuck in holding pattern," http://www.timesreporter.com/sports/x1643198420/Commentary-Proposed-Perry-Reese-movie-still-stuck-in-holding-pattern, (accessed March 3, 2010).

Derrick Thomas

Legends Live On

by Stacy Martin-Tenney

Derrick Thomas was a man capable of inciting fear and instilling hope in the hearts of men. It is hard to accept the idea of one heart embodying both compassion and brutality, but Thomas was the epitome of both. He was one of the greatest linebackers of all time on the football field, but Thomas was also a great humanitarian. Fans normally recognize football players by the number or name on the back of their jerseys. Kansas City fans knew Derrick Thomas, number 58, simply as Derrick. His contributions off the field far outweighed the significance of his record breaking performances on the field. The lives he brightened through the generosity of his kind spirit will remain as symbols of what goodness and concern for our fellow man can accomplish. Thomas truly demonstrated how sports can better this world and the value of helping someone who is less fortunate than oneself.

It would have been easy for Thomas to follow a different path in life. He never really knew his father. Captain Robert Thomas' B-52 Bomber was shot down during Operation Linebacker II in Vietnam when Thomas was only five years old. The loss that he felt was manifest in his juvenile delinquency. He was arrested for stealing a car and burglarizing a home, and his mother frequently prayed for his safe return from the Miami, Florida, streets when she heard gunshots and sirens. Thomas was one of the lucky ones. It's almost as if someone was looking out for him.

A number of adults stepped in to provide him with some guidance, or tried, at least, to deter him from his youthful transgressions. Because these individuals took the time to care about him, he survived a difficult adolescence and safely arrived at the University of Alabama to play football. He was an All-American and broke the career record for the number of sacks with 52. Even his own teammates feared him on the field, but off the field they characterized him as the social worker. He sought out opportunities to do good things for others and always wore a smile wherever he went. He was selected in the first round of the 1989 NFL Draft by the Kansas City Chiefs.

Thomas found a home in Kansas City with the Chiefs. He would play out his entire 11-year NFL career there. Soon after he arrived in Kansas City he established the Derrick Thomas Third and Long Reading Club. He nurtured this organization's mission to fight illiteracy among inner-city youth through support from the Kansas City Public Library and the Storytellers Program. Thomas could be found reading to the children at the library on Saturday mornings and frequently brought teammates with him. His contribution was not enough to satisfy him. He expected more of his teammates and encouraged them to contribute as well. Thomas had an innovative and entrepreneurial spirit, and so when he was moved by someone's hardship, he made it his cause. One particular week he decided to feed close to 800 families in the Kansas City area, so he started collecting donations from his wealthy teammates. This is when Thomas' ability to incite fear in grown men became useful off the field. He wouldn't accept less than $100 from these millionaires and typically intimidated them to donate more. When he left the locker room, he entered the front office and continued to negotiate with the organization. His drive and determination, so powerfully displayed on the football field, transitioned smoothly to his causes off the field.

Thomas had an innate ability to disrupt an offense by sacking the quarterback; it was as if he had superhuman vision. His commitment to certain individuals seemed to employ the same talent. He was actually considered small for his position on the football field, but the size of his heart was as impressive as the football stadium he played in. One young man's relationship with Thomas reveals his capacity to love and how attentive he was towards children. Thomas read the headlines about basketball tournaments being cancelled in Lone Wolf, Oklahoma because no one wanted to play with a young boy named Philip Tepe who had AIDS. The world was hysterical about the disease because they didn't understand it. Children struggle every day on the playground to get picked for a team, but it was as if Tepe wasn't even allowed on the playground. This courageous young man just wanted to play sports, so Thomas sent a limousine to bring Tepe to a Chiefs game. He took Tepe golfing, bought him a video game system, and gave him a football autographed by the legendary quarterback Joe Montana. Tepe may not have been welcomed on the court in Lone Wolf, but he was certainly a part of a charity game that included Thomas and his friends Barry Sanders and Thurman Thomas. A professional athlete's life is demanding, but Thomas knew how important it was to make time for Tepe. The illness progressed, and Tepe was enduring more pain. Thomas flew in once more to visit with his buddy and gave him his All-Pro jersey, the first one he ever gave away. It didn't ease the pain, but it brought a smile. Tepe died in March of 1994, just two days after the visit, taking a piece of Thomas with him forever. It is easy to see why Thomas was named NFL Man of the Year the season before and why he was the Kansas City Chief's MVP the following season although those committees probably knew nothing about Philip Tepe.

Tepe's story is just one of many stories about Thomas' devotion. Rahman McGill was a young student in Thomas' Third and Long Foundation. McGill describes their relationship as "a journey that was short in number of years but great in the knowledge and wisdom I gained."[1] During one of their first reading sessions, McGill told Thomas of his dream of becoming a Supreme Court Justice. Thomas admired his lofty goal and sought ways to encourage it; giving hope and confidence to a young mind will do wonders for his future. He began small by calling him "Justice" and then one day Thomas arranged a surprise visit from Supreme Court Justice Clarence Thomas.

Justice Thomas reinforced Thomas' goal setting for McGill, and promised this young man that he would secure a clerkship for him when he graduated from law school. Due to Thomas' encouragement to read, McGill speaks more eloquently today than many adults. Helping people like McGill was actually Thomas' goal in life. It was not necessarily to win football games, be MVP, go to nine consecutive Pro Bowls, or own the single game sack record in the NFL. Those were nice. To Dan LeBatard of the *Miami Herald* Thomas once said, "It's not important what I do in this game. What matters is 20 years from now, if I'm walking down the street and a doctor or lawyer or teacher said I made a difference in their life . . . I want to be remembered as someone who made a difference."[2] Thomas definitely made a difference in Tepe's life, in McGill's life, in those starving families' lives, and in the countless other lives he touched.

Although Thomas did not place great significance on his performances on the field, his career was remarkable and inspiring in a completely different way. His athletic ability was a marvel. On the field he was the kind of athlete who seemed to make time stop because his strength and quickness were unmatched by his opponents. Young boys' eyes would gleam as they got lost in their daydream of being number 58. Old men would revel in his seemingly effortless movements. He captured his fans' attention just as he did Rahman McGill's concentration when reading. Thomas' feats on the football field were staggering. He had a career total of 126.5 sacks, 728 tackles, and 45 forced fumbles, no doubt related to his well-known sack and strip maneuver. He was named consensus Defensive Player of the Year in 1989. He also won the Mack Lee Hill Award during his rookie season. He recorded the most sacks (seven) in a single game in the NFL, a performance he attributes to his father's inspiration. That game was played on Veteran's Day in 1990. When planes flew over the stadium Thomas dedicated that game to his father. The loss of his father had scarred Thomas for so long, but he was able to turn the terrible fate of Operation Linebacker II into the finest operation of a linebacker in NFL history.

His life was full. Some would say that he had lived three or four lifetimes in his mere 33 years. Thomas would only play 33 years in the game of life due to a car accident on an icy road in Kansas City on January 23, 2000. He was on his way to the airport to fly to St. Louis with two friends to watch the NFC Championship game when he lost control of his vehicle and it flipped several times throwing Thomas and one of his friends, Michael Tellis, from the car. Tellis was killed instantly. The other friend, the only one of the three to wear a seatbelt, escaped with minor injuries. Thomas was a resilient man and had taken poundings on the football field, but he had broken his neck and his spine and was paralyzed from the chest down. It is such a wicked twist of fate when a vivacious athlete becomes aware of his vulnerability. Thomas fought through the injuries and seemed indomitable even from this tragedy. He was thought to be recovering well, considering the circumstance, and his spirit was unconquerable as always. Thomas' game clock expired on February 8, 2000, when a pulmonary embolus caused cardio-respiratory arrest. Thousands poured into the Chiefs' Arrowhead Stadium to see their beloved Thomas one last time, to thank him for his kindness.

It would be easy to call Thomas' death a devastating tragedy, but it is much more appropriate to call his life illuminating. Successful football players are sometimes referred to as stars for their supreme talents. Thomas was a star that shined so brilliantly and brought hope to those in despair. Thomas truly believed in serving others and for living an exemplary life of service he was recognized by President George Bush in 1992 as his 832nd Point of Light. Thomas was the first and only NFL player to receive this honor. In 1994, he was awarded the Genuine Heroes Award by Trinity College in Chicago for service to his community. In 1995, he was awarded the Byron "Whizzer" White Humanitarian Award. Thomas had remained involved with the Veterans of Foreign Wars throughout the years. He was the keynote speaker on Memorial Day in 1993 at the Vietnam Veterans Memorial in Washington, D.C. He had also been a supporter of Project Uplink, a group that collects prepaid phone cards for soldiers overseas. In 1999, Derrick Thomas was an obvious choice as a recipient of the VFW Hall of Fame Award, an honor that would surely make his dad proud. Thomas was also inducted into the Kansas City Chiefs Hall of Fame posthumously, and the MVP award for the Chiefs has now been named the Derrick Thomas Award.

Thomas might have left this world but the light that remains is as impressive as ever. Within days of Thomas' death, more than $25,000 had been raised to promote literacy for inner-city youth through his Third and Long Foundation. Thomas' commitment to education was always apparent during his life, so it is fitting that an Edison School now bears his name. The Derrick Thomas Academy of Kansas City is in its third year and has championed Thomas' commitment to community involvement. Thomas touched so many lives during his short time. Gunther Cunningham, the Chief's former head coach, never wore his seatbelt, but thinks of Thomas every time he buckles up now. Derrick Thomas should serve as an inspiration for us all; a beacon to guide us as we work to live his dream of making this world a more equitable and caring place.

On August 8, 2009, Derrick Thomas was inducted into the Pro Football Hall of Fame. Carl Peterson, former president of the Chiefs organization, enshrined Thomas into the Hall of Fame at the request of Thomas' family. Peterson had a longtime relationship with Derrick and greatly respected his efforts in the Kansas City area. During his speech, Peterson commented on his impact, "For all Derrick Thomas fans, the light has gone back on, and it will now burn brightly in the community of Kansas City in the middle of America. And it will also burn here very brightly in the shrine to pro football, the Pro Football Hall of Fame in Canton, Ohio, and it will burn forever . . . And yes, today does culminate the life of a great NFL player, who did so much both on and off the field for his community. A life that ended too young. It must be said, my son, Derrick, you have fought the good fight. You have finished the race. You have kept the faith. Derrick, you're in the Pro Football Hall of Fame, and no one can ever take that from you."[3] Thomas' son, Derrion, proudly accepted the award on behalf of the family.

Notes

1. Adam Teicher, "KC's tribute in memory of Thomas" *The Kansas City Star*, February 15, 2000.

2. Dan Le Batard, "A bright light goes dark too soon," MacBrud Corporation of Miami Florida, http://seatbeltsafety.com/derrickedwards.htm, (accessed November 23, 2005).

3. Pro Football Hall of Fame, "Derrick Thomas Enshrinement speech transcript," posted on August 9, 2009, http://www.profootballhof.com/story/2009/8/9/derrick-thomas-enshrinement-speech-transcript/, (accessed February 28, 2010).

Reggie White

Legends Live On

by Jessica Bartter Duffaut and Jenny Yehlen

The power of sport and the power of athletes who play sports have an immense impact in our society. People want to know what athletes are doing, where they are going, where they have been, who they are dating, what they are wearing, how much money they make, and what they had for dinner last night. Every intricate little detail associated with a professional athlete's life can somehow be spun into an earth-shattering news story for consumption by a public obsessed with such trivia. But despite these excesses, the fact is that the power and appeal that sport commands among our populace can do a whole lot of good.

Reggie White was as admired as any professional player when Green Bay prepared to play Dallas for the 1996 NFC Championship. Five weeks before the game, White was scheduled to have surgery. However, on the day of the surgery, he announced that he would continue to play. He said that God gave him a miracle.[1]

A religious man, White was co-pastor of the Inner City Community Church in Knoxville, Tennessee. On Monday before the game, 18 incendiary devices were placed in his church and the walls were covered with graffiti. The original reports in Knoxville indicated the resulting fire was an accident. There was no acknowledgement of the incendiary devices or the graffiti.[2]

The incident received national attention only when the co-pastor of the church was identified as Reggie White. The three other predominantly black churches in Tennessee that were firebombed in 1995 received no national attention, nor did the three black churches in Alabama and dozens of others around the nation that were also firebombed in the months before the destruction of White's Inner City Community Church. The eyes of the entire nation were forced open because a popular athlete's church was threatened and not just that of another black pastor.[3]

White was born and raised in Chattanooga, Tennessee, and was an all-star basketball and football athlete at Howard High School. When White was 12, he told his mother and grandmother he was going to be a preacher. White was very serious about, and committed to, his religious beliefs, and just five years later, at the age of 17, he became an ordained minister. His early ability to hold an audience's attention would prove helpful in his NFL career and in his lifelong commitment to helping young people. He would be quick to say that all that he had came from God and all that he did was in the name of God.

White played football at the University of Tennessee. Coupling his religious status along with his stellar play on the field, he was nicknamed the "Minister of Defense," which would stick with him throughout his football career. White was a consensus All-American and SEC Player of the Year in his senior year. To this day, he still holds Tennessee records for sacks in a career, a single-season and a single game.[4]

White began his professional career with the Memphis Showboats of the United States Football League (USFL) in 1983. After the USFL folded in 1985, he joined the Philadelphia Eagles of the NFL. That year, he was named NFL Defensive Rookie of the Year. The 6-foot-5, 300-pound lineman became a force to be reckoned with on the field. He was quick and agile for a man of his size, and became known throughout the league for his sacking ability. Offensive linemen and quarterbacks always had to be aware of where No. 92 was on the field. Even though White was only one of 11 guys on the field playing defense, he could amazingly turn a game around all by himself. Although opponents were not very excited to see him on the other side of the line, they still appreciated having him on the field. White was greatly respected by his peers, not only for his playing ability, but also for his sportsmanlike conduct. Trash-talking was not his game. He let his actions speak for themselves. White always helped guys up, making sure they were all right. He was a genuine class act.

In his eight years with the Eagles, he recorded more sacks than games played, 124 and 121, respectively. He is the only player in NFL history to have done that.[5] In 1993, White joined the defensive efforts of the Green Bay Packers, and vastly improved a struggling team defense. After taking a year off in 1999, White finished his career by playing a year with the Carolina Panthers and then retired in 2000 at the age of 39.

But White's career went beyond the game as he worked tirelessly in the off-season with inner-city youth. Throughout his 15-year professional career in the NFL, White made it clear that it was a priority to be in a major city where he could minister to black youth.

When White concluded his career, he left the game with 198 sacks—an NFL record at the time. White was voted to 13 consecutive Pro Bowls, also a record. His focus and commitment to the inner city remained. In 1991, he opened a home for unwed mothers on his property in Tennessee. The Reggie White Foundation was developed to help the underprivileged. It primarily focuses on the needs of underprivileged children, but also works with many other groups including unwed mothers, prison inmates, and other at risk individuals.

Sadly, Reggie White passed away on December 26, 2004 at the young age of 43. Initially, his death was said to have been caused by a heart attack, but an autopsy report showed that it had been caused by respiratory problems, including sarcoidosis and sleep apnea. The NFL may have lost one of the best defenders to ever step on the field, but society also lost a wonderful humanitarian as well. There will be others who try to emulate his intimidating play on the field, but it will be harder to find someone with the passion and love he had for God, for football, and for helping people. Teammates, current players, fans, and NFL executives all had the same resounding words of praise for White, both as a player and as a person. He will always be remembered as one of the greats. Though White's life was tragically short, his positive impact on everything and everyone he touched was anything but.

Notes

1. Richard Lapchick, *Smashing Barriers: Race and Sport in the New Millennium*, (Maryland: Madison Books, 1991) 282.

2. Ibid.

3. Ibid., 283.

4. Tennessee Football Records, "Defensive Totals," University of Tennessee, Knoxville Sports, http://grfx.cstv.com/schools/tenn/graphics/football/history/2008-deftotals .pdf, (accessed January 27, 2010).

5. Reggie White's Unofficial Homepage, "Profile #92 Defensive End—Green Bay Packers," The #1 Unofficial Website of the Minister of Defense, http://olympia.fortune city.com/white/225/1regprofile.htm, (accessed January 27, 2010).

Ewing Marion Kauffman

Legends Live On

by Jenny Yehlen

Ewing Marion Kauffman was involved in the world of sports for many years, but he is more well-known as a successful businessman and a caring philanthropist. Kauffman was a very powerful man, but all those who worked with him would consider him to be the ideal co-worker, or in sports terms, an ideal teammate. Kauffman was a true team player, and he treated his co-workers as teammates, whether he was working in the business community or the world of sports. He created an atmosphere where everyone on the "team" was working toward the same goal. Even though he was usually in positions of power and authority, he would consider himself as just another player on the team.

Kauffman was born in Garden City, Missouri, in 1916, but moved to Kansas City with his family when he was a young boy. He lived in Kansas City for the remainder of his life, until he passed away in 1993. Living in the same place for so long allowed him to create a special bond with the people of the city, which motivated him to make his community a better place and really give back to the people of Kansas City.

His business skills developed at a young age with one of his first jobs selling fish and eggs door-to-door. Over the years, Kauffman honed his entrepreneurial skills to become a very successful businessman, but he never forgot where he came from or how he started. Kauffman was a strong believer and advocate of entrepreneurship and worked hard throughout his life to help others understand the very real virtues of dedication to one's goals and hard work to achieve them.

After serving in the Navy in World War II, Kauffman returned to start working in the pharmaceuticals industry, and by 1950 he had created his own pharmaceuticals company in the basement of his home. This endeavor allowed him to put his "team player" philosophy into practice. Through his philosophy, he considered himself to be just one piece of the puzzle for the success for his company. Falling in line with this philosophy is the name he chose for his company, his middle name, Marion Laboratories Inc., because he didn't want to take all the credit for the company. During the first year of his company's existence, sales reached $36,000 and the net profit was $1,000. By the time he sold his company to Merrell Dow in 1989, it had grown to $1 billion in sales and employed 3,400 associates.

In the midst of running a billion-dollar international pharmaceuticals company, Kauffman brought major league baseball to Kansas City when he bought the Royals in 1968. Kauffman used the same business strategies that he used with Marion Laboratories Inc., with the Royals, and, not surprisingly, came up with the same successful results. The team won six division titles, two American League pennants, and a World Series championship in 1985. The team's success was beneficial to the city as well. The Kansas City Royals brought economic growth to the city, thousands of job opportunities, and a sense of pride that may be unique among baseball teams in small market cities. Professional sports teams have the amazing ability to bring a community together, and that is just what the Kansas City Royals organization did for Kansas City.

Bringing professional baseball to Kansas City is not the only thing Kauffman did to improve the community. Perhaps the legacy that will last the longest when people hear of this great man is the Ewing Marion Kauffman Foundation. He created this foundation in 1966 for the purpose of encouraging entrepreneurship and improving the education of children, particularly those from economically disadvantaged backgrounds. The goals of the Foundation remain the same even unto present day.

Education is at the center of the Foundation's goals. The Ewing Marion Kauffman Foundation works with educators to create awareness of the importance of entrepreneurship and to give people the opportunity, through programs and classes, to develop those skills and abilities. The Foundation promotes entrepreneurial success at all levels. This range includes school-age students to professional business-people. The range also spans from working with individuals to families to entire companies or organizations.

During the 1980s, Kauffman made the Foundation more focused on development, education, and entrepreneurship and it began launching more specific programs in these three areas. Project STAR (Students Taught Awareness and Resistance) was the first operating program created in 1984. The goal of this program was to prevent the use and abuse of alcohol, tobacco, and other drugs among young people. In 1988, Project Choice was developed. This program was created from a deal Kauffman made with a class from his former high school. He told the high school students that if they would stay in school, remain drug-free, avoid teenage parenthood, graduate from high school, and commit to being good citizens, he would pay for their secondary education. Project Early was developed to assist families in the early stages of development of a child through child care, health care, and general family support. In 1990, Project Essential was created to develop self-esteem in children through storytelling, moral dilemma discussions, workbook lessons, and experiential activities.

Kauffman believed that entrepreneurial skills are very important skills to obtain, but not enough people have the opportunity to do so. Kauffman chose to use his expertise to teach about the importance of entrepreneurship. The Foundation is located in Kansas City and it aims to help and educate those who live in the community, but it is not limited to Kansas City. One of Kauffman's underlying goals was to make Kansas City a beautiful and pleasurable city to live in by continually updating and improving the quality of its business, educational, and cultural life.

Kauffman's name and legacy will not soon be forgotten, nor will the things he did for Kansas City. In the early 90s, Kauffman created a succession plan that was designed to keep the baseball team in Kansas City after the sale of the team and after his death. The plan also ensured that the proceeds of its sale went to local charities to benefit the city. Recently, the Ewing Marion Kauffman Foundation made a donation of $26 million to the Metropolitan Kansas City Performing Arts Center. This money came from a portion of the funds created from the sale of the team.

Currently, The Ewing Marion Kauffman Foundation's has become one of the nation's 25 largest foundations in the U.S. The Kauffman Center for Entrepreneurial Leadership, which is a portion of the Foundation, is the largest organization in the United States focused solely on entrepreneurial success at all levels. In a 2010 "State of Entrepreneurship Address," Kauffman President and CEO, Carl Schramm, presented the outlook for entrepreneurship in 2010, including the challenges facing new businesses and solutions for fueling job growth as part of the economic recovery. Also, the Foundation announced in 2003 that it would spend over $70 million in the next 20 years to put 2,300 economically disadvantaged Kansas City area kids through college. The recipients will be chosen in middle school. Even after his passing in 1993, the values and goals Ewing Kauffman instilled in his foundation are continuing to make a difference in the community of Kansas City, and it seems as though this trend will continue far into the future.

Dave Sanders

Legends Live On

by Jessica Bartter Duffaut

Dave Sanders spent his life trying to help his students and student-athletes. He gave his life trying to save them that fateful day at Columbine High School.

The teaching profession is one of the most demanding but can also be one of the most rewarding. Teachers are often overworked and underpaid, disrespected by their students, and overlooked by their administration. Parents across the country entrust teachers with their children, placing the responsibility on their shoulders to make our young people smart, responsible citizens. The best teachers gladly accept this charge and happily work to help the young people whom they hope to educate.

One such teacher was William "Dave" Sanders. A favorite among his students and the staff, Sanders was always accessible either in the classroom, on the softball field, or on the basketball court. Sanders was raised in the small Indiana community of Newtown. He excelled in basketball, baseball, and track and field at Fountain Central High School and earned a basketball scholarship to Nebraska Western University. Upon his college graduation in 1973, Sanders chose education as his career and began teaching at Columbine High School in Littleton, Colorado. Sanders taught computers and business, and he coached girls basketball and softball. He was the assistant softball coach since the sport was sanctioned by the Colorado High School Activities Association and helped the team become league champions in 1990, 1993, and 1998; district champions in 1988, 1994, and 1996; and state runners-up in 1993 and 1995. Sanders was the head basketball coach and in his first season in 1997–98, his team produced a winning record after finishing next-to-last the year before.

Sanders enjoyed teaching and was successful because he loved to help young people. He touched the lives of countless high school students during his 24 years at Columbine High, particularly on the frightful day of April 20, 1999. This day ended in tragedy when two students turned on their classmates, murdering 13 and wounding 24 more in the most devastating shooting in U.S. school history before the Virginia Tech massacre of 2007. Sanders heard the shooters coming down the halls and ran anxiously from room to room warning students to lie on the ground, seek coverage, or run and pointed them to the safe exits. Sanders searched the school securing safety for hundreds of students and faculty members without regard for his life. Just steps ahead of the heavily armed shooters, Sanders entered the cafeteria which was full of almost 500 students on their lunch break. He led the students to a stairway leading to a safe exit but rather than following them, he turned back to the school to save more students. Until Sanders entered the cafeteria, the background sounds of shots being fired were assumed to be a senior prank as it was only weeks before graduation. By the time one of the shooters entered the cafeteria, only a handful of students remained. The killers had picked lunch time hoping to come across a large number of the student body at one time and even planted two bombs in the cafeteria that easily could have killed all 488 students. Sanders most likely prevented the Columbine High School shooting from being remembered as the Columbine High School massacre.

After escaping from the cafeteria, Sanders was on his way to the library to warn more students when one of the gunmen appeared in the hallway and opened fire. Sanders was shot twice. He stumbled into a classroom where about 30 students were hiding. Though scared, the students tended to Sanders wounds and ministered to him as much as was possible under the circumstances. Two students in particular, Aaron Hancey and Kevin Starkey, held pressure on Sanders wounds and talked to him about his family. He asked them to pull out his wallet so that he could look at a picture of his wife. He often spoke of his wife, his three daughters, and his ten grandchildren. Students assured Sanders he would see them again but there was no sign of help. After a couple of hours of waiting for assistance, they held a sign up through the window trying to let authorities know that Sanders was bleeding to death. Students could see the authorities surrounding the building but they were taking necessary precautions before entering the school. Police reports later indicated that the gunmen took their own lives shortly after wounding Sanders and killing 10 students and wounding 12 more in the library, but at the time Sanders was bleeding to death there was no way of knowing. The police department was trying to secure the building and ensure safety for themselves and anyone still trapped inside. Though Sanders fought for his life for almost four hours, by the time paramedics were able to reach him, he had lost his fight. Sanders tragically died in a classroom where he had spent over half his life, living it to the fullest by enriching the lives of thousands of students.

Investigations later discovered 99 explosives planted all over Columbine High School by the two gunmen. Thirty bombs blew up in the school, but thankfully no injuries or deaths resulted from any of the explosives. The two large propane devices in the school's cafeteria could have killed everyone but thankfully were not set off since the area had been emptied by Sanders. At his funeral, over 3,000 relatives, friends, and community members mourned the loss of a hero. Both past and present students stood up to thank Sanders for changing their lives, and many thanked him for saving their lives that terrible day. Though grieving, two of his daughters agreed that had their dad lived and had Eric Harris and Dylan Klebold, the two student gunmen, lived, that he would have been the first to visit them in jail, and that he would have still believed they could be saved, a testament to this fallen hero's character.

The next fall, the Columbine softball team dedicated its field to coach Dave Sanders before its home opener. In February of 2000, ESPN presented Sanders' wife and daughters with the Arthur Ashe Courage Award in his honor. It was awarded at the ESPY Awards held at the MGM grand in Las Vegas before a tear-filled crowd of professional athletes and executives who gave a standing ovation after watching the tribute video of Sanders. Coach Sanders joined the likes of past recipients of the Arthur Ashe Award for Courage including tennis player Billie Jean King, North Carolina basketball coach Dean Smith, boxer Muhammad Ali, runner Loretta Claiborne, and broadcaster Howard Cosell.

Teachers and coaches are far too often forgotten heroes. Heroes of today's American youth are movie stars and professional athletes for their stardom, fame, and wealth. Today's heroes are stars our youth have never met and who have had no direct impact on their lives. We often forget to thank the middle school teacher who taught us the valuable lesson on integrity when caught cheating; the coach who stayed in the gym to run drills one-on-one rather than go home to his family, the high school teacher who lent his ear to us when we could not go to our parents with a teenage dilemma; or the algebra teacher who gave us extra attention until we finally understood some difficult formula or mathematical equation. Dave Sanders—teacher, coach, father, husband, grandfather, friend, and hero might have fallen, but he will never be forgotten.

Ralph Wiley

Legends Live On

by Jessica Bartter Duffaut

Far too often the world loses leaders in their prime before such figures are done doing great deeds and making this a better world. Ralph Wiley's impact on sports and society is everlasting. He was never afraid to stand-up against injustice and he left his mark despite the fact that his time on earth was much too short.

Wiley was born and raised in Memphis, Tennessee. His father died at a young age so his mother, Dorothy, worked as a humanities professor to support the family. Rooted in education, Dorothy often read to her son, planting an early seed for his love of literature. Wiley showcased his literary skill in several plays he wrote during high school. Wiley also developed a passion for sports and displayed his athletic skill on the track and football teams at Melrose High School. Wiley's football and academic prowess carried over to Knoxville College, about 400 miles east of his home in Memphis. He played wide receiver until a knee injury convinced him to drop the athlete from the student-athlete and focus his collegiate career on his studies in business and finance.

Wiley was quickly rewarded as he received his first journalism job writing for the sports section of the *Knoxville Keyana-Spectrum*, a weekly publication. Wiley's experience landed him a job in Oakland, California as a copy clerk for the *Oakland Tribune* after his college graduation in 1975. Wiley worked diligently for a year as a copy clerk until the sports editor asked him to write an article about Julius Erving. The article also involved the dissolving of the American Basketball Association and its merger with the NBA. Wiley recognized the opportunity such an article presented and he gladly accepted the challenge. His article was so well received that the *Oakland Tribune* promoted him to prep sports writer immediately. Wiley's impressive writings helped him ascend the professional ladder. He was soon promoted again, first to city beat writer and then, a year later, to sports writer. He covered boxing for the sports section where he finished almost seven years with the *Tribune*.

During the initial start of his career, Wiley became a highly regarded sports journalist in the Bay Area as a very young man. Most notably, Wiley is credited with the creation of the phrase "Billy Ball" referring to the Billy Martin managed Oakland A's of Major League Baseball. In 1982, Wiley took his skills as a columnist to New York City where he joined the staff of *Sports Illustrated*. In nine years with the prestigious magazine, Wiley wrote 139 articles, 20 of which graced the cover. He left *Sports Illustrated* as a senior writer in 1991 which surprised many who thought he was at the top of his game.

Wiley had published his first book in 1989 and devoted the next decade and a half to writing several more publications. Wiley's favorite uncle was a boxer, so Wiley found an early love for the sport. Wiley's experience with the *Oakland Tribune* and *Sports Illustrated* helped him learn about the lives of many fighters. He chronicled their struggles and triumphs in *Serenity: A Boxing Memoir*. It was published in 1989 and was well received by critics and readers. In 1991, *Why Black People Tend to Shout: Cold Facts and Wry Views from a Black Man's World* was released after it had been turned down by an estimated 25 publishers. *Dark Witness: When Black People Should be Sacrificed (Again)* was Wiley's third book which most notably offers his not-so-kind insight on O.J. Simpson. Wiley's success as an author led him to co-author *Best Seat in the House: A Basketball Memoir* and *By Any Means Necessary: The Trials and Tribulations of the Making of Malcolm X*, both written with producer, director, actor, and writer Spike Lee. He also co-wrote *Born to Play: The Eric Davis Story* and *Growing Up King: An Intimate Memoir*.

Wiley's commentaries were in high demand, and he made appearances on *Sportscenter*, *The Jim Rome Show*, *The Oprah Show*, *Donahue*, *Larry King Live*, Court TV's *Cochran & Co.*, *Nightline*, *The Charlie Rose Show*, *The Arsenio Hall Show*, *BET Talk*, ESPN Radio, *ESPN the Magazine show with Dan Le Batard*, and more. He was also an original member of NBC's *NFL Insiders* and ESPN's *Sports Reporters*. Wiley joined ESPN.com Page 2 during its inception in November 2000 where he contributed over 240 articles before his death in 2004. Wiley also wrote articles for the magazines *Premiere*, *GQ*, and *National Geographic*, as well as several national newspapers.

Known for his unique and provocative perspective, Wiley often challenged his readers to think outside the box and from inside someone else's shoes, particularly those of an African-American. Wiley had the ability to dissect an athlete to the core, presenting all sides of the person, rather than just the jock. In doing so, he did not shy away from the truth. Wiley was willing to expose the facts no matter what he discovered—good or bad, heroic or tragic—in an effort to deliver the best and most authentic stories to his readers. Wiley served an important role in the sports journalism world that was and remains largely dominated by white males.

On June 13, 2004 Wiley had just settled in for Game 4 of the NBA Finals when he died of heart failure in his home. He was just 52 years old. Wiley used his voice to better each one of us as he truly understood the impact of sports on society. Wiley is remembered for his passion, intelligence, vibrancy, honesty, humor, opinions, and, arguably most importantly, his friendship. Wiley wholeheartedly immersed himself in each piece he wrote commanding emotion out of his readers and colleagues. Some agreed and some disagreed, but he made each and every reader think.

Shortly after Wiley's death, Richard Lapchick wrote the following for ESPN.com. "As someone who writes and thinks about race and sport and social issues and sport, Ralph Wiley is a never before, never again figure. He made me rethink all that I had thought and challenged all of us to make ethics and integrity the pillars of our lives. Ralph and I talked even more often since I became an ESPN.com Page 2 columnist. I always wanted to know what he thought about what I was writing and thinking. Now I will only be able to imagine it as I will miss this special gift to humanity known as Ralph Wiley."[1]

Note

1. Page 2 et al., "Remembering Ralph Wiley," With the passing of Page 2 columnist Ralph Wiley, several of his colleagues offer moments that embody their time with Ralph. (June 14, 2004), http://sports.espn.go.com/espn/page2/story?page=mem ory/wiley (accessed January 12, 2010).

Jason Ray

Legends Live On

by Stacy Martin-Tenney

Jason Ray is a hero as much for what he did in his life as for what he did in his death. At 21 years old, Jason was killed in a car-pedestrian accident in New Jersey during a trip with the UNC Chapel Hill basketball team. The team was playing in their region for the Sweet 16 round of the NCAA tournament. Jason Ray was their mascot, Rameses. Ray was spirited and his zeal for life was infectious to all those around him. He packed more life experience into his short life than most people do in four times as many years. He was no saint, but very religious and passionate about his faith. He was not the perfect student and questioned authority and absolutes, but he was inquisitive and was about to graduate with honors from the prestigious Kenan-Flagler Business School at UNC Chapel Hill. He was not a morning person, but he rose early to study the Bible with his roommates. He was not interested in pursuing a career in business, because he wanted to pursue his passion for music and launch his band Nine PM Traffic to rock stardom. Unfortunately, Ray ran out of time to pursue all of his dreams, but he made a heroic decision as a young man that his death would give more time to others to pursue their dreams.

Jason Ray was extremely proud of his decision to become an organ donor, despite his parent's concerns. Charlotte Ray pushed back on her son's decision. "Let's be serious," Charlotte said. "Your father and I believe that you come here with all these little parts, you ought to leave here with all these parts. I'm not so sure about this."[1] After all, she considered it a miracle that Jason was even on this earth. She and his father Emmitt were high school sweethearts that had gone their separate ways for 25 years, had their own families, and found their way back to one another and then had Jason. He was certainly a gift, sharing his exuberant spirit and resilient attitude. But he was stubborn, and although respectful, he would not be told what decision he should make. So, Charlotte dropped the argument because she figured it didn't matter anyway. Jason knew it mattered. "Mom, you're crazy," he told Charlotte. "If something happens to me and I have a heart that could help save someone's life, then what good does it do to bury that heart in the ground? That doesn't make any sense at all."[2]

Ray was a character, stirring up laughter with a group of strangers or having a heartfelt conversation with someone he just met. So, when the opportunity to become a character presented itself, he tried out to be the school mascot, Rameses. The suit didn't come with instructions, and the judges just asked him to prove that he deserved to wear it. He proved it. Within a matter of minutes he had a crowd gathered on each side of the road, one chanting "Tar" and the other chanting "Heels" when he pointed in their direction. He could unite a group of fans and inspire them to cheer, he was Rameses. Tyler Treadaway shared the Rameses role with Ray and proclaimed that Ray was born to wear the Ram head and blue and white furry suit.

Ray didn't just play a character, he exhibited character. He was the student that stirred up a classroom because he questioned authority and would challenge answer after answer because he wanted to know more. His rebellion was good spirited, and so were his missions. He traveled to Haiti and Honduras on mission trips, and while he was stubborn and strong, he would return in tears from what he had witnessed. He renewed his strength through his commitment to his faith, praying for a high school girlfriend who cheated on him instead of the childish immaturity with which most youth would respond. He led a Bible study group for older men in the mornings and another study for a group of college kids in a bar.

Listening to music was a passion of his, but listening on an mp3 player was not enough for Ray. He traveled the country to hear his favorite bands in concert. It is a simple act, but everything he did, no matter how simple or how complex, he did with such passion and commitment. He even traveled to Europe to study abroad and see Michelangelo's work of art in the Sistine Chapel, because reading about it simply was not enough.

As much as he experienced life, he was very introspective and wrote about life. He carried miniature journals around with him and when he had a few moments he wrote. He wrote new lyrics for his band, Nine PM Traffic; he wrote prayers for other people; he wrote down his thoughts and questions about life. Ironically, he wrote about death too. He feared the death of his parents, of being left alone without them. One entry in his journal questioned how one should think about death. "Is it possible to have a healthy fear of death? Since Adam, all but two people have passed away. It's an inevitable end. People must see death, for ignoring it is simply lying to yourself. There are two ways to look at it: 1.) people acknowledge death and live toward it. 2.) people choose to ignore death and distance themselves away from it."[3] Maybe that is why he lived with such fervor, never knowing when, but knowing someday it would end.

The day it ended, Jason had left the hotel to walk along a sidewalk to a gas station to get something to eat before the game that night. He was struck by a Mercury Mountaineer on Route 4 in New Jersey a few hundred yards from the team's hotel. The result was catastrophic brain injury, a cracked skull, and a lifeless Jason. When the Rays received the phone call about their son, they could not believe it. Then they arrived in Jason's hospital room staring at their son, motionless, bandaged, and quiet. He was never quiet. The doctor did not inspire hope. "The doctor told me, 'Mr. Ray, I'm going to do everything I can to save your son, but I'm not God and this is going to take His intervention, because I've never seen someone injured as catastrophically as Jason make a comeback,' " Emmitt said.[4] Jason's friends, family, and Chapel Hill students filled the hospital room with the vigor and life Jason could not. It was not enough. Days after surgery, the results came back—Jason was brain dead. A nurse from the New Jersey Sharing Network was called in and found Jason's gift of organ donation amongst the paperwork. She approached the Rays about their son's decision, realizing that at this unthinkable moment, it may not be their decision to lose pieces of their son. Emmitt and Charlotte knew their son would want his decision followed, so they signed the paper granting the organ donation.

While Jason Ray had been living life to its fullest, there were four individuals waiting to face death. Ronald Griffin had been diagnosed with cardiomyopathy and congestive heart failure 13 years ago, and he had been sentenced to a Left Ventricular Assist Device (LVAD) while waiting for a heart transplant. He fought everyday for breath. The LVAD that was keeping him alive was complicating the search for a heart because it was causing strokes that would take him off the transplant list. Just when he was put back on the transplant list, Jason Ray was donating his heart.

Dennis Korzelius had lived life to its fullest in a reckless fashion, but he soon found a reason to slow down and appreciate the good in life: his new wife Pattie and the family they formed when they married. After two months together, Dennis was diagnosed with cirrhosis of the liver and end stage liver failure from hepatitis C. He needed a liver or he would only have eight months to live. Jason Ray donated his liver.

Antwan Hunter was not in pain and had a happy life, but his kidney was failing, his only kidney. Doctors had to remove his right kidney shortly after he was born due to failure, now all these years later all while feeling fine, this high school student was facing a death sentence. His mother Latisha was crushed when the doctors told her that his only hope was a kidney transplant. Jason Ray donated his kidney.

David Erving fought diabetes for 27 years, through 60 hospitalizations and 1,560 dialysis treatments. The disease took his vision, his gallbladder, caused broken bones, did not heal his broken bones properly so he walked with a limp and a cane, and finally took his remaining 22 teeth when he applied for a transplant. The doctors refused his request initially, but agreed if David would have his teeth extracted. They wanted to prevent any risk of infection through his cavities. He agreed and waited three years for a new kidney and a new pancreas, his only hope at survival. Finally, it was too much; he did not want to live this way anymore, then Jason Ray donated his other kidney and his pancreas. David would live.

Countless others benefitted from the tissues Ray donated. While transplant recipients are grateful for this gift of life, they almost always struggle to accept it emotionally because they know that someone had to die so they could live. Ronald Griffin's doctor had suggested he become a Carolina fan and during his recovery he watched Jason Ray's memorial service and the line of more than 2,500 people waiting to pay their respects. He realized that he had Ray's heart. Organ donation is a completely anonymous process, or at least it is intended to be, but there was a mix-up with Dennis' paperwork and he read through it to see that Jason Ray had donated his organs to him. "If I could, I would give it back to him in a heartbeat," Dennis said. "I knew I was dying. I had come to terms with it. Jason had no idea. And to me, that's not fair. What makes me any more special than him? I was just simply not all right with the thought that somebody had to die for this."[5]

Latisha had kept that reality from her son Antwan, knowing that he would refuse the kidney because he didn't want the surgery to begin with; he felt fine. Inside he was dying before Ray's kidney arrived. Antwan struggled quietly when he became aware, but soon he began to curiously ask what Ray liked and disliked. Ray's curiosity was alive and well. David Erving was quiet too, but quietly happy with his simple life. No more dialysis, no more diabetes. "If Jason could have picked the type of person he wanted to help, David would have been right at the top of the list," Charlotte said. "He's lived a hard life. Such a challenging, difficult life. But because of my son, he doesn't feel that pain anymore. How can that not make a mother proud?"[6]

The New Jersey Sharing Network reached out to Charlotte and Emmitt Ray to ask if they would be interested in meeting four of the men who received Ray's organs. While it was an unnerving thought to meet these men that held part of their son so close, it was something they felt compelled to do for their son. After all, if Ray were here, they would not be strangers to him. They had heard stories of the survivor's guilt recipients feel and could not bear the thought that their son's gift would come with a burden. That is not what he would want; he was never a burden to anyone. "I just had to let them know that," Emmitt said. "It bothered me. We pretty much just had a big pity party . . . everyone was crying. We probably didn't say more than 10 words. But I wanted them to know. I wanted them to understand who my son was."[7] When the Rays met Ronald, Dennis, David, and Antwan, it was like a family reunion. Ronald began to speak about his son and before he got a few words out, Ronald burst out, "I love you." It was simple, to the point and said everything all of them needed to hear. Later Ronald comforted Emmitt, who he could not imagine being in his position as a father himself. "As long as I breathe and I'm here," Ronald said, "your son is still here, too."[8] Emmitt and Charlotte are grateful for this gift of a new family that their son gave them and they have made the commitment to organ donation themselves.

Jason Ray wrote new song lyrics in his journal a week before that fateful trip to New Jersey. They were for the group's first single, "My Ordinary." Ray wrote, "A car crash grabs your attention. The white flags fly for protection. A heartbeat is a window of opportunity . . . "[9] Looking back, the lyrics are chilling, but after a closer examination of Jason Ray's life they are telling. He provided much more than a window of opportunity and it wasn't just a car crash that grabbed the world's attention, it was Ray and his simple act of human kindness. It may have been Ray's ordinary, but the world would be a better place if everyone strived for Ray's ordinary, because he was truly extraordinary.

Notes

1. Wayne Drehs, "Ray of Hope: Life, Death, Rebirth," ESPN E-Ticket, http://sports .espn.go.com/espn/eticket/story?page=rayofhope#pagetop, (accessed March 23, 2010).

2. Ibid.

3. Ibid.

4. Ibid.

5. Ibid.

6. Ibid.

7. Ibid.

8. Ibid.

9. Ibid.

Jon Blais

Legends Live On

by Stacy Martin-Tenney

Jon Blais was your average weekend warrior with a passion for life. Every day he challenged himself and those around him to pursue their passions and achieve the unthinkable. Then in 2005, Blais was diagnosed with Amyotrophic Lateral Sclerosis (ALS), also commonly known as Lou Gehrig's disease. Gehrig was a baseball legend for the famed New York Yankees for more than 14 years and known for his consecutive 2,130 game-playing streak, until the same disease stripped him of his physical prowess and ability to play the game he had dominated for so many seasons. Gehrig's square, honest persona seemed lackluster in comparison to his larger than life play on the baseball field, but it was his winning attitude and humility that made him a man we all remember. Blais shared those same character traits with Gehrig, for it was Blais' heroic performance at the Kona Ironman race in 2005 and undeletable fervor with which he pursued his fight against ALS that will make him a man we will all remember, too.

Blais competed in more than one hundred triathlons in his lifetime and enjoyed participating in almost any activity outdoors, so much so that he was inspired to move across the country from his native New England to San Diego where he could pursue those activities daily. He would swim at La Jolla Shores, hike for hours on the weekend in Balboa Park, bike in the Cuyamaca Mountains, even rock climb at Mission Trails. There was not a day that went by that

Jon Blais did not have an adventure. He challenged himself to the extreme. He would walk, for instance, 14 miles to the school he taught at with a 65 pound backpack, simply because he could. There was not an obstacle that he could not overcome and that positive attitude carried over into a belief in others.

Blais taught at the Aseltine School, a private school with a mission of helping underprivileged youth struggling with behavioral and emotional issues. Blais' mother recounted, "He always had a sense for the underprivileged student who had a difficult time, because he did."[1] Blais related to those kids in any way he could and strived to bring new and interesting things into their lives since many of them had never been exposed to things outside of their neighborhood. He brought speakers in and took them hiking and to the smoothie store. "I was also working part-time at REI, so I had friends come in and show the kids what else was out there. I had firefighters come in, arranged karate and pilates classes, and got them outfitted with climbing shoes and other gear."[2] He would take them hiking during a summer program and at first they were complaining, but then they would see the progress they made at that and began to apply themselves in other ways. "I had one student who refused to do work, but I found out he loved to cook. So he would make quesadillas every morning while the others worked. Eventually he started doing the work. It just took a little while to break those barriers."[3]

Blais was a warrior; he had suffered through some injuries before. So, when he began feeling numbness in his hand and feeling weak in the water during a swim, he brushed it off like most athletes do. Then the numbness began to spread up his arm, and he could not ignore it any longer. The physician was cautious, but Blais was crazed looking for information on the Internet about his symptoms and basically diagnosed himself before the doctor even asked him to do a spinal tap to confirm the diagnosis. The indestructible athlete without a fear or hesitation was sidelined with a fatal motor neuron disease called Amyliotropic Lateral Sclerosis. "It's crazy, my parents were always worried about me, worried about 'that phone call' since I did a lot of rock climbing. I was always careful though—didn't get on a mountain bike until I got insurance. I would joke 'Mom, it's not going to be that—it's going to be some sort of weird disease that gets me'—it's so eerie. I've had health issues, all sorts of allergies, and the growth on my nerve, but ALS is one in 50,000—I saw that on the Internet and thought to myself 'What are the chances of that?' I remember seeing that three years ago."[4]

It had been 70 years since Lou Gehrig had been diagnosed with the same awful disease, and yet there were no cures, and not even any treatments. "I read a lot about Lou Gehrig, but it's been 70 years since his death—I don't get how all this research is being done on other diseases, but there's nothing out there on ALS. It blows me away," Jon said.[5] No one knew anything. The disease itself promotes the ignorance and lack of understanding because of its stealth-like nature attacking healthy individuals without warning and quickly stripping them of their voluntary muscle function until only the disease remains. It captures the body, leaving the mind to suffer through the systemic shutdown until breathing stops.

The National Institute of Health describes ALS as an "invariably fatal neurological disease that attacks the nerve cells (neurons) responsible for controlling voluntary muscles. The motor neurons degenerate or die, ceasing to send messages to muscles. Unable to function, the muscles gradually weaken, waste away, and twitch. Eventually the ability of the brain to start and control voluntary movement is lost." Life expectancy for an ALS patient is typically between two to five years after the diagnosis. Symptoms include muscle weakness, difficulty speaking and swallowing, and results in paralysis. Blais had already been experiencing symptoms before his diagnosis and knew that the clock was ticking. He was determined to make the best of his last days and committed to raising awareness for this disease.

He moved back to Seekok, Massachusetts to live with his parents and decided that he would complete his first and last full Ironman race. "It goes back to my kids who have difficult lives, I tell them: 'You've got to face it.' If I went home to Massachusetts and did nothing about it—it wouldn't be right," he said.[6] An Ironman is comprised of three components, a 2.4-mile ocean swim, a 112 mile bike ride, and a marathon run—26.2 miles. Very few complete this challenge, no one with ALS ever had. Blais began planning to compete in the Florida Ironman race. A friend called NBC and asked the network if they would be interested in Jon's story for their coverage of the Kona Ironman. They were. Kona is a grueling course with the Pacific waters, mountainous terrain, and a run through the lava fields and the triathlete has to finish the course in 17 hours or they are disqualified. Blais accepted and began training. He made it to Kona and lined up with the rest of the athletes.

Two days before the race, Blais became right-handed because his left had succumbed to the disease. Blais took to the water with a paddle on his left hand so that he could swim. Already fatigued and slower than he had planned, he transitioned from the swim to the bike. Dealing with neurological issues and cramping he persevered through the bike ride. At mile 12 on the run, his hands went numb and he started drifting. He even vomited for a mile straight. Worried that he wouldn't make the time limit, he pushed himself. With an hour left before the course closed, Jon had reached mile 25 and relaxed a little as he neared the finish. "During a radio show with Mike Reilly, I said that if I got close enough to the finish line, they could just log roll me across," Blais said.[7] Blais approached the finish and dropped to the ground to log roll himself across the finish line. Blais was truly an Ironman.

No one lives with ALS long enough to generate significant awareness for this debilitating disease, but Jon Blais did much more than live with it. He swam, biked, and ran with it! The oxidation effects probably accelerated the affects of the disease, but Jon Blais accelerated the fight to find a cure for ALS. "On October 15, 2005, only five months after being diagnosed, Jon became the only individual with ALS to complete an Ironman, finishing in 16:28:56."[8]

Jon Blais was known as the Blazeman and has inspired a group of multisport athletes to compete in events across the country as part of Team Blazeman in an effort to raise awareness for ALS. He rolled over the finish line in Kona, and that log roll has become a symbol of hope and a means of raising awareness for ALS. The Ironman, IronGirl, and Ironman 70.3 race organizers have made Blais' number 179 honorific. They allow athletes to request the number and run on behalf of ALS and Jon Blais. After only a year the Blazeman Foundation raised over $150,000 for ALS research and there have been countless athletes rolling over finish lines. Brian Breen was one such athlete that ran Kona in honor of Blais in 2006. Blais returned to Kona in the wheelchair he was confined to, just a year after his own Ironman performance to support Breen's effort. "It was like getting to bat in place of Lou Gehrig in the actual Yankees lineup. I didn't feel an ounce of pain out there—not that there wasn't any. I just thought about

Jon the entire time, and I felt a surge of honor and pride coursing through my veins like I've never felt in my life."[9] Breen rolled across the finish line. It was a moving experience for both Breen and Blais. Blais passed away seven months later on May 27, 2007 at age 35.

Blais referred to himself as the warrior poet and though he lost his battle with ALS, he was grateful for the athletes that won their battles through racing for ALS awareness in hopes that one day the war on ALS will be won. In the words of Team Blazeman Warrior Brian Breen, "The sacrifice that Jon put forth reminds me of a patch that Pararescue Jumpers wear on their uniforms that reads, 'So that others may live.' That about sums it up. That's what Jon has done here."[10]

Notes

1. Dan Norcross, "Giving it his all," *The San Diego Union Tribune*, September 25, 2005.

2. Lonna Ramirez, "Death sentence inspires triathlete: Jon Blais hopes to finish Hawaii Ironman and raise ALS awareness," Active.com, October 5, 2005, http://www .active.com/triathlon/Articles/Death_sentence_inspires_triathlete_br____em_Jon_Blais _hopes_to_finish_Hawaii_Ironman_and_raise_ALS_awareness__em_.htm, (accessed March 21, 2010).

3. Ibid.

4. Ibid.

5. Ibid.

6. Ibid.

7. Kevin Mackinnon, "Speaking of John Blais . . ." Ironmanlife.com, November 18, 2005, http://ironman.com/columns/ironmanlife/ironmanlife.com-32, (accessed March 21, 2010).

8. Blazeman Foundation for ALS, "Jon 'Blazeman' Blais," Waronals.com, http:// www.waronals.com/about_jon.php, (accessed February 28, 2010).

9. Deanna Askin, "In memory of triathlete and hero Jon Blais, the Blazeman," Active.com/Triathlon, http://www.active.com/triathlon/Articles/In_memory_of_triath- lete_and_hero_Jon_Blais__the_Blazeman.htm, (accessed February 28, 2010).

10. Ibid.

Conclusion

by Richard Lapchick

As is evident in the stories of these 150 heroes, sport can change one's life for the better. Sport can open the door to opportunity and help young people avoid paths which are nothing but dead ends. Sport can encourage athletes to become civically engaged members of the communities in which they go to school, even as they work to succeed in their various sports. Sport teaches teamwork, commitment and accountability, all of which are crucial ingredients of a successful personal and professional life.

Sport reaches all kinds of people for all different reasons. Sport can be played competitively or recreationally or sport can be watched and enjoyed as entertainment. We watch sports we never play and we play sports we never watch. Sport can help build friendships, families, respect, confidence, and character. Sport provides health benefits some medical professionals can only begin to understand.

Most importantly, sport is unique in the boundaries it crosses with both its participants and its audience. Differences in gender, race, physical and mental abilities, age, religion, and cultures are irrelevant in the huddle, on the field, in the gym, or in the water. Sport smashes these barriers like nothing else can.

Whether one is an athlete, coach, administrator, or fan, *150 Heroes* demonstrates by example how our heroes have defied the odds and overcome obstacles; how through sport they have offered hope and inspiration to others; how they as athletes have used sport to affect meaningful social change. The possibilities athletes possess are endless.

Sport has survived and even flourished in the United States through world wars, women's suffrage, and the civil rights movement. It has evolved as Americans have evolved, always offering a form of enjoyment, a respite from the challenges of daily life. But sport can also be an important vehicle for social change.

A great deal has been achieved over the last century through sports, particularly during the last 25 years during which the National Consortium for Academics and Sports has grown from a small program in Boston to a national organization of more than 240 colleges and universities. During the last half of the 20th century, we have witnessed the integration of professional leagues, the development of women's leagues, the establishment of Title IX, the setting aside of international conflict for brief moments in sport competitions and increased funding for athletic programs for disadvantaged youth. Sports have become an even more integral part of the fabric of our social and cultural life in big cities and small towns, from Maine to Montana, from Miami to Maui.

The 150 heroes described in this volume should serve as a light, indeed, as a beacon for us all. They followed their dreams and helped us dream as well. They served others even as they succeeded on the playing field. They found hope where others believed none existed. Let us cheer their accomplishments as we follow their example and emphasize that it is more than just wins and losses that will continue the evolution of sports' positive role on society.

About the National Consortium for Academics and Sports

The National Consortium for Academics and Sports (NCAS) is an ever-growing organization of colleges and universities. The mission of the NCAS is to create a better society by focusing on educational attainment and using the power and appeal of sport to positively affect social change.

The National Consortium for Academics and Sports evolved in response to the need to "keep the student in the student-athlete." The NCAS was established by Dr. Richard E. Lapchick and since its inception in 1985, NCAS member institutions have proven to be effective advocates for balancing academics and athletics. By joining the NCAS, a college or university agrees to bring back, tuition free, their own former student-athletes who competed in revenue and non-revenue producing sports and were unable to complete their degree requirements. In exchange these former student-athletes agree to participate in school outreach and community service programs addressing social issues of America's youth.

There have been hundreds of people involved in running the NCAS and working to deliver our mission for 25 years now. Each individual has helped because of their passion for combining academics, sport, and the way we use sport to bring about social change for our youth.

The NCAS started with 11 universities in 1985 and now has 242 member institutions. Members of the NCAS have been able to bring back 30,883 former student-athletes to complete their degrees through one of our biggest programs. The Degree Completion Program was just a dream in 1985, but more than 30,000 now say that dream has become a reality.

Returning student-athletes participate in outreach and community service programs in exchange for the tuition and fees they receive when they come back to school they. They have reached over 18 million young people in cities in America, rural America, and suburban America. Wherever there are college campuses, our student-athletes are in the community helping young people face the crises of the last 25 years. Member institutions have donated more than $332 million in tuition assistance. With no athletic participation in return this time around, the biggest return possible is to the student who leaves with the degree they were promised when they first enrolled. The NCAS and its members have been able to work with children on issues like conflict resolution, trying to improve race relations, trying to reduce men's violence against women, drug and alcohol abuse, the importance of education, and the balance of academics with athletics.

The NCAS has worked with organizations and schools to help them understand issues of diversity, not only as a moral imperative, but also as a business necessity. The NCAS utilizes the Teamwork Leadership Institute (TLI) to teach our colleges, professional sports, and all of the people that sport touches the importance and value of diversity which, then in turn, reflects back on society as a whole. The mission of TLI is to help senior administrators, team front office personnel, and athletic department staff, through the provision of diversity training services, to apply the principles of teamwork to all areas of athletic departments and professional sports organizations. Challenges that stem from cultural prejudice, intolerance, and poor communication can be proactively addressed in intelligent, safe, and structured ways. TLI works with staff members to help them anticipate, recognize, and address the problems inherent to diverse teams and staff. Diversity training demonstrates that diverse people have a great deal in common. Rather than being divisive issues, racial, ethnic, and gender differences can serve as building blocks. Just as in sports, these differences can strengthen the group. TLI has facilitated over 225 workshops with the NBA, MLB , Maloof Sports & Entertainment, The Orlando Magic, the NCAA, and NASCAR.

The Mentors in Violence Prevention (MVP) National Program, founded in 1993 by Northeastern University's Center for the Study of Sport in Society, is a leadership program that motivates student-athletes and student leaders to play a central role in solving problems that historically have been considered "women's issues": rape, battering, and sexual harassment. The mixed gender, racially-diverse former professional and college athletes that facilitate the MVP National Program motivate men and women to work together in preventing gender violence. Utilizing a unique bystander approach to prevention, MVP National views student-athletes and student leaders not as potential perpetrators or victims, but as empowered bystanders who can confront abusive peers. The MVP National approach does not involve finger pointing, nor does it blame participants for the widespread problem of gender violence. Instead it sounds a positive call for proactive, preventative behavior and leadership. MVP National has facilitated sessions with thousands of high school and college students and administrators at dozens of Massachusetts schools, as well as with hundreds of student-athletes and administrators at over 100 colleges nationwide. MVP National has also conducted sessions with professional sports leagues including players and staff from the National Basketball Association (NBA), National Football League (NFL), NASCAR, and International Basketball League (IBL), as well as with every branch of the U.S. military. MVP has also trained the rookie and free agents of the New England Patriots and New York Jets, and with the Boston Red Sox minor league, as well as Major League Lacrosse (MLL).

Branded a Leader (BAL), created in 2008 by the NCAS, is a leadership program that teaches critical decision-making skills to student-athletes while challenging them to be responsible for their decisions and those of their teammates. BAL is a highly interactive training that engages student-athletes in unusually effective ways. Branded a Leader utilizes the appeal of mainstream branding strategies as a foundation for student-athletes to discuss personal decisions and difficult social situations involving teammates. The program illustrates the impact of individual and organizational decision-making on a wide range of brands through case studies of various companies and individuals. BAL trainers lead student-athletes through the "brands" that they represent (family, conference, institution, athletic department, team, community, etc.) and have them articulate how a range of good decisions and bad decisions will likely impact each of their "brands." Each segment of this training utilizes a specific aspect of decision-making skills, consequences, and accountability for self, teammates, and beyond. Student-athletes develop a success plan for enhancing their "personal brand" and share with their teammates. Branded a Leader trainers challenge the student-athletes to hold each other accountable for their espoused success goals and for making good decisions. Their role as their teammates "keeper" will be reinforced through social scenarios where they will decide the best options for intervening on a teammate's behalf.

With the alarming rate of alcohol use and abuse among students, the NCAS, in collaboration with The BACCHUS and GAMMA Peer Education Network, sought a solution through education and developed the Alcohol Response-Ability: Foundations for Student Athletes™ course in 2004. It is a 90-minute alcohol education and life skills program designed specifically for student-athletes and those who work with them in the college and university setting. In this first program of its kind, student-athletes receive a customized educational experience that is interactive, interesting, and designed to help them reduce harm and recognize the consequences associated with alcohol abuse in their campus communities. In its first year on college campuses, results came back overwhelming positive. Ninety-three percent of the students who took the course said they learned something new, and 95 percent of them said they would try at least one of the strategies they learned to lower their risk. An impressive 83 percent said they would likely make safe decisions as a direct result of the course. These figures prove more needs to be done with alcohol abuse education.

In December 2006, Dr. Richard Lapchick organized and led a group of 10 students from the University of Central Florida's DeVos Sport Business Management graduate program to volunteer in Katrina-stricken New Orleans. Also on the trip were Lapchick's wife, Ann, and daughter, Emily, and two family friends, Allyce Najimy and Smitty Pignatelli. On the first day of the trip, some of the students and Dr. Lapchick met a man named Stanley Stewart who was thinking about leaving his damaged home permanently. The entire group met Stanley the next day and took it upon themselves to help him rebuild his home. Though it would be a long, arduous endeavor, the group committed themselves to Stanley's family. More students from the DeVos program volunteered during their spring and summer breaks. They also helped spread the message that people in New Orleans were in need. The Hope for Stanley Alliance was soon formed. Thanks to special efforts by Smitty Pignatelli, the Stewart home received plumbing, electrical and drywall foundations, as well as freshly painted walls and a brand new roof. Stanley's family was able to move back home by Thanksgiving 2007. Hope for Stanley believes in the ability of sport to be an agent for social change. Individuals associated with Hope for Stanley know of the emotional, financial, and physical impact sport has on those who act as spectators and participants. It is because of this impact that there is great potential for sport to be a social tool used for the betterment of people's lives. The mission of the Hope for Stanley Foundation is to provide people in sports volunteer opportunities in areas affected by natural disasters.

Lights, Camera, Action! (LCA) is produced exclusively for the NCAS by network TV veteran Ed Berliner. The program is designed to instruct student-athletes as well as school administration, staff, and faculty on how to properly deal with all factions of media coverage with attention paid to insuring the institution is always presented and judged in a fair and positive manner by the media and the general public. Video examples from network and regional television and radio coverage are produced for a seamless integration with questions and comments designed to make the audience think and discuss. Audience members are asked their reaction to a specific instance before having the reasons and consequences of that instance explained to them, thus working from their own experiences and then explaining the reasons and thought process behind each instance. LCA is specifically designed to develop positive media habits for every individual, from the star athlete and others in the athletic community. Lights, Camera, Action! places every member of the audience in specific situations and then helps to correct any errors in judgment that may be used in a negative fashion directed at the institution, team, and/or the individual.

Each of the 150 heroes in this book was honored in celebration of National STUDENT-Athlete Day (NSAD). NSAD is celebrated annually on April 6th providing an opportunity to recognize the outstanding accomplishments of student-athletes who have achieved excellence in academics and athletics, while making significant contributions to their communities. In addition to honoring student-athletes, the Annual National STUDENT-Athlete Day program selects recipients for *Giant Steps Awards*. These awards are given to individuals on a national level who exemplify the meaning of National STUDENT-Athlete Day. Each year nominations are received from across the country, and the Giant Steps Award winners are chosen by a national selection committee in categories ranging from civic leaders, coaches, parents, teachers, athletic administrators, and courageous student-athletes. This book is a compilation of the inspiring life stories of the first 150 to be chosen in honor of the "giant steps" they have taken in sports, in society, in life, and in living.

About the Authors

Dr. Richard E. Lapchick

Human rights activist, pioneer for racial equality, internationally recognized expert on sports issues, scholar, and author Richard E. Lapchick is often described as "the racial conscience of sport." He brought his commitment to equality and his belief that sport can be an effective instrument of positive social change to the University of Central Florida where he accepted an endowed chair in August 2001. Lapchick became the only person named as "One of the 100 Most Powerful People in Sport" to head up a sport management program. He remains President and CEO of the National Consortium for Academics and Sport and helped bring the NCAS national office to UCF.

The DeVos Sport Business Management Program at UCF is a landmark program that focuses on the business skills necessary for graduates to conduct a successful career in the rapidly changing and dynamic sports industry. In following with Lapchick's tradition of human rights activism, the curriculum includes courses with an emphasis on diversity, community service and philanthropy, sport and social issues and ethics in addition to UCF's strong business curriculum. The DeVos Program has been named one of the nation's top five programs by the *Wall Street Journal*, the *SportsBusiness Journal*, and *ESPN The Magazine*.

In December of 2006, Lapchick, his wife and daughter, and a group of DeVos students formed the Hope for Stanley Foundation, which is currently organizing groups of student-athletes and sports management students to go to New Orleans to work in the reconstruction efforts in the devastated Ninth Ward. As of the fall of 2007, Hope for Stanley members have spent 19 weeks in the city in a partnership with the NOLA City Council. Lapchick was named an honorary citizen by the New Orleans City Council in October 2007.

Lapchick helped found the Center for the Study of Sport in Society in 1984 at Northeastern University. He served as Director for 17 years and is now the Director Emeritus. The Center has attracted national attention to its pioneering efforts to ensure the education of athletes from junior high school through the professional ranks. The Center's Project TEAMWORK was called "America's most successful violence prevention program" by public opinion analyst Lou Harris. It won the Peter F. Drucker Foundation Award as the nation's most innovative non-profit program and was named by the Clinton Administration as a model for violence prevention. The Center and the National Consortium for Academics and Sports created the MVP gender violence prevention program that has been so successful with college and high school athletes that the United States Marine Corps adopted it in 1997.

Lapchick also helped form the NCAS in 1985. It is a group of over 230 colleges and universities that created the first of its kind degree completion and community service programs. To date, 29,856 athletes have returned to NCAS member schools. Over 13,700 have graduated. Nationally, the NCAS athletes have worked with more than 17.5 million students in the school outreach and community service program, which focuses on teaching youth how to improve race relations, develop conflict resolution skills, prevent gender violence, and avoid drug and alcohol abuse. They have collectively donated more than 19 million hours of service while member colleges have donated more than $300 million in tuition assistance.

Lapchick was the American leader of the international campaign to boycott South Africa in sport for more than 20 years. In 1993, the Center launched TEAMWORK-South Africa, a program designed to use sports to help improve race relations and help with sports development in post-apartheid South Africa. He was among 200 guests specially invited to Nelson Mandela's inauguration.

Lapchick is a prolific writer. His 14th book was published in 2009. Lapchick is a regular columnist for ESPN.com and The *Sports-Business Journal*. He has written more than 500 articles and has given more than 2,750 public speeches.

Considered among the nation's experts on sport and social issues, Lapchick has appeared numerous times on *Good Morning America, Face The Nation, The Today Show, ABC World News, NBC Nightly News*, the *CBS Evening News*, CNN, and ESPN.

Lapchick also consults with companies as an expert on both managing diversity and building community relations through service programs addressing the social needs of youth. He has a special expertise on Africa and South Africa. He has made 30 trips to Africa, and African Studies was at the core of his PhD work.

Before Northeastern, he was an associate professor of political science at Virginia Wesleyan College from 1970–1978, and a senior liaison officer at the United Nations between 1978–1984.

In 2006, Lapchick was named both the Central Florida Public Citizen of the Year and the Florida Public Citizen of the Year by the National Association of Social Workers. Lapchick has been the recipient of numerous humanitarian awards. He was inducted into the Sports Hall of Fame of the Commonwealth Nations in 1999 in the category of Humanitarian along with Arthur Ashe and Nelson Mandela and received the Ralph Bunche International Peace Award. He joined Muhammad Ali, Jackie Robinson, Arthur Ashe, and Wilma Rudolph in the Sport in Society Hall of Fame in 2004. In 2009, the Rainbow/PUSH Coalition and Rev. Jesse Jackson honored him with "A Lifetime Achievement Award for Work in Civil Rights." Lapchick won the Diversity Leadership Award at the 2003 Literacy Classic and the Jean Mayer Global Citizenship Award from Tufts University in 2000. He won the Wendell Scott Pioneer Award in 2004 and the NASCAR Diversity Award in 2008 for leadership in advancing people of color in the motor sports industry, education, employment, and life. He received the "Hero Among Us Award" from the Boston Celtics in 1999, and was named as the Martin Luther King, Rosa Parks, Cesar Chavez Fellow by the State of Michigan in 1998. Lapchick was the winner of the 1997 "Arthur Ashe Voice of Conscience Award." He also won the 1997 Women's Sports Foundation President's Award for work toward the development of women's sports and was named as the 1997 Boston Celtics "Man of the Year." In 1995, the National Association of Elementary School Principals gave him their first award as a "Distinguished American in Service of Our Children." He was a guest of President Clinton at the White House for National Student-Athlete Day in 1996, 1997, 1998, and again in 1999.

He is listed in Who's Who in America, Who's Who in American Education, Who's Who in Finance and Industry, and Who's Who in American Business. Lapchick was named as "one of the 100 most powerful people in sport" for six consecutive years and as "one of the 100 Most Influential Sports Educators in America." He was named one of the 20 most powerful people in college sport and one of the 20 most powerful people in sport in Florida.

He is widely known for bringing different racial groups together to create positive work force environments. In 2003–04 he served as the national spokesperson for VERB, the Center for Disease Control's program to combat preteen obesity.

Lapchick has received eight honorary degrees. In 1993, he was named as the outstanding alumnus at the University of Denver where he got his PhD in international race relations in 1973. Lapchick received a B.A. from St. John's University in 1967, and an honorary degree from St. John's in 2001.

Lapchick is a board member of the Open Doors Foundation and SchoolSports which created *ESPN's RISE Magazine*. He is on the advisory boards of the Women's Sports Foundation and the Giving Back Fund. He is a founder of the Hope for Stanley Foundation. He is a consultant to the Black Coaches and Administrators association.

Under Lapchick's leadership, the DeVos Program launched the Institute for Diversity and Ethics in Sport in December 2002. The Institute focuses on two broad areas. In the area of diversity, the Institute publishes the critically acclaimed *Racial and Gender Report Card*, long-authored by Lapchick in his former role as director of the Center for the Study of Sport in Society at Northeastern University. *The Report Card*, an annual study of the racial and gender hiring practices of major professional sports, Olympic sport, and college sport in the United States, shows long-term trends over a decade and highlights organizations that are notable for diversity in coaching and management staffs.

In another diversity initiative, the Institute partners with the NCAS to provide diversity management training to sports organizations, including athletic departments and professional leagues and teams. The Consortium has already conducted such training for the NBA, Major League Soccer, NASCAR, and more than 80 university athletic departments.

In the area of ethics, the Institute monitors some of the critical ethical issues in college and professional sport, including the potential for the exploitation of student-athletes, gambling, performance-enhancing drugs, and violence in sport. The Institute publishes annual studies on graduation rates for all teams in college football bowl games, comparing graduation rates for football players to rates for overall student-athletes and including a breakdown by race. The Institute also publishes the graduation rates of the women's and men's basketball teams in the NCAA Tournament as March Madness heats up.

Richard is the son of Joe Lapchick, the famous Original Celtic center who became a legendary coach for St. John's and the Knicks. He is married to Ann Pasnak, and has three children and two grandchildren.

Jessica Bartter Duffaut

Jessica Bartter Duffaut is currently the Assistant Director of Communications and Marketing for the National Consortium for Academics and Sports (NCAS) located at the University of Central Florida. She is the co-author of three other books in this series including *100 Trailblazers: Great Women Athletes Who Opened Doors for Future Generations*; *100 Pioneers: African-Americans Who Broke Color Barriers in Sport*; and *100 Heroes: People in Sports Who Make This a Better World.*

At the University of California, San Diego, Duffaut was a member of the nationally ranked NCAA Division II volleyball team where she was elected team co-captain during her junior and senior years. The U.C. San Diego Tritons went to the playoffs every year, including a Final Four appearance her junior season. As an individual who values teamwork, Duffaut considers her "Best Team Player" award one of her greatest accomplishments.

Duffaut attributes many valuable lessons she has learned to her experiences in sport and works to apply them outside of the sports arena and into her professional life. Prior to moving to Orlando, Florida to work for the NCAS, Duffaut worked for the U.C. San Diego Recreation and Intercollegiate Athletic Departments while she earned her bachelor's degree in management science, with a minor in psychology.

Born and raised in Orange County, California, Duffaut attended Valencia High School of Placentia before becoming a Triton. Duffaut is grateful to her father who first introduced her to sports, and to her mother who taxied her to softball and volleyball practices and even dared to catch wild pitches in the backyard. Duffaut is the eldest of four siblings including Jacqueline, Brian, and Kyle, all of whom have proudly donned the jersey No. 13. Duffaut currently resides in Pasadena, California with her husband, C.J. Duffaut.

Joslyn Dalton

Joslyn Marie Dalton is currently a graduate student in the DeVos Sport Business Management Program at the University of Central Florida working toward her master's degrees in business administration and sport business management. She also works as a graduate assistant for Dr. Richard Lapchick. Prior to the DeVos Program, Joslyn attended the University of Nebraska earning an undergraduate degree in communication studies. While at Nebraska, she was a distance runner for the cross country and track and field teams. In addition to being a co-captain in her senior season on the track, Dalton was a two-time All-Big 12 performer in the 3,000-meter steeplechase. She also anchored Nebraska's distance medley relay to three separate top seven finishes at the Big 12 Championships. Her dedication in the classroom was also rewarded during her tenure for the Huskers. She was named First-Team Academic All-Big 12 on four occasions, and was named to the U.S. Track and Field and Cross Country Coaches Association's All-Academic Team for three years. Her academic and athletic success was highlighted with a 2009–10 NCAA Women's Enhancement Postgraduate Scholarship for Careers in Athletics.

Dalton was born in Fremont, Nebraska, before moving to Lincoln, Nebraska which she calls her hometown. Above all, she considers it a blessing to have had the opportunity to work on this book. She is grateful for the influence and upbringing from her parents, Robyn and the late Michael Lee Dalton, who throughout her childhood attended almost every race she ran. Joslyn has an older sister, Jordyn, and an older brother, Aaron, who is married with three beautiful children.

Stacy Martin-Tenney

Stacy A. Martin-Tenney grew up in Bloomington, Indiana, where she began her athletic career at a young age. She credits her success to her parents Maureen and Randy, both former coaches. Her parents instilled values of self worth and determination in their daughter. Stacy won two state titles her senior year with record-breaking performances and she was named the Gatorade National Female Track & Field Athlete of 1999. Auburn University offered her a full athletic scholarship in track and field. As an Auburn athlete, Stacy set new school records in the shot put, discus, hammer, and weight throw. A condition called compartment syndrome had plagued her legs for eight years and finally required surgery and extensive rehab that began with learning how to walk again. In spite of this obstacle, her numerous collegiate career accomplishments included an SEC Championship, Academic as well as Athletic All-American honors, and competing in the Junior World Championships. The pinnacle of her athletic career was qualifying for the 2004 Olympic Trials in both shot put and discus. In 2007, Martin was inducted into the Indiana Track and Field Hall of Fame for her athletic career accomplishments. She was named to the SEC Good Works Team, was a NCAA Leadership Conference Representative, president of the Student Athletic Advisory Committee, as well as being named to the SEC Academic Honor Roll all of her years at Auburn. She graduated with honors from Auburn University with a bachelor's of science in education and health promotion, and a bachelor's of science in business administration and human resource management. She has passed the torch on to her younger brother, Cory, who won two NCAA championship titles in 2008, in the hammer and the shot put and has continued his track and field career professionally.

After Auburn, Stacy entered the sports industry to work for the NCAA Beyond the Game Tour presented by CBS Sports, a promotional tour for student-athletes, and for ESPN on a summer sporting event production. She then earned a master's of sports business management and a master's of business administration at the University of Central Florida's DeVos Sport Business Management Program. She served as a graduate assistant to Dr. Richard Lapchick and The Institute for Diversity and Ethics in Sport (TIDES) and worked for the Orlando Magic during graduate school. She has participated in the Deliver the Dream weekends for families that suffer from terminal illnesses and other community service activities. Stacy was a co-author on TIDES' *2005 Racial and Gender Report Card*, and the other three books in the National Consortium for Academics and Sports' Series: *100 Heroes*, *100 Pioneers*, and *100 Trailblazers*. After graduate school, Stacy took a sports event management internship with Disney's Wide World of Sports Complex, now known as ESPN Wide World of Sports Complex at the Walt Disney World Resort. She is currently a marketing manager for Disney Sports, specifically handling the marketing efforts for the Walt Disney World Marathon Weekend, Disney's Princess Half Marathon Weekend, Disneyland Half Marathon Weekend, and Disney Wine & Dine Half Marathon Weekend. Stacy Martin-Tenney resides near Orlando, Florida, with her husband Anthony Tenney.

Austin Moss

Austin Moss II was born in Greenville, South Carolina, but moved shortly after his birth to Hopkinsville, Kentucky, which he considers home. Moss has been involved in sports throughout his life. He grew up the youngest of four children in a household that emphasized the importance of education and regularly provided opportunities to participate in sport. His older siblings, Kiyon, Naeeta, and Ravi, were very active in sports. As a result, Austin grew up traveling to their competitions and developed a profound desire to compete and be just like them. Austin and his older brother Ravi were only three years apart and they grew up playing sports together every day and pushed each other to be the very best at anything they set their minds to. Throughout childhood and into his teenage years, Moss participated in football, basketball, and baseball. From the strong values instilled by his parents, he knew the importance of succeeding in the classroom as well as on the field and how it can open many doors in life. From this mentality, Moss completed high school with a 3.5 GPA, received a partial academic scholarship from the University of Kentucky, and accepted the opportunity to join the football team as a preferred walk-on in the fall of 2005. In the spring of 2008, Austin received a full athletic scholarship from the University of Kentucky as a result of his hard work on the football field and in the classroom. During his time at the University, Moss embodied the term "student-athlete," earning Academic All-SEC honors for three consecutive years, serving as the football representative for the Student Athletic Advisory Committee, and serving as the team chapel service coordinator. He was also very active in the Lexington community speaking to local schools, mentoring young students, and participating in several community service events. As a member of the University of Kentucky football team, Moss helped turn the program around from consecutive losing seasons to winning three consecutive bowl games and finishing with a total record of 23-16 from 2006 to 2009.

In May of 2009 Moss received his bachelor of arts degree in business marketing from the University of Kentucky. From his experiences through sport, Moss was a living witness of the power and impact it can have on society and knew he had a passion to work in the industry. In the spring of 2010 Austin was accepted into the University of Central Florida's DeVos Sport Business Management Program's incoming class of 2011.

Moss is currently completing his first year in the program and working towards earning his master's in sport business management as well as a master's in business administration. He serves as a graduate assistant in The Institute for Diversity and Ethics in Sport, working alongside Dr. Richard Lapchick. Austin Moss aspires to become a director of player personnel in the NFL and holds a special interest in developing a community through the power of sport.

Brian Wright

Brian Leroy Antonio Wright was born in Takoma Park, Maryland, on April 9, 1982. As the youngest member of a large family consisting of brother Rodger and sisters, Nicole, Kahlarah, and Hillary, Brian quickly learned the concept of operating as a team from his parents Wayne and Amybelle Humphrey. This team concept captured Wright's imagination as he, at a very early age, became passionate about sports, which would help shape the rest of his young life. After lobbying between two or three different sports Wright finally decided that basketball was his sport of choice. Brian attended Takoma Academy in Takoma Park for high school and was a standout student-athlete receiving various academic and athletic awards including a McDonald's High School Basketball All-American nomination in his senior year. Brian was also an active participant in the local metropolitan community volunteering with local community service organizations in feed the homeless projects as well as an outreach program for disabled children. Upon graduation from Takoma Academy, Wright attended La Sierra University in Riverside, California. As a student-athlete, Wright excelled in the classroom and on the court and was named team captain on his team for 3 of his 4 seasons at La Sierra University. In his junior and senior campaigns, the City of Riverside Sports Hall of Fame honored Wright for his athletic accomplishments while at La Sierra University. In 2004, Wright graduated from La Sierra University with a bachelor's degree in business administration. His passion for sports and education continued after his graduation from La Sierra with his acceptance into the DeVos Sport Business Management Program. During his final semester, Wright was offered and accepted a position as a scouting coordinator with the Orlando Magic, a position that he still holds to date. His goals are to bring an NBA Championship to the city of Orlando and the Magic franchise. In his spare time Wright enjoys spending time with his family and friends, playing and teaching basketball, and reading.

Jenny Yehlen

Jenny Yehlen is a graduate of the DeVos Sport Business Management Program at the University of Central Florida. Prior to entering graduate school at UCF in 2005, Yehlen was a student-athlete at Penn State University. She earned degrees in PR/advertising and communication studies, and was a member and captain of the Lady Lion basketball team. During her tenure at UCF, Jenny worked in Academic Services for Student-Athletes (ASSA) and at The Institute for Diversity and Ethics in Sport (TIDES), where she had the opportunity to work with Dr. Lapchick on several projects. In addition to *150 Heroes*, Yehlen was also a contributing author to *100 Pioneers* and *100 Heroes*, two other books that Lapchick authored. Yehlen received an MBA and a master's in sport business management from UCF in 2007, and returned to her native state of Minnesota to work as an assistant in the University of Minnesota athletic department.

Jenny currently resides in St. Paul, Minnesota with her husband, Jarrett, and their dog, Richmond.